The Psychobiology of Curt Richter

Edited by

Elliott M. Blass

YORK PRESS
BALTIMORE

Curt Richter at His Surgical Table, 1975.

E. M. Blass

Library of Congress Cataloging in Publication Data

Richter, Curt Paul, 1894-
　The psychobiology of Curt Richter.

　"Complete bibliography of Curt P. Richter": p.
　Includes index.
　1. Psychobiology—Addresses, essays, lectures.
I. Title. [DNLM: 1. Psychology—Collected works.
2. Psychophysiology—Collected works. WL102 R535p]
QP360.R5　　1976　　599'.01'88　　75-19492
ISBN 0-912752-05-X

Copyright © 1976 by York Press, Inc.

All rights reserved, including the right to
reproduce this book or portions thereof in any
form except for the inclusion of brief quotations
in a review. All inquiries should be addressed
to York Press, Inc, 101 East 32nd Street, Baltimore,
Md. 21218

This book was manufactured in the United States of
America.

Library of Congress Number 75-19492

ISBN 0-912752-05-X

THE PSYCHOBIOLOGY OF CURT RICHTER

CONTENTS

Preface	*vii*
An Appreciation of Curt Richter, *by Eliot Stellar*	*xi*
Curt Richter: The Compleat Psychobiologist, *by Paul Rozin*	*xv*
Tribute to Curt Richter, *by Derek Denton*	*xxix*

Part I Activity and Cycles

A Behavioristic Study of the Activity of the Rat, *by Curt P. Richter*	3
Animal Behavior and Internal Drives, *by Curt P. Richter*	51
Biological Clocks in Medicine and Psychiatry: Shock-Phase Hypothesis, *by Curt P. Richter*	96
Sleep and Activity: Their Relation to the 24-Hour Clock, *by Curt Richter*	128
Some Observations on the Self-Stimulation Habits of Young Wild Animals, *by Curt P. Richter*	148

Part II Selection

Increased Salt Appetite in Adrenalectomized Rats, *by Curt P. Richter*	157

Nutritional Requirements for Normal Growth and Reproduction in Rats Studied by the Self Selection Method, *by Curt P. Richter, L. Emmett Holt, Jr., and Bruno Barelare, Jr.*   166

Salt Taste Thresholds of Normal and Adrenalectomized Rats, *by Curt P. Richter*   179

A Great Craving for Salt by a Child with Cortico-Adrenal Insufficiency, *by Lawson Wilkins and Curt P. Richter*   186

Total Self-Regulatory Functions in Animals and Human Beings, *by Curt P. Richter*   194

Self-Selection Studies on Coprophagy as a Source of Vitamin B Complex, *by Curt P. Richter and Katherine K. Rice*   227

Part III   Neurology

Decerebrate Rigidity of the Sloth, *by Curt P. Richter and Leo Henry Bartemeier*   245

The Production of the Grasp Reflex in Adult Macaques, by Experimental Frontal Lobe Lesions, *by Curt P. Richter*   264

The Significance of Changes in the Electrical Resistance of the Body during Sleep, *by Curt P. Richter*   277

Part IV   Domestication

Domestication of the Norway Rat and Its Implications for the Problem of Stress, *by Curt P. Richter*   289

On the Phenomenon of Sudden Death in Animals and Man, *by Curt P. Richter*   319

Taste and Solubility of Toxic Compounds in Poisoning of Rats and Man, *by Curt P. Richter*   330

Part V   Philosophy and Science

Experiences of a Reluctant Rat-Catcher: The Common Norway Rat— Friend or Enemy? *by Curt P. Richter*   353

Appendix: Complete Bibliography of Curt P. Richter   377

Index   389

PREFACE

Curt Richter's name is synonymous to many life scientists with outstanding scientific achievements in psychology, physiology, endocrinology and neurology. Richter has published widely in each of these disciplines; indeed many of his works are regarded as classic and definitive and serve as the very foundation for a number of contemporary scientific areas of physiobiological inquiry. Paradoxically, Richter himself has not received the recognition that his work and ideas have. Many of his best-known findings were presented during the 1920s and 1930s. While the data were often cited to buttress some theoretical notion made by this camp or that, Richter did not receive his just acclaim, so that today the findings, but not the source, are well known. Lack of appropriate recognition may also stem from the fact that Richter, because he was in the Department of Psychiatry, never had a Ph.D. student. His colleagues and students were medical students, postdoctoral fellows, visitors, and the occasional fortunate undergraduate. Consequently, after leaving Richter's Psychobiology Laboratory, they either resumed their own individual research careers or pursued more clinical pathways.

I expressed this concern to a number of colleagues, found that I had touched a responsive chord, and was encouraged to publish a tribute to Curt Richter. The traditional Festschrift was rejected because it became immediately apparent that the greatest honor that could be bestowed upon Curt Richter was to make widely available, in a single volume, his most significant contributions. This would, of course, familiarize a more general audience with Richter's enormous scope, but, even more importantly, this book provides us, through Richter's own writings, with the insights that have made his voice one of the most important in the life sciences.

A final pool of eighteen articles was divided into the categories of locomotor activity, selection, neurology and domestication; special emphasis being placed on selection—the area of Richter's research that is perhaps best known to psychologists, which embodies all of the major interests that Richter has had over the decades including behavior, endocrinology, neurology and physiology, and which is his most systematically explored area of interest. The *selection* articles start with Richter's first publication on this issue and allow the reader to follow the logical development of Richter's research strategy and insights, culminating in the 1942 Harvey Lectures.

Choosing the eighteen most important of Richter's works was an arduous task, as it was clear from the outset that eliminating any article from the text, let alone over three hundred, would make relatively unavailable many of the wonderful insights provided by Richter. After narrowing the list to about twenty-five articles, I visited Richter for the final culling process. There was an article on nest building that Richter wanted to be incorporated into the text that did not make the final list. I suggested that other articles made the major point better. Richter listened patiently, agreed with me, and then said, with his usual gentle smile, "Well, the main reason for including that one was that we had more fun doing that experiment than any of the others." Although we agreed that the article should not be included in *The Psychobiology of Curt Richter,* I promised that our discussion of it would be included. It captures the essence of Curt Richter, as a man and as a scientist. Richter's openness and enthusiasm are infectious. He combines an inordinate respect for the animal under investigation and a great capacity to work, with a childlike curiosity. Science is, therefore, an adventure, always new and exciting. The cardinal aims are to solve a biological mystery and to attempt to relate it to human behavior. Typically, Richter, has identified the behavior in question and after describing and measuring it with meticulous care, he has analyzed it, studying the internal and environmental stimuli that guide and direct it and the neurology that manages it. The analytic pathways that Richter has followed have been suggested by the animal and its relationship with its environment. Stimuli were therefore exaggerated and when the phenomenon is understood, it is certified with the counterexperiment of replacing what was removed. From this strategy of allowing the animal to dictate the analysis and from the immense joy of studying the behavior of animals, has emerged a marvelous series of simple but revealing experiments which now constitute Richter's legacy to Psychobiology.

The introductory chapter consists of three tributes that help convey this legacy. The first is by Eliot Stellar, a psychobiologist who was a colleague of Richter's at Johns Hopkins. The second is by Paul Rozin, a psychobiologist who, more than anyone else, has carried Richter's pioneering work on specific hungers, for substances other than salt, to a new level of sophistication. The third is by Derek Denton, a distinguished endocrinologist with a great interest in behavior, whose studies on the mechanisms of salt appetite in sheep are classic.

I have sought the counsel of a number of colleagues in selecting the articles that comprise this text, and wish to thank Drs. Paul Rozin, Alan Epstein and Eliot Stellar for their advice and encouragement. It is hoped that this volume has captured the essence of Curt Richter as a person and as the pioneer in psychobiology and that it allows his values to be passed on to succeeding generations of life scientists.

x

AN APPRECIATION OF CURT RICHTER

"A behaviorist with an organismic point of view, [Richter] saw that motivated behavior could be of adaptive value in the survival of the organism because of its essential contribution to the maintenance of the internal environment. Starting with the conceptualizations of Claude Bernard and with Cannon's homeostasis, Richter conceived of motivated behavior as self-regulatory behavior in the sense that it may correct deviations of the internal environment in cooperation with more automatic physiological mechanisms. . . . In his extensive investigations, Richter was able to show that the organism is actually sensitive to many of its own physiological needs and will develop motivated behavior appropriate to the correction of those needs and the maintenance of the internal environment."*

The substance of Curt Richter's major scientific contributions is presented in his own writings in this volume. I hope the spirit of the man also comes through to the reader, for in that spirit lies the explanation of his great success. It is hard to imagine the joy of scientific investigation unless you've witnessed it directly. To see curiosity and humbleness go hand in hand, to see unabashed enthusiasm for new ideas, to see excitement over little achievements that inevitably add up to a big picture, to see that weather-eye out for the new shape of understanding, all this is to see Curt Richter.

What's important about this is that it goes to the heart of scientific life, for here is a man who has spent well over fifty years in the laboratory. How else could he do it except for the sheer joy of it? All the temptations and distractions of life failed to derail Curt Richter. What a model for us all in this modern age of distractions and derail-

---

* From Alan N. Epstein, Harry R. Kissileff, and Eliot Stellar (eds.), *The Neurophysiology of Thirst*. Washington: Winston. 1973. p. 27.

ments! When I visited him in his familiar laboratory when he was in his late seventies, he said proudly, "My hand is steady and my eye is good and I operate three times a week." He was making lesions, he said, "to cut out the biological clock." I understood. He was working at the same small operating table I had seen him use almost thirty years earlier, and he had the same beautifully simple conception of what a scientific investigation was all about. It was simply the quest for big, clear phenomena of nature that instruct us so well. At that earlier time, he was cutting out endocrines and seeing the effects on specific hungers and activity. Later he was looking at wild rats, describing bait-shyness. All with the same enthusiasm.

In the biological-clock studies he had a simple, slow-moving kymograph that reset every 24 hours and showed that the onset of activity in the dark started later and later each day. The results were obvious. He could cut out the chart paper, letter it, photograph it and have a perfect illustration for publication. In the specific hunger and activity studies, he had Richter-running wheels, Richter-tubes for the various fluids, and it all got graphed on a simple chart that told the whole story.

It was beautifully simple. He delighted in the equipment he invented to solve his scientific problems. How do you handle a wild rat and inject him? You take the ribs of an old umbrella; cut it about a foot from the top; you sew a heavy sock to the cut ends; you cut the sock off at the ankle and tack the cut end around a two-inch hole in a piece of wood. (See Figure 1.) You hold the wood tightly over the wild rat's cage door and slide the door open. The wild rat leaps out through the hole in the wood, down the sock, nose up into the top of the umbrella ribs. The experimenter quickly grabs the cut end of the umbrella ribs near the sock and squeezes down hard. The wild rat is immobilized in place and the experimenter can inject him subcutaneously, intramuscularly, intraperitoneally, and even intravenously through the umbrella ribs. When the squeeze is let up, the rat leaps back into its cage.

He is just as enthusiastic about other people's gadgets. I'll never forget the first time he saw a drinkometer Harry Hill and I built, with relays going at 6–7 per second, counting off each tongue lap the rat made while drinking. "What a wonderful thing," he said, reeling off a half-dozen good experiments you could do with something like that. "I've got to have one of those. That's wonderful."

Curt Richter infected generations of students and younger colleagues. He made your ideas and findings seem worthy. He spurred you on. When he talked about his own fascinating work, as he did in the late fall of 1974 in Philadelphia, he enthralled the younger students and made their questions seem so worthwhile. Bold as ever, he proposed an evolutionary context for understanding biological rhythms. The students are still discussing it.

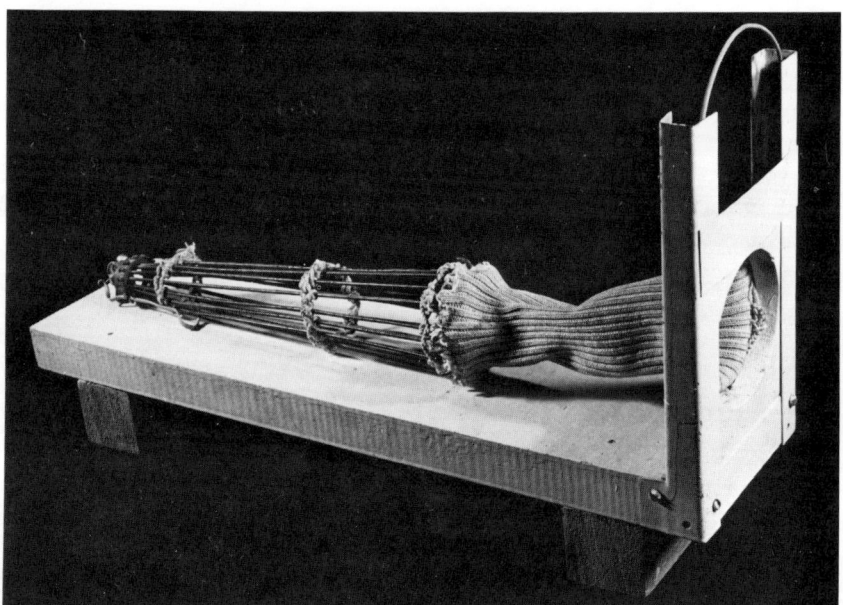

Fig. 1

Richter stories are legion and probably apocryphal. Parking his car at the Baltimore station, taking the train to New York and the boat to Europe and then getting out of the parking ticket upon his return when he explained to the police that he was an absent-minded professor. Some years ago he vaulted the six-foot-high pike fence at the Phipps clinic at Johns Hopkins late one night when Carl Pfaffmann and I had to carefully boost each other over. Even when he was eighty he beat everyone at tennis. Two or three times a week!

We dedicated the October 1974 Satellite Symposium on the Physiology of Food and Fluid Intake of the XXVI International Congress of Physiological Sciences in Jerusalem to Curt Richter and E. F. Adolph. Professor Richter didn't make it because, to his great chagrin, he slipped and fell while playing tennis and sustained a hairline fracture of the hip. Nevertheless, he functioned as honorary chairman right along with his colleague Professor Adolph, for it was clear to all of us that we were talking about the scientific problems he loved and bringing in the solutions he had forecast and set the stage for. This is the fabric of the great scientist. It is worn as a mantle by his many younger colleagues, for he has given something of himself to all of us.

Eliot Stellar
University of Pennsylvania
Philadelphia

CURT RICHTER: THE COMPLEAT PSYCHOBIOLOGIST

In the course of what he describes as an undistinguished undergraduate career at Harvard, Curt Richter was taken by the excitement of the burgeoning movement of behaviorism. And so, in the straightforward manner that always seems to characterize him, he set off in 1919 to visit the founder of behaviorism, John B. Watson. Richter's ability and enthusiasm must have impressed Watson, for he was accepted as Watson's student at the Johns Hopkins University. He was given some rats, a room in the medical school, and the general charge to find out something interesting. No graduate courses, no background biology courses. Just some animal subjects and an observant and inquiring mind. When there was something to be learned, there was a library, or the faculty. When he wanted to learn some anatomy, young Richter arranged to get a cadaver and taught himself. That is his style.

What began in that room in the Hopkins Medical School was a remarkable career. The immediate product, leading to a Ph.D. thesis in 1921, was a classic and definitive study on the nature and causation of spontaneous activity rhythms in rats (reprinted in this volume). Now, 56 years after Curt Richter entered that room in Hopkins to find something out, he is still working in the same room, and still finding things out. Descendents of the very same rats that "ran for science" in 1919 are still running in Richter's laboratory, now in widely used Richter-designed "activity wheels."

The single room has now become a few rooms. It is now and has for some time been called the Phipps Laboratory of Psychobiology. But the same young Curt Richter is inside: curious, indefatigable, original, always able to overcome technical barriers, always on to something interesting. In the course of his 56 years at Hopkins, Curt Richter has been away from his laboratory for only one extended period: a year at the Institute for Advanced Studies at Princeton. For the rest of the time, he has been exploring in the laboratory, with that unique mixture of basic scientist, practical problem solver and clinician that perhaps grows from his close affiliation with a medical school. The result has been a steady stream of high quality research papers that exemplify the best of the psychobiological approach: the study of both the mechanisms and adaptive values of biologically relevant behaviors.

The product of these years of hard work is staggering. Some 250 scientific papers and a book authored by Richter, and about 100 others authored by his students or colleagues from the Phipps Laboratory. These represent a broad scientific advance on a variety of problems. Indeed, there are few people who appreciate the full import of the work, simply because it is spread over so many diverse areas. I have had the pleasure of informing many of my colleagues that the Richter they thought had spent his whole life studying specific hungers had also made major contributions in a wide variety of other areas. Or, that the Richters of "sudden death," biological clocks, and self-selection were one and the same. This volume will surely serve to bring this point home, even as it only scratches the surface of this monumental contribution.

The diversity of Richter's interests and accomplishments is all the more remarkable because it does not come with the expected cost of superficiality. Amazing energy, dedication, and fine judgment about what to study have allowed Richter to study a substantial number of only tangentially related problems, in depth, over long periods of time. In short, Richter's accomplishment is characterized by *breadth in depth*. The breadth can be seen very clearly at the very beginning of his career. His first seven papers (1921–25) deal with the determinants of spontaneous activity, biological clocks, endocrine control of behavior, the origin of the electrical resistance of the skin, brain control of the motor system, and a device to aid in the measurement of salivation. All these beginnings developed into lifelong interests. (In these same seven papers are included studies of gastric innervation and a study of ritualized behaviors in frightened animals. These represent another side of Richter's diversity: individual incisive contributions that fall somewhat outside the main foci of interest.) The breadth of this total entry into the scientific literature is so great that none of his first seven papers refer to any of the others!

The depth of the interest and commitment to the six major themes laid down in the first papers can be seen in the fact that in 1937 and 1938, some 15 years later, Richter published at least one paper in each of these areas. And this in spite of the fact that his major preoccupation in this period was with a new interest: behavioral homeostasis as manifested in self-selection of nutrients. In subsequent years strong new commitments and contributions were made in the study of poisoning, domestication, and stress; but the initial interests are still salient today.

The sheer mass of the contribution, across a broad front of problems, can be gleaned by perusal of the bibliography published in this volume. For example, one year's work, 1938, included 12 papers; 11 with substantial empirical contributions, and one apparatus note. Seven of the papers dealt with food selection and behavioral homeostasis, including fundamental work on sodium hunger, water regulation in diabetcs insipidus, and some of the classic cafeteria experiments. Other papers dealt with spontaneous activity, the neurological basis of motor function, and biological clocks (in psychotic patients).

The hundreds of papers cover not only a broad range of topics, but an amazing variety of species. Most were done on humans (normal and diseased, of all ages) and on wild and domesticated Norway rats. However, he also worked with bullfrogs, alligators, chickens, hamsters, ground squirrels, mice, Alexandrine rats, rabbits, guinea pigs, beavers, porcupines, sloths, coatimundi, kinkajou, pigs, cats, dogs, spider monkeys, squirrel monkeys, and rhesus monkeys.

Richter truly deserves the title, the compleat psychobiologist, not so much for the breadth of his interest, but for the range and richness of his approaches. He begins his studies with careful observation of the phenomenon under study, usually a meaningful aspect of behavior. Like most psychologists, and in particular physiological psychologists, he is interested in mechanisms. He shares the general interest in accounting for behavior in the simplest possible terms: reflexes, synapses, neuro-endocrine links etc. However, he is also deeply interested in the evolutionary and developmental origins of behavior as well as in adaptive value of behavior. To understand a behavior, Richter tries to answer both evolutionary-ontogenetic and mechanistic questions: to me, this is the full psychobiological approach. Thus, in the first paper on activity, he examines the development of activity rhythms, their physiological basis in gastric contractions, the adaptive value of the activity spurts preceding feeding, their control by environmental factors, and comparative aspects of the relationship between activity, gastric contractions, and feeding in a number of species. This same psychobiological scope appears clearly in his work on domestication; physiological and behavioral analysis of the differences between wild and domestic rats go hand-in-hand with consideration of the adaptive value and evolutionary origins of domestication.

The typically brief Richter research report reveals a nose for important phenomena. From the welter of observations and research possibilities, he reliably selects those things that hold important and accessible secrets of nature. These phenomena are almost always big effects: sudden death, estrous activity rhythms, sodium hunger....

these are among the most robust phenomena in psychology. He has a talent for focusing in on the critical intersection of things that are of significance and things that are measurable. And he is a master of the art of measurement; of finding ways to reliably monitor interesting behavior, and thus make it subject to precise scientific investigation. He is the inventor of ingenious devices for measuring such things as activity, nest building, and electrical resistance of the skin. Sometimes the art of measurement shows up in an utterly simple technique, such as measuring the strength of the grasp reflex by the maximum time spent hanging from a wire by the hands. For many, a great talent for measurement would become an end in itself; how much of psychology is studying what is conveniently measured, rather than the interesting behavior behind the measurement? For Richter, ingenious measurement is just another aid in understanding. He always supplements his automated data collection with first hand observation. He keeps his eyes open.

These open eyes are always open to something new and revealing. Some of Richter's major lines of investigation originated as a result of "chance" observations. For example, observation of coprophagy by rats on a single food diet led to the coprophagy studies, observation of bizarre behavior in wild rats with their whiskers shaved led to the studies of stress and sudden death, and observations of unexplained deaths in the studies of responses to bitter tastes led to the work on poisoning. Much of this aspect of the Richter style is summed up by a quote from the French physiologist Magendie, which hangs on a plaque in Richter's laboratory: "Everyone compares himself to something more or less majestic in his own sphere, to Archimedes, Michaelangelo, Galileo, Descartes, and so on. Louis XIV compared himself to the sun. I am much more humble. I compare myself to a scavenger: with my hook in my hand and my pack on my back I go about the domain of science picking up what I can find."

Richter's research approach is individual oriented. Each subject is taken on its own terms: treatments are administered when there is an appropriate baseline, and the day-to-day behavior is monitored to determine the most opportune time for change. No lock-step designs of X days in Condition 1, and Y on Condition 2. Whenever possible, a subject is its own control. The kernel of this approach, which belongs to a classical physiology, is captured in what Richter, in a paper written in 1953, has called free, as opposed to design research. He points out that designs can limit the effectiveness of experiments and tend to discourage the opportunity for getting first hand information from the subjects. In keeping with the physiological tradition, particularly as represented by Claude Bernard, is the use of counterexperiments. After producing an effect, such as reduced activity after castration, he attempts a double confirmation (counterexperiment) by replacing the missing structure, transplanting the ovary, to see if he can recreate the original state.

The individual oriented approach means that the results from each animal are evaluated in terms of that animal. Individual differences are not accepted as statistical noise: rather they must be explained. Hence, the regular post-mortem pathology in Richter's animal experiments showing, for example, that individual differences in activity cycles after thyroidectomy can be explained in large part by the presence or absence of small residual amounts of thyroid tissue. The attention to individuals is seen clearly in most Richter experiments: the data from each animal are usually presented in tabular or graphic form. Simple descriptive statistics may or may not be used, but statistical inference is not a part of the picture. Basically, if it isn't clear in the records of individual animals, Curt Richter isn't very interested in it; he is after big game, and he always finds it.

All in all, it is a superb syle. If it needed validation, it has it in the extraordinary contribution that has resulted from it.

Richter has made major contributions in the areas of determinants of spontaneous activity, biological clocks, the neural organization of the motor system, organization and pathology of the autonomic nervous system, endocrine control of behavior, self-selection of food and specific hungers, nutrition studied through behavior, poisoning, stress, and domestication. In most of these areas, his contribution is not only large, but constitutes the pioneering work in the field. A major theme in much of the work is the adjustment of the whole organism, through behavior, to changes in the internal or external environments. Surely it is true that Richter stands as the spear carrier for the notion of homeostasis in the middle 20th century. Following on the work of Claude Bernard and Walter Cannon, he introduced the importance of behavior as a fundamental homeostatic mechanism: sometimes more sensitive than other physiological mechanisms, and absolutely fundamental in those areas of regulation such as feeding where intercourse with the environment is essential to preserve the constancy of the *milieu interne*.

Richter has faith in the appropriateness and importance of behavior as a subject for scientific investigation. He has demonstrated over and over again, the reliability and stability of behavior, and by relating it to its biological underpinnings, he has followed in the Pavlovian tradition of carving a place for the study of behavior in biology as well as psychology. The scientific validity of behavior is underlined when he uses it as a *means* to study physiological or metabolic processes. He made inferences about the functions of endocrine glands or the metabolic consequences of vitamin deficiencies from an animal's behavior. If "sloppy," "unstudyable" behavior could tell us about physiology, it must have scientific respectability. One might have hoped that the great success of psychophysics would have made the case for the power and scientific respectability of behavior, but a massive dose of evidence from Curt Richter was also required. A reading of this volume should convince anybody. As it turns out, Curt Richter's faith was contagious.

His work is also a testimony of the value of the study of animal behavior for understanding humans. Parallel studies on humans and animals were done in biological clocks, taste and the grasp reflex. Discussion of some problem in human psychology or biology appears in most of the research papers on animals. This is especially clear in the deep involvement with pathology. Pathology is used as a way to understand normal function. It is also something to be explained in itself. Many therapeutic or diagnostic insights have resulted from this work. Richter's work on alcoholism, dietary requirements in pregnancy, poisoning with anti-thyroid drugs, and damage to the sympathetic nervous system, led to clinical advances. He is also the author of a major theory of disease, the shock phase hypothesis.

Given that practically no single person is even reasonably familiar with all of Richter's main lines of work (many of which are not directly related to behavior homeostasis), I shall attempt a brief summary of the contributions, area by area, in roughly the order in which Richter began to study them. I shall emphasize those studies from the Phipps Laboratory on which Richter was actually an author; of course, in many cases, these were collaborative efforts with students and colleagues.*

Spontaneous Activity. In a way, it is remarkable that a neophyte investigator, working under the sponsorship of the leading proponent of a stimulus-response psychology, should set out to study *spontaneous* activity, that is, behavior largely under endogenous control. In fact, a major contribution of the early studies was to emphasize the importance of internal or endogenous factors in the control of behavior. This work set the stage for a full scientific study of activity by developing reliable techniques for measuring it, and showing the orderly relationship between activity and fundamental variables such as age, illumination, and temperature. Richter suggested that activity might be in part a thermoregulatory response, and noted, in this regard, a reciprocal relationship between nest building and running activity, as if they both shared a common role in temperature regulation. The powerful relationship between activity and feeding schedule was documented, and prefeeding activity spurts were related to gastric contractions. The

---

*The work described here includes substantial contributions from Wang in many areas of investigation, Langworthy and Hines in motor system neurology, Tower in sympathetic nervous system neurology, Barelare, Eckert, Hawkes, Rice and Schmidt in behavioral homeostasis and nutrition, Campbell in taste, Clisby, Dieke and Emlen in poisoning, and Mosier in domestication.

Curt Richter : The Compleat Psychobiologist xxi

secretions of the gonads, pituitary, adrenals and thyroid were all related to the maintenance of activity; removal of these glands led to decreased activity, and replacement therapy, by gland transplants or other means, led to increases in activity. Neural control was explored in a series of experiments showing a release of running activity in rats, monkeys and cats by bilateral removal of the frontal poles.

Biological Clocks. The same seminal paper that launched the studies of spontaneous activity in 1921 also initiated a lifelong study of biological clocks. The work in 1921 and the next decade or so was pioneering exploration of cyclical behavior in mammals, and was probably the first systematic study of the range of biological rhythms and their determinants in mammals, and possibly in vertebrates. Already in the 1921 studies, Richter noted that in shifting from a lighting schedule of 12 hour light, 12 hour dark to continuous darkness, the pattern of high activity in the previously dark 12 hours remained for some 12 days, strongly suggesting endogenous origins. Had Richter waited but a bit longer, he might have also discovered the circadian nature of these free-running rhythms.

Over the following 54 years, up to and including the present, Curt Richter has described an amazing variety of regular rhythms in behavior, primarily in rats and humans. For the most part, he has used activity as the eminently measurable hands for studying the biological clocks. However, he has also shown that mood changes, sleep patterns, and changes in the electrical resistance of the skin are controlled by clocks. More than anyone else, he seems to have been the person who clearly indicated the wide variety of biological rhythms in vertebrates; he himself described periods varying from a few hours to well over one year. He paid special attention to the rat's 24 hour activity rhythm, and the 4–5 day estrous activity rhythm, which he and Wang explained in terms of the ovarian endocrine cycle. He also described a fascinating 11–14 day rhythm in the rat, which appeared during pseudopregnancy or thyroid disturbance, after exposure to a number of agents or experiences that could be called general stressors. The involvement of endocrine (especially thyroid) mechanisms and stress in the emergence of new biological clocks suggested a hypothalamic control mechanism. This was confirmed by changes in rhythms consequent upon puncture lesions of the hypothalamus and represents the first clear implication of the hypothalamus in biological clocks. Richter (with his colleague, Wang) instituted a long search for the organ-basis of rhythms: through endocrine extirpations and implantations, he sought for the origin of activity rhythms in particular glands. He was most successful in uncovering ovarian control of activity rhythms; the four day estrous activity cycle was eliminated with ovariectomy, and reinstated with ovarian transplants.

In the now widely studied field of biological clocks, Richter stands out as the major figure to study the relationship between pathology and clocks. He described many cycles that appeared only in cases of human or rat pathology and developed these findings into what seems to me to be a major insight into rhythms and pathology: the *shock phase hypothesis*. Briefly, this states that in many organs or systems, individual cells go through cycles of activation which are randomly related, in phase, to the cycles of other cells in the same organ. This allows for relatively even organ function over time. In the face of various physiological insults or sudden stresses, the desynchronized cells may become synchronized, thus disclosing the presence of inherent cycles characteristic of each organ. This may lead to wide variations in the effectiveness of the organ over time, with possible pathological consequences.

Richter's contribution to the field of biological clocks is immeasurable. He was one of the major pioneers, if not *the* major pioneer, in the scientific study of biological rhythms. He developed the activity wheel, which seems to have been the first, and is certainly one of the most effective methods for continuous measurement of rhythms. Without such a tool, accurate and continuous data collection in sufficient quantity would be extraordinarily difficult. He has been one of the few people to systematically describe and study rhythms outside of the 24 hour cycle range. He was probably the first person to show the endogenous origin of rhythms in vertebrates, to relate mammalian rhythms to endocrine function, and to implicate the hypothalamus in the control of rhythms. He is the main figure in explicating the effects of a variety of pathological influences on rhythms, and the relationship of rhythms to pathology.

Neurology—The Organization of Motor Systems. Adopting a very functional adaptively oriented line of thought from the first, Richter showed the relationship between anatomical organization and function in the motor system through wisely chosen examples. He studied three species with unusual motor capacities: the porcupine with its quills, the beaver with its elaborated tail, and the sloth, with its flexor support mechanism, and showed in each case how the motor system was specialized to deal with these adaptations. The case of the sloth, reprinted in this volume, is a classic in neurology. Sherrington had shown that in the cat, decerebration produces a marked extensor rigidity—a caricature of the animal's normal posture—reflex standing. Richter showed that in the sloth, whose normal posture is hanging, decerebration produces reflex hanging—flexor rather than extensor rigidity. Thus, the consequences of decerebration can best be described functionally, as a release of activation of the muscles of support.

A series of studies on the electromyogram dealt with the fundamental issue of distinguishing voluntary from involuntary contractions, and the differentiation of a number of neuro-muscular or muscular diseases. In another, related series of experiments on humans and other primates, Richter described the disappearance of the reflexive grasp and appearance of voluntary grasping, the influence of drugs on reflexive grasping, and the release of reflexive grasping in adult animals by damage to the frontal lobes.

Neurology—The Organization of the Sympathetic Nervous System. Richter's studies of the autonomic nervous system fit with his pervasive interest in homeostasis, biological clocks, and stress. The work in this area revolved around a particularly useful technique he developed: measurement of the electrical resistance of the skin. Richter and his colleagues studied both the steady state resistance, varying slowly throughout the day and across subjects, and the rapid changes (psychogalvanic reflex) seen typically in response to sudden changes in the environment. Early work showed that the skin resistance and its changes were a function of the sympathetically controlled activity of the sweat glands. This work also provided what is probably one of the first instances of the paradigm commonly used now in psychophysiological studies of psychopathology. Richter found different diurnal patterns of skin resistance in normals as opposed to psychotics.

After these initial studies, the major focus of this research program veered off in the direction of clinical neurology. A convenient device to measure skin resistance, the dermometer, was developed and used in the diagnosis and evaluation of lesions of disturbances in the sympathetic nervous system. The increased resistance following damage to the sympathetic-innervation of a particular area permitted the mapping of sympathetic dermatomes through study of cases of selective sympathetic lesions. Extensive maps were developed, which showed a high degree of congruence between sensory and sympathetic dermatomes. The same techniques proved useful in the study of recovery of sympathetic function. Studies done with Tower traced the course of recovery after damage to the preganglionic fibers in animals, and the lack of recovery with postganglionic damage.

The Wisdom of the Whole Organism. Richter is probably most famous for his work in behavioral homeostasis. He called this whole organism involvement in homeostasis "total self-regulatory function" in the 1942 Harvey Lecture (reprinted here) which remains the most complete statement of this importance concept. Nutrient choice was the natural place to explore total organism involvement, since nutrients must ultimately be introduced from the outside environment, through ingestive behavior.

The interest in self-regulation dates back to the earliest work on activity. However, the major research program began in 1936. The study of adaptive self-selection was not itself a Richter innovation.

There were prior studies on farm animals, Davis' classic work on children, and Harris' work on specific hungers in rats. Similarly, other workers in Richter's time contributed significantly to this area: P. T. Young and E. M. Scott come immediately to mind. But it was Curt Richter who put it all together, and made a convincing, perhaps overwhelming case, for the wisdom of the total organism.

His first major set of findings was that rats suffering from sodium deficiencies showed increased preferences for sodium sources. There was a parallel finding of a remarkable sodium hunger in a human child (reprinted here) which is, to me, the most striking description in the literature of a specific hunger. On the basis of his studies, Richter theorized that sodium hunger was innate and involved some sort of change in the input from the taste receptors when they were stimulated by sodium ions. He established the critical role of taste with a technical tour-de-force in which he rendered rats ageusic by severing all three of the cranial nerves bilaterally (6 in all). Sodium hunger did not appear in these animals. The argument for innateness was based on the immediacy of the sodium preference in deficient animals, on the first occasion that they were sodium deficient, and on the fact that they showed an enhanced preference for sodium solutions with sodium levels so low that there could not be any significant beneficial effect of the ingested sodium. History has proven Richter correct on the innateness of sodium hunger. On the subject of changes in taste threshold as the basic mechanism, the verdict is uncertain, although it is clear that there must also be central factors involved.

The sodium work was followed by a large number of studies showing adaptive selection of foods under a wide variety of nutritional stresses. For most of these studies, Richter employed the cafeteria: a set of over 10 nutritional choices, including purified representatives of the major nutritional categories (e.g. protein, carbohydrate, fat, NaCl). Unlike his predecessors, he used purified rather than natural foods. The cafeteria succeeded marvelously. Rats grew extremely well on self-selection regimes, and showed growth equivalent to rats fed laboratory chow, while eating significantly fewer calories. He then used the self-selection paradigm to explore adaptive responses to a variety of nutritional stresses. In almost all cases, the rat was equal to the challenge, adjusting its intake to maximize its health and survival. Characteristic changes in selection were seen in pregnancy and lactation, including a clear increase in calcium intake in lactation, associated with the metabolic demands of milk synthesis. Parathyroidectomized rats showed the appropriate increase in calcium intake, pancreatectomized rats a drop in carbohydrate intake, adrenalectomized rats an increase in sodium intake. Vitamin deficient rats showed increases in intake of appropriate vitamin sources. Vitamin B deficient rats showed an increase in ingestion of rat feces (coprophagy), an adaptive response since the gut flora synthesize B vitamins.

Richter then turned the tables, and argued persuasively that changes in appetite that did not correspond to any presently known metabolic change were nonetheless suggestive of nutritional needs. His studies on food selection in riboflavin deficiency made direct suggestions about the role of riboflavin in metabolism. Other studies indicated a need for small amounts of galactose in fat metabolism. Along these same lines, there were studies of activity and survival time on single food choices, as a means of understanding the metabolic effects of particular nutrients. These revealing studies differed from traditional nutritional studies in that instead of removing one critical nutrient from an otherwise complete diet, the animal was studied when only this nutrient was available.

Richter also studied alcohol selection, a problem which, in fact, constituted his initiation into self-selection studies in 1926. He demonstrated that alcohol was appropriately treated as a food by rats. Unlike the human folk-wisdom of eating more food with alcohol, the rat eats less, and thus regulates caloric intake. These studies showed that rats could thrive over long periods of time with an alcohol solution (e.g. 8 percent in water) as their only source of fluids, and that addiction did not result. There are two other findings that seem to me to be of great potential importance in this area. One is that both humans (of all ages) and rats prefer low concentrations of alcohol in water to plain water, and that a small but significant minority of both species, including human children, show a preference for solutions of up to 50% alcohol. The other finding is that rats made hyperthyroid avoid alcohol. Coupled with his observation that the incidence of alcoholism is very low in hyperthyroid humans, there would seem to be promise of advances in the study and control of human alcoholism.

The emphasis in the self-selection work was primarily in showing how nutritional imbalance could be corrected by behavior. Part of the reason that Richter has had such an impact in this area comes from the sheer mass of material he has brought to bear on this issue. The nature of the mechanism underlying the food choice was often discussed, but not heavily investigated. Thus, Richter's studies focus on the steady-state adjustment to a nutritional stress, rather than the transition from one metabolic state to another. In general, Richter assumed that the rat's adjustments were innately programmed and guided by the sense of taste. In many respects, he generalized his extensive studies of sodium hunger to other specific hungers. As it happens, the rat's response to sodium is somewhat unique; it appears now that most other specific hungers have a significant learned component.

There is no doubt however that taste is a fundamental guide to nutrition independent of the role of learning. Starting with the observation that fundamental nutrients like sodium chloride and glucose had pleasant tastes to humans and were preferred by rats, Richter set out to explore the other side of the coin. Would bitter tastes, that were typically rejected, be associated with harmful substances? Supporting his view, he found that indeed many natural poisons were bitter, and instituted some studies of taste thresholds and preferences for a variety of substances in humans and rats. One result of these studies was the important observation of the similarity in the taste systems of humans and rats. Another result led to a new major research interest: poisoning.

Poisoning. A chance observation in experiments on responses to bitter tastes in rats: some phenythiocarbamide, a bitter anti-thyroid compound, was placed on the tongues of rats in order to observe their reactions. The next day, all the rats were dead. Add World War II, and governmental worries about enemy use of wild rats as vectors for the spread of disease, and so began another phase in Richter's career—the research for an effective rat poison. The search for a highly toxic but tasteless analog of phenylthiocarbamide yielded ANTU. ANTU was studied and found to be an excellent poison: highly toxic to rats but apparently with no taste, and most critically, not toxic to humans. The toxic actions of ANTU were investigated, as was the rat's response to poisoned foods: sensitization, tolerance, and poison avoidance. Cases of voluntary self-starvation was described in wild rats that, after having been poisoned a few times, refused all new foods. All this led to an ambitious rat extermination program in over 1000 square blocks of Baltimore, with census taking, development of procedures for setting out bait, estimating yields, etc. The result was a highly effective rat poison. This research program represents a superb example of the blending of basic research with the immediate needs of society. It also included one of the first two experimental studies on the effects of purified antithyroid compounds, which led to important clinical consequences for the treatment of thyroid disorders. Yet another consequence of this work was the introduction of wild rats, as experimental subjects, into the Phipps laboratory.

Domestication and Stress. An acute observer and insatiably curious investigator like Richter could hardly keep wild rats in his laboratory without being fascinated by their marked contrast with domestic rats. Possibly the most striking difference observed by Richter was the phenomenon of sudden death in wild rats. Whisker shaving, severe restraint, or forced swimming resulted in sudden death in significant numbers of wild rats. The deaths occurred much before physical exhaustion would have sufficed as an explanation. Richter showed that the death was not a result of sympathetic over-response, as one might have expected, but of parasympathetic overshoot. He suggested (in the article on sudden death reprinted in this volume) that this was consequent on a psychological feeling of hopelessness. This relates nicely to discussions by Cannon on voodoo death in humans.

The extreme response to stress in wild rats turned out to be only one of a whole catalog of differences between wild and domestic animals. These include larger adrenals, smaller gonads, a stronger tendency to attack, greater neophobia, and more successful poison avoidance in wild rats. With the establishment of a solid empirical base, typical of the Richter style, he then turned to explanation of the process of domestication. His reasonable theory, one of a few viable theories at this date, was that survival in the laboratory led to selection for lack of fierceness (handleability) and the ability to breed in the laboratory surroundings. Many of the wild-domestic differences, such as the larger gonads and lower neophobia in domesticated rats, fit with this simple explanation.

The whole enterprise of studying domestication in rats takes on more meaning when seen as a model for human "domestication." Richter has pointed out the similarities in the species: in geographical distribution, taste and food habits, and social life. The case he makes for the rat as a most opportune preparation for the study of domestication is convincing: the short life span, the great fund of knowledge on their physiology and behavior, and the ready availability of both domestic, and some would say, unfortunately, wild forms. He has pointed up some interesting parallels, such as the decrease in adrenal size in domestic rats and the parallel increase in humans of diseases related to adrenal insufficiency, such as arthritis.

Other Contributions. Richter's work includes much more, but it does not always fit easily under the topics already discussed. It includes studies on sleep and its pathology, self-stimulation in animals (reprinted here), anatomical studies, and methods for studying the nervous system. There is a distinguished contribution in the area of endocrinology, some of which has been described already under other headings, but also including studies of pituitary function and the etiology of diabetes insipidus. His behavioral studies have involved all the major endocrine glands, and physiological and anatomical studies on many of them.

An Appreciation. I have a sad suspicion that a review of Curt Richter's contribution might be accomplished more compactly by describing what he has *not* found out. There is one major area of psychobiology that he has not seriously explored: learning and plasticity. It is possibly no accident that this area is the least advanced in the field. But in recent years there has been a spurt of activity in the psychobiology of learning, based largely on the idea of specific, problem-oriented learning abilities. The most influential example of the "new" type of learning studies concerns the specialized learning abilities rats bring to bear in successfully avoiding poisons. It was Curt Richter who, in 1953, did one of the first and clearest studies demonstrating poison avoidance in the rat under controlled laboratory conditions. In 1946, in discussing some of his earliest work on poison avoidance, Richter said, "The basis for this refusal response has not been determined. It could depend on association of ill effects with the taste of ANTU or with the smell." Although Richter did not pursue this line, he laid the groundwork for this very active area.

For 54 years, Curt Richter has been providing us with a steady stream of interesting observations, well-controlled and highly repeatable experiments, new methods and devices to aid in the study of behavior, creative ideas, and instance after instance of the fertility of work on animals for the understanding of humans. He has done it within a broad psychobiological perspective, using an individual oriented style. It is a simple style: no computers, no analyses of variance.

I heard Curt Richter give a talk last year. It dealt with the consequences of the harnessing of fire by humans on their diurnal cyclicity, physiology and behavior. I just read a paper published in 1975 by Curt Richter on the effect of hypothermia on spontaneous activity rhythms. The activity cages are still clicking in the Phipps Laboratory, the nose for phenomena and open eyes are still at work, and Curt Richter, at 81, is still opening up new vistas for all of us.

Paul Rozin
The University of
  Pennsylvania

TRIBUTE TO CURT RICHTER

I first heard of Dr. Curt Richter's work when I was a medical student recently arrived in Melbourne from Tasmania in the mid-1940's. In those days with communications as they were, and Australia relatively isolated, an important event was the occasional talk by a returned traveller telling what seemed novel and exciting in the outside scientific world. One evening I went to hear a talk by Dr. F. M. Burnet, Director of the Walter & Eliza Hall Institute. He recounted what he had seen in virology, his current field of investigation. He then went on to describe what he said had interested him a great deal more than anything encountered in virology—namely, a visit to Dr. Richter's laboratory at Johns Hopkins Hospital in Baltimore, and seeing his remarkable experiments on self-regulating diet selection by animals, which Burnet recounted in some detail. And, of course, the outstanding experimental investigations of Curt Richter, widely known then, have continued to the present, and the many who have known him from other countries have always been intrigued to visit him or learn from journals or symposia what fascinating questions he was trying to answer next.

This early work on self-regulating functions was in the mainstream of a great physiological concept enunciated by Bernard and elaborated by Pflüger, Fredericq, Richet, and Cannon. What Richter proposed, as a result of his comprehensive and ingenious experiments, was that homeostasis may be maintained by the operation of behaviour regulators—responses of the total organism—as well as by the diverse physiological regulators of the internal environment. Thus, the study of drives, or some of them at least, was given a more concrete basis in terms of efforts of the total organism to maintain a constant internal environment. The pioneering experiments in rats mainly centered on the effects of endocrine gland ablations and the capacity of the organism to select and maintain life in the simple choice situation. The effect of adrenalectomy on choice of hypertonic NaCl, parathyroidectomy on the choice of calcium lactate or other calcium salts, removal of the posterior lobe of the pituitary on water intake, of hypophysectomy or thyroidectomy on nest building activity, pancreatectomy on carbohydrate and other choices in a cafeteria situation involving twelve components were studied, and the striking regulatory capacities of the organism and the importance of taste mechanisms was demonstrated. He generated the first systematic experimental consideration of self-regulatory functions in gestation and lactation, and showed the development of specific appetites. The basis of some of his observations in 1942 have only recently been partly elucidated by the demonstration, independently of the intake of body sodium balance, of direct appetite-generating effects of certain ovarian, adrenal, and pituitary hormones involved in the reproductive process. Many of his results in this area remain unexplained and will, no doubt, stimulate new studies for years to come. Characteristically his examination of the subject covered the broadest biological ground involving picas, infantiphagia, placentiphagia, geophagy, and osteophagia.

In addition to ingestion behaviour, the conditions of his experimental design with systematic record of activity of his animals revealed many aspects of cyclical behaviour which were endocrinologically determined. The baseline data initiated a wealth of intriguing investigations by him in this field ranging as widely as the long-term effects of administration of specific drugs, or acute episodes of dire stress on periodic behaviour patterns which have never been adequately explained, to the biological clocks determinant of various medical and psychiatric illness.

He has also experimentally investigated and deeply considered the behavioral, endocrinological and neurophysiological changes involved in domestication of wild species, and raised many intriguing questions in relation to the analogous transitional processes in man.

It is presumably not the role of those invited to contribute some introductory remarks to this volume of selected papers of Richter's to endeavour to catalogue the diversity of original findings involved, or for that matter to try to do so in relation to the entire contribution that is represented by his extensive bibliography. Overall, in looking at the history of endocrinology during this century, it can be said that in the field of behavioral implications of internal secretions Richter's contribution has been outstanding and the unique one. His originality and genius in demonstrating and elucidating the chemical and hormonal determination of innate behavior patterns complements, and is of comparable stature, to the contributions to understanding of the role of specific exteroceptor cues in innate behaviour which have been made over the same period by the ethological scientists.

Derek Denton
Howard Florey Institute of
  Experimental Physiology and Medicine
University of Melbourne
Parkville, Victoria, Australia

Part I ACTIVITY AND CYCLES

A BEHAVIORISTIC STUDY OF THE ACTIVITY OF THE RAT

Introduction

Interest in human psychology is moving rapidly toward problems of general adaptation involving responses of the whole organism in actual working life-situations. This change of interest is due probably in large part to the healthy impetus given to psychological research by recent work and discoveries in the allied field of psychiatry. But, undoubtedly, it is also due to the strong influences from biology, especially that part of biology which is spoken of as behavior.

This change of interest is probably more radical than it appears at first glance. It really represents an entirely different approach to things. The older psychology began with the study of the function of parts of the organisms, isolated responses (witness the work on sensations and memory) and then attempted to put these parts together. The error was made in neglecting the fact that the integration of parts often produces something—a novelty (Holt)—which could never be predicted from the study of the function of the parts alone. This older psychology was further characterized by a complete unwillingness to see the biological aspects of the organism's reactions, the place of the reactions in the life situations.

The trend of present day psychology stands in marked contrast to this older view. The tendency is now to begin with the study of the responses of the total organism—intact—and in the situation in which it ordinarily finds itself. Here the biological aspects of the problems stand

This paper was originally published in *Comparative Psychology Monographs*, Vol. 1, Serial 2, September, 1922. Reprinted by permission.

decidedly to the fore as is evidenced by the general current usage of such terms as adaptation, responses, reactions, adjustments. It is the behavior of the organism that is of most interest, what the organism *does,* and how it *works.*

By what the organism does, is meant simply the description of all of the operations and activities involved in the adjustment of the organism to its environment. This would include the description of the objects in the environment responded to, the nature and kind of responses made to these objects, the various activities elicited by these objects. Further this would include also an account of the interrelation of these different activities, hunger, sex, social and work activities, for instance, the rôle played by each, the relative importance of each in the life adjustment of the organism.

The problem of how the organism *works* deals with the more dynamic aspects of behavior. This requires in the first place the determination of the origin of the organism's activity, what it is that *drives* it, so to speak, about in the environment. Further, a knowledge of the working of an organism requires a description of how the various specific responses are set up as the organism is driven about in the environment, how these responses are knit together. Here belongs also a knowledge of how the development and knitting together of the responses are affected by such factors as early frights, shocks, trauma, distortions and limitations of activities.

At present these problems can not easily be attacked in humans for obvious reasons, despite the fact that many abnormal patients may be considered as Adolf Meyer so interestingly suggests, as "experiments of nature." In most humans the early determining factors are rarely definitely known and controlled. Because of these difficulties recourse must be had for the present to study of the behavior of animals, where the life situations are after all very much less complicated, and where the activities and reactions may be changed and distorted at will under controlled conditions.

It is largely for the solution of problems of this nature that animal psychology must be looked to for help in the future. Work in this field is at present at a very low ebb, chiefly for the reason that investigators have limited their interests almost completely to the study of the part reactions of animals (reactions to lights, colors, sounds, learning problems) and have entirely neglected the broader biological aspects of the lives of animals.

The work presented in the following pages represents an attempt to attack these problems from the angle of the life and responses of the whole organism. The attack is made on the most easily approachable and least difficult points. It includes only a small part of the total behavior problem, the study of gross bodily activity before it has become specifically connected with any of the many complicated features of the environment. The relation of this activity to certain vital factors of the environment, food, temperature, illumination is first examined. This is followed by an examination of the origin of the activity, what it is that causes the animal's activity. Finally the relation of this diffuse undirected activity to one of the animal's most important specific responses, its food-seeking activity (hunger reaction), is examined.

In making this study of the gross bodily activity of the rat the emphasis is laid throughout on what the animals do of their own accord, free from all external stimulation. For after all, there is a marked difference however not well recognized, between what an organism can be made to do and what it does of its own account (internal stimuli). The emphasis is usually placed on the former, that is on the training element—this is true particularly in the whole field of education probably even more so than in the field of animal psychology. Interest has only recently begun to be directed toward the spontaneous activities of humans and animals.

The present work was carried on in the Psychological Laboratory of the Johns Hopkins University under the direction of Dr. John B. Watson. I am deeply indebted to Dr. Watson for his help and encouragement and for the complete freedom allowed me in carrying on my work. The inspiration to this work came to a very great extent from the numerous suggestive experiments of Cannon and Carlson on the hunger problem. It came also from the behavior work of Jennings on the lower organisms and from the many stimulating experiments of Szymanski on activity problems. I am very much indebted to all of these workers. I am indebted for help and criticism to Dr. Edwin B. Holt, Dr. Knight Dunlap, Dr. H. H. Donaldson, and Dr. E. Sanford. I am also indebted to my friends Mr. Ging Wang and Mr. David Brunswick for many helpful suggestions and assistance.

I. Periodic Nature of Spontaneous Activity

For carrying out the purposes of the following experiments two things were required: (1) A situation as free as possible from all active external stimulation, and (2) an arrangement for recording the activity of animals over long periods of time without in any way stimulating the animals themselves.

The conditions of the first requirement were met in the following way. Noises were eliminated by carrying on the experiments in a room fitted with large double sound-proof doors and very thick sound-proof walls. All avoidable odours were taken care of by a very good ventilation system. The air was always fresh and free from the usual odors found in animal laboratories. The room was made completely impervious to light rays from the outside by placing heavy covering of cloth and many layers of thick opaque paper over the window. Because of the double doors and thick wall the room was also almost completely impervious to temperature changes from the outside. It was possible to maintain the temperature at one constant level for weeks at a time. The conditions of the second requirement were met by means of the construction of small triangular shaped wire cages large enough to permit the animals to move about freely. A photograph of one of these cages is shown in figure 1. This cage is 10 inches high and each side is 14 inches long. It has an aluminum bottom fastened to the cage. The bottom is supported under each corner on a rubber membrane stretched tightly over a large tambour. The tambours are connected together immediately under the cage into one tube which is led to a small Marey tambour, the lever of which records on the smoked paper of a kymograph. By this means every movement of the animal, even the slightest, is recorded on the drum with a single mark. The cage and support are rigid enough to prevent any stimulation arising from shaking of the cage or from insecurity of foot-hold.

The attack on this problem of the spontaneous gross bodily activity of the rat was begun with the simple experiment of observing what happens to activity when the animals are placed in a situation described above

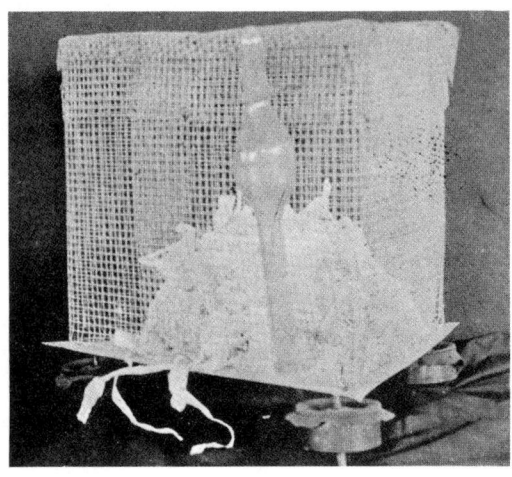

Fig. 1. Activity Cage

A Behavioristic Study of the Activity of the Rat

free from all stimulation in constant complete darkness. A typical record obtained from an animal under these conditions is shown in figure 2. It is seen that that rat is alternately active and inactive and that the regularity of the recurrence of the periods is quite striking. This regularity is brought out even better in figure 23. Frequently when the conditions of the experiments are particularly well controlled the differences in the intervals between the periods does not vary more than just a few minutes.

The rate of the periods was found to vary with the age of the animals. In very young animals this rate is most rapid, averaging about fifteen for the twenty-four hours. In old animals the rate averages about ten. The length of the activity periods also shows some variation with age, being longer in younger animals and becoming progressively shorter in older animals.

Szymanski (1) has recently also studied the activity of the rat along with the activity of many different animals, from the simplest insects to the human infant. He used an "Aktograph" for his work on rats—a device very similar to the activity cage described above, except that it is supported on springs and registers activity directly with a lever rather than pneumatically. Szymanski found that the activity of the rat is divided into ten periods per twenty-four hours. What was found in the experiment above seems to agree fairly well with this result, except that Szymanski makes no statement as to the age of the animals that he used for his experiments. He did not notice the great regularity of the recurrence of the periods probably for the reason that he made no attempt to keep the conditions of the experiment constant over longer periods of time. He did his work in an ordinary room subject to the daily changes of temperature and illumination due to the day and night on the outside.

For the reason that the rat shows a number of periods during the twenty-four hours Szymanski speaks of it as a polyphasic animal in contrast to

Fig. 2. Record of Spontaneous Activity Showing Regular Recurrence of Periods of Activity (Time in Hours.)

the monophasic animals, like the human adult for instance, which show only one long period of activity and one period of inactivity during the twenty-four hours. That this classification is of somewhat doubtful value, and that it describes their reactions to external stimuli rather than the function of any mechanism inherent in the organism itself may be brought out by the consideration of some experiments on the human infant and adults carried out in the Phipps Clinic Psychological Laboratory during the past year by Miss Tomi Wada of Columbia University (11).

Miss Wada was able to confirm on humans what was found in the experiments on rats. She used the same technique that was employed in the rat work. In the human infant she found that the same regularity of the alternation of the periods of activity and inactivity prevails. She obtained her records chiefly during the long period of sleep at night. The frequent interruptions for feeding and bathing etc. make it difficult to obtain records of activity during the day. A typical curve of the activity of a ten months infant during sleep is shown in figure 3. These periods come at the rate of one every fifty to fifty-five minutes. The regularity of these periods is very striking. Miss Wada found further that the activity of the human adult during sleep is also periodic. The interval between the periods in the adult is however considerably longer than in the infant, usually about one and one half to two hours.

Experiments are now being carried on by Mr. Ging Wang in the Hopkins Laboratory on the activity of the newly born rat before it has had any contacts with the environment, before it has ever nursed, in order to establish whether the periods are present at birth or dependent on later environmental influences. The results obtained so far seem to indicate that the activity at birth is continuous and uninterrupted by regular intervals of quiescence.

The probable relation of these activity periods to certain environmental influences (the hunger reactions) as well as to the rest of the behavior of the organism will be discussed in detail in the last two sections.

II. Relation of Spontaneous Activity to Food

It was found at the beginning of this work that the spontaneous activity of the rat is very intimately related to the food habits of the animal. This relation will now be examined in some detail from the following points of view: (1) what happens to spontaneous activity (simply the amount of activity, disregarding for the moment the peri-

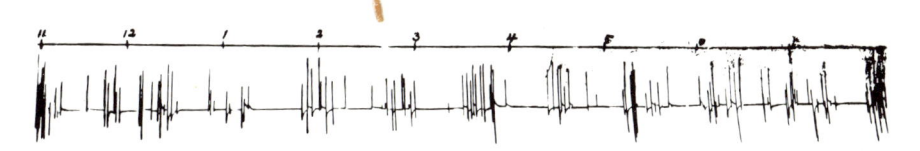

Fig. 3. Record of Spontaneous Activity of Ten Months Human Infant During Uninterrupted Sleep (Time in Hours. From Work of Miss Tomi Wada.)

ods of activity) when the animal is deprived of all food, when it is starved; (2) how spontaneous activity is distributed over the day with relation to the last feeding periods and also with relation to the time of next feeding (anticipation of feeding).

The general conditions were maintained practically the same as above. The laboratory was kept constantly either illuminated or darkened over longer periods of time. The temperature was kept constant at 23°C. All noises and odors were eliminated.

The animals were fed punctually at a certain time each day (in most of the experiments at twelve noon). Food was placed in each cage in specially arranged receptacles and left there for twenty-five minutes. Then all of the remaining food was carefully removed. This method of feeding gave each animal plenty of time to satisfy its hunger under fairly natural conditions. It also ensured an accurate control of the amount of food eaten from day to day. Actual weighing of the food showed that the amount eaten in twenty minutes remains almost constant from day to day. The animals developed normally on this method of feeding.[1]

For the first part of the experiment eight animals were used. Normal activity records were taken for five days preceding the beginning of starvation. Four of the animals of this group were also deprived of

---

[1] In this present work a synthetic diet was used after the formula of Dr. E. V. McCollum of the School of Hygiene, Johns Hopkins University. This is an excellent diet. For behavior work on the rat it is ideal.

```
Flour (graham) ............................................. 72.5
Casein ..................................................... 10.0
Milk powder (skimmed) ..................................... 10.0
Calcium carbonate .......................................... 1.5
Salt ....................................................... 1.0
Butter fat ................................................. 5.0
```

The importance of using a good diet for all animal behavior work was convincingly demonstrated by the findings of Dr. E. V McCollum in connection with work on feeding problems. He found that the maternal reactions, nest-building, caring for young, nursing, are absent in animals fed on poorly balanced diets especially diets low in proteins. These animals often eat their young.

water after the five days in order to obtain additional information on the relation of activity to water intake.

The amount of activity per day was obtained by counting the marks made on the smoked paper by each movement of the animal in the activity cage described above. The kymograph was set running just fast enough to enable the marks to be recorded individually.

Three of the animals starved but permitted to have water all the time showed a definite increase in activity for the first two to three days after the beginning of starvation and then a steady marked decrease to a point of almost complete inactivity on the eighth day. All of the animals deprived of both food and water showed a steady marked decrease in activity immediately. This group reached the point of complete inactivity already on the fifth day. The results of this experiment are shown in figure 4 where the days of the experiment are given

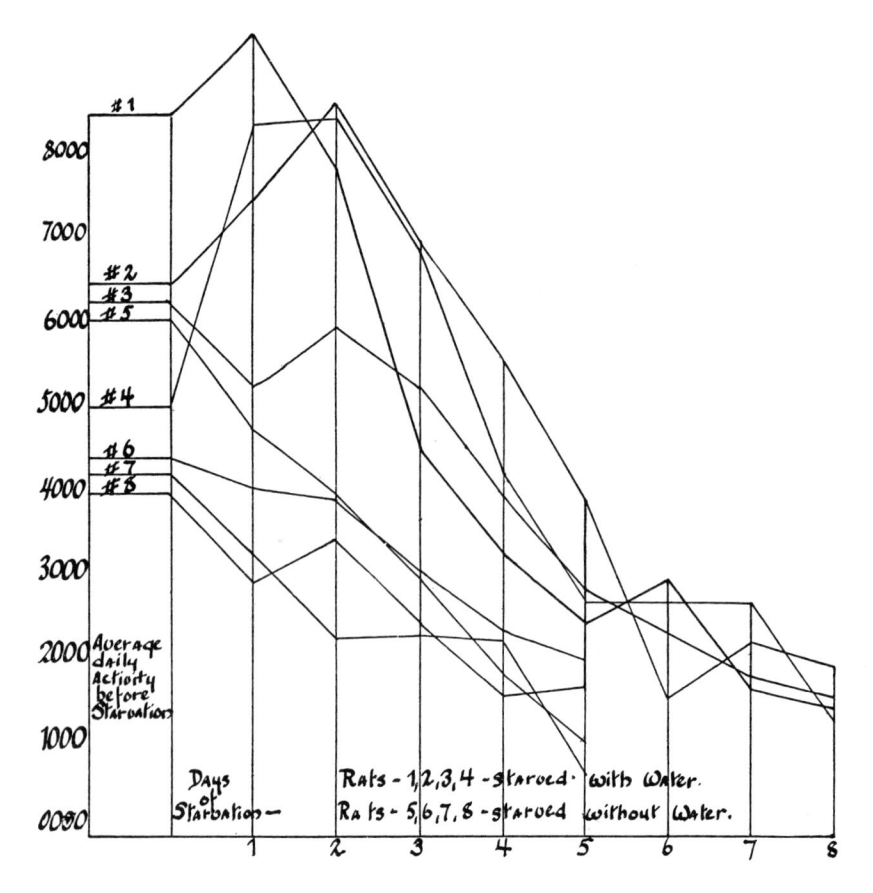

Fig. 4. Starvation Experiment

on the abscissae and the total amount of activity per day in activity units (single marks on the kymograph paper) on the ordinates. The average daily activity for the five days preceding the experiment is given on the first ordinate.

In the next experiment on the distribution of activity with relation to the time of feeding it was first undertaken to determine simply how the amount of activity of the first half of the day (the first twelve hours after the feeding period) compares with the activity during the second half. It was found that the activity during the first twelve hours is very much greater than during the second twelve. But the ratio of the amount of activity during the first twelve hours to the activity during the second was found to depend on the age of the animal. This is shown in figure 5 where the age in days is given on the abscissae and the ratio of the amount of activity during the first and second halves of the day are given on the ordinates. It is seen that the very young animals are almost twice as active during the twelve hours immediately following the daily meal than during the next twelve. In the very old animals the amount of activity during these two periods is almost evened out. This curve is based on records from thirty-five animals of three different ages.

When instead of dividing the twenty-four hours following the time of feeding into two twelve-hour periods they are divided into one hour periods, the curve of the distribution of activity has a very characteristic form. Such a curve is shown in figure 6. This curve is based on the records obtained from forty animals 250 days old. In this figure the time of the day is indicated on the abscissae in hours, while the amount of activity per hour is indicated on the ordinates. The animals were fed at 12 o'clock noon. The room was kept in constant illumination. It is

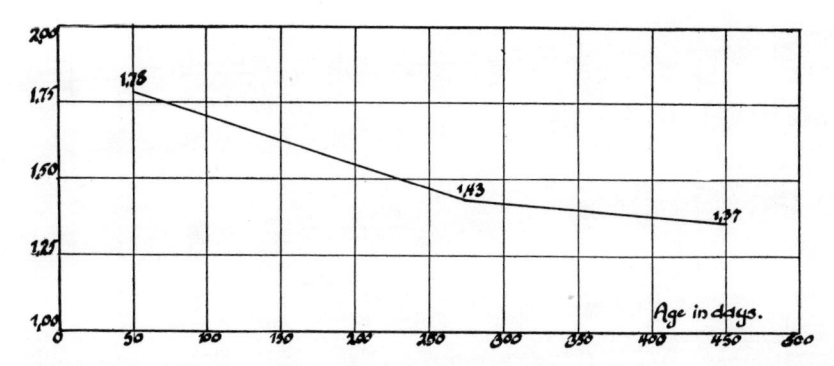

Fig. 5. Ratios of Total Amount of Activity During First and Second Twelve Hour Periods Following Single Daily Meal

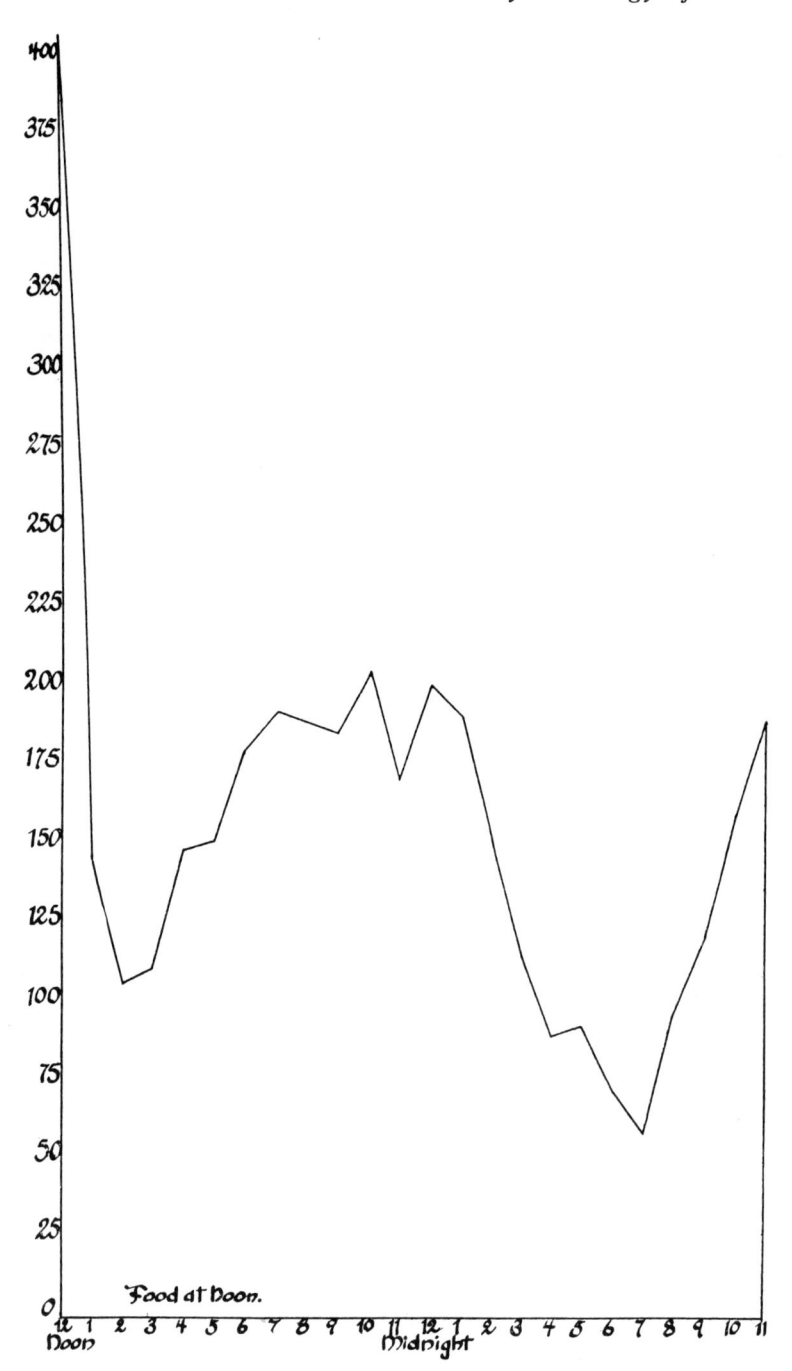

Fig. 6. Curve Showing Distribution of Spontaneous Activity During Twenty-Four Hours with Relation to Time of Feeding
    Time is given on the abscissae in hours. The amount of activity during each hour is given on the ordinates. For animal 250 days old.

seen that immediately following the daily feeding period there is a period of relative inactivity lasting from four to five hours. Then there follows a period of very intense activity for eight to ten hours. This is followed in turn by a period, lasting from five to seven hours, of almost complete inactivity. During the last two to three hours of the twenty-four the activity increases very rapidly again right up to the time of the next feeding period.

In order to avoid misunderstanding it may be well to emphasize here that this curve is a composite curve made up of the individual curves of forty animals. The individual curves of course look rather different. A typical individual curve is shown in figures 17 and 18. In these curves the alternation of periods of activity and inactivity stands out very clearly. These periods give the curves a very ragged and irregular outline. The general form of these curves corresponds however to that of the composite curve shown in figure 6. During the inactive parts of the curve the amount of activity in each activity period is relatively very small but the periods are present nevertheless. The discrepancy between Szymanski's results and the results presented in the previous section on the number of activity periods per day may be due to the fact that Szymanski failed to take these small periods into account. The importance of these small periods will be brought out in another place.

The activity distribution curve shown in figure 6 was for animals 250 days old. The form of this curve becomes very much modified in very young animals and as well in very old animals. In the former the "hump" of activity begins almost immediately after the daily feeding period, figure 7, while in the latter its onset is very much delayed. The "hump" of activity is most striking in animals about 200 days old. After that age it becomes less and less marked until in old age, over two years, the curve becomes smoothed out and the hump is obliterated. This is shown schematically in figure 8.

In order to make certain that the shape of the activity distribution curve shown in figure 6 did not depend on any external factors, for instance very slight changes of illumination imperceptible to the human eye due to the daily change of light and darkness on the outside of the laboratory, or else that the curve did not depend on the general city noises and sounds of the day, the time of feeding was changed from 12 o'clock noon to 12 o'clock midnight, also to 8 o'clock in the evening. In all cases the shape of the curve remained practically the same. This was true also when records were taken during constant illumination which seems rather conclusive evidence against changes in illumination having anything to do with results obtained.

These experiments show that the rat is naturally inactive for a time

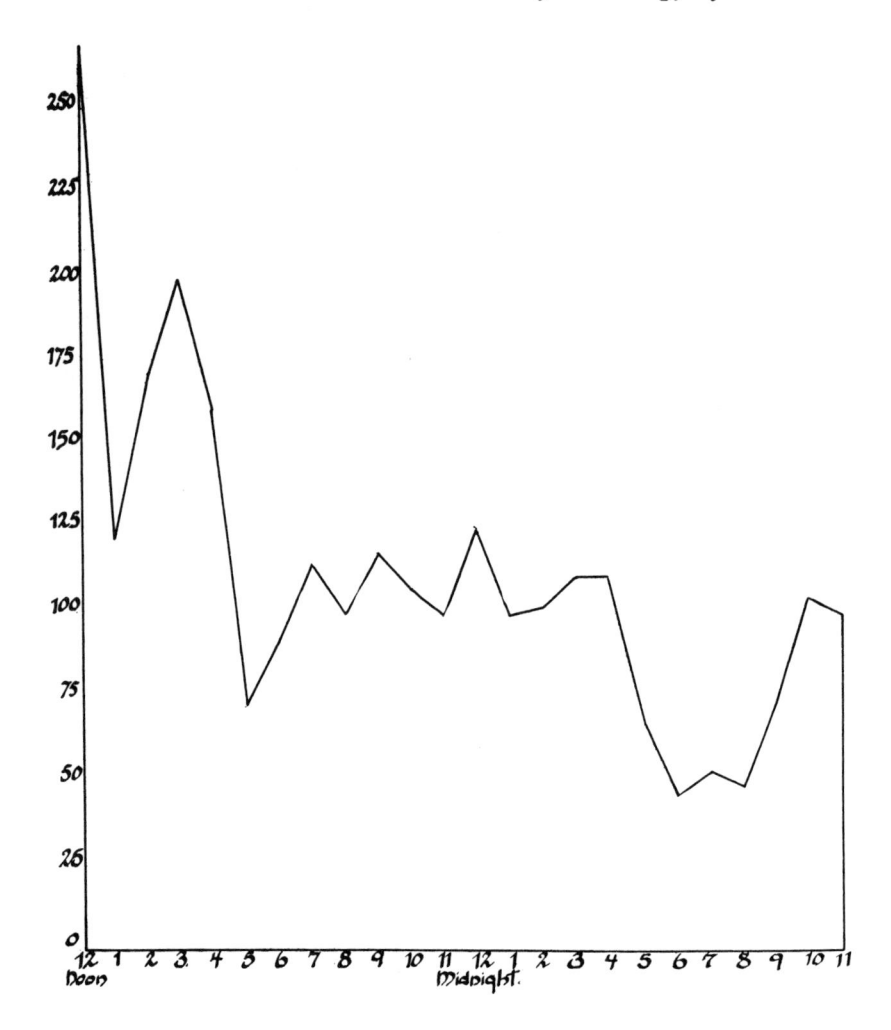

Fig. 7. Curve Showing Distribution of Spontaneous Activity with Relation to Time of Feeding. For Animals About Forty Days Old.

after eating, and that it does not become active again of its own accord for several hours afterwards. These results bear out essentially the observations man has made on his own behavior, for there is a general saying that it is not a good thing to work directly after eating. Sayings of this nature are frequently apt to be colored by fictions and superstitions, but this one seems to be based on fact. If the same curve holds for man that holds for the rat it would then seem advisable for man when he has work to do, to do it during the period of maximum spontaneous activity, that is when the body coöperates, rather than

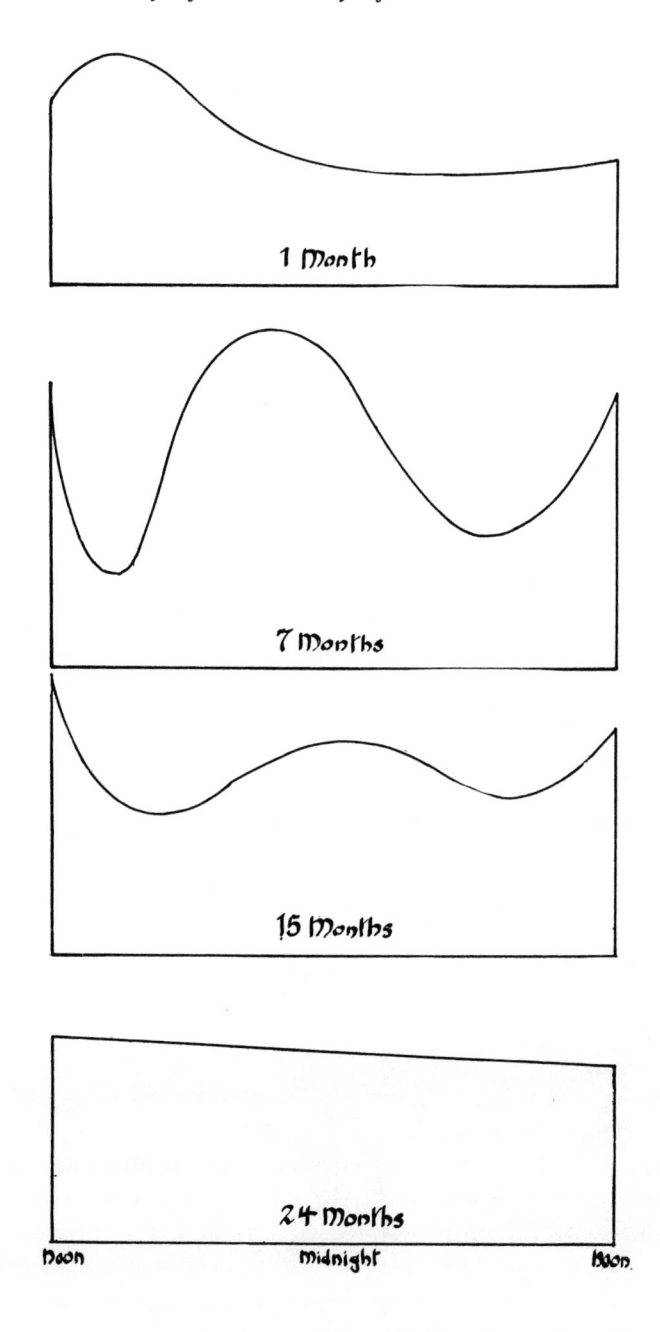

A Behavioristic Study of the Activity of the Rat 15

Fig. 8. Schematic Curves for Different Aged Animals Showing How Spontaneous Activity Is Distributed Over the Twenty-Four Hours with Relation to Time of Single Daily Feeding

during the period of natural inactivity when the body does not coöperate.

III. Relation of Spontaneous Activity to External Temperature

Temperature and illumination are factors which are present in the environment of all organisms at all times and which can never be eliminated. They are vital factors. They are present in all situations from the simplest to the most complex, so that a thorough knowledge of their relation to activity is of prime importance for the solution of any kind of behavior problems.

The difficulties of studying the relation of behavior to external temperature in animals are many. A rather highly specialized equipment and technique for obtaining and controlling temperatures at all levels are absolutely essential. Without them conclusive results are obtained only with the greatest difficulty. In the present work many different temperature experiments were tried, but with the exception of one or two all of them failed to give satisfactory results.

The following experiments deal only with the modifications of the normal activity distribution curve, described in the previous section, with relation to external temperatures. The conditions of these experiments were essentially the same as for the others. The experiments were carried out over long periods of constant illumination and constant complete darkness. Higher temperatures than the normal 23°C. were obtained by means of two electric heaters, while temperatures lower than normal were obtained from natural sources during the cold months of winter.

The results of these experiments showed that the characteristic shape of the activity distribution curve is very definitely affected by changes in external temperature. These modifications affect chiefly the position of the period of maximum activity—the "hump" in the curve. In a comparatively low temperature 10° to 15°C. this period of maximum activity begins almost immediately after the daily feeding period. The usual interval of relative quiescence following the taking of food is absent. This may be seen in figure 9. This curve is based on the records of four animals of from 200 to 300 days old, taken in an external temperature of 12° to 13°C. In a temperature considerably higher than the normal 29° to 30°C. on the other hand, the onset of the period of activity is very much delayed. The interval of quiescence following the

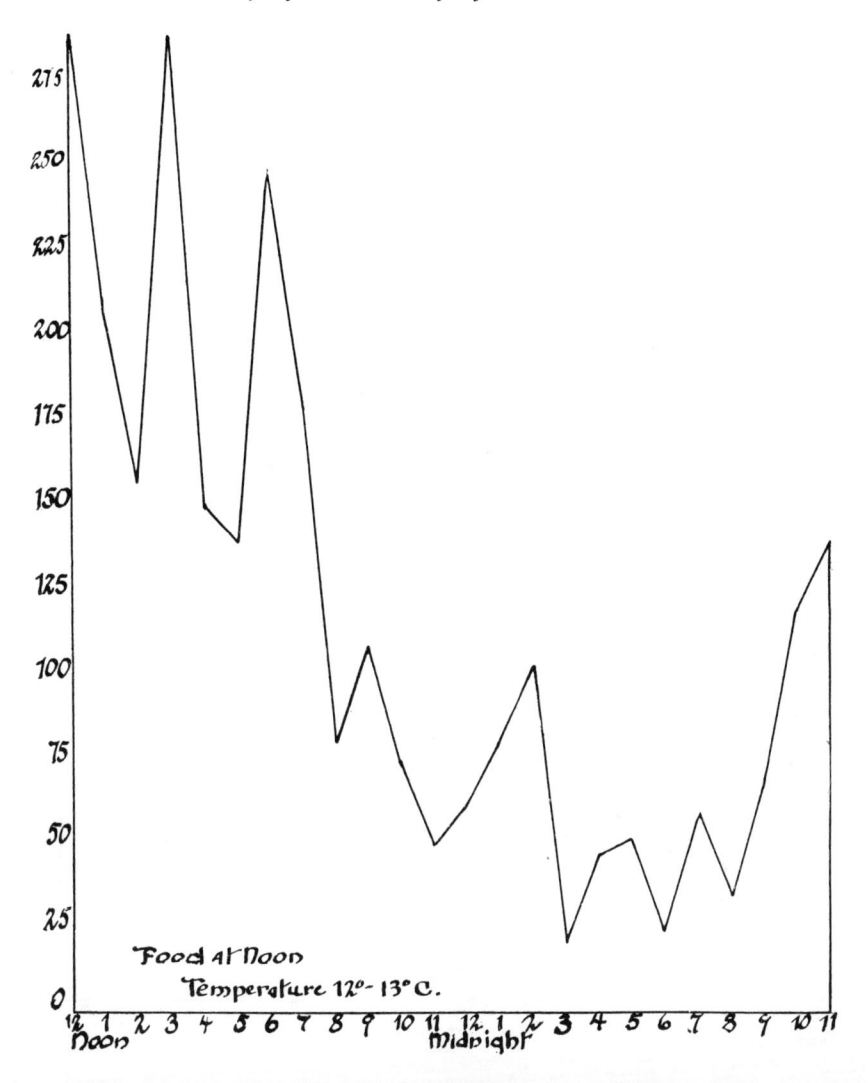

A Behavioristic Study of the Activity of the Rat 17

Fig. 9. Distribution of Spontaneous Activity with Relation to Time of Daily Feeding in a Low External Temperature. Age of Animals 200 to 300 Days.

taking of food is greatly lengthened and the "hump" of activity is not as conspicuous as before. This may be seen in figure 10 based on activity records from animals of middle age about 300 days in an external temperature of 29° to 30°C.

It will be noticed that the form of the activity curve for middle aged animals taken in a cold external temperature is very similar to the activity curve for very young animals taken at a normal temperature. In both cases the period of maximum activity begins immediately after the

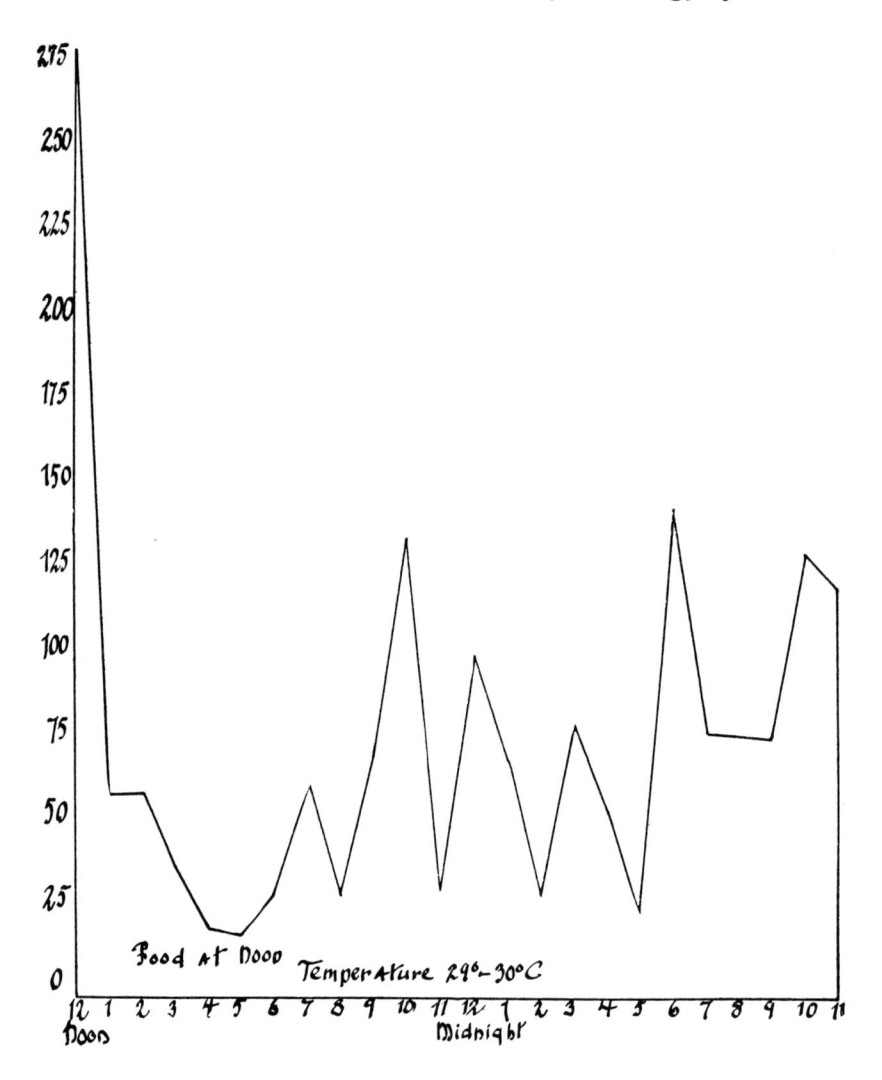

Fig. 10. Distribution of Spontaneous Activity in a High External Temperature. Age of Animals About 300 Days.

taking of food. Compare figure 8 and figure 7. Conversely in higher temperature it will be noticed that the form of the activity curve of the young animals becomes very much like the normal curve for middle aged animals. In both cases the period of maximum activity falls near the middle of the twenty-four hours.

The attempt was made to throw some light on quite another phase of the relation of activity to external temperature by the determination of the external temperature in which an organism is most active. In the previous experiments 23°C. was chosen quite arbitrarily as the normal temperature. It was found that both below (13°C.) and above (30°C.) this temperature the amount of activity per day was diminished. Somewhere between these two extremes there must be a point at which the animals are most active, a "critical" point of activity. It was not possible to make the determination of this point for the rat for the reason that the means at hand of regulating the temperature of the laboratory were not sufficient to obtain anything more than the very crudest gradations in temperature.[2]

The determination of this critical point of activity might be of help to the physiologist in solving several of the problems of animal heat. Work in this field does not seem to have progressed very much since the nineties chiefly for the reason that the behavior side of the problem—the total reactions of the organisms to different temperatures—has been neglected. This may be brought out by a consideration of the problem of the relation of metabolic processes of the body to external temperature. Physiologists speak of a critical point of the temperature of the air surrounding an organism at which the metabolism of the organism is at a minimum. The increase in metabolism below this point is brought about by chemical processes, while the increase above this point is brought about either by vaso-motor or by respiratory changes, or by muscular or glandular changes. Nothing is said however regarding the organism's activity, its total reactions to the changes in temperature. Indeed in most of the experiments on this problem the animals are confined and tied in very small chambers where not even the slightest movement is possible. Without this information of the behavior of total activity the physiologist's study of the problem must remain on a purely static level.

IV. The Relation of Spontaneous Activity to Illumination

In the environment of all animals and at all times there is some degree of illumination or else no illumination at all, that is complete darkness. It is of greatest importance in studying behavior problems to know just how these ever present factors affect the activity of organisms. On the basis of the present knowledge on this subject animals are

---

[2] The attempts that were made to correlate activity with barometric pressure and humidity were not successful. It is very difficult to control these factors without an equipment especially adapted to this purpose.

classed as being either nocturnal or diurnal, according to whether they are more active at night or during the day. This classification as it stands at present is based not only on the reactions of the animals to the light and darkness of the day and night, but also on the reactions of the animals to other factors of their environment, such for instance as possibilities of getting food, attacks from other animals, etc. This is a decided limitation. There is still a further limitation of this classification, in that it places animals in either one group or the other and does not tell just to what extent the animals are more active in the dark than in the light or the converse.

In the present experiments the attempt is made to determine whether the rat is nocturnal, and also just to what extent it is nocturnal; that is just how much more active it is in the dark than in the light.

This experiment was carried on in the following way. The laboratory in which the records were taken was alternately illuminated and completely darkened every twelve hours. The amount of activity (in activity units) in these two periods was measured. Then the ratio of the amount of activity in the dark period to the amount in the light period was taken as a numerical indication of the active extent to which the animal may be said to be nocturnal.

All conditions were kept the same in both periods, except the conditions of giving food. The animals were fed just once per day just as was done in all of the previous experiments. Records were taken in two series. In one series the animals were fed at the beginning of the dark period. In the other they were fed at the beginning of the light period. It proved necessary to take two series of records in this way because of the fact demonstrated in figure 5 above that spontaneous activity is not equally distributed over the twenty-four hours with relation to the time of feeding. There it was shown that the amount of activity in the first twelve hours following the daily meal is very much greater than during the second twelve hours. Thus in the first series of records the effect of the food is added to the effect of the darkness, while in the second it is subtracted. Records obtained in this way are shown in figure 11. Curve A gives the results in the first series in which the animals were fed at the beginning of the dark period. The ratios of the amount of activity in the dark period to the amount in the light period are given on the ordinates and the ages of the animals are given on the abscissae. The ratios for animals fed at the beginning of the light period are given in Curve B. The great discrepancy between these two curves is quite obvious.

The method by which the effect of food was eliminated may be brought out most simply by the following example. It will be noticed in

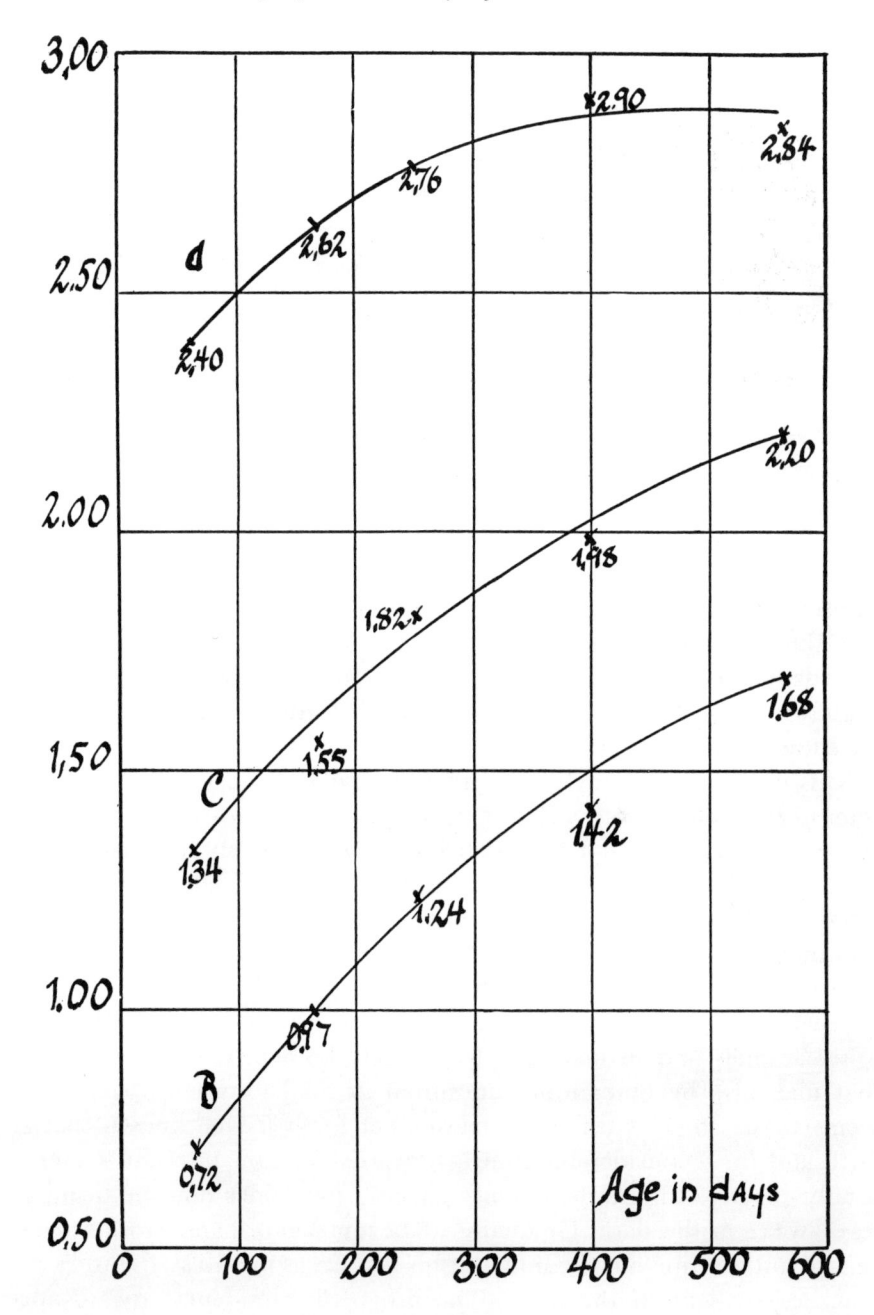

A Behavioristic Study of the Activity of the Rat

Fig. 11. Curves Showing Ratios of Nocturnal to Diurnal Activity at Different Ages. Figure Shows That These Animals Become More Nocturnal With Age.

the curves A and B in figure 11 that the animals become progressively more active in the dark than in the light as they grow older. At 400

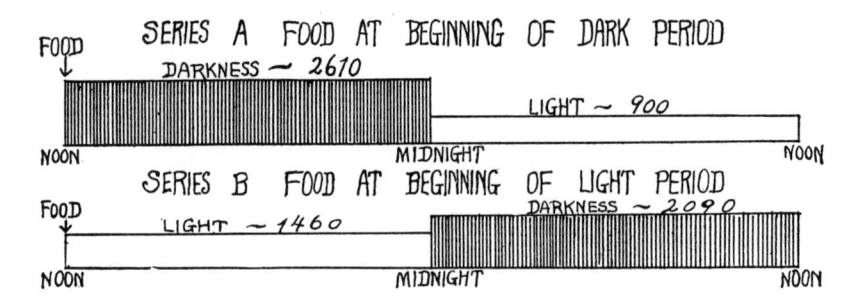

```
                SERIES A  FOOD AT BEGINNING OF DARK PERIOD
    FOOD       DARKNESS ~ 2670
     ↓       |||||||||||||||||||||||||||||
             |||||||||||||||||||||||||||||    LIGHT ~ 900
             |||||||||||||||||||||||||||||
    NOON                MIDNIGHT                              NOON
              SERIES B  FOOD AT BEGINNING OF LIGHT PERIOD
    FOOD                                DARKNESS ~ 2090
     ↓          LIGHT ~ 1460           |||||||||||||||||||||||||||||
                                       |||||||||||||||||||||||||||||
                                       |||||||||||||||||||||||||||||
    NOON                MIDNIGHT                              NOON
```

Fig. 12. Diagram Showing How Curves in Figure 11 were Obtained

days when the animals are fed at the beginning of the dark period they are 2.90 times more active in the dark than in the light. When fed at the beginning of the light period they are only 1.42 times as active in the dark. This is shown in a diagram in figure 12. In the first series the ratio of the activity in the dark to activity in the light, 2610/900 is 2.90. In the second series this ratio, 2090/1460, is 1.42. The effect of the food was eliminated then by taking the total amount of activity in the dark periods in the two series to the total amount in the light periods (2610 + 2090) 4700/(900 + 1460) 2360 or 1.99. Ratios obtained in this way are shown in curve *C* in figure 11.

This curve shows conclusively that the rat is more active in the dark than in the light, in other words that the rat is a nocturnal animal. This curve shows further that the rat becomes progressively more nocturnal as it grows older. At 60 days it is 1.34 times more active in the dark than in the light. From this age on this ratio increases rapidly until at 600 days the animal is more than twice as active in the dark as in the light.

Whether or not nocturnal and diurnal tendencies change with age in other animals and in man is not definitely known. It is generally said that man also becomes more nocturnal in his habits with age. There seems to be some truth in this statement for it is well known that at birth and for a considerable time afterwards the human infant is almost totally inactive in the dark. Only as he grows older does he begin to stay awake in the dark. Gradually he becomes more and more a night animal until in ripe old age much of his activity is manifested during the hours of twilight or the night. The progressive tendency toward nocturnal habits with age in the rat may be explained in a number of ways, all of them, however, quite unsatisfactory. First, as the animals grow older they find that they can forage and climb about more freely, with less molestation at night than during the day. This would certainly be true in part anyway for animals living in the open, but for animals living in the laboratory all the time from birth on, it seems quite questionable. Then from the point of view of the recapitulation theory, it might be said that these results would show that the Albino belongs to a species which is in the progress of changing its habitat from places on the surface of the earth, trees and bushes, to burrows and holes in the dark under the ground. According to this theory as it is generally understood the diurnal activity would represent a former stage in the life of the rat, just as it is said that the grasping reflex of the human infant belongs to an earlier stage in the development of man. Such theories do not seem to be very well-founded. A further possible explanation of the progressive change toward nocturnal activity may be sought in the changes of the structure of the eye with age, but about this very little is known.

V. Relation of Activity to Age

It was shown in the previous sections how spontaneous activity of the rat is modified by the intake of food, by temperature and by illumination. It was brought out incidentally in a number of places in these sections that the expression of activity is also dependent on age. This relation between activity and age will now be examined in more detail. In the first place a determination was made of the actual amount of activity at the different stages of the animal's life. This necessarily included also a determination of the age at which the animal is at its maximum of spontaneous activity.

These determinations were made in three different ways: (1) On the basis of the spontaneous activity in the simple stationary cages, described above. (2) On the basis of the amount of work done in the revolving drums, the total number of revolutions made at different ages. (3) On the basis of the readiness and completeness with which nests are built under normal conditions.

The technique employed in the first method was essentially the same as that described in the experiments above. For the reason that it was not possible to obtain continuous uninterrupted records on a group of rats throughout the entire period of their lives records were taken instead at frequent intervals for fifteen months on a very large group (40) of animals of all different ages (26 to 700 days). Records were taken for five to eight days at frequent intervals. In this way a sufficiently large number of records were obtained for all stages in the development of the rat. Before each series of experiments the animals were given two to three days time or longer in which to accustom themselves to the cages. Twelve of the animals of the group were left in stationary cages all the time in order to eliminate the effects on the activity which might be caused by frequent changes back and forth from the activity cages to the ordinary cages. The effects of these changes on the rest of the group did not prove to be very great. Records were taken always under the same conditions of temperature and illumination.

The relation of activity to age determined by this first method is shown in figure 14, in the curve marked "Stationary Activity Cages." In this curve the age of the animals is shown on the abscissae in days, while the average amount of activity per day in activity units is given on the ordinates in the second column labelled "Activity Units." In this curve it may be seen that at 25 days the rat is quite inactive. From this age to the age of its maximum activity, 175 days, its activity increases very rapidly. After 175 days its activity begins to fall off, slightly at first, then fairly rapidly until at 600 days it reaches the original level of inactivity from which it started.

In the second method ordinary revolving drums were used. They were 12 inches in diameter and 10 inches wide, and revolved very easily as was demonstrated by the fact that 30-gram rats were able to turn them as many as 12,000 times in twelve hours. A photograph of the

Fig. 13. Photograph of Revolving Drum

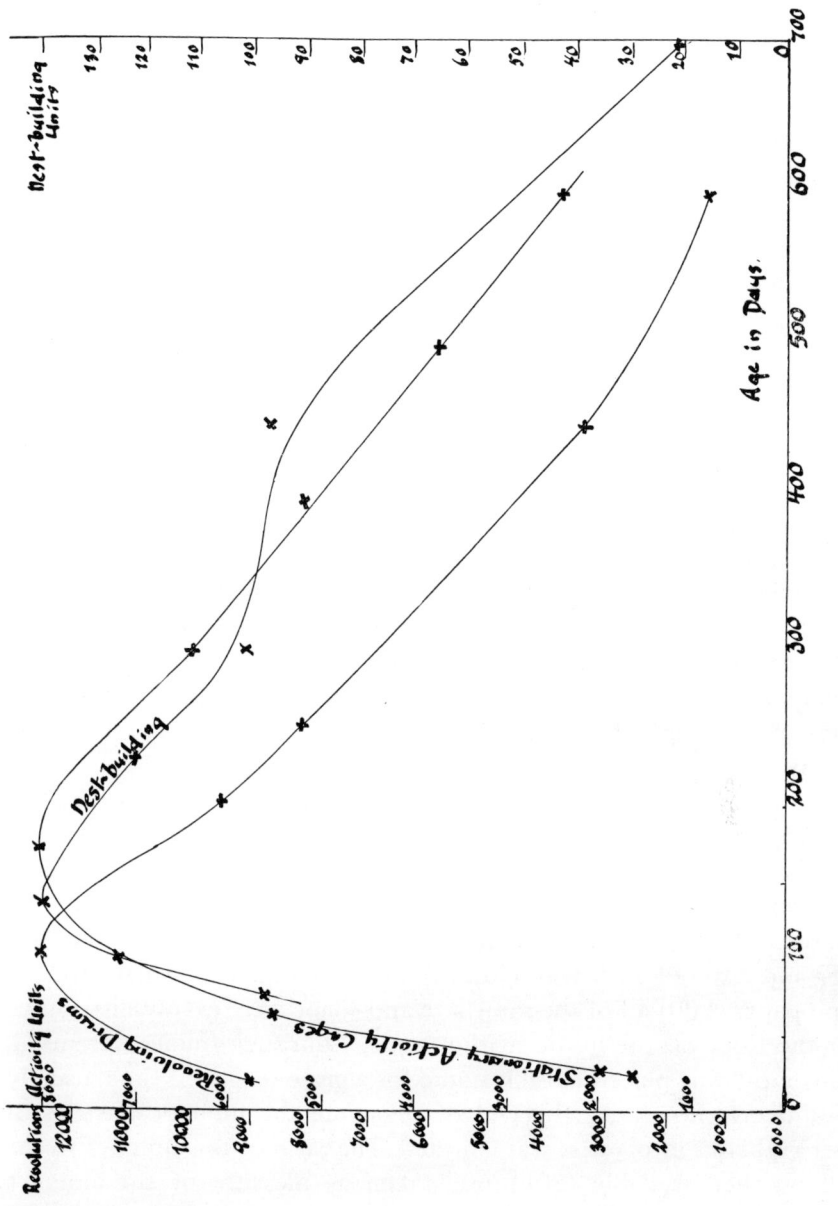

A Behavioristic Study of the Activity of the Rat

Fig. 14. Curves Showing Relation of Activity to Age According to Three Different Methods

drums is shown in figure 13. Six such drums were used in this experiment.

By placing the animals in the drums alternately every six hours it was possible to take records on twelve animals at one time. Six animals were always running in the cages while the other six rested in small separate stationary cages. In this way each animal spent twelve out of every twenty-four hours in the drums.

The animals used in this experiment were of six different ages, 30, 100, 210, 250, 450 and 600 days. Records were taken continuously for one month with the exception of an occasional day of rest. Only the scores made during the last twelve days of the experiment are included in the final record for the reason that all of the animals showed very great irregularities during the first part of the month while they were adapting themselves to the drums. A curve based on data obtained in this way is shown in figure 14 in which the age of the animals in days is given on the abscissae, and the number of complete revolutions per day are given on the ordinates.

The data from this second method gave the following results. In the revolving drums at thirty days the rat is quite active, as is demonstrated by the high average at that age of 9000 complete revolutions per day. Its activity increases however from this age until at 100 days it reaches its maximum. This confirms the work of Slonaker (2), who found period of maximum activity lies between 81 to 120 days. After 100 days the rat's activity falls off very rapidly so that at 240 days it is already less active than it was at thirty days, and at 600 days it is almost completely inactive, averaging at this age about 1000 revolutions per day.

In the third method the relation of activity to age was determined on the basis of the completeness with which the rat builds a nest for itself at different ages under ordinary conditions. For this purpose a standard situation was arranged in which the rat normally builds itself a nest. A square cardboard frame 3 feet wide and 1 foot high was placed on the floor and covered with wire cloth. A definite number of small strips of crepe paper (200) all of the same size and shape were evenly distributed over the floor on the inside of the frame. Four such frames were used. A single rat was placed in each frame for a given length of time, usually about twelve hours. At the end of this time the number of strips of paper gathered into a nest was counted. The ratio of this number to the total number available (200) was taken as measure of the animal's activity. The nests included all strips within a radius of four inches of the densest spot. During this experiment all external conditions were kept constant. It is particularly important to keep the temperature constant for it is well known how easily the nest-building activity is changed and influenced by changes of temperature.

In this way the curve marked "Nest-building" in figure 14 was obtained. The number of strips formed into a nest is given in the column headed "Nest-building Units" at the right side of the curve. This curve is based on the records for three continuous days of twelve animals of six different ages. The irregularity of this curve is very largely due to the very small number of records taken.

This curve despite its irregularities has in general the same shape as the curves obtained by the other two methods. The age of maximum activity determined in this manner lies near 135 days, which is about half way between 100 and 160 days, the ages of maximum activity determined by the other methods.

Another aspect of this problem of the relation of activity to age was brought out incidentally in connection with the experiments on the revolving drums described above.

It may be well to emphasize at this point that there is a tendency among workers interested in the activity of animals to confuse the activity of an animal due to external stimulation with the activity which manifests itself more or less spontaneously when the animal is free from all active external stimulation. Due to this confusion a number of workers say that the rat is most active at the age of thirty to forty days. They base this opinion very largely on the fact that every time they enter their laboratories they find animals of this age active, while older animals remain inactive. They fail to take into consideration that the greater activity of the younger animals at these times may be due simply to the fact that these animals may be more sensitive to any external stimulation, noise made in entering the laboratory, and that during the rest of the time when they are not stimulated they may remain quite inactive. That is to say that younger animals are spontaneously less active than older animals, but that they are more sensitive to external stimulation.

The differences between these two kinds of activity are brought out by the records of the activity of six animals of six different ages in the revolving drums. These drums both serve to stimulate the animals and at the same time to record the activity in reaction to the stimulation. The stimulating effect of the drums is well known and can easily be demonstrated, for every movement even the slightest destroys the equilibrium and causes counter compensatory movements to be elicited. How are animals of different ages affected by this stimulation?

The records of this experiment are shown in figure 15 where the abscissae give the days of the experiment, while the ordinates give the total number of half revolutions made each day and their equivalents in

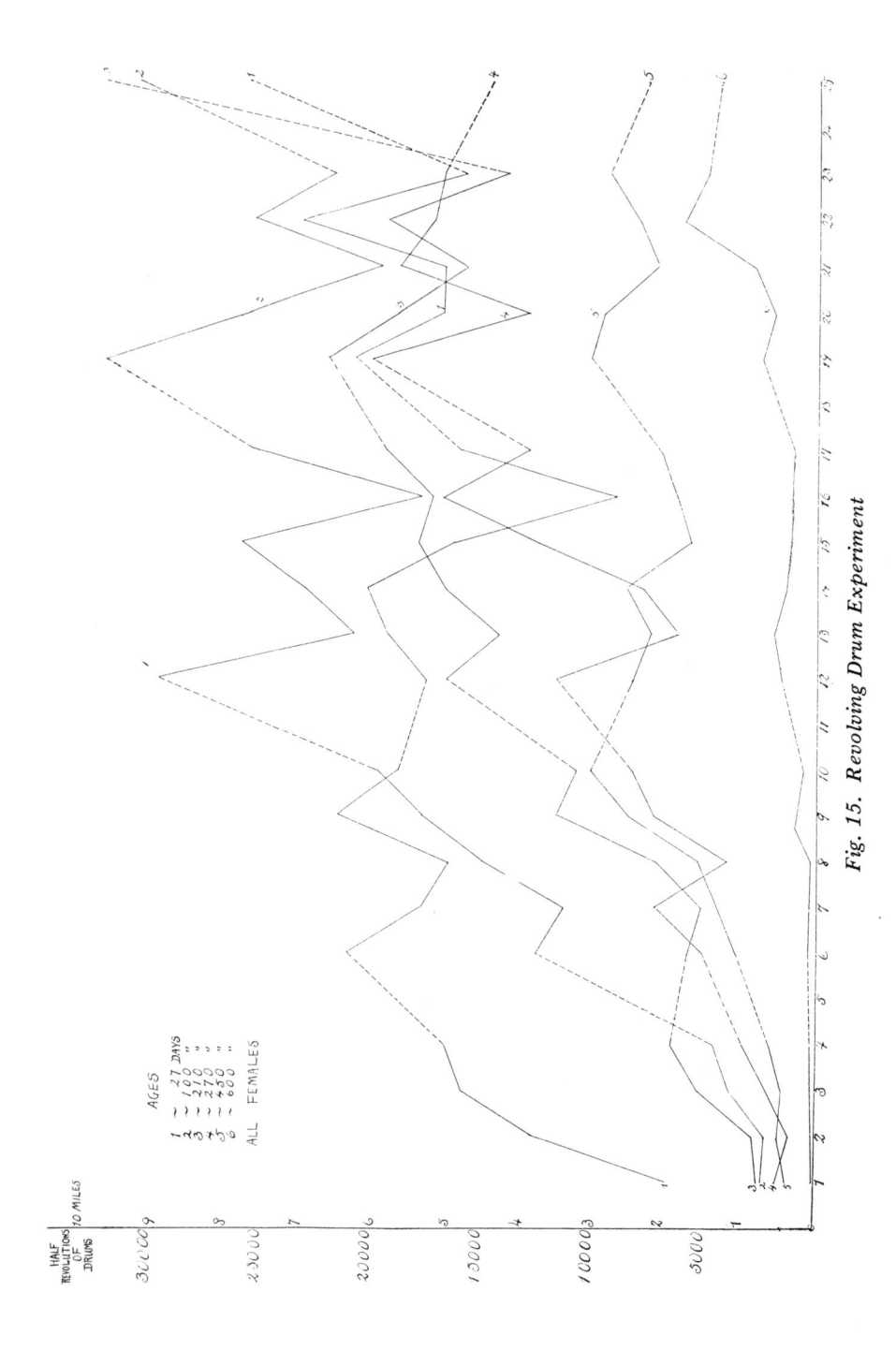

Fig. 15. Revolving Drum Experiment

miles. The dotted ordinates indicate that no records were taken on the day preceding.

It is seen that for the first day in the drums—none of these rats of course had ever been in the drums before—the youngest rat 1 begins with by far the highest number of revolutions (7000) while the second and third youngest come next with 2500 revolutions, the fourth next with 1700, the fifth next with 1200, then the last with 30. This same relation holds for the rate of increase in the daily record for the first part of the experiment. This daily increase as well as the general relation of the records of these animals is shown schematically in figure 16.

Were the higher number of revolutions made by the younger rat due to greater activity then it should continue to make higher scores throughout the experiment. But it failed to do this. It was overtaken first by the 100-day rat and then by the 210-day rat. This same thing happened in turn to the 100-day rat. It is also finally overtaken by the 210-day animal. The higher number of revolutions at the beginning of the experiment and the more rapid increase and arrival at the maximum must have been due to the greater sensitivity of the younger animals to external stimulation. The very old animals were apparently not stimulated in the least by the drums. Their increase in activity from day to

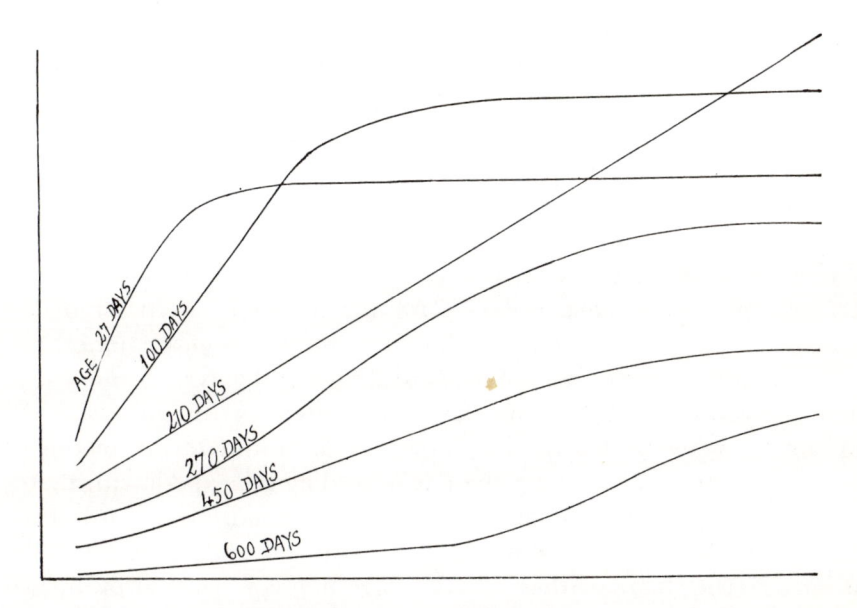

Fig. 16. Curves Showing Schematically the Results of the Revolving Drum Experiment

day was very gradual and seemed to depend almost entirely on the slow progressive adaptation and adjustment of the whole bodies to the drums.

VI. Persistence of Rhythms of Activity after Withdrawal of Rhythmic Stimulus

It may be well to add here a preliminary account of two experiments which help to throw further light on the general nature of spontaneous activity but from rather a different angle than in the previous experiments. Only a preliminary account is offered at this time because the experiments were carried out on just a few individuals and no opportunity has presented itself for confirming the results on larger groups.

The first experiment was carried out in connection with the work described in Section II on the relation of spontaneous activity to starvation. In that work the interest was limited only to the changes in amount of activity during starvation. In the present experiment the interest was focused on the changes in the manner of expression of activity changes in the form of the activity distribution curve during starvation. It will be recalled that when the rat is kept in an environment of constant temperature and illumination and fed just once per day at a definite time, the spontaneous activity is distributed in a regular way with relation to the time of the single daily meal. What happens to the shape of this curve when the factor upon which it depends is removed, that is when the animal is starved?

Two animals were used for this experiment. They were kept in the laboratory under conditions of constant darkness and constant temperature for four months preceding the beginning of the experiment. During this time they were fed very regularly and punctually at a certain time just once per day. Care was taken to keep all of the conditions just as constant as possible throughout this entire period.

The records for the two animals are shown in figures 17 and 18. In these figures the time of the day is indicated on the abscissae, the amount of activity during each hour on the ordinates. A record of normal activity was taken on the day preceding the experiment, that is on the day before the animals were deprived of food. The record of the distribution of activity on this day is shown in the top curves marked "normal." The shape of these curves corresponds in general outline to the composite distribution curve in figure 6. The records for the following days of starvation show that the general shape of this distri-

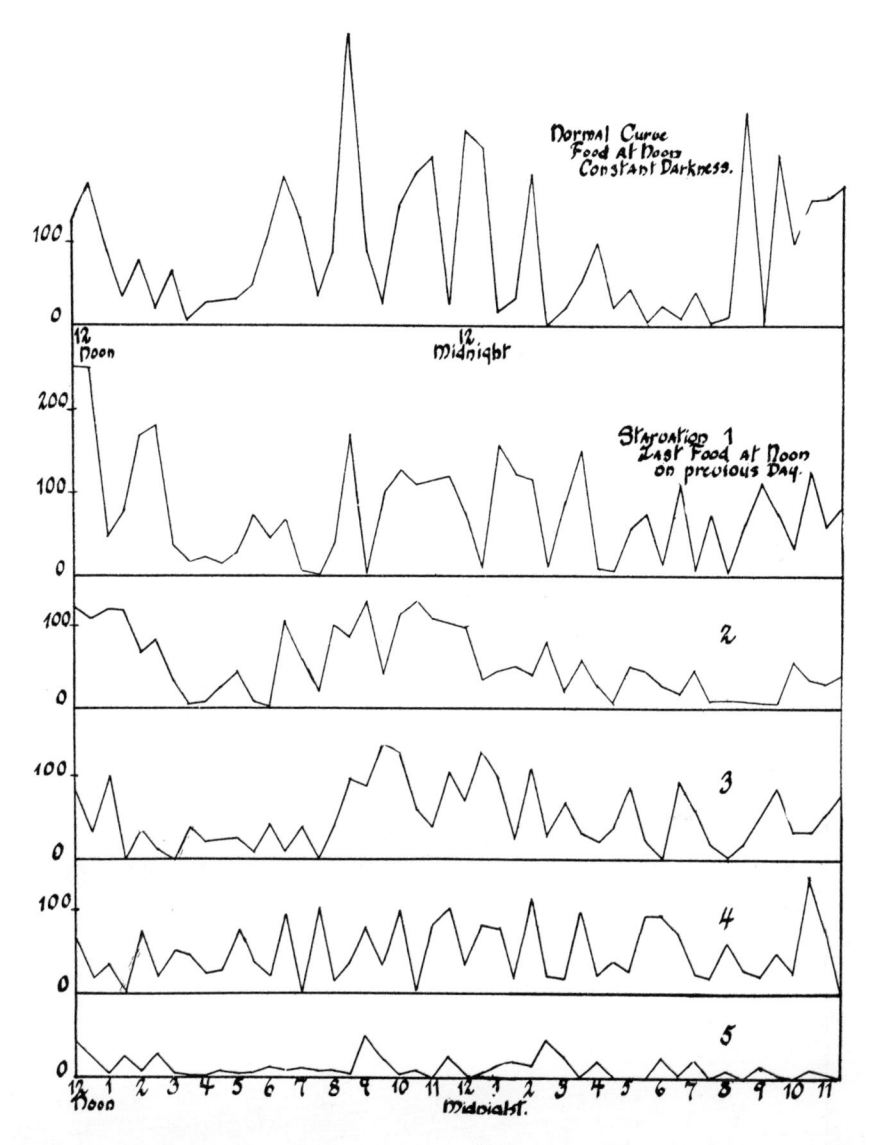

Fig. 17. Distribution of Activity During Starvation. Figure Shows the Persistence of the Typical Distribution Curve for Several Days After the Removal of Food.

bution curve is maintained for three to four days after the removal of food. The curve becomes more and more flattened out with each day of starvation until on the fifth day it is practically a straight line.

In the second experiment similar evidence was obtained. It was shown earlier that the rat is more active in the dark than in the light—and that progressively with age it becomes more and more active

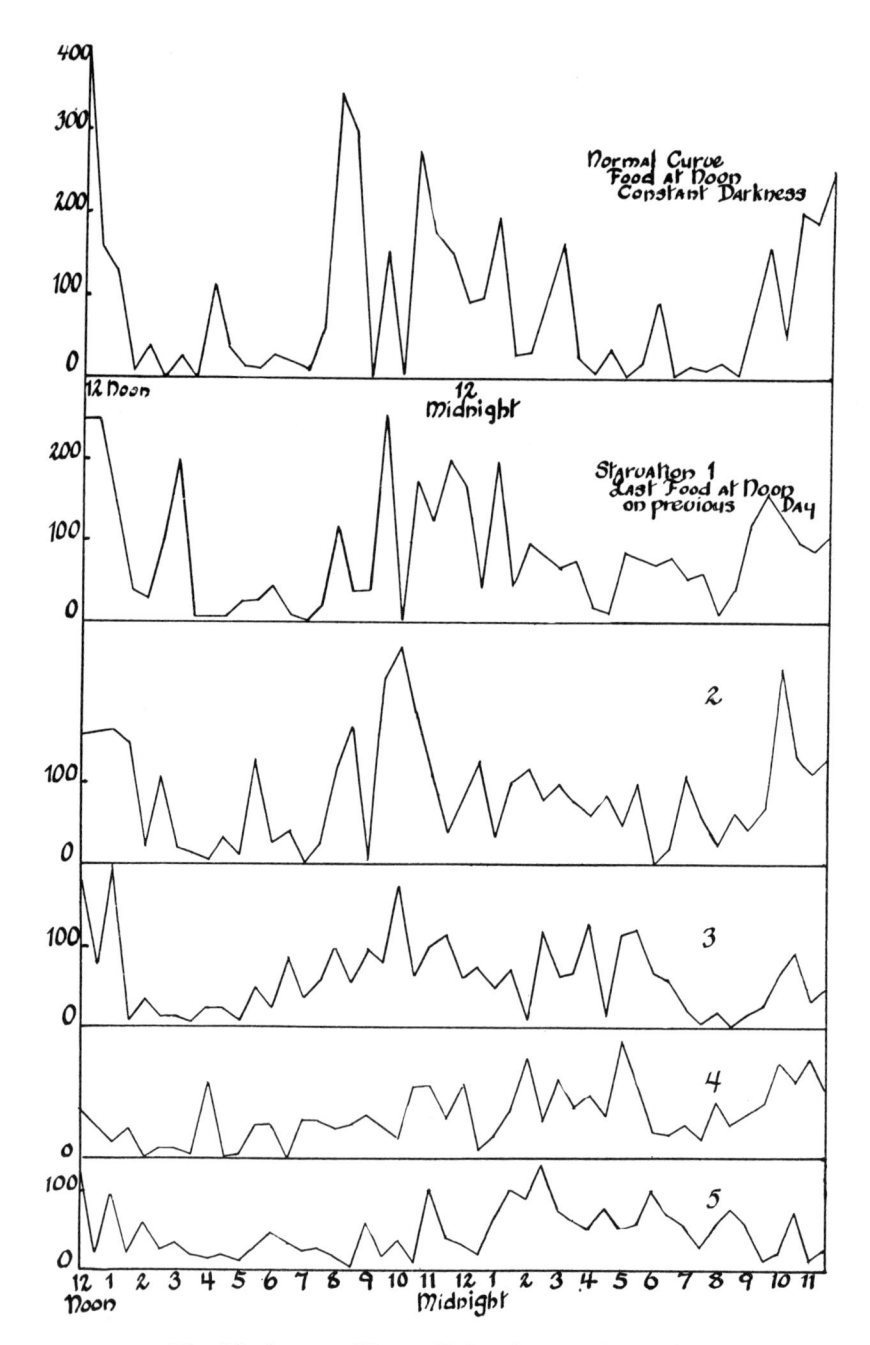

Fig. 18. Same as Figure 17, but for Another Animal

in the dark. The spontaneous activity then of animals that live in the open places where they are subjected to the daily changes of light and darkness of the day and night will not be evenly distributed over the twenty-four hours, but will be confined for the greater part to the night hours. This will depend partly of course on the time the animals are fed. When however the food factor is eliminated by leaving the food in the cage all the time, then the activity should be limited even to a greater extent to the night hours. An animal in the open then is alternately active approximately for a period of twelve hours and then inactive for a period of twelve hours throughout its entire life. What happens to these alternating periods of activity and inactivity when the animals are placed in an environment of constant darkness?

This was tried out in the following way. An animal was chosen for the experiment that was fairly old, 650 days, and which was still quite active, and which also had been subjected to the daily change of light and darkness throughout its entire life. This animal was placed in the laboratory in complete darkness. There it was confined in a cage which was somewhat larger than the ordinary triangular cages. This cage had two small exits, one leading into a revolving drum, the other into a food box in which food was left all the time. The animal could move freely from one cage to another as it chose.

What then under these conditions happens to the periods of activity and inactivity set up throughout the 650 days of the animal's life on the outside? The results of this experiment are shown schematically in figure 19. In this figure only the activity in the drums is recorded. The first line gives the alternating periods of light and darkness in twelve hour periods 8:00 p.m. to 8:00 a.m. and 8:00 a.m. to 8:00 p.m. for the 650 days of the animal's life preceding the experiment. Also it shows the period of constant darkness during the experiment. The second line gives the probable relation of activity to the animal to the changes of light and darkness for the period of life before the experiment. It also gives schematically for twelve days the time relations of the revolutions of the drum

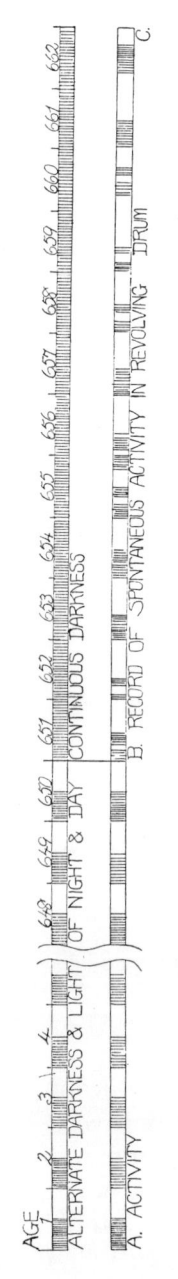

Fig. 19. Schematic Record Showing Persistence of Activity Rhythm after Withdrawal of Original Stimulus

made by the animal when placed in the environment of constant darkness. At the end of the twelve days the experiment had to be discontinued for unavoidable reasons. It may be seen that during these twelve days the regular daily alternation of activity and inactivity is fairly definitely maintained despite the constant darkness. How much longer this regular alternation of period would have continued is difficult to conjecture.

The fact of the persistence of rhythms of activity after the withdrawal of the rhythmic stimulus has been observed in a number of different animals in the past. Bohn and Keeble have interested themselves very much with this phenomenon especially with relation to the life and habits of a small animal *Convoluta roscoffensis* which has its habitat on the foreshore of the sandy beaches of Normandy and Brittany. These workers found that the habits of this animal are to a very considerable extent dependent on the movements of the tide. Just before the tide reaches them at each flow they disappear into the sand, and just as soon as they are uncovered during the ebb they come up on the surface again. In this a very regular alternation of downward and upward movement is set up. Bohn (3) and Keeble (4) found further that when these animals are scooped up in a cup with some sand and placed in the laboratory where they are no longer subjected to the periodic coming and going of the tides they still continue for several days to make the upward and downward movements just the same. Benjamin Moore (5) has also described the persistence of a rhythm in absence of the wonted stimulus in the case of phosphorescent organisms in the sea. The organisms give off their light only at night. When they are placed in a dark room this daily alternation of phosphorescence and inactivity persists over a period of fourteen days after which time the animals usually die.

VII. On the Origin of Spontaneous Activity

Throughout all of the experiments described thus far in this present study it was seen that a large part of the activity of the rat cannot be accounted for in terms of stimulation from outside sources. It was shown how some of the ever present factors, such as illumination and temperature may modify the expression of activity, but it was also shown that these factors could not be called upon to account for the activity. For this reason all that part of the activity of the rat that occurs in situations free from all external stimuli was spoken of as "spontaneous" activity. The source of this activity must lie somewhere within the organism. What organ or mechanism is there within the body of the rat which might serve to bring about this gross bodily activity?

In looking for this source of stimulation the chief characteristics of the manifestation of spontaneous activity studied above must be kept in mind; this is the very regular alternation of periods of activity and inactivity at the rate of ten to fourteen per twenty-four hours. What mechanism is there within the body which functions in this way and at this rate?

The heart and lungs although very regular and periodic in their functioning must be excluded for reason of their rate which is a matter of seconds and minutes rather than hours. The liver, rectum and bladder and intestines must be excluded because of their rate which is a matter of days, weeks or even longer intervals.

There still remains the stomach. This organ has been the subject of very thorough investigation by a number of physiologists, chiefly Cannon (6) and Carlson (7), so that its action is rather clearly understood. It has been established in the first place that the stomach when empty is not subject to continuous contractions as might be supposed, but rather that its activity is broken up into more or less clear-cut periods. During the intervals between the periods of activity this organ quite relaxed and almost completely inactive. During the activity periods it undergoes a series of contractions which may involve usually the greater part of the musculature of this organ. The rate of the recurrences of these periods differs in different species of animals, but also in members of the same species but of different ages. The average rate for most mammals when the stomach is empty is ten to fifteen per day. Under carefully controlled and regulated conditions these periods of activity may come with an astonishing regularity.

These contractions of the stomach when this organ is empty must not be confused with the contractions that occur during the process of digestion when the stomach is full. These latter contractions are known as digestion contractions, while the former are known as hunger contractions. They differ in a number of ways, first as to parts of the stomach involved, and secondly their relation in time to the last meal. The digestion contractions begin almost immediately after an ordinary meal and continue until the stomach is empty. Just as soon as any of the food is prepared for the assimilative processes in the alimentary canal below the stomach it is slowly expelled through the pylorus. The process of explusion involves the musculature from the sphyncter at the antrum to the sphyncter at the pylorus. Contractions begin at the antrum and work downward, one following another peristaltically. During the time the process of expulsion is going on the part of the stomach above the antrum is engaged in macerating and churning the food in acids preparatory to its descent below. These processes go on until the stomach is completely emptied of food. As this process nears completion a new group of contractions begin, at first almost imperceptibly, gradually increasing until finally the musculature of the entire stomach is involved. These are the so-called hunger contractions (see fig. 20). They occur only when the stomach is empty or nearly empty of food. These contractions begin at first at the lower end of the pylorus and work downward, each time however they begin farther and farther up on the wall of the stomach until they involve the entire fundus, and finally the entire stomach right up to the cardia. During these contractions marked changes take place in the entire organism, changes in blood pressure, intra-cranial pressure, reflex excitability, and in the heart-rate, while during the digestion contractions no such changes have been found to occur. The former contractions give rise to the sensations of hunger while the latter are not known to give rise to any kind of sensations.

It is with these hunger contractions that this work will concern itself at this point. It was stated above that in the empty stomach they come in regular periods at the rate of ten to fourteen per twenty-four hours. This rate corresponds very closely with the rate of the spontaneous activity periods. The fact of this close correspondence in rate may be taken then to indicate that these two phenomena occur simultaneously or nearly simultaneously.

Unfortunately it was not possible in the rat to get conclusive evidence of the simultaneity of the action of the stomach and the spontaneous gross bodily movements. Many attempts were made with the balloon method, but the difficulties of the technique due to the small size of the animals were too great. A number of animals were trained to take a very small stomach tube with a balloon attached to the end, but in every case, some time before a record was taken, either the rat destroyed the tube by biting a hole through it, or else was destroyed itself by asphyxiation. The possibility of gastrostomy was considered—that is making a small hole through the wall of the abdomen and introducing the balloon into the stomach that way, but it was feared that the effects of the operation which are necessarily quite severe in such a small animal, because of the difficulty of handling such small parts, would too greatly modify the behavior to make the experiment practicable.

In humans however, it has been possible to demonstrate this simultaneity of the contractions of the stomach and gross bodily movements. Miss Tomi Wada took simultaneous records on medical students of

A Behavioristic Study of the Activity of the Rat

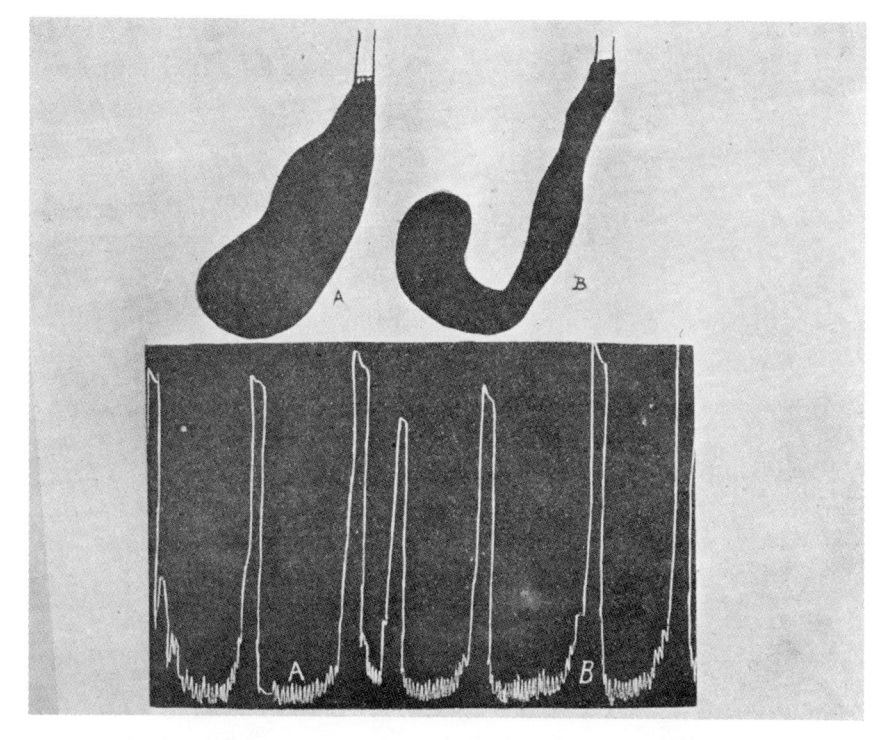

Fig. 20. Hunger Contractions of the Dog's Stomach Hours after a Meal
A, Outline of bismuth coated balloon in stomach between the gastric contractions; B, Outline of balloon at the height of a hunger contraction. (Rogers and Hardt.)

gross bodily movements and stomach contractions during sleep. The stomach contraction records were obtained by the usual method employed by Cannon and Carlson. The subjects swallowed the balloon and tube just before going to bed. The record of the gross bodily movements was obtained by means of a simple system of tambours placed under the bed. Records were taken during sleep because during the waking periods the subjects are exposed to many external stimuli, and it is not possible to differentiate the part of the activity which is due to these external stimuli from the part that is spontaneous. Miss Wada found that the spontaneous movements during sleep, what few there are, rolling over in bed, etc. come periodically in regular groups. Miss Wada found further that in every case these periods of gross bodily activity coincided with the activity periods of the stomach. During the intervals between, when the stomach is quiescent, the body is also completely quiet. These results leave little doubt about the simultaneity of gross bodily movements and the activity of the stomach.

Up to this point it has been shown that the stomach contractions and the periods of spontaneous bodily activity in all probability occur simultaneously. In any case of this kind where two phenomena occur simultaneously in this way the following possible explanations of the causal sequence may be made: (1) either both are due to some other common agent, (2) or else the bodily activity is the cause of the stomach activity (3) or finally that the stomach activity is the cause of the gross bodily activity.

One of these explanations is easily eliminated; that the stomach activity is due to gross bodily activity. It is an experimental fact easily verified that contractions of the stomach cannot be elicited in anyway by activity of the whole body, rather on the contrary bodily activity tends to inhibit the contractions (Carlson and others).

The second possibility that the stomach contractions and the activity have a common origin, a common stimulus, may be eliminated by the following evidence. (1) It is a well-known fact that the stomach when completely excised from the body still continues to contract very much as before. This excised organ will continue to function for a considerable period of time if it is kept warm and moist and given the proper nourishment of oxygen. (2) Carlson and others have shown that the stomach functions quite normally in the body after complete nervous isolation from the rest of the body, after section of both vagi and both splanchnics. Carlson sums up the evidence on this point in this way: ".... The essential point is that since the empty stomach, completely isolated from the central nervous system, does exhibit the typical hunger contractions, the primary role of the gastric nerves is that of modifying or regulating essentially automatic mechanisms in the stomach wall." (3) The autonomous function of the stomach was further demonstrated by Carlson by means of a very ingenious experiment in which he used a Pavlov accessory pouch. In this experiment he found that "when the muscularis and myenteric isthmus joining the main and accessory stomachs is relatively narrow, the two stomachs exhibit complete independence of the hunger contractions, even to the point of vigorous activity of the one during quiescence of the other...."[3]

---

[3] Carlson regards the results of this experiment as very good evidence for the independence of the stomach from the stimulation of agents in the blood-stream. Carlson argues that the blood can have nothing to do with the stimulation since the stomach and the accessory pouch function independently though they are both supplied by the same blood. In interpreting these results in this way he does not give consideration to the fact of the local rhythms of the different parts of the stomach. It is well-known that strips of muscle taken from different parts of the

There remains then the last of the three possibilities; that the spontaneous gross bodily activity is due to the activity of the stomach. This explanation seems to square best with the facts at hand at present on the activity of the stomach and the activity of the total organism. There are still so many gaps in our information regarding both of the subjects that it is not possible at this time to be quite certain of any explanations of how the organism works. The investigations in recent years of Cannon and Carlson on the sensation of hunger and its relation to the stomach contractions have rather definitely established the fact that these contractions precede the hunger sensations in time, that they are the origin of these sensations. The results obtained in the present work seem to show that the stomach contractions do not alone bring about sensations of hunger, but they also bring about movements of the entire organism by means of which, as it will be shown in the following section, the organism is brought into contact with the materials necessary for stopping the contractions.

A very important gap in our knowledge regarding the relation of the action of the viscera to the reactions of the whole organism was recently filled in by the work of Carlson and Luckhardt (8) on the visceral nervous system of frogs and turtles. In this work it was definitely established that stimulation of the visceral organs brings about reactions of the skeletal muscles, reactions of the whole organism. 1. "Mechanical or electrical stimulation of the lungs, the gall bladder, the heart, the urinary bladder and the entire intestinal tract induces skeletal reflexes both in decerebrated and purely spinal preparations. 2. These visceral skeletal reflexes, at least as regards the extremities, are essentially of the defensive or escape type."[4]

The facts obtained in the present work on spontaneous activity and the facts known from physiological work on the stomach may tentatively be formulated in the following way: There is a tendency in all living organisms to maintain a metabolic balance or equilibrium. The various substances of the body are present in a fairly definite quantitative relationship. Whenever the balance is destroyed there is an immediate reaction to reestablish it. During fasting or during any time when

---

walls of the stomach and placed in Ringer solution contract at quite different rates. Every part has its own rhythm. In Carlson's experiment then the possibility still remains that the main stomach and accessory pouch were stimulated by agents in the blood stream, but that because of their different inherent rhythms they responded independently.

[4] We found recently in a series of experiments on the behavior of foetuses (cats) still attached to the cord that stimulation of the stomach or intestine (slight pinching) elicits very vigorous movements of the entire body.

the stomach is empty and the body is in need of nourishment this balance is temporarily destroyed. There is a minus of some substances and a plus of others. The products of this deficiency—whatever they are—may be looked upon as the agents which set up the process of reestablishing the equilibrium. (This process has for its final step the movements of the entire organism about in the environment until contact with food is made and the food is ingested.) As far as is known there is no way for these deficiency products, which are probably carried in the blood stream, to stimulate the skeletal muscles directly— the muscles which bring about the movements of the entire organism. How then is the equilibrium reestablished? It is known from direct work on the stomach and from analogous work on the heart that the stomach responds to chemical stimulation, that its activity may be influenced and changed by chemical stimulation. It is safe to assume that these deficiency products stimulate the stomach, bring about in it an increase in size and rate of the contractions. These contractions in turn when they become large enough send impulses to the skeletal muscles through the vagi and central nervous system, efferent nerves, and release there the stored energy which starts the organism in operation of getting food for filling the stomach. The fact then that the energy in the muscles is only released periodically as was demonstrated above must be accounted for by the periodicity of the action of the stomach. This organ is subjected during times when the body is in need of nourishment to a continuous stimulation from the deficiency stimuli. Progressively as the strength of the stimuli increases more and more of the stomach wall responds until the entire organ from the cardia to the pylorus becomes involved. After a long series of contractions of this kind the musculature finally reaches a condition in which suddenly the deficiency stimuli are no longer able to elicit a reaction, the contractions cease and the stomach becomes quiescent. This quiescent phase which follows may be thought of as a period of fatigue in which for the time being the muscles are temporarily no longer responsive to stimulation. As the muscles recuperate the contractions begin again, and progressively as the recuperation process goes on they become larger and larger until finally the height of another period is reached and the entire reaction is repeated. This accounts for the periodicity of the action of the stomach and at the same time for the periodicity of the spontaneous gross bodily activity of the whole organism.

    Schematically this tentative formulation may be expressed in the following manner. Before presenting this schema, however, it is necessary to recall several points brought out above in Section I in the experiments which deal with the periodic nature of spontaneous activity, when the animals were kept in a small cage and fed just once per day. In these experiments it was found that the spontaneous activity comes in regular periods which are separated by intervals of almost complete quiescence and that the activity is not evenly distributed throughout each period. There is only very slight activity at first. Progressively as the period goes on the activity increases until a maximum is reached either in the middle or toward the end of the period. It must also be recalled here that the stomach contractions are not all of the same size. Each of the contraction periods begins with very small contractions which involve only a limited part of the stomach. The contractions become larger and larger until the entire stomach is involved from the cardia to the pylorus. This maximum of activity is usually maintained right up to the end of each period. Following the cessation of the contractions the stomach becomes completely quiescent. The relation of spontaneous activity to the function of the stomach is shown schematically in figure 21. In this figure spontaneous activity is given on the top line while the probable relation of the stomach contractions to this activity is given on the second line. In this schema it is intended to show that the gross bodily activity of the organism increases progressively as the activity of the stomach increases. The maximum of spontaneous activity is reached when the whole stomach becomes involved in the contractions. With the cessation of the contractions of the stomach at the end of each period the animal becomes inactive. This process repeats itself with each new period of stomach contractions.

It must be emphasized that with this tentative formulation it is not intended to imply that the stomach is the only organ in the body upon which spontaneous activity may depend. But it is true however that a larger part of the activity of the rat does fall into these regular clear-cut periods, which have been associated with the action of the stomach. Besides this activity which falls into the regular periods there still remains some activity which the limited scope of the present work did

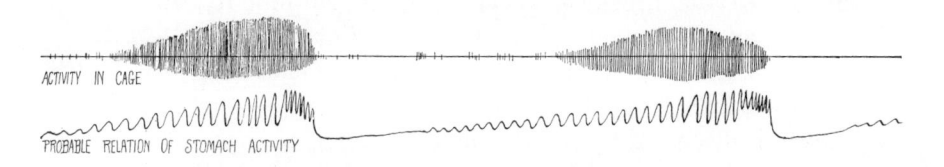

Fig. 21. Relation of Stomach Contractions to Activity

not permit to be studied in detail. Most important here is a rather considerable amount of irregular activity of females. Whether this irregular activity is related to the action of any part of the sexual apparatus was not determined. The role that the stomach mechanism plays with relation to spontaneous activity probably varies very greatly in the different species of animals. In the lower organisms it must undoubtedly account for a very much larger part if not all of the spontaneous activity. In man, on the other hand, it probably accounts for only a limited part of the activity. Still the work described above on the relation of spontaneous activity to the stomach contractions in humans during sleep would indicate that the stomach still plays a very important role in bringing about activity even in humans, however greatly covered over this activity seems to be by the flood of reactions elicited by the many different external stimuli during waking periods. In this connection it would be of importance to determine the relation of spontaneous activity to the kind and structure of the stomach. In frogs for instance the stomach happens to be so constructed that it is able to adapt itself to very large quantities of food. This animal gets its food only at rather great intervals—weeks or months—but then usually in a single large quantity, other smaller frogs or the like, which take many days to be digested. What is the relation between this kind of a stomach and the spontaneous activity of the animals? The human stomach on the other hand is so constructed that it is able to take only relatively small quantities of food at one time, but this food is digested almost immediately. A study also of the relation of activity to the action of the stomach should be very interesting in ruminants where the stomach is made up of several separate parts. What does the animal do spontaneously during the function of each of these parts?

There is still another point which argues very strongly for the prime importance of the stomach with relation to the other internal organs especially the bladder and rectum, in bringing about activity. This is the fact that in all animals, and in man living in the wilds, distention of the bladder and the rectum is relieved wherever the individual happens to be while the contractions of the stomach can only be relieved by movements of the organism about in the environment until contact with food is actually made and the food is ingested.

In light of this explanation some of the results obtained in earlier chapters especially from the work on the distribution curve of activity may now be discussed again. It will be recalled that in these experiments it was shown that when the animal is fed just once per day and under conditions of constant illumination and temperature the spontaneous activity is distributed over the twenty-four hours in a very definite way (see figure 6). The form of the activity distribution curve was shown to depend on the time of the last feeding. The two phases of inactivity and the single period of intense activity shown in this curve may be explained on the basis of the formulation given above in the following way. The first period of inactivity immediately after the daily meal occurs at a time when the processes of digestion are going on in the stomach and when the hunger contractions are absent. After the stomach empties the hunger contractions begin again and become more and more vigorous with each succeeding period. The animal is stimulated in this way only slightly at first but increasingly more intensely until it reaches its maximum of activity some twelve hours after the daily meal. At this time the nervous system and the large muscles of the body employed in making the spontaneous movements become fatigued so that although the stimulation from the stomach still continues in its periodic fashion these muscles respond only with a very small amount of activity. During this period of fatigue the attempts of the stomach to gain control of the organism, to start it to activity are clearly manifested by the small but regular periods of activity shown at this time. This may be looked upon as the period of sleep. Actual observation showed that during this period the animals are very difficult to arouse; they are curled up in balls and are as far as can be made out "sleeping." It has already been pointed out in Miss Wada's work on the activity of humans that during sleep the period of activity and inactivity come and go with great regularity synchronous with the stomach contraction periods. The stomach continues to function during this period of sleep just as vigorously as before. The amount of activity becomes larger and larger with each successive period until finally, after a condition of sufficient recuperation of the nervous system and skeletal muscles is reached, the stomach contractions again gain possession of the reactions of the whole organism and the individual awakes. The regular anticipation of the feeding periods may also be explained on the basis of the clock-like functioning of this internal organ. When all external conditions are kept fairly constant and when a regular routine of activity is gone through each day the accuracy of this time piece is quite astonishing. This is seen very well in the activity record of individual rats, but it is much better known from numerous observations from the great regularity and punctuality of the reactions of many farm animals, especially of the braying of the mule at a very definite time near noon at which it is accustomed to be fed. The ability to carry on other rhythms may be explained on this basis (9 and 10).[5]

VIII. Relation of Spontaneous Activity to Hunger

The intimate relation of gross bodily activity and the action of the stomach was pointed out in the previous chapter. There still remains the question as to the relation of this gross bodily activity to the hunger reactions of the animal. Does it follow that because this diffuse form of activity is due to the stimulation from the stomach that it must all necessarily be translated into hunger reactions, searching for food, eating, etc.? It was shown that each of the regularly recurring periods of gross bodily activity is connected with simultaneous periods of activity of the stomach. Is all of the activity in each of these periods hunger activity?

In order to answer these questions and a number of allied questions a simple construction was used, the "double cage." This arrangement consists of an ordinary triangular activity cage with a hole cut in one side large enough to permit of the easy introduction, without contact, of the snout of an inverted pipe-shaped smaller tube containing food. Both cages were supported on a separate set of tambours and the activity in each cage was registered separately. A photograph of the double cage is shown in figure 22. The small round cage contains a metal food receptacle which is so constructed that the food may be easily gotten at through the hole at the top large enough to accommodate the head of the rat, but too small to permit the rat to pick up food in its paws and to scatter it about or possibly even to take some of it back into the other cage. In this experiment food was left in the food receptacle all the time, and water was left in the waterglass attached to the outside of the triangular cage. Of course, there is an obvious possibility of the animal's entering the food box for other purposes than replenishing itself with food. In order to eliminate this possiblity

---

[5] A good example of the persistence of a rhythm of activity of an internal organ after the removal of the original exciting stimulus is found in the case of the human uterus. This organ, especially in multiparous women, continues to contract for a number of days after the birth of the child. The contractions are originally set up by the presence of the foetus. All during pregnancy these contractions go on. But interestingly in this connection they are not felt until labor begins, when they serve to expel the foetus. After labor they still continue to be felt for a number of days (that is they are still strong enough to dominate the organism).

Fig. 22. Photograph of Double Cage

the food cage was made just large enough to permit the rat to enter and to get the food, but too small to permit of very much sniffing or moving about. This arrangement was quite successful. It was possible to verify this by actual observation over rather long periods of time, after the animals had had a good chance to accommodate themselves to the particular form of cage. After the first day in the double cage, they rarely, if ever, entered the food box when just generally active and sniffing about. When they did enter they seemed to do so solely for the purpose of getting food.

The results obtained from this experiment (see figure 23) showed: (1) In this situation where the animals had free access to food all the time the periods of activity and inactivity come and go with the same regularity as before only at a slower rate—from six to ten per twenty-four hours. (2) The animals enter the food box at least once during each activity period, occasionally twice. (3) The time spent in the food box compared with the length of the entire period is very short. (4) The entrance into the food box does not take place at the beginning of the activity period but usually toward the end. Only in a few cases did any

Fig. 23. Record from Double Cage

of the animals enter the food box at the beginning of a period. No instance of an entrance between periods was recorded. (5) The amount of activity increases progressively from the beginning of each period to the point when the animal enters the food box. (6) There is always some activity after the animal returns from the food box. This activity consists chiefly in all kinds of cleansing manoeuvers very much like those of an ordinary house cat. (7) The activity which precedes the entrance into the food box is diffuse and undirected. It consists usually of such movements as jumping, climbing, playing with paper, sniffing and gnawing at the sides of the cage, etc. The element of search for food plays no rôle in this activity. The animals are so thoroughly adjusted to every part of the cage that the necessity of search drops out entirely.

In order to bring these results into relation with the activity of the stomach it is necessary to bring out some additional facts regarding the function of the stomach. (1) Each period of activity of the stomach begins with small contractions. These contractions come with a very regular rate, one every eighteen to twenty seconds. For the reason of this rate Carlson speaks of these contractions as the "twenty-second rhythm." These contractions become larger and larger as the period advances without changing their rate. (2) After these contractions have reached a certain size, quite abruptly a new series of very much larger contractions begins. These larger contractions come at a different and irregular rate, and also have a different form. These are the so-called "main hunger contractions." Whether or not there is any real difference between the small and the large contractions besides what can be explained in terms of the different extent to which the musculature of the stomach is involved in the two cases is not definitely known. (3) Cannon was the first to show that these large contractions give rise to the sensation of hunger and (4) Carlson has shown that the intensity of the hunger sensation is roughly proportional to the size of the contraction.

The relation of the results obtained in the "double cage" to these facts is brought out in figure 24. In this figure the diffuse spontaneous activity in the double cage is shown on the top line. The entrances into the food box are shown on the second line. The probable relation of the stomach contractions to the diffuse activity and to the entrances into the food box is shown on the bottom line. The small contractions serve only to stimulate the animal to diffuse activity, restlessness. It is not until the onset of the large contractions, the main hunger contractions, that the animal enters the food box. With the introduction of

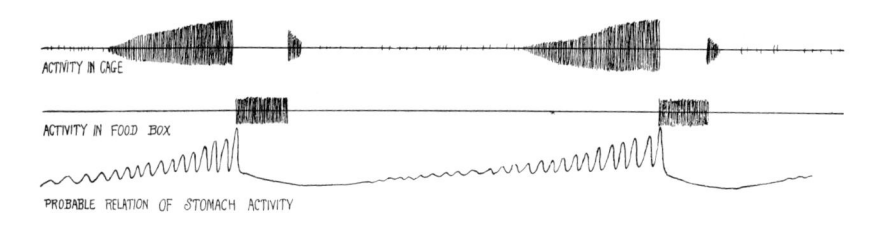

A Behavioristic Study of the Activity of the Rat

Fig. 24. Relation of Stomach Contractions to Activity in Double Cage

food into the stomach the contractions cease. Once started at eating, however, the animal continues until the stomach is filled. The activity in the cage following the return from the food box is made up entirely of cleansing manoeuvres elicited by the various kinds of external stimulation connected with eating.

The fact that the animal does not enter the food box until the onset of the large contractions may be explained in the following way: At birth the members of all mammalian species are known to have contractions of the stomach almost continuously (Carlson). Driven then by these contractions the animals are active diffusely and remain active until either stomach contractions are in some way stopped, or else due to gross exhaustion the animals are no longer able to move. They move and toss their heads about here and there, suck at everything that happens to stimulate their lips, bits of straw, hair of the mother's body, feet and ears of sisters and brothers, and finally the teats of the mother. It is only the last of these activities that brings about a change within the organism. When the teats touch the lips sucking movements are elicited; a warm stream of milk flows down the animal's throat; the stomach contractions are stopped; hunger pangs are relieved; the animal lies down and goes to sleep. Each time the contraction periods begin again the animal becomes active; begins moving about and sucking at everything and the whole process is repeated. As this trial and error process goes on, the onset of the stomach contractions gradually becomes more and more definitely associated with the sucking of the teats, becomes the main motor outlet, while the others fall into disuse. This process goes on for a time; in the rat it is a matter of days (as near as I could determine by observation, eight or ten days); in the human infant it is a matter of months until the stomach contractions elicit the one reaction of crying and actually seeking food. This process is somewhat complicated by the fact that the stimulus to activity is not at all times the same, for, as was shown above, the stomach contractions vary considerably in amplitude, also possibly even in their nature during different parts of the contraction period. If the animal happens to find the teats during the part of its activity which is caused by the milder contractions it will nurse just as at any other time; but the changes that take place within the organism when milk or food is taken during this part of the contraction period are so slight that no definite associations can be built up between them and the sucking at the teats and the taking of food. When however, the animal happens to find the teats during the period of main stomach contractions things are quite different. Now the changes resulting from the taking of the milk are strong enough to become associated with the stomach activity, and form the basis of the cycle: stomach contractions—going out to teats—nursing—inhibition of contractions—relief. There are further reasons why these reactions become associated more readily during the period of strong contraction: first the fact that during the period of strong contractions the animals are more active and vigorous than during the period of milder contractions; secondly chances and the frequency on a simple trial and error basis of finding the teats during the former period will be much greater. Then also for the reason that milder contractions are more easily stopped the animal will nurse for a shorter time during this part of the period. Besides these simple factors of frequency, duration, recency of stimulation, there will be other rather more situational factors which will help to build up the association; such things as odor of the teats, the warmth of the mother's body, etc., and, of course, the encouraging reaction of the mother herself.

Gradually the main stomach contractions and the sucking of the teats become permanently associated and there is less tendency for the animal to suck at the teats during the period of weaker contractions. The onset of the main stomach contractions comes to serve as a signal for the taking of food and the animal no longer hesitates but goes directly to the teats. Later on, after the animals are weaned, as was the case in the double cage, the onset of the main contractions served as a signal for the animal to go to the food box.

It is hoped that further light may be thrown on the origin of these specific food reactions by work that is now being carried on by Mr. Ging Wang on the activity of the newly born of rats and cats before they have ever been fed. Mr. Wang is attempting to find out when the periodicity begins, whether or not it is present at birth, and what relation it has to the times of feeding, and the time required for the complete emptying of the stomach. He also hopes to get some information on these reactions during the period of the animal's life before it is born. It is astonishing how little definite information is available at present regarding the activities during this very important time of development.

The facts on hand from work on the activity of the human infant present certain difficulties which are not easily explained. Miss Wada found in her work that the gross bodily movements of the infant during sleep come in periods at the rate of one every fifty-five minutes. It is difficult to see how this rhythm could have been set up by any external stimuli in as much as the infant on which these records were taken was fed once every four hours from birth on. In adults the periods of activity come at the rate of one every two hours. But in adults we have shown definitely that these periods occur simultaneously with the periods of activity of the stomach. Here again, however, the relation of the food habits to the periods of activity is difficult to explain. The solution of these problems must wait for further evidence.

References

1. Szymanski, J. S.: Versuche ueber Aktivitaet und Ruhe bei Saeuglingen. Pfluegers Archiv, 1918, clxxii, p. 424.
   Szymanski, J. S.: Die Verteilung der Ruhe und Aktivitaetsperioden bei einigen Tierarten. Pfuegers Archiv, 1918, clxxii p. 430.
   Szymanski, J. S.: Aktivitaet und Ruhe bei Tieren und Menschen. Zeit. f. Allgemeine Physiologie, 1920, xviii, p. 105.
2. Slonaker, J. R.: The normal activity of the white rat at different ages. J. Comp. Neur. and Psychol., 1907, xvii, pp. 342–359.
   Slonaker, J. R.: The normal activity of the albino rat from birth to natural death, its rate of growth and the duration of life. J. Animal Behaviour, 1912, ii, pp. 20–42.
3. Bohn, G.: Sur les movements oscillatoires des Convoluta roscoffensis. C. R. Ac. Sc., Oct., 1903.
4. Keeble, Frederick: Plant-Animals, Cambridge Manuals of Science and Literature, Cambridge, 1910.
5. Moore, Benjamin: Origin and Nature of Life. Home University Library.
6. Cannon, W. B.: The Mechanical Factors of Digestion, New York, 1911.
   Cannon, W. B.: Bodily Changes in Pain, Hunger, Fear and Rage. New York, 1920.
7. Carlson, A. J.: The Control of Hunger in Health and Disease. The University of Chicago Press, Chicago, 1916.
8. Carlson, A. J., and Luckhardt, A. B.: Studies on the sensory nervous system. VII. Skeletal reflexes induced by stimulation of visceral afferent nerves in the frog and turtle. Am. Jour. of Physiol., 1921, lv, p. 306.
9. Froehlich Fried. W.: Ueber die rhythmische Natur der Lebensvorgaenge. Zeit. f. Allg. Physiologie, 1912, xiii.
10. Boldyreff, W.: Function periodique de l'organisme chez l'homme et les animaux superieur. Quart. Jour. of Exper. Physiol., 1916, x, p. 175.
11. Wada, Tomi: An experimental study of hunger in its relation to activity. Arch. of Psych., 1922, lvii.

ANIMAL BEHAVIOR AND INTERNAL DRIVES

One of the most fundamental of all the phenomena which characterize animal life and distinguish it from plant life is the spontaneous motility of the animal organism. A few plants, to be sure, especially certain forms of marine vegetation, do move about, but these few are exceptions in the plant kingdom. The activity of animals, on the other hand, although it varies widely in form and extent from species to species, is an ordinary phenomenon which one always anticipates under normal circumstances. We may ask, then, what it is that sets off the diverse performances which animals display. Ordinarily we think of most of their activity as being due to some form of external stimulation. We know, however, that all animals, from the lowest uni-cellular organism to man, are active even when all external stimuli have been eliminated. And since this spontaneous motility, just as any other kind of motility, must have a definite cause, it must be due to some natural factor within the organism. Many workers have chosen to call it "voluntary" activity, presumably because of the common belief that the "will" to do is the origin of the action. We believe, however, that spontaneous activity arises from certain underlying physiological origins. We shall attempt to show from studies chiefly on the white rat what some of these origins are, and how they fit into the general biological picture of the animal's life.

The investigations described below have been made by Ging H. Wang, Elaine F. Kinder, Tomi Wada, and the present writer in the Psycho-

---

This paper was originally published in *The Quarterly Review of Biology*, Vol. II, No. 3, September 1927. Reprinted by permission.

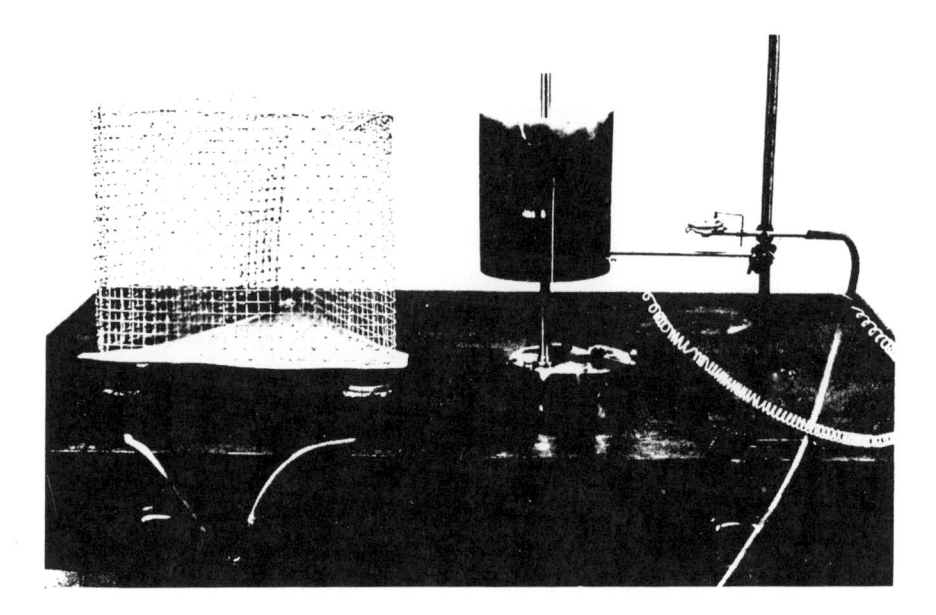

Fig. 1. Photograph of Cage Used in Studying Gross Bodily Activity
The cage is triangular in shape, 12 inches high and 12 inches wide. Each corner is supported on a rubber tambour through which all movements are transmitted to a recording Marey tambour. The time is recorded on the smoked paper in half hour intervals by means of an eight day clock.

biological Laboratory of the Phipps Psychiatric Clinic during the past six years. Some of the experiments have already been reported elsewhere, but we have taken this opportunity to collect also numerous observations that are as yet unpublished. Of the extensive work on animal "drives" done by Hoskins (1925), Moss (1924), Slonaker (1924, 1925, 1926), Stone (1924, 1925, 1926), Szymanski (1920, 1922), and Tracy (1926) we shall incorporate in this review only that part which bears directly on our own method of approach or on our own experimental findings.

Periodic Nature of Spontaneous Activity—Two-Hour Rhythm

We may begin our review with the rat confined just after feeding in a small cage of the type shown in figure 1. The walls and floor of the cage are absolutely bare and the room in which the experiment is performed is kept constantly illuminated and free from all disquieting noises and odors. If we observe the animal for a while we see that it moves about most of the time, doing many things. It sniffs and claws at the walls of

Animal Behavior and Internal Drives

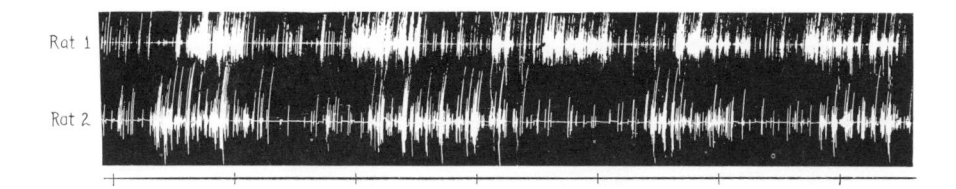

Fig. 2. Records from Two Adult Rats Showing the Periodic Nature of Their Spontaneous Activity. Time is given in hours below the record.

the cage, it climbs, and gnaws and scratches; but from all these observations, however interesting at first sight, we learn nothing of what makes it active. If, however, we arrange the cage so that every movement therein, even the slightest, is recorded over a period of ten to twelve hours on a smoked drum, a remarkable fact comes to light: this diffuse gross bodily activity occurs rhythmically, active periods alternating with periods of almost complete quiescence. The active periods occur at intervals varying from one to two hours. Moreover, the records show further that the activity within each active period is slight at the beginning, but increases as the period advances and reaches its maximum usually near the end (Richter, 1922). Typical records obtained from two rats in triangular cages are shown in figure 2. The record in figure 3, obtained from a guinea pig in the same type of cage, is representative of a similar rhythm found in other animals. Had the motility been irregular and non-periodic we should have accomplished nothing in our investigation of its origin. On the contrary, however, it is very significant that such well defined periods of activity, recurring at such regular intervals, are found when external conditions are as nearly constant as is practically possible. This fact would indicate that the

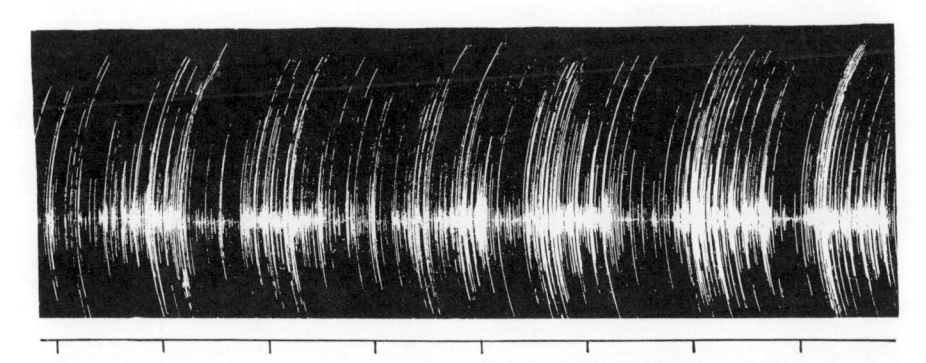

Fig. 3. Record of Spontaneous Activity of an Adult Guinea Pig. Time in hours below the record.

motility rhythm must be set up from within the animal in some organ which functions at a similar frequency of one and a half to two hours.

Origin of the Two-Hour-Activity Rhythm

A review of the periodicity of the different viscera eliminates at once the heart and lungs and the sex glands, since the two former organs function at a frequency much higher and the latter at a frequency much lower than that of the bodily activity rhythm. In the stomach, however, we know that active periods alternate with quiescent intervals every hour and a half to two hours. In 1904 Boldireff was able to show that contractions occur in the walls of the empty stomach, but several years elapsed before Carlson (1916) demonstrated the periodic nature of this activity. Carlson, working with guinea pigs, dogs, and monkeys, found that from one to two hours after a meal, when the stomach is nearly empty, contraction waves begin passing downward over the stomach walls. These waves, small at first, gradually become larger and larger until they finally involve the whole lower half of the organ, and the gastric musculature often passes into a condition of semi-tetanus. Then, quite suddenly, the contractions cease and an inactive interval of an hour or more ensues. After this period of quiescence the small waves begin again, and the entire process is repeated. Thus one period follows another as long as the stomach remains empty

Gastric movements in both animals and man have been studied by means of the apparatus shown in figure 4 (Martin and Rogers, 1927). A balloon attached to the end of a tube is passed through the oesophagus

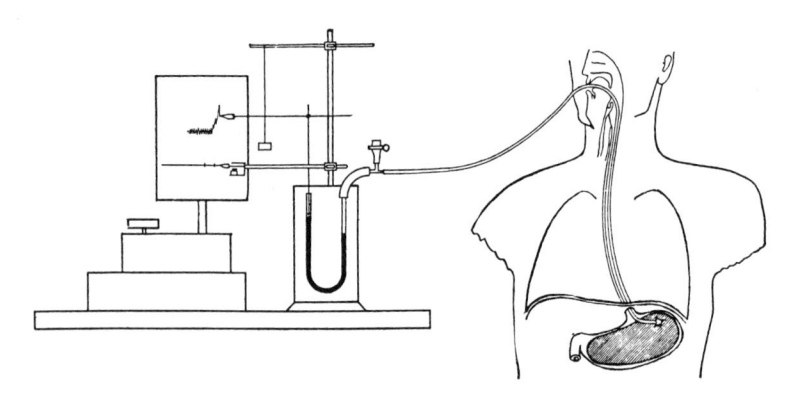

Fig. 4. Diagram Showing the Method of Recording the Hunger Contractions of the Empty Stomach (Martin and Rogers, 1927)

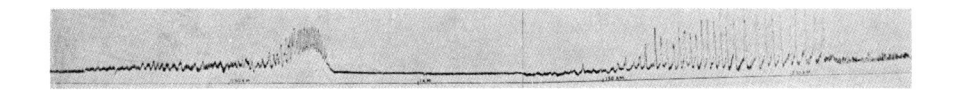

Fig. 5. Record of Stomach Contractions of a Human Adult Taken during Uninterrupted Sleep

into the stomach and inflated, and a manometer is fastened to the other end of the tube. The contractions of the stomach change the pressure on the balloon, so that some of the air is pushed up into the tube, and the level of the water in the manometer is changed. As the water rises and falls with the contraction waves, the movement is recorded by a floating pointer on a smoked drum. A record obtained by this method with similar apparatus is shown in figure 5. The record was taken in this laboratory on a human adult during a night of normal sleep. The portion presented—that portion registered between 12.30 and 2.30, when the last meal had certainly been assimilated—illustrates very clearly the cyclic nature of the movements of the empty stomach.

According to the recent observations of Rogers and Martin (1926), the stomach takes the shape shown in figure 6 A at the height of each of the single contractions near the end of the active period and that shown in figure 6 B when it is inactive and relaxed. With each of these large waves, then, we see that the lower part of the stomach contracts to such an extent that the lumen practically disappears, whereas the upper part may show a contraction wave near the middle.

Cannon and Washburn (1912) and Cannon (1915) have shown that with these large contractions the sensation of hunger arises, and from the work of Rogers and Martin we know that these "hunger" contractions are set up in the lower third of the stomach. The hunger sensation is not produced until the end of the active period is nearly reached,

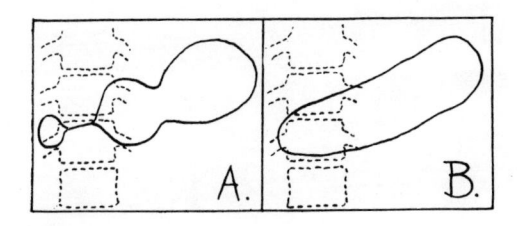

Fig. 6. A. Shape of the Stomach at the Height of a Contraction Wave. B. Shape of the Relaxed Stomach
(Roentgenographic observations by Rogers and Martin, 1926.)

when the waves have become very large, but even then it increases in intensity to some extent with the magnitude of the contraction, and it disappears entirely when the contractions cease. The inference, therefore, is quite logical that the two-hour periods of gross bodily activity in the rat are associated with periods of gastric movement and have to do with the hunger responses of the animal.

Correlation between the Two-Hour Activity Rhythm and the Hunger Response

In order to test this hypothesis we recorded simultaneously the bodily activity of the animal and the intervals at which it sought food and ate. This experiment was performed in the type of cage shown in figure 7. The larger compartment was simply the usual triangular activity cage shown in figure 1; the smaller compartment contained a cup filled with a powdered food mixture (McCollum diet). The corners of each cage were supported on rubber tambours and so arranged that the activity in the two cages was recorded separately. In this way the curve in figure 8 was obtained, where the activity in the large cage is registered on the first line, and that in the food-box on the second, with

Fig. 7. Photograph of Combined Food and Activity Cage
The two compartments are supported on separate sets of tambours so that the activity in each is recorded separately.

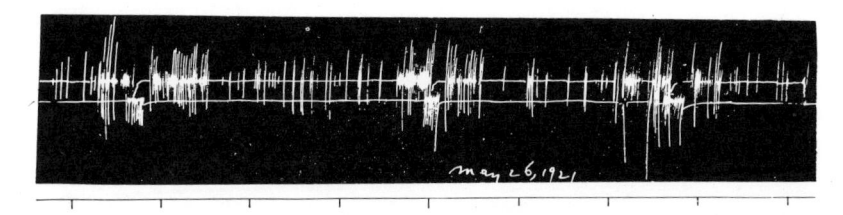

Fig. 8. Record Showing the Relation Between Gross Bodily Activity and Feeding Periods.

Activity in the large cage is given on the upper line, and entrances into the food-box on the lower. Time in hours is indicated below the record.

the time in hours below. It will be seen immediately that the animal always enters the feeding-cage and eats once during each activity period, that it enters usually near the end of the period and rarely at the beginning, and that it does not enter during a quiescent interval. Moreover, we have found through prolonged personal observation, that an adult animal rarely approaches the food-box *except to eat,* and that the vibrations recorded in the activity cage for a short time after it leaves the food-box are produced almost entirely by an extensive cleansing performance which always follows feeding. In these experiments the activity periods, recurring invariably with the entrance into the food-box, are even more regular than they were in the earlier work when no food was available. With this greater regularity, the quiescent intervals are much longer, so that the lapse between periods is three to four hours instead of one to two, as found in the activity cage with no food-box attached. The significance of the lengthened intervals will be discussed below.

We may now attempt to show in more detail how the gross bodily activity, the feeding habits, and the stomach contractions seem to be correlated. The simultaneous records of activity and feeding suggest that a close relationship must exist between the periods observed in the simple activity cage and the hunger "drive" of the animal. From the experimental data compiled above we know that the motility rhythm and the stomach contraction rhythm have three features in common: the frequency of both varies between one and two hours; the active phases of both begin at slight intensity and increase gradually, reaching a maximum near the end; and in both the active period ends abruptly and is followed by a quiescent interval. If we represent the two rhythms as in figure 9 *A*, drawing a diagrammatic activity record directly above a diagrammatic record of gastric movement, so that the active phases of the two coincide, we find that the small stomach contractions occur

58   *The Psychobiology of Curt Richter*

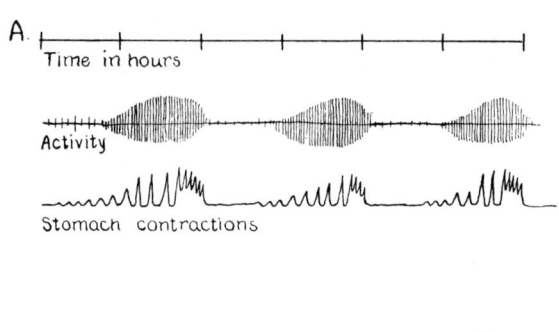

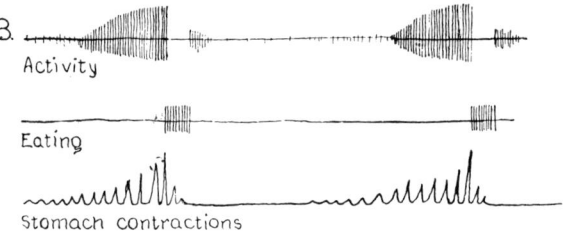

Fig. 9. Schematic Representation of the Relation Between Periods of Gross Bodily Activity and Stomach Contractions.
  A. Simple activity cage without food. B. Double cage with food.

simultaneously with the beginning of the motility period, and that as the magnitude of the contractions increases the animal becomes more and more active. But how can we justify our representation in terms of the hunger response? It is very probable that as long as the animal experiences the hunger sensation which accompanies the stomach movements, it seeks for food, unsuccessfully, of course, in the single cage without a food-box. When the gastric contractions stop, however, the hunger disappears and the animal becomes quiet again.

On this basis one might expect that when food was available all the time, the rat would enter the food-box as soon as the contractions began. Actually, however, we know that it moves about in the main cage for some time before it approaches the food-box. How, then, can we explain this preliminary diffuse activity? Here again, as in figure 9 *A,* the relationship may be represented schematically. In figure 9 *B,* a record taken simultaneously from the activity cage and the food-box is shown in diagram on the first and second lines, and a stomach contraction record on the third. Thus we see that the small contractions give rise to the diffuse activity in the large cage. The animal seems at first simply to be annoyed and becomes more and more restless as the contractions grow larger, until the "main" contractions set in and the general discomfort becomes centralized in the hunger sensation. This stimulus dominates the behavior of the organism and it enters the food-box to eat. When its appetite has been satisfied, it passes into a period of quiescence which lasts until the stomach has become empty and the contractions have started up again. And since time is required for the contents of the stomach to be digested, the interval between contraction periods is three to four hours instead of one to two hours as observed in the earlier experiments.

We had hoped to establish this relationship in more detail in the rat by means of records taken simultaneously of stomach contractions and gross bodily activity, but all of our attempts to introduce balloons into the stomach of this animal were unsuccessful. It is very difficult to keep it from biting a hole in the tube in the first place. Furthermore, its throat is apparently too small to admit even the finest tube without a severe asphyxia resulting. Because of this failure, we turned our attention to other animals from which Carlson and his associates had already obtained good records of stomach contractions.

Since the stomach tube can be introduced and fastened very easily in the bullfrog, we experimented on this animal, using the technique of Patterson (1915). The tube and bulb were pushed into the stomach through a small hole made in the skin beneath the throat, and the frog was placed in an activity cage enclosed in a box which could be almost completely darkened. Water from a faucet dripped through on the animal at all times in order to keep it in good condition. In this way we obtained stomach contractions which showed no periodicity at all. In one individual, in fact, both the frequency and the amplitude remained constant for eighteen days. The lack of periodicity partly defeated the purpose of the experiment, but not as much as the fact that the frogs remained perfectly still at all times, never making even the slightest movement.

The pigeon seemed more promising for our purposes, since we had previously found its activity to be definitely periodic. The intervals between the periods are somewhat shorter here than they are in the rat, but they are just as regular. The cage used in these experiments was cylindrical in shape, two feet in diameter and three feet high. The circular bottom, made of cardboard, and small enough to fit inside the wire wall without touching it at any point, was supported on tambours so that all movements of the pigeon were recorded on a smoked paper. A wooden rod pushed through the wire wall half-way up, pivoted on a nail at one end and supported on a tambour at the other, served as a

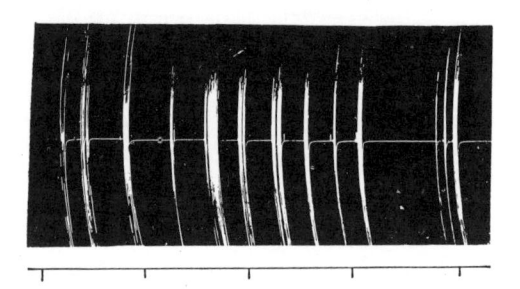

Fig. 10. *Record Showing the Periodic Activity of a Pigeon, Kept in a Large Cage with a Perch.*

The bird spent most of its time on the perch, but at quite regular intervals it jumped down to the floor for a few minutes. This record shows the activity on the floor. Time is given in hours below the record.

perch from which activity could also be recorded. Figure 10, a record of the activity on the bottom of the cage when no food was available, shows that the bird left the perch about once every 20 minutes; and by attaching a recording food-box filled with corn, we found that every time it jumped down it invariably stopped to eat. Rogers (1916) has demonstrated a thirty-minute average rate for the active period of the crop of the pigeon, observing at the same time that it was most restless when its crop was contracting. We attempted, therefore, to record simultaneously the crop contractions and the activity in the larger cage, but the bird always managed to expel the tube no matter how carefully it had been inserted and fixed.

We sought our relationship next in experiments on the human infant. Wada (1922) found that in a child ten months old, during a continuous uninterrupted sleep lasting eight hours, the activity, as recorded by a tambour and sping placed beneath the crib, was definitely periodic, the interval between the periods averaging forty-five minutes. This seemed to offer us an excellent opportunity, especially since Carlson and Ginsburg (1915) had found that the stomach tube could be passed quite easily into infants. Our plan was to take simultaneous records of the stomach contractions and the activity periods during sleep. In six babies used for these experiments we succeeded in passing the tube without too much difficulty, but then either the babies would not go to sleep, or else the tube was completely blocked by strong spasms of the cardiac sphincter. After many unsuccessful attempts this method of attack had to be abandoned.

Meanwhile, Wada, taking records on medical students while they slept, succeeded in obtaining some very conclusive results. The students swallowed the stomach tube at ten o'clock in the evening, just before retiring, and simultaneous records were taken throughout the night of the stomach contractions and bodily movements. Besides diffuse activities such as turning over, smaller movements were recorded whenever

Animal Behavior and Internal Drives 61

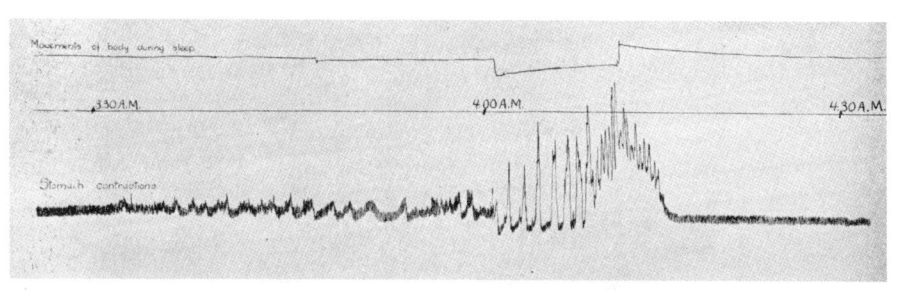

Fig. 11. Simultaneous Record of Gross Bodily Movement and Stomach Contractions of a Human Adult Taken during Deep Sleep

possible. Adult activity during sleep, just as infant activity, proved to be periodic, but the interval between the periods is much longer, varying between two and three hours. The stomach contractions, of course, are also rhythmical, much more so than they are during the waking state. And the periods of these two phenomena coincide very well; when the stomach is quiescent the gross bodily activity is reduced to a minimum, but during the contraction periods frequent movements occur, the largest coinciding with the "main" hunger contractions. The record in figure 11 illustrating this fact is similar to those obtained by Wada. The body movements indicated on the top line in this figure were recorded by means of a tambour and spring attached from beneath to the spring of the bed. Since only large movements such as turning over are registered in this way, it can be seen that just before the "main" hunger contractions set in, the subject became very active, and again almost simultaneously with the largest contraction wave there was an even greater amount of activity.

The results of most of our supplementary experiments, therefore, while not conclusive, would seem to uphold our theory that the two-hour activity rhythm in the rat is dependent on gastric function.

Feeding Habits of the Rat

Starting from our observations on the relation between activity and the feeding periods of the rat, we decided to extend our investigation to a study of its food habits, with special reference to their regularity. For this purpose cages shown in figure 12 were constructed. They consisted of individual compartments large enough for the animals to take plenty of exercise, with a small tunnel on one side at the top leading to the food-box. This tunnel was built in an inconvenient position in order to discourage the rat as much as possible from entering it except when

Fig. 12. Cages Used for Studying Food-Habits

driven by hunger. The food-cup was placed at the end of the tunnel under the wire cloth floor, and a hole was made in the floor just large enough for the rat to insert its head. Whenever it reached in for food, the balance of the cup on a large tambour was disturbed and a mark was made on a smoked drum.

The records obtained in these cages bring out clearly the great constancy of the feeding habits of the rat. The record in figure 13, taken on an adult animal from 8 p.m. to 8 a.m., shows that the feeding period recurred about once every three hours throughout the day, and when the experiments were extended over a longer time, it was found that the rhythm persisted very constantly from day to day (see fig. 14). Similar experiments on other animals confirmed these results. A rat may eat seven times a day or it may eat eight or ten times, but in any case it maintains a constant average from one day to the next. The degree of variability of the feeding response is shown very clearly by the curve in figure 15, compiled from records taken on four animals for

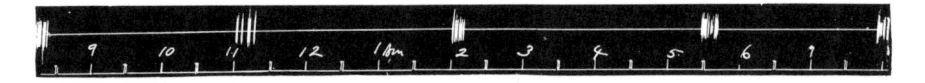

Fig. 13. Record Showing the Feeding Periods of An Adult Rat. Time is registered at half-hour intervals.

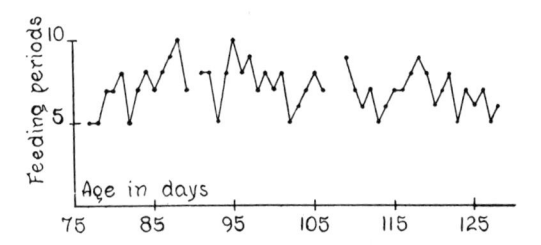

Fig. 14. Graph Showing the Regularity of the Feeding Periods of an Adult Rat from Day to Day
The number of periods per day is given on the ordinates and the age of the animal in days on the abscissae.

twenty successive days. The abscissae represent the length of the intervals recorded between feedings, and the ordinates indicated the number of times each interval was recorded from any one of the four individuals. The curve is evenly balanced with a mode of two hundred and fifty minutes, or approximately four hours. The few longer intervals, we believe, may be identified entirely with periods during which the rat, like the human being, slept in spite of the stomach contractions.

From the above experiments it seems fairly well established, then, that the hunger contractions stimulate the organism to activity, but what the details of the mechanism are we are not prepared to discuss. We do believe, however, that somehow, with each new hunger contraction period, impulses are sent up the afferent nerves from the stomach to the brain and out to the striped muscles, to release the energy stored up there.

Genesis and Development of the Feeding Habits

But how does the activity produced in this way become associated finally with the eating process? We cannot assume that the new-born

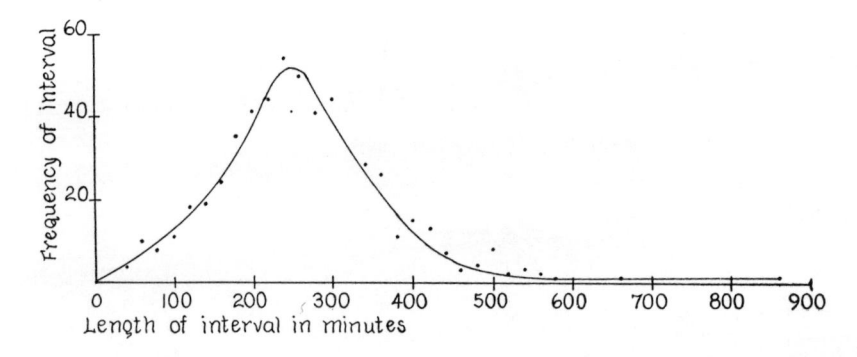

Fig. 15. Frequency Curve of Intervals of Various Lengths between Feeding Periods in Four Adult Male Rats for Twenty Days

animal seeks food when the contractions begin. Indeed it would seem more probable that the relationship is built up by the usual trial and error method. In order to solve this problem one must learn more about the activity of the very young animal. Does it show the periodic motility of the adult individual?

The activity of the new-born rat was recorded from the cages shown in figure 16. The bottom of the cage consisted of a wooden frame 6 inches square with a sheet of rubber dam stretched taut across it. The rubber was covered with pieces of flannel and the sides of the cage, made of paper, were pasted on the wooden frame. Every movement of the animal in the cage was transmitted through the rubber membrane to a lever which recorded on a smoked paper drum. The young rats were left in the cages for twelve hours at a time, and then returned to their mothers for twelve hours.

Records obtained in this way showed that the motility of the rat immediately after birth is continuous rather than periodic (see fig. 17). For the first ten days it remains constant; then a rhythm begins to appear, and by the sixteenth day clear-cut and very regular intervals are

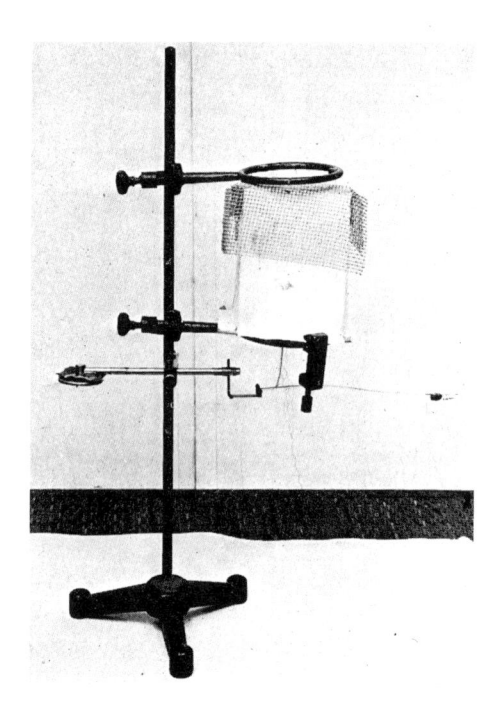

Fig. 16. Photographs of Cages Used in Recording Activity of New-Born Rats

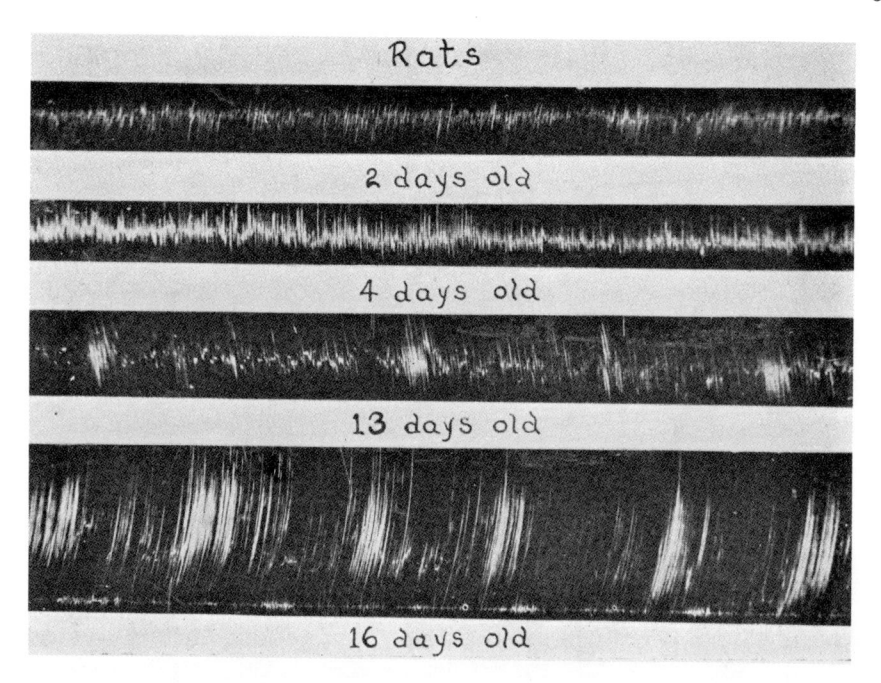

Fig. 17. Record of the Activity of a New-Born Rat Two, Four, Thirteen, and Sixteen Days after Birth
Up to the tenth day the activity is continuous, then it gradually breaks into periods, which, by the seventeenth day, stand out very clearly in the records.

present. This result is consistent with the fact that the new-born of some animal species show stomach contractions with almost no indication of periodicity (Patterson, 1914). On the basis of this knowledge, then, we may picture how the diffuse activity of the new-born rat resolves itself into a search for food.

In its almost continuous motility, the very young animal sucks at everything with which its mouth comes into contact—the feet and legs of its litter mates, the straw of the nest, hair on its mother's body, and, eventually, the mother's teats. When it sucks at anything other than the teats, nothing results; the stomach contractions persist and the activity continues as before. When it sucks at the teats, on the other hand, an entirely different situation arises; milk fills the stomach, the contractions cease, and the animal grows quiet. Then as the stomach becomes empty again, the process will be repeated. The animal may happen upon the teats at the very beginning, or it may reach them after a prolonged active interval. In either event, the excursion always ends with the feeding process. The young doubtless frequently find the teats through the intervention of the mother, but largely by the trial and

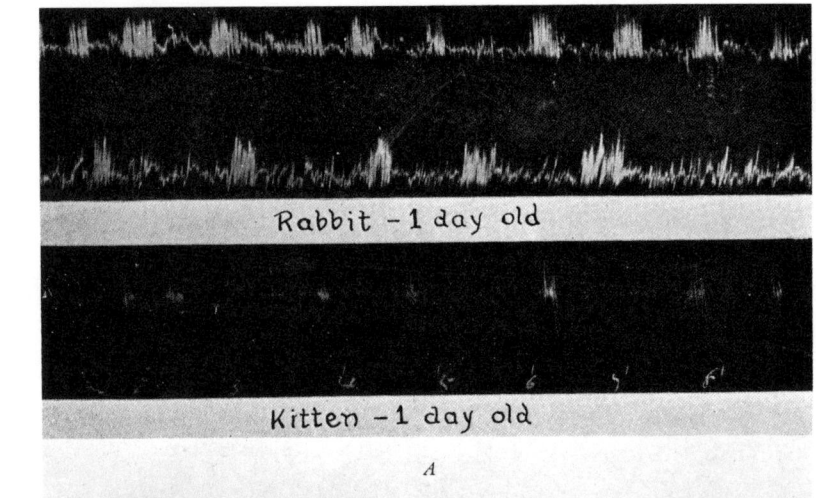

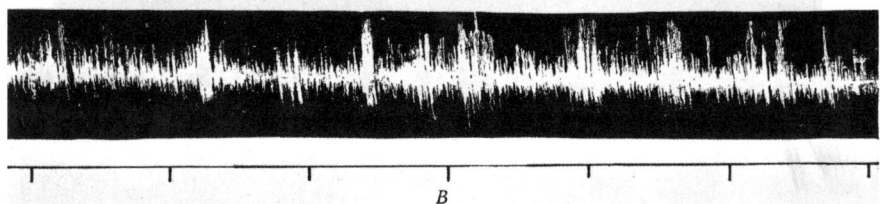

Fig. 18. Activity Records of New-Born Animals
A, *rabbit and kitten.* B, *chicken. Time in hours below the record.*

error method there is gradually established, on a conditioned reflex basis, an association between discomfort due to stomach contractions, feeding, and subsequent relief. In the adult rat, the preliminary restlessness which occurs during the time of small contractions is diverted at once into specific food seeking activities as soon as the main contractions begin.

It is interesting in this connection that the new-born guinea pig, rabbit, kitten, and chick, unlike the rat, show periodic activity at birth (see fig. 18 *A* and *B*). But how may this fact be brought into relation with the view developed above? It is important to note that while the rat is still in a comparatively embryonic condition at birth, these other animals are all fairly well developed and coördinated. The rat, for several days after birth, progresses much as a worm does, crawling and wriggling its way about; the new-born guinea pig, on the other hand, actually walks almost at once. In keeping with their periodic bodily activity, the more highly developed individuals probably show periodic stomach contractions at birth. We have as yet done no experiments to test this theory, but we hope soon to observe in detail the feeding

Animal Behavior and Internal Drives 67

habits of these animals to determine how the habits differ from those of the rat with regard to their genesis and development.

Further Observations on the Periodic Nature of Spontaneous Activity. Four-Day activity Rhythm in the Female

So much for the three to four-hour activity rhythm apparent in records taken during twelve to twenty-four hour periods. Our observations must now be extended over days and weeks instead of hours. The small triangular cages are impractical for this purpose because of the length of time required to count the individual marks on the smoked drum record. Activity for long periods can be measured more simply and much more accurately in the type of cage shown in figure 19,

Fig. 19. Apparatus Used for Measure Spontaneous Running Activty
The living compartment with the food cup and water bottle, and the cyclometer and lever, can be seen on one side of the partition, and the revolving drum on the other side (Richter and Wang, 1926).

which consists of a small living compartment just large enough to accommodate a food-cup and an adult animal, and a revolving drum to which the animal has free access at all times. By means of a cyclometer connected with the axle of the drum by an excentric lever, all revolutions, clockwise and counter clockwise, are recorded. A detailed description of the complete apparatus and method employed is given elsewhere (Richter and Wang, 1926; Richter, 1926; Wang, 1927). The rat, like many other small rodents, seems to enjoy running and spends much of its time in the drum. Although the daily activity averages between five and ten miles for most of the animals, as many as twenty-seven miles have been recorded for one individual in twenty-four hours.

Here again, casual observation of the running activity discloses nothing of its origin. Continuous records over long periods of time, however, reveal a fact far more striking than the tri-hourly rhythm described above. In the female rat the activity falls into a regular four-day cycle, most females running eight to ten miles every fourth day and but a fraction of a mile on the three days intervening. In the record in figure 20, in which activity measured in the number of revolutions is indicated

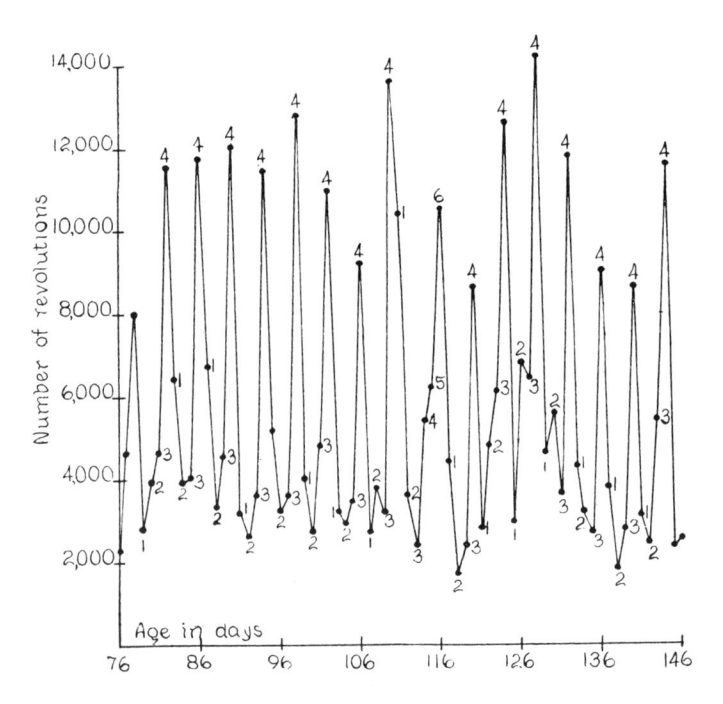

Fig. 20. Running Record of a Normal Female Showing the Four-Day Cycle

Animal Behavior and Internal Drives 69

on the ordinates, and the days of the experiment on the abscissae, the regular four-day peak is very evident. Since this rhythm, which was described independently by Wang (1923) and Slonaker (1924), occurs in an environment free from any cyclic disturbance, it, too, must have its origin within the organism. But what organ functions in the rat at a four-day rhythm?

Four-Day Activity Rhythm and the Ovulation Cycle

Observations of the ovulation cycle of the rat made by Long and Evans (1922) answer this question at once. These workers have shown, by the methods of Stockard and Papanicolaou (1917), that the length of the oestrous cycle in the rat is four days, with individual variations above and below this average. As is well-known, this was determined by histological studies of cast-off cells scraped with a small spatula from

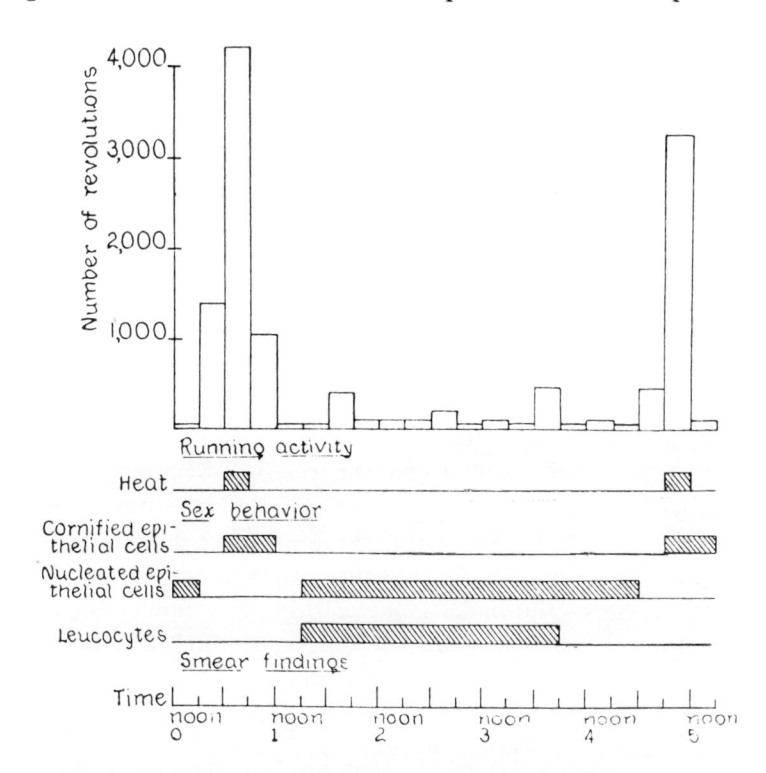

Fig. 21. Exact Temporal Relationship between Running Activity and the Ovulation Cycle, Established by Means of Six Hour Records (after Wang, 1923).

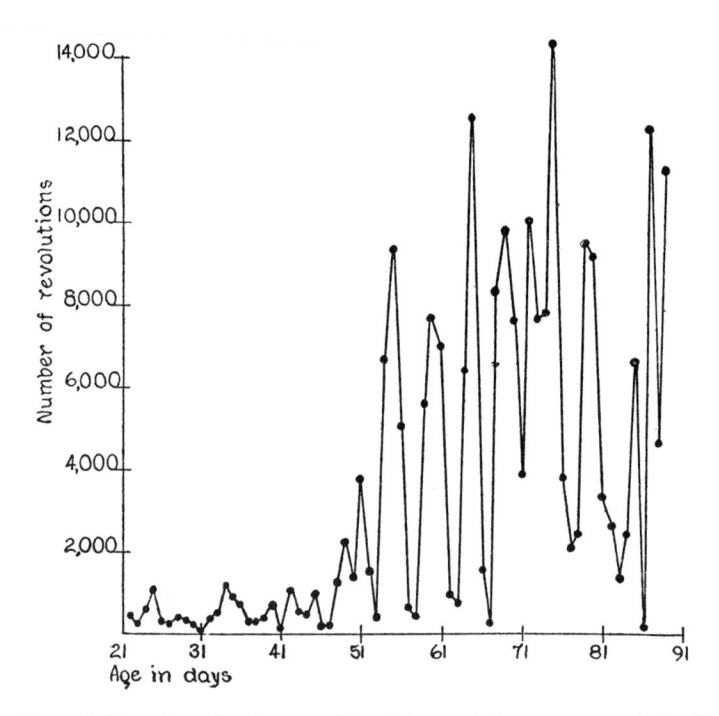

Fig. 22. Record Showing the Burst of Activity and Appearance of the Four-Day Cycle at Puberty (after Wang).

the vaginal mucosa. During the dioestrum nucleated epithelial cells and leucocytes are present, whereas during the periods of oestrus and ovulation only cornified cells appear.

Wang and Slonaker have been able to show by means of simultaneous smear and activity records, that the peak of running activity every fourth day just precedes ovulation. This is undoubtedly one of the most interesting correlations that have been made in animal behavior.

The question arises then, as to the relation between the running activity and the sex "drive" of the animal. Wang has found that females will mate for a short time just before and just after the peak of running activity is reached, while at all other times they are completely indifferent or even averse to the male. The exact relationship between running activity, vaginal smears, and sex activity, as worked out by Wang, is shown in figure 21. Records taken every six hours on all three phenomena showed that the great burst in running activity recorded on the day of oestrus is confined almost entirely to the six-hour interval which immediately precedes the appearance of cornified cells in the vaginal smear.

Animal Behavior and Internal Drives 71

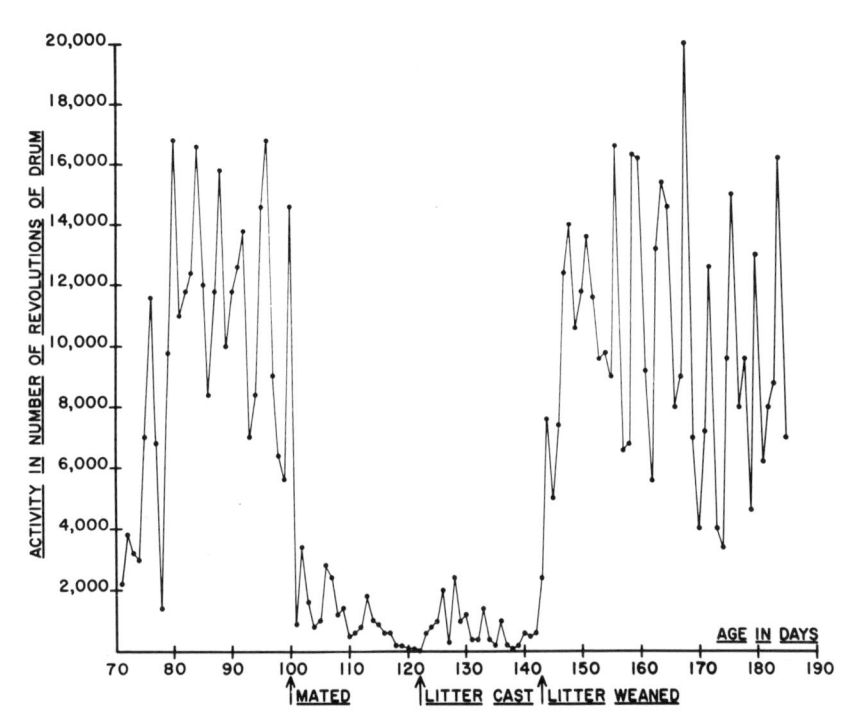

Fig. 23. Record Showing the Effect of Pregnancy and Lactation on Spontaneous Activity. The four-day cycle is absent during pregnancy and lactation, appearing again a short time after the litter is weaned (after Wang).

Obviously, therefore, the spontaneous activity is dependent on ovarian function. The degree of dependence can be demonstrated directly by numerous experiments performed on animals in which the ovaries were not functioning. Pre-pubescence, senility, pregnancy, pseudo-pregnancy, lactation, and castration all show a clear-cut effect in the activity readings. In figure 22, a typical normal record is presented to show the low running level before puberty and the sudden pubescent burst.

Pregnancy causes a 60 to 95 per cent decrease in activity which lasts through the entire gestation and lactation period (Slonaker, 1925; Wang, 1923. See fig. 23). Pseudo-pregnancy, produced when the tip of the uterus is stimulated with a glass rod introduced through the vagina, results in an immediate decrease which persists for fifteen days (Wang, 1923. See fig. 24), and sterile copulation performed by a vasectomized male has the same effect (Slonaker, 1925).

Similar results were obtained in a series of experiments in which a normal female had constant access to a cage containing a vasectomized

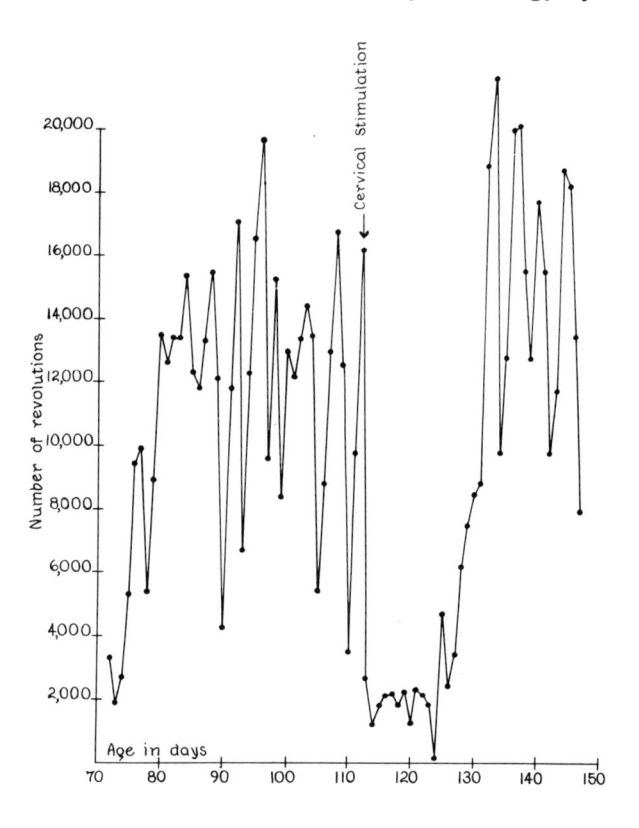

Fig. 24. *Effect of Pseudo-Pregnancy on Activity (after Wang).*

male. In these experiments a sex-box attached to the usual living cage connected with the revolving drum, was so arranged that the female could pass freely back and forth to visit the male, but the male could not get into the living cage and revolving drum. This separation was achieved quite simply by means of a board partition with a hole just large enough to admit the female, but too small for the male. A typical record obtained in this way is shown in figure 25. In order that we might differentiate running activity changes caused by the extra compartment from those caused by the presence of the male, we attached the sex-box a week before the male was introduced. The record shows that the mere addition of the sex cage produced no effect. When the male was placed in it, however, there was an immediate and prolonged decrease in activity which persisted for eight to ten days after he was removed again.

Figure 26 shows the effect of complete removal of the ovaries: the activity drops (60 to 95 per cent) to a flat, low level and the four-day

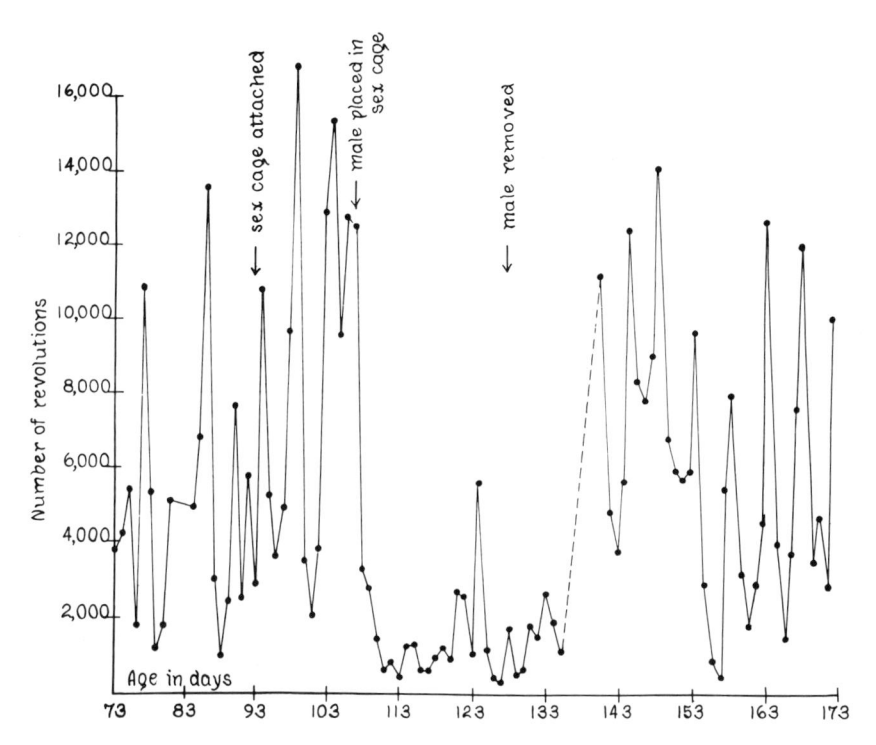

Fig. 25. Record Showing how the Presence of Male Affects the Activity of Female.

cycle disappears completely. When an animal is spayed before puberty its activity always remains low and nonrhythmical (Wang, 1923; Slonaker, 1924).

Finally the dependence of the running activity on the ovaries may be demonstrated most strikingly by the effects of ovarian implantation in spayed animals. Whenever the grafts "take," the activity begins to increase almost immediately, and it grows gradually higher until the normal running level of the female is reached. Then, if the grafted ovary is removed, the activity drops about 60 to 95 per cent, just as it does in the normal female after spaying.

These experiments show definitely that the high running level is dependent upon some substance secreted by the ovaries into the blood stream. The question now arises as to what part of the ovaries produces this substance. Bugbee and Simond (1926) have thrown some light on this problem by experiments in which the extract from pigs' follicles was injected into spayed rats. Such a procedure produces the same effect that successful implantation of an ovary would have produced— the activity shows a marked increase from the low spayed level to the

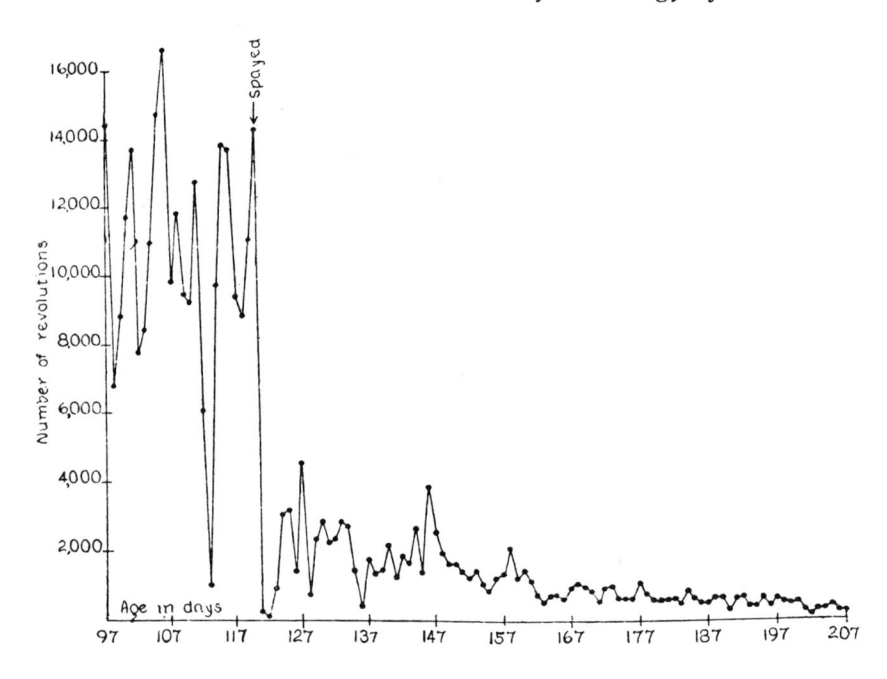

Fig. 26. Record Showing the Effect of the Complete Removal of Both Ovaries

level of normal animals and the genital tract resumes its normal condition.

Wang also has obtained these results by the injection of follicular extracts (Unpublished results. See fig. 27). He found that the smear changes are usually detected several days before the activity changes become well defined, and in many instances the activity and smear changes occur independently of each other. Accordingly he has concluded that there may be in the ovarian secretion one specific substance for furthering the growth and development of the genital tract and another for the production of activity. And on the basis of experiments in which he traumatized the ovaries (Wang and Guttmacher, 1927), this suggestion becomes even more plausible. It was found quite by chance that a small remnant of ovary left in the body produces very striking changes in both smear and activity findings. The activity, except for a drop of short duration immediately following the operation, usually regains its original level, but the four-day cycle is entirely absent. Coincident with the high irrhythmic activity level, the vaginal smears usually show cornified cells, the indication of oestrum in the normal animal. In some individuals, however, the other types of cells, as well as cornified cells, appear and disappear with very little relation to the changes in activity.

Animal Behavior and Internal Drives 75

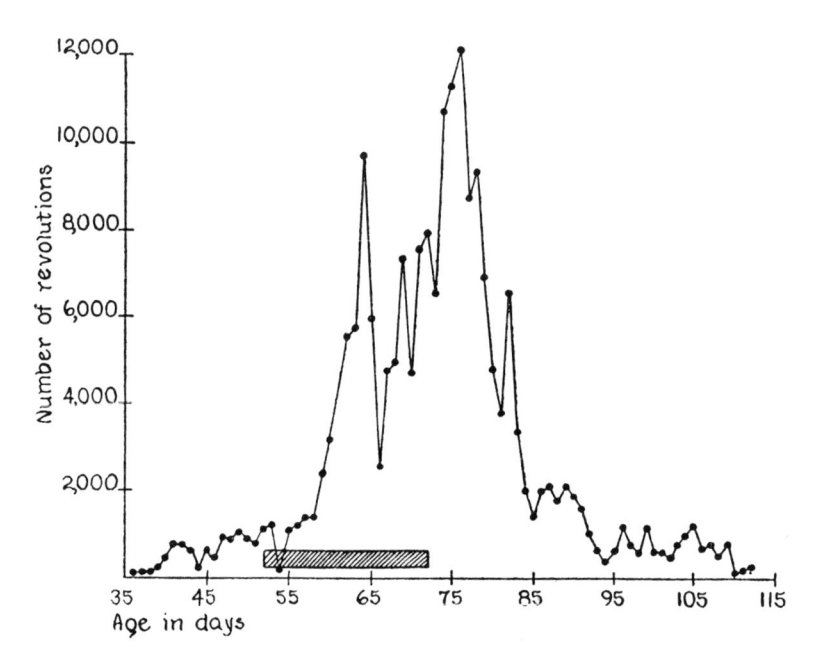

Fig. 27. Record Showing the Effect of Daily Injections of Follicin on the Running Activity of a Spayed Female. The shaded area indicates the period over which the extract was administered.

The question as to how and where the secretion acts to produce the activity has not yet been answered. We thought at first that, just as the three to four-hour rhythm was set up by stomach contractions, so the four-day cycle might have its origin in the contraction of some similar hollow viscus in the sex-apparatus, probably the uterus. Contrary to our expectations, however, Wang found that removal of the uterus affects neither the level of activity nor the four-day cycle (fig. 28), and Hoskins (1925, II) has recently confirmed these observations. The secretion, then, must take effect in some part of the central nervous system, either by simply increasing the irritability of the centers in the brain and spinal cord, or by actually stimulating those centers. Although definite evidence is lacking at present, we are inclined to hold to the latter possibility.

Spontaneous Running Activity of the Male

In the male the spontaneous running activity does not show the four-day cycle of the female, and the general average is somewhat lower. However, it is dependent on the sex glands, for when the animal

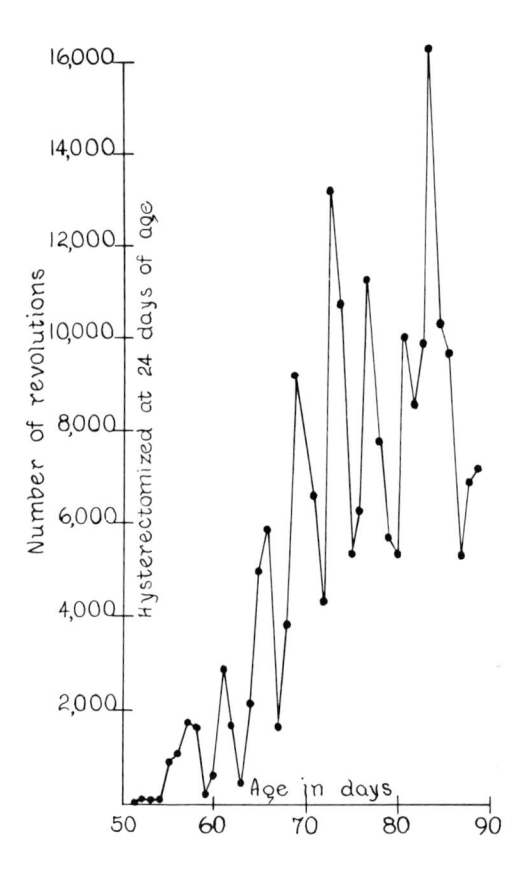

Fig. 28. Record Showing that Removal of the Uterus Affects Neither the Level of the Running Activity nor the Appearance of the Cycle

is castrated the activity drops about 60 per cent to the low level of the spayed female (fig. 29). Hoskins (1925, IV) was able to demonstrate no change in activity when testes were transplanted to the castrate, but we have found that the activity immediately increases to the normal running level (Richter and Wislocki, 1927). And transplantation of ovaries brings about an even greater increase (Wang, Richter, and Guttmacher, 1925). The activity then reaches the high level of the female, and, what is more interesting, it also shows the four-day rhythm (see fig. 30). When the grafts are removed the castrate effects appear again.

That the relation of running activity to the sex "drive" is not so clear-cut in the male as it is in the female, is demonstrated in a series of experiments in which each male was removed from the running cage for a half hour each day and placed with a female in "heat" in a large stock

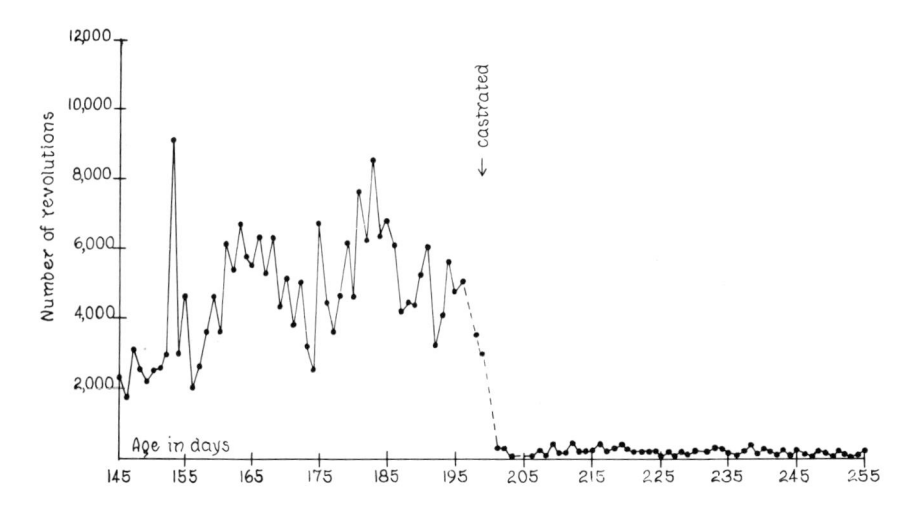

Fig. 29. Spontaneous Running Activity of a Male, Showing the Effect of Castration

cage. We found in this way that males showing a low running activity took no interest in the females and made no effort to copulate, whereas males with a high running activity copulated frequently. Contrary to the effect on the females, however, copulation, even when repeated as many as thirty times, produced no noticeable change in the running

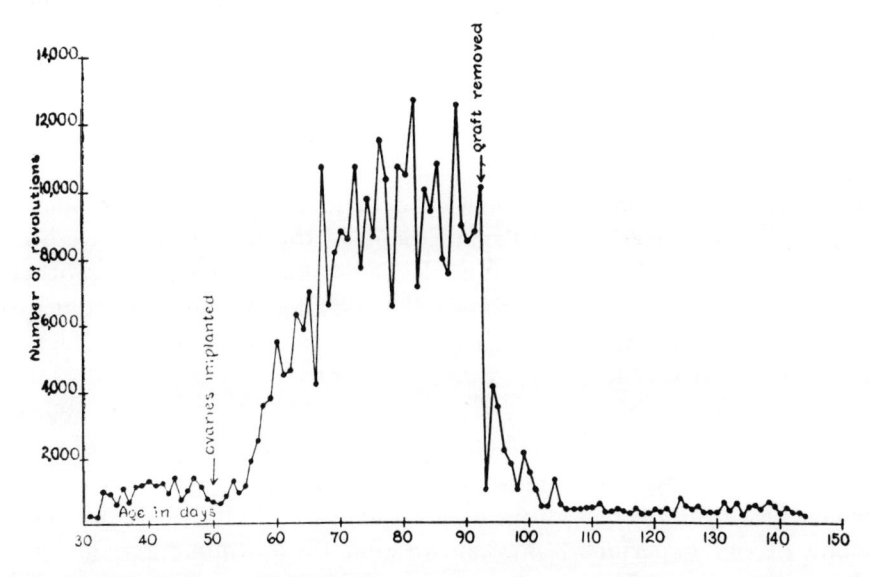

Fig. 30. Record Showing the Effect of Implantation of Ovaries into a Castrated Male

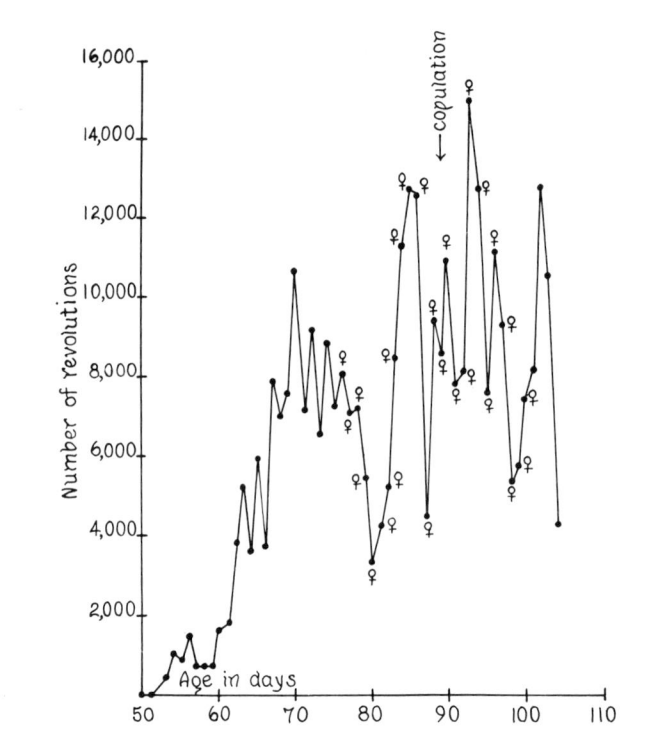

Fig. 31. Effect of Copulation on the Running Activity of a Male

level of the male on the following day. An activity curve of one of these animals, typical of the entire group, is presented in figure 31.

Nothing is known regarding the mechanism involved in the production of the activity of the male. That the removal of the seminal vesicles produced a no more noticeable effect than did the removal of the uterus in the female is shown in figure 32. We are trying to discover on what part of the testes the activity is dependent by a method similar to that used by Stockard and Papanicolaou in the female. We have been extirpating the testes in some animals at a peak of activity and in others at a depression with the expectation that detailed histological studies of these organs may disclose what parts are responsible for the fluctuations in activity. Although we have obtained no conclusive data the approach is promising.

It must be borne in mind before we pass on to a discussion of other rhythms that the work reported above has simply demonstrated to what extent the overt bodily activity *is dependent* on the sex hormone. None of our experiments has shown that the hormone actually *produces* the activity. Very probably a number of other organs are equally

Animal Behavior and Internal Drives

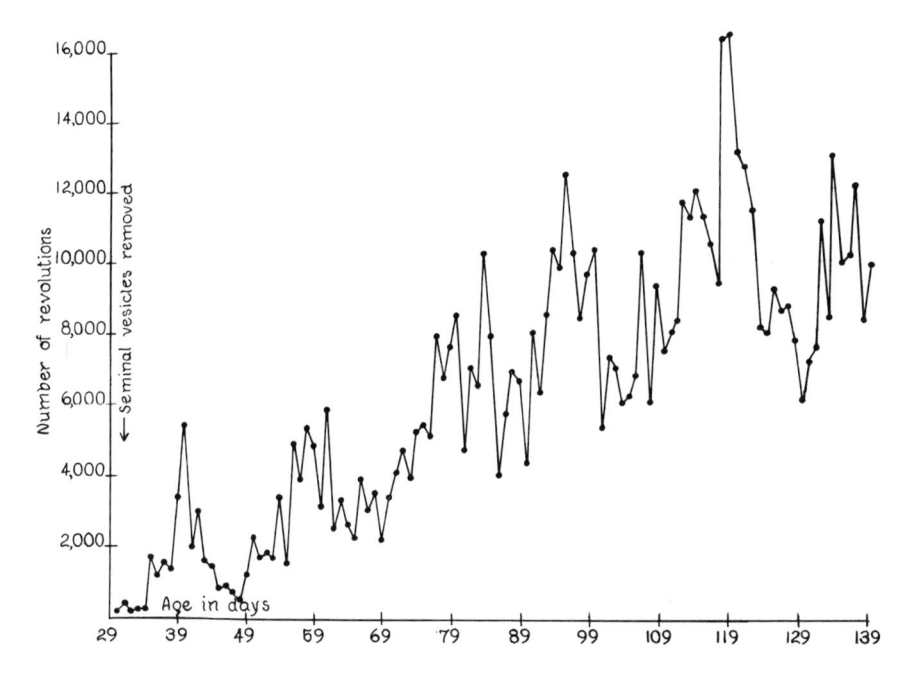

Fig. 32. Record of the Running Activity of a Male, Showing the Effect of Removal or Both Seminal Vesicles

The record differs in no way, so far as we have been able to determine, from that of a normal animal.

important, so that the elimination of any one of them would be sufficient to bring about the large decrease in activity which follows spaying or castration. We have tried removing the thyroid, parathyroid, and the pituitary, but in so far as our operations were successful, they produced no change in activity. Removal of the adrenals, on the other hand, causes a decrease in the running average, although the sex cycle still remains (See fig. 33). It can be seen, then, that we still do not have complete knowledge of the mechanism which determines the composite picture of the spontaneous activity.

Other Activity Rhythms

With a knowledge of the cyclic fluctuations in activity we may learn a great deal about changes which occur in the different organs within the body, when outwardly or without sacrifice of many animals nothing could be learned. The discovery of the four-day activity rhythm in the female rat, for instance, would have led very quickly to the

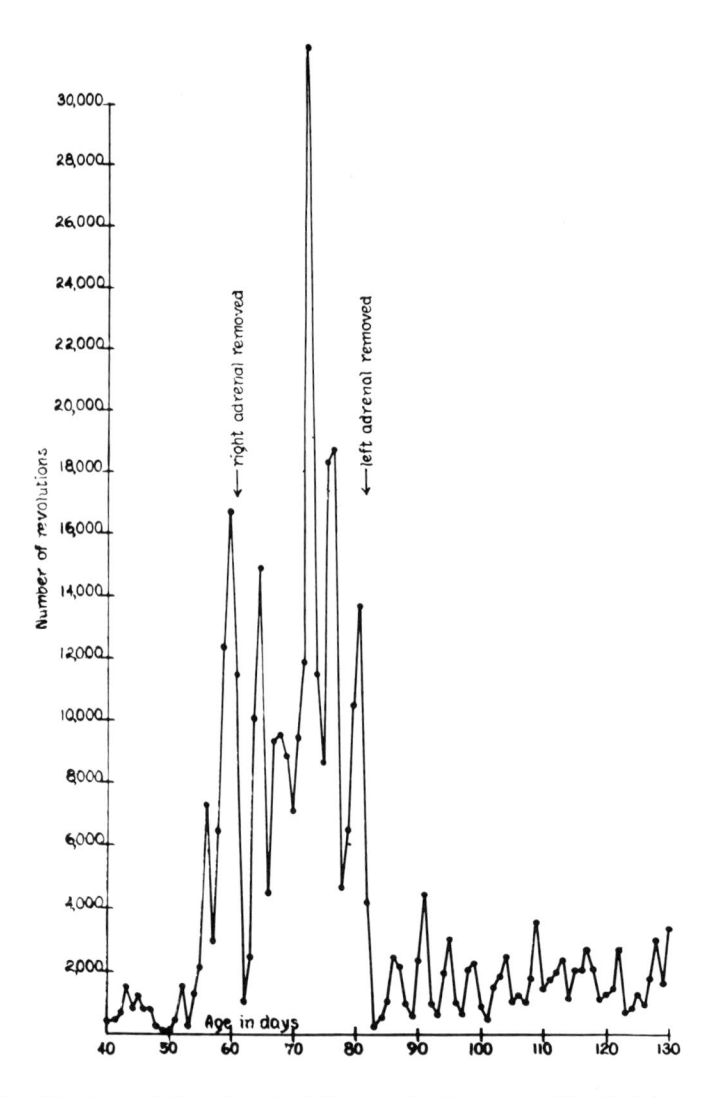

Fig. 33. Record Showing the Effect of the Removal of Both Adrenals

discovery of the oestrous rhythm had it not been already detected by other means. This same principle may be applied in a search for cyclic changes in other internal organs, since we have found periods of activity longer than four days in both males and females after the sex organs have been removed. There are at least two other fairly well-defined rhythms, one of from seven to ten days (fig. 34), and one of from sixteen to thirty days (figs. 35 and 36). Besides these two rhythms a number of others varying between forty and one hundred and twenty days have occasionally been observed by Slonaker (1926) and by us.

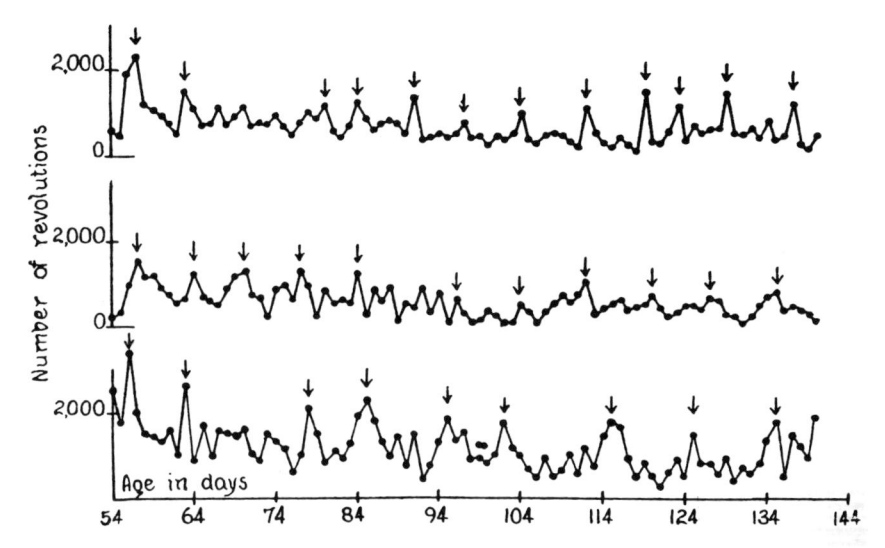

Fig. 34. Records from Two Castrated Males and One Spayed Female, Which Show Rhythms Varying from 5 to 8 Days

These rhythms have been observed in normals, but they are found most often in castrated or spayed animals probably because of the much lower running activity level.

Figure 37 shows the activity record of one animal in which a small remnant of one ovary remained.

The question arises now as to the origin and significance of these rhythms. The other internal glands, the thyroid, the parathyroid, the pituitary and the adrenals, suggest a possible source. We have been

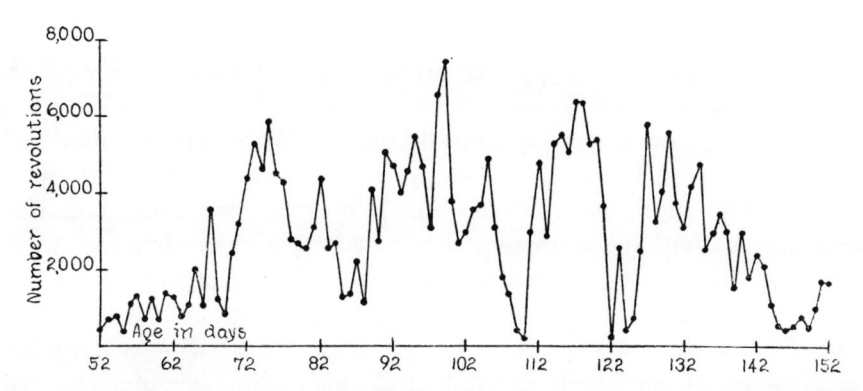

Fig. 35. Record of a Normal Male Showing a 16 to 20 Day Cyclic Change in the Running Activity Level

The cycles are much more irregular than the four-day cycle, but they are clearly present nevertheless.

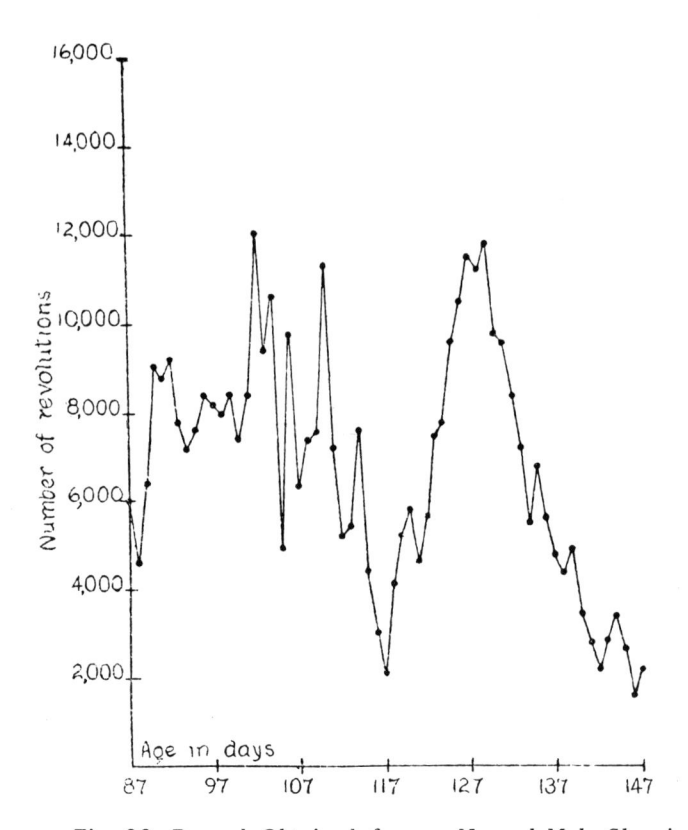

Fig. 36. Record Obtained from a Normal Male Showing One Very Striking Cycle of 29 Days Duration
The activity mounts steadily for 12 days, then decreases again equally steadily for the next 17 days. Such regular cycles often appear in the midst of an otherwise very irregular record.

removing each of these organs at various phases of activity but we have been unable as yet to make a study of the histological sections.

So much for the origin of these rhythms. What is their significance? Are they associated with some specific performance just as the three to four-hour and the four-day cycles are? It may be that, coinciding with these slower fluctuations of running activity, changes in such pursuits as burrowing, climbing, gnawing, fighting, nest-building, and other specific activities can be demonstrated. However, before we take up the question of these more complicated behavior patterns, we must consider briefly some of the purely physiological mechanisms in order that we may comprehend the complete activity picture presented by the organism.

Animal Behavior and Internal Drives 83

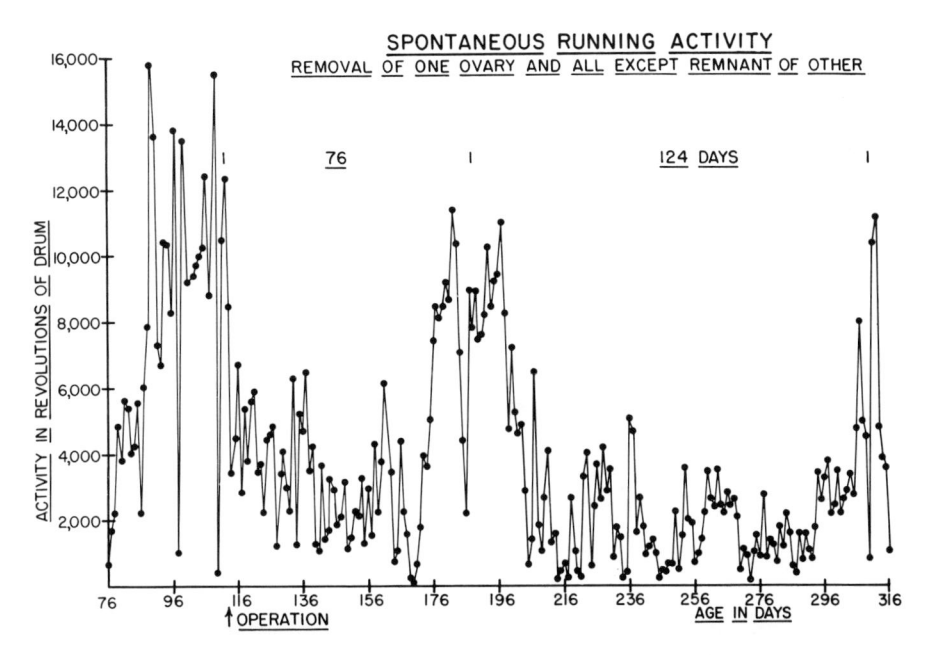

SPONTANEOUS RUNNING ACTIVITY
REMOVAL OF ONE OVARY AND ALL EXCEPT REMNANT OF OTHER

Fig. 37. Graph Showing Cycles of Much Larger Duration—90 to 120 Days
This record was obtained from a female with one ovary completely removed and the other partially cut away. The animal did not show the low activity of the spayed animal. On the contrary it showed cyclic fluctuations during which it reached a level nearly as high as that present before the ovary was traumatized.

Overt Responses of a Purely Physiological Nature

For this reason we have studied drinking, urination, and defecation, to determine whether these functions, too, are periodic. Records of the time interval at which these three responses occur show that they are all rhythmical.

Thirst was studied by means of the cages shown in figure 38. A recess large enough for the animal to enter and drink, but too small for it to lie down or turn around, was built on one side of the cage and an inverted watering tube was placed at the end away from the cage. The bottom of this recess was made of a piece of aluminum pivoted at one end and supported on a tambour at the other, so that whenever the animal entered to drink a mark was recorded on a smoked drum. The records, as may be seen in figure 39, show that the rat drinks about ten times a day at intervals of two and a quarter hours. The periodicity of the thirst response is quite as remarkable as that of the hunger response,

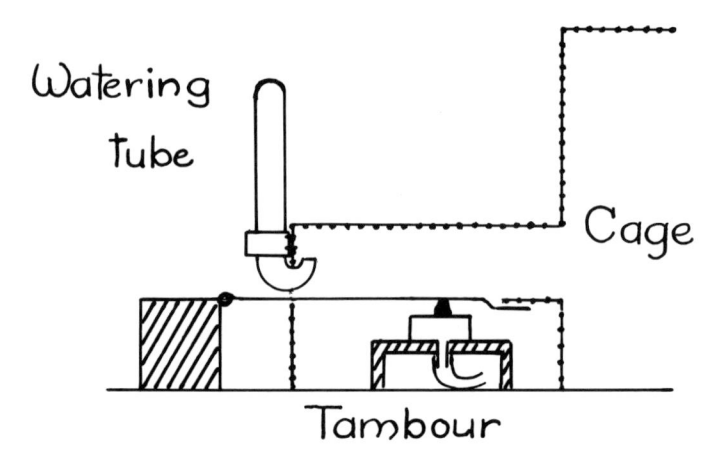

Fig. 38. Diagram of the Cage Used in Recording the Thirst Rhythm

in view of the current conception that the rats eat and drink at very frequent and irregular intervals.

Urination and defecation were recorded in the apparatus illustrated in figure 40. The small cage with a ½-inch mesh wirecloth bottom, rested over an 8-inch paraffined tin funnel. When the rat defecated, the feces slipped through the wire floor into the funnel and on to an inclined trough of fine-meshed wire below. As they dropped from the end of this trough they struck a small paper disc fastened to the end of a tambour, and the process was recorded as in figure 41. Urine was also collected in the funnel but it passed directly through the wire trough to another paper disc attached to another tambour. A record of urination is shown in figure 42.

From simultaneous records of urination and defecation obtained by this method, it was found that although these two functions are very regular, they are quite independent. Urination occurs approximately every two hours; defecation, every five hours, but the group of animals studied up to the present time is not sufficiently large to permit accurate statements of the time interval, nor can we show how these rhythms vary with age and sex.

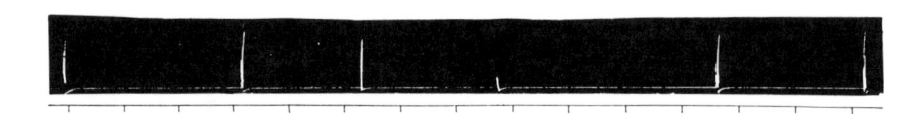

Fig. 39. Record Showing the Thirst Rhythm of an Adult Animal Time in hours below.

Animal Behavior and Internal Drives 85

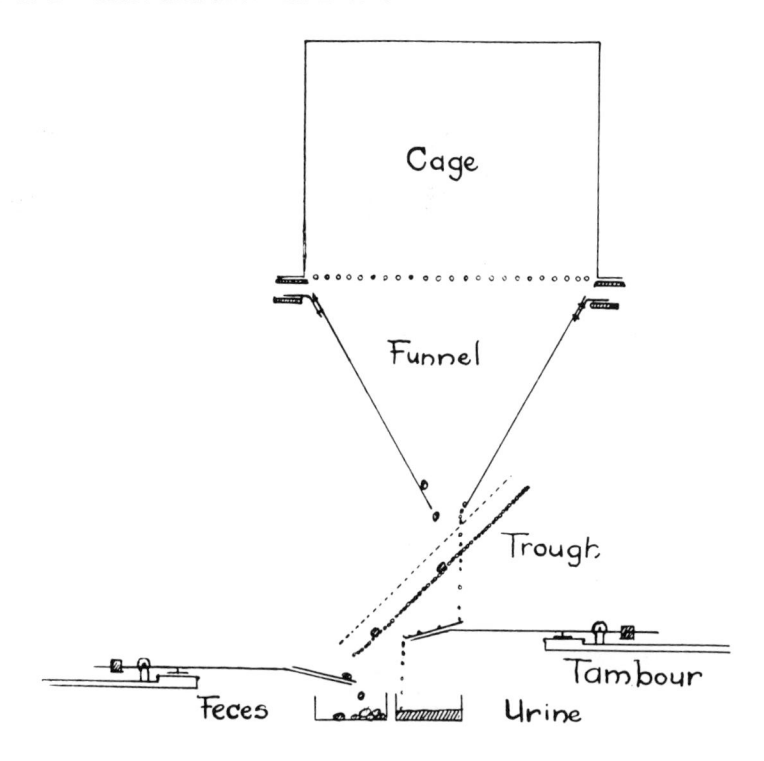

Fig. 40. Diagram of Apparatus Used to Record Urination and Defecation Rhythms.

These phenomena must reveal the periodicity of the bladder and rectum, but so far we do not know in what organ thirst is localized. Possibly through our knowledge of its periodicity we may obtain some clue as to its origin.

The results of all the experiments discussed above have shown how largely the spontaneous activities of the rat are periodic in nature, and are associated with periodically functioning organs. From these results, we see the animal as an organism carrying within itself various mechanisms discharging at different rates, to a great extent independently of one another. By way of summary we have listed in Table I the different

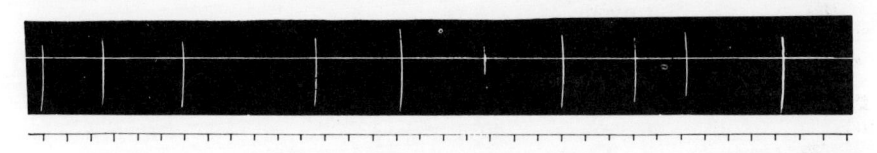

*Fig. 41. Record of the Defecation Rhythm of an Adult Rat
Time in hours below*

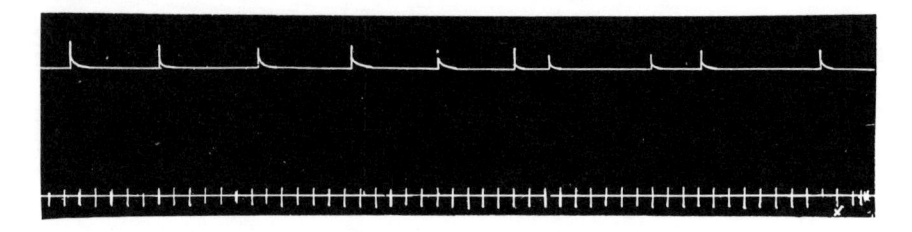

*Fig. 42. Record Showing the Urination Rhythm of an Adult Rat
Time in half-hour intervals.*

activities according to their periodicity and the organ with which they are associated.

Constructive Activities

With this work on the simpler forms of spontaneous behavior as a basis, we may now single out for study the more complicated and specific performances of the rat, such as burrowing, gnawing, nest-building, and social activities. At the present time nest-building is the only constructive activity which has been quantitatively studied. We may ask, then, what it is that makes the rat build nests. In order to answer this question we must arrange our experiment so that nest-building is practically the only outlet for the animal, and all other activities are either kept constant or eliminated. Such a situation in which

TABLE I

Activity	Periodicity	Associated Organ
Urination	2–3 hour	Bladder
Drinking	2–3 hour	?
Defecation	3–5 hour	Rectum
Eating	3–4 hour	Stomach
Mating ♀	4 day	Ovaries
Nest-building	?	?
Gnawing	?	?
Burrowing	?	?
Fighting	?	?
Migrating	?	?
?	7 days	?
?	18–22 days	?
?	40–120 days	?
?	?	Adrenal
?	?	Pituitary
?	?	Thyroid
?	?	Parathyroid

spontaneous nest-building can be measured has been worked out very satisfactorily by Kinder (1927), in two different types of cages.

In these cages the activity is measured in terms of the number of strips of crêpe paper used each day by the rat in building its nest. The method of presenting the paper differed in the two types of cages. In the first type 600 strips, one-half inch wide and 6 inches long, were scattered each day evenly over the floor, and the animals built their nests by pushing the strips into heaps. In cages of the second type, (fig. 43 *A* and *B*) 250 strips, 12 inches long, were hung over the sides so that

Fig. 43. One Type of Cage Used in Measuring Next Building Activity.
    A *shows the cage assembled without nest-building material. The walls are of galvanized iron and the top of wire cloth. The diameter of the cage is 36 inches and the height 18 inches.*
    B *shows the arrangement of the strips of crêpe paper over the sides of the cage. The strips were hung so that the rats could reach them comfortably only by standing on their hind feet (after Kinder, 1927).*

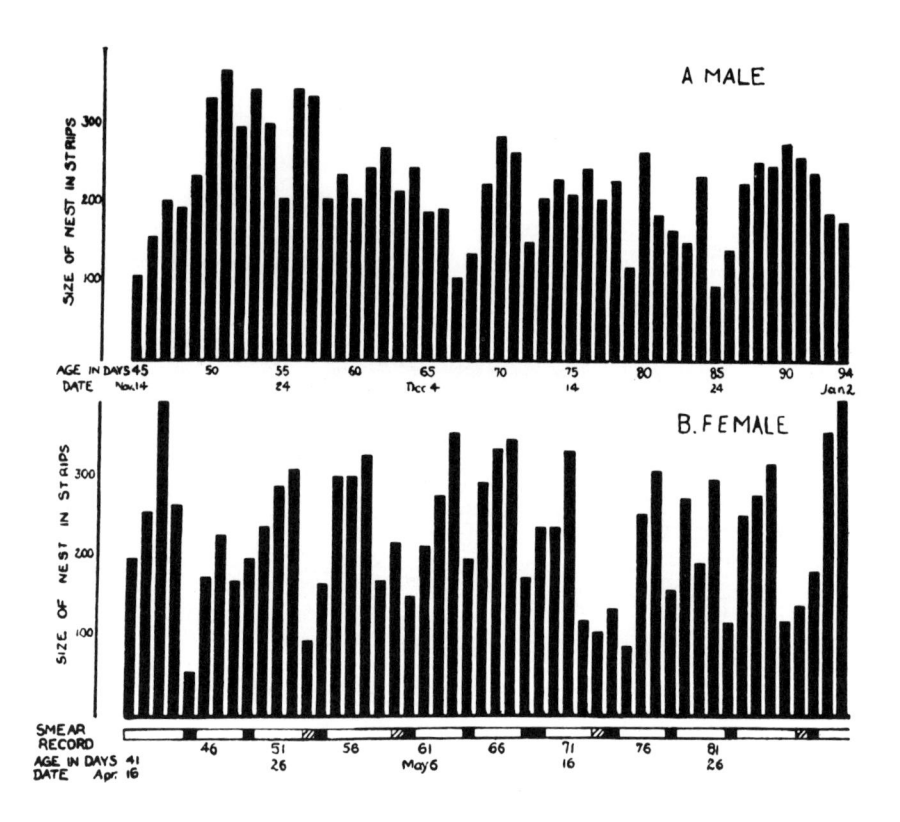

Fig. 44. Daily Records of the Nest-Building Activity of A, *a Male, and* B, *a Female, over a Period of 50 Days*

the animal had to pull down one strip at a time and take it to the nest. With these cages Kinder found that if the nests are removed each day rats of all ages will build a fresh nest within the following twenty-four hours. That the activity is present and equally strong in both sexes is shown by the records of the daily nest-building activity of a male and female given in figure 44 *A* and *B*. Moreover, nest-building is practically independent of experience, since young rats thirty days old raised in sawdust build perfect nests out of the crêpe paper the first time it is presented to them. But what is it that drives the rat to build nests? Again observations for short intervals tell us nothing about the mechanism involved. Observed over long periods of time under controlled conditions, will it also be periodic like the running activity? Here

Animal Behavior and Internal Drives 89

NEST-BUILDING AND RUNNING ACTIVITY
FEMALE RAT

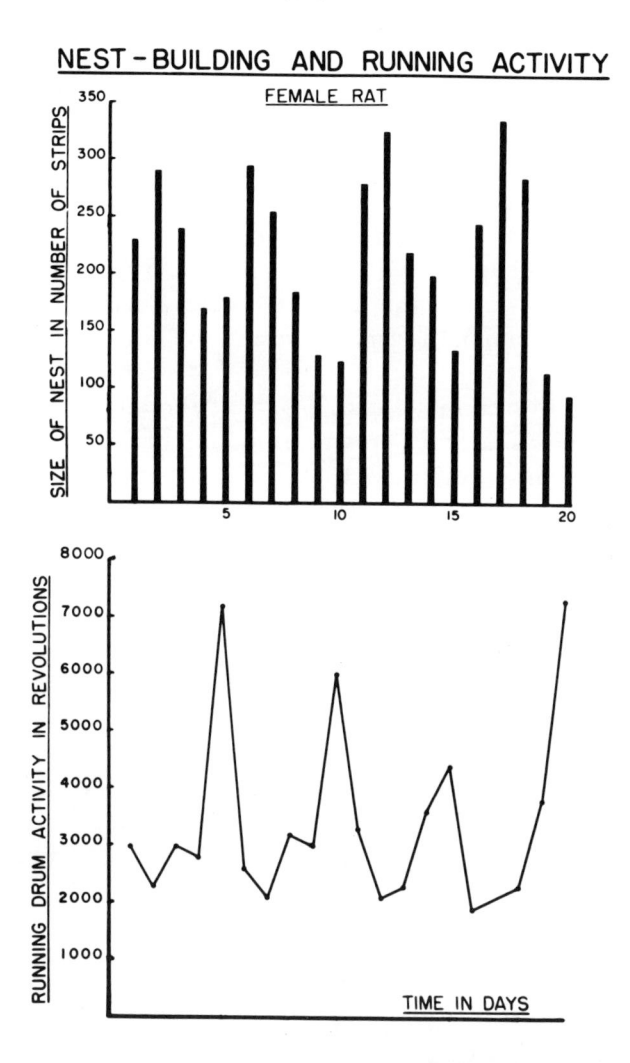

Fig. 45. Record Showing the Relation between Nest-Building and Running Activity (after Kinder)

Kinder found that the four-day rhythm of the female is present just as it was in the running activity (fig. 45), but it has a very different relation to the cycle. Nest-building is greatest in the dioestrous interval of low running activity and lowest during oestrus when the running activity is highest. At parturition and during lactation the nests are very large, but the controlling mechanism is obviously not an essential part of the reproductive activity since the males often built nests as large as those of the mother rats.

Kinder found that all phases of the nest-building phenomenon have one feature in common that indicates the origin of the activity: every phase can be understood as a part of the heat-regulating mechanism by means of which the body-temperature is maintained at a constant level. The activity increases in low temperatures and decreases in high temperatures. It is high when there is a tendency for the body temperature to decrease, before puberty, during the inactive dioestrous interval, during pregnancy and lactation, and during starvation; it is low at oestrus, when the animal is very active and the body temperature tends to increase.

We may regard nest-building as a part of the heat-regulating mechanism, just as we consider the growth of fat and hair during cold weather a part of the more primitive physiological manifestations of heat conservation. Nest-building, like the building of shelters and the wearing of clothing, is a much more highly developed method of maintaining a normal body temperature, but it is nevertheless an expression of the same impetus that produces the increase in fat and hair in more primitive animals (C.J. Martin 1901). The mechanism of the drive involved here, therefore, is very different from that present in either the hunger or the sex activities.

Allied to nest-building in the rat are probably burrowing, the tendency of the animal to wedge itself into small spaces with contact on all sides, and its desire to huddle together with several of its mates. These activities also tend to conserve heat, in contrast to running, climbing, and jumping, which contribute to the maintenance of a constant body-temperature through heat production.

The various performances which, although associated with other drives, may be considered as contributing to the heat-regulating process, can be grouped as follows:

$$\left.\begin{array}{l}\text{Nest-building}\\ \text{Burrowing}\\ \text{Huddling into small spaces}\\ \text{Huddling together—social contact}\end{array}\right\} \text{conserve body heat}$$

$$\left.\begin{array}{l}\text{Running}\\ \text{Climbing}\\ \text{Jumping}\end{array}\right\} \text{increase heat production}$$

Thus far we have investigated the different activities of the rat separately under more or less isolated and controlled conditions. We believe that it is possible, however, to study the animal under normal

Animal Behavior and Internal Drives

conditions, when it can indulge in any of the activities present in its usual outdoor environment. For this purpose we have constructed the set of cages shown in figure 46, in which a record can be obtained of the time spent each day by the rat in climbing, running, burrowing, gnawing eating, drinking, and mating. This cage makes it possible to account for the activity of the animal each day during every minute of the twenty-four hours. The large triangular central cage and all of the smaller cages at the side, except the revolving drum and the climbing tower, are supported on tambours. Running activity is recorded both graphically and with a cyclometer; climbing activity, by counting the number of times the animal goes up and down the tower each day. Both the entrance to the tower and the top part are supported on tambours, so that a record is made on smoked paper each time the animal starts up the tower and when it reaches the top.

Because of the fact that we had only one cage we were not able to gather enough data to be of statistical value, but we have made sufficient observations to know that with some refinement of this method the behavior of the rat can be thoroughly studied in the laboratory. Certainly with this type of cage we can obtain a normal environment for the animal, in so far as it has an outlet for most of its different drives, and if we can judge how normal the environment is by the type of rat that it produces, the success of the method is unquestionable. An individual brought up in the multiple cage is far more intelligent than one raised in the ordinary running cage. Within the multiple cage the animal shows all kinds of constructive and imaginative activities, rarely, if ever, seen in an ordinary laboratory rat, and on occasions when it escapes it avoids recapture with extraordinary success. We may note in passing that were rats of this environment used for experiments on extirpation of the different areas in the cortex of the brain, much more noticeable defects in behavior might possibly be demonstrated as a result of the injuries than have appeared thus far in the rat kept under the usual laboratory conditions.

Individual differences are quite striking in the multiple cage if we may judge from our small number of animals. One rat will spend most of its time in the climbing tower, passing up and down as many as thirty or forty times a day; another will spend all of its time in the sex box; and another will gnaw all day long. None of our records have been taken over sufficiently long periods to permit us to give any perspective on either the constancy and fluctuations or the importance of the different activities in the life of the rat, but we do know that in this cage the running activity in the drum is reduced in every case to a few hundred revolutions per day. It is very interesting also, that in these

Fig. 46. Multiple Activity Cage

cages where the animal has many different diversions the frequency of its eating period is greatly reduced. It enters the food-box once every five or six hours, and sometimes even less frequently, but whether it actually eats less food we have not yet determined.

That even the most complicated form of the rat's behavior may be studied in this cage is brought out by the following observations. In experiments on one animal a liberal supply of building material—sticks, rope, stones, and cloth—was placed in the large central cage. This animal had habitually deposited its feces in the water-cup. Usually the water was changed every day, but on one occasion, by some neglect, it was not changed for several days, so that the resulting odor became very unpleasant. At this point the animal started to cover the hole over the water-cup. It first removed part of the upper layer of the cardboard bottom of the large central cage, and dragged it into the water-box. It placed the cardboard over the cup and smoothed it down on all sides until the hole was perfectly covered. Then from the bottom of the central cage it lifted stones larger than its head three inches into the drinking cage and placed them over the cardboard cover. Besides the large stones numerous pebbles and sticks were used until the water-box was completely blocked. The animal had cut off its only water supply by this performance. Since we wished to see what it would do when it became very thirsty, the material was left undisturbed and no other water was given. After three days, the animal pushed all of the sticks and stones from the drinking cage into the large central cage, tore up the cardboard seal, and drank its fill of the polluted water. This observation is certainly comparable to those made in the field. Had our apparatus been working better just at this time we should have obtained a complete biological record of this very interesting incident.

Another performance likewise constructive but less complicated was frequently observed. The rats plug up the entrance to any of the smaller cages whenever they have been frightened on entering them. This is the only explanation that can be offered for the frequency with which adult rats closed the entrance to the running drum shortly after they were placed in the cage. In one instance the opening was plugged up so tightly with nest-building material that a knife had to be used to open it up again.

Many similar examples could be given to demonstrate that in our artificially constructed environment practically every variety of behavior observable in a natural environment is obtained. And with a record of the way in which the animal spends its time before and after such episodes much more light will be thrown on their origin.

List of Literature

Boldīreff, V. N. 1904. [Periodic work of the digestive apparatus on an empty stomach.] Arch. biol. nauk., S. Peterb., 11, p. 1. Transl. 1905. Arch. c. sc. biol., 11, p. 1.

Bugbee, E. P., and Simond, A. E. 1926. The increase of voluntary activity of ovariectomized albino rats caused by injections of ovarian follicular hormone. Endocrinology, 10, p. 349.

Cannon, W. B. 1915. Bodily Changes in Pain, Hunger, Fear, and Rage; an Account of Recent Researches into the Function of Emotional Excitement. New York.

—— and Washburn, A. L. 1912. An explanation of hunger. Amer. J. of Physiol., 29, p. 441.

Carlson, A. J. 1916. The Control of Hunger in Health and Disease. Chicago.

—— and Ginsburg, H. 1915. The gastric hunger contractions of the newborn. Amer. J. of Physiol., 37, p. 29.

Hoskins, R. G. 1925. Studies on vigor. II. The effect of castration on voluntary activity. Amer. J. of Physiol., 72, p. 324.

——. 1925. Studies on vigor. IV. The effect of testicle grafts on spontaneous activity. Endocrinology, 9, p. 277.

Kinder, E. F. 1927. A study of the nest-building activity of the albino rat. J. of Exp. Zool., 47, p. 117.

Long, J. A., and Evans, H. M. 1922. The oestrous cycle in the rat and its associated phenomena. Mem. Univ. of Calif., Berkeley, 6.

Martin, C. J. 1901. Thermal adjustment and respiratory exchange in monotremes and marsupials. A study in the development of homeothermism. Philosophical Transactions, 195, B, p. 1.

Martin, C. L., and Rogers, F. T. 1927. Hunger pain. Amer. J. of Roentgenology and Radium Therapy, 17, no. 2, p. 222.

Moss, F. A. 1924. Study of animal drives. J. of Exp. Psychology, 7, p. 165.

Patterson, T. L. 1914. The variations in the hunger contractions of the empty stomach with age. Amer. J. of Physiol., 33, p. 473.

——. 1915. The cause of the variations in the gastric hunger contractions with age. Amer. J. of Physiol., 37, p. 316.

Richter, C. P. 1922. A behavioristic study of the activity of the rat. Comp. Psychology Monographs, 1, no. 2.

——. 1926. A study of the effect of moderate doses of alcohol on the growth and behavior of the rat. J. of Exp. Zool., 44, p. 397.

—— and Wang, G. H. 1926. New apparatus for measuring the spontaneous motility of animals. J. Lab. and Clin. Med., 12, p. 289.

—— and Wislocki, G. B. 1928. Activity studies on castrated male and spayed female rats with testicular grafts in correlation of the activity with the histology of the grafts. *Am. J. Physiol.* 86, p. 651.

Rogers, F. T. 1916. The hunger mechanism of birds. Proc. Soc. Exp. Biol. and Med., 13, p. 119.

—— and Martin, C. L. 1926. X-ray observations of hunger contractions in man. Amer. J. of Physiol., 76, p. 349.

Slonaker, J. R. 1924. The effect of pubescence, oestruation and menopause on the voluntary activity in the albino rat. Amer. J. of Physiol., 68, p. 294.

——. 1925. The effect of copulation, pregnancy, pseudo-pregnancy, and lactation on the voluntary activity and food consumption of the albino rat. Amer. J. of Physiol., 71, p. 362.

———. 1926. Long fluctuations in voluntary activity of the albino rat. Amer. J. of Physiol., 77, p. 503.

Stockard, C. R., and Papanicolaou, G. N. 1917. The existence of a typical oestrous cycle in the guinea pig with a study of its histological and physiological changes. Amer. J. of Anat., 22, p. 225.

Stone, C. P. 1924. Delay in the awakening of copulatory ability in the male albino rat incurred by defective diets. I. Quantitative deficiency. J. of Comp. Psychology, 4, no. 2, p. 195.

———. 1925. The effects of cerebral destruction on the sexual behavior of rabbits. I. The olfactory bulbs. Amer. J. of Physiol., 71, no. 2, p. 430.

———. 1925. Delay in the awakening of copulatory ability in the male albino rat incurred by defective diets. II. Qualitative deficiency. J. of Comp. Psychology, 5, no. 2, p. 177.

———. 1925. The effects of cerebral destruction on the sexual behavior of rabbits. II. The frontal and parietal regions. Amer. J. of Physiol., 72, no. 2, p. 372.

———. 1925. Preliminary note on the maternal behavior of rats living in parabiosis. Endocrinology, 9, no. 6, p. 505.

———. 1926. The initial copulatory response of female rats reared in isolation from the age of twenty days to the age of puberty. J. of Comp. Psychology, 6, no. 1, p. 73.

Szymanski, J. S. 1920. Aktivität und Ruhe bei Tieren und Menschen. Zeitschr. f. allg. Physiol., 18, p. 105.

———. 1922. Aktivität und Ruhe bei den Mensch en. Zeitschr. für angewandte Psychologie, 20 p. 192.

Tracy, H. C. 1926. The development of motility and behavior reactions in the toadfish (*Opsanus tan*). J. of Comp. Neurology, 40, p. 253.

Wada, T. 1922. An experimental study of hunger in its relation to activity. Arch. of Psychology, no. 57.

Wang, G. H. 1923. The relation between "spontaneous" activity and oestrous cycle in the white rat. Comp. Psychology Monographs, 2, no. 6.

———. 1927. The effect of thyroid feeding on the spontaneous activity of the albino rat and its relation to accompanying physiological changes. Bull. of the Johns Hopkins Hospital, 40, p. 304.

——— and Guttmacher, A. F. 1927. The effect of ovarian traumatization on the spontaneous activity and genital tract of the albino rat, correlated with a histological study of the ovaries. Am. J. Physiol. 82, p. 335.

———, Richter, C. P., and Guttmacher, A. F. 1925. Activity studies on male castrated rats with ovarian transplants, and correlation of the activity with the histology of the grafts. Amer. J. of Physiol., 73, p. 581.

BIOLOGICAL CLOCKS IN MEDICINE AND PSYCHIATRY: SHOCK-PHASE HYPOTHESIS*†

Biological clocks in medicine and psychiatry we think of as devices of the body that keep time with relative independence of external conditions and events: each in its own units and with varying degrees of accuracy.

What are these clocks? And where are they located? By all odds the best-known example is the ovarian clock, which for several decades of a woman's life determines the time of ovulation, usually at about 28-day intervals.

What other clocks are there? Why aren't they more readily apparent? What makes them run? What part do they play in our lives? Of what interest are they to medicine in general and psychiatry in particular?

Study of these clocks produces new perspectives on the normal and abnormal functioning of various organs of the body, such as peripheral organs, endocrine glands, and the brain.

It is true that normal human beings give little indication of possessing

---

This paper was originally published in the *Proceedings* of the National Academy of Sciences, Vol. 16, No. 11, November 1960, and later in the *Bulletin of the Johns Hopkins Hospital*, Vol. X, No. 12, September 1954. Reprinted by permission.
* This material was presented in part in the Thomas Salmon Lectures delivered in New York City, December 2, 1959. The published lectures give a full account of our observations of biological clocks not only of man but of animals; much of the present material was presented in a symposium on "Biological Clocks" organized by the Long Island Biological Laboratories and held at Cold Spring Harbor in June, 1960. Drs. E. A. Park and K. K. Rice made many helpful criticisms and suggestions.
† Studies carried out under grants from the National Institute of Public Health and the National Science Foundation, and through the opportunities offered by a year's membership at the Institute for Advanced Study in Princeton, New Jersey, 1957–1958.

biological clocks—other than the 24-hour clocks of men and women and the 28-day menstrual clocks of women. But many other timed mechanisms are present, as becomes unmistakably clear under certain abnormal conditions.

These clocks manifest their existence through the appearance of one or more of a number of physical and mental symptoms. Let me give a few examples: first, of clocks manifesting themselves through primarily physical symptoms; and second, of others that become evident through primarily mental or emotional symptoms. (I shall in each case present them in order of the lengths of the units in which the clocks measure time, beginning with the shortest intervals we have detected so far.)

Clocks That Manifest Their Presence Through Primarily Physical Symptoms

Evidence for the existence of a clock that measures time in the shortest units (12 hours) is presented in the temperature chart of a 19-year-old girl in Figure 1 (1). Ordinates show body temperature readings taken at frequent intervals throughout the day and night. Peaks of 104.2–105.3°F were reached twice every 24 hours. With ascending temperatures the patient was increasingly ill; once the peak

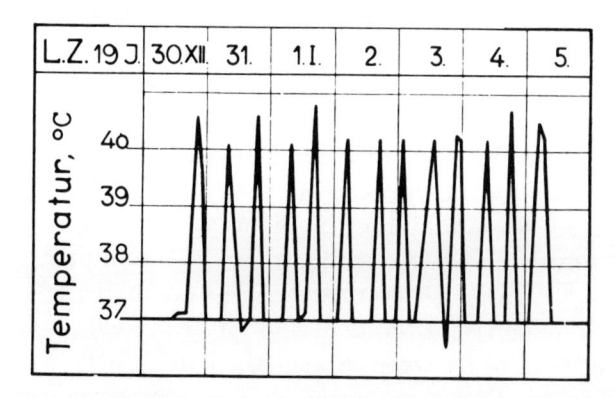

Fig. 1. Hourly temperature readings showing 12-hour spikes of body temperature in a 19-year-old girl (Hitzig, 1955). These peaks came in a series of 20–28 fairly regular intervals of 5 months. It is noteworthy that these temperature cycles had been present in this patient from early childhood; further that almost identical cycles subsequently appeared in her daughter at the age of 9 months and were still definitely present at the age of 6 years—at the time of the publication of Hitzig's report. During the intervals between each series of temperature peaks, both mother and child were entirely free from all abnormal symptoms.

FOOD ALLERGY
ROWE, 1948

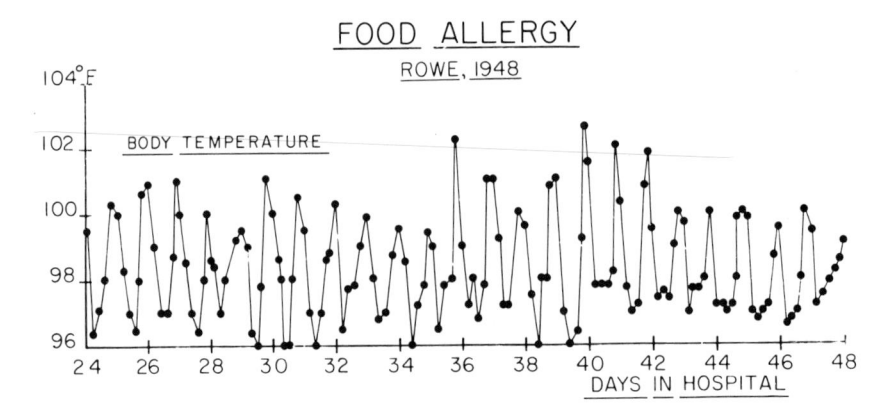

Fig. 2. Graph showing part of daily records (24–48th day) of 130-day stay in hospital of an 18-year-old girl suffering from food allergy and showing 24-hour cycles. Rowe's cereal-free elimination diet, started on the 122nd day of the patient's stay in the hospital, promptly interrupted the 24-hour fever cycles. (Redrawn from Rowe, 1948.)

had been passed she felt a remarkable relief from symptoms. Blood and other studies failed to explain the fever.

The presence of a clock that measured time in units of 24 hours may be seen in the temperature chart of an 18-year-old girl in Figure 2 (2). This patient suffered from a food allergy. Ordinates show body temperature recorded at frequent intervals during the day and night. Body temperature fluctuated at 24-hour intervals not only far above but far below the normal level. During periods of fever the patient experienced cramping in the mid-abdomen and in the rectum; at other times she was free of discomfort.

Evidence for the existence of a clock that measured time in units of 48 hours is presented in the daily records of body temperature and pulse rate of an 8-year-old boy in Figure 3 (1). Since the age of 4 months this boy had shown attacks of fever, severe pain in head and chin, polyuria, neutropenia, every 48 hours and lasting 3–5 hours. The original attack occurred after a period of high fever subsequent to small-pox vaccination. Between attacks the patient played and was free of all disturbances. From the presence of an enlargement of the third ventricle, polyuria, and other symptoms, Hitzig concluded that the patient probably suffered from a lesion in the diencephalon.

The existence of a clock that measured time in still longer units (9 days) was manifested in a 43-year-old man by periodic swelling of the right knee (Fig. 4) (3). Solid black areas indicate times during which the right knee was swollen. Intervals between onsets of succeeding attacks

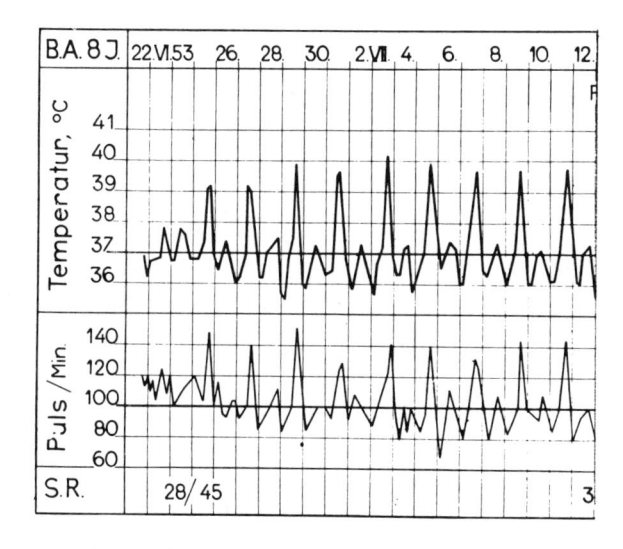

Biological Clocks in Medicine and Psychiatry 99

Fig. 3. Graph showing daily records of body temperature and pulse rate of 8-year-old boy (Hitzig, 1955).

are shown in days. In each attack the knee remained swollen 3–5 days; during the remainder of the cycle there was no evidence of abnormality. The synovial spaces that become filled with fluid during episodes of hydrarthrosis are illustrated in the drawing in Figure 5 (4). Many of these patients state that at the start of an attack they have the sensation of water literally rushing into the knees.

Evidence for the existence in one individual of two independent clocks that measured time in units of 7 or nearly 7 days is shown in the record of a 47-year-old man also with intermittent hydrarthrosis (Fig. 6) (5). In this case the chart gives daily measurements of the circumference of each knee in centimeters for a period of 140 days. In many instances the swelling in one knee was at a maximum while it was at a minimum in the other. Thus, at the start of the record, maximum peaks came on Tuesdays and Wednesdays in the left knee and on Fridays and Saturdays in the right.

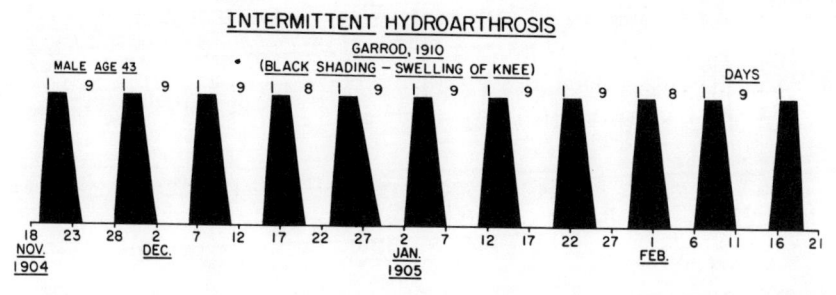

Fig. 4. Daily records showing periods of swelling of knee in a 43-year-old man with intermittent hydrarthrosis. Lengths of intervals between attacks are shown in days. (This 95-day chart was redrawn from Garrod, 1910.)

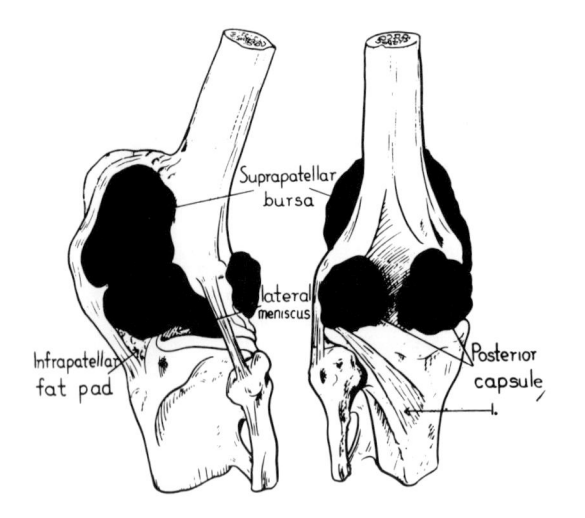

Fig. 5. Drawings showing the synovial spaces (solid black shading) of the knee. (Modified from Brantigan and Voshell, 1941.)

The presence of a clock that measured time in still longer units (17–19 days) was manifest in the blood count of a 41-year-old woman suffering from cyclic agranulocytosis as seen in Figure 7 (6). The number of polymorphonuclear cells fluctuated between 4,000 and zero every 17–19 days. Lip and cheek ulcers appeared during each cycle just

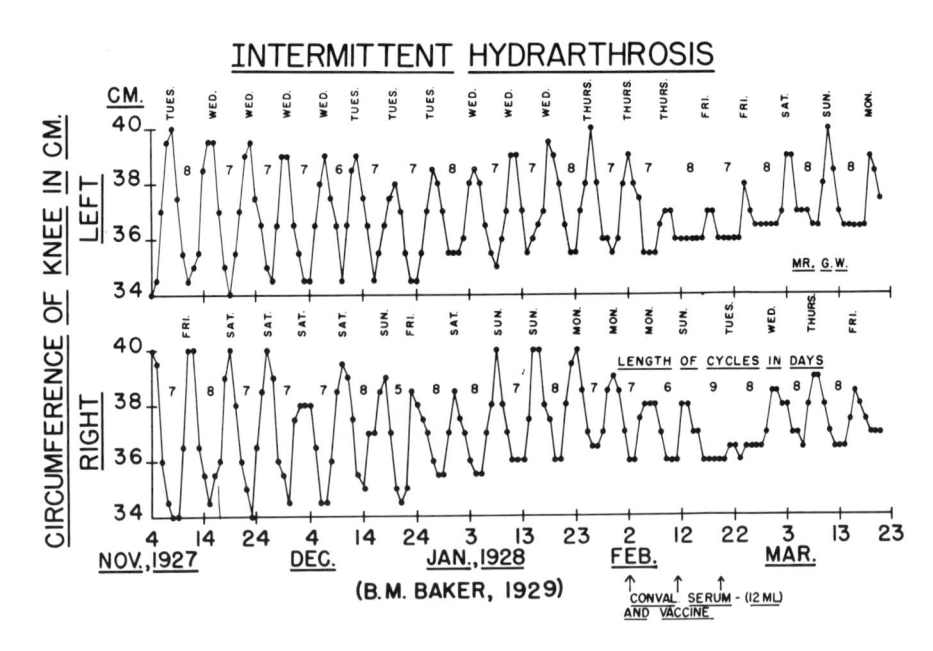

Fig. 6. Daily records of circumferences of the right and left knees of a patient with intermittent hydrarthrosis. Ordinates give circumference of each knee in centimeters. (Redrawn from Baker, 1929.)

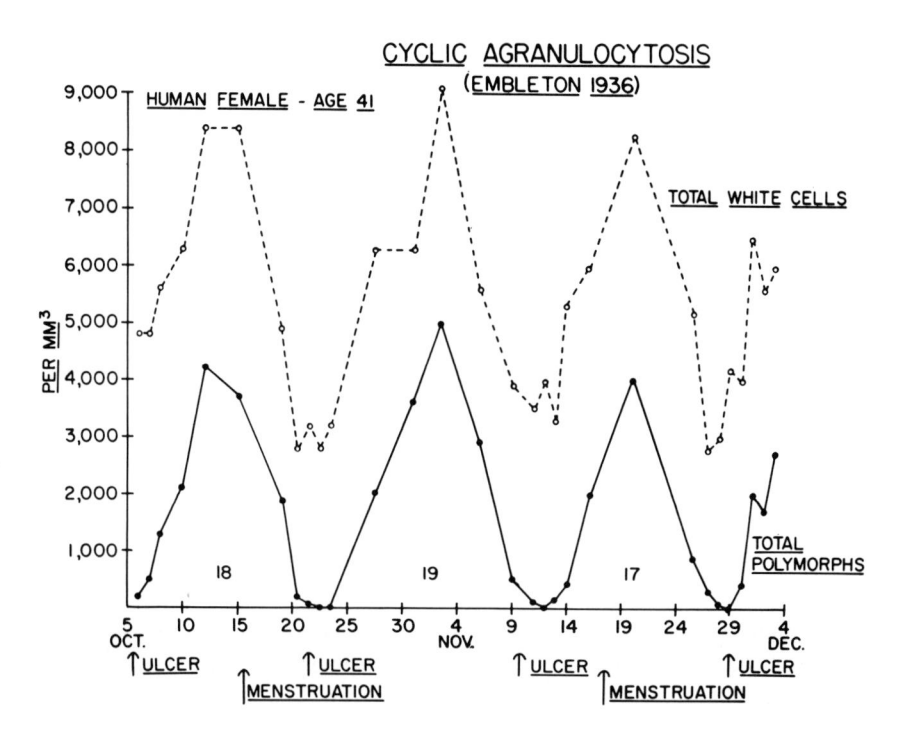

Biological Clocks in Medicine and Psychiatry 101

Fig. 7. Graph showing daily records of total white cells and polymorphonuclear cells per cubic mm of blood in a 41-year-old woman with cyclic agranulocytosis. The lengths of the cycles are indicated in days. Arrows indicate appearance of mouth ulcers and of menstrual periods. (Redrawn from Embleton, 1936.)

before the number of neutrophils, important defenders of the body against infection, reached these zero levels. The patient experienced malaise coincident with the agranulocytosis. There is evidence here also of the existence of a second clock, the menstrual clock, in this case measuring time in units of 34 days and entirely independently of the other.

Evidence for the existence of a clock that measured time is still longer units (24, or nearly 24, days) is shown in the temperature chart of a 19-year-old boy with Hodgkin's disease (Fig. 8) (7). This chart gives daily morning-evening temperatures over a 240-day period. During the periods of elevated temperatures the patient complained of tiredness, headache, loss of appetite, and abdominal pain and showed increased pulse and respiratory rates, loss of weight, splenomegaly, and lymphadenopathy.

The existence of a clock that measured time in units of 52 or nearly 52 days is demonstrated in the chart in Figure 9 which shows the

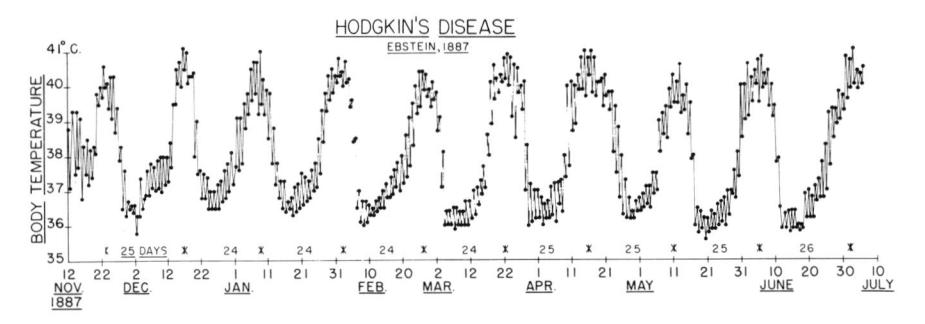

Fig. 8. Graph showing daily body temperature records of a 19-year-old boy with Hodgkin's disease. The numbers over the base line give the lengths of the temperature cycles in days. (Redrawn from Ebstein, 1887.)

occurrence of attacks of acidosis in a young girl, aged eight and one-half years at the time of the first attack (8). Beginning at an age of one and one-half years this child showed definite symptoms of pituitary, thymic, and calcium disturbances, growth abnormalities, and attacks of allergy consisting of skin eruption, asthma, gastrointestinal upsets, and fever. Later, acidosis became the chief symptom of the attacks which persisted up to her 13th year. Treatment with pituitary substance, thyroid powder, and calcium lactate, helped to reduce the number and severity of attacks. Two other of Timme's patients also had attacks of 50–60 days in length.

The presence of a clock that measured time in still longer units (four and one-half months on the average) is demonstrated in the chart in Figure 10 which shows the occurrence and duration of attacks of benign duodenal ulcers over an 8-year period in a man who was 29 years old at the onset of the illness (9). During these attacks, each lasting 10–15 days, the patient suffered from postprandial pain.

Clocks That Manifest Their Presence Through Primarily Mental and Emotional Symptoms

Now let us turn to examples of clocks that manifest their presence through primarily mental and emotional symptoms. Evidence for the presence of a clock that measured time in units of 24 hours was seen in a 28-year-old woman suffering from Parkinsonism subsequent to an attack of encephalitis early in childhood (10). During each day up to nine o'clock in the evening the patient was bed-ridden, unable to walk, or to feed herself because of a marked rigidity and tremors of her legs

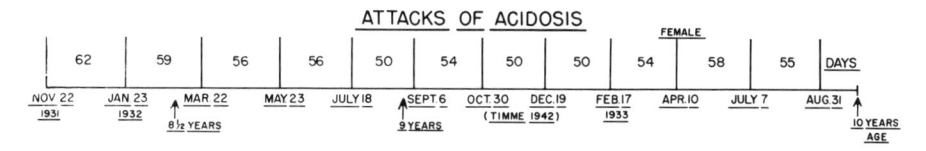

Biological Clocks in Medicine and Psychiatry 103

Fig. 9. Graph showing record of attacks of acidosis in a young girl and length of intervals between attacks. (Chart made from data taken from paper by Timme, 1942.)

and arms. Her handwriting was indecipherable, her speech unclear; but she was euphoric. Quite sharply near nine o'clock in the evening she showed a sudden change in her whole personality. Rigidity and tremors disappeared; she was able to walk, feed, and otherwise take care of herself; her speech and handwriting became perfectly clear; the euphoria disappeared to leave in its place a state of apathy. Figure 11 shows a graph of these changes. These 24-hour cycles were present during the nine-year observation period in the hospital.

The presence of a clock that measured time in units of 48 hours is evidenced in the excerpts of a so-called behavior chart (Fig. 12) kept by trained nurses for a 64-year-old woman from the Phipps Clinic (11). The two top rows of squares are marked for normal behavior and mood: reading, cheerful; the two squares in the second row are marked for abnormal behavior: fearful, sad (actually suicidal). Here we see a 48-hour cycle, 24 hours of normal and 24 hours of abnormal behavior. This same cycle is clearly reflected in hours of sleep and definitely, but less clearly, in pulse rate. In this case transition from one phase to the other was very sharp—often occurring within a few minutes—and at almost exactly the same time on successive nights. This is the same cycle seen in the patient with primarily physical symptoms whose record is shown in Figure 3.

Evidence for the existence of a clock that measured time in slightly

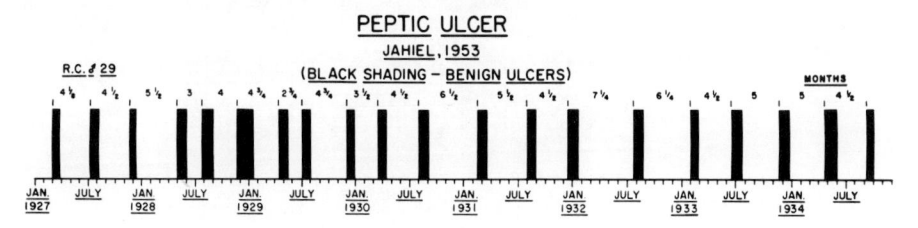

Fig. 10. Graph for 29-year-old man showing record of appearance of recurrent duodenal ulcers. Solid black shading indicates appearance and duration of ulcers. Numbers at the top show intervals in months between onset of successive attacks. (Redrawn from Jahiel, 1953.)

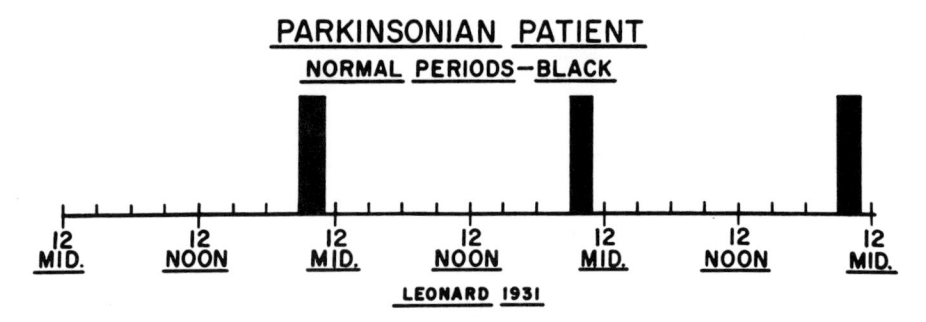

Fig. 11. Graph made from the clinical report (Leonard, 1931) of a 25-year-old woman with Parkinsonism. The black shaded areas lasting 2–3 hours each 24 hours are periods during which the patient was able to walk, feed herself, talk and write clearly, but was apathetic.

longer units (5 days) comes from another Phipps Clinic patient, a 30-year-old woman diagnosed as "constitutional inferiority with hypomaniac features" (12). In Figure 13, which shows hours of sleep, we see the presence of a clock that measured time in units of 5 days. One to two days of excitement and sleepless nights were followed by periods of 2–3 days of sluggish behavior and nights of normal sleep.

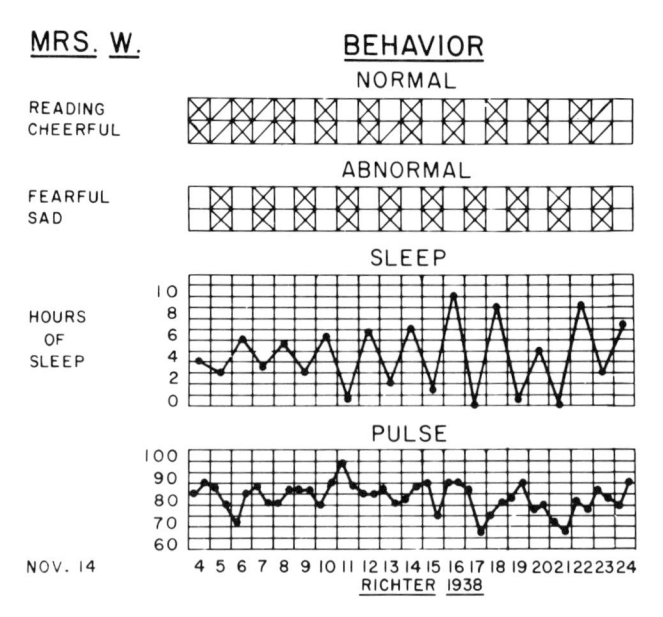

Fig. 12. Part of behavior chart of 61-year-old woman showing presence or absence of normal and abnormal behavior and mood; also body temperature and pulse rate. A 48-hour cycle is clearly shown in behavior and mood, hours of sleep, and pulse rate. (Richter, 1938.)

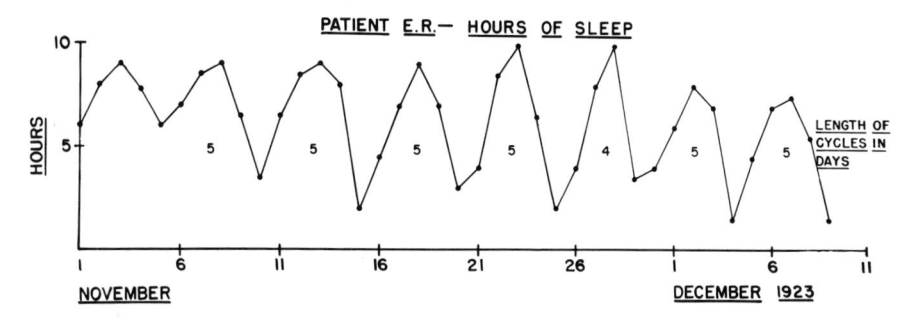

Biological Clocks in Medicine and Psychiatry 105

Fig. 13. Graph showing daily record of hours of sleep of a 30-year-old woman diagnosed as "constitutional inferior with hypomanic features." (Richter, 1934.)

The presence of a clock that measured time in still longer units (19–24 days) is evidenced in the daily records of a 22-year-old male catatonic-schizophrenic patient with recurrent periods of excitement (Fig. 14) (13). The top graph represents estimates of mood; the second, a measure of the patient's ability to concentrate; the third, total urinary nitrogen. The record extends over a 110-day period. Throughout the entire time, the patient was kept in bed and on a constant diet. This patient was alternately wild and excited, so much so that he had to be forcibly restrained, and then normal or slightly depressed. Here again the transition between the two phases occurred within a very short period. During the excited phases the patient had difficulty in concentration. Sinusoidal cycles of the same lengths appeared in total nitrogen metabolism.

Evidence for the existence of a clock that measured time in units of 40 days may be seen in the excerpt from the daily behavior chart for a Phipps Clinic patient a 56-year-old schoolteacher (Fig. 15) (14). Mark-

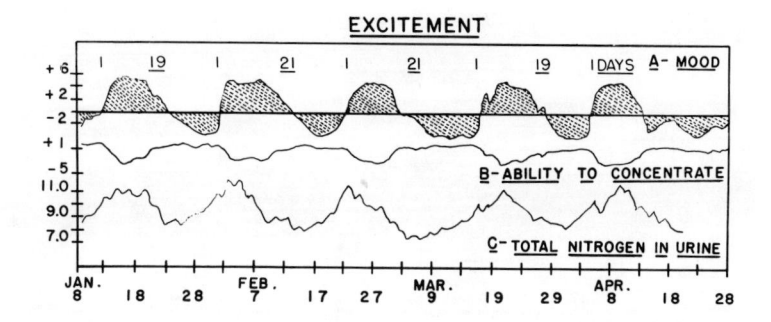

Fig. 14. Graph showing daily records for 22–year-old male catatonic-schizophrenic patient with periodic excitement. (Redrawn from Gjessing, 1936.)

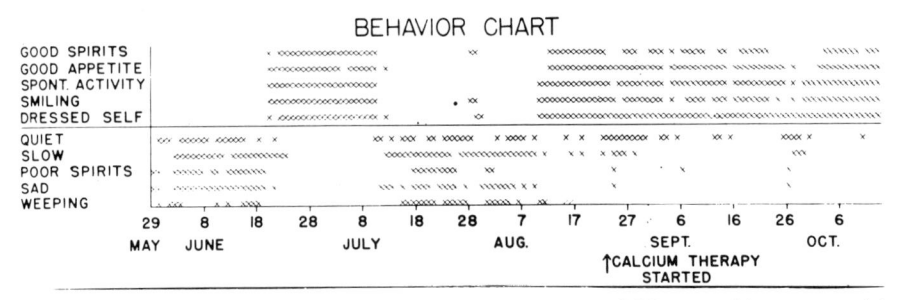

Fig. 15. Graph showing part of daily behavior chart of 56-year-old woman with apparent parathyroid deficiency. (Redrawn from Richter, Honeyman and Hunter, 1940.)

ings for normal behavior and mood are indicated above the center dividing line; markings for depressed behavior and mood, below the line. The depressed and normal phases both lasted about 20 days. The change from one phase to another was quite sharp. This patient suffered from an apparent parathyroid deficiency. Treatment with calcium lactate solution and AT_{10} (Dihydrotachysterol) corrected the calcium deficiency and abolished the attacks.

The existence of a clock that measured time in units of 52, or nearly 52, days is demonstrated in the excerpt of the daily behavior chart of a 14-year-old boy (Fig. 16) (15). Markings for manic behavior and mood are shown on the top third of the chart; for normal behavior and mood, on the middle third; and for depressed behavior and mood, on the bottom third. At the age of 14 years this boy suddenly began showing circular attacks that followed a succession of changes in behavior and mood from manic to normal, to depressed, to normal, to manic, etc. He was observed in the Phipps Clinic for eight and one-half months and in another hospital for nine months, at the end of which time the attacks still occurred with the same regularity. It will be noted that in this

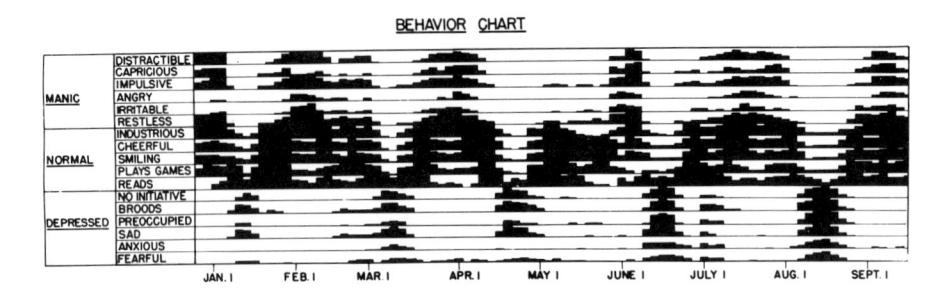

Fig. 16. Part of behavior chart showing daily record of behavior and mood of 14-year-old boy. (Redrawn from Rice, 1944.)

BODY WEIGHT
PERIODIC MANIC-DEPRESSIVE PSYCHOSIS
(PILCZ)

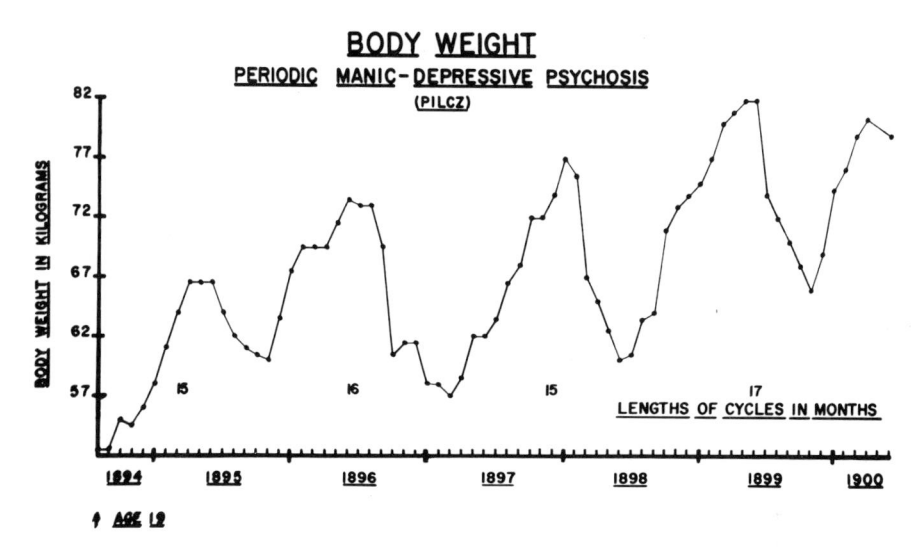

Fig. 17. Graph showing body weight at monthly intervals of a manic-depressive patient in the Municipal Hospital of Vienna. (Redrawn from Pilez, 1901.)

patient with primarily mental and emotional disturbances, the lengths of the cycles were exactly the same as those of the three patients with primarily physical attacks described by Timme (8).

The presence of a clock that measured time in much longer units, 15–17 months, was seen in a manic-depressive patient during 6 years of her life spent in the Municipal Hospital in Vienna (Fig. 17) (16). The ordinates give weight in kilograms, abscissas time in months. During manic periods the patient lost weight, which she more than regained in each successive period of normal or depressed behavior.

Characteristics of Biological Clocks

Over the course of years I have collected records of more than 500 patients whose symptoms have occurred with clock-like regularity. Some of the records came from the medical and psychiatric departments of the Johns Hopkins Hospital, some from other hospitals, but most of them came from the literature. I have combed the world literature of medical and psychiatric publications from the XVIIth Century to the present time for reports of cyclic clinical phenomena, particularly for charts showing actual daily measurements. This is the first time all this material has been correlated from the point of view of a biologist rather than that of a clinician, and with special emphasis on the cycles themselves, their duration, and other characteristics. Most records were obtained during the past century and the early part of the present century, when medical men, including psychiatrists, were concerned with obtaining careful detailed records of the clinical course of illnesses rather than with effects of various forms of treatment.

From the standpoint of research it is to be regretted that our increased knowledge and greatly improved means of treatment have led to the elimination of much of the characteristically detailed early reports. Some of the most significant recent records on psychiatric patients were made by a biochemically-minded psychiatrist, Gjessing in Norway, and by his followers in Germany, the United States, and New Zealand. Gjessing kept his patients under strictly controlled situations and kept daily records of many different metabolic and mental functions over long periods of time. Many good records of patients with primarily physical records were made or collected by Reimann (17).

That we deal here with true "internal" clocks is shown by the fact that the various physical and mental manifestations recurred with great regularity, in most instances over long periods of time despite marked changes in external conditions to which the patients must have been exposed such as temperature, humidity, barometric pressure, and other external influences—and despite reactions to the many day-to-day emotionally charged events and occurrences. The attacks occurred with such great regularity that in many instances the person was able to predict months ahead the exact day of an attack—in some instances, not only the day but the hour and even the minute. One man, an insurance company officer, who had alternate days of depressed and normal behavior, showed me his appointment book with alternate days crossed off his calendar many months ahead. Under controlled conditions of a clinic this man had shown 48-hour cycles of metabolic function as well as of behavior and mood. At Cambridge University the schedule for soccer games over a season was specifically arranged so that no game fell on days when their best player, who suffered from hydrarthrosis of an injured knee every 9 days, would be incapacitated.

These various clocks measure time in different units ranging from 12 hours to several years. In many instances each unit consists of two phases; either the one is abnormal and the other normal, or they may both be abnormal. Either may be longer; the transition from one phase to the other is often strikingly abrupt. The relative lengths of the two phases, as well as the nature of the transition from one to the other, may vary from person to person. In some instances the cyclical curve may be sinusoidal. In any one patient the length and characteristics of the cycles tend to remain exactly the same.

These biological clocks may manifest themselves with equal frequency in males and in females and they may appear at any age from shortly after birth to old age. They may persist for months, years, or a lifetime, or they may be evident for only short periods, either to disappear forever, or to return again later.

Further, these biological clocks may manifest themselves with equal frequency in patients whose symptoms are primarily physical and those with primarily mental or affective symptoms—and the units in which their clocks measure time have much the same range, 12 hours to a year or more. Not only do the units have much the same ranges but in a number of instances so far they have been found to have the same lengths. This is most notably true of patients with 48-hour clocks; two such records were presented at the beginning: one showing primarily physical symptoms (Fig. 3), the other primarily mental symptoms (Fig. 12). Instances were also presented in which clocks that measured time in units of approximately 52 days were present in both groups of patients (Figs. 9 and 16 respectively). A number of other such instances are at hand. The further analysis of our data will undoubtedly bring out still others.

In every instance in which examinations of physical functions were made in patients with primarily mental and emotional symptoms, definite evidences were also found for the presence of physical symptoms. This indicates that in the one group clocks manifest their presence by physical signs; in the other, through both physical and mental signs and symptoms.

It may be noted that many psychiatrists have long denied the existence of inherent clock mechanisms in their patients in the belief that recurrences of abnormal mental and affective states result from reactions to recurring emotional stimuli and disturbing life situations. The close similarity between the clocks of the two types of patients—established here for the first time—indicates that both kinds depend on the operation of inherent cyclic mechanisms.

It is significant that with few exceptions the clocks may manifest themselves through various forms of periodic pathological changes without leaving any detectable lasting physical or mental effects even after years or an entire lifetime of recurrences. In other words, between attacks the individual remains normal, thus providing his own normal baseline for comparison of changes that occur during attacks.

It must be mentioned here that thorough examinations made in many of the patients have failed to reveal the presence of any infectious organisms, the cyclic multiplication of which could account for the periodic changes. It is true that infectious diseases have been found in some of these patients with periodic illnesses, but elimination of the infection did not interfere with the cycles.

It may be mentioned at this point that the results of studies on the experimental production of abnormal cycles of behavior and metabolism in animals carried on since 1921 have helped to provide a more general perspective on the biology of clock phenomena. Results of these studies were summarized in my Salmon Lectures and will be referred to here only in passing.

Nonspecific Symptoms of Presence of Clocks

The presence of clocks may be manifested by cyclic changes in almost any organ of the body, as may be seen in Table 1 which lists the organs that in one patient or another have been reported to show cyclic changes—joints, bone marrow, lymph glands, stomach and duodenum, etc., and the respective clinical manifestations; or by cyclic changes in almost every mental or emotional function—stupor, depression, elation, excitement, etc., as may be seen in Table 2, which lists the various symptoms that have been reported to occur in one or the other of patients with periodic psychiatric illnesses.

It must now be pointed out that some of these symptoms may be specific for a certain clock unit or for a definite disease, others may not

TABLE 1. ORGANS AFFECTED IN PERIODIC ILLNESS, AND ASSOCIATED CLINICAL MANIFESTATIONS

Organs	Clinical manifestations
Joints (synovial spaces)	Intermittent hydrarthrosis, pain
Bone marrow	Cyclic neutropenia, agranulocytosis (ulcers) thrombocytopenia (bleeding, reticulocytopenia, anemia)
Lymph glands	Cyclic lymphocytosis, monocytosis, fever, Hodgkin's
Stomach and duodenum	Cyclic peptic ulcers, vomiting, diarrhea, fever
Peritoneum	Benign paroxysmal peritonitis, pain, fever
Salivary glands	Cyclic excessive secretion
Sweat glands	Cyclic excessive sweating
Spleen	Cyclic neutropenia, fever
Kidney	Cyclic hematuria, oliguria, polyuria, fever
Muscles	Familial periodic paralysis
Eyes	Cyclic iritis, polyserositis
Skin	Cyclic purpura, urticaria, angio-neurotic edema, erythema, fever
Brain	Cyclic epilepsy, hypo- and hyperthermia, insomnia, hypersomnia, headache, migraine

TABLE 2. MENTAL AND EMOTIONAL
STATES IN PERIODIC ILLNESSES

Stupor	Hallucination
Depression	Hypo-or hypersomnia
Elation	Bulimia
Excitement	Dipsomania
Mania	Actual changes of personality
Paranoia	Hypochondriasis

be. The outstanding example of nonspecific physical manifestations is fever. Thus the chart in Figure 18 shows that fever may be an indicator of the presence of any one of the clocks that measure time in units ranging from 12 hours to 30 days, or more. This chart shows the average length of cycle for each of the 123 individuals in whom the presence of a clock was manifested by periodic peaks of body tem-

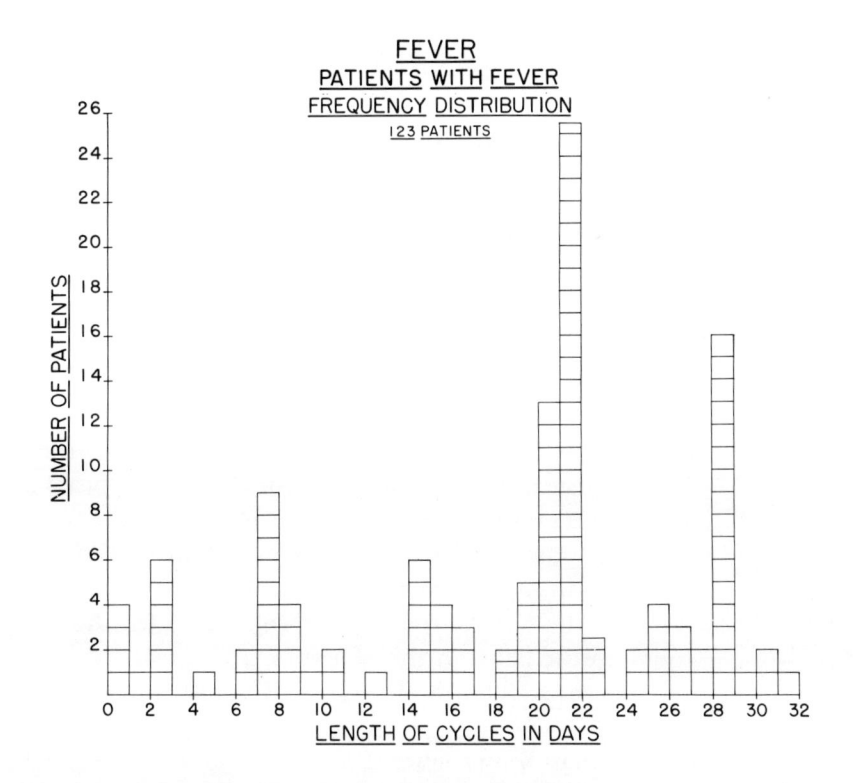

Fig. 18. Distribution chart from 123 patients in which fever was one of the outstanding symptoms. Abscissas show length of fever cycles in days; ordinates number of patients with each length of cycle.

perature. Abscissas give the length of the units in days; ordinates show the number of individuals having each length of cycle.

It is noteworthy that the fever chart shows maxima of numbers of individuals at 7 days and multiples of 7, namely 14, 21, and 28 days. The possible significance of this remarkable pattern will be discussed at another time.

Data for pulse rate and number of leucocytes are not available for the same large number of individuals but, since in all instances in which data are available, an increased pulse rate and leucocytosis so closely followed fever, it is likely that these two functions follow the same pattern as in Figure 18.

It is possible that most mental and affective symptoms may be nonspecific: thus stupor may be a symptom of a 48-hour or of a 43-day clock; depression maybe a symptom of a 48-hour, or of a 15-month clock, etc.

How the mental symptoms come to be nonspecific can be learned from histories of patients with a 48-hour clock, 24 hours each of a "good" and "bad" day. These histories show that a fairly close relationship exists between behavior and mental status on "good" and "bad" days and the more or less chronic behavior and mental conditions present before the superimposition of the 48-hour cycle. Thus, in a normal person the presence of the 48-hour clock may manifest itself only through physical symptoms, cycles of body temperature, pulse rate, edema, etc., whereas a schizophrenic may show marked schizophrenic reactions on the "bad" day, reduced or no schizophrenic symptoms on the "good" days, and a depressive patient may be deeply depressed on his "bad" day, cheerful, communicative, etc. on the "good" day.

Of special interest here is the fact that in patients suffering from a fairly constant state of psychotic or neurotic symptoms, the appearance of the clock suffices not only to break up the mental and affective states into 48-hour periods, but to return the patient to a normal or nearly normal condition in the 24-hour period of the cycle.

A full knowledge of the mechanisms of the 48-hour clock—how the clock works—would throw light on the control of the great variety of psychotic and other states which it is able to modify in such remarkable fashion.

We may conceive that fever, leucocytosis, and other nonspecific symptoms have the same relation to the internal clocks that the hands have for an ordinary clock—they are simply indicators of the clock's running.

Specific Symptoms of the Presence of Clocks and Possible Sites of Clock Mechanisms

Now let us turn to instances in which a symptom or illness is associated with a definitely limited range of clock units, instances in which the symptoms may be a part of the clock mechanism itself. I shall start with intermittent hydrarthrosis, a condition in which we have records for the largest number of patients and also an illness which, as will be seen, offers almost ideal experimental conditions for our purposes: there is no fever, no leucocytosis, no changes in pulse rate, no mental or emotional symptoms—in most instances swelling of the joints constitutes the sole abnormal symptom. In any one patient the lengths of the cycles of swelling of a joint tend to remain so constant over periods of months or years that we are able to speak of a characteristic rather than an average length of cycle. Figure 19 presents the distribution curve of the characteristic lengths of cycles for 128 patients with

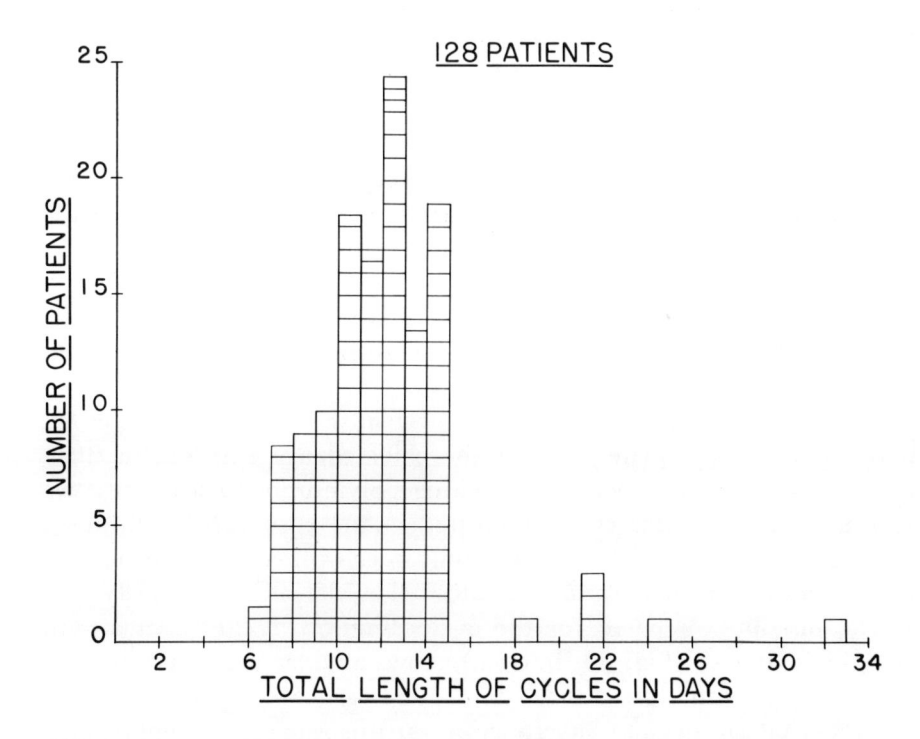

Fig. 19. Distribution chart for 128 patients with intermittent hydrarthrosis. Abscissas give lengths of cycles in days; ordinates, number of patients with each length of cycle. In most instances the lengths of cycles for any one patient remained the same over long periods of time with only an occasional variation of a day or two.

intermittent hydrarthrosis—all of the patients for whom we have definite records of lengths of cycles. The ordinates record the number of patients showing characteristic cycles of each duration as measured in days. As can be seen, the lengths of these cycles almost all fall within a very narrow range, 7–14 days inclusive. Thus, in keeping with our thinking in the cases already discussed, we assume that these patients harbour clocks that keep time in units coming within this range.

The striking facts concerning the periodicity in this particular syndrome are that although in most patients with multiple joint involvement, swelling occurs at the same time in all joints—that is, all joints have the same lengths of cycles and all are in phase, in some patients, as we have seen, the lengths of cycles may be the same in two or more joints, but the swelling may reach maxima at different times in the respective joints. That is, although the cycles have the same lengths, they are out of phase. In still other patients with multiple joint involvement, the cycles of swelling in three or more joints may not only be out of phase but have different lengths; that is, in one joint it may be 8 days, in another 9 days, in another 10 days. This means that the joints may function quite independently of one another—still, however, within the range of 7–14 days. These observations make it unmistakably clear that the joints function not only independently of one another but of any central control, since it is difficult to imagine influences of these different rates arriving from the brain. Here the clock mechanism must be located in the periphery, presumably in the cells of the joints that secrete synovial fluid.

In similar manner, the distribution curve of the duration of the cycles in 38 patients with cyclic agranulocytosis (Fig. 20, top) shows an even much narrower range at 21 days. The conclusion seems to be inescapable that some mechanism or mechanisms must function in the body with this frequency. Since the chief change observed in these patients is in the number of circulating polymorphonuclear cells, we may presume that this clock is located in the tissue producing these cells. Until now, their life span has only been estimated on the basis of indirect measurements. These estimates fall as high as 13 days (18).

The distribution curve for the cycle duration of 20 patients with Hodgkin's disease (Fig. 20, bottom) shows a wider but still definitely limited range with a peak at 20 days. Here again we are led to assume some mechanism in the body functions at this rate. The lymph glands and spleen are the organs most obviously affected in these patients; they are also the organs specifically involved in the production of lymphocytes. We would, therefore, expect to find the clock controlling

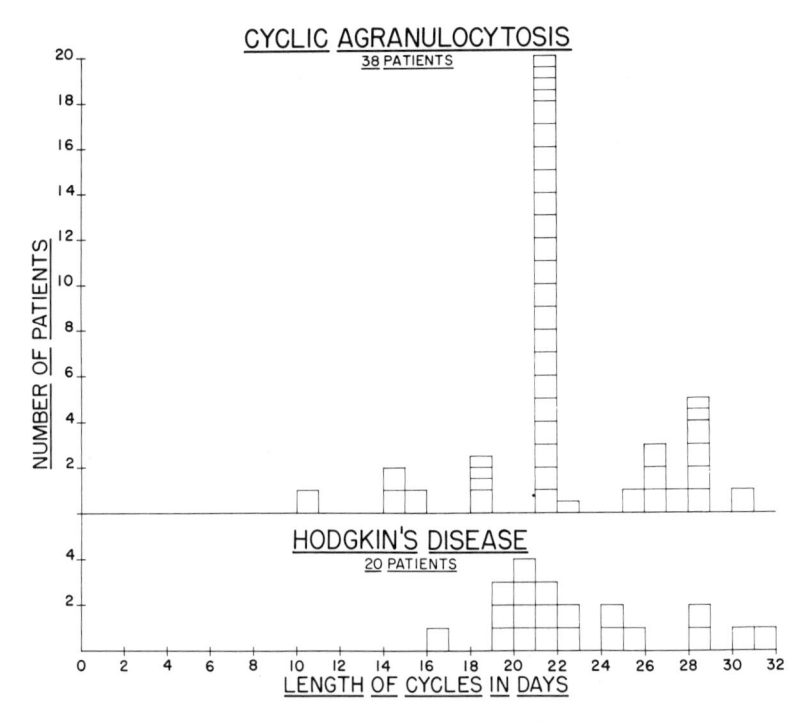

Biological Clocks in Medicine and Psychiatry 115

Fig. 20. (Top) Distribution chart for 38 patients with cyclic agranulocytosis. Abscissas give lengths of cycles in days, ordinates number of patients with each length of cycle. (Bottom) Distribution chart for 20 patients with Hodgkin's disease.

Hodgkin's disease located in these tissues. Of interest here is that the life span of lymphocytes has been calculated to be 20–21 days (19), which coincides almost exactly with the units of the postulated clocks.

Figure 21 shows the distribution curve for the cycle duration of 31 catatonic-schizophrenic patients. As before, the abscissas give the average length of cycle for each patient. The lengths of the cycles for any one individual tended to remain quite constant. Here again we see a delimited distribution, only one patient with a cycle length below 20, and only 2 above 48 days. It seems reasonable to assume that there is a mechanism within the body which in different individuals functions at different levels within this range. The finding that most of these patients responded to administration of thyroid powder, thyroxin, or triiodothyronine (13, 20–23), suggests that a deficiency of circulating thyroid is important in the development of this illness. This is also suggested by our finding that very similar cycles of spontaneous activity, food and water intake, have been produced in rats by removal or

CATATONIC SCHIZOPHRENIC FREQUENCY DISTRIBUTION 31 PATIENTS

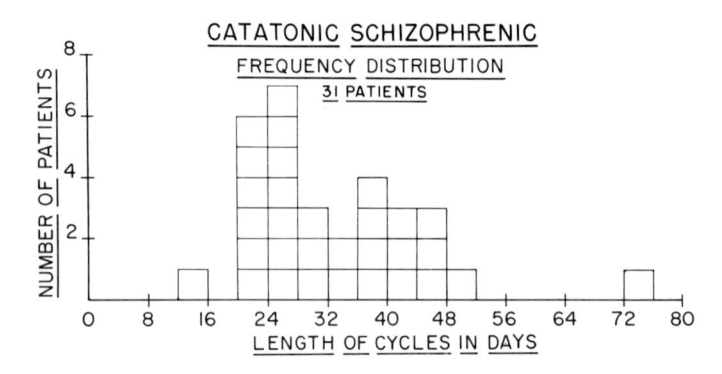

Fig. 21. Distribution chart for 31 catatonic-schizophrenics. Abscissas show length of cycles in 4-day periods; ordinates number of patients with length of cycles falling within each 4-day period.

destruction of large parts of the thyroid; further that treatment of these animals with thyroid preparation eliminated the abnormal cycles (24, 25). Noteworthy also is that on the basis of daily observations of follicles of thyroid tissue auto-implanted to the ear of rabbits, Williams (26) reported many years ago that the individual follicles undergo regular cyclic changes. The longest cycle was found to be 20 days.

Figure 22 shows the number of psychiatric patients (108) whose cycles had lengths falling respectively at 48 hours (78 patients), 72 hours (4 patients), 96 hours (11 patients), 120 hours (15 patients). Therefore we might expect also to find mechanisms within the body functioning at these rates. According to their histories many of these patients have suffered severe head injuries, illnesses with high fever, great stress in one form or another. They showed a variety of corresponding cyclic autonomic disturbances in pulse rate, hours of sleep, blood chemistry, appetite, thirst, etc. Thus, it seems likely that the clocks involved may be located in the hypothalamus, which is the site of the nuclei controlling these functions. Head trauma seems apt to be followed by symptoms occurring in 48-hour cycles, while lethargic encephalitis is more often followed by 120-hour cycles (27).

It must be pointed out here again that evidence at hand indicates that an individual may display symptoms of the presence of several clocks at one time. We have already seen instances in which a patient with intermittent hydrarthrosis harboured a clock in each of two or three or more joints, each clock measuring time in its own unit. We have also seen instances in which individuals displayed the presence of several different types of clocks—in one case an 18-day cycle of neutropenia and a 34-day cycle of menstruation. There are other instances in which individuals have shown three or more such different types of clocks, for instance a 9-day swelling of the knees, a 7-day cycle of abdominal pain, and a 14-day cycle of renal disturbances. In such patients the peaks of body temperature may not show any obvious periodicity, thus giving the impression of a noncyclic phenomenon; however, plotting of the various specific symptoms that accompany the nonspecific fever peaks often bring out clearly the presence of several independent cycles.

Three Types of Biological Clocks

In reviewing all the data collected in these patients with various kinds of cyclic disturbances in behavior, mood, and metabolism, it appears that the human body harbours at least three different types of biological clocks:

Type I: *Peripheral Clocks.* These are located, for instance, in the synovial fluid-producing tissue in the joints, in the cell-producing tissue in bone marrow, etc. They are to a large degree independent of influences arising elsewhere in the organism, particularly in the pituitary gland and the hypothalamus. Thus, for instance, as was mentioned above, cyclic swelling of the joints is generally the only pathological

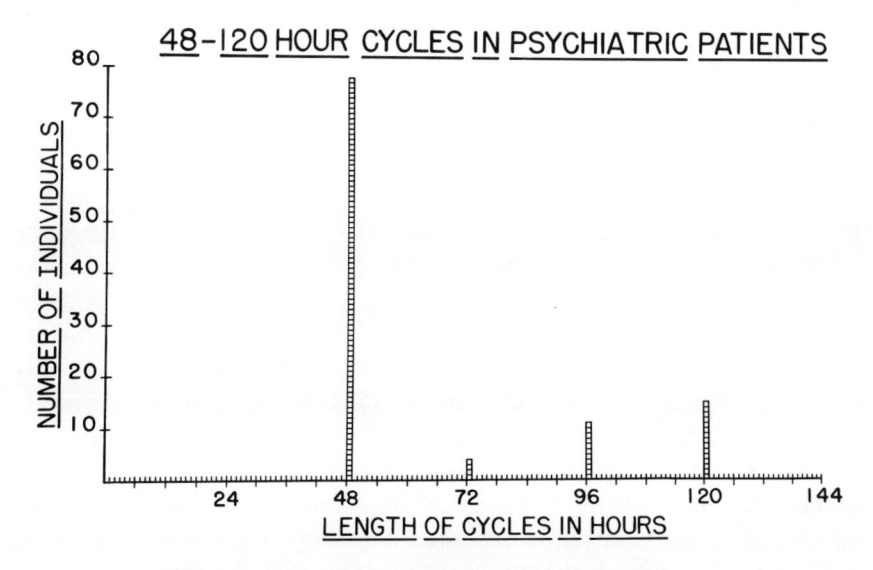

Fig. 22. Distribution chart for 108 psychiatric patients with length of cycles of 48, 72, 96, and 120 hours respectively.

change demonstrable in patients with intermittent hydrarthrosis. There is no fever, no increase in pulse rate, no leucocytosis. Pain may be the only accompanying symptoms. But that these clocks are not completely independent of the rest of the organism is shown by the fact that most of them can be temporarily stopped by pregnancy. However, because of their high degree of independence of other parts of the organism, these clocks are very accurate.

Type II: *Central Clocks*. These clocks are located in the central nervous system. On the basis of our present knowledge we assume they are most likely to be found in the thalamus, hypothalamus, reticular formation, or in the posterior lobe of the pituitary gland.

I have included the posterior lobe of the pituitary gland as a possible harbourer of a clock, or clocks, of this type, since it actually is part of the brain, and since in animal experiments damage to this structure brought out extraordinarily regular but abnormal cycles in running activity, food and water intake, and functioning of the reproductive tract (28). From results of our own animal experiments we can conclude that the region of the infundibulum contains more cyclic mechanisms than any other part of the brain or body. But just which structures in this intricate region are the actual sites of such clock mechanisms is not known. Nor do we know to what extent they are controlled through neuro-hormonal secretion in the hypothalamus. At least some of these central clocks keep time with a high degree of accuracy and, again, independently to a large extent of influence from other parts of the body. Thus, as an instance, in one patient a 48-hour clock operated without a miss for over 30 years, despite all the many influences, external and internal, to which he must have been exposed during this time (29).

Many observations reported in the literature on animals, insects, and plants have established the high degree of accuracy of the functioning of the 24-hour clock, the chief representative of this type of clock (30–34).

Type III: *Homeostatic Clocks*. These are part of the homeostatic mechanisms that include the interaction between the target glands of internal secretion—the thyroid, parathyroids, gonads, adrenals, and the anterior lobe of the pituitary gland and/or the hypothalamus. An example would be the ovarian or menstrual clock that depends on the homeostatic relationship between a target endocrine gland, the ovary, and the pituitary and hypothalamus. Another example would be the presumably thyroid clock of catatonic-schizophrenics which would be regulated by the homeostatic mechanism including the thyroid, pituitary, and hypothalamus.

MENSTRUAL CYCLES DISTRIBUTION CURVE

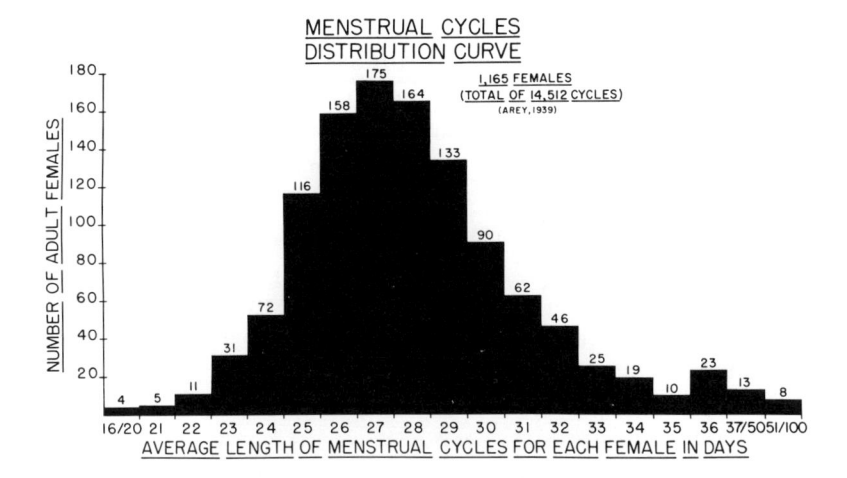

Fig. 23. Distribution chart of average lengths of menstrual cycles for 1,165 females—a total of 14,512 cycles. (Redrawn from Arey, 1939.)

Compared to the Type I (peripheral) clocks and to Type II (central) clocks, these are much less accurate and operate over a much wider range of variation. Thus, for example, the ovarian or menstrual clock measures time most frequently in units of 27–28 days but the length of the units ranges from 14 to 100 days, as may be seen in the distribution chart of the characteristic duration of the menstrual cycles of 1,165 "normal" women (Fig. 23) (35). The ordinates give the number of women with characteristic cycles of each duration (indicated on the abscissas). Similar curves have been obtained by others, both in human beings and monkeys (36,37).

In these clocks the actual timing mechanisms are probably located in the target glands but they are very definitely under the influence of secretion from the anterior lobe of the pituitary, as well as being controlled by specific centers in the hypothalamus and thalamus. It is possible that impulses from the sympathetic and the parasympathetic components of the autonomic nervous system may also play a part in the regeneration of this clock mechanism.

Conditions Under Which These Three Types of Clocks Are Revealed. Shock, trauma, and allergy (38) are probably the most common forerunners of the appearance of Type I and Type II clocks. Prolonged spells of fever, prolonged treatment with any one of a variety of drugs or hormones, and presence of arteriosclerosis or of lues have been reported as antecedents of these two types of clocks. However, instances are also on record in which these clocks made their appearance apparently spontaneously.

Particular susceptibility to cyclic manifestations may also play a part since instances are known in which individuals—even within the first few months of life—show evidence of harbouring not only one but several clocks, each measuring time in quite different units, and all independent of one another. This is true especially of the large groups of patients who from early ages suffer from the so-called Mediterranean disease, otherwise known as paroxysmal peritonitis, or periodic abdominalgia (39). Evidence at hand indicates that this particular susceptibility has a definitely genetic origin, as Armenians and Jews show a high incidence of cyclic proneness and also because, in a number of instances, abnormal cyclic phenomena have appeared in as many as five generations of a family (40).

In contrast to the other two types of clocks, the usual condition for the appearance of Type III clocks must be either a great reduction of functional activity in the target gland or of the cells of the anterior pituitary that secrete the corresponding trophic hormone. Another possibility which can be anticipated to result in the manifestation of this Type III clock would be consequent upon functional or structural changes in hypothalamic centers resulting from prolonged attempts of the organism to maintain homeostasis in the face of a great reduction in amounts of functioning tissue of the target glands (24). The results of our studies in experimental production of abnormal cycles of behavior and metabolism in rats indicate that loss of function of the frontal lobes and presumably of the resultant loss of inhibitory influences on lower centers may be followed by the appearance of Type III clocks (25). The results of these studies on rats have likewise shown that conditions of general debilitation are conducive to the appearance of abnormal cycles.

Treatment of Individuals with Cyclic Manifestations of Illness

It was hoped that light might be thrown on the operation of the clock mechanisms by the study of methods of treatment that have resulted in disappearance of abnormal cycles. However, this study did not reveal much useful information since only a very few effective treatments for any of the cyclic conditions are known. Up to the present time no consistent treatment has been found for patients showing any of the Type I (peripheral) clocks, but a great variety of treatments at different times in one patient or another have resulted in the loss of all signs of the presence of a clock. Thus, for example, in the case of patients suffering from intermittent hydrarthrosis, temporary or permanent cures have been achieved by the following: cauterization of synovial membranes, drainage of the synovial spaces, puncturing or washing out of these spaces with mercuric chloride or carbolic acid, injection of iodine into the synovial spaces, or the oral administration of drugs such as arsenic and quinine.

Many patients showing Type II (central) clocks have made spontaneous recoveries, but to my knowledge none has been helped by any form of treatment.

Symptoms evidencing the presence of Type III (homeostatic) clocks have responded to treatment with thyroid hormone, extract of thyroid, thyroxin, or triiodothyronine. One of our patients suffering from parathyroid deficiency and showing very regular 40-day cycles in mood and behavior lost all signs of periodic changes after treatment with AT-10 and oral ingestion of large amounts of solutions of calcium lactate.

Pathological Findings in Patients Manifesting Clocks

As stated earlier, remarkably few pathological changes have been demonstrated in any patients revealing the presence of biological clocks of any type. Thus, in patients with intermittent hydrarthrosis many examinations of synovial fluid or membranes have yielded very few if any evidences of pathological changes.

The many laparotomies performed in patients with paroxysmal peritonitis have revealed the presence of peritoneal inflammation, but nothing more; inflammation disappeared at the end of each attack.

Examination of the brains of patients with cyclic disorders similarly have not revealed any patholotical changes—with the exception of patients with histories of earlier specific central nervous system disorders, such as lethargic encephalitis, progressive paralysis, etc.

Evolution of Clocks

Evidence at hand indicates that the 24-hour clock—which is found not only in man but in other animals, birds, insects, and plants—is the most primitive clock. How and when the other clocks appeared in different animals, what significance and selective value they had in the life of the animals, remains unknown. It would appear that cyclic phenomena are more readily visible in lower animals than in man. It is possible that, in the process of evolution, clocks that once may have played a part in the animal's life are gradually becoming concealed until in many only two clocks, the 24-hour and 28-day menstrual clocks, are still visible, and that they too may ultimately become concealed, to make their appearance only under various forms of pathological conditions.

In summary, thus far, the results of this study have shown that the body harbours a number of clocks—some located in peripheral organs, for instance in the joints; some located in endocrine glands, for instance the thyroid; some located in the nuclei of the hypothalamus and near-by parts of the brain. It may now be asked how these clocks work; how the various organs of the body undergo such marked periodic changes over long periods of time without showing signs of damage—either on gross or histological examination; how shock, trauma, or other agents elicit cyclic responses; how an assortment of agents may cause the cyclic responses to disappear?

Shock-Phase Hypothesis

From the prolonged consideration of these questions an idea emerged that may provide an answer to at least some of these questions. This idea came partly from the detailed study of the case histories of the large variety of patients possessing clocks, especially those seen in patients with intermittent hydrarthosis, and partly from the study of a phenomenon that has been observed in the common fruit fly (41–45). It has been reported that the pupa of the common fruit fly has an inherent 24-hour emergence rhythm; further, that when a large number of pupae are kept together in the absence of any outside stimuli, that is, in constant darkness, at a constant temperature, etc., the flies emerge at all times of the day and night, giving a fairly constant emergence rate until all pupae have emerged; it has further been reported that a shock, short flash of light or thermal stimulus, may serve to bring all of the pupae into phase so that they emerge at 24-hour intervals until all have pupated. It occurred to me that what happens to the individual members of a colony of flies in response to a strong shock might also happen to the individual units of an organ that are physically closely bound together into an integrated whole. This idea has taken shape as the "shock-phase" hypothesis.

This hypothesis consists of the following postulates:

1. That each one of the functioning units of the organism—cells, follicles, glomeruli, neurons, etc.—has an inherent cycle, the length of which is characteristic of that organ.

2. That these units, although physically closely bound together, may operate independently of one another. Thus, they may all be active, or inactive, or at various stages between activity and rest.

3. That in a normal healthy organ these units function out of phase, that is, some are active while others are resting or at various intermediate stages, thus insuring a fairly constant level of productivity.

4. That under certain circumstances these randomly functioning units of an organ may all be synchronized by a shock or trauma, or by other forms of interference, thus revealing the lengths of the inherent cycles of the individual units.

5. That under certain circumstances the synchronized units of an organ may be desynchronized by various forms of interference, thus restoring the organ to its normal noncyclic productivity.

According to this hypothesis, for instance, the fluid-producing organs of the joints are composed of individual units, each one having its own inherent cycle, ranging in length from 7–14 days. For most individuals the lengths of the cycles of the units are the same in all joints; in other individuals the units within different joints have cycles of different lengths. Under normal conditions some of the units are active, others are resting, others in between, thus maintaining production of a fairly constant amount of synovial fluid from day to day and so concealing all signs of the presence of cyclic phenomena in the individual units. After local injury, allergic shock, etc., the units are brought into phase to produce the great swelling of the joints at 7–14 day intervals. Various forms of nonspecific treatment as was pointed out above, may then desynchronize the units to return the joints to their normal condition.

Further, according to this hypothesis, in normal individuals the neutrophil-producing units in the bone marrow, likewise, have their inherent rhythm of 21, or nearly 21, days, and are capable of independent functioning. Under normal conditions some of these units are producing neutrophils, others are resting, others are at various stages between. Under abnormal conditions these units may all be brought into phase, so that at one time all functioning units are producing cells, at another, none.

According to this theory the same principles apply to: the lymph-producing units in the lymph glands or spleen; the hormone-controlling neurons of the various nuclei in the brain stem; likewise the acid-producing cells of the gastric mucosa; or to the fluid-producing cells of the peritoneal membranes in the abdominal and thoracic cavities, etc.

Evidence for Hypothesis. At the present time we know of a number of organs the functioning units of which may under normal conditions be in all stages of activity, some very active, some completely inactive, the others at various stages between.

It is a common observation that the follicles of the thyroid in a normal animal or person are at any one time apt to be in all stages of activity and rest, and that under pathological conditions they may likewise all be in a state of hyperactivity, or in a state of complete inactivity. In his studies on follicles of autotransplants of thyroid tissue, Williams found that individual follicles pass through definite cycles of growth—and quite independently of one another (26).

It is known on the basis of studies of the activity of the cells of the gastric mucosa made by means of special dyes that these cells at any one time may be at all stages of activity and inactivity (46).

Further, it is known that the uterus of normal females shows all stages of activity and inactivity and independence of the rest of the organism (47).

Some evidene at hand indicates that the glomeruli of the kidneys may likewise function quite independently of one another (48). However, we have no idea whether the glomeruli have an inherent cycle, and if so of what length.

Evidence is also at hand indicating that the individual neurons of the various centers of the brain may function independently of one another (49).

Summary

1. Human beings harbour many clocks—far more than hitherto has been suspected, most of which manifest their presence only under pathological conditions.

2. These clocks may manifest their presence either through physical signs or symptoms, involving in one individual or another almost every organ of the body, or in primarily mental and emotional symptoms, involving almost every form of abnormal behavior, or mood, and thinking.

3. The clocks show an apparent degree of independence of all external physical influences—temperature, humidity, barometric pressure, etc.—as well as of day-to-day emotional situations or disturbances, and so depend on inherent mechanisms.

4. These various clocks keep time in units that range in length from 12 hours to several years; but for each clock the units tend to remain quite constant.

5. Our records indicate the existence of three types of clocks:

> I. Peripheral—those located for instance in the blood-forming tissues in the bone marrow, etc.
> II. Central—those located in the brain, particularly in the hypothalamus and reticular formation.
> III. Homeostatic—those mechanisms involving target organs, endocrine glands, the pituitary, and hypothalamus.

6. A "shock-phase" hypothesis in agreement with the observed clinical phenomena has been proposed to explain how the clocks work. It is assumed that the functioning units of every organ of the body—cells, follicles, neurons, glomeruli, etc.—have an inherent cycle, characteristic of the organ. Under normal conditions these units of any given tissue function out of phase; under abnormal conditions they may function in phase, thus disclosing the length of the inherent cycle of the organ. The units may be put in phase by shock, trauma, allergy, etc.; similarly, they may be put out of phase again by a variety of agents and forms of treatment.

7. Patients with cyclic phenomena offer an excellent opportunity for the study of the physiology of individual organs as well as of the functioning of the total organism, particularly as seen in various abnormal mental and emotional conditions.

References

1. Hitzig, W. H. Periodische Krankheit. Kasuistische Mitteilung von vier typischen Fällen, *Helvetica Paediatrica Acta*, 10, 649 (1955).
2. Rowe, A. H. Fever due to food allergy, *Ann. Allergy*, 6, 252 (1948).
3. Garrod, A. E. Concerning intermittent hydrarthrosis, *Quart. Jour. Med.*, 3, 207 (1910).
4. Brantigan, O. C., and A. F. Voshell. The mechanics of the ligaments and menisei of the knee joint, *Jour. Bone & Joint Surg.*, 23, 44 (1941).
5. Baker, B. M. Undulant fever presenting the clinical syndrome of intermittent hydrarthrosis, *Arch. Int. Med.*, 44, 128 (1929).
6. Embleton, D. Rhythmical agranulocytosis, *Brit. Med. Jour.*, 2, 1258 (1936).
7. Ebstein, W. Das chronische Rückfallsfieber, eine neue Infectionskrankheit, *Berl. klin. Wchnsch.*, 24, 565 (1887).
8. Timme, W. Periodicity in endocrinopathic states, *Jour. Mt. Sinai Hosp.*, 9, 818 (1942-1943).

9. Jahiel, R. Concept of periodicity in natural history of peptic ulcer and its consequences, *Am. Jour. Dig. Dis.*, 20, 257 (1953).
10. Leonard, K. Eigenartige Tagesschwankungen des Zustandbildes bei Parkinsonismus, *Zeit. für die ges. Neurol. & Psychiat.*, 134, 76 (1931).
11. Richter, C. P. Two-day cycles of alternating good and bad behavior in psychotic patients, *Arch. Neurol. & Psychiat.*, 39, 587 (1938).
12. Richter, C. P. Cyclic manifestations in the sleep curves of psychotic patients, *Arch. Neurol. & Psychiat.*, 31, 119 (1934).
13. Gjessing, R. Beiträge zur Kenntnis der Pathophysiologie der Katatonen Erregung. III Mitteilung. Über Periodisch Rezidivierende Katatone Erregung, mit Kritischem Beginn und Abschluss, *Arch. f. Psychiat. & Nervenkrankh.*, 104, 355 (1936).
14. Richter, C. P., W. Honeyman, and H. Hunter. Behavior and mood cycles apparently related to parathyroid deficiency, *Jour. Neurol. and Psychiat.*, 3, 19 (1940).
15. Rice, K. K. Regular forty to fifty day cycle of psychotic behavior in a 14-year-old boy, *Arch. Neurol. and Psychiat.*, 51, 478 (1944).
16. Pilez, A. *Die Periodischen Geistesstörungen*, (Jena: Verl. G. Fischer, 1901).
17. Reimann, H. A. Periodicity in disease, *New Engl. Jour. Med.*, 256, 652 (1957).
18. Patt, H. M., and M. A. Maloney. Control of granulocyte formation, in *Homeostatic Mechanisms* (Brookhaven Symposium in Biology 10, Brookhaven National Laboratories, 1957).
19. Hamilton, L. D. Control of lymphocyte production, *ibid.*
20. Gornall, A. G., B. Eglitis, A. Miller, A. B. Stokes, and J. G. Dewan. Long-term clinical and metabolic observations in periodic catatonia, *Am. Jour. Psychiat.*, 109, 584 (1953).
21. Mall, G. Beitrag zur Gjessingschen Thyroxinbehandlung der Periodischen Katatonien, *Arch. f. Psychiat. and Nervenkrankh.*, 187, 381 (1951–1952).
22. Danziger, L., and J. A. Kindwall. Thyroid therapy in some mental disorders, *Dis. Nerv. System*, 14, 3 (1953).
23. Lindsay, J. S. B. Periodic catatonia, *Jour. Ment. Sci.*, 94, 590 (1948).
24. Richter, C. P. Hormones and rhythms in man and animals, *Rec. Prog. in Hormone Res.*, 13, 105 (1957).
25. Richter, C. P., G. S. Jones, and L. T. Biswanger. Periodic phenomena and the thyroid: Abnormal but regular cycles in behavior and metabolism produced in rats by partial radiothyroidectomy, *Arch. Neurol. and Psychiat.*, 81, 233 (1959).
26. Williams, R. G. Microscopic studies of living thyroid follicles implanted in transparent chambers installed in the rabbit's ear, *Am. Jour. Anat.*, 62, 1 (1937–1938).
27. Aiginger, J., and E. Neumayer. Über Periodische, Paroxysmale, Pseudoneurasthenische Zustandsbilder bei Postencephalitikern, *Wien. klin. Wschr.*, 61, 314 (1949).
28. Richter, C. P. Abnormal but regular cycles in behavior and metabolism in rats and catatonic-schizophrenics, in *Psycho-Endocrine Symposium with Special Reference to Schizophrenia*. 2nd International Congress of Psychiatry. Zurich, Switzerland, 1957.
29. Starobinski, A. Un Cas de Psychose Maniaque Depressive a un Jour d'Alternance, *Ann. Medico-Psychologiques*, 11, 344 (1921).
30. Aschoff, J. Tierische Periodik unter dem Einfluss von Zeitgebern, *Ztsch. f. Tierpsychologie*, 15, Heft. 1 (1958).
31. Bykow, K. M. *Studien über Periodische Veränderungen Physiologischer Funktionen des Organismus.* (Berlin: Akademie-Verlag, 1954.)

32. Bünning, E. *Die Physiologische Uhr.*, (Berlin: Springer-Verlag, 1958).
33. Halberg, F. Some physiological and clinical aspects of 24-hour periodicity, *Journal-Lancet*, 73, No. 1, 20 (1953).
34. Bruce, V. G., and C. S. Pittendrigh. Endogenous rhythms in insects and microorganisms, *Am. Naturalist*, 91, 179 (1957).
35. Arey, L. B. The degree of normal menstrual irregularity, *Am. Jour. Obstet. and Gyn.*, 37, 12 (1939).
36. Corner, G. W. Ovulation and Menstruation in Macacus Rhesus, in *Contributions to Embryology* (Washington: Carnegie Institution, Publ. 332, 1923), vol. 15, p. 75.
37. Hartman, C. Studies in the reproduction of the monkey, Macacus (Pithieus) Thesus, with special reference to menstruation and pregnancy, in *Contributions to Embryology* (Washington: Carnegie Institution, Publ. 433, 1932), vol. 23, p. 1.
38. Rowe, A. H. *Clinical Allergy due to Food, Inhalants, Contactans, Fungi, Bacteria, and Other Causes: Manifestations, Diagnosis, and Treatment* (Philadelphia: Lea and Febiger, 1937).
39. Heller, H., E. Sohar, and L. Sherf. Familial Mediterranean fever, *Arch. Int. Med.*, 102, 50 (1958).
40. Reimann, H. A., J. Moadié, S. Semerdjian, and P. F. Sahyoun. Periodic peritonitis—heredity and pathology: report of seventy-two cases, *J.A.M.A.*, 154, 1254 (1954).
41. Kalmus, H. Periodizität und Autochronie (Ideochronie) als Zeitregelnde Eigenschaften der Organismen, *Biologia Generalis*, 11, 93 (1935).
42. Kalmus, H. New research in the diurnal periodicity of animals, *Acta Med. Scand. Suppl.*, 108, 227 (1940).
43. Bünning, E. Zur Kenntnis der endogenen Tagesrhymik bei Insekten und bei Pflanzen, *Ber. dtsch. bot. Ges.*, 53, 594 (1935).
44. Pittendrigh, C. S. On temperature independence in the clock-system controlling emergence time in Drosophila, *Procs. Nat. Acad. Scs.* 40, 1018 (1954).
45. Brett, W. J. Persistent diurnal rhythmicity in Drosophila emergence, *Ann. Entom. Soc. Amer.*, 48, 119 (1955).
46. Bradford, N. M. and E. R. Davies. The site of hydrochloric acid production in the stomach as determined by indicators, *Biochem. Jour.*, 46, 414 (1950).
47. del Castillo, E. B. and G. di Paola. Cyclical vaginal response to the daily administration of estradiol in castrated rats, *Endocrinol.*, 30, 48 (1942).
48. Smith, H. W. *Principles of Renal Physiology* (New York: Oxford University Press, 1956).
49. Franck, U. F. Models for biological excitation processes, *Progress in Biophysics and Bio-physical Chem.*, 6, 171 (1956).

SLEEP AND ACTIVITY:
THEIR RELATION TO THE 24-HOUR CLOCK

The concept of the constancy of the internal environment as announced in 1859 by Claude Bernard (2) or of homeostasis as expressed by Walter Cannon (3) in 1932 has come to play an all important role in physiology and medicine. Bernard and Cannon described the many physiological regulators that serve to maintain fixity of the internal environment despite great and threatening changes in the external environment.

In a series of studies on self-regulatory functions in animals and man carried on from 1935 to 1950, it was found that constancy of the internal environment is maintained not only by physiological regulators but by behavioral regulators as well (5). Thus, for example, the adrenalectomized rat lacking its physiological regulator for maintaining a fixed salt level of the blood will, if given the opportunity, ingest enough salt to keep itself alive and free from symptoms of insufficiency. Many other such instances of behavioral regulators were found. As a result of these findings and particularly those of Cannon, I had come to believe that almost all aspects of behavior can be fully understood in terms of the concept of homeostasis.

I bring this up because, during the past 10 years, results of our studies on periodic phenomena in animals and man have disclosed the existence of mechanisms that likewise involve almost every function of the body and also play an all important part in the regulation of

---

This paper was originally published in *Sleep and Altered States of Consciousness*. Copyright 1967, Association for Research in Nervous and Mental Diseases, Inc. Reprinted by permission.

behavior and emotions—but which are entirely independent of homeostasis. These are biological clocks that exert important influence and control over many life processes, such as sleep, but which are in no way affected by changes that they produce in these processes—in brief they are free of all feedback (6, 7).

To illustrate what is meant by such nonhomeostatic mechanisms and the part that they play particularly with reference to the regulation of sleep, I give a brief summary of results of our studies on only one such mechanism—the 24-hour clock. This is one of the most interesting of all biological phenomena and is present in almost every form of life—mammals, birds, insects, plants and even in unicellular organisms. A detailed account of all our experiments on the 24-hour clock will appear in a monograph (8).

Let us start with the question, what is the 24-hour clock? What are its characteristics; how does it operate?

To answer these questions I use our observations made on the common laboratory rat, an ideal animal for studies on periodic phenomena, largely because of its spontaneous activity which can so readily be registered and measured, and because of the constancy and reliability of its physiology and behavior.

To aid in the understanding and evaluation of our observations, I give a brief account here of the experimental technique and conditions. A full account is given elsewhere (6).

Fig. 1 shows a few of the 80 individual cages used for these experiments. Each cage consists of a small living compartment containing a nonspillable food cup and a graduated water bottle on one side of a metal partition and a revolving drum on the other. A 3-inch opening connects the two. A cyclometer on the front end of the axle of the drum registers every single revolution, thus giving a record of total amount of activity per 24 hours; an eccentric cam (see fig. 2) on the rear end of the axle opens and closes a microswitch registering each revolution on a 20-pen operation recorder in another room. Six recorders were used. Each pen of a recorder registers revolutions of the drum for one animal. The paper moves at a rate of 18 inches per 24 hours. The sheets for 24 hours are cut into strips by means of a specially designed machine; the strips for any one animal are mounted consecutively on large cardboard sheets. Each record extends from 12 noon to 12 noon. The laboratory was completely dark from 6 p.m. to 6 a.m. and fully illuminated from 6 a.m. to 6 p.m. Records were taken each morning at 9 a.m. of revolutions of the drums and of food and water intake.

Fig. 1. Individual activity cages showing revolving drums, living compartments with water bottle and cyclometer. Nonspillable food cup (not visible) fits into recess at opposite end of living compartment.

Important here is that the rats are not in any way forced to run; they run on their own accord, in some instances as much as 30 to 40 miles per 24 hours.

For these studies, carried on intensively since 1957, over 900 wild and domesticated rats have been used, many of them followed by daily readings for over 2 years.

Under conditions of alternating 12-hour periods of light and darkness, normal rats have one fairly continuous active period lasting 12 hours or less every 24 hours as may be seen in the records of two rats in fig. 3. These show distribution of activity (*dark areas*) from 12 noon to 12 noon over a 47-day period. The dates of the individual days are given at the *left* of the records. Daily onsets of activity of the first rat occurred with some regularity almost at once after the start of the 12 hours of darkness; onsets of activity of the second rat occurred with equal regularity 2 hours after the start of the dark period. In other animals onsets occurred at various constant intervals—up to 3 hours—

Fig. 2. Rear view of an activity stand showing drums, an eccentric cam on the end of each axle, microswitches and wires connecting to recorder in another room.

after start of the dark period. Here we have our first evidence for the presence of a 24-hour clock.

Constant temporal relationship of onsets of activity to the start of the dark period shows that the clock is set by the 24-hour changes of light and darkness.

To eliminate this effect of light, rats were blinded—in most instances by section of the optic nerves; in some by enucleation. These operations have practically no detectable effect on the rat, either on running activity, food or water intake, body weight or reproductive cycles.

Fig. 4 shows the effect of blinding. Preoperatively this rat was kept under conditions of alternating 12-hour periods of light and darkness. A shows that, for the 30 days before blinding (O.N.), onsets of daily activity periods occurred at 7:15 p.m. and terminated at 6 a.m. at the start of the light period. Almost at once after blinding, onsets and

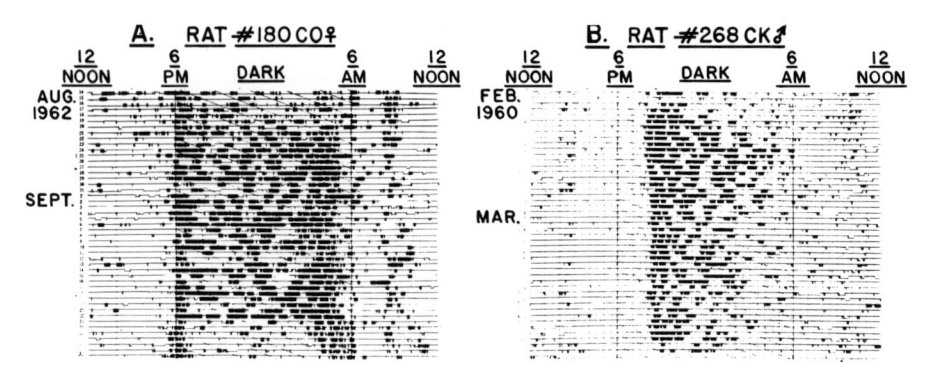

Fig. 3. Activity distribution charts of two normal rats. They show spontaneous running activity with relation to the time of day for a 47-day period. Dates are shown at the left of the charts. The laboratory was totally dark from 6 p.m. to 6 a.m.

terminations began coming later each day. After 1 month they came exactly 20 minutes later each day and continued to do so for the next 7 months (B, C, D) with truly incredible accuracy. Terminations of the active periods occurred 12 hours and a few minutes after the onsets,

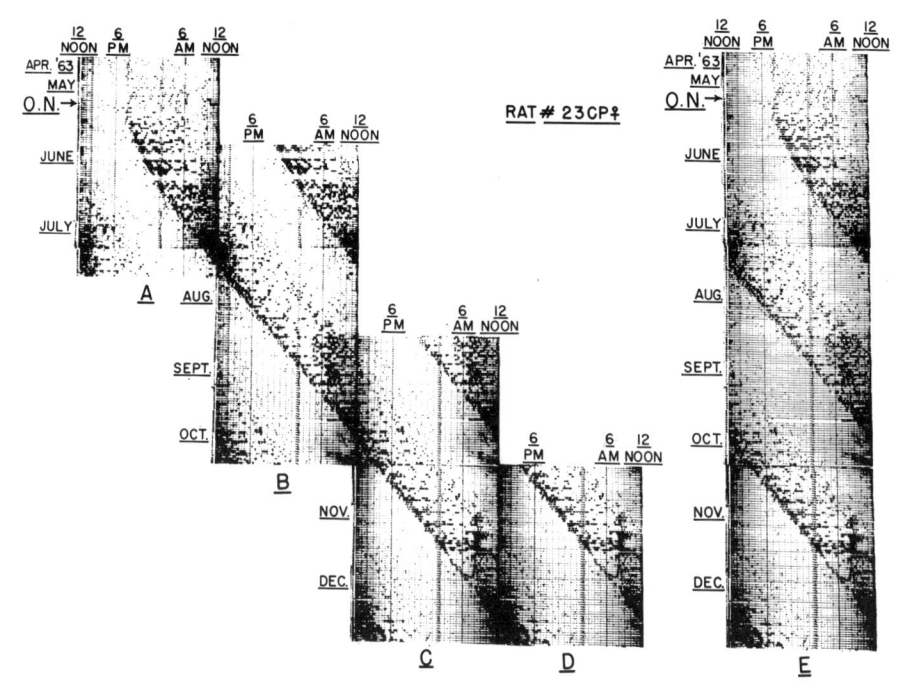

Fig. 4. Charts showing effects of blinding (O.N.) on distribution of spontaneous running activity of an ordinary laboratory Norway rat.

Sleep and Activity: Their Relation to the 24-Hour Clock   133

showing that the clock measures not only 24-hour but 12- or nearly 12-hour intervals. E shows how, in order to conserve space, records are placed one under the other, giving a series of parallel lines of onsets rather than a single straight line.

Complete independence of the clock of external and internal events and the high degree of accuracy and constancy of the clock are illustrated in fig. 5. This 20-month record belongs to a fierce, suspicious

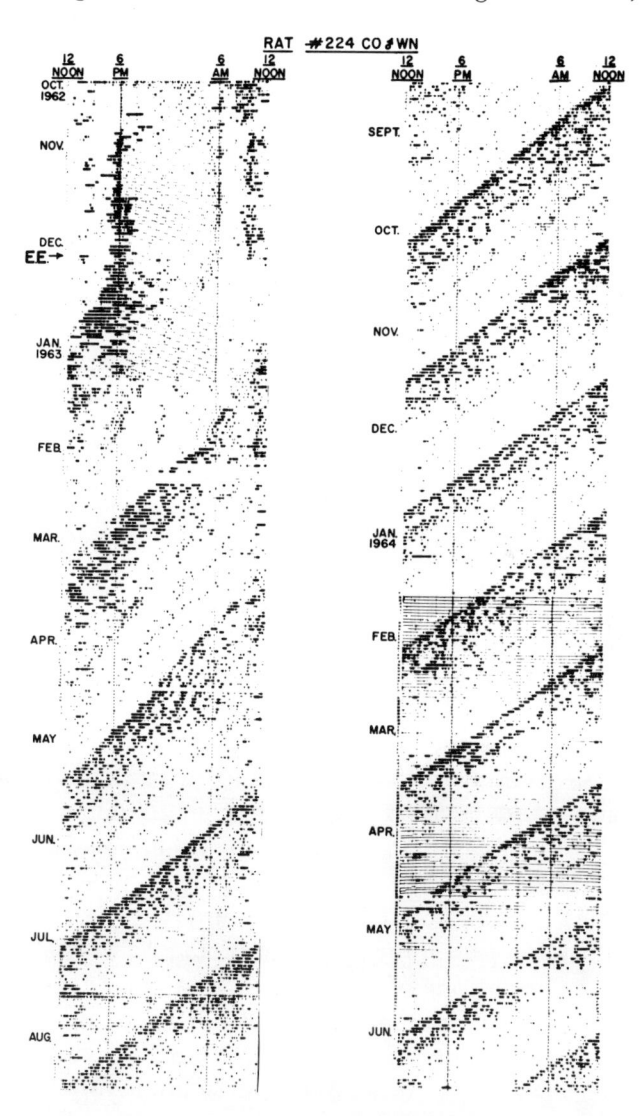

Fig. 5. Spontaneous running activity distribution chart for a wild Norway rat (trapped in Baltimore) over a 20-month period before and after blinding (E.E.).

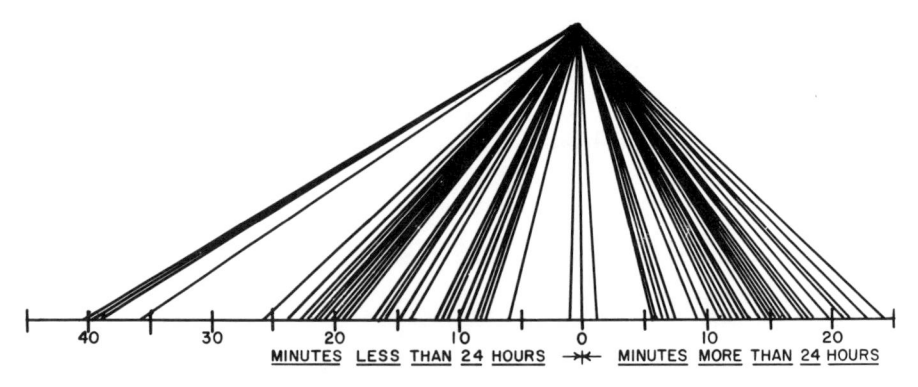

Fig. 6. Chart showing lines of onsets of the active periods of 60 blinded rats on stands at the same time, 1958 to 1959.

wild rat trapped in an alley in Baltimore. We have activity records on it for over 2 years. Shortly after blinding (E.E.) it started to run earlier each day. After 5 months it was running 37 minutes earlier with extraordinary accuracy. If this clock had been used to tell time it would have been in error by not many minutes over a 7-month period. This is remarkable when we consider that during the 7 months this wild rat was exposed to all kinds of disturbances—daily changes of food and water bottles, weekly removal from living cage for weighing, cleaning of cages, talking of assistants, seasonal changes in temperature, humidity and others.

Independence of atmospheric, climatic and other disturbances is further illustrated in fig. 6, which shows lines of onset of active periods of 60 rats that were on the stands at the same time. The onsets ranged from 41 minutes shorter than 24 hours to 28 minutes longer. No two rats had exactly the same periods. The periods could not possibly correspond to any cosmic influence. The record also shows that rats on the stands had no influence on one another: in adjoining cages one rat might have a period longer than 24 hours; the other one shorter than 24 hours.

When it starts running either earlier or later, the clock usually continues at the same period for many months.

The clock's independence of internal stimulation and disturbances is now illustrated. I start with the endocrine glands. For these experiments we only used blinded rats whose clocks had been running with great regularity either faster or slower than 24 hours for at least several weeks. Thus, the record in fig. 7A shows onsets of activity had been occurring 18 minutes later each day for several weeks before the rat was

Sleep and Activity: Their Relation to the 24-Hour Clock

TABLE 1. ENDOCRINOLOGICAL
INTERFERENCES THAT HAD NO EFFECT
ON CLOCK

Gland	Method	No. of Rats
Gonads	Gonadectomy	15
	Mating	17
	Pregnancy and lactation	15
Adrenals	Total removal	25
Hypophysis	Total removal	15
	Posterior lobectomy	8
Pineal	Total removal	26
Pancreas	Partial removal	4
	Alloxan injection	6
Thyroid	Thyroid powder in food	12
	Antithyroid compound	7
	Injection of I-131	4

adrenalectomized. It shows that adrenalectomy had no effect on the clock. Fig. 7B shows likewise that hypophysectomy had no effect. Hypophysectomy made the rat inactive for 10 days, but that it had no effect on the clock is shown by the fact that resumption of activity occurred at the predicted time. Fig. 8 shows that pinealectomy also had no effect on the clock. Table 1 summarizes the results. It shows complete independence of the clock of all of the endocrine glands.

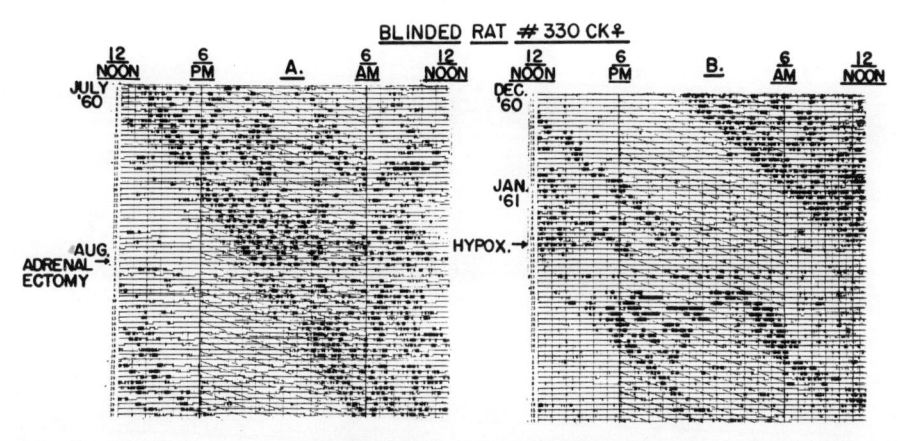

Fig. 7. Spontaneous running activity distribution charts showing lack of effect of adrenalectomy (A) and of hypophysectomy (B) on the clock.

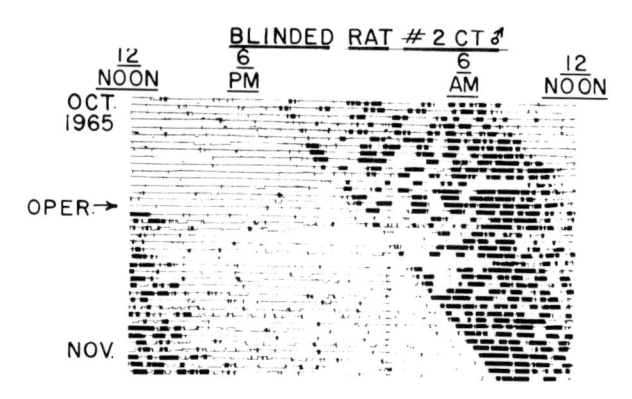

Fig. 8. Spontaneous running activity distribution chart showing that pinealectomy had no effect on the clock of this animal.

Our observations showed that the clock is independent of metabolic changes such as starvation, dehydration and hypothermia. Stopping respiration and heartbeat for 50 minutes had no effect in rats; in some hamsters stopping the heart by hypothermia for over 2 hours had no effect.

Further, almost every conceivable form of interference with the nervous system had no effect, as may be seen in Table 2. In all instances drug dosages were very high, close to the LD50 (lethal dose that kills half of the number of animals).

That the clock is inborn and not dependent on exposure of an animal to alternating 12-hour periods of light and darkness is shown by the clearcut manifestation of the clock in rats that had been blinded a few days after birth—a time when the eyes are still covered with a thick layer of skin and long before they have begun to function—and in congenitally blind microphthalmic rats (kindly sent by Dr. L. G. Browman, Montana State University, Missoula, Montana), as may be seen in the records of two rats in fig. 9.

We know that the clock is not located in any of the endocrine glands because removal of the glands had no effect on the clock.

Ablation of almost every part of the brain down to the hypothalamus had no effect on the clock, which means that the clock probably is located somewhere in the hypothalamus. It is not possible to give a detailed account here of our results on well over 200 rats with all types of lesions in this area. Fig. 10 shows the effect produced in a blinded rat by a lesion in the hypothalamus. The 24-hour cycle is no longer present in activity.

TABLE 2. DISTURBANCES OF THE NERVOUS SYSTEM THAT HAD NO EFFECT ON THE CLOCK

Conditions	Manner Produced	No. of Rats
Anoxia	Nitrogen	8
Convulsions	Electroshock	18
	Caffeine—4th ventricle	23
Tranquilization	Chlorpromazine	6
Poisoning	Lysergic acid diethylamide	11
	Serotonin	8
Anesthesia	Ether	20
	Pentobarbital	11
	Carbon dioxide	5
	Nitrous oxide	7
	Urethane	5
Intoxication	Alcohol	14
Deep sleep	Phenobarbital	5
	Barbital sodium	9
Acute stess	Forced swimming	32
	Restraint	5
	Electric shock	2
Hypo- and hyperactivity of autonomic nervous system	Atropine	7
	Acetylcholine	5
	Epinephrine	4
	Superior cervical ganglionectomy	16
Analgesia	Colchicine	8
Catalepsy	Bulbocapnine	7

We have not actually seen the clock itself. On the basis of our observations we assume that it is constituted of many cells, each one of which is programmed to function at a rate of 24 or nearly 24 hours, that under ordinary conditions in the rat these cells all function together but that under certain conditions they may become desynchronized at least to some extent (6). The location of the timing mechanism in the individual cells—the anatomy of the mechanism—is at present unknown.

In the rat this clock has two functions: 1) a timing device that tells the rat when to emerge from its burrow to find its prey or to avoid its enemies, and 2) a coordinator of autonomic and behavioral functions.

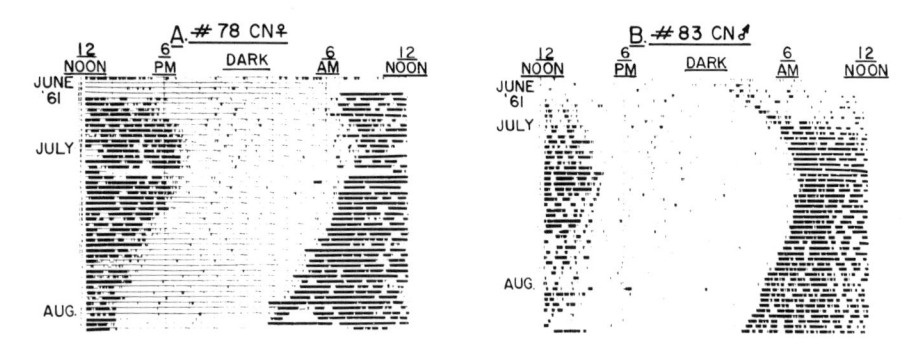

Fig. 9. Spontaneous running activity distribution charts showing presence of clock in two congenitally blind microphthalmic rats.

These various results have established the independence of the clock of influences—particularly from the autonomic nervous system—that play such an important part in maintenance of homeostasis. Elsewhere I have said that the clock is as independent of the rat as a wrist watch is of its wearer (6). This is not strictly true because, although independent of influences from the rest of the organism, it exerts a great influence

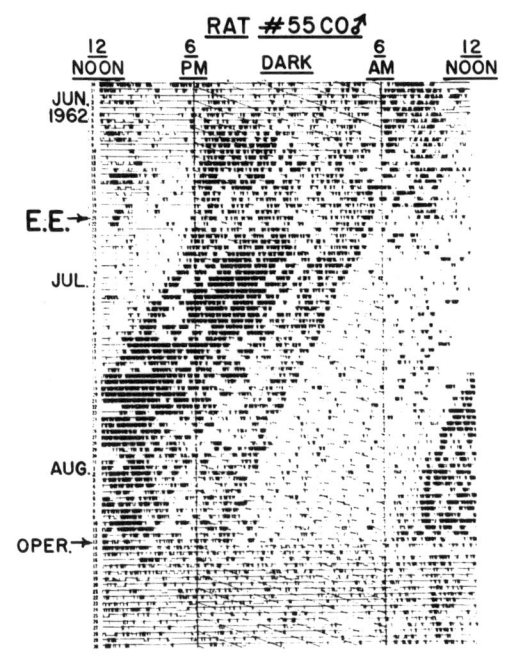

Fig. 10. Spontaneous running activity chart showing effect of hypothalamic lesions on the clock of a blinded (E.E.) rat.

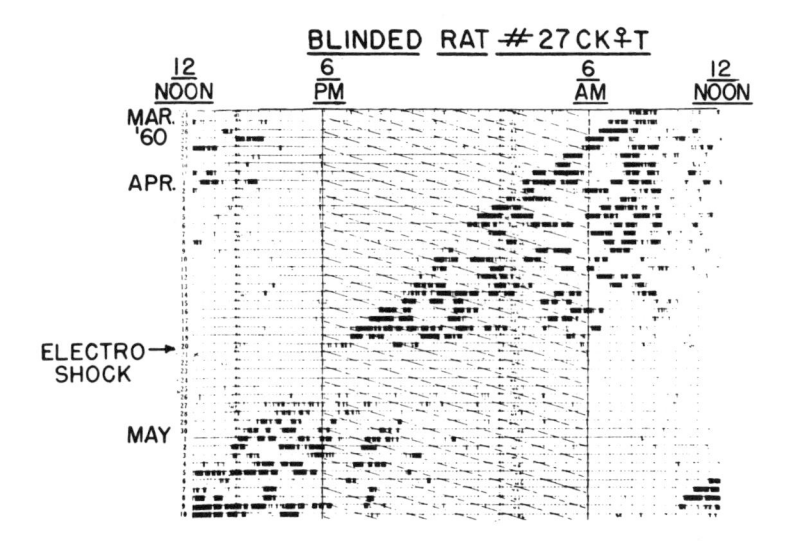

Sleep and Activity: Their Relation to the 24-Hour Clock 139

Fig. 11. Spontaneous running activity distribution chart showing lack of effect of electroshock on the clock.

on the organism. It is a one-way relationship that we now examine in a few special instances such as eating, drinking and sleeping.

Before presenting these results, I must call attention to the fact that activity is only a hand of the clock; it shows that the clock is running and at what rate. It can be removed without interfering in any way with the function of the clock, as illustrated in fig. 11. In this blinded rat electroshock produced severe convulsions lasting several minutes and a period of total inactivity lasting 9 days. That, however, the clock continued to run and at the same rate during the 9 days is shown by the fact that resumption of activity occurred at the predicted time. Thus, removal of the hand had no effect on the clock.

With few exceptions, the 24-hour clock manifests itself by the onsets of the active period, and in many instances by terminations of the active period 12 hours later, as may be seen in figs. 4, 7B, 8, 9 and 10. However, as shown in figs. 3B, 5 and 7A, very often activity dwindles out during the active period, leaving it uncertain whether the clock is still measuring the length of the active period. That probably in most instances the clock does measure the 12- or nearly 12-hour period, even though not shown in the activity record, is demonstrated by results of experiments on the effect on the clock of frontal lobectomy, or removal of the septum, as may be seen in fig. 12. Removal of the olfactory bulbs and undercutting the frontal lobes have the same effect.

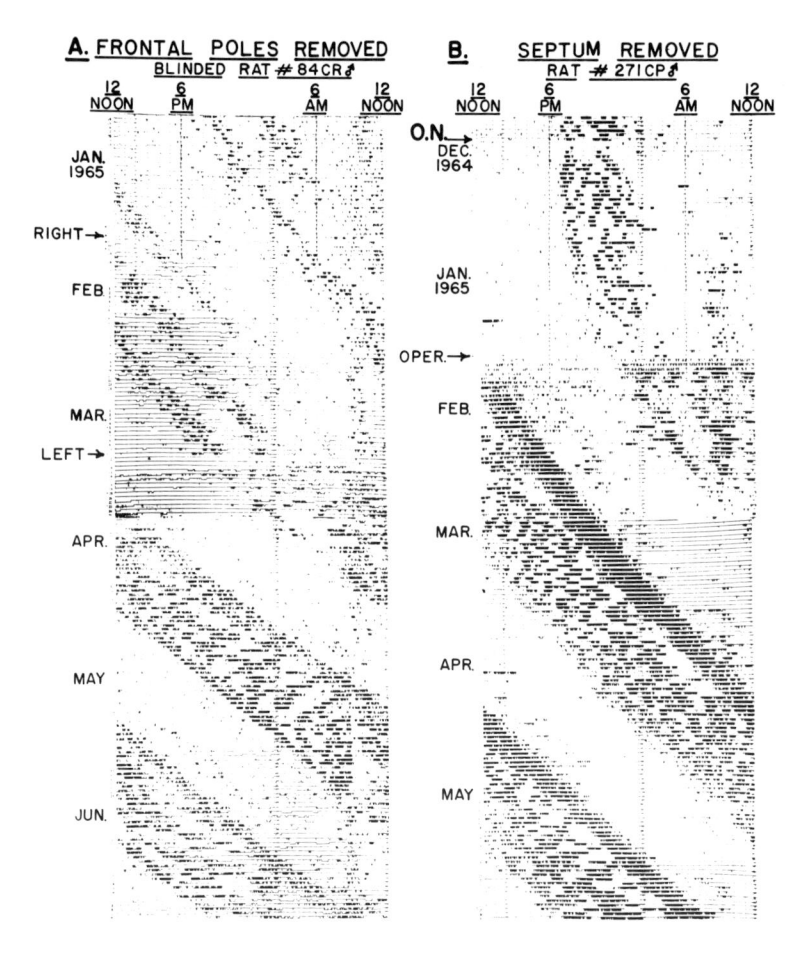

Fig. 12. Spontaneous running activity distribution chart showing effects produced by frontal lobectomy (A) and removal of the septum on onsets and terminations of the active period (B).

None of these operations has any effect on the period. These operations make the rat more active throughout the active period right up to the sharply defined terminations. In the record of the blinded rat in fig. 12A, bursts of activity occurring later each day and lasting a few minutes constituted the only definite evidence of the presence of the clock. Some irregular activity occurred about 8 hours later. Removal of the right frontal pole brought out times of onsets and terminations of the active period but still not very clearly. Subsequent removal of the left frontal pole about 2 months later made the rat very much more active throughout the active period and very clearly established times of onsets and terminations. During the inactive intervals the rat was totally

Fig. 13. Schematic drawing showing sharp onsets of active period and sharp termination and maintenance of activity of a fairly constant level throughout the period.

inactive. Sharp onsets and terminations of the active period made it possible to measure its lengths with accuracy—12 hours and 20 minutes. Thus, the mechanism for production of activity seemed literally to be turned on sharply at one point and off sharply 12, or nearly 12 hours later, and on again sharply 12 hours and 20 minutes later, etc. Fig. 12B shows that removal of the septum also made this blinded (O.N.) rat much more active and brought out the times of onsets and terminations of the active periods. Here again, the rat was almost totally inactive during the inactive phase. Thus, the clock appears to affect activity-producing mechanisms in a series of "on" and "off" periods as shown schematically in fig. 13.

The chart in fig. 14 shows very close correspondence between distribution patterns of spontaneous activity and eating times. Activity patterns are shown at the *left,* eating times patterns are shown at the *right.* During the active period the rat ran for 5 to 10 minutes, then ate, then ran again, thus circulating between the drum and the eating cage almost continuously. The same type of record was obtained on many other rats.

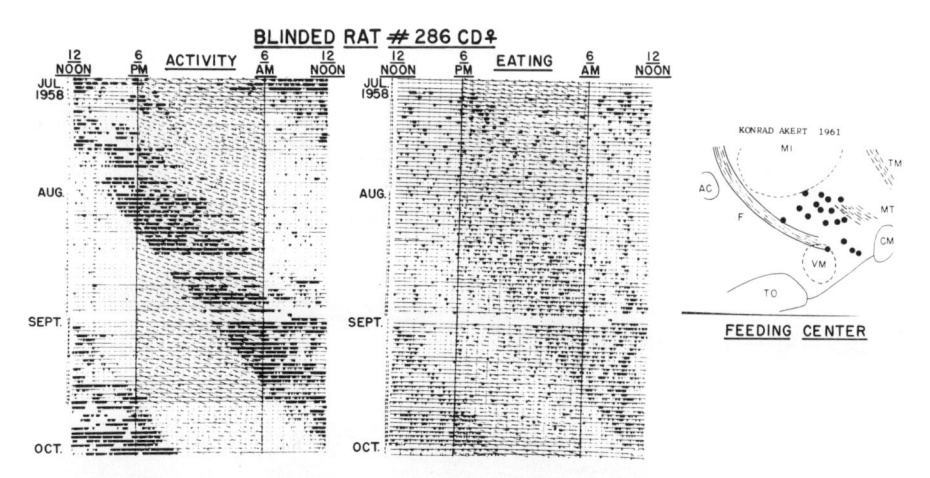

Fig. 14. Distribution charts showing close temporal relationship between activity and eating times of a blinded rat. (Drawing showing feeding center was taken from Akert [1].)

142   The Psychobiology of Curt Richter

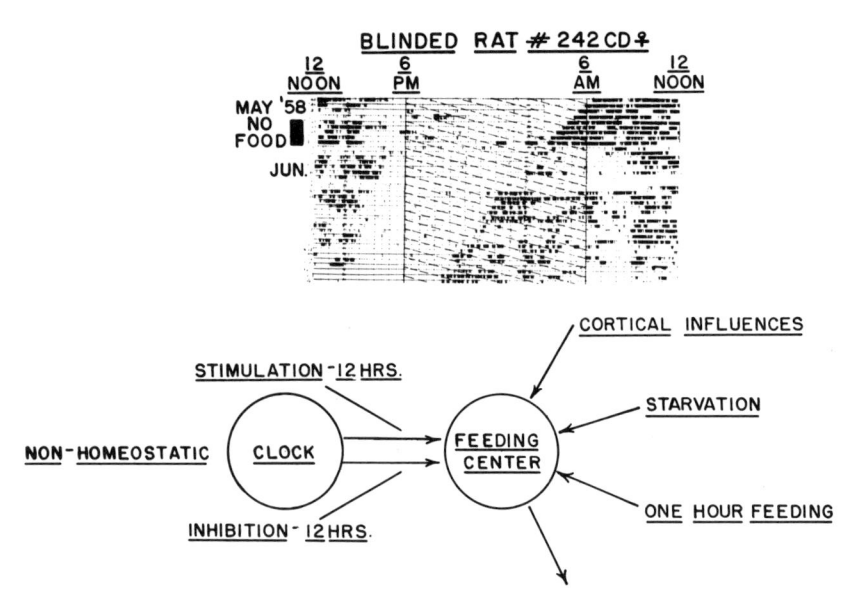

Fig. 15. Top, spontaneous running activity distribution chart showing lack of effect of 7-day starvation on the clock. Bottom, schematic diagram showing one-way relationship between clock and the feeding center.

This means that the clock must act on the feeding center (9) shown at the *right* in fig. 14, to produce the same effects that result from electrical stimulation.

Impulses either direct or indirect do not feed back to the clock from the feeding center. We know this from the observation that starvation of 7 days, which must have a powerful action on the center, had no effect on the clock. (See record at the *top* in fig. 15.) One-hour daily feeding periods and high food intake produced by feeding thyroid extract likewise had no effect on the clock. The diagram in fig. 15

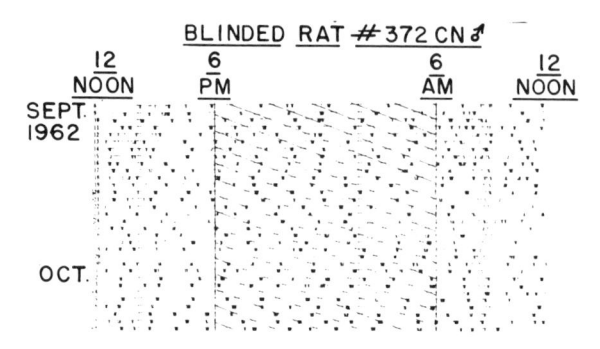

Fig. 16. Distribution chart of eating times of rat with hypothalamic lesion.

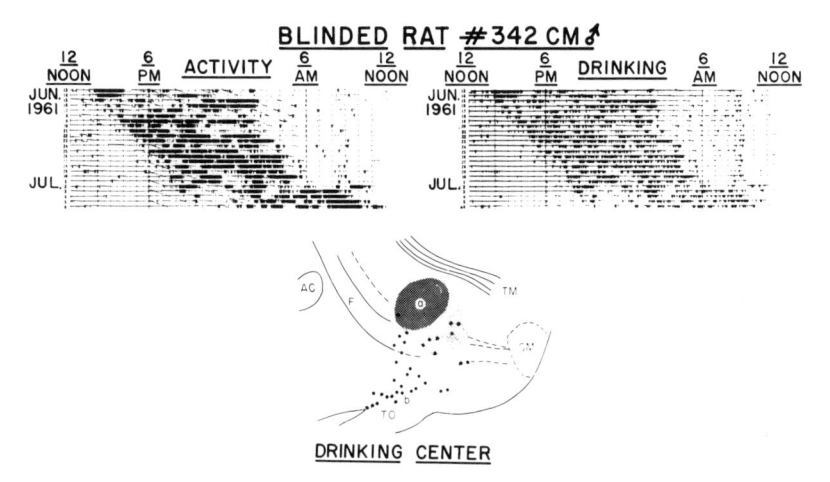

Sleep and Activity: Their Relation to the 24-Hour Clock 143

Fig. 17. Charts showing close temporal agreement between activity and dehydration of a blinded rat (A), and location of drinking center (B). (Taken from Akert [1].)

(*bottom*) shows that this is a strictly one-way relationship. It shows alternating 12-hour periods of stimulation and inhibition of the feeding center. Destruction of the clock by a hypothalamic lesion eliminated all manifestations of the clock in the record of eating times as may be seen in fig. 16. The rat ate at intervals of 40 to 60 minutes throughout the 24 hours.

By means of another simple device, a "drinkometer," a modification of a device designed by Stellar and Hill (9), we recorded drinking times of our rats. Every lap of water by the rat was registered on the recorder.

The charts at the top in fig. 17 show the close agreement between distribution patterns of activity and drinking times. This rat drank over 100 times on the average during the 12-hour active period and only a few times in the inactive period. This could mean that here also impulses from the clock produce the same effects on the drinking center that result from electrical stimulation.

That a strict one-way relationship exists between the clock and the drinking center is demonstrated by the fact that severe dehydration of 67 hours had no effect on the clock has may be seen in the record of one of the rats shown in fig. 18. A schematic drawing of this one-way relationship is shown at the bottom. It shows the alternating 12-hour periods of stimulation and inhibition. After hypothalamic lesions rats drank every few minutes throughout the 24-hours, as may be seen in fig. 19.

Finally, we may now consider the effect of the clock on sleep. We

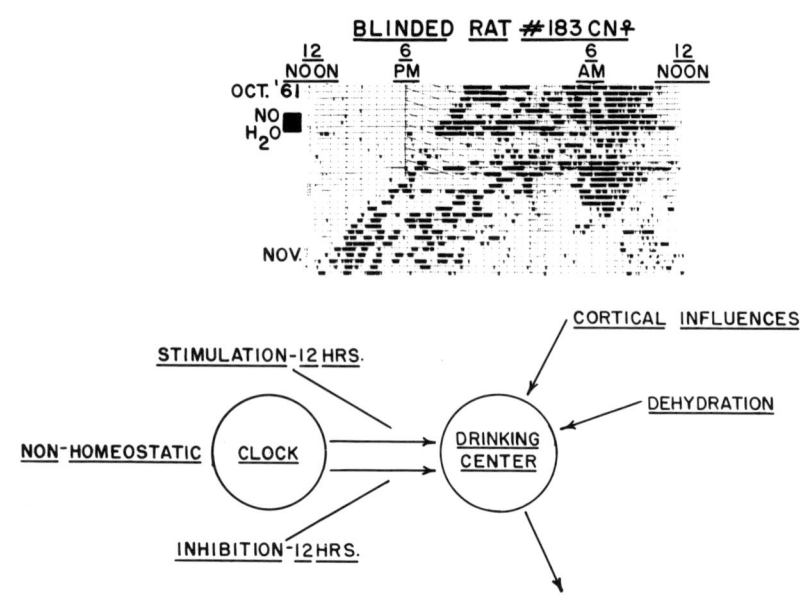

Fig. 18. Top, *spontaneous running activity chart showing that severe dehydration (67 hours) had no effect on the clock.* Bottom, *schematic diagram showing one-way relationship between the clock and the drinking center.*

were not able to devise a method of recording sleeping times, so we had to watch them—a tedious occupation. For this purpose we are now using blinded rats that can be observed under full illumination in our large laboratory; we also replaced wire fronts of the cages with clear glass to facilitate observations. We record sleeping, grooming and resting, and eating, drinking and activity are registered on the recorder. We have records for two full 24-hour periods on 18 rats and for the 3 hours immediately before the onsets of the daily activity period for 7 successive days on nine animals. We do not as yet have enough data to prepare

Fig. 19. Distribution chart showing drinking times of rat with hypothalamic lesion.

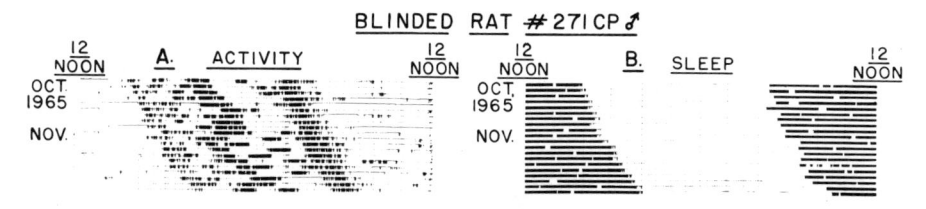

Sleep and Activity: Their Relation to the 24-Hour Clock 145

Fig. 20. Spontaneous running activity distribution charts showing probable relationship between spontaneous activity and sleeping. Sleeping chart was constructed from observations made on sleeping patterns over short periods on many other rats.

definite sleep distribution patterns. We do know that rats spend much of the inactive period in sleep, not continuous sleep, but sleep interrupted at irregular intervals every 2 to 5 hours by a few minutes spent in eating, drinking and grooming, and that rats wake up 10 to 30 minutes or more before the start of the active period, and spend most of this time in grooming, some in eating and drinking and resting. The onsets and terminations of sleep conform in an inverse pattern to activity, but do not appear to be quite as regular. Fig. 20 shows a partially schematic record of the relationship between activity and sleep. *A* shows 20-day activity distribution record of rat 271CP; *B* shows the same record with sleeping times filled in on the basis of knowledge obtained from the aforementioned observations on sleep.

The clock must act on the sleep-activity center, which is probably the reticular formation, in much the same way that electrical stimulation results in arousal and lack of stimulation or inhibition results in sleep.

Here a strictly one-way relationship apparently exists between the clock and the sleep-activity center. We know this from the observations that: 1) deep sleep lasting 12 to 15 hours and followed by a stuporous condition of another 16 to 20 hours produced by large doeses of phenobarbital had no effect on the clock (see fig. 21) although pheno-

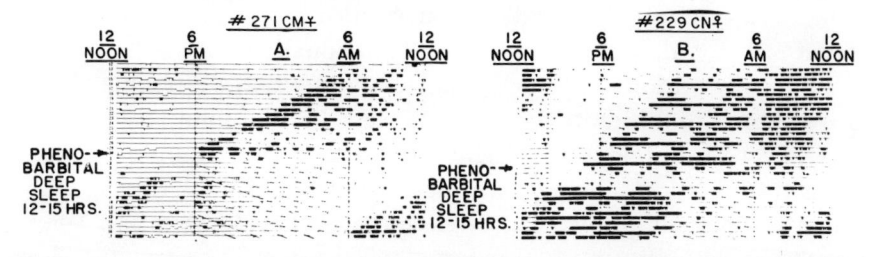

Fig. 21. Spontaneous running activity distribution charts of two rats showing lack of effect on the clock of deep sleep produced by intraperitoneal injection of phenobarbital.

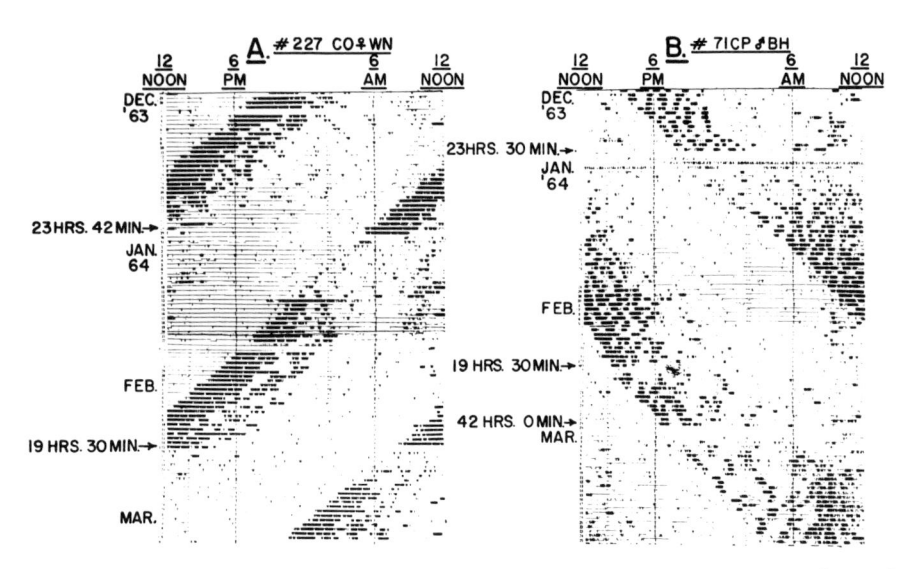

Fig. 22. Spontaneous running activity distribution charts of two rats showing lack of effect of prolonged lack of sleep (19 to 42 hours) on clock produced by forced swimming in tank.

barbital has such a profound effect on the reticular formation; and 2) loss of sleep of 19 to 42 hours produced by forced swimming had no effect on the clock. (See fig. 22.)

Fig. 23 shows a schematic drawing of this one-way relationship which illustrates the one-way relationship between the clock and the sleep-activity center. Elimination of the clock by hypothalamic lesions results in a more or less continuous inactive stuporous condition interrupted by frequent regular drinking and eating times.

Thus, we have seen that this nonhomeostatic 24-hour clock plays an all-important role in regulation of sleep, of eating and drinking and probably of many other functions.

It is not possible to discuss here the role played by the 24-hour clock in man. It can only be said that man also possesses this clock; its presence is not detectable in normal individuals, but is very clear in patients with various types of brain diseases or brain trauma. Man's discovery of fire 400,000 years ago produced a profound change in the functioning of the clock (4). Light from his hearth fire protected him during the night and reduced his need of telling time, with the result that in the process of evolution the clock lost its function as a timing device. Timing ability no longer has survival value. However, the clock still serves to integrate and coordinate autonomic and behavioral functions such as sleep just as it does in the rat.

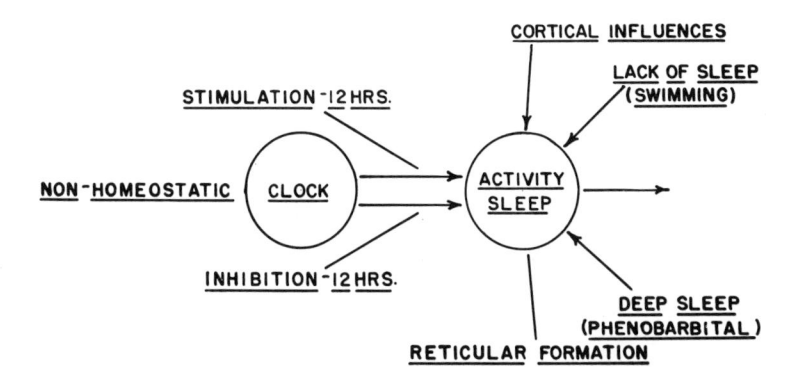

Sleep and Activity: Their Relation to the 24-Hour Clock 147

Fig. 23. Schematic drawing showing one-way relationship between clock and sleep activity center (reticular formation).

Thus, results of these studies have disclosed existence of a remarkable mechanism—the 24-hour clock—that plays an important role in the lives of animals and man but in complete independence of homeostasis; however, homeostasis must still, of course, be taken into consideration with the clock in our thinking about factors involved in the regulation and control of sleep.

References

1. Akert, K.: Diencephalon. In *Electrical Stimulation of the Brain*, edited by D. E. Sheer. University of Texas Press, Austin, 1960.
2. Bernard, C.: *Leçons sur les propriétés physiologiques et les altérations pathologiques des liquides de l'organisme*, Bailliers, Paris, 1859.
3. Cannon, W. B.: *The Wisdom of the Body*. W. W. Norton, New York, 1932.
4. Coon, C. S.: *The Origin of Races*. Alfred A. Knopf, New York, 1963.
5. Richter, C. P.: Total self regulatory functions in animals and human beings. Harvey Lect., 38:63–103, 1942–1943.
6. Richter, C. P.: *Biological Clocks in Medicine and Psychiatry*. Charles C Thomas, Publisher, Springfield, Ill., 1965.
7. Richter, C. P.: *Psychopathology of Periodic Behavior in Animals and Man*. Samuel W. Hamilton Lecture. Presented at the 55th Annual Meeting of the American Psychopathological Association, New York, 1965.
8. Richter, C. P.: The 24-hour clock of animals and man (in preparation).
9. Stellar, E. and Hill, J. H.: The rat's rate of drinking as a function of water deprivation. J. Comp. & Physiol. Psychol., 45:96, 1952.

SOME OBSERVATIONS OF THE SELF-STIMULATION HABITS OF YOUNG WILD ANIMALS

During the past summer in Panama I had opportunity to make a few observations on several forms of self-stimulation habits of three wild animals: a coatimundi, a kinkajou and a spider monkey. I had become accustomed to consider self-stimulation habits as confined to the human race in the form of thumb and finger sucking and erotic habits. It was therefore of considerable interest to observe these habits in young wild animals, all of which had started their lives in the jungle. It may be that some of our difficulties in understanding such self-stimulation habits in human beings are due to failure to consider their general biologic setting. It is hoped that the present limited observations may stimulate an attack on these problems from a more biologic point of view.

The first animal was a young female coatimundi. It belongs to a group called "small bears" by the Germans. These animals have some of the characteristics of bears but are often mistaken either for raccoons or, because of their long noses, for ant-eaters. They are, however, much higher developed than the latter. Their curiosity is scarcely equaled by that of monkeys. They poke their long noses into everything, and their prehensile feet are able to manipulate and investigate things with the greatest agility.

My coatimundi had been caught in the jungle when about 3 months old, taken to the home of Mr. Molina of David (who gave it to me) and given the freedom of the patio. It seemed to get along very well under conditions of semicaptivity and made no effort to escape.

This paper was originally published in the *Archives of Neurology and Psychiatry*, Vol. 13, June 1925.

Observations on Self-Stimulation Habits of Young Wild Animals 149

It was while taking the four day boat trip from David to the Canal Zone with the coatimundi that I observed its peculiar habit of taking its left knee into its mouth and sucking and chewing it. At first I thought this little more than a cleansing habit, but I found that it occurred regularly when the coati went to sleep, was hungry or was thwarted in attempts to explore its surroundings, and especially when it became entangled in its ropes (Fig. 1). When given its freedom or when played with, the sucking activity immediately stopped. The indulgence was so frequent that the hair was almost completely worn away from the part of the knee that the coati took into its mouth.

Fig. 1. Several Typical Knee-Sucking Postures of the Coatimundi

Observations over several months have shown that this special form of self-stimulation always occurs when the animal is going to sleep, but disappears whenever it gains its freedom and is able to forage in the ground and look for beetles. No effort has been made to break the habit.

The second animal was a male kinkajou, about 3 months old. The kinkajou is closely related to the coatimundi, but looks like a cross between a bear, a monkey and a cat. The picture of my young kinkajou is shown in Figure 2. Because of its supposed great predilection for honey it is often known as a honey bear.

This young kinkajou had been captured in the jungle shortly after birth, and had been brought up on a bottle by a physician. At 3 months of age, it had a habit of autofellatio so firmly fixed that the physician was unable to break it. This habit, like the knee-sucking of the coatimundi was indulged in when the animal went to sleep, when it was hungry or when it was thwarted in any of its activities. The act was made possible by the extreme flexibility of the neck and trunk of the animal. When it was curled up, the head was in close contact with the abdominal wall. The penis, which consists of a flap of skin about one

Fig. 2. Kinkajou.

cm. long, is situated unusually high on the ventral surface, so high that it might be mistaken for an abnormal formation of the umbilicus. When the animal is indulging in this activity, it is curled up into a perfect ball.

The third animal was a male spider monkey about 6 years old, which had been kept in the home of Dr. E. Currie in the Canal Zone since its capture in the jungle after the mother was shot. It was brought up on a bottle, its diet carefully regulated, and it was given a daily bath. When old enough it was permitted to eat at the table and to sleep with members of the family, and seemed to be perfectly adjusted to its human environment. It had always been well-behaved until the past year, when with the onset of puberty it occasionally showed entirely unprovoked outbursts of rage. In one of these, it bit its master rather severely so that it was given to me to be taken to Barro Colorado Island Laboratory on Gatun Lake.

On the way to the laboratory, I noticed that it sucked its fingers very much as many children do, especially when its activities were thwarted or when it was prevented from escaping. Sudden noises along the road or jarring of the car caused it to suck its fingers vigorously, and once during the trip it so fell asleep. The animal had had this habit since its capture, and no attempt had been made to break it. Unfortunately, the animal soon escaped.

This escape was interesting as illuminating the comparative strength of different cravings. When we reached the laboratory, the monkey was released a few feet from the edge of the jungle. It quickly made its way to the top of one of the tallest trees, where it dangled from one of the branches, making sounds of unmistakable joy. Then it suddenly turned and made its way through the treetops into the jungle, never to return. All of Dr. Currie's efforts to recall the animal with familiar calls and whistles were futile. A most firmly wrought attachment made during six or seven years of most intimate association with its master, and with marked dependency, could be dissolved without the slightest indication of a struggle by something which the tall trees of the jungle offered; a something which, because of the previous condition of semicaptivity, this animal had never before experienced.

I should like to note that in all three animals the self-stimulation activity was sucking, but the area involved was different for each animal. It would seem that the sucking was the important thing, not the part of the body involved; that there is no reason to believe that the penis because it happened to be a sex organ played any different role in the kinkajou than did the knee in the coatimundi. It would appear to be a matter more of what part is most easily reached by the mouth and how well this part fits the mouth. This factor is important in the knee-sucking of the coatimundi whose mouth is long and narrow and pointed. The sharp-edged flat knee fits it very well, and the lips of the animal everywhere are in close contact with it. The paws of the coatimundi with their sharp, nonretractile claws would not fit nearly so well as the knee. In the case of the kinkajou, the feet are considerably too large for the mouth and here, too, the sharp nonretractile claws would make it difficult to keep the paws comfortably in the mouth. In the spider monkey, the fingers of the hand are really the only parts of the body it can reach with its mouth and which can be left there without danger of injury. The body, although more flexible than the human body, has still a limited scope of movement compared to that of the coatimundi or the kinkajou. Its mouth can reach only a few parts of its own body, and these parts happen to be so shaped that they are not suitable to be taken into the mouth. The fingers of the hand reach the mouth easily and also form a snug contact with the lips on all sides.

In discussing the origin of these habits, one must start with the all-important role played by the sucking habit. It is probably the most primitive of all mammalian habits. Preyer has observed the sucking activity in rabbit and guinea-pig fetuses and also in the human fetus. Schotti, Soltmann and Scheel also observed this activity in the human fetus. I have observed it in a number of rabbit fetuses about twenty days old. Because of the presence in utero of sucking activity, one must consider the possibility that self-stimulation sucking habits have their origin during this stage of the animal's development. I have made several observations on new-born human infants that seem to me to establish definitely the intra-uterine origin of these habits. In one infant especially, I noticed within one hour after birth, vigorous finger-sucking. There were blisters on the fingers that were sucked, and there was reason to believe that these blisters were raised before birth. This infant showed a well coordinated finger-to-mouth movement without the presence of random or trial and error attempts. I have learned from obstetricians that finger-sucking and thumb-sucking are observed occasionally in the first few minutes of postnatal life.

I believe that formation of these habits in utero depends, in the first place, on the ease and frequency with which the mouth comes into contact with the part of the body involved. The frequency of contact will depend largely on the activity of the fetus, the strength of the sucking activity itself will be a factor. Both the general bodily activity and the sucking activity will depend on the nourishment of the fetus. An under-nourished fetus will probably be much more active and suck very much more vigorously than a well-nourished fetus. Stimulation of the outside of the mother's body and the activity of the mother herself are also factors to be considered. It is my impression that most of these self-stimulation habits do have their origin in the intra-uterine stages of development, and that many which appear some time after birth are only to be regarded as revivals of earlier habits.

One important factor in the origin of self-stimulation habits of these wild animals is the fact that they were kept under conditions of captivity or semicaptivity without association with other animals of their own kind. The element of consolation probably played an important role here.

Part II SELECTION

INCREASED SALT APPETITE IN ADRENALECTOMIZED RATS

Adrenalectomized rats are known to have a definitely increased salt need, inasmuch as the administration of large quantities of salt either greatly reduces or eliminates the symptoms of insufficiency, and actually increases the survival incidence (Rubin and Krick, 1933; Gaunt, Tobin and Gaunt, 1935; Kutz, McKeown and Selye, 1934). But is this need accompanied by an increased salt appetite, and will the adrenalectomized rat, if given free access to salt take sufficient quantity to keep itself alive and free from symptoms of insufficiency? In an effort to answer these questions the following experiments were undertaken.

Methods

It was necessary for this purpose to devise a method by which salt could be given freely, under circumstances which made possible measurement of the actual amount ingested. It would have been simplest, of course, to present granular salt in a separate container. However, the small amount ingested daily and the comparatively large amount spilled or carried away on the paws definitely ruled out a quantitative measure by this method. For this reason salt was offered in solution in the drinking water. At the outset a 1 per cent salt solution was used because Rubin and Krick obtained their successful results from a solution of approximately this strength; but since, with only the salt

---

This paper was originally published in *The American Journal of Physiology*, Vol. 115, No. 1, March 1936. Reprinted by permission.

solution available, the rat's intake would depend partly on the salt need and partly on the thirst for water, access was given at the same time to tap water presented in a second container. In this way the rat could satisfy its thirst and its salt appetite independently.

In the first series of experiments with the 1 per cent salt solution and water, the animals also received the usual amount of salt in the McCollum diet (approximately 0.145 gm. per day). Inasmuch as the normal rats did not distinguish between the salt solution and the water, a second series of experiments was started with the strength of the salt solution increased to 3 per cent and no salt give in the food. It was found then that the normal animals did differentiate very definitely between the 3 per cent salt solution and the water.

The rats were kept in individual cages containing a food cup, and two inverted graduated bottles, one with salt solution, the other with tap water. The water and salt solutions were changed at the same time to avoid any difference in the freshness of the two liquids. The fluid intake was recorded daily and the body weight was recorded weekly.

To establish the effects produced by the salt solution two control groups of animals were adrenalectomized and kept under exactly the same conditions, except that one received only the salt contained in the food, while the other received no salt, either in the drinking water or in the food.

The adrenalectomy was done by the technique in which the surrounding fat, connective tissue and also about one-quarter inch of the pedicle are removed with the gland (Pencharz, Olmsted and Giragossintz, 1931; Firor and Grollman, 1933). In order to make certain that the effects produced depended specifically on adrenalectomy, a third group of control experiments was performed to determine the relation of gonadectomy and hypophysectomy to salt appetite.

Results

Survival rate of adrenalectomized rats on a saltless diet and on a standard McCollum diet. Fifteen animals that had previously been on the standard McCollum diet were adrenalectomized and placed on a saltless diet. All of these animals immediately developed symptoms of insufficiency with a loss of weight, appetite, and death after an average of 11 days. None of the animals survived.

Twenty-six animals raised on the McCollum mixture were adrenalectomized and continued on this standard diet from which they received approximately 0.145 gram of salt per day. Sixteen of these animals died at an average interval of 17 days, while ten animals, or 39 per cent, gave signs of living their normal span of life, and were killed about forty-five days after adrenalectomy.

Increased survival rate of adrenalectomized rats with access to 1 per cent or 3 per cent salt solution and tap water. Thirteen animals on the regular McCollum diet given the choice of drinking 1 per cent salt solution or tap water, drank enough of the former to increase very markedly their chances of survival. Nine, or 69 per cent, showed all signs of living indefinitely and only four, or 31 per cent, died. This is a marked increase in the survival rate over that of the animals which received only the salt contained in the McCollum diet. Moreover the average duration of life of the animals that died was 19 days, which is greater than that of animals on either saltless diet or on only the McCollum mixture.

Five animals given the choice of 3 per cent salt solution or tap water showed a survival rate of 80 per cent. One animal lived 38 days, the others showed a normal gain in body weight and no signs of insufficiency except a slightly decreased appetite.

Further proof that the animals were actually kept alive by the salt which they ingested voluntarily, is shown by the effects produced on survival when the 1 per cent salt solution was removed leaving only tap water available. The nine animals which gave every indication of living indefinitely on the 1 per cent salt solution were deprived of the salt solution at intervals ranging from 33 to 77 days after adrenalectomy but were still kept on the McCollum diet. (See the last two columns in table 1.) Eight out of the nine animals died after an average of 5.1 days with a range of variation of 4 to 7 days, while the ninth animal was still alive on the 36th day.

Amount of increase of salt intake in adrenalectomized rats. A marked effect produced by adrenalectomy on the salt appetite is shown very clearly in figure 1. It will be seen that before adrenalectomy the tap water averaged 20 cc. per day, the intake of 1 per cent salt solution only 10 cc. per day; and that almost immediately after adrenalectomy the intake of tap water began to decrease, while the intake of salt solution showed a sharp increase. Forty days after adrenalectomy, when the animal was killed, the salt solution intake had reached a level of 45 cc. per day and was still increasing while the water intake had decreased to less than 4 cc. per day.

The results of these experiments are summarized in table 1. It will be seen that the average daily intake of tap water decreased from 16.5 cc.

TABLE 1. CHOICE OF 1 PER CENT SALT SOLUTION OR WATER (DRY DIET CONTAINING 1 PER CENT SALT)

RAT NO.	AGE	Ave. Daily Tap Water Intake 10 days before adrenalectomy	Ave. Daily Tap Water Intake 20–30 days after adrenalectomy	Ave. Daily Intake of 1% Salt Solution 10 days before adrenalectomy	Ave. Daily Intake of 1% Salt Solution 20–30 days after adrenalectomy	Ave. Daily Salt Intake from 1% Salt Solution 10 days before adrenalectomy	Ave. Daily Salt Intake from 1% Salt Solution 20–30 days after adrenalectomy	Ave. Daily Salt Intake in Food 10 days before adrenalectomy	Ave. Daily Salt Intake in Food 20–30 days after adrenalectomy	Total Ave. Daily Salt Intake 10 days before adrenalectomy	Total Ave. Daily Salt Intake 20–30 days after adrenalectomy	Body Weight Day of adrenalectomy	Body Weight 30th day after adrenalectomy	Ave. Daily Salt Intake per Kilogram Body Weight 10 days before adrenalectomy	Ave. Daily Salt Intake per Kilogram Body Weight 20–30 days after adrenalectomy	Survival After adrenalectomy	Survival After salt removal
	days	cc.	cc.	cc.	cc.	gms.	gms.	gms.	gms.	gms.	gms.	gms.	gms.	gms.	gms.	days	days
1	78	3.0		7.9		0.079		0.120		0.199		145	140	1.45		15 D†	
2	78	15.1		19.9		0.199		0.120		0.319		150	141	2.13		16 D	
3	78	14.9		11.9		0.119		0.120		0.239		145	125	1.65		14 D	
4	83	16.4	4.7	10.8	33.2	0.108	0.332	0.120	0.110	0.228	0.442	165	173	1.38	2.55	33 +	4 D
5	98	26.3	4.8	35.1	44.6	0.351	0.446	0.121	0.096	0.470	0.552	214	230	1.67	2.40	34 +	5 D
6	67	15.6	1.6	10.0	21.4	0.100	0.214	0.100	0.153	0.320	0.367	188	207	1.70	1.77	77 +	36 K*
7	80	19.4	1.4	6.7	19.3	0.067	0.193	0.143	0.110	0.210	0.303	220	223	0.95	1.30	40 +	4 D
8	83	12.2	1.9	37.7	26.7	0.377	0.267	0.120	0.110	0.497	0.377	181	181	2.92	2.08	49 +	7 D
9	83	22.6	3.6	8.9	35.0	0.089	0.350	0.120	0.110	0.209	0.460	170	180	1.23	2.55	47 +	6 D
10	89	23.0	4.5	9.1	27.0	0.091	0.270	0.120	0.110	0.211	0.380	182	195	1.16	1.95	48 +	6 D
11	82	9.2	3.1	19.3	19.6	0.193	0.196	0.107	0.093	0.293	0.295	151	168	1.94	1.75	42 +	5 D
12	73	30.6	6.9	5.7	25.5	0.057	0.255	0.163	0.099	0.220	0.354	234	215	0.94	1.64	31 D	
13	64	6.6	1.2	37.4	24.1	0.374	0.241	0.120	0.110	0.494	0.351	217	205	2.28	1.71	46 +	4 D
Av.	80	16.5	3.4	16.9	27.6	0.169	0.276	0.123	0.110	0.301	0.388	181	183	1.65	1.98		

* Killed.
† Died.

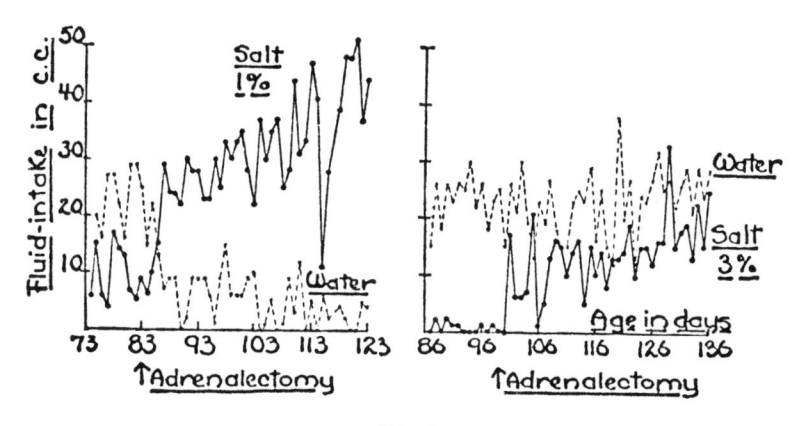

Fig. 1

for the 10 days before adrenalectomy to 3.4 cc. for the 20 to 30 day period after adrenalectomy, while the intake of the 1 per cent salt solution increased from 16.9 cc. for the 10 day pre-operative period to 27.6 cc. for the 20 to 30 day post-operative period. These daily averages of 27.6 cc. of salt solution and 3.4 cc. of tap water indicate definitely that the animals differentiated between these two fluids. However, before adrenalectomy the average daily intake was practically identical for tap water and for the 1 per cent salt solution (16.5 cc. as compared to 16.9 cc., respectively). This must mean that before operation the animals did not differentiate between the two fluids. In keeping with this view is the fact that some of the animals drank more water while others took more salt solution, a fact which suggests that it was largely a matter of chance which bottle was selected. It seems probable that had a definite distinction been made between these two fluids, the salt solution intake before adrenalectomy would have been much lower, consequently the percentage increase in the salt need after adrenalectomy would have been much greater than was found in these experiments.

The failure of the rats before operation to distinguish between the tap water and the 1 per cent salt solution may have been due either to the fact that the salt solution was too weak or to the fact that the salt which they received in the diet was sufficient to satisfy the salt need as well as to dull the sensitivity of the salt appetite.

Because of this failure of the animals to differentiate definitely between the 1 per cent salt solution and water before adrenalectomy, a 3 per cent salt solution was substituted. This was not too concentrated to be measured accurately in the water bottles used in these experiments, and it was of sufficient strength that the five animals which had

TABLE 2. CHOICE OF 3 PER CENT SALT SOLUTION OR WATER (DRY DIET WITHOUT SALT)

Rat No.	Age	Average Daily Tap Water Intake 10 days before adrenalectomy	Average Daily Tap Water Intake 20–30 days after adrenalectomy	Average Daily Intake of 3% Salt Solution 10 days before adrenalectomy	Average Daily Intake of 3% Salt Solution 20–30 days after adrenalectomy	Average Daily Salt Intake from 3% Salt Solution 10 days before adrenalectomy	Average Daily Salt Intake from 3% Salt Solution 20–30 days after adrenalectomy	Body Weight Day of adrenalectomy	Body Weight 30th day after adrenalectomy	Average Daily Salt Intake per Kilogram Body Weight 10 days before adrenalectomy	Average Daily Salt Intake per Kilogram Body Weight 20–30 days after adrenalectomy	Survival
	days	cc.	cc.	cc.	cc.	grams	grams	grams	grams	grams	grams	days
14	99	24.4	23.9	0.6	16.5	0.018	0.495	383	370	0.047	1.33	65 K
15	93	10.0	14.1	1.8	4.1	0.054	0.123	162	174	0.341	0.71	67 K
16	93	17.0	16.7	2.7	11.4	0.081	0.342	170	175	0.476	1.98	38 D
17	91	24.6	20.3	3.0	18.1	0.090	0.543	265	268	0.353	2.04	65 K
18	91	39.0	27.7	2.7	12.5	0.081	0.375	292	318	0.284	1.19	65 K
Av.	93	23.0	20.5	2.2	12.5	0.065	0.376	254	261	0.300	1.45	

the choice of drinking it or tap water differentiated between the two before adrenalectomy as well as afterwards. A record from one of these animals is presented in figure 1. It will be seen that the intake of the 3 per cent salt solution increased from a level of less than 2 cc. per day before adrenalectomy to 20 cc. afterwards, while the water intake remained practically the same.

The results as summarized in table 2 show that before adrenalectomy the average daily water-intake was 23.0 cc. while the intake of 3 per cent salt solution was 2.2 cc. It will be noted that this marked difference in the consumption of salt solution and water was present in all five animals. The intake of the 3 per cent salt solution for the 20 to 30 day period after adrenalectomy was 12.5 cc., almost six times as high as the intake before. This, undoubtedly, is a much more correct estimate of the salt needs of the adrenalectomized animals than was obtained in the experiments with the 1 per cent salt solution.

Effect of gonadectomy and hypophysectomy on salt appetite. It was found that gonadectomy and hypophysectomy have no effect on salt appetite. The average daily intake of 3 per cent salt solution of four gonadectomized rats was 3.0 cc. for the 10 days before adrenalectomy and 3.9 cc. for the 20 to 30 days after; and for the six hypophysectomized rats it was 3.6 cc. before and 1.5 cc. afterwards, a decrease proportional to the general decrease in metabolism.

It may be assumed, then, that the increased salt appetite which follows adrenalectomy is specific for the deficiency created by the loss of the secretions of the adrenal gland. It is of interest that the atrophy of the adrenals found in the hypophysectomized rats was not associated with an increase in salt appetite.

Salt appetite of normal rats. In the above experiments it was shown that the amount of salt taken voluntarily by adrenalectomized rats gave an indication of their salt need. It seemed likely that the voluntary salt intake could also be a measure of the salt need of normal animals. It was of interest to know, then, how the salt need determined in this way compares with the salt that the animals receive in the standard McCollum diet.

This diet contains 1 per cent salt which according to the calculations of Wang (1925), of an average daily food intake of 14.5 gram in adult rats would mean an average daily salt intake of 0.145 gram or 0.659 gram per kilogram body weight.

Records taken on a group of nineteen normal animals on a saltless diet with a choice of either 3 per cent salt solution or tap water gave a daily voluntary salt intake of 0.123 gram or 0.577 gram per kilogram body weight, which is very nearly the same as the amount received in the McCollum diet. It was thus determined by a very different method that the salt present in the McCollum diet is an adequate amount for normal animals.

Discussion

The fact that the salt appetite of adrenalectomized rats has such a close relationship to the salt deficiency indicates that appetite may be used as a measure of the deficiencies produced by endocrine disturbances, or by pathological changes in other parts of the body.

It has been observed on the medical wards of the Johns Hopkins Hospital that patients with Addison's disease have spontaneously expressed a great appetite for foods rich in salt, particularly ham and herring. It is also known that during pregnancy, when the greatest changes take place in the entire endocrine system, appetites may also change considerably. Thus it may be that even in man a closer study of the appetite might throw more light on the actual needs and deficiencies present in such conditions as pregnancy or in acute or chronic disturbances of the endocrine system.

Summary

1. The survival rate of thirteen animals adrenalectomized and put on a saltless diet was zero per cent and the average length of life after adrenalectomy was 11 days.

2. The survival rate of twenty-six animals adrenalectomized and continued on the standard McCollum diet (approximately 0.145 gram of salt per day) was 39 per cent and the average duration of life of the animals that died was 17 days.

3. Thirteen rats kept on the standard diet and given the choice of tap water or 1 per cent salt solution ingested a larger quantity of salt solution after adrenalectomy and their survival rate was increased to 69 per cent.

4. Five rats kept on a saltless diet but given the choice of a 3 per cent salt solution or tap water ingested six times as much salt solution after adrenalectomy and showed a survival rate of 80 per cent.

5. It was thus determined that the salt appetite is greatly increased by adrenalectomy and by virtue of this appetite the survival rate is also greatly increased.

6. The salt needs of the nineteen normal rats determined by the choice method on the 3 per cent salt solution was shown to be approximately the same as the amount calculated empirically by McCollum; that is, 0.577 gram per kilogram body weight per day as compared to 0.659 gram for the McCollum diet.

References

Firor, W. M. and A. Grollman. Amer. J. Physiol. 103: 686, 1933.
Gaunt, R., C. E. Tobin and J. H. Gaunt. Amer. J. Physiol. 111: 321, 1935.
Kutz, R. L., T. McKeown and H. Selye. Proc. Soc. Exper. Biol. and Med. 32: 331, 1934.
Pencharz, R. K., J. M. D. Olmsted and G. Giragossintz. Physiol. Zool. 4: 501, 1931.
Rubin, M. I. and E. T. Krick. Proc. Soc. Exper. Biol. and Med. 31: 228, 1933.
Wang, G. H. Amer. J. Physiol. 71: 729, 1925.

NUTRITIONAL REQUIREMENTS FOR NORMAL GROWTH AND REPRODUCTION IN RATS STUDIED BY THE SELF-SELECTION METHOD

The ability of animals and humans to make dietary selections which are conducive to normal growth and reproduction has not received much attention in modern nutrition studies. The survival of animals and humans in the wild state in which the diet had to be selected from a great variety of beneficial, useless, and even harmful substances is proof of this ability. It would be of interest to know the ingredients of this self-selected diet; the percentage of fat, carbohydrate, and protein, and the mineral and vitamin content. This knowledge would probably throw an entirely new light on the nutritional requirements for growth, health, and reproduction.

In the wild state, quantitative studies of the food intake of animals and humans would be impractical. It is necessary, therefore, to try to reproduce the essential features of field conditions in the laboratory.

A few attempts have been made to study the self-selection of diets under controlled conditions. Animals were given a choice of a number of foods which were present either in their natural habitat or which on theoretical grounds might play a part in their nutrition. Most of these experiments were undertaken in agricultural stations with the hope of finding a cheap and simple method of feeding animals. Evvard (1915) gave pigs a free choice of whole corn grain, meat meal (containing 60 per cent protein), whole oats, linseed oil meal, wheat middlings, char-

---

This paper was originally published in *The American Journal of Physiology*, Vol. 122, No. 3, June 1938. Co-authors were L. Emmett Holt, Jr., and Bruno Barelare, Jr. Reprinted by permission.

coal, limestone, salt, and water. The animals showed remarkably rapid growth. One animal was the largest pig of its age ever raised at the Iowa Experimental Station. He also found that young pigs, given free access to salt, showed better growth than pigs which received varying amounts of salt in their regular diet. With Dox (quoted by Evvard, 1915), he showed that a free choice of calcium carbonate also produced increased growth in pigs. Osborne and Mendel (1918) gave rats a choice of two diets, one with a superior, and one with an inferior mixture. A number of such pairs of diets were used, some with high and low protein content, some with proteins poor and rich in amino-acid content, etc. Ultimately, the rats always chose the superior mixture and showed normal or nearly normal growth. By similar but more extensive experiments on rats and mice, Mitchell and Mendel (1921) confirmed these results. Kon (1931) reported that, given a choice of sucrose, casein, and a salt mixture offered separately, rats did not thrive as well as when these substances were offered in a composite mixture. Pearl and Fairchild (1921) reported that, given a choice of a large variety of natural foods, chickens showed better growth than was obtained under a system of man-controlled mass feeding. Recently Dove (1935) also reported that chickens were able to make advantageous selections from a variety of natural foods. According to him, this ability varied from animal to animal and was dependent on genetic factors. Davis (1928) found that three young children, given a choice of a large number of foods, grew normally and became more healthy. Sweet (1936) found that children made better dietary selections on the basis of appetite than when guided by their parents.

These experiments had in common several shortcomings due to the use of natural foods or synthetic food mixtures. It was believed by most of the workers that appetite could be a guide only when foods were presented in their natural form. However, because of the complexity of the ingredients in natural foods, it was never possible to determine whether an animal was attracted to a single component or to the combination of substances.

These difficulties were overcome to a great extent in self-selection experiments in which purified or nearly purified substances were used (Richter, Holt, Barclare, 1937). The possibility that rats could make selections from purified substances was suggested by the results of experiments on the changes in mineral appetite of adrenalectomized and parathyroidectomized rats. It is well known that adrenalectomized rats die within 10 to 15 days after the operation, apparently because of the excessive loss of salt. It was found that when given free access to salt solutions, adrenalectomized rats voluntarily took a sufficient amount to keep themselves alive and free from symptoms of insufficiency (Richter, 1936). In some animals, the salt intake increased fifteen-fold after adrenalectomy. Parathyroidectomized rats which ordinarily lose weight, show symptoms of tetany, and eventually die, took large amounts of solutions of calcium lactate, 2.4 per cent. Consequently they remained free of tetany and grew normally. The calcium lactate intake was increased twelve fold in one animal after parathyroidectomy. Parathyroid implants to the anterior chamber of the eye caused the calcium appetite to return to its normal level (Richter and Eckert, 1937).

It was decided then that if the deficient rats could select these two minerals to such great advantage, it might be worth while to determine whether normal rats could make wise selections of other minerals as well as of protein, carbohydrate, fat, and vitamins. The ideal method of determining this would have been to give the rats a choice of all substances which are known to have anything to do with nutrition; however, this would be impractical at this point.

In order to simplify the situation, it was decided to restrict the selections to one representative of most of the substances known to play an important part in the nutrition of the rat, that is, protein, carbohydrate, fat; the minerals, sodium, calcium, phosphorus, potassium; vitamins A, B, D, and E. It has been reported that the rat can produce its own vitamin C (Parsons and Hutton, 1924); therefore, this substance was not offered.

The immediate problem was to select the representative of each group. The fact that this experiment depended entirely upon appetite suggested that the rats themselves should select the representatives. Obviously, this was better than making a priori selections on the basis of our theoretical knowledge of the nutritional value of the foodstuffs. A series of well known fats, carbohydrates, and proteins were offered singly and with no other substance except water. Under these conditions, the survival time was taken as a measure of the nutritional value of the food. The selection of the mineral solutions and their concentrations was also left to the rat. Rats kept on the McCollum diet were given a choice of water and a mineral solution. The ingestion of a small amount of the solution each day was taken to indicate that the mineral was needed and should be included in the multiple food choice experiments. A similar system was used in selecting the substances containing the vitamins, except that the choice was smaller.

Methods

The rats were kept separately in cages consisting of a revolving drum, a cyclometer, and a living compartment containing food and fluid receptacles. In the preliminary single food choice experiments, the living compartments contained one bottle for water and another bottle or cup for the food to be tested. In the multiple choice experiments, the cages were made large enough to contain 3 cups for solids and 8 bottles for fluids.

The rats were placed in the cages at an average age of 49.5 days and kept on the McCollum diet for 10 days or more before being changed to one of the experimental diets. The McCollum diet contained 725 grams of graham flour, 100 grams of casein, 100 grams of skimmed milk powder, 50 grams of butter, 10 grams of sodium chloride, and 15 grams of calcium carbonate. Lettuce (10 grams) was given weekly.

Daily records were made of activity, intake of solids and fluids, and of vaginal smears; weekly readings were made of body weight. The bottles were cleaned and refilled twice weekly. The animals were kept under constant observation for the appearance of any deficiency symptoms.

The animals were autopsied; the endocrine glands were removed and preserved for histological study.

Seventy-two animals were used in the preliminary single food experiments; 8 animals were used in the multiple food choice experiments. Since these records were obtained, observations have been made on 40 additional animals with essentially the same results.

Results

Preliminary experiments with choice of single foodstuffs, fat, carbohydrate, and protein. Fat. Six fats were tested: olive oil, lard, cod liver oil, wheat germ oil, perilla oil, and peanut oil. Groups of 4 animals were kept on each of these fats plus water. Records were made of activity, body weight, and solid and fluid intake.

For the present purposes, only the survival time will be reported. The results are summarized in figure 1. The rats lived longest on olive oil, averaging 46.5 days; next longest on lard, 27.5 days; and shortest on perilla oil, 11 days. Olive oil was thus selected for the multiple food choice experiments.

Carbohydrate. Six carbohydrates were tested: dextrose, sucrose,

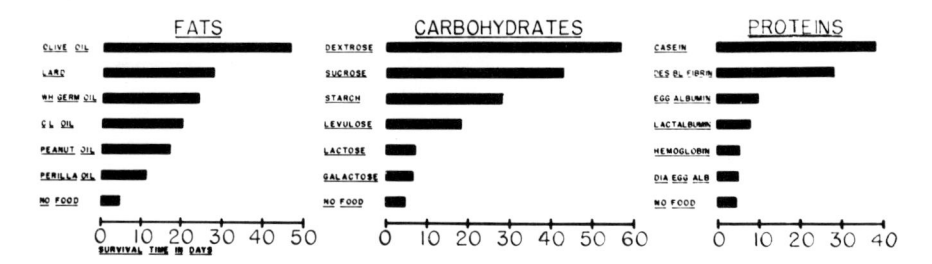

Fig. 1. Survival Times of Rats on Single-Choice Experiments

starch levulose, lactose, and galactose. The animals lived longest on dextrose, 57 days, next longest on sucrose, 43 days, and shortest on galactose, 6.5 days. Sucrose, rather than dextrose, was chosen for the multple choice experiments, because it had already been used in a number of our experiments and because animals lived nearly as long on it as on dextrose.

Protein. Six proteins were tested: casein (autoclaved and purified), desiccated blood fibrin, egg albumin, lactalbumin, hemoglobin, and dialyzed egg albumin. The animals lived longest on casein, 38.5 days, next longest on desiccated blood fibrin, 28.5 days, and shortest on dialyzed egg albumin, 5.0 days. Casein was selected for the multiple food choice experiments.

These survival times must be regarded as only rough estimates to serve the present purposes. With records on a larger number of animals, data obtained from this type of experiment should help to throw more light on the fundamental nutritional differences between these various substances.

Minerals: Sodium. From the afore-mentioned adrenal experiments it was known that normal as well as adrenalectomized rats show a definite appetite for sodium chloride offered either in 1 per cent or 3 per cent solutions. Due to the fact that often the 1 per cent solution was not concentrated enough to be distinguished from tap water, the 3 per cent solution was used in the multiple choice experiments.

Calcium. It was observed in the parathyroid experiments that normal rats show an appetite for calcium lactate solution and consequently will drink a small amount from day to day. A 2.4 per cent solution was used in the following experiments.

Phosphorus. The rats showed a definite appetite for phosphorus in the form of dibasic sodium phosphate. The concentration easily distinguished from water was 8 per cent.

Potassium. The preliminary experiments indicated that rats would take potassium chloride in concentrations varying from 1 to 2 per cent. Solutions of 1 per cent were used in the present experiments.

Vitamins: Cod liver oil. It was found that rats would take a small amount of cod liver oil each day when it was offered in a container separate from the McCollum food. Due to the fact that vitamin D could not be obtained separately from vitamin A, cod liver oil had to be used to test the appetites for both.

Vitamin B Complex. At the time these experiments were started, dried baker's and brewer's yeast were the only practical sources of vitamin B. It was found that, given either separately or with the McCollum diet, yeast was readily taken by rats. Dried baker's yeast was chosen for these experiments because of its powdered form.

Vitamin E. The only practical available source of vitamin E was wheat germ oil. The rats drank it quite freely when it was offered either separately or with the McCollum diet.

Thus, in summary, the following substances were used: olive oil, casein, sucrose, sodium chloride, 3 per cent, calcium lactate, 2.4 per cent, dibasic sodium phosphate, 8 per cent, potassium chloride, 1 per cent, yeast, cod liver oil, wheat germ oil, and water. The casein, yeast, and sucrose were offered in the food cups; the solutions were offered in the graduated inverted bottles.

Multiple food choice experiments: Effect on growth. The growth curve for 8 females is presented in figure 2. For purposes of comparison, growth curves are shown also for 19 females on the McCollum diet, and for 50 females kept on a diet of table scraps in the Wistar Institute

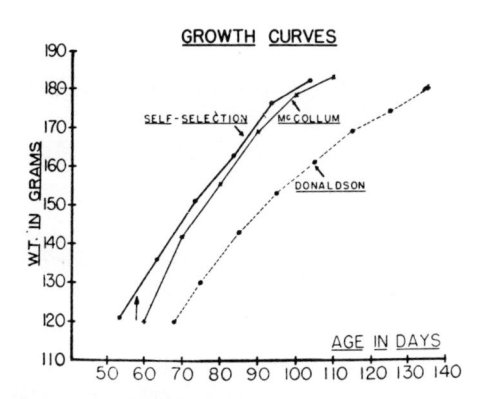

Fig. 2. Growth curves of 8 female rats on self-selection diet, 19 animals on McCollum diet, and 50 animals on the table scrap diet at the Wistar Institute. The arrow at 59 days indicates the average age at which the experimental rats were changed from the McCollum to the self-selection diet.

(Donaldson, 1915). After an initial slight reduction in weight, probably produced by the change from the McCollum diet, the growth of animals on the self-selection diet paralleled almost exactly that of the animals on the McCollum diet. On both of these diets, growth was far better than on the Wistar diet.

Reproduction. The 4- to 5-day oestrous cycles, studied by the vaginal smear method, showed a very striking regularity. They were considerably more regular than on the McCollum diet.

The rats mated, conceived, gave birth to normal litters, and nursed their young quite as well as on any of the synthetic diets. A detailed study of the changes in appetite during pregnancy and lactation on the self-selection diet has been made (Richter and Barelare, 1938).

Activity. The average daily activity of the 8 animals on the self-selection diet was essentially the same as that of 19 animals on the McCollum diet. See figure 3. The self-selection curve is slightly lower, but when the great individual variations of animals on both diets are taken into account, this difference is negligible.

Average Daily Intake of the Various Solids and Fluids. The average daily intakes recorded for the 8 animals are presented in table 1. They are based on a 10 day period after the animals had been on the self-selection diet for at least 40 days and had shown normal growth and regular oestrous cycles. The average age of the animals was 100 days. The total solids (including oils) ingested weighted 8.91 grams, which is 36.4 per cent less than the 14.0 grams average for animals of the same age on the McCollum diet. The total fluids imbibed amounted to 22.6 cc. which is about the same as the average water intake of animals on the McCollum diet.

Total Calories and Percentage of Fat, Carbohydrate, and Protein. The average daily total caloric intake on the self-selection diet was 46.3

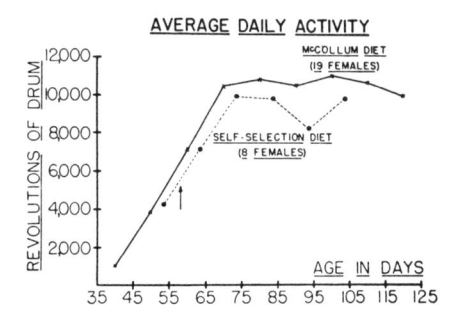

Fig. 3. Curves showing daily activity of 8 female rats on self-selection diet and 19 female rats on McCollum diet.

TABLE 1. TABLE SHOWING AVERAGE DAILY INTAKE OF SOLIDS, FLUIDS, AND CALORIES ON THE SELF-SELECTION AND MCCOLLUM DIETS

	Solids	Calories	Fluids
	(grams)		*(cc.)*
Self-selection:			
Casein	1.30	6.7	
Yeast	1.40	1.5	
Sugar	2.30	8.5	
Olive oil	1.70	14.6	
Cod liver oil	0.14	1.2	
Wheat germ oil	1.60	13.8	
NaCl (3 per cent)	0.04		1.3
KCl (1 per cent)	0.03		2.5
Na_2HPO_4 (8 per cent)	0.23		2.9
Ca lactate (2.4 per cent)	0.17		7.2
Water			8.7
Total	8.91	46.3	22.6
McCollum	14.00	56.0	23.0

calories. See table 1. This is 18.7 per cent less than the average total caloric intake of 56.0 calories of animals of the same age on the McCollum diet.

Fat contributed 64.0 per cent, protein 16.0 per cent, and carbohydrate 20.0 per cent of the total calories as compared to 14.1 per cent, 26.7 per cent, 59.2 per cent respectively on the McCollum diet (table 2). Thus it is seen that the animals on the self-selection diet ingested far larger proportions of fat and less of protein and carbohydrate. This explains in part the smaller bulk of the self-selection diet.

Daily Mineral Intake. The mineral content of the self-selection diet is shown in table 3. The average daily intake of sodium was 0.090 gram which is slightly higher than the amount (0.066 gram) ingested on the McCollum diet. The average daily calcium intake on the self-selection

TABLE 2. TABLE SHOWING CALORIC PERCENTAGES OF FAT, PROTEIN, AND CARBOHYDRATE ON THE MCCOLLUM AND SELF-SELECTION DIETS

Diet	Fat	Protein	Carbohydrate
	per cent	*per cent*	*per cent*
Self-selection	64.0	16.0	20.0
McCollum	14.1	26.7	59.2

TABLE 3. TABLE SHOWING DAILY INTAKE OF MINERALS ON THE MCCOLLUM AND SELF-SELECTION DIETS

	Self-Selection	McCollum
	(grams)	(grams)
Na from NaCl	0.015	
Na from Na_2HPO_4	0.075	
Total sodium	0.090	0.066
Ca from Ca lactate	0.032	
Ca from yeast	0.001	
Ca from casein	0.010	
Total calcium	0.043	0.127
P from Na_2HPO_4	0.051	
P from yeast	0.010	
P from casein	0.020	
Total phosphorus	0.081	0.074
K from KCl	0.013	
K from yeast	0.029	
Total potassium	0.042	0.074

diet was 0.043 gram which is about one third as much as is taken on the McCollum diet (0.127 gram). The average daily phosphorus intake was approximately the same for both diets, 0.081 as compared to 0.074 gram. The potassium intake on the self-selection diet was lower than on the McCollum diet (0.042 as compared to 0.074 gram).

Daily Vitamin Intake. Vitamins A and D. With an average daily intake of 0.14 cc. of cod liver oil containing 600 I. U. of vitamin A and 85 I. U. of vitamin D per gram, the average daily intake of the rats was 84 I. U. of vitamin A and 12 I. U. of vitamin D. See table 4. The

TABLE 4. TABLE SHOWING AVERAGE DAILY VITAMIN INTAKE ON THE SELF-SELECTION AND MCCOLLUM DIETS

	A	B	C	D
	I. U.	Sh. U.	Sh. U.	I. U.
Self-selection	84	31	24	12
McCollum	18	18	17	1

averages were considerably higher than those calculated for the McCollum diet.

Since cod liver oil contains both vitamins, it is not possible to draw any definite conclusions regarding the appetite for either A or D. We do know that rats with all the signs of vitamin A deficiency will drink large quantities of cod liver oil, as much as 5 cc. per day, and as a result show an almost immediate recovery. Furthermore, we know that normal rats will ingest small amounts of carotene (Smaco) daily with considerable constancy.

Vitamin B Complex. With an average daily intake of 1.4 grams of dried baker's yeast containing 8.6 Sherman units of vitamin B_1, and 44 Sherman units of vitamin G per gram, the daily vitamin intake from this source was 12 Sherman units of vitamin B_1 and 19 Sherman units of G. With an average daily intake of 1.6 cc. of wheat germ oil containing 12 Sherman units of B_1 and 3 Sherman units of G per gram, the daily intake from this source was 19 Sherman units of B_1, and 5 Sherman units of G. The totals are given in table 4. These values are only slightly higher than those calculated for the McCollum diet.

Vitamin E. We were unable to determine the vitamin E content of wheat germ oil intake. Since the rats showed such a great craving for fat, and since their appetite for wheat germ oil is almost as great as for olive oil, it may be assumed that a large part, if not all of the appetite for wheat germ oil was for fat, rather than for any of its other components.

Vitamin C. It was mentioned above that rats apparently are able to synthesize their vitamin C from their food and that for this reason it was not offered for choice. It is interesting to report, however, that given free access to ascorbic acid (Cebione, Merek), rats will drink small amounts daily with considerable regularity. It is possible, of course, that they may be attracted to the acid rather than to the vitamin content.

Individual Differences. The selections made by the 8 animals were strikingly similar, except for sucrose and olive oil. Two animals chose larger amounts of sucrose and smaller amounts of olive oil ("sugar burners"); six chose more fat than carbohydrate ("oil burners").

The "sugar burners" usually become "oil burners" after several months. No instances have been recorded in normal animals of a change in the opposite direction. In general, there appears to be a tendency for animals to use more fat as they grow older. This explains the higher carbohydrate intake of younger animals in our preliminary report.

Discussion

The results of these experiments demonstrate the ability of rats to select from purified substances a diet which is conducive to normal growth and reproduction. The difficulties present in some of the previous self-selection studies thus must have been due to the complex nature of the natural foods or of the food mixtures offered for choice.

Despite the fact that ingredients of natural foods rarely appear separately, animals apparently are able to recognize them in their isolated forms. There must be some mechanism by which animals are able to recognize not only sugar and salt, but other minerals, vitamins, proteins, and fats. The existence of special appetites for these substances was suggested by Turro (1910-1911) on the basis of theoretical speculations regarding the underlying mechanisms of appetite and hunger.

How the animals are able to make such advantageous dietary selections is not known. There are those who believe that all self-selection choices are based on experience, or a trial and error process. This might apply in vitamin B deficient rats in which the beneficial results of yeast (vitamin B) ingestion appear almost at once, in fact, within less than an hour (Harris et al., 1933). But certainly this does not apply to normal animals in which the effects of eating any substance, except possibly a strong poison, do not appear usually for many hours or even days. The fact that all of the rats made essentially the same choices, and without any apparent experimentation, indicates that some other mechanism must be involved. The consistent selections made by different species also suggests another explanation. To explain the specific food choices, Turro (1910-1911) postulated a "trophic center" in the basal ganglia, but there is little evidence to substantiate such a theory. It would seem more likely that nutritive deficits produce physiochemical changes throughout the entire body, including the taste mechanisms in the mouth, and that these changes may entirely alter the taste for different substances. In response to these changes an animal may be stimulated to seek certain substances in much the same way as dehydrated animals are stimulated by a dry throat to seek water. On the basis of theoretical considerations on appetite and hunger, Mursell (1925) arrived at very similar conclusions. Thus he states, "the best hypothesis covering these facts is that of certain positive chemotropisms which operate to set up cravings for specific substances."

This problem will have to be solved experimentally by studying the effects produced on the various appetites by division of the taste nerves, or destruction of the taste buds on the tongue and in the mouth.

It may be pointed out that in this method we have for the first time a real tool for the study of gustatory localization in the cortex and brain stem. Experiments are now in progress on the effects produced on dietary selections by removal of different parts of the cortex.

These experiments have several shortcomings. In the first place, the diet did not contain some of the most important minerals: iron, manganese, magnesium, copper, and cobalt. It is undoubtedly true that the lack of these would have eventually produced some defect. We do know from preliminary experiments using the technique described in the present paper that rats have an appetite for all of these minerals. In addition, the diet did not contain vitamin C.

Another shortcoming of the experiments is the use of yeast which contains at least three important substances with different functions, vitamin B_1, riboflavin, and nicotinic acid, in addition to large amounts of protein and carbohydrate.

Summary

1. A study was made of the ability of rats to select their diet from a number of purified foods.

2. The assortment offered in separate containers to the animals included one representative each of the more important nutritional substances: olive oil, casein, sucrose, cod liver oil, wheat germ oil, yeast, sodium chloride, calcium lactate, sodium phosphate, and potassium chloride.

3. The 8 animals used in these experiments made selections conducive to normal growth and reproduction. They grew as rapidly and were as active as animals on the standard McCollum diet and showed strikingly regular oestrous cycles. They mated, gave birth to normal sized litters, and nursed them until the time of weaning.

4. Despite the same rate of growth, the average daily caloric intake was 18.7 per cent less than on the McCollum diet, 46.3 calories as compared to 56.0 calories.

5. The weight of the solids (including oils) was 36.4 per cent less, 8.91 grams as compared to 14.0 grams on the McCollum diet.

6. The results showed that the rat has a special appetite not only for salt and sugar, but also for protein, carbohydrate, sodium, calcium, phosphorus, potassium, and the vitamins.

References

Davis, C. M. Am. J. Dis. Child. 36: 651, 1928.
Donaldson, H. H. Mem. Wistar Inst. Anat. and Biol. 6: 69, 1915.
Dove, W. F. Am. Naturalist 69: 469, 1935.
Evvard, J. M. Proc. Iowa Acad. Sci. 22: 375, 1915.
Harris, L. J., J. Clay, F. J. Hargreaves and A. Ward. Proc. Royal Soc. B. 113: 161, 1933.
Kon, S. K. Biochem. J. 25: 472, 1931.
Mitchell, H. S. and L. B. Mendel. Am. J. Physiol. 58: 211, 1921.
Mursell, J. L. Psychol. Review 32: 317, 1925.
Osborne, T. B. and L. B. Mendel. J. Biol. Chem. 35: 19, 1918.
Parsons, H. T. and M. K. Hutton, J. Biol. Chem. 59: 97, 1924.
Pearl, R. and T. E. Fairchild. Am. J. Hygiene 1: 253, 1921.
Richter, C. P. Am. J. Physiol. 115: 155, 1936.
Richter, C. P. and B. Barelare, Jr. Endocrinol. 1938.
Richter, C. P. and J. F. Eckert. Endocrinol. 1: 50, 1937.
Richter, C. P., L. E. Holt, Jr. and B. Barelare, Jr. Am. J. Physiol. 119: 388, 1937.
Sweet, C. J. A. M. A. 107: 765, 1936.
Turro, R. Ztschr. f. Sinnesphysiologie 44: 330, 1910; 45: 217, 327, 1911.

SALT TASTE THRESHOLDS OF NORMAL AND ADRENALECTOMIZED RATS[1]

The results of previous self-selection experiments showed that removal of the adrenals in rats greatly increased the appetite for sodium chloride (1, 2). In some instances the appetite as reflected in the voluntary salt intake increased 10 to 18 times over the preoperative level. Incidental observations indicated that adrenalectomy also lowered the taste threshold for salt. With a slightly modified self-selection technic a special study has now been made of salt taste thresholds of normal as well as of adrenalectomized rats.

Methods

At the outset each rat had access to 2 graduated inverted bottles filled with distilled water. After 8 to 16 days when the intake from each bottle had reached a fairly constant level, one bottle was filled with a sodium chloride solution of an estimated subliminal concentration. Each day thereafter the concentration was increased in small steps until the rats manifested a consistent preference for the salt solution. The concentration of the salt solution at the point of divergence of the

---

This paper was originally published in *Endocrinology*, Volume 24, No. 3, March 1939. Reprinted by permission.

[1] Investigation supported by a grant from the Committee for Research in Endocrinology of the National Research Council.

water and salt solution intake curves was taken as a measure of the taste threshold.

In order to make certain that any distinction made by the rats between the salt solution and the distilled water depended entirely on the salt content and not on any extraneous factor, the following precautions were observed: the two bottles were cleaned and refilled each day; the distilled water used for the salt solution and for the water bottles was always taken from the same source of supply; the fluids in both bottles were kept at the same temperature; the same two bottles were used throughout the experiment, one bottle for distilled water, the other for salt solution; and each bottle was kept in its original position in the cage.

The rats had constant access to the standard McCollum diet which contains 1 per cent sodium chloride.

In the experiments dealing with the taste threshold of adrenalectomized rats, the operation was performed when the intake from each of the two distilled water bottles had reached a fairly constant level. On the day following adrenalectomy one bottle was filled with the salt solution of estimated subliminal concentration.

Results

Salt Taste Threshold of Normal Rats

Series 1. In this experiment each rat had access to two bottles of distilled water for a period of 8 days. Then, one bottle was filled with a 0.05 per cent salt solution and thereafter on each successive day the concentration was increased in steps of 0.01 per cent.

During the preliminary period on distilled water the rats drank almost equal and constant amounts from both bottles. On the first day after the salt solution was offered most of the rats drank more salt solution than distilled water. Table I-A summarizes the results of this experiment on 8 rats. Apparently, the initial concentration of the salt solution in this series was either at or above the taste threshold.

Series 2. In this experiment distilled water was offered in both bottles for a period of 14 days. Then one bottle was filled with a salt solution of a concentration of 0.005 per cent, and each day thereafter increased as follows.

Salt Taste Thresholds of Normal and Adrenalectomized Rats

1. 0.005 per cent	11. 0.040 per cent
2. 0.006 "	12. 0.045 "
3. 0.007 "	13. 0.050 "
4. 0.008 "	14. 0.060 "
5. 0.009 "	15. 0.070 "
6. 0.010 "	16. 0.080 "
7. 0.015 "	17. 0.090 "
8. 0.020 "	18. 0.100 "
9. 0.030 "	19. 0.200 "
10. 0.035 "	20. 0.300 "

Fig. 1A gives the average daily intake for 12 normal animals for 5 days when both bottles were filled with distilled water and for 30 days when one bottle was filled with salt solution. The concentrations of the salt solution are shown in the small graph at the bottom. During the preliminary 5-day period the intake of distilled water from each bottle averaged approximately 13 cc. per day. After the salt solution was started the intake from the two bottles remained the same until the concentration of the salt solution reached 0.05 per cent. On that day, indicated by the arrow, the intake of salt solution increased slightly. Thereafter it increased fairly steadily reaching a peak of 33 cc. on the 24th day. At this time the daily distilled water intake still averaged 12 cc.

TABLE 1. SALT TASTE THRESHOLD OF NORMAL RATS

	A Series I			B Series 2	
Rat no.	Age at beginning of exper. (*days*)	Threshold salt sol. (%)	Rat no.	Age at beginning of exper. (*days*)	Threshold salt sol. (%)
1	105	0.05	1	102	0.04
2	105	0.05	2	102	0.05
3	105	0.06	3	117	0.05
4	105	0.06	4	102	0.08
5	102	0.05	5	98	0.06
6	102	0.05	6	98	0.07
7	105	0.05	7	92	0.06
8	102	0.07	8	102	0.035
			9	102	0.05
			10	102	0.06
			11	92	0.05
			12	98	0.06
Averages	104	0.055		101	0.0554

AVERAGE DAILY FLUID INTAKE

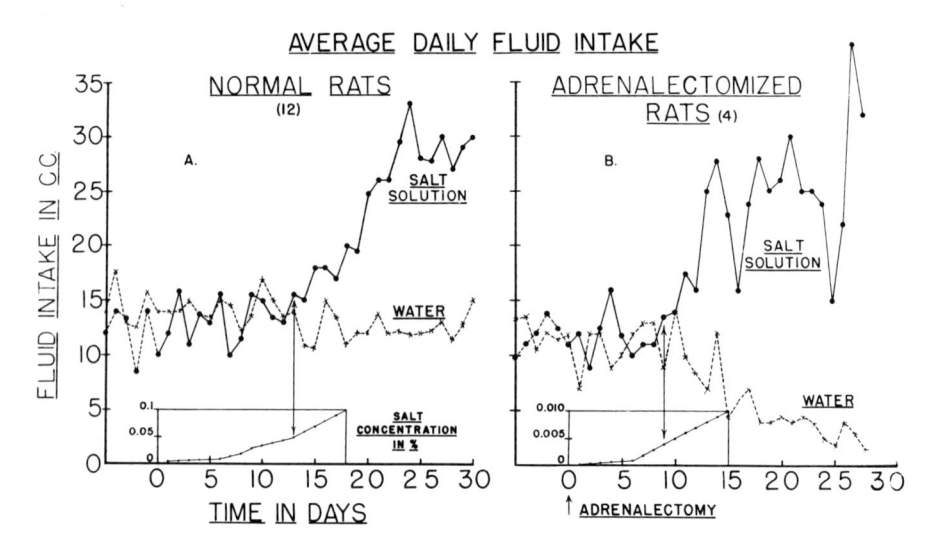

Fig. 1. (A) Daily Intake of cc. of Water and Salt Solutions of Increasing Concentration for 12 Normal Rats (series 2) and, (B), for 4 Adrenalectomized Rats (series 3). Threshold concentration is designated by the arrow.

Table 1B summarizes the results for the 12 rats. The taste threshold averaged 0.0554 per cent and ranged from 0.035 to 0.08 per cent. In summary, normal rats began to distinguish salt from water in concentrations of 1 part of salt to nearly 2,000 parts of water.

Salt Taste Threshold of Adrenalectomized Rats

Series 1. Each animal had access for 16 days to two bottles which contained distilled water. The rats were then adrenalectomized and on the same day one bottle was filled with a 0.010 per cent salt solution. Each day thereafter the concentration was increased in steps of 0.001 per cent. On the first day almost all of the rats drank more of the salt solution than of water. Table 2A summarizes the results for 8 animals. Just as in Series 1 of normal animals the initial concentration of salt solution was at or above the threshold.

Series 2. In this series the salt solution was started in a concentration of 0.001 per cent on the day of adrenalectomy and increased daily in steps of 0.001 per cent. Here again, on the first day most of the adrenalectomized rats drank more salt solution than water. Apparently the initial concentration was still too close to the threshold. Table 2B summarizes the results for 4 rats.

Salt Taste Thresholds of Normal and Adrenalectomized Rats

TABLE 2. SALT TASTE THRESHOLD OF ADRENALECTOMIZED RATS

	A Series 1			B Series 2			C Series 3	
Rat no.	Age at operat. days	Threshold	Rat no.	Age at operat. days	Threshold	Rat no.	Age at operat. days	Threshold
1	139	0.011	1	136	0.002	1	377	0.004
2	139	0.010	2	139	0.003	2	355	0.003
3	139	0.010	3	122	0.002	3	355	0.004
4	139	0.010	4	136	0.002	4	305	0.004
5	132	0.011						
6	136	0.011						
7	139	0.014						
8	136	0.010						
Averages	137	0.0109		133	0.0023		348	0.00375

Series 3. In these experiments salt solutions were started on the day of adrenalectomy in concentrations of 0.0001 per cent, and increased as follows:

 1. 0.0001 per cent   9. 0.0040 per cent
 2. 0.0003   "   10. 0.0050   "
 3. 0.0005   "   11. 0.0060   "
 4. 0.0007   "   12. 0.0070   "
 5. 0.0009   "   13. 0.0080   "
 6. 0.0010   "   14. 0.0090   "
 7. 0.0020   "   15. 0.0100   "
 8. 0.0030   "

Fig. 1-B shows the average water and salt solution intake of 4 adrenalectomized animals for a preliminary period of 8 days in which both bottles were filled with distilled water, and for the postoperative period of 27 days in which one bottle was filled with salt solution. The concentrations of the salt solution are shown in the small graph.

In the 8-day preliminary period the intake of distilled water for the two bottles averaged approximately 12 cc. per day. For 8 days after adrenalectomy and after the salt solutions were started the intake of water and salt solution remained equal. When a concentration of 0.004 per cent was reached the rats started to drink more salt solution and less water. On the 27th day the salt solution intake had reached a peak of 38 cc. while the water intake had dropped to 3 cc. per day.

Table 2C summarizes these results. The salt taste threshold for the 4 animals averaged 0.0037 per cent and showed practically no individual variations at all. In other words, the adrenalectomized rats began to distinguish salt solution from water in concentrations of 1:33,000.

Discussion

These experiments show that normal rats have a definite and consistent taste threshold for sodium chloride. Most of the animals distinguished salt solution from water in concentrations as low as 1 part of salt to 2,000 parts of water. The taste thresholds were markedly lowered by adrenalectomy. The adrenalectomized animals distinguished salt solution in much smaller concentrations, 1 part of salt to 33,000 parts of water.

In human beings only one report of a lowered salt threshold has come to our attention. Darley and Doan (3) reported a lowered salt taste threshold (0.092 per cent as compared to 0.185 per cent for normals) in a 20-year-old patient who also had a greatly increased salt appetite. She had manifested the signs and symptoms of obstruction of the lesser circulation since childhood and at autopsy marked pulmonary arteriolar sclerosis was found. Unfortunately the adrenals were not studied. However, the changes in appetite and taste threshold for salt strongly suggest some derangement of these glands.

The reason for the preference of normal rats for salt solution is not clear. It may be that the salt content of the McCollum diet does not fulfill all of their salt needs. The great preference for salt solution shown by adrenalectomized animals is clearly dependent in some way on the greatly increased salt need.

The adrenalectomized rats showed a preference for extremely small amounts of salt before having the opportunity to discover the beneficial effects of ingesting large amounts. This indicates that the increased salt intake must have depended on an altered appetite for salt rather than on a trial and error process resulting in relief from insufficiency symptoms or discomfort after ingesting salt. It may be noted also that the amount of salt received in the salt solution at the threshold level, 0.0005 gm. per day, is very small compared to the amount of salt received each day from the McCollum food, approximately 0.1 gm. In adrenalectomized rats the taste receptors of the oral cavity must undergo chemical changes which alter the taste for salt.

Summary

The salt taste threshold of 20 normal rats averaged 0.055 per cent, that is, the animals detected salt in solution of approximately one part of salt to 2,000 parts of water.

Removal of the adrenals in 8 rats (Series 2 and 3) greatly reduced the salt taste threshold. It averaged 0.003 per cent, that is, the animals distinguished between water and salt solution in a concentration of 1:33,000.

The adrenalectomized rats showed a craving for salt offered in amounts which could not possibly have had any beneficial effect.

The results indicate that adrenalectomized rats ingest more salt, not because they learn that salt relieves their deficiency discomforts, but because of chemical changes in the taste mechanisms in the oral cavity, giving rise to an enhanced salt discrimination.

References

1. Richter, C. P.: *Am. J. Physiol.* 115: 155. 1936.
2. Richter, C. P., and J. F. Eckert: *Endocrinology* 22: 214. 1938.
3. Darley, W., and C. A. Doan: *Am. J. M. Sci.* 191: 633. 1936.

A GREAT CRAVING FOR SALT BY A CHILD WITH CORTICO-ADRENAL INSUFFICIENCY

Special food cravings or aversions have received only passing interest in modern medicine and have been almost entirely neglected in modern nutrition. This is due to the prevalent view that appetite cannot be trusted as a guide to the proper selection of foods. Results of experiments on rats using the self-selection technic indicate, on the contrary, that a very close relationship exists between appetite and nutritional needs of minerals and vitamins, as well as of fats, carbohydrates and proteins. In human beings there are only a few instances which throw light on the relationship between appetite and dietary needs. Davis[1] reported that when very young normal children were given free access to a large number of natural foods they made selections which resulted in normal growth and development. She also reported that a child with vitamin A deficiency took large amounts of cod liver oil and thereby caused the deficiency symptoms to disappear.

During the past year we had occasion to make in this hospital a clinical observation which demonstrates in a very striking way the close relationship between appetite and nutritional needs. The endocrinologic aspects and the full medical history of this case have been reported in detail by Wilkins, Fleischmann and Howard.[2] The following data were taken from their history:

This paper was originally published in the *Journal of the American Medical Association*, Vol. 114, March 9, 1940. The authors were Lawson Wilkins, M.D. and Curt P. Richter. Ph.D. Reprinted by permission.

These observations from part of a study of the "Influence of Hormones on Appetite," supported by the Committee on Research in Endocrinology of the National Research Council.

Report of Case

D. W., a boy aged three and one-half years, admitted to the Harriett Lane Home for Children, showed a marked development of his secondary sex organs. His penis and testes were as large as those of a 12 year old boy. The prostate was fairly well developed; spermatogenesis was absent. Over the pubis there was a rather abundant growth of long dark hair. The voice was deep and the laryngeal cartilage was as prominent as that of a full grown man.

The skin on his scalp and body had a slightly brownish hue; the alveoli of the nipples were pigmented and the gums over the upper incisors showed a patch of brownish pigmentation.

His blood had a low sodium and a high nonprotein nitrogen content. Other physical observations were negative.

In the hospital the boy did not seem to be especially ill. He behaved like a very defective child, growling and snarling in an incoherent manner when attempts were made to examine him. He was offered the regular ward diet. His appetite was poor and he ate but little of the food. When feedings were forced, he vomited on several occasions. Seven days after admission he suddenly died.

Postmortem examination revealed that both adrenals were large. There was hyperplasia of the androgenic or prenatal zone cells, with marked diminution of the normal cortical cells. The testes were composed of similar cells crowding out the seminiferous tubules. Otherwise no pathologic changes were found. The precocious development of the secondary male sex characteristics was thought to be due to the embryonic hyperplasia of the androgenic zone of the adrenal. It appeared that death from adrenal insufficiency resulted from destruction of the electrolyte-controlling elements of the adrenal cortex.

One of the interesting features of this case was the presence of a great craving for salt. After his death it was learned that from the age of 12 months the child had eaten salt in large quantities. In addition, he had been given saline enemas every second or third day because of constipation. Subsequently a full account was obtained from the parents concerning the onset and development of this craving. The following letter, which is one of the most extraordinary documents on behavior on record, was written by the parents in response to a few questions regarding their child's special appetites:

> Dear Dr. ____:
> Since receiving your letter it has been on my mind constantly to remember as nearly as possible the correct answers to all of your

questions. We want to thank you for your very nice letter and are glad to help in any way we can.

Some of the things I am writing you I know are not direct answers to your questions, but indirectly I feel that they may be of some help to you and perhaps explain how we had studied D—— and his peculiarities. Of course, in the beginning we knew that he was very sick, but did not know his true condition or what to expect.

We had such a hard time trying to find milk to agree with him that I remembered exactly when each kind was changed; but when he first started eating salt I didn't think it was so important until later when he started craving it.

With his feeding problems we only gave one new food at a time and took particular notice of the reaction it had on him. At six months we still didn't have any one milk to agree with him for any length of time except mother's milk. At this time Dr. —— told us to start giving him strained vegetable soup and beef broth. He liked it, but as soon as it touched his tongue he would gag and bring up everything he had in his stomach unless I made it very thin with the beef broth. About a month later we started giving him strained vegetables; but, no matter what it was, he would bring it all up immediately unless it was very thin, practically liquid. At this time the doctor told us to give him crackers and zwieback; but as soon as he got any crumbs or little pieces of food on his tongue he would gag and bring up everything else. I would keep trying him from time to time thinking that perhaps the next time he would do better.

When he was around a year old he started licking all the salt off the crackers and always asked for more. He didn't say any words at this time, but he had a certain sound for everything and a way of letting us know what he wanted. This was the first we had noticed his wanting the crackers or salt. Finally he started chewing the crackers; but he only chewed them until he got the salt off, then he would spit them out. He did the same with bacon, but he didn't swallow the pieces. When he was about sixteen months old, crackers were the first food he chewed and swallowed; but it was quite a while after that before he would chew up and eat a whole cracker. He would usually just make a mess of them eating the salt off.

In an effort to try to find a food that he would like well enough to chew up and swallow, we gave him a taste of practically everything. So, one evening during supper, when he was about eighteen months old, we used some salt out of the shaker on some food. He wanted some, too. We gave him just a few grains to taste, thinking he wouldn't like it; but he ate it and asked for more. This was the beginning of his showing that he really craved salt, because this one time was all it took for him to learn what was in the shaker. For a few days after that, when I would feed him his dinner alone at noon, he would keep crying for something that wasn't on the table and always pointed to the cupboard. I didn't think of the salt, so I held him up in front of the cupboard to see what he wanted. He picked out the salt at once; and in order to see what he would do with it, I let him have it. He poured some out and ate it by dipping his finger in it. After this he wouldn't eat any food without having the salt, too. I would purposely let it off the table and even hide it from him until I could ask the doctor about it. For it seemed to us like he ate a terrible lot of plain salt. But when I asked Dr. —— about it, he said, 'Let him have it. It won't hurt him.' So we gave it to him and never tried to stop it altogether. After we gave it to him all the time he usually didn't ask for it with his dinner; but he wouldn't eat his breakfast or supper without it. He really cried for it and acted like he had to have it. Foods that he ordinarily wouldn't touch he would eat all right if I added more salt to them. He would take the shaker and pour some out on his plate and eat it with his finger, but we always tried to keep him from getting what we thought would be too much for him. He never did care much for zwieback, toast or bread or for cooked potatoes, but he did like raw potatoes, raw carrots, celery, tomatoes, lettuce and different other foods if he could dip them in salt. If I didn't give it to him, he always asked for it. At eighteen months he was just starting to say a few words, and salt was among the first ones. We had found that practically everything he liked real well was salty, such as crackers, pretzels, potato chips, olives, pickles, fresh fish, salt mackerel, crisp bacon and most foods and vegetables if I added more salt. We never tried to force him to eat a food; I always tried to prepare the same food in a way that he would like it. Spinach and green beans were his favorite vegetables. By letting him taste different foods he learned to like quite a variety, although he was three years old before he really ate a good meal by chewing it and swallowing it. In the meantime, I kept feeding him strained foods with the beef broth.... As he grew older and ate better, he very seldom brought up his meals any more. But he always wanted a lot of vegetable juice on his foods before he would eat them. If I didn't give it to him, he would ask for it and would eat everything good; but he wanted the salt too. By the time he was three years, I could reason with him and make him understand when he had enough of anything. At the time we had no idea as to the amount of salt he ate, or what the result would be if he didn't have it; but we have measured it now and would say that he ate between three quarters to one teaspoon of plain table salt a day *in addition* to all foods being saltier than ours. If he ate a food without it, I let him go; but if he wanted more salt in it, I added a little more. Many times I tried to make him think I added it, but he always knew the difference with the first taste. Some days he may have had a little more or less than the amount stated, which is, as we would judge, the average.

He would not eat anything sweet, though. Mostly everything with much sugar in it he would either bring back up or *just wouldn't eat it.* He would not eat cereal with sugar and milk on it. I would always strain his cereal into his glass of milk and let him drink it. Wheaties, or any small amount of dry cereal I tried to give him, he would not eat with sugar and milk but wanted it dry with salt sprinkled on. He *did not* like candy, cake, custards, puddings, etc. He did eat a little ice cream or jello.

He was a very observing baby and, even in his sickly condition, started noticing pictures in books when he was six months old. He always liked books, and we would read to him quite a lot. When he was about two years old he began reading the pictures himself. He would get out one book after another and never seemed to grow tired of reading them. Many times he surprised us by knowing and recognizing things in the pictures we hadn't even noticed. And by the time he was three and a half he knew a few words by sight. When he was two and a half he loved to hunt for the attractive pictures of the good foods in the magazines. He learned to know what all the foods were and made believe he ate them. It was surprising to us to see how this improved his appetite at meal time, for it was at this time that he started chewing his foods better and acted like he really enjoyed them. Another thing that helped him learn to eat was because he became interested in cooking. Many times he would play for an hour or more making believe he was cooking his Daddy's supper and imagining all kinds of foods he was cooking.

There was no other one food that he seemed to crave like salt, except water. Many people seemed to think this was because he ate so much salt, but he liked lots of water to drink from the time he was four months old. At six months, if we showed him a bottle of water and one of milk, he would take the water in preference to the milk *every time.* And in studying him, we found that by giving him lots of water he would be able to belch easier and so keep his milk down better. He learned to know himself that it helped him. As soon as he knew what the word 'water' meant, he would cry for it every time he heard the word mentioned. And when he saw the river or the ocean, he always thought he had to have some to drink until we were finally able to explain to him that it wasn't drinking water. But up until the time we took him up there he still wanted water every time he saw anybody else drink it. He always asked for it many times between meals; and if there was water on the table at meal time he would rather drink it than eat his meal. And if we let him drink and eat too much without making him stop to belch in between, his food would come back up almost every time. Also, if we let him cry much, he could not keep anything in his stomach.

At home he acted and played the same as any perfectly normal child. But the doctor had told us not to take him anywhere among people because of contracting contagious diseases, which he didn't think D—— could pull through. The result was that he was afraid of strangers; and when we brought him up there it was the first time that he was among complete strangers and strange surroundings. We had never been away from him ourselves before. Either my husband or I were always with him to take care of him.

I hope that I have answered all of your questions satisfactorily and also that at least part of what I have written will be of some help to you. In order to remember the answers as nearly correct as possible, it was necessary for me to recall D——'s whole life. If there is anything at all that I have omitted don't hesitate to let us know. We will be glad to answer it if we can. As for the different kinds of milks we gave him and the age when each one was changed, also his growth and development, I had those recorded on the backs of the pictures I sent you sometime after we returned from up there.

Hoping we have been able to help you in your studies and perhaps some children in the future, we are,

Yours very truly,

Mr. and Mrs. ———.

Comment

The full significance of the craving for salt by this child can be obtained from a review of our knowledge of salt craving by adrenalectomized animals.

It is well known that in rats kept on the ordinary stock diets symptoms of insufficiency develop and the rats die within ten to fifteen days after adrenalectomy. Death occurs largely because of the excessive loss of sodium chloride in the urine and the resulting changes in the internal osmotic conditions.[3] It is known that the survival time can be increased and the mortality rate decreased by increasing the salt content of the food until it approximates the amount of salt lost in the urine. Further, it was shown that when adrenalectomized rats have access to salt in a container separate from the food they will ingest large amounts of salt and, as a consequence, keep themselves alive and free from symptoms of insufficiency.[4] Some of the rats ingested from fifteen to twenty times as much of a 3 per cent salt solution thirty days after adrenalectomy as they had in the last ten day preoperative period. That the increased salt appetite depended on the loss of the adrenals was demonstrated by the observation that adrenals successfully implanted to the anterior chamber of the eyes caused the craving to disappear entirely.

This increased craving for salt manifested by adrenalectomized rats is not an isolated instance of a mineral or food craving which is closely related to dietary needs. We[5] have reported that parathyroidectomized rats have an increased appetite for calcium, magnesium and strontium salts, which are known to decrease parathyroid tetany, and that they have a decreased appetite for phosphorus. We found also that pregnant and lactating rats given free access to a large selection of minerals, vitamins, purified (or nearly purified) fats, proteins and carbohydrates, all in separate containers, make selections in accordance with their needs. They increased their intake of calcium, phosphorus, protein and fat.

There can be little doubt, then, that with his increased salt craving the three and one-half year old boy with deficient adrenal cortical tissue made an effort to maintain a normal internal salt balance. Apparently he started as early as eleven months after birth. During the two and one half years previous to his entrance to the hospital he must have kept himself alive by eating large amounts of salt. In the hospital he was not given free access to salt but was given the regular ward diet, which contains the normal amount of salt and, as a result, died suddenly.

The basis for special cravings has not yet been established. We do not know whether the adrenalectomized rats eat large amounts of salt because the ingestion of salt makes them feel better or because their taste for salt has changed—in other words, that in their salt deficient state they become chemotropically attracted to salt. In favor of the latter view is the observation that adrenalectomized rats have a greatly decreased threshold for salt. They distinguish distilled water from salt solution in a 1 : 33,000 concentration, while normal rats do not make this distinction until the salt solution reaches a concentration of 1: 2,000.[6] Such minimal amounts of salt as are received in drinking a few cubic centimeters of a 1 : 33,000 solution could not possibly have any physiologic effect. This boy also showed a positive reaction to salt when he first tasted it in pure form in very small quantities on the top of soda crackers. It is not readily conceivable that such a small amount of salt could have had any detectable effect on his deficiency condition.

Summary

A boy aged 3½ years with deficient adrenal cortical tissue, manifesting various symptoms of adrenal insufficiency, had a marked craving for salt. On the basis of observations made on adrenalectomized rats, it would seem that this boy, by increasing his salt intake, kept himself alive for at least two and one half years.

References

1. Davis, Clara M.: Self Selection of Diet by Newly Weaned Infants, Am. J. Dis. Child. 36: 651 (Oct.) 1928.
2. Wilkins, Lawson; Fleischmann, W., and Howard, J. E.: Macrogenitosomia precox associated hyperplasia of the androgenic tissue of the adrenal. Endocrinology 26: 385–295, 1940.
3. Loeb, R. F.: Proc. Soc. Exper. Biol. & Med. 30: 808 (March) 1933. Harrop, G. A.; Soffer, L. J.; Ellsworth, Read, and Trescher, J. H.: J. Exper. Med. 58: 17 (July) 1933. Rubin, M. I., and Krick, E. T.: Proc. Soc. Exper. Biol. & Med. 31: 228 (Nov.) 1933.
4. Richter, C. P.: Am. J. Physiol. 115: 155 (March) 1936.
5. Richter, C. P., and Eckert, J. F.: Endocrinology 21: 50 (Jan.) 1937. Richter, C. P., and Eckert, J. F.: Am. J. M. Sc. 198: 9 (July) 1939.
6. Richter, C. P.: Endocrinology 24: 367 (March) 1939.

TOTAL SELF REGULATORY FUNCTIONS IN ANIMALS AND HUMAN BEINGS[1]

In 1859 Claude Bernard (1) first described what he called the internal environment of the body, consisting largely of the body fluids, and showed that in mammals the properties of this internal environment ordinarily vary within fixed limits, variation outside of these ranges endangering life. He described many of the physiological mechanisms by means of which the body keeps these properties at fixed levels, and pointed out that it is by virtue of the existence of these mechanisms that mammals are able to live and thrive under widely varying external conditions.

Cannon (2), in a long series of remarkable experiments, collected in 1932 in his book "The Wisdom of the Body," not only confirmed Bernard's concept but greatly extended it. Largely through his efforts this concept has become almost an axiom of modern medicine. Cannon speaks of a constant state or homeostasis. Thus he states: "The constant conditions which are maintained in the body might be termed equilibria. That word, however, has come to have a fairly exact meaning as applied to relatively simple physico-chemical states, in closed systems, where known forces are balanced. The coordinated physiological processes which maintain most of the steady states in the organism are

---

This paper was originally published in *The Harvey Lectures Series* Vol. XXXVIII, 1942–1943. Reprinted by permission.

[1] This work was carried out with the following collaborators: Doctors Bruno Barelare, John E. Eckert, Dr. Clarence Hawkes, L. Emmett Holt, Elaine Kinder, Katherine Rice, Edward C. H. Schmidt, Jr., and Mr. John Birmingham, Miss Alice MacLean and Mrs. Kathryn H. (Campbell) Clisby.

so complex and so peculiar to living beings—involving, as they may, the brain and nerves, the heart, lungs, kidney, and spleen, all working cooperatively—that I have suggested a special designation for these states, homeostasis. The word does not imply something set and immobile, a stagnation. It means a condition—a condition which may vary, but which is relatively constant."

Both Bernard and Cannon concerned themselves almost entirely with the physiological and chemical regulators of the internal environment. They showed, for instance, that when an animal is placed in a cold external environment and is consequently threatened with a decrease in body temperature, loss of heat is minimized by decreased activity of the sweat glands and constriction of the peripheral blood vessels, and more heat is produced by increased burning of stored fat and by shivering. These are all physiological or chemical regulators.

The results of our own experiments have shown that behavior or total organism regulators also contribute to the maintenance of a constant internal environment. The existence of such behavior regulators was first established by the results of experiments in which it was found that after elimination of the physiological regulators the animals themselves made an effort to maintain a constant internal environment or homeostasis. I will give you a few examples which are taken mainly from experiments on the endocrine glands. Thus, operative removal of the adrenal glands from animals eliminates their physiological control of sodium metabolism, and as a result large amounts of sodium are excreted as salt in the urine and the internal environment is greatly disturbed (3). If given access only to a stock diet, such animals die in 8–15 days. However, if given access to salt in a container separate from their food they will take adequate amounts to keep themselves alive and free from symptoms of insufficiency. Figure 1 shows a photograph of the cages used for these experiments. Each cage contained a food cup and two graduated inverted bottles. One bottle was filled with tap water, the other with a 3 per cent solution of sodium chloride. The special stock food was made without added sodium chloride. In order to establish base lines, daily records of the intake from each bottle were taken for several weeks before the adrenals were removed. Figure 2 gives two typical records. The first graph gives the water intake and body weight records of a control rat which had access only to tap water and not to any sodium chloride solution. After adrenalectomy the water intake and body weight dropped sharply and it died in 7 days. The second graph shows the record of one of the experimental animals. Before adrenalectomy the intake of water averaged 22 cc., that of salt

Fig. 1. Three Individual Cages of the Type Used for Mineral Appetite and Taste Threshold Experiments. Each cage is equipped with one food-cup and two inverted graduated 100-cc. bottles.

solution, 2 cc. Almost at once following adrenalectomy the intake of salt solution increased and after 12 days reached a level near 13 cc. Body weight continued to increase at its normal rate and the rat was in good health when it was killed 48 days after operation. Similar observations have been made on several hundred adrenalectomized animals. We have found that, when offered a variety of mineral solutions at the same time, the adrenalectomized rats increased their intake of all the sodium salts, and did not show an appetite for other chlorides (4).

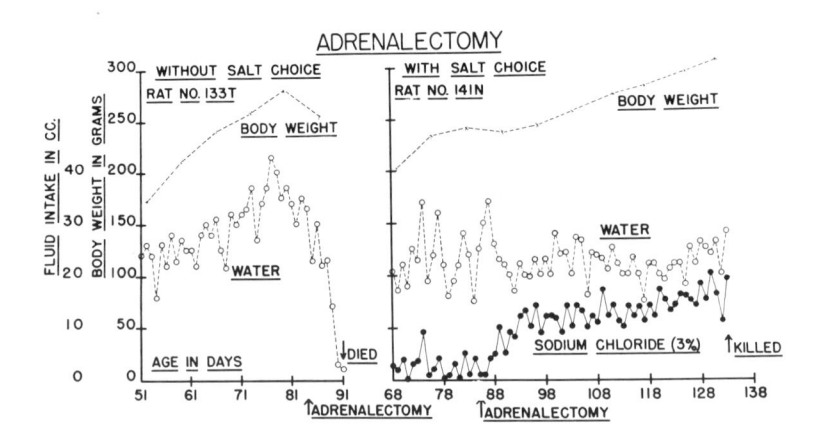

Fig. 2. Increased Sodium Chloride Appetite After Adrenalectomy: a. Control rat without access to sodium chloride. b. Experimental rat with choice of water or sodium chloride solution.

We found further that parathyroidectomized rats, which on a regular diet develop tetany and usually die within a few days, will, when given access to a calcium solution, take sufficiently large amounts to keep themselves alive and free from tetany (5). Figure 3 gives a typical record of a rat which had access to two bottles, one filled with tap water and the other with a 2.4 per cent solution of calcium lactate. Almost immediately after parathyroidectomy the rat began to drink more of the calcium lactate solution and less of the water. In 15 days its calcium lactate intake had increased from a preoperative average of 3 cc. to 17 cc. Parathyroid implants made to the anterior chamber of the eye after 45 days reduced the calcium appetite to its normal level almost at once. It was found further that the parathyroidectomized rats had an increased appetite for other calcium solutions, the acetate, the gluconate, the nitrate, and for the chemically closely related metals strontium and magnesium, but not for other metals. It is noteworthy also that the parathyroidectomized rats manifested a reduced appetite for phosphorus solutions, which is in keeping with the well-known decreased rate of excretion of phosphorus in hypoparathyroidism (6).

In the same way, pancreatectomized rats, which have lost their physiological means of regulating carbohydrate metabolism, ingest large

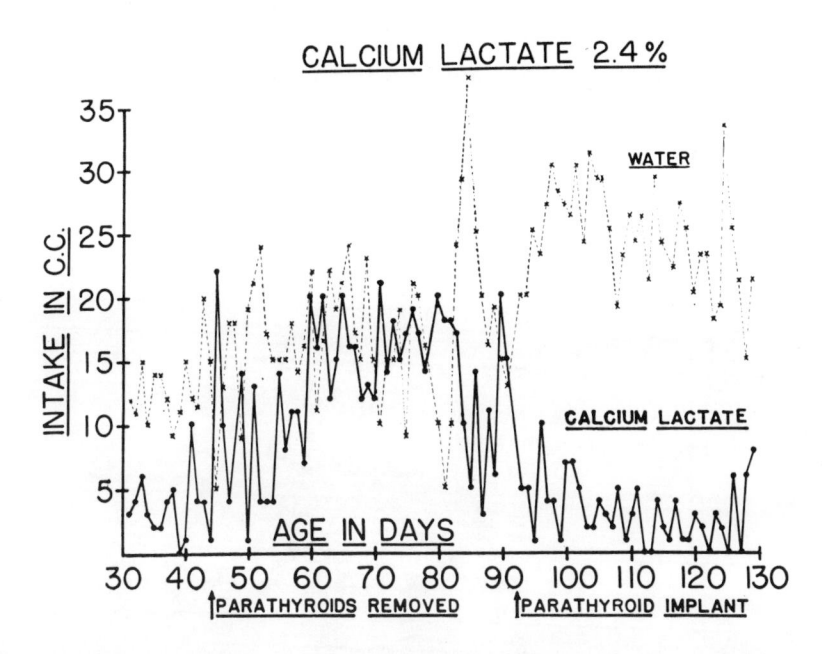

Fig. 3. Increased Appetite for Calcium Lactate Following Parathyroidectomy and Its Decrease Following Successful Grafting of Parathyroid Tissue.

amounts of water, presumably to assist in eliminating the unoxidized glucose. Further, when kept on a regular mixed diet with a high carbohydrate content, they manifest a marked polyphagia, apparently in an effort to obtain needed amounts of substances that can be utilized. They have a high blood sugar and do not gain weight at a normal rate. We have found that when pancreatectomized rats with marked diabetes were offered a carbohydrate, a fat, and a protein in separate containers, in place of the mixed diet, they refused the carbohydrate and ate large amounts of fat and protein (7). As a result they lost their symptoms of diabetes, i.e., their blood sugar fell to its normal level, they gained weight, ate less food, and drank only normal amounts of water.

Similarly, removal of the posterior lobe of the pituitary gland eliminates one of the chief physiological regulators of water metabolism. Without the antidiuretic hormone from this gland animals excrete large amounts of urine and as a result become dehydrated and soon die. When not given access to water some of the experimental rats lost as much as one sixth of their body weight in urine during the first eight hours after the gland was removed. However, when given access to unlimited amounts of water such animals began to drink large amounts soon after the diuresis had become well established (8). They continued to show a high water intake, in some instances taking almost twice the body weight in water per day, and kept themselves not only alive but in

Fig. 4. Side View of Nest Building Cage, Showing Paper Roll and Cyclometer.

Total Self-Regulatory Functions in Animal and Human Beings 199

good health. We must regard the great thirst of animals with diabetes insipidus not as a primary symptom produced by an injury to a so-called thirst center in the brain stem, but as a secondary symptom, an effort made by the total organism to compensate for the abnormal fluid loss (9, 10).

One more example should suffice for the present purpose. It is taken from the field of body temperature regulation and is concerned with the rat's effort to maintain a constant body temperature after the physiological heat regulating mechanisms have been seriously disturbed (11, 12). The individual cages used for these experiments were each equipped with a roll of soft paper one-half inch wide and 500 feet long, with the free end readily accessible to the rat within the cage. Figure 4 shows a cross-sectional view of one of these cages. By means of a cyclometer and a scale to compensate for the progressively decreasing diameter of the roll, the amount of paper used each day was measured, and interpreted as an effort made by the rat to conserve heat by covering itself. All used paper was removed each day at noon. It was found that normal male and female rats used approximately equal

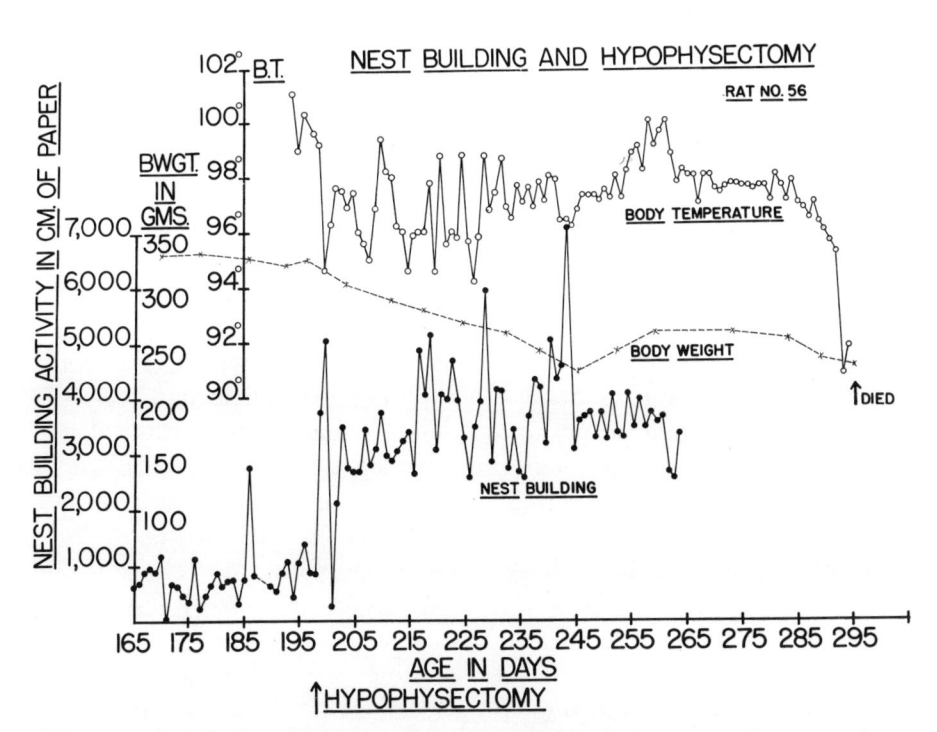

Fig. 5. Increased Nest Building Activity after Hypophysectomy, and Fall in Body Temperature with Consequent Death, after Removing Nesting Paper.

amounts of paper to build nests which varied in size with changing external temperatures, for example, a drop in room temperature from 80 to 45 degrees increased the amount of paper used daily from 500 to 6000 centimeters. With this method we were also able to show that hypophysectomized rats built much larger nests than normal animals, as a result of their inability to produce adequate amounts of heat, which consequently threatened them with a fatal reduction in body temperature. Figure 5 shows the effect produced on nest building activity of a rat by hypophysectomy. The length of paper used daily increased from 700 to 3500 centimeters. When nest building paper was no longer made available, the rat died after 35 days, with a body temperature more than 15 degrees below normal. Thyroidectomized rats, which likewise have lost their ability to produce adequate amounts of heat, also built very large nests in an effort to cover themselves and thus to conserve heat. Both thyroidectomized and normal rats treated with large amounts of thyroid extract stopped building nests altogether. Some of the hypophysectomized and thyroidectomized rats used the entire roll of 15,000 centimeters (500 feet) of paper in 24 hours. Thus we have another instance in which, after removal of the physiological regulators, homeostasis was maintained by a total organism response.

On the basis of the results of these different experiments, it would seem very likely that in the normal, intact animal the maintenance of a constant internal environment depends not only on the physiological or chemical regulators, but also on the behavior or total organism regulators. We do not yet know, however, the relative parts played by each: whether, for instance, the physiological responses take care of most of the regulation, or whether they function only when the behavior mechanisms have failed or broken down, or whether both are constantly and simultaneously in action. We may discuss as an example the regulation of sodium metabolism. When an animal lives in a region in which the available food does not contain an adequate amount of salt, it may either seek salt by migrating to a salt lick, or its adrenal cortex may become more active and as a consequence less salt will be lost in the urine. On the other hand, an animal may be forced to take a high amount of salt in its food: in this case it may either decrease its food intake, or increase the excretion of salt by drinking large amounts of water, or its adrenal cortex may become less active and as a consequence more salt will be lost in the urine. I will return later to the problem of the relation of these processes.

The question of the basis of these self regulatory abilities has undoubtedly already come to your minds. Does experience determine the dietary choice? Do rats eat certain substances because the ingestion of these substances makes them feel better, and avoid others because their ingestion produces discomfort or pain? Or does the taste of the substance determine the choice? In other words does appetite serve as a guide to the selection of a beneficial diet? It is not possible to give definite answers to these questions at the present time. Certainly the selections may depend on both factors. The evidence at hand, however, indicates that taste plays a very important part. In the first place, section of the taste nerves (glossopharyngeal, chorda tympani and lingual) apparently abolishes the ability of rats to make beneficial dietary selections. In one series of experiments it was found that after combined section of all three pairs of nerves, thus eliminating taste sensation from the entire surface of the tongue, adrenalectomized rats no longer increased their salt intake and as a consequence died just as they would have done had they not had access to any salt at all (13).

Further evidence for the significance of taste sensation in making dietary choices comes from experiments on the taste thresholds of rats. In order to determine the concentration at which rats could first distinguish between water and a given solution we again used the small cages containing a food cup and two graduated inverted bottles shown in Figure 1. Base lines were obtained with both bottles filled with distilled water. After 8–16 days, when the intake from each bottle had become relatively constant, one bottle was filled with a solution of subliminal concentration of the substance to be examined, and each day thereafter the concentration was increased in small steps. Such determinations have now been made with various substances (14, 15, 16). Figure 6 gives the average dextrose intake curve for 8 rats under these conditions. Over a period of 29 days the concentration of the dextrose solutions was increased from 0.01 to 11.0 per cent. It will be noted that the rats first indicated a definite preference for the dextrose solution when the concentration reached 0.2 per cent. With increasing concentrations up to 11 per cent the preference constantly became more marked. All of the other substances tested so far, such as sucrose, maltose, sodium chloride, potassium chloride, calcium lactate, etc., which gave this same type of record, are known to have nutritional value. Since the amounts of the substances obtained by the rats at the threshold concentrations were certainly not sufficient to have any physiological value, the preference must have depended entirely on taste.

With poisons, or any harmful substances, the type of curve is quite different (17). In such cases the first indication the rats gave of the

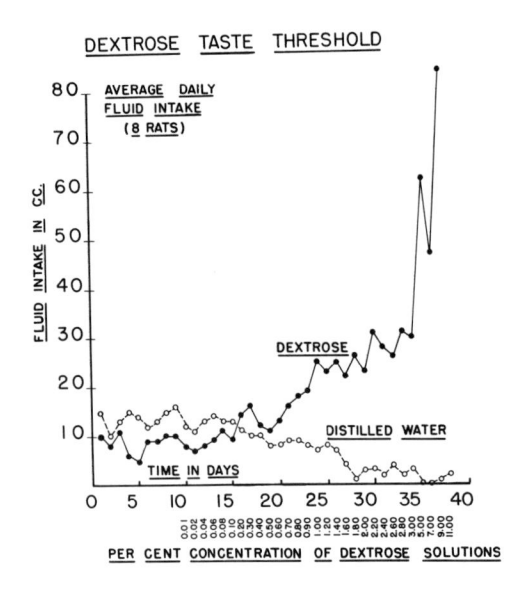

Fig. 6. Curves Showing Average Dextrose Taste Threshold for 10 Rats.

recognition of the substance was a preference for water over the solution. This may be seen in Figure 7 which gives a typical record of a rat which received increasing concentrations of mercuric chloride. This rat suddenly decreased its intake from the mercuric chloride bottle when the concentration reached 0.003 per cent, or 3 parts in 100,000 parts of water. At this level the total amount of the drug ingested was too small to have any detectable physiological effect.

Using the same technique, we have found that adrenalectomized rats, which have a greatly increased need for salt, have a much lower salt taste threshold than normal rats (18). For 12 normal rats the average taste threshold was 0.055 per cent, and for 4 adrenalectomized rats it was 0.0037 per cent, about 15 times lower. Here again the minute amount of salt obtained from the solutions for which the adrenalectomized rats first manifested a preference for salt solution over water could not have had a physiological effect.

At present, then, the processes involved in the selective activity of the rat can be formulated as follows, using the salt appetite of adrenalectomized rats as an example. In such animals there is a sodium deficiency in all the tissues of the body, including the taste buds of the tongue; consequently a salt solution of a given concentration brought into contact with the taste buds in such an animal would encounter a different situation from that found in the normal rat, with the higher salt content. In particular, the sodium ion would be expected to diffuse

MERCURIC CHLORIDE TASTE THRESHOLD

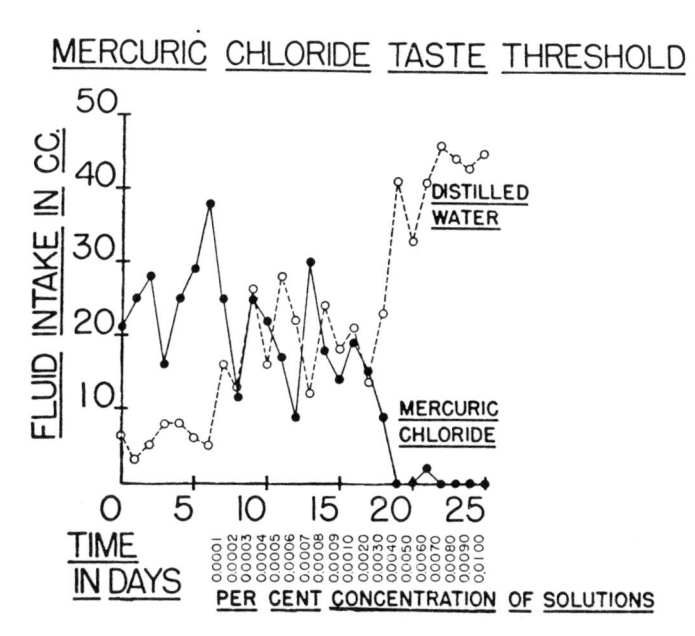

Fig. 7. *Typical Individual Curves Showing Mercuric Chloride Taste Threshold.*

through the membrane more readily and thus stimulate the taste buds at a lower concentration. More detailed studies are necessary before the mechanism of taste recognition can be more fully understood: osmotic pressure relationships must be investigated, as well as the rôle of the amount and composition of the saliva, and more knowledge is required of both taste bud and central nervous system processes.

I would like now to point out that knowledge of the behavior regulators offers us a new method of attacking a great many different problems, especially those concerned with the relationships between the endocrine glands and nutrition. Thus we can often determine the function of a gland by observing the adjustment that the animal makes to its removal. Had this method been available we could have determined the sodium regulatory function of the adrenal glands many years ago, long before the advent of modern biochemical methods, in particular the excellent studies of Loeb and others (19, 20). It would only have been necessary to give some adrenalectomized rats access to a variety of mineral solutions, and by their selections they would have indicated at once that removal of the adrenals produces primarily a change in sodium metabolism. In the same way we might have determined the calcium regulatory function of the parathyroids long before the biochemical studies of MacCallum (21) and others.

I will give you a few illustrations of the different uses which have

TABLE I

A	B
1. Sucrose	1. Dextrose
2. Casein (vitamin-free)	2. Casein (vitamin-free)
3. Olive oil	3. Olive oil
4. Sodium chloride—3%	4. Sodium chloride—3%
5. Potassium chloride—1%	5. Potassium chloride—1%
6. Calcium lactate—2.4%	6. Calcium lactate—2%
7. Dibasic soidum phosphate—8%	7. Dibasic sodium phosphate—4%
8. Cod liver oil	8. Magnesium chloride—0.5%
9. Wheat germ oil	9. Cod liver oil
10. Baker's yeast (dried)	10. Thiamine hydrochloride—0.02%
11. Water (tap)	11. Riboflavin—0.00125%
	12. Nicotinamide—0.01%
	13. Calcium pantothenate—0.01%
	14. Choline chloride—0.3%
	15. Pyridoxine hydrochloride—0.02%
	16. Biotin—0.05% (= 5γ/cc.)
	17. Water (tap)

been made of this method. We have applied this technique to the determination of the normal dietary requirements of the rat (22). For this purpose the rats were given access to an assortment of 11 substances, one source of each of the substances known to play an important part in nutrition, as listed in Table I, A. Large cages of the type shown in the photograph in Figure 8 (cage 75) were used in these experiments. The cages contained several food cups for solids and from 8–20 graduated inverted water bottles with capacities of either 30 or 100 cc. for fluids.

Fig. 8. Cages Used for Single Food Choice and Self Selection Experiments Showing Graduated Inverted Bottles for Fluids and Food-cups for Solids

GROWTH CURVES

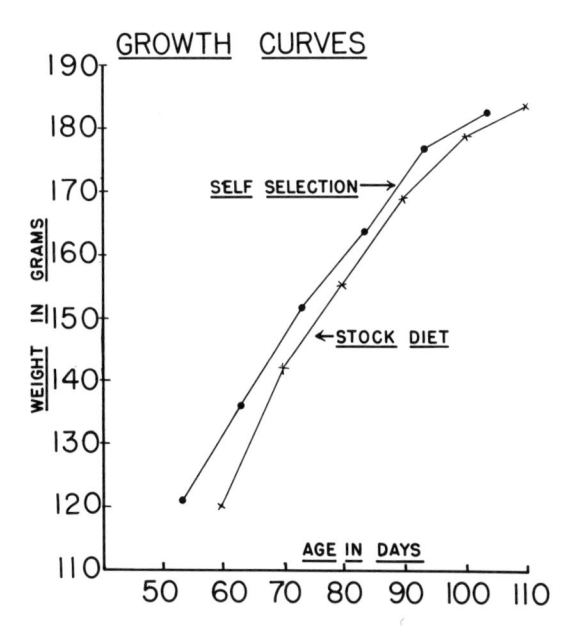

Fig. 9. *Average Growth Curves for 8 Rats on Self Selection Diet and 19 Rats on Stock Diet.*

On the selections made from these substances the rats grew at a normal rate, were normally active, reproduced, and showed no signs of deficiency, actually thriving for as long as 500 days, at which time the experiment was discontinued. Figure 9 gives the average growth curves for 8 rats on the stock diet[2] and for 19 rats on this self selection diet. That the rats actually made very efficient choices from this assortment is shown by the fact that, although they grew at the same rate, their total food intake as measured in grams was 36 per cent less than that of the control rats kept on our stock diet. The difference in total caloric intake was less great, 46 and 56 calories on the self selection and stock diets respectively, by virtue of the higher fat content of the self selection diet. In terms of the total caloric intake the self selection diet consisted of 64 per cent fat, 16 per cent protein, and 20 per cent carbohydrate.[3]

In later experiments, the yeast was omitted from the list of sub-

---

[2] The stock diet used contained graham flour 725, skim milk powder (Breadlac) 100, casein (No. 30, Labeo) 100, calcium carbonate 15, sodium chloride 10, and butter 50.

[3] Small amounts of magnesium and trace elements such as iron, copper, iodine, were undoubltedly contained in the tap water, casein, and yeast.

stances offered for choice, and replaced by the various components of the vitamin B complex, singly and in different combinations, thus offering a means of determining metabolic interrelationships between these and other constituents of the diet. (See Table I, B.) When given access to all of the substances, without either yeast or any of the members of the vitamin B complex, the rats took high amounts of fat, little or no carbohydrate, and no protein (23, 24). They thus indicated that without any vitamin B they could use fat, but not carbohydrate or protein. When given access to thiamine hydrochloride as the only member of the vitamin B complex the rats reversed their fat and carbohydrate appetites, taking more carbohydrate and less fat, but still no protein. The appetite for fat was greatest in the group receiving riboflavin as the only representative of the B complex. This observation is in agreement with the work of Mannering, Lipton, and Elvehjem, who demonstrated that the growth of young rats on a riboflavin low ration was increasingly stunted as the fat content of the ration was increased, and that the deleterious effect of the high fat rations was entirely overcome by the addition of riboflavin to the diet (25). Progressively as each member of the vitamin B complex was added in our experiments, riboflavin, nicotinamide, pyridoxine, calcium pantothenate, biotin and choline chloride, in addition to the thiamine (Table I, B, gives the full list of all the substances offered for choice), the rats took more carbohydrate and protein and less fat; also, the number of rats which made successful choices increased, as was evidenced by more nearly normal growth curves, more regular oestrous cycles, and more normal endocrine weights. Almost without exception, however, the success of the selections depended on whether the rats showed an active appetite for protein: unless they ate protein freely they did not thrive. By controlling the individual components of the vitamin B complex offered for choice we could almost at will make an animal eat large amounts of fat or little or no fat, similarly we could influence the appetite for carbohydrate and protein. From such experiments we have learned that rats are able to make beneficial selections from purified foods quite as well as from natural foods. Further, since all of the substances are offered in purified form, it becomes possible with only one or two exceptions, by removing any one bottle or food cup to eliminate all of any one substance from the diet. For instance, removal of one bottle eliminates all thiamine chloride from the diet, or the removal of one food cup all carbohydrate.

We have used this method also to study the nutritional needs of the rat during pregnancy and lactation (26). The rats were given access to the 11 substances listed in Table I, A, with yeast as the source of the vitamin B complex. The daily intake of each substance was recorded for several weeks before mating, during pregnancy, for 25 days of lactation, and for several weeks after the litters were weaned. A special cage was devised to prevent the young from eating and drinking from the mother's food cups and bottles. The rats showed quite definite and consistent changes in appetite for each of the different substances offered, especially during the lactation period. Figure 10 gives the average daily intake of the four mineral solutions in 5-day periods for 20 days before mating, 20 days of pregnancy, 25 days of lactation, and 10 days after the litters were weaned. Figure 10, A, shows that the ingestion of sodium chloride increased during the first five days of pregnancy to a definitely higher level, and increased still more during the second half of the lactation period, dropping to its original level almost at once after weaning. The sharp increase in salt appetite during the first 3–5 days of pregnancy was one of the most constant of all the changes in appetite. Figure 10, B, shows that the calcium lactate intake increased slightly during pregnancy, but very markedly during lactation, at the height of which it reached peaks which were 30–40 times as high as the average daily intake present before mating. After the litters were weaned the calcium intake did not decrease at once to its original level

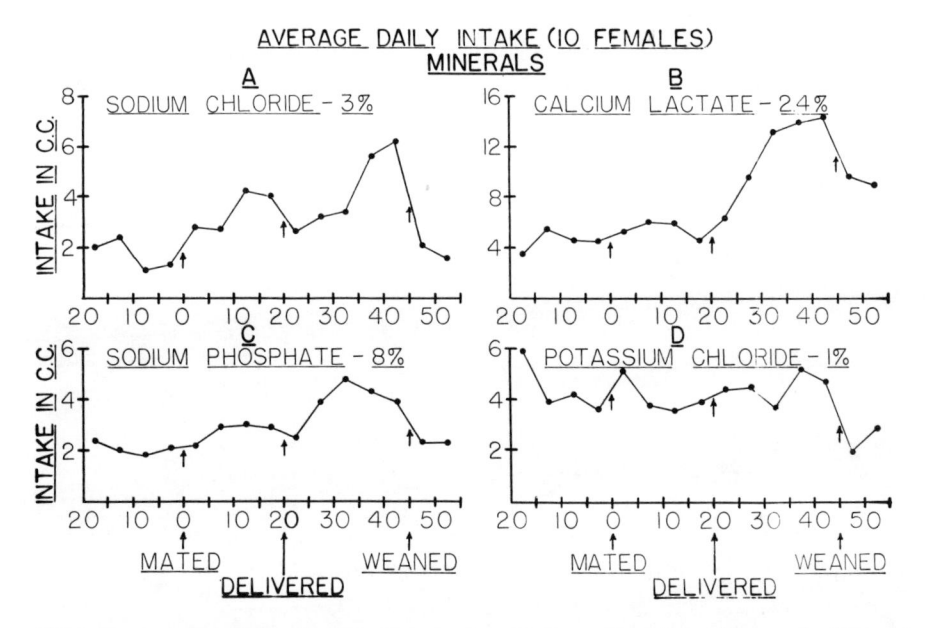

Fig. 10. *Average Daily Intake Curves for 10 Rats Showing Changes in Mineral Appetite during Pregnancy and Lactation.*

but only after several weeks. Figure 10, C, shows that the sodium phosphate appetite increased slightly during pregnancy and very definitely during lactation, dropping to normal at once after the litters were weaned. Figure 10, D, shows that no changes in potassium chloride intake occurred during pregnancy and lactation. However the intake decreased sharply after the litters were weaned.

Figure 11 summarizes the observations made on the changes in appetite for fat (olive oil), protein (casein), and carbohydrate (sucrose). The fat intake showed a small but definite increase during pregnancy and a very large increase during lactation. It decreased fairly rapidly after the litters were weaned. The protein intake gave much the same record. In marked contrast the intake of carbohydrate remained essentially unchanged throughout all of the periods. That the rats made very efficient selections is shown by the records in Figure 12, which gives the average daily food intake in grams, in 5-day intervals, for 10 rats on the self selection diet and for 10 rats on the stock diet, both groups of mothers nursing the same number of babies. In spite of the fact that the babies produced on the self selection diet weighed as much as those of stock rats and were apparently in as good health, the food intake, measured in grams, was about 20 per cent lower during pregnancy and almost 50 per cent lower at the height of lactation. The smaller intake of the self selection rats must be explained by the fact that they could satisfy their increased appetite for minerals without ingesting a large amount of other, unneeded, foodstuffs. On the stock diet, for instance, the rats that wanted a high amount of calcium had to take a large amount of the entire diet along with the calcium.

Thus, in these self selection experiments the pregnant and lactating rats have indicated with their appetites that they need increased amounts of fat and protein, as well as of sodium, calcium, phosphorus,

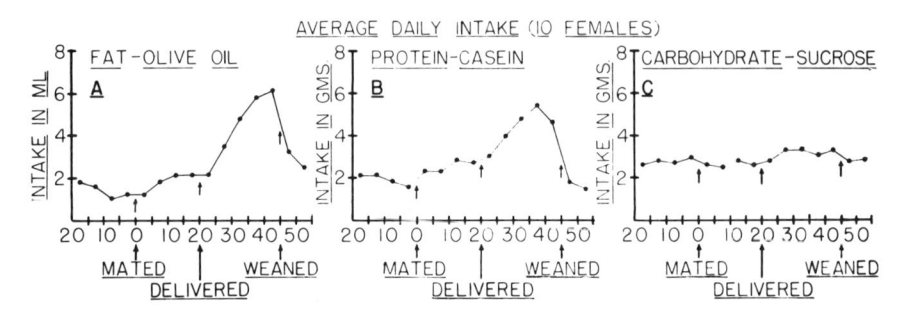

Fig. 11. *Average Daily Intake Curves for 10 Rats Showing Changes in Fat, Protein, and Carbohydrate Appetites during Pregnancy and Lactation.*

Total Self-Regulatory Functions in Animal and Human Beings 209

DAILY FOOD INTAKE DURING PREGNANCY AND LACTATION
AVERAGE FOR 5 DAY INTERVALS

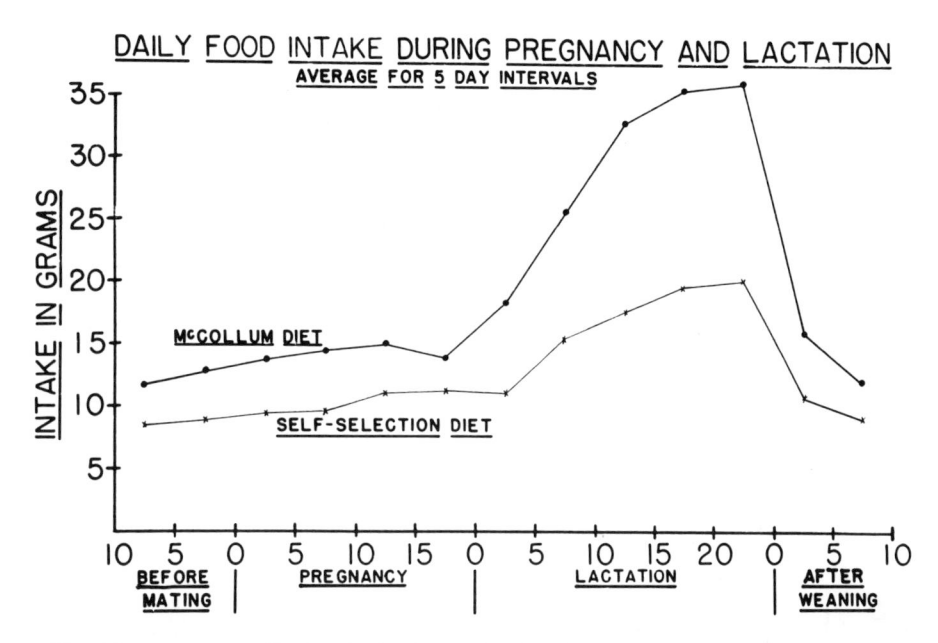

Fig. 12. Average Daily Intake in Grams for 10 Rats on the Self Selection Diet and for 10 Rats on our Stock Diet (modified McCollum diet).

and possibly potassium. These results are closely in agreement with knowledge derived from biochemical studies regarding the needs present during these conditions, except for the sharp increase in salt appetite which occurs during the first few days of pregnancy. With this method we may determine not only the substances that are needed by the animals under special conditions, but also the relative amounts of each.

These and similar experiments have brought out one of the most important self selection principles, namely the inverse relationship between the appetite for carbohydrate and fat. Invariably, when a rat eats high amounts of fat it eats little or no carbohydrate, and the reverse is also true. One example will suffice for the present purpose. Figure 13 shows the olive oil, sucrose, and casein intake curves of a rat placed on the self selection diet listed in Table I, A, but without yeast and wheat germ oil, that is, entirely lacking in all vitamin B. For the first 11 days large amounts of sucrose were taken and only a small amount of olive oil. Then, when the vitamin B deficiency began to manifest itself, the intake of sucrose decreased and that of olive oil increased. After 2 weeks the rat showed almost no appetite at all for the sucrose. Thirty-six days after the start of the diet dried baker's

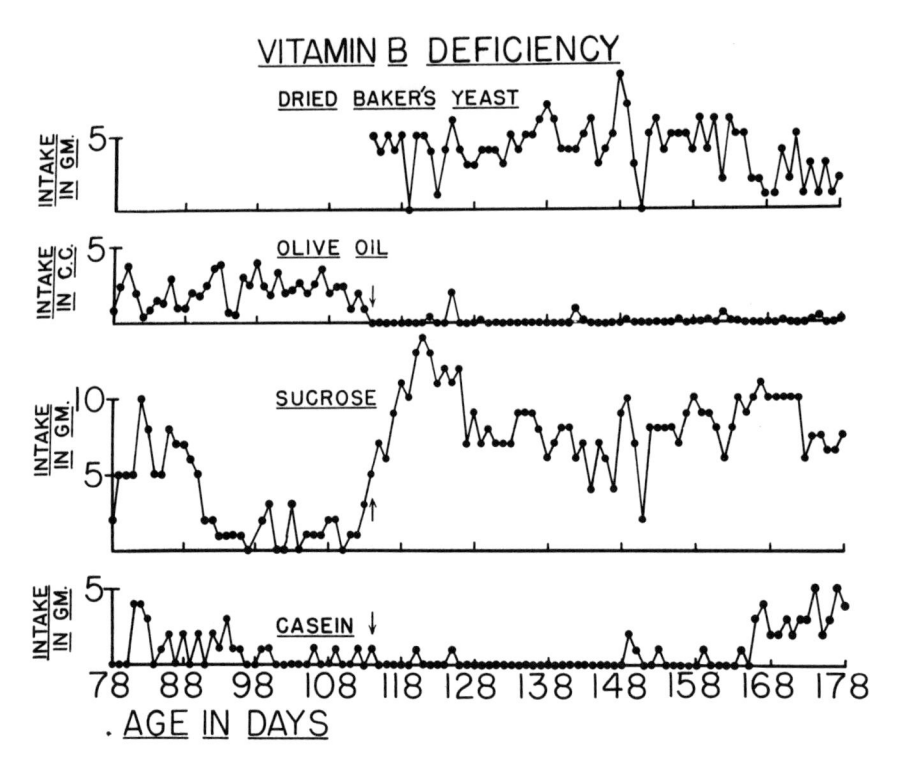

Fig. 13. *Typical Individual Record Showing Inverse Relationship between Carbohydrate and Fat Appetites, and their Dependence on the Vitamin B Complex Content of the Diet.*

yeast was offered; large amounts were eaten at once, with the result that the animal immediately manifested a great appetite for sucrose and stopped taking olive oil. It may be noted incidentally to the present purposes that progressively as the vitamin B deficiency developed the rat took less casein and after several weeks refused it almost entirely. After yeast was made available its appetite for casein did not return for over 45 days. Presumably in the meantime the protein obtained from the large amounts of yeast ingested satisfied the animal's requirements for this foodstuff.

Another self selection principle brought out by these experiments is that rats will make every effort to maintain their daily caloric intake at a fixed level. Thus, when rats are kept on the stock diet and are forced to take additional fat by stomach tube, or additional sugar or alcohol in their drinking water, they will reduce their intake of the stock diet almost exactly by the equivalent caloric value received from the additional substances. For instance, three groups of rats which could satisfy

Total Self-Regulatory Functions in Animal and Human Beings 211

their thirst only from 8, 16, and 24 per cent solutions of alcohol respectively, reduced their food intake directly in proportion to the caloric value of the ingested alcohol, so that the total caloric intake still remained the same as when the rats received the stock diet (27). In some of the rats on the 24 per cent colution of alcohol, the daily intake of alcohol averaged from 45 to 50 per cent of the total caloric intake. In spite of their high intake of alcohol and the consequent great reduction in the intake of vitamins and minerals, the rats were in excellent shape when they were killed and autopsied after nine months on the experimental diets.

We have also used the self selection technique for a further study of the functions of the adrenal gland. In one series we offered rats access to a 40 per cent solution of dextrose, and a 3 per cent solution of sodium chloride, in addition to a salt-poor stock diet and tap water (28). As shown in the typical record in Figure 14, after adrenalectomy the rats started at once to drink more of the salt solution and less of the sugar solution; however, their food and water intake remained essentially unchanged. Thus these rats indicated that they needed, or could use, the salt but not the carbohydrate. Parenteral administration of percorten (desoxycorticosterone) quickly reduced the salt appetite to its normal level, and increased the dextrose intake very markedly.

In another series of experiments we studied the changes in appetite for dextrose of normal rats produced by daily injections of protamine

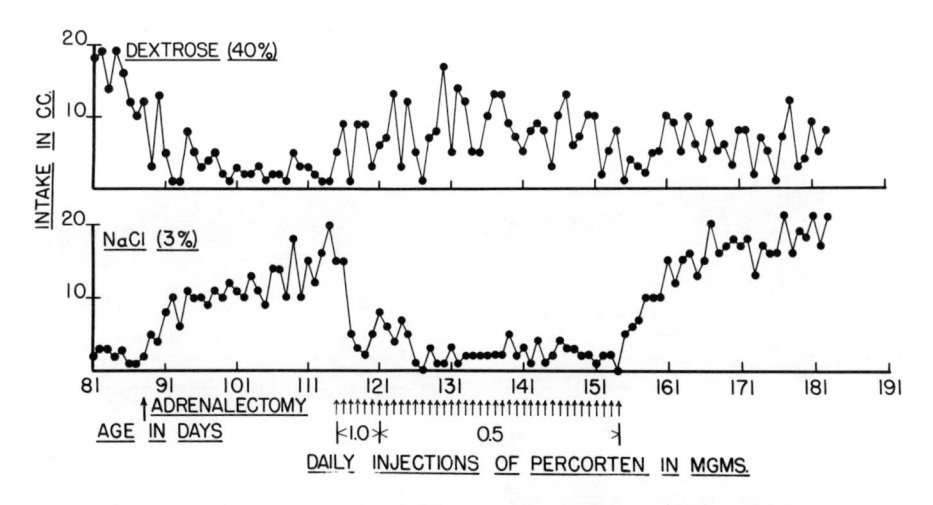

Fig. 14. Typical Individual Record Demonstrating Effects of Adrenalectomy and of Subsequent Percorten Injections on the Daily Intake of Dextrose and Sodium Chloride.

zinc insulin (29). In these experiments the rats had access to the stock diet, a 40 per cent solution of dextrose, and tap water. The initial dosage of 2 units was increased by increments of 0.4 unit each day either until the rats died or a level of 16 units was reached. As shown in a typical record in Figure 15 the dextrose intake increased steadily, more than doubling during treatment, while the intake of the stock diet increased only very slightly, thus indicating that the increased appetite of insulin treated rats is specifically directed toward carbohydrate. Of special interest was the precipitous drop in dextrose appetite which occurred immediately after cessation of the insulin injections. For about a week the rats scarcely touched the dextrose solution. Thereafter the dextrose intake increased again, first reaching the pre-experimental level, and finally surpassing it. The maintenance of the abnormally high level must indicate changes of some sort in the carbohydrate-insulin balance, the nature of which we cannot explain at the present time.

Preliminary results of some of our experiments indicate that the appetite method may also be used to bioassay various biological prepa-

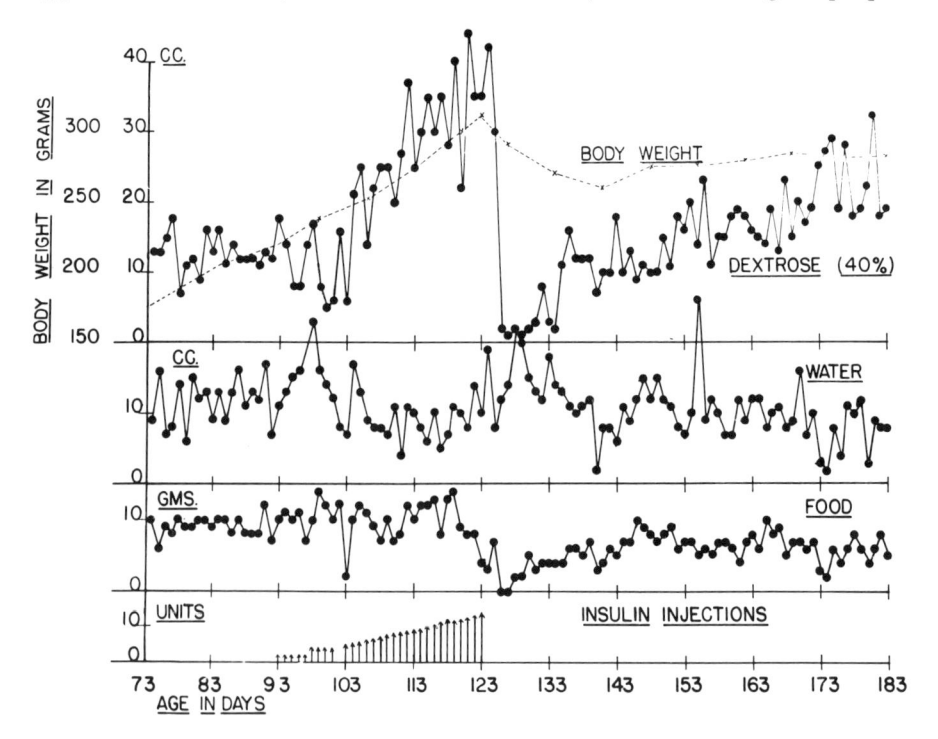

Fig. 15. *Typical Individual Record of the Daily Dextrose, Food, and Water Intake of a Normal Rat Treated with Increasing Doses of Insulin.*

Total Self-Regulatory Functions in Animal and Human Beings 213

rations. For example, it was found that substances which influence calcium metabolism all affect the calcium lactate intake of parathyroidectomized rats (30). For such an experiment the substances to be tested were incorporated in the food, which was a modification of our usual stock diet made without the skim milk powder and calcium carbonate. It was found that the presence of even very small amounts of the various vitamin D preparations or of dihydrotachysterol (A.T. 10) placed in the food could be detected by an immediate decrease in the intake of the calcium solution. For assay studies the amounts of the test substances mixed with the food were increased or decreased until the calcium lactate intake returned to its normal preoperative level. Figure 16 shows an assay record for A.T. 10. In this animal parathyroidectomy had increased the intake of 2 per cent calcium lactate from 3 cc. to a fairly constant level near 16 cc. Forty days after parathyroidectomy the drug was first added to the diet at the rate of 5 mgm. per 100 grams of food. As can be seen this amount had an immediate effect on the calcium intake, but was toxic, as indicated by the prompt weight drop. In successive periods, 0.5 and 0.05 mgm. per 100 grams of food were tried, allowing intervening time for recovery; the larger dose had a marked effect while the smaller dose had none at all. Finally, a dose of

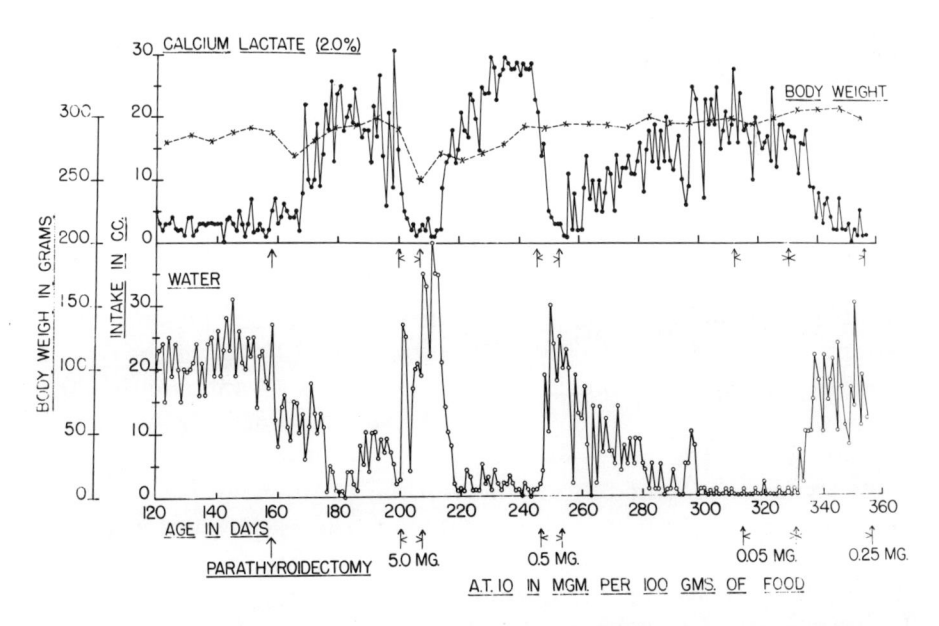

Fig. 16. Typical Individual Record Showing the Effects Produced on Increased Calcium Lactate Appetite by Varying Doses of Dihydrotachysterol (A.T. 10) Added to the Food.

0.25 mgm. per 100 grams of food was tried and was found to bring the calcium lactate intake gradually down to its preoperative level. Thus the minimum effective dose of A.T. 10 for a parathyroidectomized rat must lie between 0.05 and 0.25 mgm. per 100 grams of food, or between 5 and 25 micrograms per day when measured in terms of actual intake. Using the same technique we have assayed vitamins D_2 and D_3, as well as irradiated ergosterol and irradiated cholesterol. It was further found that parathormone, which is known to act primarily on phosphorus metabolism, had only a slight effect on the calcium lactate intake of parathyroidectomized rats, even when given in toxic amounts.

Some of the most fruitful applications of the study of the rat's appetites have been made in so-called single food choice experiments, in which the rats have access to only one purified food, a fat, carbohydrate or protein, or to a single whole food such as corn, graham flour, peanuts, etc., either alone or with access also to one or more of the different vitamins, enzymes or minerals (31). Figure 8 (cage 74) shows one of the small cages used for these experiments. Each cage contains a food cup and either one or two graduated inverted bottles. Under the conditions of such an experiment specific dietary interrelationships can often be more clearly brought out than when mixtures of foodstuffs are fed. I will give you only a few examples. It was found in confirmation of some preliminary observations made by Holt and Kajdi (32) that, while young adult rats kept on no food at all, but with free access to water, survived only 4–6 days, when kept exclusively on dextrose and water they survived 36 days, and when given access also to a 0.02 per cent solution of thiamine hydrochloride they lived more than twice as long, 76 days (33). Thus, under the simplest conditions, these experiments showed the marked effect which thiamine hydrochloride has on the metabolism of dextrose. Of special interest from the point of view of the possible use of these data in planning emergency rations, was the extreme activity for more than 20 days of the rats on dextrose alone, some animals running as much as 15 miles on the 25th day, while on dextrose and thiamine hydrochloride a high level of activity persisted as long as 60 days.

Applying this method to the study of the nutritional value of various single whole foods we have found that on an exclusive diet of yellow or white corn rats maintained their original weights for more than 3 months (34). However, after approximately 60 days on the diet they became inactive, and the yellow corn-fed rats showed only dioestrous vaginal smears, while the white corn group began to show a vitamin A deficiency, as evidenced by constantly cornified smears, after about 50

Total Self-Regulatory Functions in Animal and Human Beings 215

days. The voluntary ingestion of cod liver oil produced remarkable results on the yellow corn-fed rats. Within only 4 days they all again showed regular 4-day oestrous cycles; almost at once they ate more corn, gained weight, and became much more active. After 15 days they reached approximately their pre-experimental levels of running activity, averaging 10–15 miles per day. Figure 17 shows a typical record of the activity, food intake, body weight, and vaginal smears of a rat kept on the single food yellow corn diet, and later given access to cod liver oil.

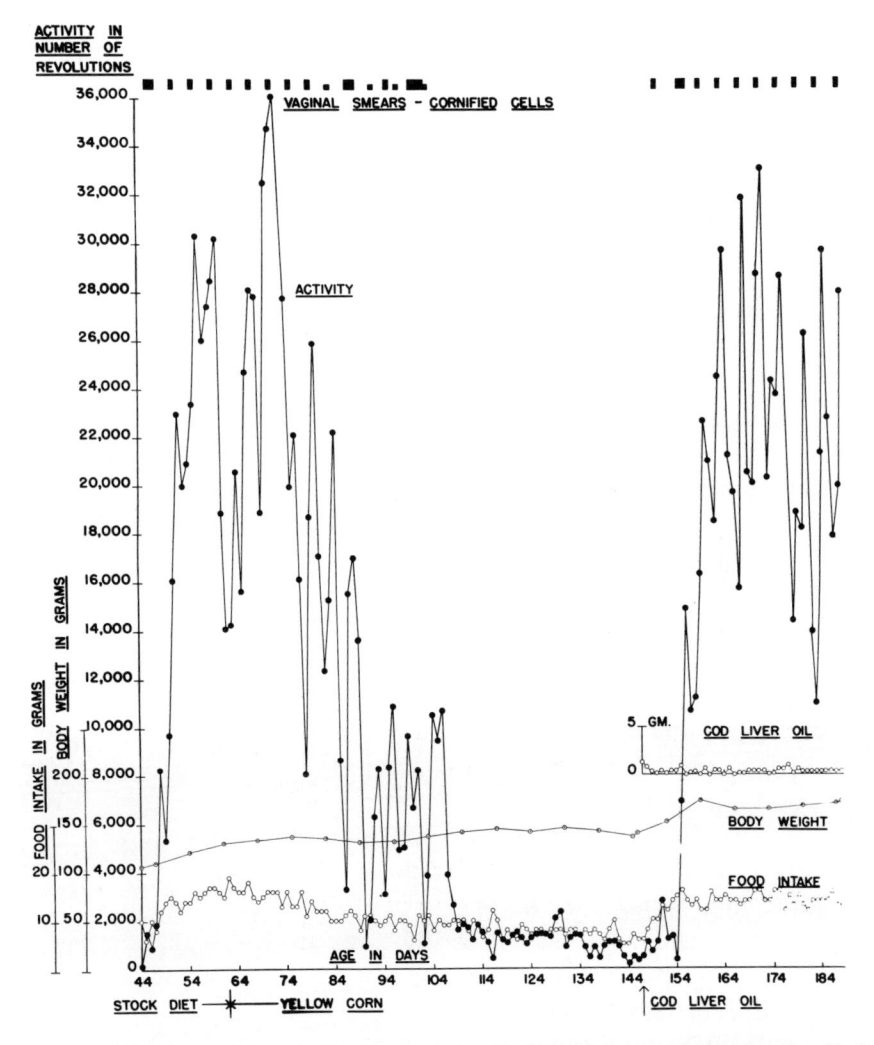

Fig. 17. Typical Individual Graph Showing Daily Activity, Food Intake, Body Weight, and Vaginal Smears of a Rat Kept on an Exclusive Diet of Yellow Corn and the Effects Produced by the Ingestion of Cod Liver Oil.

The results of these experiments indicate that, under the conditions of this experiment, yellow corn when supplemented with cod liver oil becomes an excellent food. In marked contrast, the rats on white corn failed to respond to the ingestion of the cod liver oil, except with an immediate change of their vaginal smears from a condition of constant cornification to a persistent dioestrous condition. They remained inactive and did not show an increased appetite, or gain weight. These results demonstrate that white corn must lack some essential nutriment that is present in yellow corn, and not supplied by cod liver oil.

Other animals besides the rat have also been reported to make beneficial selections of diets from natural and semi-natural foodstuffs. In 1914 Evvard tried a "free choice" system of feeding pigs, and concluded that "the appetite of the pig appears to be a very good guide as to its bodily needs" (35–38). One such experimental animal grew to be the largest hog ever raised at the Iowa Agricultural Experiment Station. Nevins found that dairy cows made beneficial selections of diet, as evidenced both by milk output and weight gains (39). Godden stated that sheep grazing in hill pastures in which some areas were deficient in minerals, consistently left the deficient herbage untouched (40). Orr has reported numerous further instances of beneficial selections of diet made by livestock (41). Similarly, Price reported that chickens given a choice between three varieties of butter, one with a high content of vitamin A and D, another high in the A factor but poor in D, and a third variety poor in both factors, unerringly selected the first sample, though neither taste nor odor indicated any differences to the human observer (42). Pearl and Fairchild also found that chickens made more efficient choices of food on self selection diets than on mixed diets (43). Similarly, Stearns and Hollander successfully used a "cafeteria" system of feeding for pigeons (44). We have found that monkeys, given access to the same selection of foods as the rats, with the single exception that vitamin C was also available to them, thrived throughout the three months of the experiment. Guinea pigs, ferrets, and mink did less well, perhaps owing to a deficiency of vitamin K, which was not offered for choice; these species consistently showed intestinal hemorrhages at autopsy after several months on the diet, though there was never any gross bleeding from the gastro-intestinal tract.

If it is true that rats have such a remarkable ability to select beneficial foods and to avoid harmful foods, it may be asked how it is possible to poison them. In our experiments it was found that when poisons such as arsenic trioxide, mercuric chloride, or morphine sulfate

Total Self-Regulatory Functions in Animal and Human Beings 217

were offered separately in solution the rats avoided them in extremely low concentrations, far below the level at which they might have had any physiological effect. Franke and Potter found that rats made clear cut differentiations between diets which contained varying amounts of selenium (45). It has been our experience that rats can be made to take poisons only under two conditions: (1) when the poisons are sufficiently thoroughly mixed with their food to mask most of the taste, and then usually only when the rats are very hungry; or (2) when the poisons are too highly insoluble in the saliva to be tasted. In this connection it may be pointed out that the inability to vomit may explain the great caution with which rats approach their food. Dogs and many other animals that are able to vomit are usually less cautious. We have found, however, that monkeys and chimpanzees, despite active vomiting responses, can be made to take soporifics orally only with the greatest difficulty. They detect the presence of the drugs even when very thoroughly mixed with their food or powdered and hidden in bananas.

I would like to call your attention also to the possibility that various phenomena, ordinarily spoken of as perverted appetites, such as coprophagy, infantophagia, autophagia, placenta eating, and bone eating, may be regarded as instances of self regulatory activities. We are now making special studies of some of these phenomena, determining how they fit into the picture of the total nutrition of animals. Coprophagy, or feces eating, is frequently observed, especially among animals on deficient diets. That it serves a useful purpose, and is actually a form of self regulatory activity, is evidenced by the fact that rats on a single food dextrose diet lived more than half again as long (54 as compared with 34 days) when given access to their feces (33). Similarly, it may well be that urine drinking, or ouronodypsia, is of comparable significance with coprophagy. Thus, Orent-Keiles and McCollum have reported a pica exhibited by rats on diets low in potassium (46). The animals showed a marked tendency to lick their genitals, especially after urinating, while coprophagy was not observed. Since potassium is excreted almost entirely through the kidneys, it seems likely that the rats were attempting to recover this deficient element from the urine. It may be of interest that we have found that rats have an active appetite for cancer tissue (47). Recently, for example, 3 almost moribund tumor-bearing rats were kept in one cage, each rat carrying more than 100 grams—very nearly half the body weight—of neoplastic tissue. After the first rat died, the other two were observed avidly eating the tumor off its body and by the following morning not a trace of tumor remained on the dead rat. On occasion the rats will even eat large portions of the tumors off their own bodies. This appetite may not be as extraordinary as it seems at first glance when we consider that the tumors are constituted of young, extremely rapidly growing tissue. Nash has reported the autophagia of wounded paws or tails in 50 per cent of starved traumatized rats (48). Since neither injury nor hunger alone were sufficiently strong stimuli to induce self eating, it was concluded that the mouthing of wounds practiced almost universally among animals only leads to actual autophagia in the presence of a very strong hunger drive.

There are many reported instances in which animals manifest special appetites as a result of dietary deficiencies. Theiler, Green, and Viljoen found that the osteomalacia so prevalent in South African cattle was associated with a phosphorus deficiency in the soil and vegetation of the regions in which the disease was prevalent, and that such animals were confirmed bone eaters (49). When the bones were infected with the bacillus para botulinus, the cattle developed acute botulism, so-called Midland Disease or Lamsiekta, with its consequent high mortality. An adequate supply of phosphorus eliminated the disease. Similarly, Jones found that the sheep at Burrowa, in New South Wales, cured themselves of "weakness" by eating the earth in certain paddocks (50). On analysis, the earth from these natural lick holes proved to be unusually rich in iron (7.1 per cent Fe_2O_3). Orr also mentions a disease of oxen in Kenya known as Nakuruitis, characterized by emaciation, anemia, "running at the eyes," and in the advanced stages by loss of power and coordination of the limbs, which was cured when the animals were allowed to lick ad libitum a mixture of equal parts of common salt and ferric oxide (51). According to Orr, horses in Victoria, Australia, circumvent the natural consequences of grazing on inferior pasturage by eating the bark of "grey-box" trees, which on analysis is shown to be exceedingly rich in lime, containing 53.7 per cent as compared with 2.7 per cent in native grasses (41).

McCollum has observed that hens on experimental diets designed to determine whether birds could synthesize lecithin, developed such a strong habit of egg eating that they had to be carefully watched in order to secure the eggs immediately after they were laid (52). Since egg yolk is an unusually rich source of this phospholipin it seems very likely, at least, that the animals were making an effort to correct the deficiency.

Before I give you the results of observations that have been made on self selection ability in humans, I would like to point out the astonishingly close relationship that exists between the dietary requirements of rats and human beings. With the exception of the needs for vitamin C their requirements have proved to be almost identical. It is of interest, then, that actual measurements of the taste ability have shown that rats and human beings have almost exactly the same taste thresholds for all of the substances so far tested, with the difference that human beings show a wider range of individual variation. The methods used for determining taste thresholds were essentially the same in both cases, with the exception that the human subjects used words to describe their taste reactions. It is not astonishing that humans recognize a difference in taste between distilled water and the solution being tested at a consistently lower concentration than that at which they can definitely characterize the taste of the solution. Thus, the average concentration at which adult humans first recognized a difference between salt solution and distilled water was 0.010 per cent, while the average concentration at which they first definitely recognized the salty taste was 0.065 per cent (53). This latter figure agrees very well with the 0.055 per cent taste threshold of rats for sodium chloride. Similarly, the human sweet taste threshold for sucrose solutions falls at an average of 0.41 per cent, while the average taste threshold of rats for sucrose is 0.50 per cent (54). In the case of the bitter tasting toxic compound, phenylthiocarbamide, there is even closer agreement, as seen in Figure 18. The taste difference threshold and the bitter taste threshold of human beings both averaged 0.0003 per cent, while the average taste threshold for rats also fell at this same concentration (55).

We may now discuss self regulatory functions in human beings. To what extent do behavior regulators manifest themselves in human beings? That we must have essentially the same ability as animals to make beneficial dietary selections is attested by our very existence. Certainly in the wild state, when man was dependent for his food on selections made from a great variety of nutritious, harmless, and poisonous substances, he did not have the guiding hand of the modern nutritionist to help him select his diet. Appetite must have been his chief guide then, and today appetite must still play a far more important role than many nutritionists seem willing to admit.

Davis has reported many interesting examples of infants who thrived and grew on diets which they selected from a wide assortment of natural foods, even citing one child who overcame the symptoms of a marked vitamin D deficiency by voluntarily drinking large amounts of cod liver oil (56–60). In Davis' experiments with children, when natural foods were offered for choice, there was a wide fluctuation in appetite

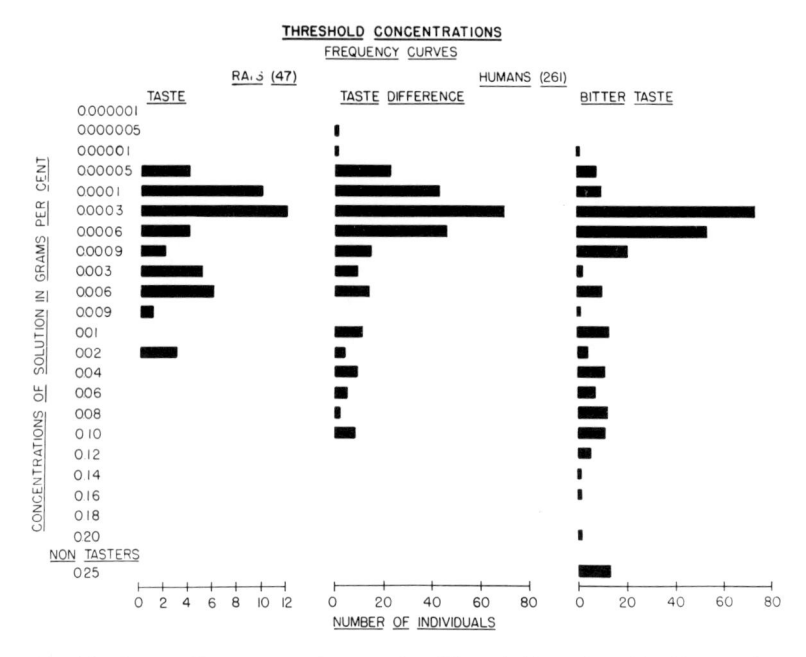

Fig. 18. Maximum Frequency Curves for Phenylthiocarbamide Taste Thresholds for Rats and Human Beings.

for the different foods from day to day and from week to week. This seems readily understandable in view of the fact that each food may be used to satisfy any one of several appetites at different times. However, when rats are kept on a full self selection diet of purified substances, their appetites remain surprisingly constant over long periods of time. Sweet has also adduced evidence to show that children thrive better when allowed to select their own food and meal times, than on a fixed regime (61).

Along this same line I would like to mention the results of some preliminary observations that we have made on the cod liver oil appetite of children at different ages (62). We have now tested over a thousand children from 5 to 14 years of age simply by letting them taste a small spoonful of the unadulterated oil. At 5 years almost all of the children liked cod liver oil; progressively with increasing age more and more of them manifested a dislike for it. This was found to be true regardless of whether or not they had had cod liver oil before. Thus, as shown in Figure 19, of 328 children tested in one of the schools near the Johns Hopkins Hospital, in the 5-year-old group, 100 per cent of the girls and 92 per cent of the boys liked cod liver oil, while in the 14-year-old group only 36 per cent of the girls and 28 per cent of the

Total Self-Regulatory Functions in Animal and Human Beings 221

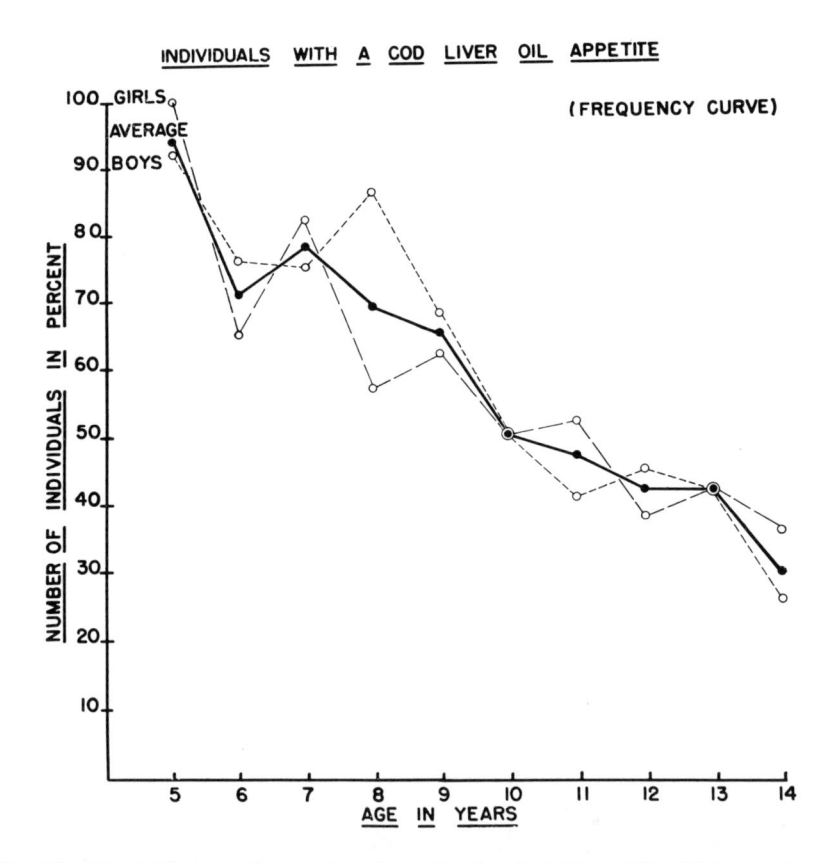

Fig. 19. Chart Showing Decreasing Appetite for Cod Liver Oil with Increasing Age in 328 School Children.

boys still liked it. Some children at 14 years had an almost insatiable appetite for cod liver oil. When allowed to satisfy their craving they took as much as 16 tablespoonsful in one day, and continued to take high amounts for 5–10 days. After that they took only small amounts, and finally stated that they no longer liked it. Rats kept on diets deficient in vitamins A or D responded in much the same way when offered cod liver oil. Our results thus suggest the possibility of using the cod liver oil appetite as a means of detecting deficiencies of vitamin A or D or some of the fatty acids.

We do have a few instances in which in human beings just as in the rats, the physiological regulators have been either completely or partially eliminated. Thus, in Addison's disease, in which there is a destruction of the adrenal cortex, we have found many patients who manifested a marked craving for salt—either for salt itself or food with a high salt content, such as ham, sauerkraut, etc. In the latter instances the patients themselves did not in any way associate the craving for these foods with their high salt content. All they knew was that the food had an unusually pleasant taste to them. Doctor Lawson Wilkins and I have described a three-and-a-half-year-old boy with destruction of adrenal cortical cells by hyperplasia of the androgenic zones of the glands, who kept himself alive for more than two years by eating large amounts of salt, literally by the handful (63). When his salt intake was restricted to the amounts present in a regular hospital diet he promptly developed symptoms of insufficiency and died. Another patient, a 34-year-old man with marked Addison's disease, put approximately 1/8-inch layer of salt on his steak, used nearly 1/2 a glass of salt for his tomato juice, used salt on oranges and grapefruit, and even made lemonade with salt. As a matter of fact, a salt craving is so often an early manifestation of Addison's disease that it is of considerable diagnostic significance.

Similarly, children with parathyroid deficiency have been reported to show a craving for chalk, plaster, and other substances with a high calcium content. Instances have also been reported in which patients with pernicious anemia have kept themselves in good health as a result of the satisfaction of a strong craving for liver. Similarly, dietary anemias may be at the root of the clay-eating habits commonly practiced in the poorer sections of the South (64). The high water intake of patients with diabetes insipidus may also be regarded as an effort to prevent dehydration, which is threatened by the loss of physiological regulation of the posterior lobe of the pituitary gland. In the same way, we may regard the high water intake of the diabetes mellitus patient as a means of diluting the urinary sugar and avoiding a consequent dehydration. The high food intake may also be regarded as an effort to supply the necessary calories, the ability to utilize sugar having been lost. Similarly, the voracious appetite of the hyperthyroid patient is presumably the direct result of the increased metabolic rate, which would soon produce cachexia if the food intake were limited to normal amounts.

Other instances of self regulatory functions not in the field of nutrition might also be cited. We may regard the great physical activity of many normal individuals, the play activity of children, and perhaps even the excessive activity of many manic patients, as efforts to maintain a constant internal balance by expending excessive amounts of energy. On the other hand, the low level of activity seen in some apparently normal people, the almost total inactivity seen in depressed patients, again may be regarded as an effort to conserve enough energy to maintain a constant internal balance.

Those who do not believe that self regulatory ability still exists in man cite various instances of individuals who failed to make advantageous selections, instances in which individuals have eaten the wrong foods, or too much or too little food. We can offer several points which must be taken into account in considering these failures. In the first place, the use of natural foods instead of purified chemical substances will certainly frequently confuse the choices, since the selections depend so largely on taste; and in order to get adequate amounts of needed substances it may be necessary to take other harmful or unneeded substances. In the second place, with the present prevalence of highly refined foods, the necessary vitamins, minerals, etc., may not be available in sufficient amounts, so that no matter how adequate the self regulatory ability, the individuals could not make satisfactory selections. In the third place, inherited and acquired defects of the sensory mechanisms may also account for some of the poor dietary selections. Thus, from the work of Blakeslee and Fox and of Snyder and others, it is known that a small percentage of individuals are unable to taste the bitter-tasting substance, phenylthiocarbamide, and that this inability is inherited as a Mendelian recessive (65, 66). Likewise, we have found some individuals who are unable to taste other bitter substances, and some who are unable to taste sweet substances. We have found further that, although most children dislike alcohol solutions above 10–15 per cent, about 8 per cent of a large group of children were either indifferent to, or actually liked, solutions of alcohol in concentrations as high as 50 per cent (27). This observation may perhaps account for the excessive drinking of some individuals. However, cultural influences probably account for most failures to make beneficial dietary selections. Most children are brought up by their parents to distrust their own appetites. Often when they like a food they are told not to eat it, and when they dislike it they are equally often told that it is nourishing and good for them. In later life such persons are much more apt to depend on food faddists than on their own taste sensations.

Finally in this connection I want to draw your attention to the possibility that self regulatory functions may undergo a partial or total breakdown. Some of the instances of dietary failures just mentioned may be instances of such a breakdown. The total regulators may wear down or age just as Cannon has reported that the physiological regulators do (2). A breakdown of the total self regulators would depend in the first place on disturbances in the sense organs—the heat, cold, pain, taste receptors, etc.—or in the parts of the brain involved in the ability to observe sensations of fatigue, pain, taste, etc., and to react to them.

Thus, Ruch, Brobeck, and Blum have shown that monkeys with lesions of the arcuate nuclei are no longer able to make advantageous taste differentiations (67). The fact that animals deprived of the frontal poles of their brains may become so active that they literally run themselves to death would indicate that this part of the brain also plays an important part in the total self regulatory functions (68–71). The great overactivity seen in some psychiatric patients may result from a breakdown of the self regulatory systems. Further instances would be seen in catatonic patients who no longer react to external or internal stimuli and unless cared for by tube feeding, etc., would not live; and in anorexia nervosa patients who when left to their own devices would gradually let themselves starve to death. Many other instances might be explained on this basis.

Thus, in summary, I have tried to show that the maintenance of a constant internal environment depends not only on the physiological or chemical regulators, but as well on behavior or total organism regulators. Proof of the existence of the behavior regulators was taken from experiments in the field of endocrinology and nutrition. It was shown that disturbances created in the internal environment by removal of one or the other of the endocrine glands were corrected by the animals themselves. It was demonstrated that the ability to select diets with relation to internal needs seems to depend more upon taste sensations than on experience, and it was pointed out that this knowledge of the ability of animals to make beneficial selections can be used to study a variety of problems in the fields of endocrinology and nutrition. Evidence was further presented for the existence and successful operation of similar behavior regulators in human beings. Thus, we believe that the results of our experiments indicate that in human beings and animals the effort to maintain a constant internal environment or homeostasis constitutes one of the most universal and powerful of all behavior urges or drives.

Bibliography

1. Bernard, C., Leçons sur les propriétés physiologiques et les altérations pathologiques des liquides de l'organisme, Paris, Bailliers, 1859.
2. Cannon, W. B., The wisdom of the body, New York, Norton and Company, Inc., 1932.
3. Richter, C. P., *Am. Jour. Physiol.*, 1936, 115, 155.
4. Richter, C. P., and Eckert, J. F., *Endocrinology*, 1938, 22, 214.
5. Richter, C. P., and Eckert, J. F., *Endocrinology*, 1937, 21, 50.

6. Richter, C. P., and Eckert, J. F., *Am. Jour. Med. Sci.*, 1939, 198, 9.
7. Richter, C. P., and Schmidt, E. C. H., Jr., *Endocrinology*, 1941, 28, 179.
8. Richter, C. P., *Am. Jour. Physiol.*, 1935, 112, 481.
9. Richter, C. P., and Eckert, J. F., *Am. Jour. Physiol.*, 1935, 113, 578.
10. Richter, C. P., *Proc. Assoc. Res. in Nerv. and Ment. Dis.*, 1936, 17, 392.
11. Kinder, E. F., *Jour. Exp. Zool.*, 1927, 47, 117.
12. Richter, C. P., *Cold Spring Harbor Symposia on Quant. Biol.*, 1937, 5, 258.
13. Richter, C. P., *Trans. Am. Neurol. Assoc.*, 1939, 65, 49.
14. Richter, C. P., and Campbell, K. H., *Am. Jour. Physiol.*, 1940, 128, 291.
15. Richter, C. P., and Campbell, K. H., *Science*, 1940, 91, 507.
16. Richter, C. P., and Campbell, K. H., *Jour. Nutrition*, 1940, 20, 31; also unpublished data.
17. Richter, C. P., and Clisby, K. H., *Am. Jour. Physiol.*, 1941, 134, 157.
18. Richter, C. P., *Endocrinology*, 1939, 24, 367.
19. Loeb, R. F., *Science*, 1932, 76, 420.
20. Loeb, R. F., Atchley, D., and Stahl, J., *Jour. Am. Med. Assoc.*, 1935, 104, 2149.
21. MacCallum, W. G., and Voegtlin, C., *Jour. Exp. Med.*, 1909, 11, 118.
22. Richter, C. P., Holt, L. E., Jr., and Barelare, B., Jr., *Am. Jour. Physiol.*, 1938, 122, 734.
23. Richter, C. P., Holt, L. E., Jr., Barelare, B., Jr., and Hawkes, C. D., *Am. Jour. Physiol.*, 1938, 124, 596; also unpublished data.
24. Richter, C. P., and Hawkes, C. D., *Am. Jour. Physiol.*, 1941, 131, 639.
25. Mannering, G. J., Lipton, M. A., and Elvehjem, C. A., *Proc. Soc. Exp. Biol. and Med.*, 1941, 46, 100.
26. Richter, C. P., and Barelare, B., Jr., *Endocrinology*, 1938, 23, 15.
27. Richter, C. P., *Quart. Jour. Studies on Alcohol*, 1941, 1, 650.
28. Richter, C. P., *Endocrinology*, 1941, 29, 115.
29. Richter, C. P., *Am. Jour. Physiol.*, 1942, 135, 781.
30. Richter, C. P., and Birmingham, J. R., *Endocrinology*, 1941, 29, 655.
31. Richter, C. P., *Am. Jour. Physiol.*, 1941, 133, 29.
32. Holt, L. E., Jr., and Kajdi, C. N., *Am. Jour. Dis. Child.*, 1939, 58, 669.
33. Richter, C. P., and Rice, K. K., *Am. Jour. Physiol.*, 1942, 137, 573.
34. Richter, C. P., and Rice, K. K., *Am. Jour. Physiol.*, 1943, 139, 147.
35. Evvard, J. M., *Proc. Am. Soc. Anim. Prod.*, 1941, p. 50.
36. Evvard, J. M., *Proc. Iowa Acad. Sci.*, 1915, 22, 402.
37. Evvard, J. M., *Modern Farming*, 1922, 7, nos. 3, 4, 5.
38. Evvard, J. M., Snell, M. G., Culbertson, C. C., and Snedecor, G. W., *Proc. Am. Soc. Anim. Prod.*, 1927, p. 85.
39. Nevins, W. B., *Univ. of Ill. Agr. Expt. Sta. Bull.* 289, 1927.
40. Godden, W., *Jour. Agr. Sci.*, 1926, 16, 78.
41. Orr, J. B., Minerals in pastures, London, Lewis and Co. Ltd., 1929.
42. Price, W. A., *Certified Milk*, 1929, 4, 8.
43. Pearl, R., and Fairchild, T. E., *Am. Jour. Hyg.*, 1921, 1, 253.
44. Stearns, G. L., and Hollander, W. F., *American Pigeon Jour.*, Dec. 1939 issue.
45. Franke, K. W., and Potter, van R., *Jour. Nutrition*, 1935, 10, 213.
46. Orent-Keiles, E., and McCollum, E. V., *Jour. Biol. Chem.*, 1941, 140, 337.
47. Rice, K. K., unpublished data.
48. Nash, C. B., *Science*, 1940, 91, 342.
49. Theiler, A. H., Green, H. H., and Viljoen, P. R., 3rd and 4th *Reports Div. of Vet. Res.*, 1915, 1, 68.
50. Jones, L. G., *Queensland Agric. Jour.*, 1918, 9 and 10, 48.
51. Orr, J. B., *Report on Pasture Investigation in Kenya*, 1927.

52. McCollum, E. V., Orent-Keiles, E., and Day, H. G., The newer knowledge of nutrition, 1939, p. 577.
53. Richter, C. P., and MacLean, A., *Am. Jour. Physiol.*, 1939, 126, 1.
54. Richter, C. P., and Campbell, K. H., *Am. Jour. Physiol.*, 1940, 128, 291.
55. Richter, C. P., and Clisby, K. H., *Am. Jour. Physiol.*, 1941, 134, 157.
56. Davis, C. M., *Am. Jour. Dis. Child.*, 1928, 36, 651.
57. Davis, C. M., *Am. Jour. Dis. Child.*, 1933, 46, 743.
58. Davis, C. M., *Jour. Am. Dental Assoc.*, 1934, 21, 636.
59. Davis, C. M., *Am. Jour. Dis. Child.*, 1935, 50, 385.
60. Davis, C. M., *Canad. Med. Assoc. Jour.*, 1939, 41, 257.
61. Sweet, C., *Jour. Am. Med. Assoc.*, 1936, 107, 765.
62. Richter, C. P., unpublished data.
63. Wilkins, L., and Richter, C. P., *Jour. Am. Med. Assoc.*, 1940, 114, 866.
64. Abbott, O. D., *Milbank Memorial Hospital Report*, 1940, 53.
65. Blakeslee, A. F., and Fox, A. L., *Jour. Hered.*, 1932, 23, 97.
66. Snyder, L. H., *Ohio Jour. Sci.*, 1932, 32, 436.
67. Ruch, T. C., Brobeck, J., and Blum, M., Read before the Society of Physiological Neurology (Atlantic City, June 1941).
68. Richter, C. P., and Hines, M., *Brain*, 1938, 61, 1.
69. Richter, C. P., and Hawkes, C. D., *Jour. Neur. and Psych.*, 1939, 2, 231.
70. Beach, F. A., *Jour. Comp. Psychol.*, 1941, 31, 145.
71. Langworthy, O. R., and Richter, C. P., *Am. Jour. Physiol.*, 1939, 126, 158.

SELF-SELECTION STUDIES ON COPROPHAGY AS A SOURCE OF VITAMIN B COMPLEX

Many observers have noted that under conditions of dietary deficiency animals will eat their own feces or feces from other animals and that this ingestion of the feces prevents the appearance of deficiency symptoms (1, 2). Thus, for studies on the effects of dietary deficiencies the eating of feces, or coprophagy, must be rigidly eliminated. For purposes, however, of studies on the ability of rats to make beneficial dietary selections it becomes a phenomenon not to be eliminated but to be investigated in its own right (3). Hitherto only a few attempts have been made to single out eating of feces for special experimental study. Roscoe who collected feces from vitamin B deficient rats and returned them to their cages found that the rats ate from 40 to 100 per cent of the feces and lived for long periods of time (4). Guerrant and Dutcher collected feces from rats kept on diets in which either sucrose or dextrin constituted the source of carbohydrates and fed them to vitamin B deficient rats (5). The rats ate the feces from the dextrin group but not from the sucrose group, presumably because the sucrose did not support the intestinal bacterial synthesis of vitamin B while the dextrin did support this synthesis.

An attack on the problem has now been made with the self-selection technique. In the following experiments rats kept on a diet which lacked all components of the vitamin B complex were given access to feces from normal animals. We wished to determine whether the rats

---

This paper was originally published in *The American Journal of Physiology*, Vol. 143, No. 3, March 1945. The authors were Curt P. Richter and Katherine K. Rice. Reprinted by permission.

would eat the feces, and if so in what amounts and with what consistency over long periods of time, and the extent to which the ingestion of the feces would replace the entire vitamin B complex.

For these experiments the rats had access to one representative of each of the most important foodstuffs in purified or nearly purified form and in separate non-spillable containers. From the results of previous experiments it was known that most rats show normal growth on selections made from the following substances:

1. Dextrose
2. Olive oil
3. Casein (vitamin free)
4. Dried brewer's yeat or liver powder
5. Cod-liver oil
6. Sodium chloride 3 per cent
7. Dibasic sodium phosphate 4 per cent
8. Potassium chloride 1 per cent
9. Calcium lactate 2 per cent
10. Magnesium chloride 0.5 per cent
11. Tap water

It will be noted that in this assortment of substances yeast or liver powder is the only source of the vitamin B complex. The rats did less well on liver powder than on yeast in that fewer rats showed normal growth curves. When the rats refused to eat either the yeast or liver powder they lost weight at a rapid rate. Very few rats refused to eat the yeast powder, while a fair number refused to eat the liver powder, presumably because of its bitter taste.

Important for the present purposes is the observation made in some of the previous self-selection experiments that the appetites for carbohydrate, fat and protein depended on the components of the vitamin B complex which the rats received (6, 7). Without access to any of the components, that is, without yeast, the rats ate large amounts of fat, little or no carbohydrate, and no protein. With access to thiamine as the sole source of the vitamin B complex, the rats ate less fat, more carbohydrate, but still almost no protein. Progressively as the other components, riboflavin, niacin, pyridoxine, pantothenic acid, and choline chloride were made accessible in separate containers, the rats ate larger amounts of carbohydrate, more protein, and smaller amounts of fat; and progressively the body weight curves more closely approached the normal. Thus the proportions of the carbohydrate, fat, and protein intakes give a rough indication of the presence of the aforementioned six components of the vitamin B complex in the diet. Accordingly when on the self-selection diet the rats have access to yeast, which contains all of the six vitamin B components at least in small amounts, most rats show a great carbohydrate and protein appetite and small appetite for fat.

In the following self-selection experiments yeast or liver powder were omitted from the ten substances offered for choice and were replaced by feces collected from normal rats. This meant that the only vitamin B that could have been present in the diet must have been contained in the feces. Comparisons were made of the body weight curves and of the proportions of the carbohydrate, fat, and protein intakes when yeast, liver, or feces constituted the sole source of the vitamin B complex.

Methods

Previous reports contain a full description of the individual cages and the technique used for self-selection experiments. Each cage was equipped with a screened bottom and contained three non-spillable cups for the solids and eight graduated inverted bottles for the fluids.

The intake of each substance was recorded daily. The bottles were cleaned and refilled twice weekly. The animals were weighed weekly.

The experiments were carried out in three series. In the first the rats were given access for a period of 50 days to the assortment of substances listed above in which yeast constituted the sole source of the vitamin B complex. Then for a period of 54 days feces from normal rats replaced the yeast. After that the feces were omitted leaving the diet entirely free from all vitamin B. In the second series the conditions were essentially the same except that the rats had access first to liver powder rather than to yeast. They had access to liver for 38 days and to feces for 65 days. In the third series the rats were given access to feces from normal rats for a period of 40 days. Then for a period of 66 days yeast replaced the feces. After that the yeast was omitted.

The feces were collected daily from healthy young adult rats which were given our stock diet[1] and were kept in screened bottom cages. The feces were ground in a meat grinder before they were given to the rats. Each day all of the feces remaining from the previous day were removed.

---

[1] This diet contained graham flour 72.5 per cent, casein 10.0 per cent, butter 5.0 per cent, skim milk powder 10.0 per cent, calcium carbonate 1.5 per cent, sodium chloride 1.0 per cent.

230   The Psychobiology of Curt Richter

Results

First Series

Body Weight. Figure 1A shows the body weight curves of the four rats used in this series. Until these rats were 96 days of age they received only our regular stock diet. They were then placed on the self-selection diet with access to the 11 different substances. For the first 50 days yeast represented all of the components of the vitamin B complex; for the next 54 days yeast was omitted and replaced by the freshly ground feces; after that the feces were removed, leaving the rats on a diet which lacked all components of the vitamin B complex. On the yeast diet two rats gained at a normal rate; two at a reduced rate. When changed to the feces diet, three rats continued to gain at approximately their previous rate, one rat lost weight temporarily and then quickly caught up with the other rats. After the removal of the feces all 4 rats lost weight at a rapid rate. Two rats died after 38 days and 48 days on the B-free diet respectively. The other two were killed after 25 and 32 days respectively. Thus, when given access to feces the rats grew quite as rapidly as on yeast, and when deprived of feces they lost weight at a very rapid rate.

Dietary Selections. Figure 2 shows a typical self-selection record for one of the rats. The chart shows the daily intake of dextrose, casein, cod-liver oil, and olive oil during the three periods when the rat had

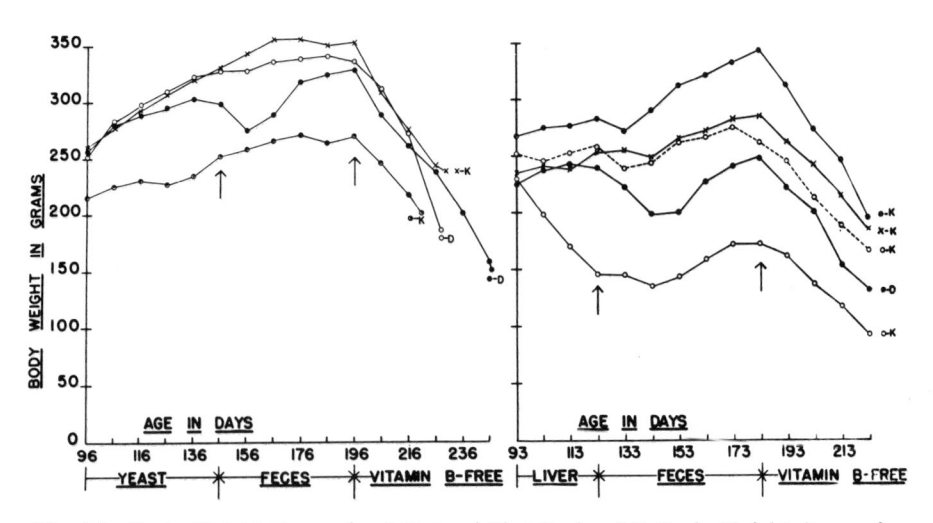

Fig. 1A. Body Weight Curves for 4 Rats of First Series. 1B. Body Weight Curves for 5 Rats of Second Series.

Self-Selection Studies in Coprophagy as a Source of Vitamin B

access to yeast, feces, and no vitamin B respectively. It also shows the body weight curve. During the 50-day period on yeast the intake of the various substances remained fairly constant, except for a gradual increase in the intake of dextrose and simultaneous decrease in oil consumption. At the end of this period the rat ate about 2 grams per day of yeast, about 5 grams of dextrose, 2 grams of casein, and almost no cod-liver oil or olive oil. When feces replaced the yeast there was almost no noticeable change in the body weight curve. The rat ate the feces at once and after a few days in slightly larger amounts than it had previously eaten the yeast. Its dextrose intake increased while the casein intake decreased slightly. The rat still took only minimal amounts of the oils. When the feces were removed, leaving no source of vitamin B, the animal began losing weight at once, stopped eating dextrose and casein, and started at first to take cod-liver oil, later olive oil in large amounts. Still later when the rat was failing generally, it also stopped taking fat.

Intake of Yeast and Feces. The first two columns in table 1 show the average daily intake of yeast and feces for the 4 rats for the last 20 days of the period on yeast and on feces. The yeast intake averaged 2.2 grams; the feces intake 4.5 grams. Thus, the rats ate about twice as much of the feces as of the yeast.

Almost at once after the feces were made available the rats ate them

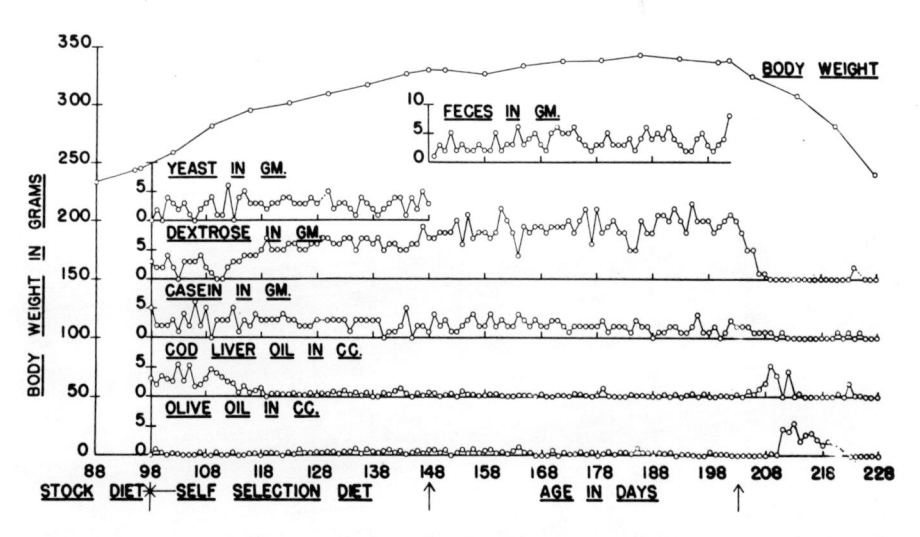

Fig. 2. Body Weight Curves and Daily Dietary Selection of Rat 3 of the First Series. This rat had access to yeast for 50 days (ages 98–148 days); then to feces for 54 days (ages 149–202 days); after that it had access to no vitamin B (ages 203–228 days).

TABLE 1. AVERAGE DAILY FOOD INTAKE FOR LAST 20 DAYS ON YEAST, LIVER, AND FECES DIET, AND FOR 11–30 DAYS ON VITAMIN B-FREE DIET

	Sources of Vitamin B Complex in Grams		Dextrose in Grams				Casein in Grams				Olive-Oil and Cod-Liver Oil in CC.			
	Yeast	Feces	Yeast diet	Feces diet	Vitamin B-free		Yeast diet	Feces diet	Vitamin B-free		Yeast diet	Feces diet	Vitamin B-free	
First series (4 rats)	2.2 (0.9–3.3)	4.5 (3.8–5.7)	6.0 (2.4–10.6)	8.0 (5.7–10.9)	0.4 (0.2–0.5)		2.7 (2.1–4.2)	2.9 (1.7–4.3)	0.2 (0.1–0.3)		1.2 (0.4–2.3)	0.7 (0.3–1.3)	2.2 (1.6–2.8)	
	Liver		Liver diet				Liver diet				Liver diet			
Second series (5 rats)	2.2 (0.1–3.1)	5.4 (3.7–7.2)	5.7 (0.6–9.5)	8.7 (7.3–9.9)	1.4 (0.5–2.0)		0.5 (0.1–0.9)	2.0 (0.1–3.4)	0.3 (0.2–0.6)		0.9 (0.2–1.6)	0.3 (0.1–0.5)	1.6 (0.6–2.4)	
	Feces	Yeast	Feces diet	Yeast diet			Feces diet	Yeast diet			Feces diet	Yeast diet		
Third series (5 rats)	3.0 (1.6–3.9)	2.4 (1.2–3.8)	6.4 (1.3–8.3)	4.4 (1.8–6.1)	1.7 (0.3–5.4)		1.4 (0.6–2.1)	1.6 (0.1–3.9)	0.2 (0.1–0.3)		0.6 (0.3–1.8)	0.8 (0.3–1.9)	1.1 (0.5–1.5)	

Self-Selection Studies in Coprophagy as a Source of Vitamin B

freely and in large amounts. They continued to eat constant and large amounts throughout the experimental periods. They seemed to accept the feces as readily or even more readily than yeast and definitely more readily than the liver powder.

From observations made on the daily output of feces of rats kept on our stock diet we were able to determine how many rats were required to supply the feces eaten daily by these rats. The feces of 28 adult rats were collected and weighted daily for 15 days. Their individual daily output averaged 1.6 grams with only minor variations from rat to rat. Thus the 4.5 gram intake of feces per rat represented the output of 2.8 rats on the stock diet.

Intake of Carbohydrate, Protein and Fat. Table 1 also gives the average daily intake of dextrose, casein, and of olive oil and cod-liver oil for the 4 rats. The average daily intake of dextrose increased from 6.0 grams for the last 20 days on the yeast diet to 8.0 grams for the last 20 days on the feces diet. From the 11th to 30th days on the vitamin B free diet (no yeast or feces) the dextrose intake dropped sharply to 0.4 gram. Casein intake remained essentially the same on the feces as on the yeast diet but decreased almost to zero during the vitamin B free period. The combined intake of olive oil and cod-liver oil decreased during the period when the rats had access to feces but increased very definitely during the vitamin B free period. All 4 rats showed essentially the same changes in appetite.

Table 2 shows that the average daily total caloric intake was 51.7 during the yeast period and 49.5 during the feces period and dropped to 20.4 after removal of the feces. The table also shows the percentage intake of carbohydrate, fat, and protein. The intake of carbohydrate increased on the feces diet from 52.8 to 64.7 per cent while the fat intake decreased sharply and the protein intake decreased only slightly. After removal of the feces the carbohydrate intake dropped from 64.7 to 7.9 per cent while the intake of fat increased from 12.7 to 88.2 per cent and the intake of protein decreased from 22.6 to 3.9 per cent.

Intake of Minerals. Table 3 gives the average daily intake record of the five mineral solutions for the rats in the three series of experiments. In the first series it was found that the rats decreased their calcium lactate intake when changed to feces, and increased it again when the feces were removed. The intake of sodium phosphate showed just the reverse changes. The intake of potassium chloride decreased on the feces diet and also when the feces were removed. The intake of magnesium chloride was very high on both yeast and feces and showed a very sharp drop after removal of the feces. The intake of sodium chloride gradually decreased.

TABLE 2

	Average Daily Total Caloric Intake-Last 20 Days of Each Period	Caloric Percentages of		
		Carbohydrate	Fat	Protein
First series (4 rats)				
Yeast period (50 days)	51.7	52.8	19.8	27.4
Feces period (54 days)	49.5	64.7	12.7	22.6
Vitamin-B-free period*	20.4	7.9	88.2	3.9
Second series (5 rats)				
Liver period (38 days)	40.8	55.2	25.2	19.6
Feces period (65 days)	45.5	76.5	5.9	17.6
Vitamin-B-free period*	20.3	27.6	66.5	5.9
Third series (5 rats)				
Feces period (40 days)	36.6	69.9	14.8	15.3
Yeast period (66 days)	38.0	56.0	17.5	26.5
Vitamin-B-free period†	15.4	44.1	51.4	4.5

* 10th to 30th days.
† 30th to 50th days.

Second Series

Body Weight. Figure 1B shows the body weight curves of the 5 rats used in the series in which the rats had access to powdered liver in place of yeast. None of the rats grew as well as on yeast. Four showed only a slight gain during the 38 day period and one showed a marked loss. During the 65 day interval in which the feces replaced the liver, the 4 rats which had previously shown a slight gain lost weight temporarily, then gained at a more rapid rate than on liver. The fifth rat stopped losing weight, maintained its weight at a flat level for about 40 days, then started to gain at an almost normal rate. When the feces were no longer offered to them, all of the rats lost weight at a constant and very rapid rate.

Intake of Liver and Feces. The second part of table 1 summarizes the results. The daily intake of liver averaged 2.2 grams and intake of feces averaged 5.4 grams which is almost 2½ times the intake of the liver. On the basis of an average output of 1.6 grams of feces per day for a rat on the stock diet, it would require 3.4 normal adult rats to supply this amount of feces. It will be noticed that one rat ate practically no liver. This is also the rat which showed the large loss in weight.

Intake of Carbohydrate, Casein and Fat. The second part of table 1

TABLE 3. AVERAGE DAILY INTAKE OF MINERAL SOLUTION IN CUBIC CENTIMETERS FOR LAST 20 DAYS ON YEAST, LIVER, FECES AND FOR 10–20 DAY PERIOD ON VITAMIN B-FREE DIET

	Calcium Lactate (2%)			Sodium Phosphate (4%)			Potassium Chloride (1%)			Magnesium Chloride (0.5%)			Sodium Chloride (3%)		
	Yeast diet	Feces diet	Vitamin B-free	Yeast diet	Feces diet	Vitamin B-free	Yeast diet	Feces diet	Vitamin B-free	Yeast diet	Feces diet	Vitamin B-free	Yeast diet	Feces diet	Vitamin B-free
First series (4 rats)	2.6	0.9	4.5	4.5	12.1	4.3	4.6	2.7	1.6	14.7	12.0	3.4	4.2	2.1	2.0
	Liver diet			Liver diet			Liver diet			Liver diet			Liver diet		
Second series (5 rats)	1.9	1.2	2.6	2.1	6.1	3.7	1.8	2.0	2.9	5.8	5.2	3.0	3.5	2.6	3.2
	Feces diet	Yeast diet		Feces diet	Yeast diet		Feces diet	Yeast diet		Feces diet	Yeast diet		Feces diet	Yeast diet	
Third series (5 rats)	1.5	2.7	3.1	4.4	5.5	9.3	1.8	2.6	4.4	6.6	3.6	3.9	3.5	3.9	4.0

gives the average daily intake of dextrose, casein, olive oil and cod-liver oil for the 5 rats for the last 20 days of each of the three periods. The changes were essentially the same as in the first series. The average daily intake of dextrose increased from 5.7 grams on liver to 8.7 grams on feces and decreased to 1.4 on the unsupplemented diet. The casein intake increased from 0.5 gram to 2.0 grams on feces and decreased to 0.3 on the vitamin B free diet. The fat intake decreased from 0.9 gram on liver to 0.3 gram on feces and increased to 1.6 grams when no vitamin B was available to the animals.

The dietary selections of the rat which consistently refused to eat the liver powder are worthy of special comment. Figure 3 shows the liver, feces, dextrose, casein, cod-liver oil and olive oil intake of this animal, also the weekly records of body weight. This rat was placed on the self-selection diet at the age of 93 days. During the following 33 days it ate no liver powder and showed the constant sharp loss in body weight typical for rats of this age on a vitamin B free diet. Progressively during the first twenty days it ate less dextrose, more fat, and no casein. After that when the animal began to fail it also ate less fat. At an age of 132 days feces were made available in place of liver powder. They were offered in the same container. On the very first day the rat ate a large amount of feces, approximately 5 grams, and continued to eat as large or even larger amounts during the following 65 day period. Of special interest is the sudden return of the appetite for dextrose that occurred on the day after feces were offered. Over a 20 day period the daily dextrose intake increased from 0 to 10 grams. The rat stopped losing

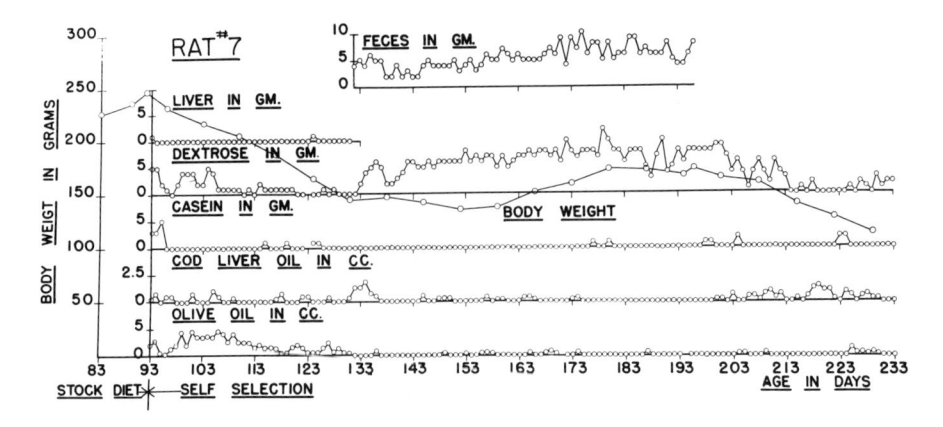

Fig. 3. Body Weight Curve and Daily Dietary Selection of Rat 7 of the Second Series. The rat had access to liver powder for 38 days; then to feces for 65 days, and thereafter to no vitamin B.

weight but did not start to make a definite gain until approximately 30 days later. After that it recovered a part of its original weight loss. After the feces were removed the dextrose intake gradually decreased again and the cod-liver oil intake increased. The failure of the rat to take casein at any time after the feces were made available was most probably due to the advanced stage of emaciation reached by the rat during the vitamin B free period while the rat did not eat liver powder.

Table 2 shows that the average daily total caloric intake increased on the feces diet from 40.8 to 45.5 and decreased to 20.3 after removal of the feces. The percentage intake of carbohydrate increased from 55.2 on the liver diet to 76.5 on the feces diet and dropped to 27.6 after removal of the feces. Fat intake showed the opposite changes. It decreased from 25.2 on the liver diet to 5.9 on the feces diet and increased to 66.5 after removal of the feces. The protein intake decreased only after removal of the feces.

Intake of Minerals. The changes in appetite for the mineral solutions were less constant than in the first series, but in general they were similar. See table 3.

Third Series

In this series the rats started on the feces diet and were later changed to the yeast diet. The results are not strictly comparable to those

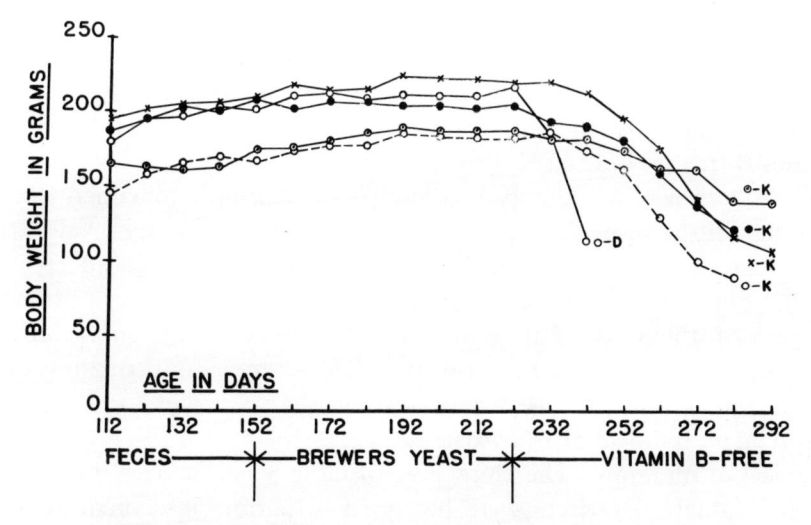

Fig. 4. Body Weight Curves of 5 Rats of the Third Series.

obtained on the 9 males of the first and second series, since the 5 rats used were females which weighed considerably less and furthermore were about 20 days older.

Body Weight. Figure 4 shows the body weight curves of these 5 rats. During the 40 days on the feces diet these rats gained at a slow but steady rate. During the 66 days on the yeast diet they continued to gain at approximately the same rate. The change from feces to yeast was not reflected in these curves. After removal of the yeast 4 of the rats began to lose weight but less rapidly than after the removal of feces in the first and second series. One rat lost weight very rapidly and died after 10 days.

Feces and Yeast Intake. The third part of table 1 summarizes the results of these experiments. The feces intake averaged 3.0 grams for the last 20 days on the feces diet, while the yeast intake for the last 20 days averaged 2.4 grams. According to our previous calculations the feces intake represents the average daily output of approximately 2 rats. It will be noticed that one animal ate only half as much of the feces as did the other four.

Intake of dextrose, casein and oils. Table 1 summarizes the results. The dextrose intake was higher on the feces than on the yeast diet but decreased only a small amount after removal of the yeast. The intake of fats remained very low throughout and failed to show the large increase present in the first and second series after removal of the feces. The average for the rat which ate the small amount of liver deviated considerably from those of the other animals. In all of the animals the changes in appetite which are characteristic for the vitamin B deficiency did not appear until after 30 days on the vitamin B free diet. This is in keeping with the observation that these animals lost weight at a less rapid rate than did the rats of the first and second series during the vitamin B free period.

Table 2 shows that the average daily caloric intake remained low in all 5 rats on the feces and yeast diets and decreased after removal of the yeast. Carbohydrate averaged 69.9 per cent on the feces diet, decreased to 56.0 per cent on the yeast diet, and decreased to 44.1 per cent after removal of the yeast. Fat intake showed the reverse changes on the feces diet and yeast diet but also increased after removal of the yeast. The protein intake increased definitely on the yeast diet and decreased sharply after removal of the yeast.

Intake of Minerals. The third part of table 3 summarizes the results. The individual differences were too great to permit any conclusions to be drawn.

Discussion

The results of these self-selection experiments on coprophagy showed that rats on a vitamin B deficient diet ate large amounts of feces freshly collected from normal rats. Measured in grams they constituted one-fourth to one-third of the entire diet. They started to eat the feces at once, definitely more readily than they ate liver powder, and quite as readily as they ate yeast powder. Particularly noteworthy was the constancy of the intake from day to day during the 40 to 50 day experimental periods.

That the rats on the feces diet grew or maintained their body weight as well as the rats on the yeast diet makes it seem very likely that the feces must contain the same growth promoting components of the vitamin B complex which are present in yeast.

The effects produced by the ingestion of feces on the carbohydrate, fat and protein appetite also indicate that the feces probably contained not only thiamine but riboflavin, niacin, pyridoxine, pantothenic acid and choline chloride. That in most instances the rats on feces had a higher carbohydrate appetite than the rats on yeast suggests that feces may contain even greater amounts than yeast of some of the vitamin B components, particularly of thiamine.

The comparison, however, of the results of the first and third series brings out a difference between yeast and feces. In the first series omission of the feces from the substances offered for choice after the rats had had access to them for 54 days was followed by a sharp decrease in body weight and death within a few weeks' time. In contrast in the third series the omission of yeast after the rats had had access to it for 66 days was followed by a slower decrease in body weight. Thus it would appear that on the yeast diet the rats were better able to store some of the vitamin B components.

It may be noted here that we do not know whether the rats ate the feces exclusively to supply the needed vitamin B. It is possible also that they ate the feces for other substances, some of them which may not even be present in yeast or liver powder. That under these conditions in which a number of other substances were available at the same time rats ate the feces at once and did not have to be starved into eating them, indicates that the feces do not contain any bitter tasting or otherwise unpleasant tasting and probably toxic substances. They differ in this respect from yeast and particularly liver powder which for some rats must have such a bitter taste that they refuse to eat them although in doing so they develop a serious vitamin B deficiency.

That the feces of rats contain vitamin B we know from the observations made by numerous workers starting with those of Osborne and Mendel who conducted the first experiments on the effects of a diet consisting in part of feces (8). Later experiments were carried out by Steenbock, Sell and Nelson (1), Dutcher and Francis (9), Heller, McElroy and Garloch (10), Smith, Cowgill and Croll (11), Roscoe (4), Guerrant and Dutcher (2), Kennedy and Palmar (12), Moore, Phymate and White (13), and others. The last named workers reported that the feces from 10 rats on a diet supplying 1 per cent yeast were found sufficient to keep the majority of 25 young rats alive for over eight months when used as the sole source of vitamin B. The use of wheat germ oil in the diet however probably invalidates their results.

The source of the vitamin B contained in the feces still remains doubtful. The results of our self-selection experiments throw no new light on this question. We do not know whether the vitamin B in the feces represented an undigested excess which passed through the intestinal tract unchanged or whether it was synthesized in the intestinal tract by bacteria. Most of the evidence at hand however favors the latter explanation.

Summary

1. Rats kept on a self-selection diet completely lacking all components of the vitamin B complex ate 3 to 5 grams per day of feces collected from normal adult rats. The daily output of feces from 2 to 4 normal adult rats supplied all of the needed vitamin B components for one rat on an otherwise B deficient diet.

2. Feces-fed animals continued to grow at normal rates and showed no signs of specific deficiency. Their appetites for carbohydrate, fat and protein were essentially the same as they had been when given access to yeast or liver powder.

3. When no longer given access to feces the rats at once lost weight at a rapid rate. They showed the changes in appetite which are characteristic of vitamin B deficiency, namely, a substitution of fat for most of the carbohydrate and protein previously taken.

4. Thus it is concluded that for at least 40 to 50 days feces satisfactorily replaced all the components of the vitamin B complex found in yeast or liver powder.

5. That the rats ate the feces at once and in large amounts and over

long periods of time without any ill effects would indicate that the feces did not contain any bitter tasting or toxic substances.

References

(1) Steenbock, H., M. T. Sell and E. M. Nelson. J. Biol. Chem. 55: 399, 1923.
(2) Guerrant, N. B. and R. A. Dutcher. J. Biol. Chem. 98: 225, 1932.
(3) Richter, C. P. Harvey Lectures Series xxxviii, 63, 1942–1943.
(4) Roscoe, M. H. Biochem. J. 25: 2056, 1931.
(5) Guerrant, N. B. and R. A. Dutcher. Proc. Soc. Exper. Biol. and Med. 31: 796, 1933–1934.
(6) Richter, C. P., L. E. Holt, Jr. and B. Barelare, Jr. Am. J. Physiol. 122: 734, 1938.
(7) Richter, C. P. and C. D. Hawkes. Am. J. Physiol. 131: 639, 1941.
(8) Osborne, T. B. and L. B. Mendel. Carnegie Inst. of Washington, no. 156, 61, 1911.
(9) Dutcher, R. A. and E. Francis. Proc. Soc. Exper. Biol. and Med. 21: 189, 1923–1924.
(10) Heller, V. G., C. H. McElroy and B. Garlock. J. Biol. Chem. 65: 255, 1925.
(11) Smith, A. H., G. R. Cowgill and H. M. Croll. J. Biol. Chem. 66: 15, 1925.
(12) Kennedy, C. and L. S. Palmer. J. Biol. Chem. 76: 607, 1928.
(13) Moore, C. U., H. B. Phymate and V. White. Am. J. Physiol. 102: 593, 1932.

Part III   NEUROLOGY

DECEREBRATE RIGIDITY OF THE SLOTH.[1]

Sherrington has shown that in quadrupeds like the cat, dog, guinea-pig and monkey, transection of the brain-stem near the level of the anterior colliculi produces a marked rigidity of all the muscles which normally assist the animal in maintaining its standing posture against the pull of gravity. These are chiefly the extensor muscles of the limbs and spine, the retractor muscles of the head and tail, and the elevator muscles of the jaw. An animal that has been decerebrated in this way stands without support when it is placed on its feet, and because of the dependence of this posture on proprioceptive impulses Sherrington termed it "reflex standing."

Our knowledge regarding this interesting phenomenon is limited almost entirely to observations made on quadrupeds which normally stand upright on all four feet. It occurred to one of us while studying the behaviour of the sloth, that this animal, because it has just the opposite posture and normally hangs rather than stands, would offer an

---

This paper was originally published in *Brain*, Vol. 49, 1926. The authors were Curt P. Richter and Leo Henry Bartemeier. Reprinted by permission.

[1] The experimental part of this work was done by Dr. Richter, with the aid and suggestions of Dr. George B. Wislocki, in Panama at the Institute for Research in Tropical America. Dr. Richter wishes to express his indebtedness to the Institute for the assistance and facilities offered for carrying on this and other work during the summer months of 1924 and 1925. Thanks are due especially to Mr. James Zetek, custodian of the laboratory, and to Dr. Ignanzio Molino, assistant custodian, for their tireless efforts in helping to procure the necessary materials and animals. The histological work was done in the Neurological Laboratory of the Phipps Clinic by Dr. Bartemeier. The work both in Panama and in Baltimore was greatly aided by the interest and encouragement of Dr. Adolf Meyer.

excellent opportunity for establishing the general applicability of our present knowledge regarding decerebrate rigidity. Would decerebration in the sloth produce extensor rigidity as in the cat and dog, or flexor rigidity in keeping with its normal hanging posture? Would not the decerebrate sloth show "reflex hanging" rather than "reflex standing"? The results of our work answer these questions quite definitely, and at the same time suggest what posture one might expect in decerebrate man.

The Normal Behaviour and Posture of the Sloth

Since the sloth is very little known either through first-hand contact or the literature, we wish to give a short account of its normal behaviour and posture before presenting the results of our experiments. It is a strictly arboreal animal, living in the tropical rain forests of Central and South America. For most of its life it hangs back downward from the branches of trees, and its behaviour in this posture is characterized by marked inactivity, occasionally interrupted by slow and deliberate movements.

It is well equipped for this inverted hanging position with large

Fig. 1A. Two-toed Sloth Hanging from Lattice. This photograph shows it in an active posture, in contrast to the resting or sleeping posture in the next figure.

Decerebrate Rigidity of the Sloth 247

Fig. 1B. Two-toed Sloth in Sleeping Posture. The head is tucked in between the forelimbs, but is still just visible at the left end in the photograph. The hair was shaved from the right fore-limb. The bands around the fore-arm and the attached wires were used in some electromyographic experiments.

strong claws from 6 to 10 centimetres long on all four legs. The action of these claws is entirely dependent on neuro-muscular activity, not on any mechanical arrangement of the tendons or ligaments which would enable the animal to hang with no expenditure of energy. This is demonstrated most clearly by the fact that the claws of the dead sloth are flaccid and toneless, quite unable to support the weight of the body.

In describing the details of the normal posture of this animal it is necessary to deal separately with the two common species, both of which were used in the following experiments. There is the *Choloepus didactylus,* Linn., species (see fig. 1A), commonly called two-toed sloth from the number of claws on the fore-feet, and the three-toed *Bradypus griseus griseus* species (see fig. 2).

Both species have two normal postures, one assumed when resting or

Fig. 1C. Two-toed Sloth. Same as 1B.

sleeping, the other when in motion or on the alert preparatory to moving. In the resting or sleeping postures of the two-toed sloth (see figs. 1B and 1C) the limbs and trunk are flexed, the head and tail are flexed ventrally. In this posture the head is almost completely con-

Fig. 1D. Two-toed Sloth in the Prone Position on a Paved Surface, Unable to Lift Its Weight from the Ground.

Fig. 2. Active Hanging Posture of Three-toed Sloth.

cealed between the limbs, so that it becomes difficult to determine its location in the photograph. In the resting posture the animal appears as a large hairy ball. Its moving posture (see fig. 1A) is somewhat different. The hind-limbs, although still flexed, are less so than in the resting posture, and the fore-limbs are almost fully extended. The claws, of course, are very markedly flexed. The head remains nearly in line with the axis of the body.

The helplessness of the animal on the ground is demonstrated in Fig. 1D. It has become so highly specialized for its arboreal existence that when it does leave the trees on rare occasions it is scarcely able to raise its body from the ground and literally has to drag itself along.

The three-toed sloth normally exhibits resting and active postures which are very similar to those of the other species. In addition, however, it assumes a second resting posture when it sits at the top of a tree, clinging to the trunk (see fig. 3). We have described this attitude as "holding" rather than as "hanging," although the same muscles, the flexors, are involved in both. The hind-limbs, elevated at the thigh, spread apart, rotated outward, and flexed at the knee, form a plane nearly perpendicular to the longitudinal axis of the body. The depression of the head and the right-angle flexion of the elbow-joint further contribute to the general equilibrium, but the animal merely holds on to the tree with the claws of the fore-limbs, whereas it literally embraces the trunk with the hind-limbs. These are essential for the maintenance of the holding posture and anatomically well adapted to it, since they are short and stocky, and so strong that the animal searching for food can completely release the fore-limbs and lean backwards. The entire body is supported in this awkward position by the hindlimbs and the abdominal muscles.

Fig. 3. *Three-toed Sloth in its Resting or Sleeping Posture, Holding on to the Trunk of a Tree. It will be noticed that most of the work of holding is done by the hind-limbs which are elevated before the body. (Photographs by James Zetek.)*

Methods

In decerebrating the sloths the technique used by Bazett and Penfield on cats was followed. In the sloth, however the complete operation could be performed by one man alone. After the animals were anesthetized a mid-line incision was made in the skin of the neck and the common carotids exposed. A loop of silk thread passed carefully around each vessel was permitted to hang freely from the incision. Just before the transection of the brain-stem was performed, a small weight, a mosquito hæmostat or a similar object, was attached to the end of each loop and allowed to hang freely so that the flow of blood to the brain was temporarily stopped. Then the skull was trephined; an area of the brain about three-quarters of an inch in diameter was exposed just over the occipital region, and the plane was located through which the transection was to be made. During the operation the head was held in a horizontal position in the left hand, with the tips of the forefinger and thumb compressing the vertebral arteries between the wings of the atlas. The transection was effected by a single quick thrust through the hemispheres and brain-stem with a sharp scalpel. The severed part of the brain was immediately scooped out with the handle of the scalpel and the resulting cavity filled with cotton wool. The pressure on the vertebral arteries was then gradually released and the weights attached to the loops around the carotids were removed. Because the slight bleeding in the animals stopped just as readily when no effort was made to prevent the flow of blood to the brain, the precautions for occluding the arteries were gradually disregarded. This greatly simplified the procedure, making unnecessary the incision in the skin of the neck and the search for the carotids. The entire operation was performed in two to three minutes, most of the time being consumed by trephining the skull. Chloroform was used as an anæsthetic in three of the animals; ether, in the other thirteen, since ether was found to be far more satisfactory. Contrary to current conceptions, it was found that the sloths became deeply anæsthetized very quickly, often in less than a minute.

Sixteen animals were decerebrated, three two-toed and thirteen three-toed sloths. The plane of transection varied between the lower level of the locus coeruleus (see fig. 4A), in the upper hind-brain and the retroflex bundle of Meynert (fig. 4), in the anterior end of the mid-brain. We were fairly successful in our efforts to transect the brain-stem of each successive sloth at a slightly higher level. A normal and decerebrate brain of each of the two species is photographed in fig. 5.

From the work on other animals, especially cats, it is known that the success of keeping decerebrate preparations alive and in good condition

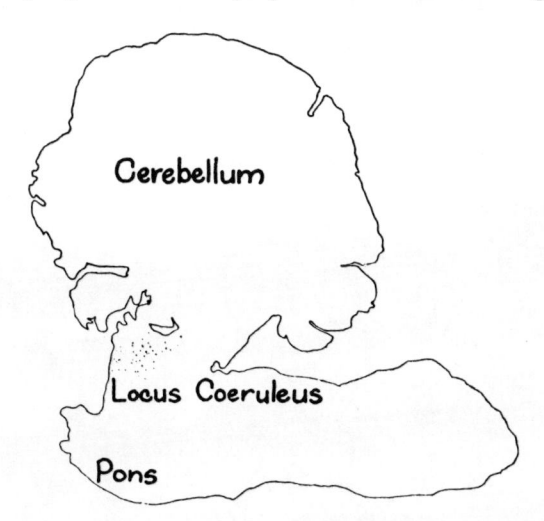

Fig. 4A. Ink Tracing of Sagittal Section, Showing One of the Brain-stems with the Lowest Transection. The section shows the cerebellum and indicates the position of the lower portion of the locus coeruleus; it is well below the red nuclei.

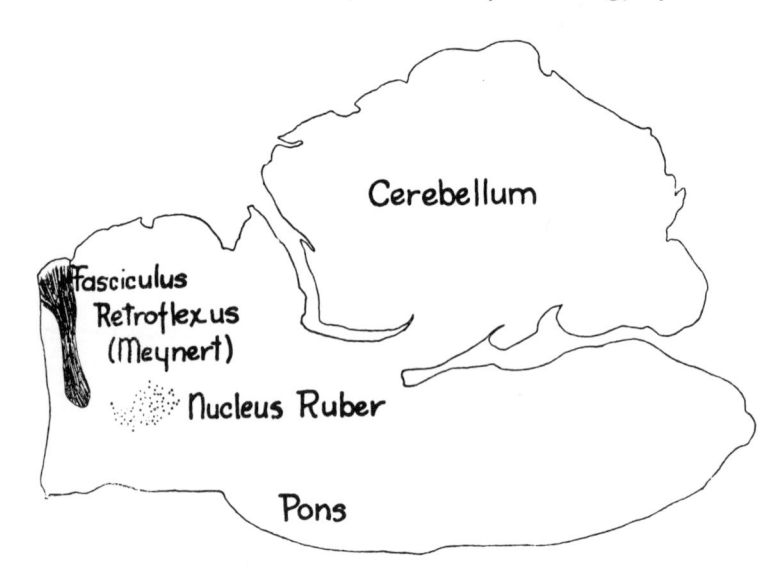

Fig. 4B. Ink Tracing Made from Section, Showing Level of Highest Cut Made in Any of the Sixteen Animals. The red nucleus and retroflex bundle of Meynert are indicated.

depends very largely on how well the body temperature is maintained at or near the normal level. Since one of the most important characteristics of a decerebrate animal is its loss of temperature control, it is necessary to provide artificial heat regulation for decerebrate specimens. This is done either by heating the surrounding medium to the normal temperature, as was done by Bazett and Penfield (1), or, less

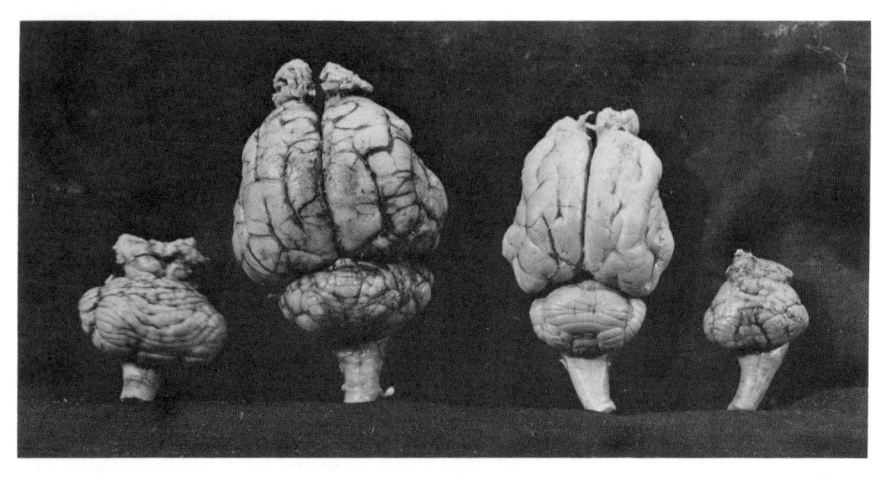

Fig. 5. Photograph of an Intact Brain of a Two-toed and of a Three-toed Sloth; also a Brain-stem of a Decerebrate Individual of Each Species.

elaborately, by using an electric pad or hot-water bottle and blankets. In Panama, where our sloths were decerebrated, the temperature of the air averaged about 85°F.; the normal body temperature of the animal is 85–91°F. The temperature of the air, then, served to maintain the body temperature of the sloths very near the normal level and greatly simplified the post-operative precautions. The excessive humidity of the tropics also aided in keeping the decerebrate animals in good condition.

Results

In the sloth decerebration produces flexor rigidity of the limbs and trunk, and "reflex hanging" instead of extensor rigidity and "reflex standing" as in the decerebrate cat (see figs. 6, 7, 8, 9).

The intensity of the flexor rigidity and the ability of the animals to hang reflexly varied with the levels at which the brain-stem was transected, but especially with the position of the transection in relation to the red nuclei.

The five animals in which the red nuclei were entirely removed showed a very close reproduction of the sloth's normal resting or sleeping posture. Fig. 6 gives two views of one of the three-toed sloths in this group. The hind-limbs were held before the body, flexed at the knee and hip just as they are normally when encircling the trunk of a tree; the fore-limbs were flexed at the elbow and resisted forward movements at the shoulders; the trunk tended to become curled up and

Fig. 6. Two Views of a Decerebrate Three-toed Sloth (Brain Transection below Red Nuclei) Showing Flexion of Limbs, Depression of Head, Marked Flexion of Trunk. This posture is an almost perfect reproduction of the normal resting posture.

Fig. 7. Photograph Showing Posture of Three-toed Sloth in Which the Brain Stem was Transected above the Red Nuclei.

offered strong resistance to efforts to straighten it; the head and the short stubby tail were flexed ventrally; the claws also showed flexor rigidity. When the claws were hooked over a rod held horizontally, or when the limbs were placed around the trunk of a small tree, the animal hung for several minutes without falling. The fore-limbs were invariably the first to let go, while the hind-limbs still maintained a fairly good grip. Thus it was shown that the animals without the red nuclei exhibited strong flexor rigidity of the extremities and trunk, closely reproducing normal resting or sleeping posture, but because of the poor tonus of the claws they were not able to maintain their normal hanging posture very long before they fell.

The eleven sloths with the transection either through or above the red nuclei showed less rigidity, especially of the fore-limbs and trunk, but a much more marked rigidity of the claws, so that they were able to hang much more steadily and longer than the animals in the first group. One of the three-toed sloths with the high transection is seen lying on its back in fig. 7. The fore-arms are flexed at the elbows; the hind-limbs are flexed at the knee and show strong resistance to being spread apart, but are not drawn up before the body as they are in the other sloths; the head is bent neither forward nor backward, but tends to remain in line with the axis of the body. When hanging, these animals very closely

Fig. 8. Reflex Hanging Posture of Three-toed Sloth Decerebrated above Red Nuclei.

reproduced the sloth's normal active posture. (See the photograph of the decerebrated three- and two-toed sloths in figs. 8 and 9.) The fore-limbs are almost fully extended, although before the animals were placed in the hanging position they were flexed; the hind-limbs are flexed, but not so much as in the resting posture; the head is held in good position. Even when hanging by only two limbs, as in fig. 10, the animals were able to maintain their hanging posture very well. Thus it was demonstrated that these animals with the higher transection show less rigidity of the limbs and trunks but more of the claws, so that they are much better able to maintain their normal hanging posture.

One animal remained hanging for over thirty hours after the operation. After that time the grip of its fore-limbs gave way, while that of the claws of the hind-limbs was still as strong as before.

These results demonstrate that to a large extent the rigidity of the limbs and trunk is distinct from the rigidity of the claws upon which "reflex hanging" depends. The animals in which the red nuclei were removed showed strong rigidity of the limbs and trunks, but were scarcely able to hang, while those in which the nuclei were left intact showed much less marked rigidity of the limbs and trunk but were able to hang very well for long periods of time without showing any fatigue.

This observation is essentially in agreement with the results of Magnus and Rademaker (2, 3), in their experiments on the red nuclei and their relation to postural tone. They found that cats decerebrated below the red nuclei show a marked rigidity of the limbs and trunk. In

Fig. 9. Reflex Hanging Posture of Two Decerebrated Two-toed Sloths. The level of transection was above the red nuclei in both. The animal at the right remained hanging for over thirty hours after the operation. The hair was clipped from the limbs to show their posture.

this respect they are like the sloths with similar transection. Magnus and Rademaker showed, however, that the standing posture of the decerebrated cats is only a caricature of the standing posture of a normal animal, because of the exaggerated tone in the extensors and the almost complete absence of tonus in the flexors. From some of our own observations made on thirty cats we have concluded that much of the discussion regarding the exaggerated nature of the standing posture of decerebrated cats is overdrawn. It is true that when these animals are examined lying on their sides they show a very strong extensor rigidity of the limbs, but when they are placed in the standing position they can maintain it for a few minutes only. The same was true of the sloths without the red nuclei; in spite of the marked rigidity of their limbs they were able to hang but a few minutes.

It seems likely that the failure to distinguish between rigidity of the limbs and ability to stand may explain some of the differences in experimental results obtained by different workers.

Furthermore, Magnus and Rademaker found that animals in which the red nuclei were left intact showed less rigidity but a normal

Fig. 10. Two-toed Sloth Decerebrated above the Red Nuclei. It is shown hanging from two legs.

distribution of tone and a normal standing posture. The sloths with the transection above the red nuclei also showed less rigidity but were able to hang much longer than the animals of the other group.

Reproduction of normal posture in the decerebrate sloth is shown further by the order in which the different parts of the total posture appear and disappear after operation. It was pointed out above that in the normal individual the hind-limbs play the most important role, since by them alone the animal is able to maintain its position. It is an interesting fact, then, that in the decerebrate sloth the hind-limbs are the first to become flexed and rigid and the last to lose their rigidity. They usually show good flexor tonus almost immediately after the brain-stem is transected. The flexion of the claws of the hind-feet appears about the same time. Whether the knee or hip becomes rigid first we were not able to determine. Usually soon after decerebration the hind-limbs, showing right-angle flexion, are held as if fastened around a tree, and offer resistance to spreading. Flexor tone of the claws on the fore-limbs, relatively less essential for the normal animal to preserve its equilibrium, appears next. Then the elbows show rigidity. We were unable to discover when the tonic contractions of the trunk muscles appeared.

Thus it is shown that the most important effects of decerebration appear in the different parts of the animal in the order of their importance for the maintenance of the normal posture. It is of interest to recall here that the decerebrate cat, which normally uses its fore-

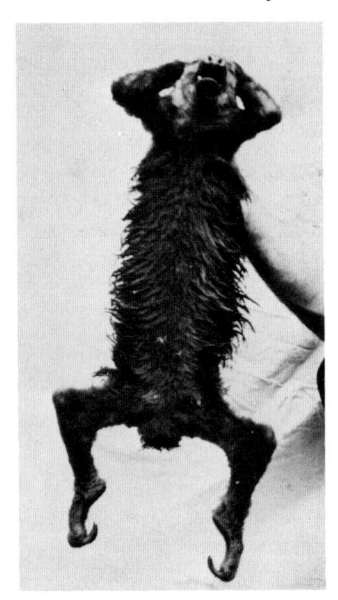

Fig. 11. Photograph of Two-toed Sloth, Showing Well-directed Response of Forelimbs to Slight Touch on Incision at Back of Head. This animal often actually succeeded in tearing the sutures and in pulling out cotton swabs from the incision.

limbs most in preserving its erect posture, shows extensor rigidity in the fore-legs earlier and to a greater degree than in the hind-legs.

Further light is thrown on the relation between the characteristic attitude of the normal and decerebrate sloths by postural differences existing between the two species and concerning chiefly the hind-limbs. In the three-toed sloth, as has been pointed out, the hind-limbs may be held up before the body with the thigh elevated and the leg abducted and rotated outward. In the two-toed sloth the hind-limbs, which are much longer than those of the three-toed species, are used more distinctly for hanging than for holding, so that they show neither spreading nor rotation. This difference is present likewise in the decerebrate animals.

The flexor rigidity of the sloths exhibits, in common with extensor rigidity, inhibition due to phasic reflexes. Almost any tactual stimulation around the head will cause the flexor tonus of the fore-limbs to disappear in favour of an extending and clasping movement, often directed with marked accuracy to the point of stimulation (see fig. 11), or as though it were attempting to catch the offending object in its arms.

It may be pointed out in this connection that a study of the phasic reflexes and their resulting effect on the flexor rigidity disclosed, quite by chance, the fact that these animals react also to at least one acoustic stimulus. We had previously made repeated vain attempts to elicit responses by using all kinds of instruments for producing noises. On one occasion, however, when a normal baby sloth was examined in the presence of a decerebrate adult sloth, it was found that every time the baby squealed the adult raised its body off the table and turned its head slowly from side to side. This observation was repeated many times always with the same result. It was a noteworthy fact that a response could be obtained by this one acoustic stimulus and no other.

Although phasic reflexes affect the fore-limbs very readily, it is an interesting fact, in keeping with the account given above regarding the importance of the hind-limbs in the posture of the animal, that these reflexes have very little, if any, effect on the hind-limbs. Were their flexor tone to become inhibited and the hind-limbs relaxed under normal conditions, the animals would fall to the ground.

The lengthening and shortening responses characteristic of extensor rigidity are present with some modifications in flexor rigidity. This may be demonstrated by an examination of the rigidity of the fore-limb. We start with the limb in a fully flexed position and extend it slowly. The extension movement meets with almost no resistance until the fore-arm reaches a position in which it is nearly perpendicular to the upper arm. Then suddenly, as though a string from the shoulder to the wrist had become taut, marked rigidity appears; and from then on the usual lengthening response is present. This result seems to be partly in disagreement with the recent findings of Liddell and Sherrington (2) on the so-called myotatic or muscle-stretch reflexes; they have shown that even the slightest pull on an extensor muscle of a decerebrate cat is sufficient to produce a reflex contraction of the muscle, and they explain the phenomenon as follows. The stretching of the muscle stimulates sensory endings within itself, which set up impulses that are carried from this muscle to the cord and then back again to the muscle. In the sloth, however, as has just been shown the fully flexed fore-arm can be extended until the upper and lower parts are nearly at right angles to each other before the rigidity begins. This means that during this time the biceps muscle is being subjected to a considerable amount of stretching without eliciting the reflex contractions which would be expected on the basis of Liddell's and Sherrington's work. It is not clear at present how these results can be explained. We may consider in this connection the fact that the right-angle position of the fore-arm and upper-arm occurs most frequently in the normal animal and affords the greatest mechanical efficiency.

Discussion

These experiments clearly establish the general applicability of the conclusions regarding decerebrate rigidity arrived at by Sherrington. He has shown that decerebrate rigidity is a postural reflex involving the muscles used by the animal in maintaining its normal posture against the pull of gravity. The decerebrate sloth, just as one would expect on the basis of Sherrington's conclusions, shows "reflex hanging" with flexor rigidity of the limbs, trunk, and especially the claws. To explain this phenomenon, however, simply by saying that the muscles showing rigidity are anti-gravity muscles, gives only a part of the picture. It does not explain how they are affected. The limitations of this interpretation come out much more clearly in the sloth with its general state of flexion than in animals with extended limbs and body. It is true that in the decerebrate sloth the anti-gravity muscles, the flexors, are involved, but this does not explain why the fore-limbs, for instance, happen to be flexed almost exactly to a right angle. One might have expected to see them fully flexed, just as the limbs of a cat are fully extended. It does not explain why the hind-limbs of a decerebrate sloth without the red nuclei are also held in a position of semi-flexion, with the thighs elevated at the hip until they are nearly at right angles to the axis of the body, rotated outward and spread, with the right angle flexion at the knee-joint. An understanding of the origin of these special postures is obtained when we learn that they reproduce in almost every detail the animal's habitual posture. Sherrington somewhat indirectly has also called attention to this point. We should like to emphasize further its significance.

On the basis of our present knowledge regarding decerebrate rigidity, derived on the one hand from animals which use their extremities for standing, and on the other from those which use them for hanging or for holding, it seems possible to foretell what kind of posture would be produced by a similar operation in man. His normal posture has, in common with that of standing animals, the extensor rigidity of the legs used in supporting the body, and with that of hanging animals, the flexor rigidity of the arms and hands used in lifting, holding, and carrying activities. Then, following the principle of the close reproduction of habitual posture by decerebrates, it seems reasonably certain that in man this operation would produce extensor rigidity of the legs, and flexor rigidity of the arms and hands.

This conclusion is of some importance for the study of conditions of decerebrate rigidity produced in man by lesions at different locations.

Kinnier Wilson (7) described a number of cases which he believed showed the same features present in decerebrate rigidity produced experimentally in animals. For him this meant chiefly extensor rigidity of all extremities, as it is found in the decerebrate cat or dog.

Walshe (5, 6) thinks that Wilson's cases, with possibly one or two exceptions, do not show true decerebrate rigidity, but that they are instances of generalized muscular spasms such as are seen in tetanus and strychnine tonic fits and similar conditions.

In Walshe's opinion, true experimental decerebrate rigidity must show, besides Magnus-de Kleijn reflexes, reflex inhibition due to phasic reflexes, shortening and lengthening responses, extensor rigidity of the legs, and *flexor* (not extensor) rigidity of the arms and hands.

We were so fortunate as to be able to see a case of hemiplegia through the kindness of Dr. Frank R. Ford, of the Neurological Department, affecting chiefly the upper-arm, examined by Walshe during his stay at the Johns Hopkins Hospital in 1925. It was a paralysis of long standing and was described by him as showing all of the physiological features of typical experimental decerebrate rigidity. Our examination showed the presence of marked flexor rigidity of the forearm and the lengthening and shortening reaction, Magnus-de Kleijn reflexes, and the reflex inhibition due to phasic reflexes. But what from our point of view was especially interesting was that this patient showed the 90-degree flexion of the elbow-joint and the grasping reflex. An examination of the arm showed that, just as in the sloth, the rigidity began suddenly when the lower arm was nearly at right angles to the upper arm. Voluntary movement of the fingers was almost entirely lost, but reflex grasping was present just as it is in the new-born infant and in the decerebrate sloth. A rod placed in the hand of the patient caused the fingers to contract around it so firmly that strong effort was required to detach it again.

These experiments definitely explain the appearance of flexor instead of extensor rigidity in the arms of man, showing true decerebrate rigidity, and clearly bear out Walshe's conclusions arrived at from a somewhat different angle.

This principle of habitual posture may throw some light on the differences in the position of the fore-limbs obtained by Sherrington and Riddoch in their work on monkeys. In some animals the fore-limbs were extended and in some way they were flexed. It would be important to know whether the kind of monkeys used in their experiments normally employed their fore-limbs as props for supporting the body weight, or for holding and gripping. The *Rhesus* monkeys use their fore-limbs as props, while monkeys of some other species—for instance, the spider monkey, which we have had under observation for several months—do most of their walking with their hind-limbs and restrict the use of their fore-limbs to gripping and manipulating. It may be pointed out here that it is possible also that the differences in the habits of the individuals of each species may show up after decerebration.

Summary

(1) The decerebrate sloth shows flexor rigidity of the limbs, claws and trunk, and reflex hanging in keeping with its normal posture. This is to be expected on the basis of the principle arrived at by Sherrington in his work on quadrupeds with an upright standing posture.

(2) The posture of the decerebrate sloth varies with the level of transection. When the red nuclei are removed the posture closely reproduces the animal's resting posture. In these animals the rigidity is marked in the trunk and limbs, but is not so strong in the claws. For this reason they are not able to hang very well. When the cut is made above the red nuclei, the rigidity of the limbs and trunk is less marked, but the ability to hang is much greater. The hanging posture closely corresponds to the animal's normal active posture. The agreement of this work with that of Magnus and Rademaker is pointed out.

(3) Similarities in the physiological characteristics of flexor and extensor rigidity are discussed. They show in common the lengthening and shortening responses, reflex inhibition from phasic reflexes and lack of fatigue.

(4) The dissimilarities have to do chiefly with spastic quality. For a certain range of movement the limbs do not exhibit any rigidity. In the fore-limbs the rigidity does not manifest itself until the lower part of the limb is nearly at right angles to the upper part; then it appears very suddenly and in full strength. This is discussed at length and is referred to as the right-angle flexor phenomenon.

(5) It is pointed out that the posture of the decerebrate sloth cannot be completely explained by stating that the anti-gravity muscles were involved. It is necessary to refer also to the habitual posture of the animal.

(6) On the basis of this principle it is shown what posture might be produced by a similar operation in man. Since in normal man the legs are extended in supporting the body, and the arms and hands flexed in

lifting and holding, decerebate man would probably show extension of the legs and flexion of the arms and fingers.

An example is given of a case of hemiplegia which showed all of the criteria of true experimental decerebrate rigidity, Magnus-de Kleijn reflexes, lengthening and shortening responses, and reflex inhibition due to phasic reflexes. In addition, it showed extensor rigidity of the legs and flexor rigidity of the arms, thus confirming Walshe's conclusions arrived at from a somewhat different angle.

Bibliography

[1] Bazett, H. C., and Penfield, W. G. A Study of the Sherrington Decerebrate Animal in the Chronic as well as the Acute Condition, *Brain*, 1922, 45:185.
[2] Liddell, E. G. T., and Sherrington, C. S. Reflexes in Response to Stretch (Myotatic Reflexes), *Proc. Roy. Soc.*, B, 1924, 96:212.
[3] Magnus, R., and Rademaker, G. G. J. Die Bedeutung des Roten Kernes für die Körperstellung, *Schweiz, Arch. f. Neurol. u. Psychiat.*, 1923, 13:408.
[4] Rademaker, G. G. J. Der Rote Kern, die Normale Tonusverteilung und die Stellfunktion, *Klin. Wochenschr.*, 1923, 2:404.
[5] Walshe, F. M. R. The Decerebrate Rigidity of Sherrington in Man, *Arch Neurol. and Psychiat.*, 1923, 10:1.
[6] *Idem.* A Case of Complete Decerebrate Rigidity in Man, *Lancet*, 1923, 2:644.
[7] Wilson, S. A. K. On Decerebrate Rigidity in Man and the Occurrence of Tonic Fits, *Brain*, 1920, 43:220.

THE PRODUCTION OF THE "GRASP REFLEX" IN ADULT MACAQUES BY EXPERIMENTAL FRONTAL LOBE LESIONS

The grasping reflex described as the result of rather discrete injuries to the frontal lobe is gradually being proved of fundamental phylogenetic and ontogenetic importance. The first scientific study of the grasping response in the human newborn was made by Robinson in 1891. He found that the human infant would reflexly grasp any object placed in the palm of its hand. This response was strong enough to permit the infant to hang from a horizontal bar entirely unsupported as long as two minutes. Robinson considered this reflex similar to the clinging activity of the newborn monkey, who holds on to the undersurface of its mother's body while she swings from limb to limb. Reflex grasping is present in the human infant for the first few months of life, and disappears gradually, during the time when voluntary grasping is developing. Later, although the reflex may not be strong enough to support the infant's weight, difficulty in releasing at will small objects held in the hand can be observed. As a phenomenon, reflex grasping has been noted in the young of all the primates so far studied. Just how characteristic this is of them as a whole, is not known. And of late, studies of cortical injury have described the return of this infantile reflex, as associated with lesions of the premotor area of the cerebral cortex. This fundamental phenomenon of reflex grasping offers the experimental neurologist a new field for exploring primate relationships as well as an opportunity of elucidating the underlying neural mecha-

---

This paper was originally published in *Proceedings of the Association for Research in Nervous and Mental Disease,* Vol XIII, 1932. The authors were Curt P. Richter, Ph.D. and Marion Hines, Ph.D. Reprinted by permission.

nisms, with the hope that such an elucidation will better the understanding of its appearance in cerebral lesions in adult man.

In 1909 Janischewsky described a return of this infantile grasping in outspoken Parkinsonism, and five years later (1914) he found it as a symptom of tumor in the left frontal lobe. An analogous phenomenon was observed by Bechterew as the "Beugereflex der Hand." Since then, similar observations have been made by many clinicians including Schuster and his co-workers, Adie and Critchley, Lhermitte, Freeman and Crosby. Attempts to use the reflex in the localization of brain tumors have been somewhat frustrated by the discrepancies in observations. Nevertheless, some believe that the presence of the reflex indicates a lesion in the frontal lobes or in its underlying tissue. There are, of course, others who think forced grasping is a phenomenon associated with lesions in the thalamus (Kleist) or with such generalized conditions as hydrocephalus (Janischewsky). Or it may appear with lesions of the subcortical ganglia and in post-encephalic Parkinsonism. It is, however, more or less agreed that whatever the site of the lesion, it is located somewhere in the prosencephalon on the side opposite the hand showing the reflex.

Our knowledge of the cortical and subcortical mechanisms involved in this phenomenon is still very limited, in spite of the careful study of many clinical cases. An adequate understanding of the relations of Brodmann's area 6 has not been given, either by the detailed descriptions of change of reflexes following removal of tumors, the presence of which had resulted in the grasping and groping phenomena (Adie and Critchley), or by the anatomical studies of Schuster and Casper, who observed a diminution of nerve fibers in the occipito-frontal bundle subsequent to lesions in the premotor area.

Brodmann (1912) divided the frontal lobe of primates into two parts, a posterior area, the regio precentralis, which contained the motor cortex (area 4) and Campbell's premotor (area 6); and an anterior area, the regio frontalis. The former, the regio precentralis is characterized by the possession of an agranular cortex, and the latter, the regio frontalis by a granular cortex. The regio frontalis of man has been called the prefrontal cortex by Feuchtwanger and by Goldstein, and this term was used in the discussion of this region by Hines. As a name, prefrontal cortex carries a significance not found in Brodmann's regio frontalis, because the adjective frontal has been associated with the noun lobe, for many years. In his regio frontalis Brodmann (1909) identified in monkeys areas which he considered homologous to 8, 9, 10, 11 and 12 of man. The areas 4, 6, 8 and 9 are not only found upon the lateral surface of the frontal lobe, but in a manner similar to the arrangement in man, they pass over the crest of the cortex to lie upon the medial surface as far ventrally as the sulcus cingulus.

Although Brodmann did not make a detailed study of the frontal lobe of this species, similar areas have been identified in this macaque by one of us (Hines) and in particular the upper part of Brodmann's area 6 (Campbell's premotor) has been delimited, and used as a guide in the operations.

This particular research was begun in the hope that it would be possible to delimit a region, which by its ablation in the brain of the macaque (*Pithecus rhesus*) would give a result similar to the grasping phenomenon in man.

Methods

All operations were performed under ether anesthesia, preceded and followed by injections of morphine and atropine. The skull was trephined and the bone removed with rongeurs. The dura mater was reflected with care, sparing the underlying blood vessels. The anterior boundary of the motor area was delimited by unipolar faradic stimulation. The ablation was made with slender sharp knives after the larger blood vessels supplying the region to be removed were ligated by silk thread. In closing, the dura mater was sutured in place. The periosteum, the subcutaneous fascia, the subcutaneous connective tissue and the skin were separately sutured with interrupted stitches. After the operation (Department of Anatomy), the monkey was taken to the Phipps Psychiatric Clinic. The following morning it was examined to determine the length of time it would hold on to a bar with either hand. The technique of measuring the duration of the time interval which a monkey would support its weight by its grasp upon a bar has been described by one of us (Richter, 1931). Some forty-one operations were performed upon seventeen macaques (*Pithecus rhesus*). With the exception of two animals (hand area of motor cortex, and bilateral area 17 of occipital lobe) this study was confined to the exploration of the frontal lobe anterior to the motor cortex.

Results

The results of these ablations of various parts of the frontal lobe can be divided into two groups: first, those which did not bring out the hanging response in either hand; and second, those which did. As far as the elicitation of the hanging response is concerned the ablation of regions other than the frontal lobe fall into the former class.

I. Lesions Which Did Not Elicit the Hanging Response

a. Of the Frontal Lobe. When the group of four macaques (E, JI, K, and C), each of which had suffered well circumscribed superficial lesions of parts of the frontal lobe, anterior to the motor cortex (before June, 1930) were first examined for the presence of the grasp reflex in November of 1930 none of them showed any variation from the normal as defined by previous experiments on unoperated animals. In three of these animals, the two subsequent operations on each never involved the medial surface of the cortex opposite the lateral part of area 6. That is, all ablations except one (JI, April 23, 1931) were confined either to removal of more cortical surface of the frontal region anterior to the motor cortex, or to a slight increase in depth of removal of the white matter underlying the lateral distribution of area 6. The depth of such operations precludes the passage of collateral fibers through the deeper cortical layers so that no long association fibers could have reached the motor cortex from the more anterior part of the frontal lobe via area 6.

The other group of operations which also gave no results was performed upon the frontal lobe. No hanging reflex was found in JII after the ablation of all of the left frontal lobe except area 6 and area 4 (June 24, 1932) nor after an exactly similar removal on the right (July 28, 1932). The bilateral presence of area 6 was capable of preventing the appearance of the grasp reflex in either hand. This type of result was also found in no. 19 (February 24, 1932) in which area 6 of one side was separated from area 6 of the other by cutting the corpus callosum.

The most difficult of explanation are the unilateral ablations of the total frontal lobe anterior to the motor cortex. There were two of these; one, which following a previous extensive removal of the lateral surface of the left frontal cortex had shown a transient heterolateral hanging reflex, after ablation of the remainder of this same frontal lobe minus area 4, demonstrated a hanging response, which was even of less intensity and of shorter duration than that found after the first operation. The other one was a removal of the same amount of tissue at one operation (February 10, 1932). This animal (no. 16) did not show even a transient hanging until after the second operation, when the prefrontal and premotor areas were removed on the left, together with a small piece of the tip of the caudate nucleus.

b. *Lesions of Other Parts of the Brain Which Failed to Bring Out Any Grasping Phenomena.* These two types of lesions, removal of the total arm area (no. 9) and bilateral ablation of the occipital lobe including the total area striata (no. 20) failed to change the negative response which these monkeys showed toward the horizontal bar, before operation. The first lesion resulted in the paresis typical of removal of the motor cortex in monkeys. In the removal of the total area striata, no portion of either the thalamus nor the basal ganglia was taken out, so that the resulting changes were confined entirely to optic phenomena, and gave negative results as far as hanging was concerned.

II. Lesions Which Did Bring Out the Hanging Response

The unilateral removal (nos. 1, 5 and 14) which always elicited the unequivocal hanging response in the opposite hand was that of area 6 through to, and including, the medial surface as far ventrally as the corpus callosum. Such ablations removed the gyrus cingulus ventral to area 6 and left in the thin strip of tissue belonging to the ventral portion of area 6 anterior to the lower arm and face area of the motor cortex. Such lesions did not produce permanent results. However, when this operation was performed after the corpus callosum (no. 19) had been cut the hanging time was short in seconds and endured only a few days.

On the other hand, certain unilateral lesions always result in bilateral increase of hanging time. These ablations have certain combinations of removal in common. When the cortex of area 8, immediately anterior to area 6 (no. 3, E and JI) and that of area 6 are removed, the time of hanging is markedly increased in the hand opposite the lesion and only slightly in the homolateral hand. To obtain this result from the combination of areas 8 and 6, it is not necessary to perform the operation simultaneously; nor is this result modified by an inclusion also of either the superficial cortex from the contiguous leg region or of the cortex about the sulcus rectus. If the cortex is superficially removed from the lateral surface of the entire area 6 (F) including that part which lies anterior to the leg, arm and face regions of the motor cortex, the results are reversed, the longest hanging time is found in the homolateral hand and the shortest, in the heterolateral. Both hands were found to show an equal hanging time in no. 18 in which area 6 was isolated from the surrounding cortical areas and the corpus callosum cut, so that the only connections remaining for this region were those it makes subcortically.

The Production of the Grasp Reflex in Adult Macaques 269

Among the bilateral ablations, there was only one type which gave what could be considered permanent results. This occurred when area 6 was removed through to, and including the medial surface bilaterally (no. 14) or when this operation was preceded by the removal of the more dorsal parts of the opposite areas 6 and 8 together with the cortex about the sulcus rectus (no. 3). Although the reflex in both these macaques had been lost in the right hand subsequently to the removal of area 6 on the left it was brought out again in both hands stronger, however, in the left which was opposite the second removal (right area 6). In both these animals the reflex persisted in both hands throughout the remaining length of life (no. 3, 162 days, and no. 14, 155 days).

In the removal of the left prefrontal and premotor areas from no. 16 the very tip of the head of the caudate nucleus was nipped. There was no interruption of the pyramidal tracts because movement could be produced by electrical stimulation of the motor cortex on that side after the operation. This ablation (March 9, 1932) produced a marked increase in hanging time in both hands although the previous removal of the right frontal lobe, without area 4, gave no results at all. In this animal, however, the longest hanging time in seconds and the duration of the reflex were greatest in the hand homolateral to the second ablation. At present writing this operation has not been repeated.

The only bilateral extirpation, which did not affect both hands, was that produced at a second operation (F, April 22, 1931), when the superficial cortex of area 6 anterior to the arm and face regions of area 4, together with the lateral surface of area 6, anterior to the leg region of the motor cortex, through to and including the medial surface, down to the corpus callosum were removed on the right. The reflex was present in the heterolateral hand for a short time only. A third operation which produced on the left a condition of cortical loss similar to that on the right (F, April 22, 1931) did not cause a reappearance of the reflex.

In one animal the prefrontal and premotor areas were completely removed on the left (C, March 30, 1932) after the lateral surface of area 6 and the cortex of area 9, anterior to 8, had been removed on the right almost two years previously (May 16, 1930). Hanging from the bar appeared in both hands, stronger on the left (homolateral to new lesion) than on the right. The reflex disappeared from the heterolateral hand within nine days and persisted in the homolateral until she was killed (August 4, 1932).

The further operations upon nos. 18 and 19 present interesting results. After the removal of area 6 through to and including the medial surface on the right, the heterolateral hand gave the longest hanging time in seconds and the reflex appeared in the homolateral also. But unlike the double operation in no. 14, the reflex again disappeared. A similar result was found after the fourth operation on no. 18, when the actual removals of brain tissue in the two animals were equivalent. Moreover the result of removal of area 6 (from lateral to medial surfaces) in no. 18 on the left was similar to that of area 6 and area 8, in that the hanging response was bilateral with the greatest length of time in seconds to be found in the homolateral hand. It must be remembered that also upon the right, area 6 had been isolated from the surrounding cortex. The result of this was hanging by both hands for the same length of time in seconds and only one day difference in days, a finding similar to the first operation on the left, as reported.

In summarizing then, the lesion which results in the hanging response on the part of the heterolateral hand is the removal of area 6, anterior to the leg region, of the motor cortex, through to and including the medial surface. The removal of the comparable area in the opposite hemisphere brings out the reflex in the heterolateral hand as well as in the homolateral. Such bilateral lesions have produced a continuance of the reflex for as long as six months, a result not found when both the frontal lobes, anterior to the motor cortex are removed. The relative permanence of the reflex is destroyed, however, by adding to the bilateral removal of upper area 6, the cutting of the corpus callosum, although cutting the corpus callosum alone produced no results. Again, unilateral removal of upper area 6 plus cutting the corpus callosum gave as transient and unimpressive results as unilateral removal of the frontal lobe anterior to the motor cortex. As far as the hanging response is concerned, either unilateral or bilateral removal of area 6 and cutting the corpus callosum is equivalent to unilateral and bilateral removal of the frontal lobe anterior to the motor cortex.

Unilateral removal of the superficial cortex of upper area 6, either medial or lateral surface together with superficial removal of area 8 or 9 results in bilateral hanging, with the longest time in seconds on the heterolateral hand.

Isolation of area 6 plus the cutting of the corpus callosum produced hanging equally from both hands (no. 18), whether the lesion was unilateral or whether it had become bilateral (in the first case a contrast to the results obtained at the first operation upon no. 19). Subsequent removal of each of these isolated areas gave hanging longer in the heterolateral hand than in the homolateral. The results of increased hanging time after the first ablation vanished to return after the second, to vanish again.

Discussion

The production of reflex hanging in monkeys by removal of the total dorsal part of the premotor cortex is similar to the classic reports of the lesion necessary to produce the grasping and groping phenomena in man. An homologous area is injured and the pathological reflex appears in the opposite hand. But unlike the condition in man, cutting the corpus callosum modifies both the appearance and the duration of the reflex in macaques. Further, dissimilar to the findings in man (Adie and Critchley, 1927; Schuster and Casper, 1930) simultaneous removal of this area and the motor cortex in monkeys (Fulton, Jacobsen and Kennard, 1932) does not prevent the appearance of forced grasping. The implication of this finding is not at variance with the data presented. For, if the presence of two intact motor cortices does not prevent the subsequent disappearance of reflex hanging, initially produced by bilateral ablation of the frontal lobe anterior to the motor cortex, then that cortex alone, uninhibited by the action of the regions anterior to it, cannot maintain the grasping phenomenon as demonstrated in these animals.

In certain of the operative combinations described, reflex hanging appeared bilaterally after unilateral lesions, in others, after bilateral (second operation on the opposite side) lesions. The lesions of the first group are of three varieties; (1) area 6 plus some other part of the frontal lobe, generally the medial surface anterior to area 6, either 8 or 9 or both; (2) total lateral surface of area 6; (3) complete isolation of area 6 from surrounding cortex. The bilateral lesions are of two varieties, removal of the frontal lobe anterior to the motor cortex and isolation or removal of upper area 6 with or without cutting the corpus callosum.

Since the inclusion of the upper part of area 6 in the more extensive operations did not result simply in the development of a heterolateral grasping phenomenon, the appearance and duration of the hanging reflex in the macaque are not a direct function of the loss of the upper part of area 6, as such. Apparently then, the results of loss of upper area 6 are modified by the inclusion in the operation of other areas of the frontal lobe. It is these results which confuse the picture and contribute to the complexity of any interpretation which attempts to collect them into a whole working hypothesis.

At the present state of this work, the grasping activity could be explained, similar to the clinical reports of loss of regions homologous to upper area 6 in man, as the removal of an inhibition upon the motor cortex—an inhibition however which is modified by subsequent or simultaneous removal of other parts of the same frontal lobe. This modification creates the necessity of viewing the development of the reflex in question as an inhibition-loss which is the end-product of an imbalance within the frontal lobe. This imbalance is not developed when one prefrontal and premotor area is simultaneously removed or when one upper area 6 is ablated together with a previous cutting of the corpus callosum. Under these conditions the intact opposite frontal lobe is sufficient. The two lesions in question have only two elements in common, loss of upper area 6 and the interruption of the adjoining callosal fibers. The inclusion in the operation of the callosal fibers appears to have prevented the imbalance produced by the removal of upper area 6, alone. The removal of this imbalance by the ablation of one frontal lobe (anterior to the motor cortex) may allow the uninjured member of the opposite side to inhibit the appearance of the reflex in either hand through the homolateral cortico-spinal tract or through some unknown extra-pyramidal system. To be sure, it is not impossible that the control of the opposite motor cortex might be effected via the callosal fibers which lie adjacent to the two paracentral lobules.

The bilateral appearance of the grasping phenomenon after unilateral ablations, which include other parts of the frontal lobe than upper area 6, may be explained by the emergence of a bilateral imbalance. Such a bilateral imbalance could be conceived as produced by the loss (1) of inhibitory fibers passing from area 6 to the motor cortex of the same side and (2) of similar fibers crossing from lower area 6 or from areas 8 or 9 to the opposite motor cortex through the corpus callosum. There is nothing in this particular group of experiments which suggests that the hanging reflex operates through any other tract than the cortico-spinal.

If, however, the cortico-spinal tract were the only efferent system used by this reflex, the removal of upper area 6 plus the cutting of the corpus callosum should give results similar to the complete isolation of the premotor cortex. The former as already noted is attended by a most transient hanging reflex in the heterolateral hand only and the latter by an appreciable grasping equal in both hands for a week's duration. Such a difference suggests that the neurones which remain in the isolated cortex have the ability to create a bilateral imbalance which releases the reflex. This interpretation is rather convincing; for a similar result appeared when the opposite premotor cortex was similarly isolated, but did not reappear later when each isolated area was in turn subsequently removed. After each of these two ablations the heterolateral reflex became pari passu the prominent one. Of course, it is not impossible that the neurones remaining in the isolated area 6 reached the motor cortex of both sides. Nevertheless, it is highly improbable, for the cut of isolation was similar to that which precedes ablation. On the other hand these results suggest the release of the inhibition of this interesting reflex in some region other than the motor cortex.

The imbalance necessary for the production of a permanent grasp reflex is not created by removal of all of both frontal lobes anterior to the motor cortex. After the ablation of the second lobe the hanging reflex appears bilaterally; strongest in the homolateral hand. The latter part of this result was found following two other operative combinations. When the total lateral surface of area 6 (F) was removed, or when the remainder of the premotor and prefrontal areas was removed (C had lost opposite cortex from lateral surface of area 6, plus the medial surface of areas 8 and 9), the hanging reflex appeared bilaterally, strongest on the homolateral hand. Although these three operations produced a comparable result (the strongest grasp in the homolateral hand) the neural mechanisms involved are not comparable. For that reason more operative combinations (now in progress) are necessary to converge the routes taken by the reflex in question. In the first procedure, the second ablation of the frontal lobe (anterior to the motor cortex) included the tip of the caudate nucleus but did not touch the pyramidal tract, because immediately after the removal the motor cortex was sensitive to unipolar faradic stimulation. If the removal of the tip of the caudate nucleus produced the prominent homolateral hanging reflex, the inhibition of the reflex works through some other center than the motor cortex. Anyway, whatever this removal was capable of producing for the time being, later the reflex disappeared in both hands, although it lasted for one month in the homolateral one. In the second, the inclusion of lower area 6 anterior to the arm and hand region may have removed the inhibition of the reflex bilaterally either by removal of the region from which cruciate fibers originate and thus produce an imbalance within the opposite motor cortex or fibers may pass through the deeper layers of this area destined for some subcortical region which aids in the inhibition of the reflex. That the former is the more plausible interpretation is supported by the fact that subsequent ablation of the total opposite area 6 (lateral through to medial surface in dorsal part) resulted only in heterolateral hanging which was not permanent.

The third instance of homolateral hanging is most satisfactorily explained by the release of an imbalance within the opposite frontal lobe dependent upon the old lesion, by the new removal of the total prefrontal and premotor areas. And here, this pathological reflex endured until the animal was killed four months later.

Apparently in man large ablations of the frontal lobe sparing the motor cortex do not produce the grasp reflex. Certainly large lesions of the frontal lobes are described without taking cognizance of that reflex (see Feuchtwanger's monograph, 1923). And in Goldstein's excellent review (1927) this phenomenon is not discussed under results of lesions of the frontal lobe nor in those of the corpus callosum is its name mentioned. Here, however, the patient is described as being unable to open the closed hand; the hand continues to hold against opposition, generally until another innervation follows. Apparently, in man also the lesion must be somewhat discrete, producing here also an imbalance, such that the grasping reflex is not inhibited when the gyrus frontalis superior, the gyrus fornicatus (gyrus cingulus), as well as the entire medial surface of the frontal lobe are injured (Schuster and Casper, 1930). Schuster and Casper's study of brains of individuals, who in life were characterized by the pathological reflex under consideration, showed that fibers from the gyri listed above traveled via the occipitofrontal bundle and the corpus callosum to both motor cortices. Their cases always showed the reflex in the hand opposite the lesion, so that the bilateral influence of one frontal lobe as considered to be generally true for other types of lesions within this region of the human brain (Goldstein, 1927) has not been recognized for the grasping phenomenon. On the other hand Schuster and Casper believe that a bilateral lesion can produce an unequivocal unilateral Zwangsgreifen.

Certainly, in monkeys neither cutting the corpus callosum adjacent to the medial surface of area 6 nor bilateral removal of the prefrontal cortex produces the reflex. Only bilateral removal of the dorsal part of area 6 from the lateral surface through to and including its medial surface and the gyrus cingulus will produce in this beast enduring (six months) bilateral reflex hanging. And apparently unlike the clinical studies concerning the homologous area in man the second operation producing a bilateral removal of upper area 6 results in a bilateral reflex, stronger on the opposite hand. And again lesions of the medial surface anterior to area 6 (8 and 9) in the macaque contribute a factor to the total picture of the reflex, but of themselves alone, unlike man, are not able to produce the phenomenon.

Whether or not the premotor area in the intact macaque prevents the appearance of the reflex by an inhibition which works through the motor cortex cannot be gainsaid. Indeed, as a reflex, grasping will appear in the macaque when the motor cortex and upper area 6 are simultaneously removed (Fulton, Jacobsen and Kennard) and will disappear subsequent to its appearance following the bilateral ablation of the premotor and prefrontal cortices. The inhibition of this reflex under these conditions is either taken over by something else or the motor cortex becomes adjusted to its balanced loss. Consequently, at the present writing there is no proof that for the maintenance of the grasping reflex in the macaque an inhibition of the motor cortex only must be removed. Rather, an imbalance within the frontal lobe anterior to the motor cortex must be maintained by the bilateral ablation of upper area 6. But the exact motor pathway or pathways through which this imbalance works, cannot as yet be delimited.

Summary

The grasp reflex, as measured by the length of time an adult *Pithecus rhesus* will hang by its hand from a horizontal bar, is not produced either by cutting the corpus callosum adjacent to the medial surface of area 6 or by bilateral removal of the prefrontal cortex. Only bilateral removal of the dorsal part of area 6 from the lateral surface through to and including its medial surface together with the gyrus cingulus just ventral to the cortical area in question will produce in this beast enduring (six months) bilateral reflex hanging. And unlike the clinical studies concerning the homologous region in man, the grasp reflex produced by unilateral removal of the cortical tissue just described vanishes after a few days to return in both hands following the second operation removing a comparable region in the opposite frontal lobe, stronger in this instance in the hand opposite the second lesion. And again lesions of the medial surface anterior to area 6 (8 and 9) in this macaque contribute a factor to the total picture of the reflex; but ablation of the medial surface of areas 8 and 9, unlike man, are not able to produce the grasping phenomenon.

Reflex hanging will disappear subsequent to its appearance following the bilateral ablation of the premotor and prefrontal cortices. Under these circumstances the inhibition of this reflex is either taken over by some other nerve center or the motor cortex becomes adjusted to its balanced loss. At the present writing there is no proof that for the maintenance of the grasping reflex in the macaque an inhibition of the motor cortex only must be removed. Rather, an imbalance within the frontal lobe anterior to the motor cortex must be maintained by the bilateral ablation of upper area 6. The exact pathway through which this imbalance inhibits the grasping phenomenon has not as yet been delimited.

Bibliography

Adie, W. J., and Critchley, M. 1927. *Brain*, 1, 142.
Bechterew, W. V. 1916. (Quoted by Janischewsky.)
Brodmann, K. 1909. Vergleichende Lokalisationslehre der Grosshirnrinde Leipzig.
_____. 1912. *Verhandl. d. anat. Gesellsch. München.*
Freeman, W., and Crosby, P. T. 1929. *J. A. M. A.*, xciii, 7.
Feuchtwanger, E. 1923. Die Functionen des Stirnhirns. Berlin.
Goldstein, K. 1927. Handbuch der normalen und pathologischen Physiologie, x, 842.
Fulton, J. F., Jacobsen, C. F., and Kennard, M. A. 1932. *Brain*, lv, 524.
Fulton, J. F., and Keller, A. D. 1932. The sign of Babinski. A study of the evolution of cortical dominance in primates. Baltimore.
Hines, M. 1929. *Physiol. Rev.*, ix, 462.
Janischewsky, A. 1928 *Deutsche Ztschr. f. Nervenh.*, cii, 177.
Kleist, K. 1927. *Monatschr. f. Psychiat. u. Neurol.*, lxv, 317.
Lhermitte, J. 1929. *L'Encephale*, xxiv, 87.
Mayer, C. 1923. *Ztschr. f. d. ges. Neurol. u. Psychiat.*, lxxxiv, 464.
Richter, C. P. 1931. *Arch. Neurol. & Psychiat.*, xxvi, 784.
Richter, C. P., and Paterson, A. S. 1932. *Brain*, lv, 3, 391.
Robinson, L. 1891. *Nineteenth Cent.*, xxx, 831.
Schuster, P. 1923. *Ztschr. f. d. ges. Neurol. u. Psychiat.*, lxxxiii, 586.
Schuster, P. 1927. *Ztschr. f. d. ges. Neurol. u. Psychiat.*, cviii, 715.
Schuster, P., and Casper, J. 1930. *Ztschr. f. d. ges. Neurol. u. Psychiat.*, cxxix, 739.
Schuster, P., and Pineas, H. 1926. *Deutsche Ztschr. f. Nervenh*, xci, 16.

THE SIGNIFICANCE OF CHANGES IN THE ELECTRICAL RESISTANCE OF THE BODY DURING SLEEP

Our knowledge regarding the changes which take place in the body during sleep is still very limited. Like most other things common to our daily life, sleep has always, except on a few occasions, enjoyed almost complete immunity from experimental investigation, and at the same time it has been the topic of an almost endless number of theories and speculations. Some experiments on blood pressure, pulse rate, and respiration and a few measurements of the intensity of sleep have been made. Of these the experiments on the intensity of sleep were most interesting and promising. The first investigations along this line were undertaken in 1863 by Kohlschütter (1), a student of Fechner; and since then a few other investigators, Monninghoff and Piesbergen (2), Michelson (3), Howell (4), have either repeated or slightly extended the original experiments. Depth of sleep was measured in terms of the intensity of acoustic stimulus necessary to awaken the subjects. The stimuli were repeated at short intervals and in progressively increasing intensities. The results of these experiments showed that the intensity or depth of sleep increases very quickly, reaches a maximum before the end of the second hour, and then decreases again equally rapidly to a low level at which it remains, with small fluctuations, until the end of the sleep period. This result is obviously not in agreement with general experience. It is a fact of common observation that there are the widest individual differences in the depth of sleep at different times after the onset. Some individuals sleep just as soundly and are awakened with as

---

This paper was originally published in the *Proc. of the National Academy of Sciences,* Vol. 12, 1928. Reprinted by permission.

great difficulty after eight as after two hours' sleep; some awaken easily at any time. A part of the fallacy of this experimental work must probably have been due to the fact that the subjects were constantly under a strain waiting to be awakened, and the sleep accordingly was never normal. It may be said that any experiments on the depth of sleep which require the awakening of the subject are very liable to similar errors and misinterpretation.

In the present work a different approach to this problem will be described, one which does not involve the interruption of sleep and all of the resulting complications. At the same time it will be shown how the quality of sleep, an aspect hitherto neglected, may also be measured and studied experimentally.

Our observation made several years ago that the electrical resistance offered by the body to a galvanic current is markedly increased during sleep (in one individual from 30,000 to 500,000 ohms), was the point of departure for the following experiments. Waller (5) had made a similar observation many years before. He found, while taking resistance records of the diurnal variation of the electrical resistance of his own body, that the resistance was very much higher in the morning just after waking than it was the night before. More recently Pieper (6) in Germany working on infants, and Chambers and Farmer (7) in England working on students, found a marked increase in resistance during sleep.

Our records were obtained by measuring the resistance offered to the passage of an imperceptible constant galvanic current usually from one hand to the other. Electrodes were especially devised for this purpose (8). They were made of solid pieces of zinc covered with a thick paste made by mixing kaolin with saturated zinc sulphate solution. These electrodes have the advantage that they are non-polarizable, that they make intimate contact with the skin without injuring or irritating it, and that they can be easily attached and removed, usually without interrupting sleep. The resistance was measured with a string galvanometer.

As a basis for an understanding of the results of our sleep experiments, it is necessary first to present the results of several experiments which show what factors are involved in the electrical resistance of the body. By means of a fairly simple experiment we were able to demonstrate conclusively that the resistance is localized almost entirely in the skin. It was found that a puncture through the skin with a hypodermic needle, even of the finest bore, reduces the resistance instantaneously from any level however high, practically to zero, as may be seen in the graph in figure 1. In this experiment the electrodes were attached to the

Changes in the Electrical Resistance of the Body During Sleep 279

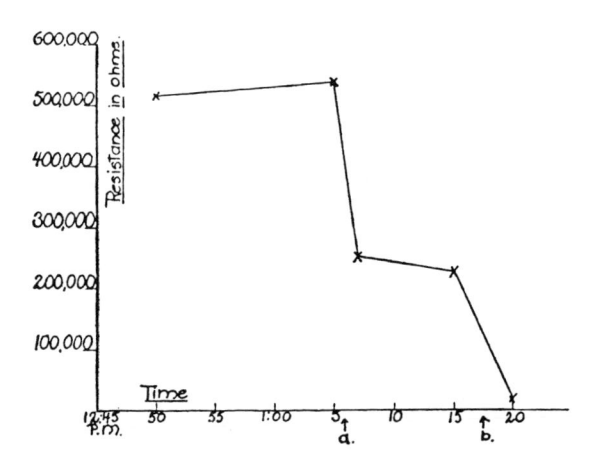

Figure 1

back of each hand and the resistance offered to the passage of a current from one hand to the other was measured before and after the punctures were made. At the beginning the resistance was 540,000 ohms. A hole through the skin of the left hand, indicated at "*a,*" caused a drop to 250,000 ohms, a hole in the right hand, indicated at "*b,*" a drop to 15,000 ohms. This result was confirmed by numerous other observations.

With this fact definitely established, that the electrical resistance is localized in the skin, it became important to determine whether the porous area of the palm of the hand and the relatively non-porous area of the back of the hand contribute equally to the resistance. Other experiments showed that the resistances of these two parts of the skin are very different and respond differently to various physiological stimuli. These determinations were made by taking simultaneous readings of the resistance offered to the passage of a current from the palm of one hand to the palm of the other, and from the back of one hand to the back of the other. In the present connection it is sufficient to point out a few of the differences. Subcutaneous injections of atropin (1/100 to 1/50 grains) at a point distant from the electrodes, increase very markedly the resistance of the palms. The results are recorded in figure 2. Here resistance in ohms is given on the ordinates, and the time of day in hours on the abscissae. Several readings were made between 11 A.M. and 1 P.M., before the atropin was injected. During this time the palm–palm resistance averaged about 20,000 ohms; the back–back resistance was gradually decreasing. After the injection the former increased steadily up to 460,000 ohms, while the latter continued to decrease at about the same rate as before, giving no evidence whatso-

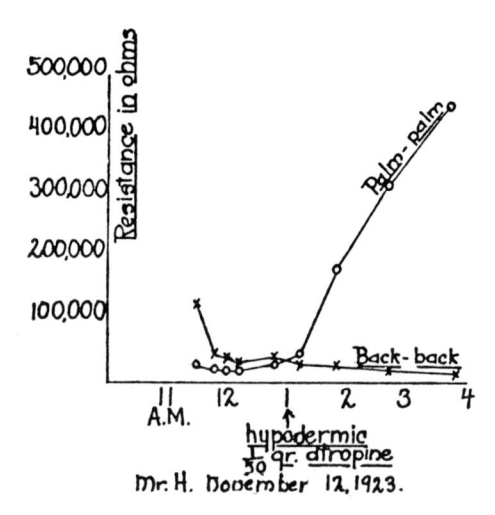

Figure 2

ever of having been affected by the atropin. A similar result was obtained in a number of other individuals. Because of the well known paralytic action of atropin on the nerves of the sweat glands, the inference appears likely that the increase in resistance on the palmar surfaces, where we know that sudoriparous glands are extremely abundant, is due to the effect of atropin on these glands. However, we are forced to conclude further that the effect of the drug on the sweat glands of the back of the hand must be masked in some as yet unanalyzable way. The action on the back of the hand may eventually be explained by the determining role of structural arrangements other than sweat glands and different from those of the palmar surface.

A very similar result was obtained in monkeys by actually cutting the nerves to the hands and feet. In three monkeys the sciatic and anterior crural were sectioned. This operation was followed by an enormous increase in the palm–palm resistance, without any change whatsoever in the back–back resistance, as may be seen in the record of one of the animals in figure 3. The resistance is given in ohms on the ordinates; the duration of the experiment is given in days on the abscissae. In this graph the resistances of the skin of the sole and back of the two feet are given separately. It will be seen that for the two days before the operation, the resistance of all four areas was nearly the same. Then immediately following the section of the sciatic and anterior crural of the left leg, the resistance of the sole of the foot increased within three days to 990,000 ohms, and still retained approximately this high level of resistance after a month. These with the atropin experiments, demonstrate conclusively that the resistance of the palmar surface of

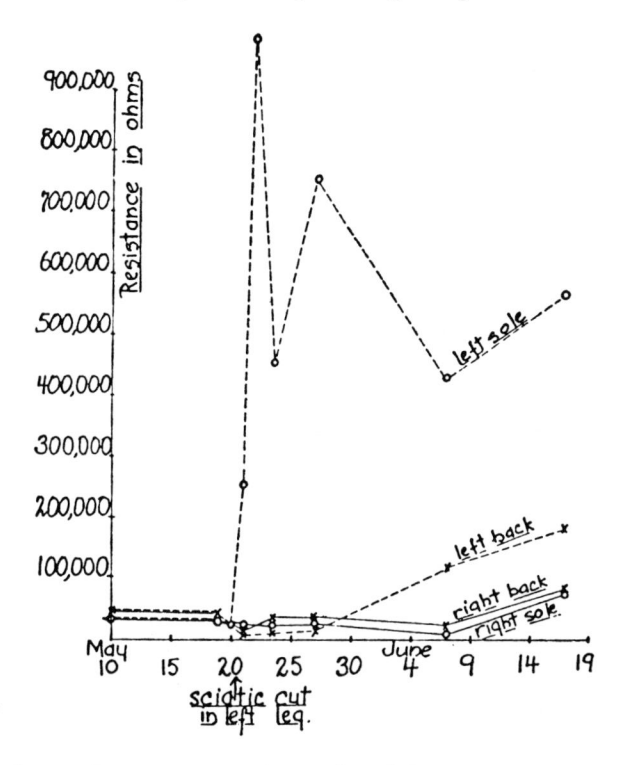

Changes in the Electrical Resistance of the Body During Sleep

Figure 3

the hand and foot is dependent upon and regulated by nervous impulses, while that of the dorsal surface is not dependent on nervous impulses. Although we do not know definitely just how the resistance of the nonporous areas is regulated, we have a considerable amount of evidence which suggests that it is dependent on the changes in the epithelial cells of the skin in agreement with the results of Ebbecke's interesting experiments (9). Ebbecke showed that the skin, with its many cells, responds to stimulation with an increase in permeability, very much the same as the semi-permeable membrane of a single cell. Thermal, galvanic, mechanical and chemical stimuli bring about local changes in resistance.

Previous workers, attaching one electrode over a porous and the other over a non-porous area of skin, or dipping the entire hand in salt solution, failed to make the distinction in the physiological function of the palm and back which has been brought out in the present work.

In the sleep experiments also, the first point to be established was that the backs and palms of the hands are affected very differently so far as changes in resistance are concerned, as is demonstrated in the graph in figure 4. Here the resistance is given on the ordinates in ohms, and the duration of the experiment in hours on the abscissae. There are

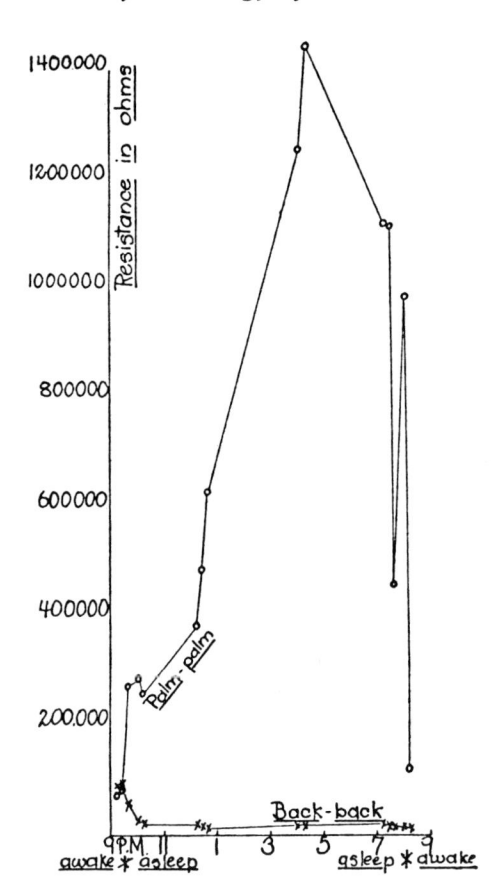

Figure 4

two curves, one for the palm–palm, the other for the back–back resistance. The former shows a very marked increase during sleep, from 70,000 ohms to 1,450,000 ohms; the latter shows a slight decrease. In the sixteen individuals on whom sleep records have thus far been taken, we have found in all cases without exception the palm–palm record increased, usually quite markedly, while the back–back resistance increased in some, decreased in others. How do these changes in resistance correlate with other conditions present in the subjects?

It was found that the changes in the resistance of the palms follow closely the depth or intensity of sleep. As soon as the individual drops off to sleep, the resistance begins to increase slowly in some, very rapidly in others. Those in whom it reaches a high level, as for instance, the patient whose record is shown in figure 4, sleep very heavily and can be aroused only with great difficulty. This patient did not show the least response to loud noises around the laboratory and seemed completely oblivious to having the electrodes attached and removed. In

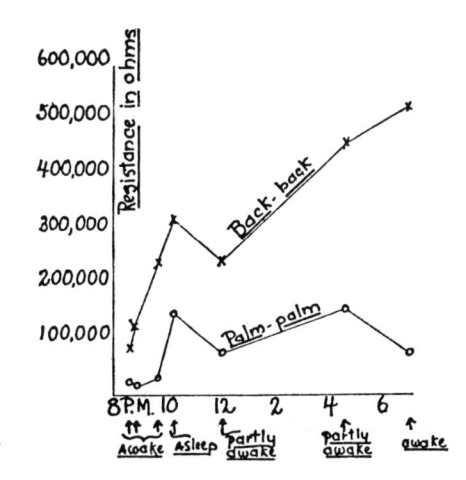

Figure 5

contrast to these individuals are those in whom the increase in palm–palm resistance is not so great. In the patient in figure 5, for example, the sleep is light, as is shown by the fact that he responded to even slight noises and tactual stimuli with changes in respiration, sighs, changing of position in bed, etc. It may be mentioned here that in most of these experiments the subjects were under continuous observation throughout the night so that all responses and activity could be noted.

This close correspondence between the depth of sleep and the resistance is shown further very clearly by the records of the following experiments. It was found that awakening, however suddenly brought about, is followed instantly by a drop of the resistance from any level to the waking level. This can be seen in the graph in figure 4. At 8 A.M. the patient was deeply asleep, and his resistance was 980,000 ohms. Five minutes later he was awakened as suddenly as possible, and his resistance decreased to 120,000 ohms.

Several similar observations were made on a monkey which, while held in the lap of an assistant in a darkened room, slept fitfully. The resistance followed the change in sleep so closely that it was possible to state quite accurately, without seeing the animal at all, whether it was awake, drowsing or asleep, simply on the basis of the resistance readings.

This, then, offers a new method of measuring the depth of sleep and has the marked advantage that its successful use does not require the interruption of sleep. Because the individual variations are too great we are not able to give an average normal curve for the intensity of sleep. This can be done only with a much larger group of individuals and under standard conditions. The curve of the intensity of sleep is not nearly so uniform or simple as the results of the experiments of Kohlschütter and the later workers would lead one to believe.

It is a fact of considerable importance that sleep has the same effect on palm–palm resistance as paralysis or complete section of the nerves in this part of the skin. It is not known at present, however, whether in sleep we deal also with an interruption of the nervous impulses, or with the effect of an inhibitory process.

A very different aspect of sleep was illuminated by the investigation of the changes of resistance in the non-porous skin of the back of the hand. It was pointed out above that physiologically this skin differs very much from the porous skin of the palms and also that during sleep it responds differently, showing an increase in some individuals, a decrease in others. What is the origin of these contrary results? It was found that the individuals with an increase in back–back resistance during the night were able to relax more or less completely during sleep, and were refreshed in the morning. That those with a decrease were often obviously strained was shown by their gritting the teeth, talking, groaning, etc., activities possibly connected with dreaming. These individuals awakened in the morning feeling tired. The results suggested that we were dealing with two different kinds of sleep, a quiet, relaxed sleep, and a strained sleep connected with muscular activity. They are in agreement with the results obtained in other experiments carried on during the day on the relation between resistance and tenseness in different types of patients and normals. It was found that in early schizophrenics and normals who are usually obviously tense and strained, the back–back resistance is low, while in cases of stupor and normals who are obviously free from tenseness the resistance is high.

Attention has recently been called in a very conclusive way to the difference between these two kinds of sleep by MacWilliam (10) in his work on the changes of blood pressure during sleep. Contrary to the result of previous investigators this work showed that sleep is not necessarily accompanied by a decrease in blood pressure, that often there is a marked increase. Thus he says: . . . ."there are two entirely different conditions in question in sleep—1, sound sleep with lowering of pressure; 2, disturbed sleep, dreaming, etc., which may be attended by remarkable elevations of pressure, e.g., systolic pressure raised from 125 to 182 mm., or from 130 to 200, etc.; diastolic pressure raised from 75 to 105 mm., etc. These changes were much greater than were induced in the same individuals by moderate exertion (cycling, walking, stair climbing, etc.), straining, abdominal efforts, dose of atropin to remove vagus control over the heart, mental excitement, etc. In view of the rapid development of such changes in sleep, especially in dreams of motor effort, nightmares, etc., it is evident that a formidable strain—harmless in the young and healthy person—may thus be thrown on the weak points of the circulatory system, whether these be cardiac with susceptibility to anginal attacks or to ventricular fibrillation and sudden death, or arterial with risk of hemorrhages, cerebral (especially in the recumbent posture), gastro-intestinal or pulmonary. The conception of sleep as a period of quiescence and recuperation has thus to be qualified by the contingency of disturbed sleep with active calls on the nervous system the heart and the blood vessels. The mechanism of the rise of pressure in disturbed sleep differs in some respects from that present in ordinary muscular exertion, since in the former the pumping action of working muscles, greatly augmenting the venous return to the heart, is absent. The above-mentioned disturbances may occur during disturbed sleep when there is after waking no recollection of definite dreaming."

This method of measuring the changes in resistance may throw some light also on the differences between normal sleep and certain pathological conditions which closely resemble sleep. We have had occasion to measure the resistance of a number of patients in catatonic stupors, some of which so closely resembled sleep that it was impossible to tell by looking at the patients that they were not asleep. They remained in the same position in their beds for hours at a time, without giving any sign of being in contact with their surroundings; they showed no responses to stimuli; generally they gave the impression of being completely relaxed and inert. It is an interesting fact that these stupors which so closely resembled sleep, should give such very different electrical resistance records. A typical record of one patient is shown in figure 6. This gives hourly readings of resistance throughout an entire day, during which time the individual seemed to be asleep. The palm—palm resistance, which we have shown invariably increases during normal sleep, remained on a flat low level varying from 8000–13,000 ohms. This is even considerably below the average palm—palm resistance for normals (45,000 ohms) during the waking state. If we keep in mind the fact that the resistance of the palm is dependent on nervous stimulation, that it follows closely the dropping out of mental activity during sleep and its return on awakening, we may conclude that in these patients the unusually low palm—palm resistance indicates an increased nervous activity, an amount even greater than is found in normal during the waking state. The back—back resistance on the contrary is very high, in some individuals as high as a million ohms. This result is in keeping with the results of the sleep experiments where a high back—back resistance was also found to be associated with freedom

Figure 6

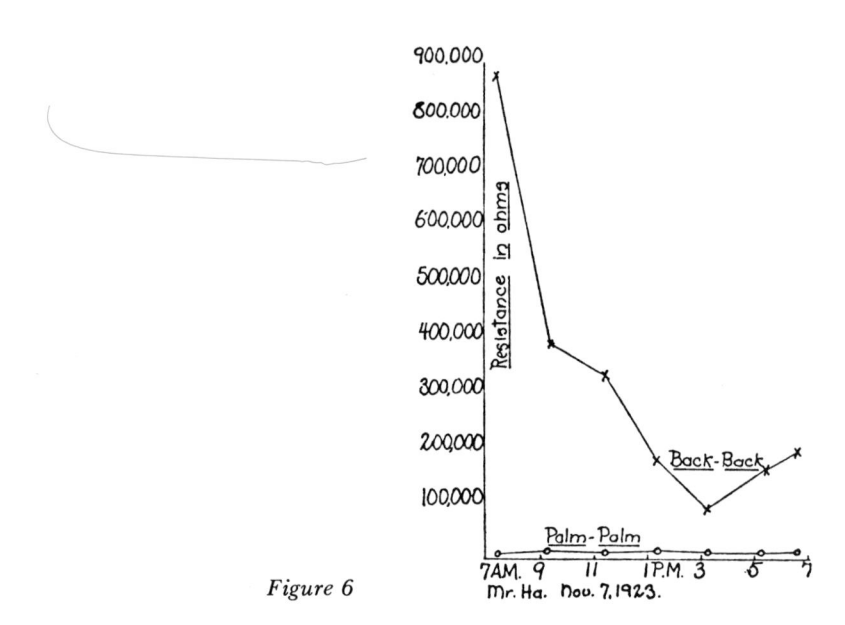

from muscular strain and a generally relaxed condition. In these patients, then, we have evidence for heightened nervous activity and a diminished muscular activity. It would seem that the nervous activity somehow is not permitted to reach, or is blocked from reaching the muscles. We have good reason to believe, on the basis of clinical observation, that in this condition there is much nervous activity and that the individuals are in contact with what is going on, as is demonstrated by their ability after coming out of the stupor to recount in detail, with considerable accuracy, everything that happened around them during the stupor, and by the appearance of entirely new and widely elaborated phantasies.

References

1. Kohlschütter, *Ztsch. f. rat. Med.*, 1863.
2. Monninghoff and Piesbergen, *Ztsch. f. Biol.*, 19, 1, 1883.
3. Michelson, "Dissertation," Dorpat, 1891.
4. Howell, *J. of Exper. Med.*, 2, 313, 1897.
5. Waller, *Proc. of Roy. Soc. B.*, 90, 90, 1918.
6. Pieper, *J. f. Kinderheilk.*, 107, 57, 1925.
7. Farmer and Chambers, *Brit. J. of Psych.*, 15, 1924–25.
8. Richter, *Amer. J. of Psychol.*, Vol. 68, No. 1, Mar., 1924.
9. Ebbecke, *Pflügers Archiv.*, 190, p. 230.
10. MacWilliam, *Physiol. Rev.*, Vol. 5, No. 3, July, 1925.

Part IV DOMESTICATION

DOMESTICATION OF THE NORWAY RAT AND ITS IMPLICATIONS FOR THE PROBLEM OF STRESS[1,2]

An experiment unwittingly started about 100 years ago by a scientist in France and since then carried on by innumerable scientists all over the world, has produced results that may have a direct bearing on this symposium on life stress and bodily disease. This experiment concerns the domestication of the Norway rat.[3]

The first animal tamed for purely scientific purposes, the Norway rat today offers an incomparable opportunity for study of the effects of that domestication. We know more about its anatomy, physiology and behavior than about any other animal except man; and its wild ancestor is still present in large numbers and readily available, literally at our

---

This paper was originally published in *Life Stress and Bodily Disease*, 1950, Vol. XXIX of the 1949 *Procs., Association for Research in Nervous and Mental Disease.* Reprinted by permission.

[1] This work has begun under a grant from the Rockefeller International Health Board for work on the biology of the wild rat and continued under a research grant from the Division of Research Grants and Fellowships of the National Institute of Health, U.S. Public Health Service.

[2] I wish to acknowledge the help received from Dr. Sally H. Dieke and Dr. Charles A. Jarvis who prepared many of the graphs used in this paper; also to Mr. John O. Neustadt, Mr. Henry N. Wagner, Jr., and Dr. Sally H. Dieke for their suggestions and criticisms in the preparation of the manuscript. Thanks are due also to the following who took an active part in the experimental work: Dr. Miguel R. Covian, Dr. Harold S. Fish, Dr. William J. Griffiths, Jr., Dr. Philip V. Rogers, Dr. Charles E. Hall, Mrs. Kathryn Clisby, Miss Susan Pardee, Mr. James W. Woods, Mr. David Mosier, Mr. Harold A. Collins and Mr. Elias Cohen.

[3] In 1855, Addison published his classical book on the syndrome that now bears his name; in the following year Brown-Séquard adrenalectomized rabbits in an effort to test experimentally in animals some of Addison's clinical observations on

doorsteps. We have here the opportunity to study not only the anatomical changes that domestication has produced but also the changes in physiology and behavior.

Darwin (1868), the great pioneer in the study of the variations produced by domestication, had for the most part to content himself with domesticated animals whose ancestors had long since departed from the world scene. These ancestors were known to him only through written records, drawings, or paleontological specimens, and even then only in their anatomical features such as shape and size of skull and skeleton, or type and kind of hair. In addition, not much was known at that time about the domesticated animals beyond their anatomical characteristics.

With the Norway rat a very different situation exists today. There is a great fund of knowledge about the domesticated form, not only about the anatomy of its so-called "hard parts"—its teeth, skull and skeleton—but also about its so-called "soft parts"—its glands, muscles, viscera and blood—and about its physiology and behavior.

The wild Norway lives chiefly in burrows in cellars, yards, alleys, and fields, a life situation in which it has to search for its food and water, provide its own shelter, fight for its mates, and protect itself from its many natural enemies, dogs, cats, snakes and man. In short it must live under almost constant stress. In marked contrast the domesticated Noway lives in a protected environment in laboratory cages under conditions in which food and water are always available, relatively luxurious shelter from heat and cold is provided, mates are readily accessible, and no natural enemies threaten its existence.

Now what are the differences between these two strains of the

---

patients. These were the first deliberate adrenalectomies performed on animals. Within a few months Philipeaux, testing the validity of Brown-Séquard's observations on rabbits, adrenalectomized some albino and hooded rats. This is the first record we have been able to find on the use of rats in the laboratory. Philipeaux does not state in his paper how he obtained these rats so it is not known if they were freshly caught or came from a pre-established colony. During the rest of the Nineteenth Century, sporadic reports appeared indicating that Norway rats were being used in European laboratories. The ancestry of these rats and their modern descendants has not been traced, but it is probable that the first rats used were mostly albino or hooded sports and that there was some subsequent interbreeding with wild Norway rats. Domesticated rats were apparently not readily available in France at the end of the century, since in 1894–97 Boinet used wild Norways (rats d'égout) for observing the effects of adrenalectomy. Domesticated Norways were first brought to the United States shortly after 1890 by H. H. Donaldson.

To our knowledge H. H. Donaldson was the first to recognize the existence of the phenomenon of the domestication of the Norway rat and to make studies on the differences between the wild and the domesticated forms. His book on "The Rat" gives a full account of the results of his valuable and interesting studies.

Norway rat? To answer this question comparisons were made between wild Norway rats recently (10–20 days) trapped in Baltimore[4] and domesticated Norways from our laboratory colony.

This study was made possible as a result of the development of simple effective methods for trapping (Richter and Emlen, 1945) and handling (Emlen, 1944) wild rats in large numbers. With these methods, many thousands of captured live wild rats have been studied in our laboratory during the past 8 years.

Our colony of domesticated Norways was started (1922) with albino rats from the Wistar Institute; a few hooded, tan and black rats from the colony of Dr. E. V. McCollum were introduced in 1927. Throughout the 28-year existence of the colony, the conditions involved in the care and handling of the rats have changed very little. The two rooms in which the rats are kept are well ventilated and always maintained at a fairly constant temperature of 77°F; outside light has been excluded and artificial light is used only in the daytime when the rats are being fed and records are being taken. Only one stock diet[5] has been used throughout and it has been mixed fresh at least once a week. Care has been taken to make food and water available at all times. Almost from birth all of the rats have been handled at least once a week when being transferred to clean cages and when being weighed.

No conscious effort has been made to select and breed rats with any special characteristics, except occasionally a few females that proved to be very active in the revolving drums were returned to the stock colony for breeding. The number thus restored to the colony has formed only a small part of the entire colony, which usually ranges between 400 and 600 animals.

For breeding purposes 3 females are placed in a cage and a different male is placed with them every week. As the females become pregnant they are removed and placed in separate cages. Females that do not become pregnant after about four weeks are removed from the breeding cages. This system gives the rats a wide range of choice of mates and leaves the selection largely to them. It does mean, however, that to some extent the females are selected for fertility.

---

[4] The wild rats used in this study came from all parts of the city. In our experience wild rats tend to remain in one place very consistently over long periods of time and do not change their domiciles except under pressure of starvation or other calamities. In spite of the great differences in their various habitats—city blocks, granaries, factories, farms—they show a surprising homogeneity in their anatomical and physiological characteristics.

[5] This diet contained graham flour 72.5 per cent, casein 10.0 per cent, butter 5.0 per cent, skim milk powder 10.0 per cent, calcium carbonate 1.5 per cent and sodium chloride 1.0 per cent.

Anatomical Differences

In external appearance, skeletal structure and growth rate, these domesticated rats differ only slightly from their wild ancestors. Absence of skeletal differences between the domesticated and wild rats is indicated by their almost identical relationship of body-weight to body-length as shown in Fig. 1.[6] In confirmation of the data in this figure we have found that under laboratory conditions both rats gain weight at about the same rate for the first 200—300 days, after which the wild rat grows faster and finally attains a much higher weight level.

Wide differences between the two strains were found in the weights of the "soft parts"—the glands and other internal organs. Table 1 summarizes these results.

TABLE 1. CHANGES PRODUCED BY DOMESTICATION (ON BASIS OF BODY WEIGHT)

\multicolumn{3}{c}{Weights of Organs}		
Decreased	Increased	Showing Earlier Development
Adrenals	Hypophysis	Ovaries
Preputials	Thymus	Uterus
Liver		Testes
Spleen		Seminal vesicles
Heart		Prostate
Kidneys		
Brain		
Thyroid (?)		
Pancreas (?)		

\multicolumn{3}{c}{Number of Organs}		
Decreased	Increased	No Change
Fungiform papillae	Peyer's patches	Foliate papillae

---

[6] This figure and most of the following figures are based on observations made on 100 (47 male, 53 female) recently trapped wild rats and 105 (64 male, 41 female) domesticated rats from our colony. For these curves rats were selected that were apparently in good health and with body weights evenly distributed over the entire weight range for each strain. Curves are fitted to the data by the method of least squares. Dotted lines at plus and minus one standard error indicate the degree of scattering around the lines.

In dissecting and preparing the organs for weighing we closely followed the instructions as given by Donaldson in his book on "The Rat" (1924).

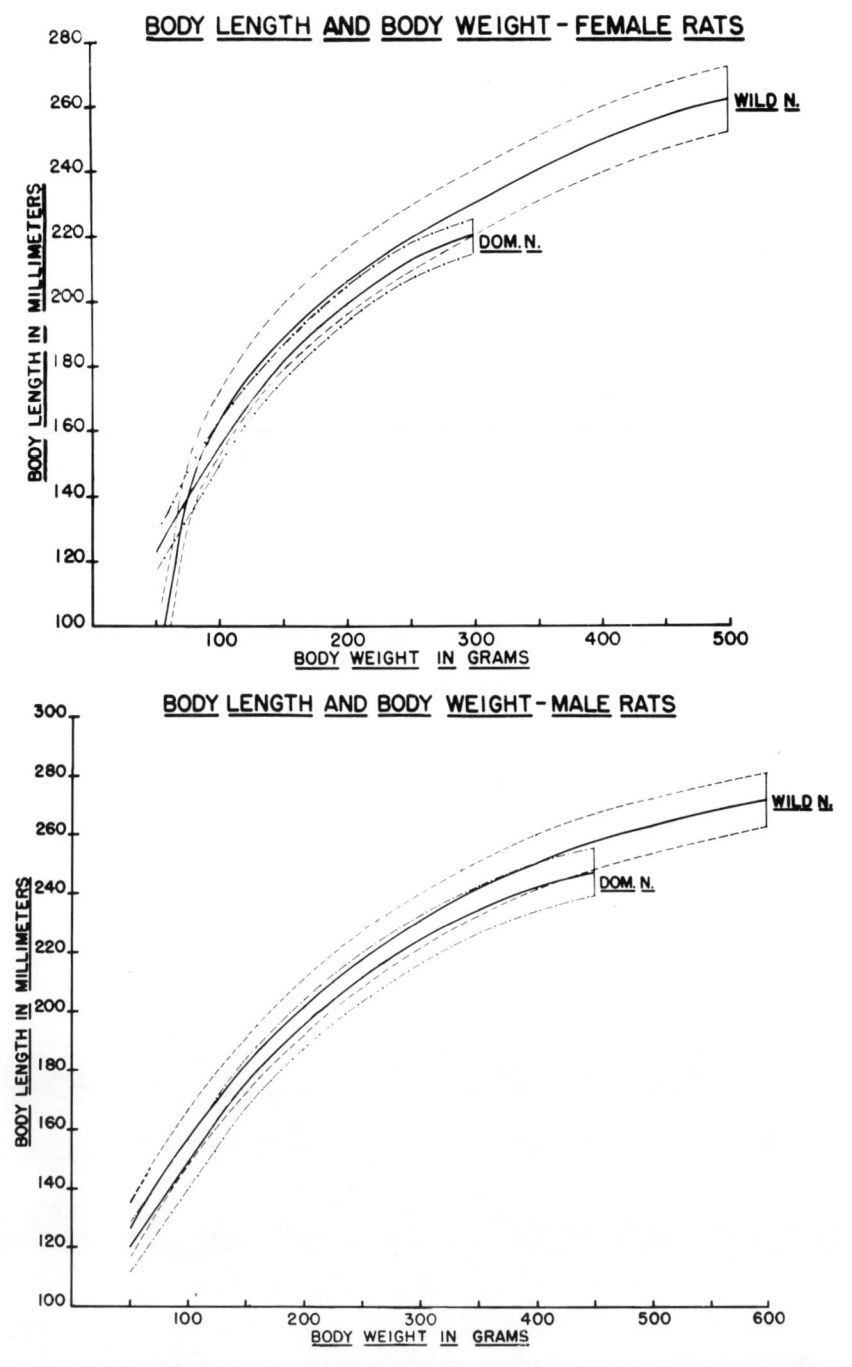

Fig. 1. Graphs Showing the Relationship between Body Length and Body Weight in Wild and Domesticated Rats

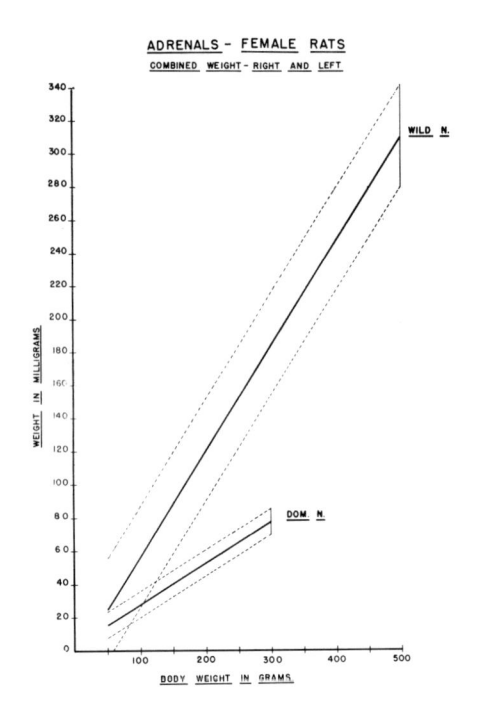

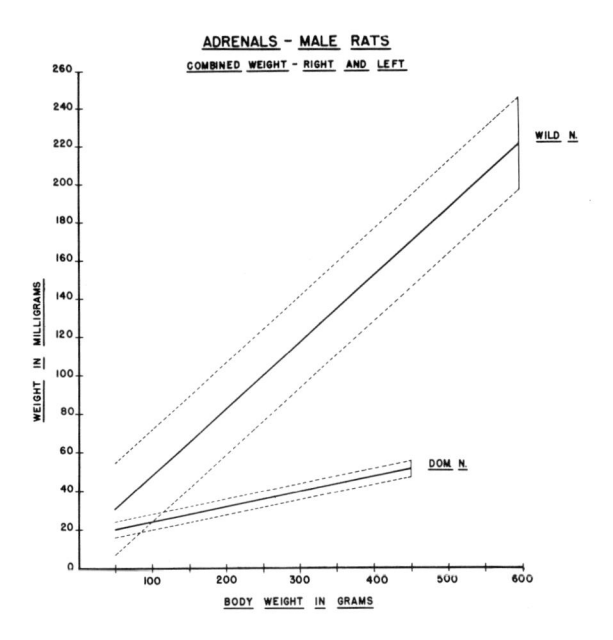

Fig. 2. Graphs Showing the Relationship between Weights of the Adrenal Glands and Body Weight in Wild and Domesticated Rats

Organs Weighing Less in Domesticated Rats

Of most interest from the point of view of this symposium is the great reduction in weight that has occurred in the adrenal glands of the domesticated rats. This reduction in weight probably constitutes the greatest of any of the anatomical changes that have been produced by domestication of the Norway rat. The reduction in weight is entirely limited to the cortex (Donaldson, J. C., 1928, Rogers and Richter, 1948) since the weight of the adrenal medulla relative to body weight is the same in both strains. Fig. 2 gives adrenal weights with relation to body weight for female and male rats and shows that on the average the wild rats' adrenals weigh proportionately two to four times as much as those of the domesticated rats. In individual cases we have found some wild rats with adrenals as much as 10 times heavier than those of the domesticated rats. Fig. 2 also shows that the adrenal glands in females of both strains weigh considerably more than those of the males and that the difference between the strains is most marked in the males.

Adrenals from domesticated rats of other colonies are in general equally small. The atrophy of the adrenal glands of the domesticated rat was first reported in 1907 by C. Watson and confirmed by J. C. Donaldson (1928), H. H. Donaldson (1924) and Rogers and Richter (1948).

This difference in size is so great that even when domesticated rats' adrenals are made hypertrophic by the most severe form of stress their weights only begin to approach those of adrenals from wild rats.

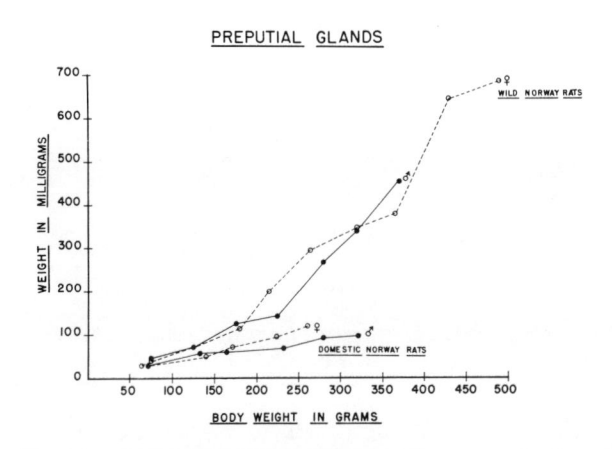

Fig. 3. Graph Showing the Relationship between Weights of Preputial Glands and Body Weight in Wild and Domesticated Rats (data taken from Hall, 1948)

Hall (1948) found that an almost equally great decrease in weight has occurred in the preputial glands. The preputial weights with relation to body weight are shown in Fig. 3 which is based on a study by Hall (1948) on 121 wild and 78 domesticated rats. There was no sex difference in either strain.

The spleen, liver, heart and kidneys[7] are also definitely smaller in the domesticated rats. See Figs. 4–7. The brain weight is slightly smaller in the domesticated rats. See Fig. 8. Donaldson's data (1924) on the weights of these five organs in domesticated rats agree fairly well with the weights reported here; he did not weigh these organs in wild rats.

Thyroid gland weights were found by us to be definitely smaller in the domesticated rats at all body weight levels. However, Donaldson (1924) reported that he found little difference in his studies on the weights of thyroids in both strains, although he did find in his colony of domesticated rats that the weights of the thyroid glands had become progressively smaller over a 20-year period. Because of these discrepancies in the two sets of data, we have listed the difference in thyroid weights as doubtful.

We have no definite information on the parathyroids since it is not possible to remove them intact for weighing. However, our impression from several series of parathyroidectomies is that they are considerably smaller in the domesticated than in the wild rat.

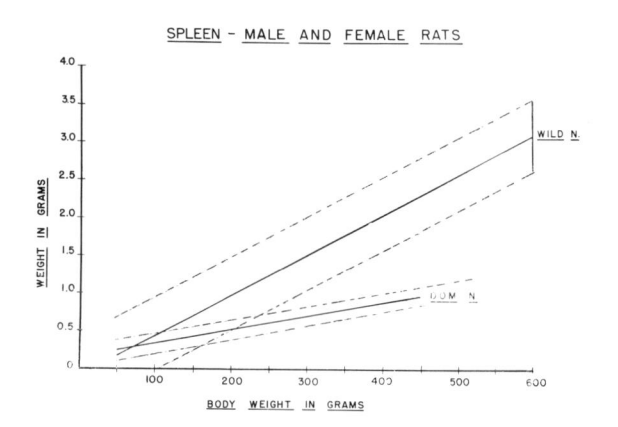

Fig. 4. Graph Showing the Relationship between the Weight of the Spleen and Body Weight in Wild and Domesticated Rats

---

[7] The break in the curve for wild rat kidneys, occurring at body weight of about 400 grams may be due to a diseased condition of the kidneys of older rats. The wide scattering of the kidney weights in this range makes it impossible to calculate a standard error for this part of the curve. Mention should also be made that at least 75 per cent of the livers showed signs of helminth infestation.

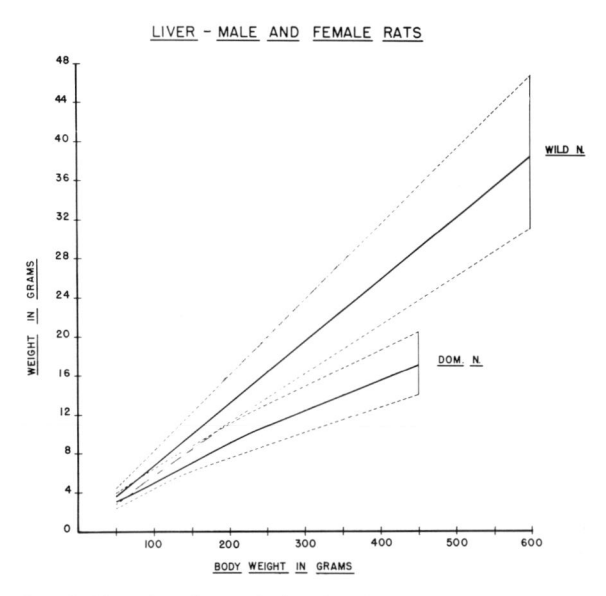

Fig. 5. Graph Showing the Relationship between the Weight of the Liver and the Body Weight in the Wild and Domesticated Rats

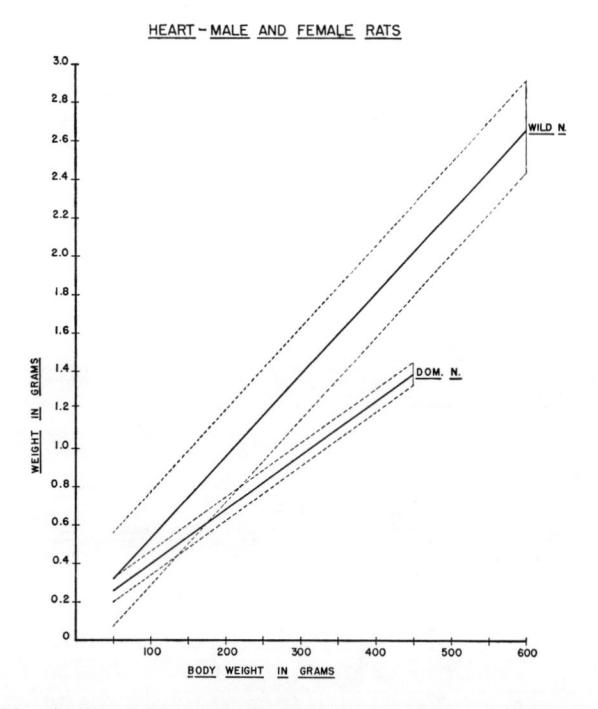

Fig. 6. Graph Showing the Relationship between Weight of the Heart and Body Weight in Wild and Domesticated Rats

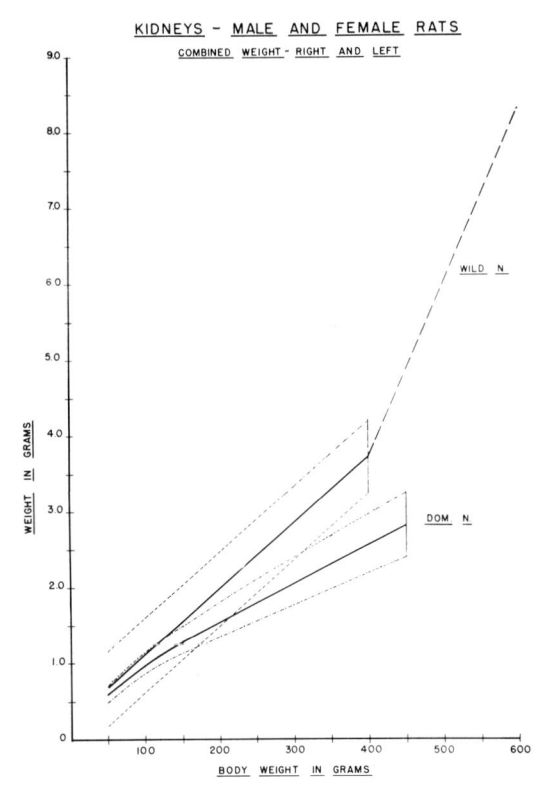

Fig. 7. Graph Showing the Relationship between Weight of the Kidneys and Body Weight in Wild and Domesticated Rats

Our results indicate that the pancreas is only slightly smaller in the domesticated than in the wild rat. Since the weights of this organ in our domesticated rats are less than those reported by Donaldson (1924) for his domesticated rats, we have also listed the decrease in the pancreas weight as doubtful.

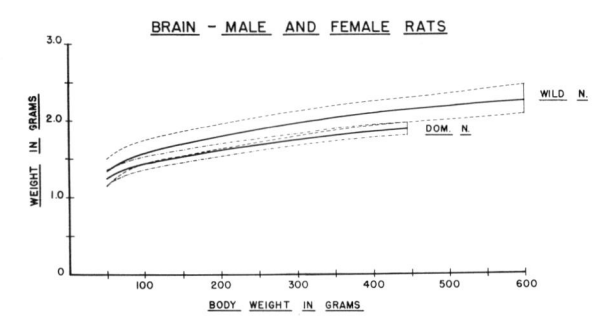

Fig. 8. Graph Showing the Relationship between Weight of the Brain and Body Weight in Wild and Domesticated Rats

Organs Weighing More in Domesticated Rats

In marked contrast to all the organs discussed above, the hypophysis is larger in domesticated rats than in wild rats. See Fig. 9. The contrast is more marked in the female where the difference is almost double. Donaldson (1924) reported a similar difference.

The thymus gland weights are also larger in the domesticated rats, with the greatest differences existing between the males of both strains.

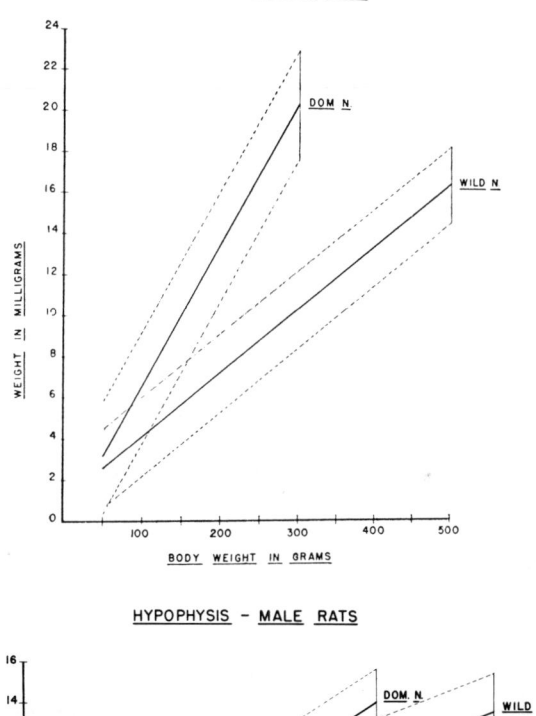

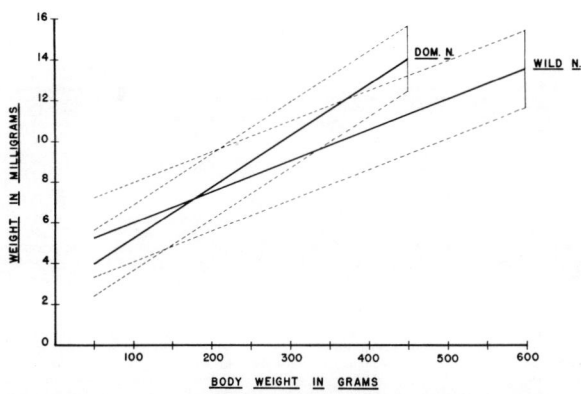

Fig. 9. Graph Showing the Relationship between Weight of the Hypophysis and Body Weight in Wild and Domesticated Rats

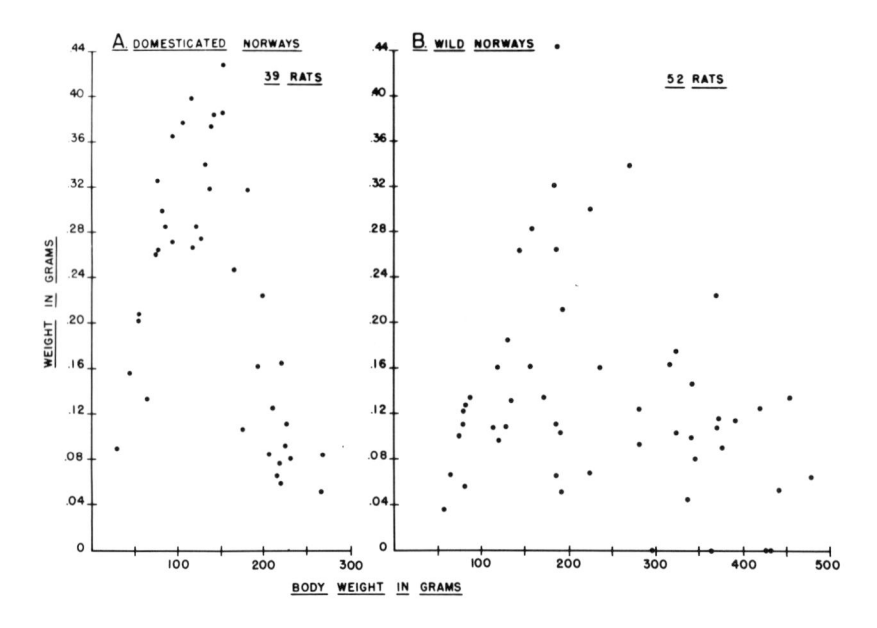

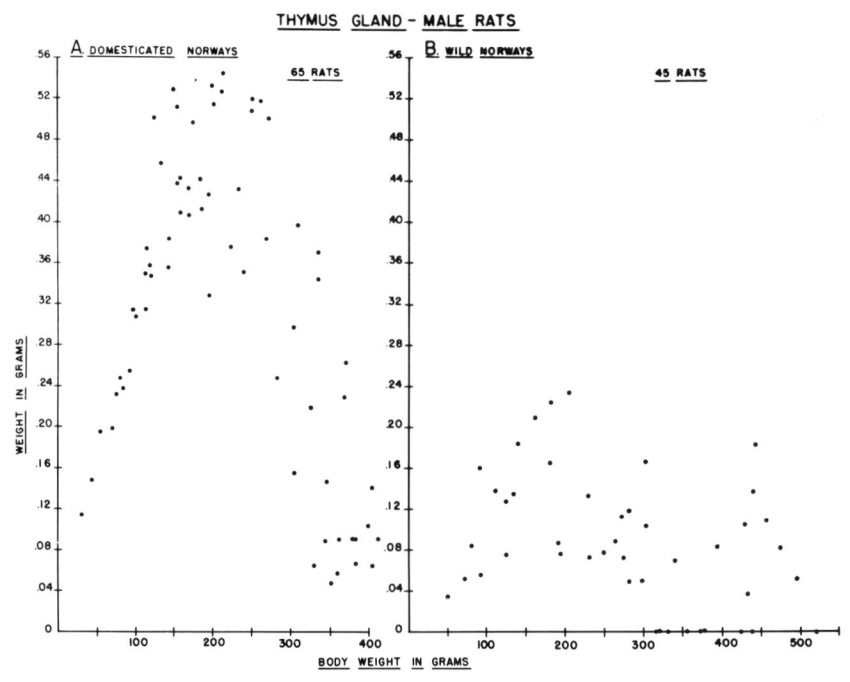

Fig. 10. Scatter Graphs Showing the Relationship between Thymus and Body Weight in Wild and Domesticated Rats

Because of the wide scattering of weights in the wild rats studied, it was not possible to construct curves but Fig. 10 gives scatter graphs for domestic and wild rats of both sexes. Some wild rats were found to be without any thymus tissue at all.

Organs Showing Earlier Development in Domesticated Rats

Relative to body weight, the testes, ovaries and secondary sex organs are larger in the domesticated rats during the early part of life but eventually they are exceeded in weight by the corresponding wild rat organs. Fig. 11 shows that until the rats reached a body weight of about 300 grams the testes were somewhat larger in the domesticated rats. The seminal vesicles, coagulating glands and prostate glands gave essentially the same type of curve.

Likewise the ovaries were larger in the domesticated rats until the body weights reached a level around 200 grams (Fig. 12). The uterus weights gave the same type of curve.

These changes in the reproductive organs agree with the observation

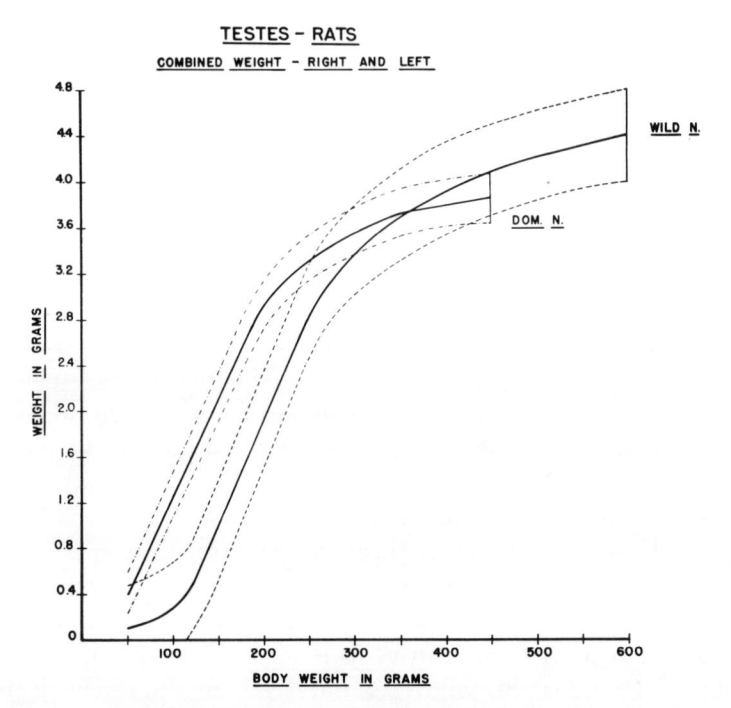

Fig. 11. Graph Showing the relationship between Weight of Testes and Body Weight in Wild and Domesticated Rats

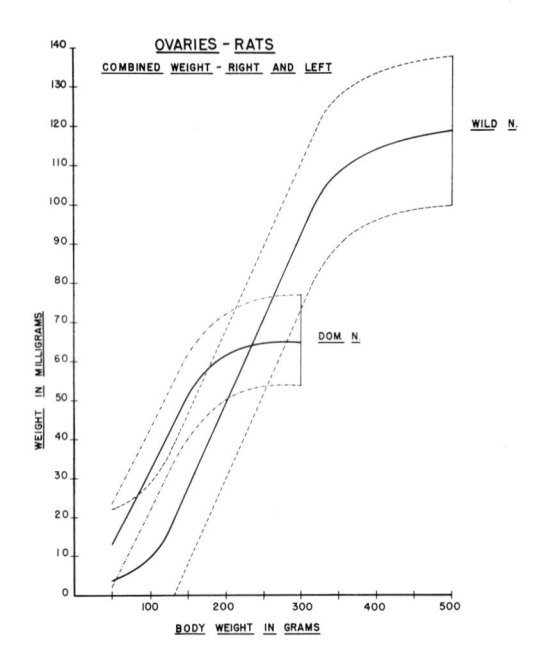

Fig. 12. Graph Showing the Relationship between Weight of Ovaries and Body Weight in Wild and Domesticated Rats

made on many different colonies that, as the rats become domesticated, the vagina opens at progressively earlier ages and litters are born to younger and younger females.

Organs Differing in Number

Not only have the weights of glands and organs changed during domestication but the number of some of the organs have changed. Fig. 13 gives frequency distribution curves for the number of fungiform and foliate papillae on the tongues of wild and domesticated rats; ordinates give the number of tongues and abscissae the number of papillae per tongue. The foliate papillae number the same in both strains but the fungiform papillae are fewer in the domesticated rats—178.3 as compared to 217.9 in the wild rats (Fish and Richter, 1946).

The number of Peyer's patches has also increased during domestication. Fig. 14 is a frequency distribution curve for the number of Peyer's patches found in the small intestines in the two species, showing an average of 16.3 for the wild rats and 18.9 for the domesticated rats. (Richter and Hall, 1947). The greater number of these lymphoid

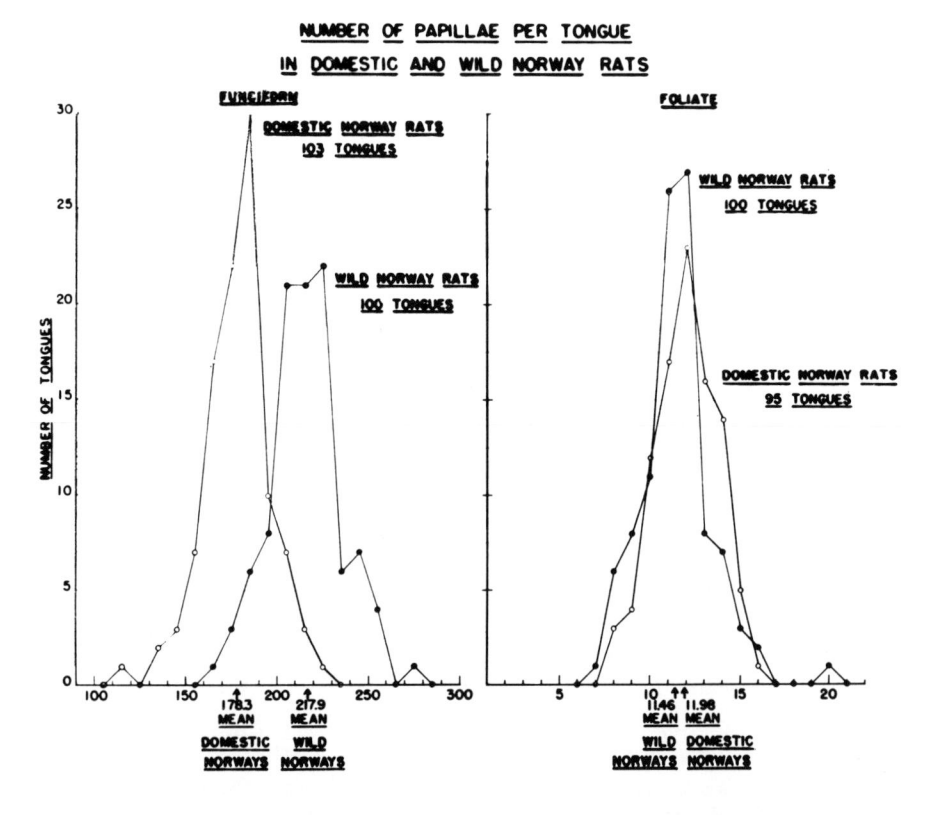

Fig. 13. Frequency Distribution Curves Showing Number of Papillae per Tongue in Wild and Domesticated Rats (data taken from Fish and Richter, 1946.)

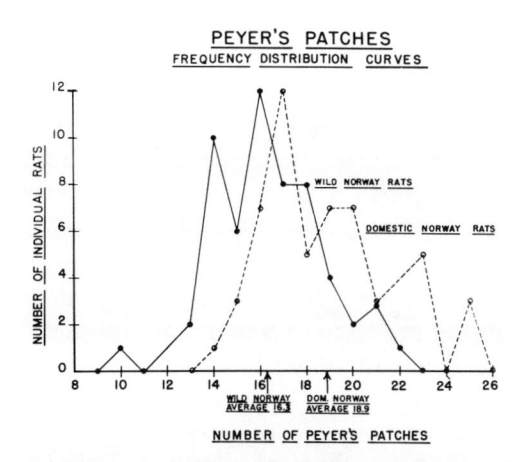

Fig. 14. Graph Showing Frequency Distribution Curves for the Number of Peyer's Patches on Small Intestines in Wild and Domesticated Rats

patches in the domesticated rats agrees with the finding that they also have more of the lymphoid thymus tissue.

No differences were found in the length of either the large or small intestine in the two strains (Richter and Hall, 1947).

Physiological Differences

Marked physiological differences also exist between the two strains of Norway rats. Only a few of these differences will be mentioned at this time.

In agreement with the finding that the adrenal glands are much smaller in the domesticated than in the wild rat, it was found that after adrenalectomy, domesticated rats have a much smaller replacement need. Thus, while 87 per cent of a group of domesticated rats survived on salt therapy alone, only one out of 50 wild rats survived and this one may have had an accessory body (Richter, Rogers and Hall, 1950). Fig. 15 shows records of 3 of the wild rats. The rat whose record is presented in Fig. 15A was kept on a salt-poor diet but had access to a 3 per cent salt solution and water. Despite the fact that it increased its intake of salt solution, it died at the end of 18 days. Fig. 15B shows the record of a rat that received a diet with a 3 per cent salt content. It died suddenly at the end of 7 days. Fig. 15C shows the record of a rat that had access to a diet with a 4 per cent salt content (stock diet plus 3 per cent salt) and also to a one per cent salt solution. It died suddenly at the end of 18 days. The sudden loss of appetite and death of these animals closely resembled the crises seen in Addison's disease in man.

Treatment with desoxycorticosterone acetate (by pellet) and cortical extract (corticosorbate in food) in addition to salt therapy did not suffice to keep more than a small portion of the adrenalectomized wild rats alive. Many of them died the same sudden death described for the rats on salt therapy alone. It seems likely that the treatment did not suffice to take care of stress caused by disturbances in the laboratory. To test this possibility Covian (1949) made a study in this laboratory of the effects produced on the survival time of adrenalectomized wild rats by experimentally induced stress. For this purpose he used a "fighting chamber" (to be described below) in which two adrenalectomized wild rats at a time were stimulated to fight one another.

Covian found that in some instances the rats died while fighting even though no observable injuries had been inflicted; in most instances they died within a day or two after fighting. Fig. 16 gives the record of one

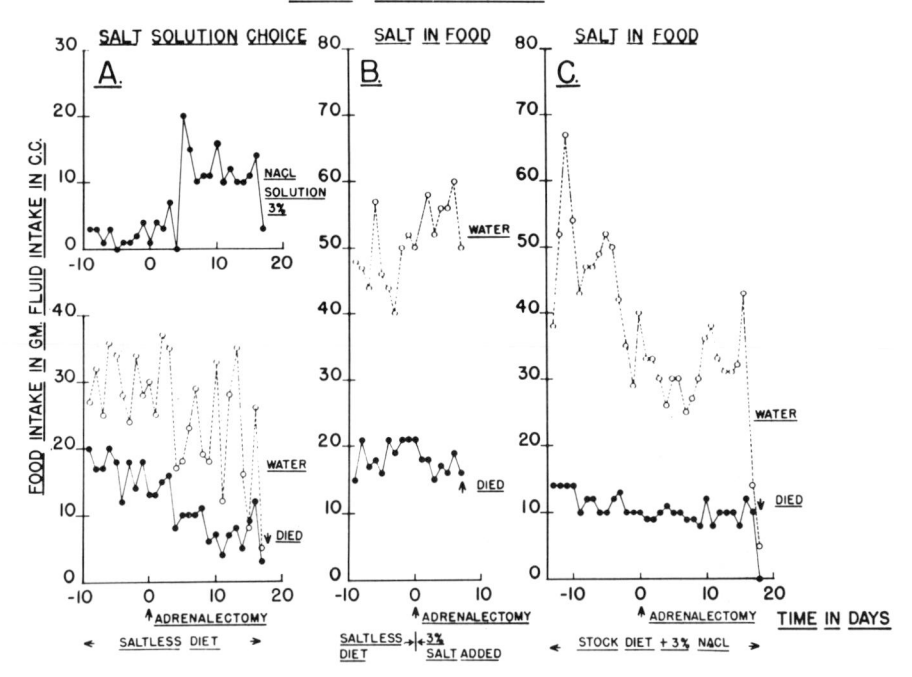

Fig. 15. Graph Showing the Effects of Three Forms of Salt Treatment in Three Adrenalectomized Wild Norway Rats
(A) Rat with access to a 3 per cent salt solution (no salt in diet).
(B) Rat with 3 per cent salt added to "salt-poor" diet.
(C) Rat with 3 per cent salt added to stock diet and with drinking water with 1 per cent salt

of his adrenalectomized wild rats in which he had implanted a DOCA pellet and given a high salt-content diet. With this treatment the rat's food intake quickly regained its normal level; after adrenalectomy its water intake increased rather than decreased and its body weight showed a small increase. By the 25th day it gave all indications that full replacement had been achieved. On the 29th day it was placed for 5 minutes in the fighting chamber with another wild rat. It fought vigorously during this time. Its food and water intake dropped off at once and on the 3rd day it died. At autopsy the implanted pellet was recovered. Since normal wild rats can be fought repeatedly over long periods of time without fatal effects, it is clear that none of the replacement therapies that were tried sufficed to produce full replacement of the secretion from the normal adrenal.

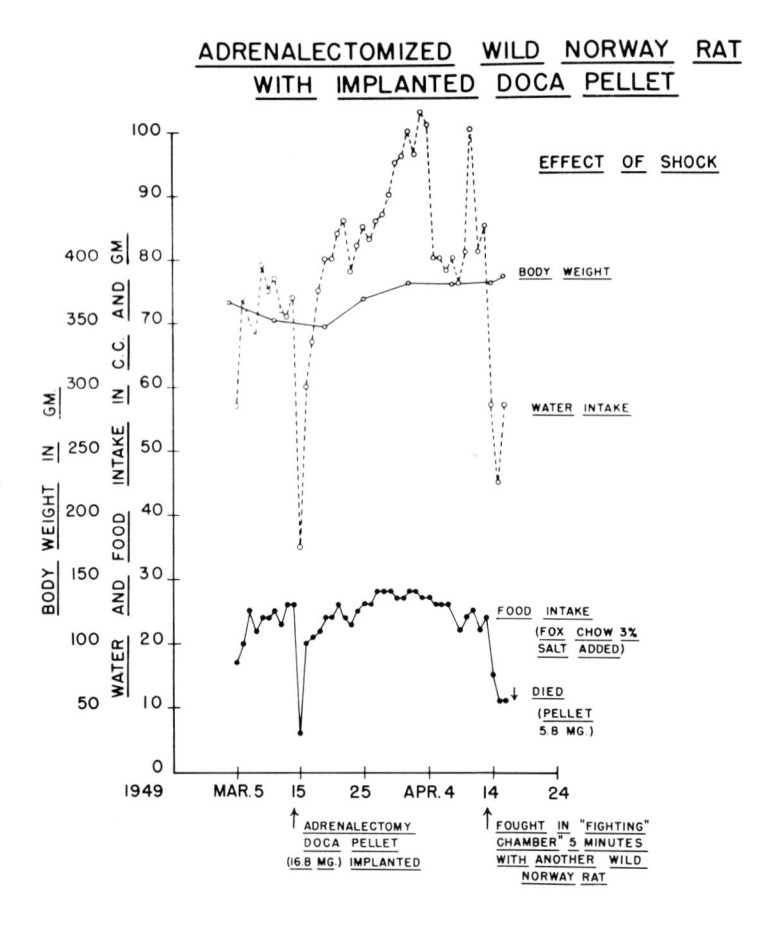

Fig. 16. Graph Showing the Effect of Stress in Adrenalectomized Wild Norway Rat Treated with a DOCA Pellet and Salt

An equally startling physiological difference between the wild and domesticated rats came out in studies on the resistance to thiourea poisoning. This drug was found to be practically non-toxic to wild rats (LD50, 1800 mg/kg), but highly toxic to domesticated rats (LD50, 5 mg/kg). Thus a 360-fold difference in toxicity exists between the two strains (Dieke and Richter, 1945). To our knowledge this is the greatest difference in toxicity known to exist between strains of any animal species.

Studies made by Griffiths (1944) on the production of running fits by high frequency sounds brought out a further difference between the domesticated and wild rats. High frequency sounds produced seizures in more than 20 per cent of the domesticated rats from our colony, but failed to produce them in any of several hundred wild rats that were

Domestication of the Norway Rat and Its Implications for Stress 307

tested. In this set of observations the rats were kept on the regular stock diet.

In later experiments the rats were kept on a magnesium-deficient diet which is known to bring out audiogenic seizures. Griffiths (1947) found that although wild rats on this diet showed the characteristic signs of magnesium deficiency, such as reddening of the ears, they showed only comparatively few convulsions when subjected to high frequency auditory stimulation and in no instance died. In marked contrast, all of the domesticated rats on the same diet had convulsions almost every time they were tested, that is after the other signs of magnesium deficiency manifested themselves. Furthermore, all of the domesticated rats died during the course of a fit, in most instances within 10 to 15 days after the start of the magnesium-deficient diet. Fig. 17 gives typical records of a domesticated and a wild rat. It gives the daily food intake; weekly readings of body weight; the days on which the rats were tested with the high frequency sounds; and the appearance of convulsions. The domesticated rat had no fits when tested for 10 days on the stock diet and showed its first fit on the 10th day after the start of the magnesium-deficient diet, at about the time when other signs of deficiency developed. It survived this fit but died while being tested two days later. The wild rat had its first fit on the 6th day of the deficient diet. It continued to show running fits during the next 16 days but thereafter it

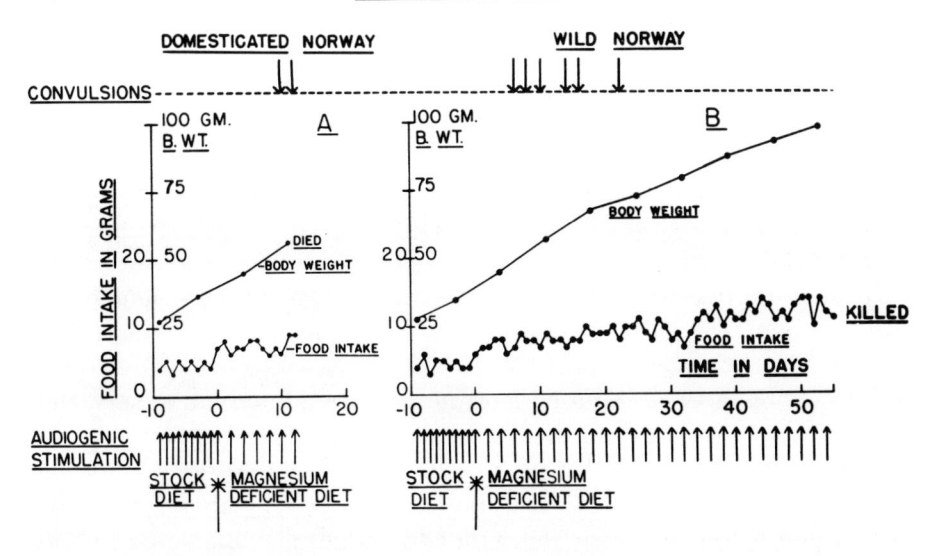

Fig. 17. Graph Giving the Record of Audiogenic Convulsions or Running Fits for a Domesticated and a Wild Norway Rat, Both on a Magnesium-Deficient Diet.

had no more seizures for the remaining 32 days it was tested. It was killed on the 54th day after the start of the diet.

Some observations made by Hammett in 1922 on the effects of parathyroidectomy in wild (second generation) and domesticated rats indicates that the parathyroid, like the adrenals, may be more necessary to the wild rat than to the domesticated rat. He found that only 10 per cent of wild rats (second generation) and 21 per cent of untamed albinos, survived parathyroidectomy while the survival rate in tame, gentle albinos was 87 per cent. He did not attempt to weigh the parathyroids, nor did he indicate whether they appeared larger in the wild form. As mentioned previously, it is our impression that they are larger in the wild form.

Behavior Differences

There are striking differences in behavior between the two forms. The wild Norway is fierce, aggressive, suspicious, and constantly on the alert for an attack. In captivity it always tries to escape; it breeds very poorly and often eats any young that are born. The domesticated Norways are tame, gentle, and apparently entirely content with captivity, rarely trying to escape even when being transported in open top cages. They breed readily and seldom eat their young. Papers by Yerkes (1913), Sadovnikova-Koltzova (1926), and Stone (1932), pioneer workers on the behavior of wild rats give a fuller account of the behavior differences between the two strains.

During the 28 years of the existence of our colony the rats have become progressively more tame. In the early years of the colony, workers were frequently bitten when handling the rats; now it is a rare occasion when anyone is bitten, and then usually it is an inexperienced worker who through fear handles the rats roughly.

Several differences in behavior can be experimentally demonstrated by exposing the two strains of rats to the same stress situation. One of the best devices for this purpose is the "fighting chamber" mentioned above. This is a wooden box $9 \times 16 \times 9$ inches with a glass front, and a grid floor connected to an inductorium, so wired (alternating bars) that rats may be given electric shocks. When two wild rats are placed in this chamber and are given a shock they turn on each other at once and begin fighting. Apparently each one holds the other responsible for the shock and if left in the chamber for a long time they may even fight to the death.

In striking contrast, when two domesticated rats are placed in this chamber and are given a shock they merely jump into the air and do not in any way indicate that they hold each other responsible for the shock. When subjected to repeated shocks they often huddle together in a corner. It may be noted that the domesticated rats, not being distracted by the necessity of warding off an attacker, often discover that they can avoid the shocks by standing up with their two hind feet on the same or alternate bars.

Our dietary self-selection cages can also be used to illustrate behavior differences. In these cages the rats have access to 15 purified or nearly purified substances, all offered in separate containers; glucose, casein (purified), olive oil, sodium chloride, calcium lactate, potassium chloride, sodium phosphate, magnesium chloride, thiamine, riboflavin, niacin, pantothenic acid, pyridoxine, cod liver oil, and water. From these substances adult domesticated rats make selections that result in normal growth and development. Some domesticated rats have thrived on such self-selection diets for over 800 days. In marked contrast, adult wild Norways do not thrive in this situation. They refuse to taste the unfamiliar substances and so literally starve themselves to death in 40 to 50 days. Usually they take only fat, a substance with which they are presumably familiar from their garbage pail days (Richter, 1946).

Owing to their high degree of suspiciousness the wild rats are far more difficult to poison than are the domesticated rats; and once having survived a poisoning they become even more wary of being poisoned a second time—that is, if the poison has a recognizable taste or odor. In contrast the domesticated rats readily accept poisoned baits and so can be killed without much difficulty.

How strongly the wild rats react to the danger of poisoning was brought out by experiments in which the rats were allowed to eat a food that contained enough poison to make them very sick, but not to kill them. Later over a period of several weeks or months, the poison was incorporated in the food in first one and then another of the several food cups in an irregular order, and the kinds of food containing the poison were changed in an equally irregular manner. After being subjected for some time to this life-threatening procedure, some of these wild rats reacted by refusing to touch any food at all, unpoisoned as well as poisoned, and so died of starvation just as the other wild rats did when offered the various new foodstuffs contained in the self-selection diet. Others still continued to eat unpoisoned food but developed very peculiar behavior, standing or sitting upright almost continuously over periods lasting several months (Richter, 1948).

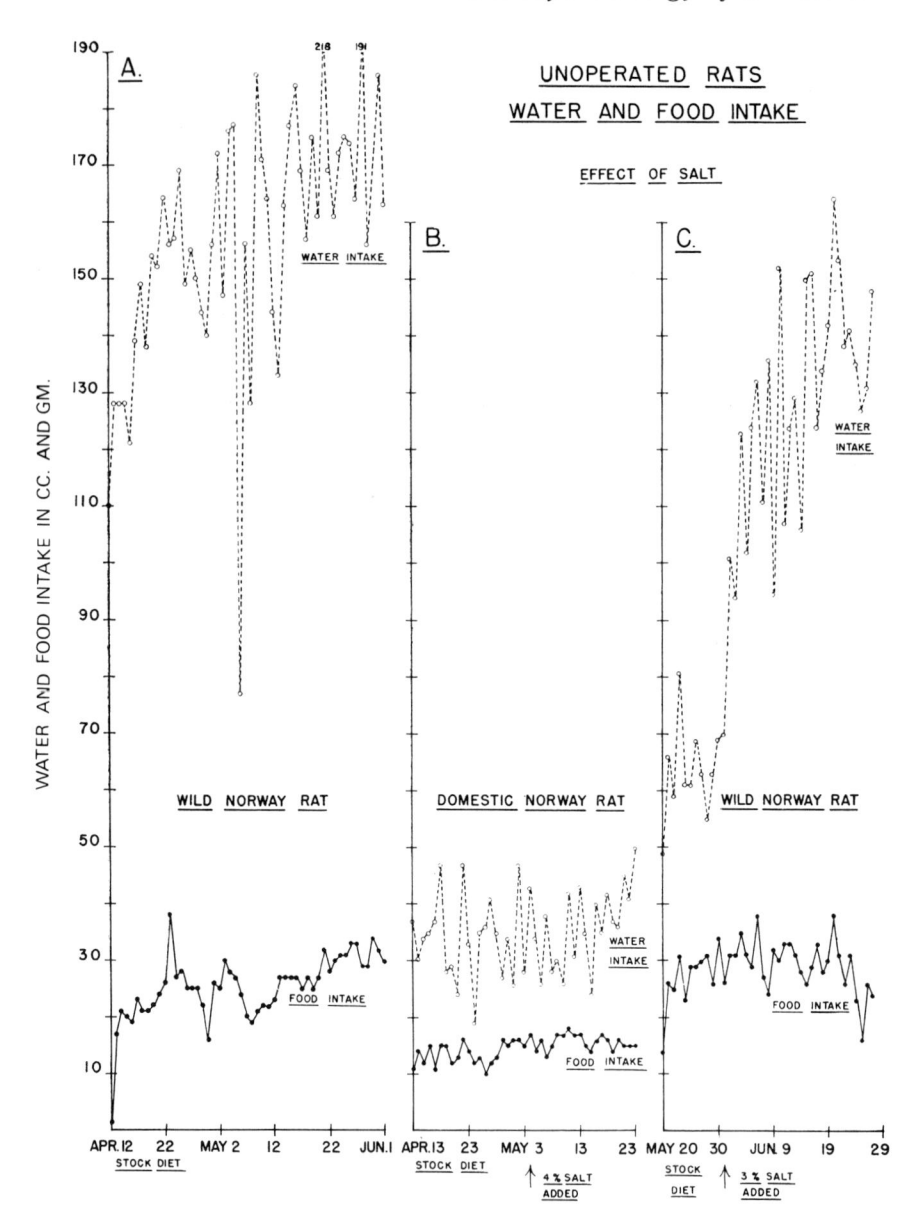

Fig. 18. Graph Showing the Water and Food Intake for Two Wild Norways and One Domesticated Norway Rats
(A) Record showing high water intake of a wild Norway rat kept on the stock diet.
(B) Record showing that the addition of 4 per cent salt had no effect on the water intake on the domesticated rat.
(C) Record showing the large increase in water intake that the addition of 3 per cent salt to the stock diet produced in the wild rat.

Discussion

The results of these studies have demonstrated the existence of marked differences—anatomical, physiological and behavioral—between the domesticated Norway rat and the recently-trapped wild Norway rat. These differences are the ground-work with which our understanding of domestication may begin. But before considering how domestication might have caused these differences, we must first consider the validity of using the recently trapped or captive wild rat as a standard of reference. The wild rat living free in its native habitat is the proper control animal for the study of domestication, but we have studied it only indirectly through the study of the trapped wild rat. Hence we need to know what changes, if any, are produced in our reference animal by its trapping and captivity, the stresses involved, and the possible effects of alterations in diet and external conditions.

Several observations have been made showing how the stress of captivity and the change from the field to the laboratory diet may produce a profound change in the behavior, physiology and anatomy of the wild rat. One of these observations that show an effect on the behavior and physiology will be given here in some detail. We found that about 30 per cent of captured wild rats have a very great thirst, drinking 3 to 4 times as much water per day as do domesticated rats of the same weight except those with diabetes insipidus or mellitus. Fig. 18A gives a typical water intake record of one of these animals. On the basis of a variety of tests made on these rats, it appears that differences in basal metabolic rate could not account for the differences in water intake; similarly studies on the specific gravity and sugar content of the urine ruled out the possibility that the rats suffered from either form of diabetes. In the absence of evidence of kidney dysfunction it seems likely that the thirst resulted either from the higher salt content of the laboratory stock diet, or from the stress of captivity, or from both. It is reasonable to assume that rats in the field eat a diet rather low in salt, and that the amount of salt present in the stock diet represents a large increase. Since desoxycorticosterone acetate injections in the normal rat are known to increase thirst in direct proportion to the amount of salt in the diet, (Rice and Richter, 1943) this combination in the wild rat of a great amount of adrenal secretion and the high salt content of the diet might explain their great thirst. The results of preliminary experiments have shown indeed that wild rats respond with an increased thirst to increased amounts of salt in their diet more readily than do domesticated rats. Fig. 18 B and C shows that salt (3 and 4 per cent respectively) added to the stock diet greatly increased the water intake of a wild rat but had no effect on the water intake of the domesticated rat. The fact, however, that when kept on a diet with a very low salt content some recently trapped wild rats still drank large amounts of water may indicate that the stress of captivity plays a significant part in the production of their increased thirst.

It is possible that in the wild rat the stress of captivity might also have produced anatomical changes, especially of the adrenals which are known to hypertrophy with stress. To obtain the weights of the glands of the wild rats living in the wild state requires killing wild rats suddenly in their natural habitat and then autopsying them within a few minutes in order to get the gland weights before any changes could have occurred. Nichols (1949) has already made such observations on the adrenals. He shot rats on the city dump and removed the adrenals at once. He also trapped rats and killed them at various intervals after capture. The adrenals taken from rats killed in the field weighed much more than those of domesticated rats of the same body weight; also they had a higher cholesterol content. Rats killed at intervals after capture showed increasingly heavier gland averages during the first 24 hours; their adrenal weights did not return to the normal (rats killed in field) level for about 7 days. In any case the adrenals of the rats killed in the field were still far above the weight levels of domesticated rats and the levels present after 7 days were much the same as those present in the rats killed in the field. Since the adrenals are among the most labile of all the organs it is likely therefore that the gland and organ weights as given in the previous sections of this paper correspond closely with those of glands for rats in the field. However it will be important to repeat all of these anatomical observations on rats killed in the field. Here the thymus weights will be of major interest, since this organ responds very readily to stress.

The results indicate that definite differences exist between the present day domesticated rat and its wild ancestor. Our knowledge of the progress of these changes from the wild ancestor to the present day domesticated rat is very limited. That such changes probably progressed at a gradual rate is likely from observations made by ourselves and others who have had colonies for any length of time. Over the course of years the rats become tamer, less fierce, less apt to bite, or to escape. The most valuable information on the probable progress of events in this interval comes from observations made by King and Donaldson (1929, 1939) in which they attempted to reproduce the entire domestication process under controlled conditions. They started with 6 wild rats and bred them through 25 generations. They found that from one generation to the next gradual changes in organ weights and behavior occurred that were all in the direction of the present day domesticated animal but at the 25th generation only approached the average levels of the domesticated rats.

Thus the use of the captive wild rat as validly representing the completely wild animal in its free state is supported by Nichols' experiments, and the direction of the differences we have observed between it and the domesticated rat are borne out by domesticating experiments. Hence it seems reasonable to conclude that the anatomical, physiological and behavioral differences we have observed are actually changes brought about in the Norway rat as a result of domestication.[8]

We may now inquire into the possible causes of the changes and consider the environmental and genetic factors concerned. Environmental factors would include the effects of eating the stock diet over long periods of time; living in a room with a fairly constant temperature of 77°; being handled at regular intervals by laboratory helpers. For instance, the daily ingestion of large amounts of salt almost from birth might have a consistently depressant (but not genetic) effect on the adrenals of each generation. If this dietary factor were the only cause involved, the effect should disappear when the rats are put on another diet.

Other environmental factors to be considered are those acting on the rats during their lifetime to produce behavioral differences, such as differences in life experiences of the wild rat and the domesticated rat. To analyze these differences, it will be necessary to bring up baby rats caught in the field, or first generation offspring born in the laboratory to captured pregnant wild rats with a control group of domesticated rats under identically the same conditions, same diet, same amount of handling, and so forth. Some studies have already been made on such first generation captive wild rats. We know that they grow up to be less suspicious, less fierce, and more tractable than their parents, but they are very nervous, bite readily, and still make use of any opportunity to escape. Their reactions to the self-selection diet are very different from those of their parents. H. Wagner, a student working in this laboratory, has shown that the first generation wild rats readily sample all of the substances offered for choice and grow normally on their selections.

---

[8] The domesticated Norway rat like other domesticated animals has shown many mutations (Castle, 1947).

Similarly it would be profitable to study the effects produced on organ weights and behavior by placing domesticated rats in the environment of the wild rat in city blocks and farms. Recapturing them at a later date and studying any changes produced should add to our knowledge of the effects of lifetime environmental influences.

Both of these suggested experiments to control the environment could also serve to isolate the genetic factors of the two strains of Norway rat. Cross-breeding experiments may also be used for this purpose. It has been found that the weights of the adrenals and preputials of the hybrids are nearly the same as are those of domesticated rats (Rogers and Richter, 1948; Hall, 1948). Yerkes (1913) and Stone (1932) have used hybrids of wild and domesticated Norway rats for the genetic studies on the inheritance of savageness, timidity, and other behavior characteristics.

Selection seems to have played the most important part in the production of the differences between these two strains. By selection we mean here not the natural selection of wild rats in their natural habitat where the wildest, fiercest and strongest—the fittest for that environment—survive, but selection in the artificial environment of the laboratory, where the fittest for this type of environment survive—those that are most tame, gentle, and fertile. The two stages in the lives of rats at which this selection process has most effect are mating and during care of the young. In captivity wild rats do not mate well. In only a few out of many instances when rats are put together does a pregnancy result. In each instance it is likely that it is the tamest rats of any group that mate. This will be true of mating in each successive generation, so that the tamer rats will be more apt to propagate their own characteristics. After the young are born, wild mothers frequently eat their entire litter, especially if they are disturbed, so that at this stage an even more severe screening for tameness occurs. The rats that do survive these two stages must have the tamest characteristics and through successive generations should produce progressively tamer animals.

In our colony this selection process was carried out almost exclusively by the rats themselves. It is true that a rat that bit the helper, or escaped very often, was perhaps less apt to be used for breeding, but that is the extent of any selection that was practiced by us.

The results of these studies have demonstrated the wide differences between the domesticated Norway and its wild ancestor. The domesticated rats have long been used for all types of experiments, including those on the effect of stress. Owing to its defective equipment this animal may respond very differently to stress or other changes than does its more vigorous and possibly more physiologically competent ancestor. It may then be wondered whether the "diseases of adaptation" as reported by Selye (1946) would occur in wild rats, whether in fact these syndromes are not simply an indication that the domesticated rat has an inadequate equipment for meeting stress. Studies are now in progress on the reactions of these two strains of rats to various forms of stress-producing factors: cold temperature, swimming, fighting, etc.

On the other hand, since captivity is naturally a very severe form of stress for the wild rat, it should serve as an excellent situation for the study of the effects of stress on all types of function. Nichols who made the first studies on the freshly captured rat, measured the cholesterol content of the adrenals. He found a sharp drop during the first 24 hours. Studies are in progress in this laboratory on the ascorbic acid content of the adrenals and the eosinophil count in recently trapped wild rats.

At this point it seems reasonable to consider whether the process of domestication that we have followed in the Norway rat may not to some degree parallel the development of man in society.[9] It seems likely that man, like the wild rat, originally lived in an environment where his fitness, hence his survival, was measured by his physical activity, aggressiveness, and ability to withstand violent change. But with the growth of communities and the consequent increase in daily peace and stability for the individual—a transformation like that undergone by the rat in his introduction to colony life in the laboratory—the qualities of physical strength, fierceness and aggressiveness would no longer be at such a premium. Hence would result the increase and perhaps even predominance of the progeny of the weaker, milder, "better adjusted" individual.

---

[9] Attention may be drawn at this place to the fact that the Norway rat that has long lived in intimate association with man, often sharing the same houses of shelter, has several characteristics in common with man which may be of special interest in the study of the effects of domestication: (1) *A world wide distribution and a large population.* It has been stated that in many localities there is at least one rat for every man; and that the rat and human population increase at essentially the same rate; (2) *Diet.* The fact that most of our modern knowledge of human nutrition comes from the work on Norway rats, attest to the similarity of dietary needs. Furthermore rats and man have almost the same taste ability as is shown by the observation that their taste thresholds are the same for a variety of nutritional and poisonous substances: salt (Richter and MacLean, 1939), sugar (Richter and Clisby, 1940), phenyl-thiourea and other poisons (Richter and Clisby, 1941; Richter, 1950); (3) *Reproductive cycles.* The reproductive cycles in rats and man occur at frequent and regular intervals throughout the year.

In the light of such a development, changes in the adrenals and other organs might be expected to occur in man as we see they have in rats. Of course we lack data on the endocrine organs of aboriginal man to compare with those of our contemporaries.[10] But we have presumptive evidence of widespread deficiency of the adrenal secretion in modern man in the high incidence of rheumatoid arthritis, asthma and many other diseases which seem to yield to treatment with adrenal extracts and ACTH (Hench and collaborators, 1949).

In summary, the experiment started 100 years ago with the domestication of the Norway rat may help to throw some light on trends of development of animals that live in a controlled environment and of the factors involved in the production of these trends. It may also give us data that will help us to study the effects that the controlling of the environment may have had on man.

References

Addison, T. 1855. On the Constitutional and Local Effects of Disease of the Suprarenal Capsules. London: Highley.

Brown-Séquard, C. E. 1856. Experimental Research on the Physiology and the Pathology of the Adrenal Capsules. Comp. Rend., 43: 422–425, 542–546.

Boinet, E. 1895. Ablation des capsules vraies et accessoires chez le rat d'egout. Comp. Rend. Soc. de Biol. S.47, 498–500.

Boinet, E. 1896. Maladie d'Addison experimentale chez le rat d'egout. Comp. Rend. Soc. de Biol. T.48, 164.

Boinet, E. 1897. Dix nouveaux cas de maladie d'Addison experimentale chez le rat d'egout. Comp. Rend. Soc. de Biol. 8th and 15th of May, 439 and 473.

Cohen, J. and D. P. Ogdon. 1949. Taste Blindness to Phenyl-thio-carbamide and Related Compounds. Psych. Bull. 46: 490.

Covian, M. R. 1949. Role of Emotional Stress in the Survival of Adrenalectomized Rats Given Replacement Therapy. Jour. Clin. Endocrinology 9: 678.

Castle, W. E. 1947. The domestication of the Rat. Proc. Nat. Acad. Sc. 33: 109.

Darwin, Charles. 1868. The Variation of Animals and Plants under Domestication. London: J. Murray.

Dieke, S. H. and C. P. Richter. 1945. Acute Toxicity of Thiourea to Rats in Relation to Age, Diet, Strain and Species Variation. J. Pharmacol. & Exp. Therap., 83: 195.

---

[10] One physiological difference between modern Europeans and aborigines from various lands is known to exist. This is reflected in the reduction in the number of individuals who are able to taste a compound, phenyl thiourea, that has a very bitter taste for most persons and none at all for others. The inability to taste this substance is inherited as a Mendelian recessive. Whether any other anatomical and physiological changes are genetically linked with this characteristic is not known. Cohen and Ogden (1950) have summarized the findings of many workers on this topic.

Donaldson, H. H. 1924. The Rat. Memoirs of Wistar Institute, 2nd Ed., p. 372.
Donaldson, J. C. 1928. Adrenal Gland in Wild Gray and Albino Rat: Cortico-Medullary Relations. Proc. Soc. Exp. Biol. & Med., 25: 300.
Emlen, J. T., Jr. 1944. Device for Holding Live Wild Rats. J. Wildlife Manag. 8: 264.
Fish, H. S. and C. P. Richter. 1946. Comparative Number of Fungiform and Foliate Papillae on Tongues of Domestic and Wild Norway Rats. Proc. Soc. Exp. Biol. & Med. 63: 352.
Griffiths, W. J., Jr. 1944. Absence of Audiogenic Seizures in Wild Norway and Alexandrine Rats. Sciene 99: 62.
Griffiths, W. J., Jr. 1947. Audiogenic Fits Produced by Magnesium Deficiency in Tame Domestic Norway Rats and in Wild Norway and Alexandrine Rats. Am. Jour. Physiol. 149: 135.
Hall, C. E. 1948. Comparison of the Preputial Glands in the Alexandrine, the Wild, and the Domestic Norway Rat. Proc. Soc. Exp. Biol. and Med., 69: 233.
Hammett, F. S. 1922. Studies of the Thyroid Apparatus. V. The Significance of the Comparative Mortality Rates of Parathyroidectomized Wild Norway Rats and Excitable and Non-excitable Albino Rats. Endocrinology, 6: 221.
Hatai, S. 1907. On the Zoological Position of the Albino Rat. Biol. Bull., 12: 266.
Hench, P. J., E. C. Kendall, C. H. Slocumb and H. F. Polley. 1949. The Effect of a Hormone of the Adrenal Cortex (17-hydroxy-11-dehydro corticosterone: Compound E) and of Pituitary Adenocorticotropic Hormone on Rheumitoid Arthritis; Preliminary Report. Proc. Staff Meet. Mayo Clinic, 24: 181.
King, H. D. 1939. Life Processes in Gray Norway Rats During Fourteen Years of Captivity. Am. Anat. Memoirs, No. 17.
King, H. D. and H. H. Donaldson. 1929. Life Processes and Size of the Body and Organs of Gray Norway Rat During Ten Generations in Captivity. Am. Anat. Memoirs, No. 14.
Nichols, J. (Personal Communication).
Philipeaux, J. M. 1856. Note sur l'extirpation des capsules surrénales chez les rats albinos (Mus rattus). C. R. Acad. Sci., 43: 904.
Rice, K. K. and C. P. Richter. 1943. Increased Sodium Chloride and Water Intake of Normal Rats Treated with Desoxycorticosterone Acetate. Endocrinology, 33: 106.
Richter, C. P. 1946. Further Observations on the Ability of Rats to Make Beneficial Selection from Purified Substances. Read at the Annual Meeting of the Friends of the Land, Athens, Ohio.
Richter, C. P. 1948. Psychotic Behavior Produced Experimentally in Recently Trapped Wild Rats, Apparently by Fear of Food Poisoning. Sec. International Symposium, Mooseheart Laboratory for Child Research.
Richter, C. P. 1950. Taste and solubility of Toxic Compounds. Jour. Comp. Physiol. Psych. 43: 358–374.
Richter, C. P. and K. H. Campbell. 1940. Sucrose Taste Threshold of Rats and Humans. Am. Jour. Physiol. 128: 291.
Richter, C. P. and K. H. Clisby. 1941. Phenylthiocarbamide Taste Thresholds of Rats and Human Beings. Am. Jour. Physiol. 134: 157.
Richter, C. P. and J. T. Emlen, Jr. 1945. A Modified Rabbit Box Trap for Use in Catching Live Wild Rats for Laboratory and Field Studies. Publ. Health Rep. 60: 1303.
Richter, C. P. and C. E. Hall. 1947. Comparison of Intestinal Lengths and Peyer's Patches in Wild and Domestic Norway and Wild Alexandrine Rats. Proc. Soc. Exp. Biol. & Med., 66: 561.

Richter, C. P. and A. MacLean. 1939. Salt Taste Thresholds of Humans. Am. Jour. Physiol., 126: 1.

Richter, C. P., P. V. Rogers, and C. E. Hall. 1950. Failure of Salt Replacement Therapy in Adrenalectomized Recently Captured Wild Norway Rats. Endocrinology, 46: 233–242.

Rogers, P. V. and C. P. Richter. 1948. Anatomical Comparison Between the Adrenal Glands of Wild Norway, Wild Alexandrine and Domestic Norway Rats. Endocrinology 42: 46.

Sadovnikova-Koltzova, Mary P. 1926 Genetic Analysis of Temperament of Rats. Jour. Exp. Zool. 45: 301.

Selye, H. 1946. The General Adaptation Syndrome and the Diseases of Adaptation. Jour. Clin. Endocrinology 6: 117.

Stone, C. P. 1932. Wildness and Savageness in Rats of Different Strains. Studies in the Dynamics of Behavior. Edited by Karl S. Lashley. The University of Chicago Press. Chicago, Illinois.

Watson, C. 1907. A Note on the Adrenal Gland in the Rat. Jour. Physiol., 35: 230.

Yerkes, R. M. 1913. The Heredity of Savageness and Wildness in Rats. Jour. Animal Behavior, 3: 286.

ON THE PHENOMENON OF SUDDEN DEATH IN ANIMALS AND MAN

"Voodoo" death—that is the title of a paper published in 1942 by Walter Cannon.[1] It contains many instances of mysterious, sudden, apparently psychogenic death, from all parts of the world. A Brazilian Indian condemned and sentenced by a so-called medicine man, is helpless against his own emotional response to this pronouncement—and dies within hours. In Africa a young Negro unknowingly eats the inviolably banned wild hen. On discovery of his "crime" he trembles, is overcome by fear, and dies in 24 hours. In New Zealand a Maori woman eats fruit that she only later learns has come from a tabooed place. Her chief has been profaned. By noon of the next day she is dead. In Australia a witch doctor points a bone at a man. Believing that nothing can save him, the man rapidly sinks in spirits and prepares to die. He is saved only at the last moment when the witch doctor is forced to remove the charm. R. Herbert Basedow in his book *The Australian Aboriginal*[2] wrote in 1925:

> The man who discovers that he is being boned by an enemy is, indeed, a pitiable sight. He stands aghast with his eyes staring at the treacherous pointer, and with his hands lifted to ward off the lethal medium, which he imagines is pouring into his body. His cheeks blanch, and his eyes become glassy, and the expression of his face becomes horribly distorted. He attempts to shriek but usually the sound chokes in his throat, and all that one might see is froth at his mouth. His body begins to tremble and his muscles

---

This paper was originally published in *Psychosomatic Medicine* Vol. XIX, No. 3, May-June 1957. Reprinted by permission.

twitch involuntarily. He sways backward and falls to the ground, and after a short time appears to be in a swoon. He finally composes himself, goes to his hut and there frets to death.

Cannon made a thorough search of reports from many primitive societies before he convinced himself of the existence of voodoo deaths. He concluded:

> ... the phenomenon is characteristically noted among aborigines—among human beings so primitive, so superstitious, so ignorant, that they feel themselves bewildered strangers in an hostile world. Instead of knowledge, they have fertile and unrestricted imaginations which fill their environment with all manner of evil spirits capable of affecting their lives disastrously....

Having, after a painstaking search of the literature, convinced himself of the reality of this phenomenon, Cannon next addressed himself to the question "How can an ominous and persistent state of fear end the life of man?" To answer this question he had recourse to his experimental observations on rage and fear in cats. He believed that while rage is associated with the instinct to attack and fear with the instinct to flee, these two emotions have similar effects on the body. Thus, when either of these instincts is aroused the same elemental parts of the nervous system and endocrine apparatus are brought into action, the sympathicoadrenal system.

> If these powerful emotions prevail, and the bodily forces are fully mobilized for action, and if this state of extreme perturbation continues in uncontrolled possession of the organism for any considerable period, without the occurrence of action, dire results may ensue.

Thus, according to Cannon, death would result as a consequence of the state of shock produced by the continuous outpouring of adrenalin. Voodooed individuals would, therefore, be expected to breathe very rapidly, have a rapid pulse, and show a hemoconcentration resulting from loss of fluids from the blood to the tissues. The heart would beat faster and faster, gradually leading to a state of constant contraction and, ultimately, to death in systole.

Cannon expressed the hope that anyone having the opportunity to observe an individual in the throes of voodoo influence would make observations on respiratory and pulse rates, concentration of the blood, etc., to test this theory.

I bring this up here not because I have had opportunity to examine human victims—I have not—but because I have observed what may be a similar phenomenon in rats and because our studies may throw light on the underlying mechanisms of sudden unexplained death in man, not only in voodoo cultures. We are still actively at work on the problem and consequently this communication must be considered simply as a report of work in progress.

As so often happens, this phenomenon was discovered accidentally, as it were, during the course of other experiments. The first observation was made with Dr. Gordon Kennedy in 1953 while studying the sodium metabolism of rats on very high salt diets. To determine the amount of sodium excreted, three animals on a diet containing 35 per cent NaCl were kept in metabolism cages over large glass funnels. The urine was collected in a cylinder. To prevent contamination of the urine with this salt-rich food, the food-cup in each cage was placed at the end of a passageway, as far as possible from the neck of the funnel; however, despite our precautions, food was still dragged over the funnel, apparently on the whiskers or hair of the snout. In a further attempt to prevent this contamination the whiskers and hair were trimmed away with electric clippers. One of the three rats at once began to behave in a very peculiar manner, incessantly pushing its snout into the corners of the cage or into the food-cut with a corkscrew motion. Although before the clipping procedure it had seemed entirely normal, eight hours afterwards it was dead.

This observation was recalled a year or two later, while we were studying differences in the response to stress of wild and domesticated Norway rats. For these studies we measured endurance by means of swimming survival times, using specially designed tanks—glass cylinders 36 inches deep, standing inside glass jars 8 inches in diameter and 30 inches in depth (Fig. 1). A jet of water of any desired temperature playing into the center of each cylinder precluded the animals' floating, while the collar of the cylinder itself prevented escape. The study was started with observations on our domesticated rats. Figure 2 shows the relationship between swimming time (drowning) and water temperature. The ordinates show average (7 rats at each point) swimming time in hours, and the abscissas water temperature in degrees Fahrenheit. As can be seen, the average survival times were directly related to the temperature of the water; thus, the swimming times ranged from 10–15 minutes at 63–73° F., to 60 hours at 95° F., to 20 minutes at 105°.

The significance of this average curve was greatly reduced by the marked variations in individual swimming times. At all temperatures, a small number of rats died within 5–10 minutes after immersion, while

Fig. 1. Glass Swimming Jars, Water Jets, Cold and Hot Water Faucets, Pressure Gauge, and Pressure Regulator.

in some instances others apparently no more healthy, swam as long as 81 hours. The elimination of these large variations presented a real problem, which for some time we could not solve. Then the solution came from an unexpected source—the finding of the phenomenon of sudden death, which constitutes the main topic of this communication. On one occasion while I was watching rats swim it occurred to me to investigate the effect of trimming the rat's whiskers on its performance in water. Would a rat swimming without whiskers show the peculiar behavior of the original rat in the metabolism cage?

Our observations were started with twelve, tame, domesticated rats. Using electric clippers, the whiskers and hair of the facial area were trimmed before the animals were placed in water at 95° F., a temperature at which most intact, control rats swim 60 to 80 hours. The first rat swam around excitedly on the surface for a very short time, then dove to the bottom, where it began to swim around nosing its way along the glass wall. Without coming to the surface a single time, it died 2 minutes after entering the tank. Two more of the twelve domesticated

On the Phenomenon of Sudden Death in Animals and Man 323

SWIMMING TIME
WITH RELATION TO WATER TEMPERATURE
DOMESTICATED NORWAY RATS
AVERAGES FOR SEVEN RATS AT EACH POINT

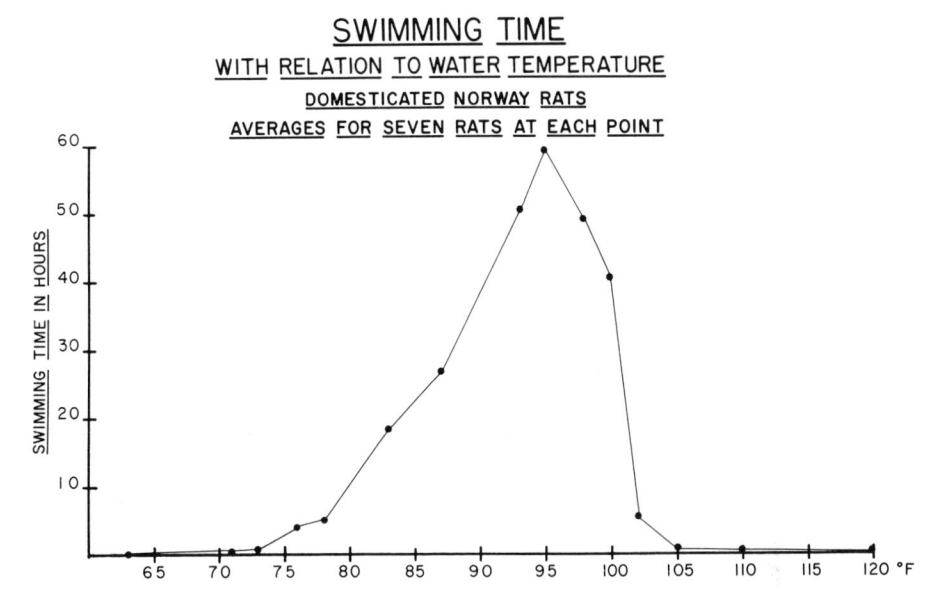

Fig. 2. Curve Showing Average Swimming Time (end point, drowning) of Unconditioned Tame Domesticated Norway Rats with Relation to Water Temperature. Averages for 7 rats at each point.

rats tested died in much the same way; however, the remaining 9 swam 40 to 60 hours.

Five of 6 hybrid rats, crosses between wild and domesticated rats, similarly treated, died in a very brief time. We then tested 34 clipped wild rats, all recently trapped. These animals are characteristically fierce, aggressive, and suspicious; they are constantly on the alert for any avenue of escape and react very strongly to any form of restraint in captivity. All 34 died in 1–15 minutes after immersion in the jars.

From the results we concluded that trimming the rats' whiskers, destroying possibly their most important means of contact with the outside world, seemed disturbing enough, especially to wild rats, to cause their deaths. However, when we began analyzing the various steps involved in transferring the fierce, wild rats from their cages to the water jars without the use of any anesthetic, it became obvious that a number of other factors had to be taken into account. To evaluate the relative importance of these factors, it became necessary to follow the rats from the time they left their cages until they finally died at the bottom of the swimming jars.

Figure 3*A* shows the type of metal cage used for the wild rats. The bevelled end contains a hinged door, the flat end a sliding door. Figure

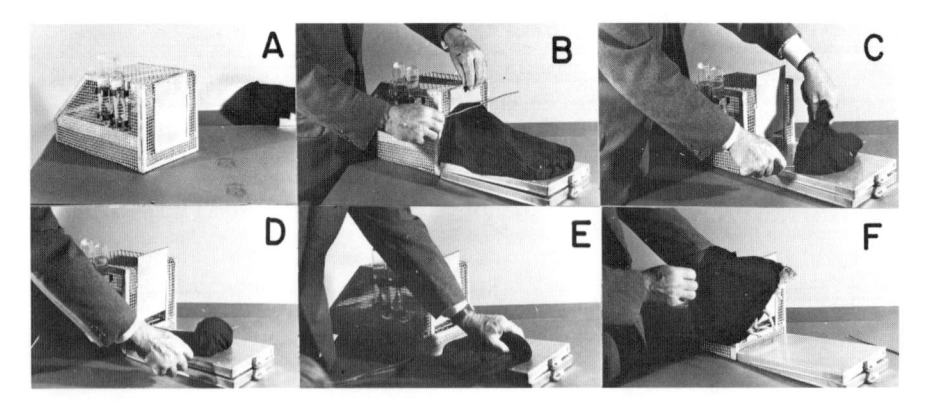

Fig. 3. Steps Involved in Transferring Wild Rat from Holding Cage to Black Bag.

3B shows the black opaque bag used for catching and holding the rat. The open end is held over the sliding door at the flat end of the cage. When the sliding door is opened, the rat sees the dark opening—an avenue of escape—and usually within seconds, almost "shoots" in. The instant the rat is out of the cage its retreat is cut off by a rod pressed down across the mouth of the bag as shown in Fig. 3C. Figures 3D and E show how, by means of the rod, the rat is then pushed into the end of the bag, where it is firmly but gently prevented from turning. The head is located by palpation and is held between the thumb and fingers, with care not to exert any pressure on the neck, while the body is held in the palm of the hand. Over 2000 rats have been held in this way, and none has ever made an attempt to bite through the bag. The rat is then lifted and the black cloth is peeled back exposing its head and body. (See Fig. 3F.) Held in this way the rat can neither bite nor escape; its whiskers can be trimmed, it can be injected, or it can be dropped directly into a swimming jar.

Thus, in evaluating the possible causes of the prompt death of the wild rats in this experiment, account must be taken of the following factors:

1. Reaction of the rat to confinement in the holding bag.
2. Reaction to being held in the experimenter's hand, while being prevented from biting or escaping.
3. Peripheral and cerebral vascular reactions to being held in an upright position. (The upright posture is reported to be fatal to wild rabbits.)[3]
4. Peripheral and cerebral vascular reactions to possible unavoidable pressure on the carotid sinus, carotid body, or larynx, exerted by the tips of the forefinger and thumb in holding the

rat. (Prolonged pressure on the carotid sinus can produce syncope and even death in man as well as animals through its effect on vascular and respiratory mechanisms.)[4]
5. Reaction to the process of being clipped.
6. Reaction to confinement in swimming jar, with no avenue of escape.
7. Reaction of the clipped rats to a new situation, determined by the loss of stimulation from whiskers.
8. Respiratory reaction to immersion in water. (Diving produces marked slowing in heart rate.)[5]
9. Peripheral and cerebral vascular reactions to immersion in water at a temperature of 95° F. (Immersion in water of this temperature could produce a marked drop in pressure, resulting in cerebral anemia.)
10. Vascular reaction to nearly upright swimming posture. (Similar to, but presumably more marked than in No. 3.)

At present it appears that of all these factors, two are the most important: the restraint involved in holding the wild rats, thus suddenly and finally abolishing all hope of escape; and the confinement in the glass jar, further eliminating all chance of escape and at the same time threatening them with immediate drowning. Some of the wild rats died simply while being held in the hand; some even died when put into the water directly from their living cages, without ever being held. The combination of both maneuvers killed a far higher percentage. When in addition the whiskers were trimmed, all normal wild rats tested so far have died. The trimming of the whiskers thus proved to play a contributory, rather than an essential, role.

What kills these rats? Why do all of the fierce, aggressive, wild rats die promptly on immersion after clipping, and only a small number of the similarly treated tame domesticated rats?

On the basis of Cannon's conclusions and under the influence of the current thinking about the importance of the part played by the adrenals and the sympathetic nervous system in emotional states, and especially under stress, we naturally looked first of all for signs of sympathetic stimulation, especially for tachycardia and death in systole. Accordingly we were first interested in measuring the heart rate.

Electrocardiographic records were taken by means of electrodes consisting of short pieces of sharpened copper wire, each with a very fine insulated wire soldered to the blunt end. The pointed copper wires were dipped into electrode jelly and inserted under the skin of the two hind legs and one foreleg. They were inserted up the legs and the connecting wires were bent back up over the legs. A piece of plastic

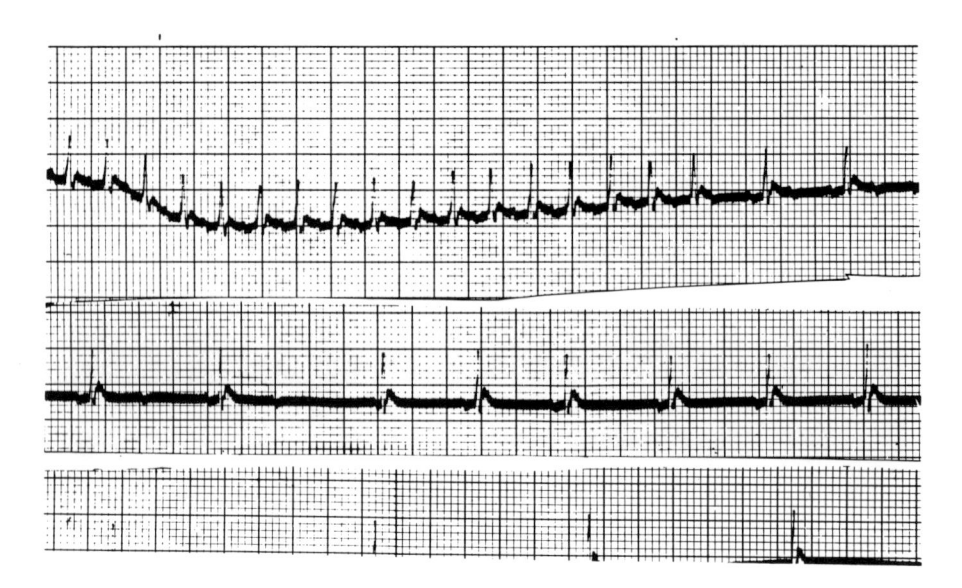

Fig. 4. Part of Electrocardiogram on Wild Rat Taken a Few Minutes after the Rat's Immersion in the Water Jar.

adhesive tape wrapped around the leg held the electrode and wire in place, insuring that a force exerted on the connecting wire would pull the electrode further under the skin rather than dislodge it. The connecting wires were brought together over the animal's back. In this way the rat could swim without getting itself entangled. Surprisingly, records taken under water were indistinguishable from those taken in air.

Contrary to our expectation, the EKG records indicated that the rats succumbing promptly died with a slowing of the heart rate rather than with an acceleration. Figure 4 shows portions of the underwater EKG record typical of a rat dying promptly after immersion. Terminally, slowing of respiration and lowering of body temperature were also observed. Ultimately the heart stopped in diastole after having shown a steady gradual decrease in rate. As expected, autopsy revealed a large heart distended with blood. These findings indicate that the rats may have died a so-called vagus death, which is the result of overstimulation of the parasympathetic rather than of the sympathicoadrenal system.

It should be pointed out that the first response to stress, whether that of restraint in the hand or confinement in the water jars, was often an accelerated heart rate; only subsequently, with prolongation of the stress situation, was this followed by slowing. In some rats the latter response developed very promptly, in others not for a few minutes.

On the Phenomenon of Sudden Death in Animals and Man

The following additional facts are in agreement with such a preliminary formulation: (1) pretreatment with atropine prevented the prompt death of 3 out of 25 clipped wild rats. By increasing the dose or by varying the interval between the injections and the test it might have been possible to achieve a higher survival rate; (2) domesticated rats injected with definitely sublethal amounts of cholinergic drugs (morphine, physostigmine, mecholyl), i.e., of parasympathetic stimulants, died within a few minutes after being put in the swimming jars. Thus, one-tenth of the LD 50 of morphine sufficed to bring out the sudden death response in these rats, in effect eliminating this distinction between domesticated and wild rats; (3) so far all the adrenalectomized wild rats tested still showed sudden-death response, indicating that the deaths were not due to an overwhelming supply of adrenalin. Thyroidectomy likewise did not prevent the appearance of the sudden-death phenomenon.

The situation of these rats scarcely seems one demanding fight or flight—it is rather one of hopelessness; whether they are restrained in the hand or confined in the swimming jar, the rats are in a situation against which they have no defense. This reaction of hopelessness is shown by some wild rats very soon after being grasped in the hand and prevented from moving; they seem literally to "give up."

Support for the assumption that the sudden-death phenomenon depends largely on emotional reactions to restraint or immersion comes from the observation that after elimination of the hopelessness the rats do not die. This is achieved by repeatedly holding the rats briefly and then freeing them, and by immersing them in water for a few minutes on several occasions. In this way the rats quickly learn that the situation is not actually hopeless; thereafter they again become aggressive, try to escape, and show no signs of giving up. Wild rats so conditioned swim just as long as domestic rats or longer.

Another observation worthy of record concerns the remarkable speed of recovery of which these animals are capable. Once freed from restraint in the hand or confinement in the glass jars, a rat that quite surely would have died in another minute or two becomes normally active and aggressive in only a few minutes. Thus, in order to measure the maximum swimming time, we now try to free the rats of all emotional reactions to restraint or confinement by successively exposing them to these situations and freeing them several times beforehand. In this way we have succeeded in eliminating most of the individual variations and are now obtaining quite constant, reproducible, endurance records for both domesticated and wild rats.

It is interesting that a few wild rats have also been protected by pretreatment with chlorpromazine, without other "conditioning."

That the wild rats as compared to the domesticated rats seem much more susceptible to this type of death would suggest that they have a higher vagus tone. In agreement with this thought are the well-known observations that vagus tone is higher in healthy, vigorous individuals than in weaker ones; also that vagus tone is higher in wild than in domesticated animals in general.[6]

Other wild animals—rabbits, shrews, and pigeons—as well as some domesticated animals—ewes—are known to show a sudden-death response; whether of the same kind as we have described here is not known at present.

How can these results be applied toward the understanding of the voodoo-death response in man? Apparently the "boned" victim, like the wild rat, is not set for fight or flight, but similarly seems resigned to his fate—his situation seems to him quite hopeless. For this reason we believe that the human victims—like our rats—may well die a parasympathetic rather than a sympathicoadrenal death, as Cannon postulated.

Like the wild rat, primitive man, when freed from voodoo, is said to recover almost instantaneously, even though he had recently seemed more dead than alive. These observations suggest that the sudden-death phenomenon may be a one-time occurrence both in rats and man—in any particular circumstances, ending either in death or in immunity from this particular kind of death. In human beings as well as in rats we see the possibility that hopelessness and death may result from the effects of a combination of reactions, all of which may operate in the same direction, and increase the vagal tone.

There is the further suggestion that the incidence of this response varies inversely as the degree of civilization, or domestication, of the individual, since it occurs more frequently in wild than in domesticated rats and so far certainly has been described chiefly in primitive man, that is to say, in creatures living in precarious situations.

However, some physicians believe that this phenomenon exists also in our culture. Thus, according to Cannon, Dr. J. M. T. Finney, the well-known surgeon at the Johns Hopkins Hospital, apparently believed in it, since he absolutely would not operate on any patient who showed a strong fear of operation. Many instances are at hand of sudden death from fright, sight of blood, hypodermic injections or from sudden immersion in water.

During the war a considerable number of unaccountable deaths were reported among soldiers in the armed forces in this country. These men died when they apparently were in good health. At autopsy no pathology could be observed.[7]

Of interest here also is that, according to Dr. R. S. Fisher, Coroner of the City of Baltimore, a number of individuals die each year after taking small, definitely sublethal doses of poison, or after inflicting small, nonlethal wounds on themselves; apparently they die as a result of the belief in their doom.

Summary

A phenomenon of sudden death has been described that occurs in man, rats, and many other animals apparently as a result of hopelessness; this seems to involve overactivity primarily of the parasympathetic system. In this instance as in many others, the ideas of Walter Cannon opened up a new area of interesting, exciting research.

References

1. Cannon, W. B. "Voodoo" death. *Am. Anthrop.* 44:169, 1942.
2. Basedow, H. *The Australian Aboriginal.* Adelaide, Australia, 1925.
3. Best, C. H., and Taylor, N. B. *Physiological Basis of Medical Practice.* (Fifth Ed.) Baltimore, 1950.
4. Weiss, S. Instantaneous "physiologic" death. *New England J. Med.* 223:793, 1940.
5. Irving, L. The action of the heart and circulation during diving. *Tr. New York Acad. Sc.* 5:11, 1942.
6. Clark, A. S. *Comparative Physiology of the Heart.* London, Cambridge, 1927.
7. Moritz, A. R., and Zamchek, N. Sudden unexpected deaths of young soldiers. *Arch. Path.* 42:459, 1946.

TASTE AND SOLUBILITY OF TOXIC COMPOUNDS IN POISONING OF RATS AND MAN[1]

The art of poisoning with murderous intent was widely practiced from the earliest historical times up to the middle of the last century. Professional practitioners, who favored arsenic compounds, raised this art to great heights during the Middle Ages, and particularly during the Renaissance. Since then the development of methods for detecting poisons in tissues and the development of effective antidotes have gradually discouraged the professionals, so that now the art is practiced only infrequently and half-heartedly by amateurs.

During and after the First World War, a renewed interest in poisoning developed—this time not as applied to human beings but for controlling the large populations of destructive, disease-bearing, wild rodents that progressively infested more and more of our cities, towns, and farms. Several factors may account for this. First, workers in different fields became aware that chemical compounds had many potential uses both

---

This paper was originally published in *The Journal of Comparative and Physiological Psychology*, Vol. 43, No. 5, October, 1950.

[1] Started under a contract between the Office of Scientific Research and Development and the Johns Hopkins University and completed under a contract between the Medical Division, Chemical Corps, U. S. Army and the Johns Hopkins University. Under the terms of this contract the Chemical Corps neither restricts nor is responsible for the opinions or conclusions of the author. Reported in part in 1944 at a meeting of the Rodent Control Subcommittee, the division of Chemistry, Committee on Medical Research, of the Office of Scientific Research and Development; carried out with the assistance of Romaine Randall and Paul T. Condit. Much help was received from Dr. Tracy I. Storer of the University of California in the collection of the historical data on the discovery and use of the various poisons.

for the treatment and for the destruction of biological organisms and particularly for the control of insects. Second, the synthesis in industrial and university laboratories of an almost limitless number of chemical compounds of every conceivable structure made many new compounds available for biological testing. Third, with the greatly reduced incidence of cases of homicidal poisoning, people in general became less afraid of the widespread use and distribution of poisons—in fact, poisons of one sort or another have become a part of the collection of drugs that fill most medicine cabinets.

Before the First World War only four rodenticides were in common use—strychnine, arsenic trioxide, barium carbonate, and red squill.[2] After that war two new poisons, thallium sulphate and zinc phosphide, were introduced. Both of the latter proved to be more effective but also more dangerous to use.[3]

During the Second World War, owing to the enemy's control of the supplies of red squill, strychnine, and thallium sulphate, the search for substances that would be effective against noxious rodents was re-

---

[2] Certain arsenic compounds appear free in nature and so were probably discovered at a very early date in man's history. Written records appear as early as 340 B.C. when Aristotle reported on the results of his examination of arsenic compounds that Alexander had brought back from his campaigns (13, 29). Although in ancient and medieval times man used these poisons to kill his fellow man, he used them also to kill rodents. Lewin mentions that in 1384 (14) arsenic compounds were used to poison rats. In a book published in 1590 Mascall mentions the use of arsenic as a rat poison (17).

Barium carbonate was first used as a rodent poison by Crampe in 1878 (5). Red squill is a large bulb with pink scales (*Urginea scilla*) that grows along the Mediterranean seaboard. The inhabitants of this region have known since early historical times that the fresh bulbs could be used to poison rodents. The first actual report of such a use was made by the Arabian investigator, Muhammed Elgafaki, at the beginning of the 13th century (6). In the Middle Ages the fresh bulb scales, chopped and mixed with fat or food, were used as baits (7). Extracts of the bulbs were made and analyzed by M. P. Orfila in 1818 (20). This material was tested before the First World War in England by Boulenger and Mitchell (3) and later was recommended for use in the United States in 1917 by Lantz (12); owing largely to its reputed low toxicity for man red squill was the most widely used rodenticide between the wars. Lewin reports, however, that it has been known to kill man (14). White squill is non-toxic for man and rats and was used for a long time as a heart stimulant, as well as an expectorant, emetic and diuretic.

[3] Lamy in 1862–63 first described the high toxicity of thallium compounds (10, 11). Thallium sulphate was used as a rodenticide in Germany in 1920 and was marketed as "Zelio" paste. Hartnack brought it to this country in 1922–1923. Owing to its high toxicity for man it has had only a limited use (19). Zinc phosphide was developed in Italy (8). It has been widely used in Germany and England, and less widely by the U. S. Fish and Wildlife Service. It is highly toxic to man.

newed. Among the many substances tested, sodium fluoroacetate (Compound 1080) was found to be an especially effective rodenticide. It proved more toxic than any of the previous poisons, but because of its universal toxicity, and the lack of an antidote, even more hazardous to use.[4] Alpha-naphthyl thiourea (ANTU)[5] which was developed in this laboratory in the course of this search, was shown to have a high toxicity for both the domestic and the wild Norway rat, while it is relatively non-toxic for a variety of other animals, probably including man.

The reasoning which led to the discovery of ANTU was based on observations that rats are able, on their own initiative, to make beneficial selections from among various substances offered to them. It seemed clear that the rats based their choice on the sense of taste. Accordingly, when we found that phenyl thiourea, a highly toxic but also very bitter substance, was not sufficiently well accepted by wild rats to be an effective rodenticide, we looked for a related, equally toxic, but less soluble compound, on the assumption that lowered solubility would mean reduced bitterness and hence a more efficient poison. ANTU, which is considerably less soluble than phenyl thiourea, proved indeed to be less bitter and was readily accepted in lethal amounts by wild rats.

The success of this type of reasoning made us decide to examine other common poisons, to see whether we had discovered a general

---

[4] The high toxicity of methyl fluoroacetate was discovered in 1939 by three Polish scientists working in the Polish Anti-Gas Institute. After the German invasion of Poland one of the discoverers transmitted this information to the British, who confirmed the original work and developed the sodium salt as a water poison. These facts were made available to the O.S.R.D. and through Dr. Walter R. Kirner, Chief of Division of Chemistry, to the Fish and Wildlife Service. It was given the number 1080 on the latter's list of toxic compounds, which accounts for its common name. The public disclosure of the toxicity of sodium fluoroacetate and its high efficiency as a rat poison was made by Dr. E. R. Kalmbach of the Fish and Wildlife Service (9). This compound has a very high toxicity for rats as well as for most other animals including man. To date several children and adults have died from accidental poisoning with compound 1080. Closely related compounds (potassium salts) have been found to be present in a plant, *Dichapetalum cymosum*, known in South Africa as "Gifblaar" (15, 16). The leaves of this plant are very poisonous to stock animals; only a few leaves have killed an ox (26). Various preparations of this highly toxic plant have long been used with great success by the natives for mass poisoning of rival tribes. A recent government bulletin gives a full account of the dangers involved in the use of compound 1080 and of the precautions that must be observed by those who work with it (22).

[5] The methods of using alpha-naphthyl thiourea as a rodenticide were developed during the last war, under a contract with the Committee on Medical Research of the Office of Scientific Research and Development (25).

principle. Do all toxic substances carry with them a warning taste, bitter or otherwise? And if so, is this detectable only by rats or is there some correlation between the taste sensations of rats and of men? The fact that rats cannot regurgitate food once it is swallowed presumably accounts for their cautious, mincing eating habits, but the question arises whether they are also, perhaps, equipped with more sensitive taste perception. The present paper resulted from our attempts to answer these questions. We have examined the seven poisons mentioned above, and also four other known toxic substances, three on the basis of their unpleasant taste to man (strychnine sulphate, mercuric chloride and phenyl thiourea) and one other derivative of thiourea, namely thiosemicarbazide, which was recently found by Dr. Emmanuel Waletzky of the American Cyanamid Company to be very toxic to rats (21).

Methods

Table 1 lists the eleven poisons that were used. It gives the median lethal doses (LD50's) in mg/kg. body weight for domestic and wild Norway rats and the estimated minimum fatal doses for man, likewise expressed in mg/kg. The table also lists the sources from which we obtained these poisons, and the approximate solubilities of each in water in mg/100 ml. of water at room temperature.

The rats were housed in individual wire mesh cages containing a food cup (filled with a stock diet[6]) and two graduated drinking bottles placed in symmetrical position at either side of the front wall of the cage (23, 24). Each bottle was plainly labelled and was kept in the same corner of the cage throughout the experiment. Daily at 11 A.M. readings were made of the fluid intake from the two bottles. The rats were weighed at weekly intervals.

Both bottles contained distilled water for the first 10 to 15 days, or at least until the intake from each bottle had become fairly constant. Most of the rats showed a consistent preference for one or the other bottle. Previous observations have demonstrated that this preference can be either for the bottle itself (because of smoothness of lip or some other characteristic) or for its position in the cage.

After the initial control period, a subliminal concentration of one of the poison solutions was placed in whichever bottle the rat had consis-

---

[6] Graham flour 72.5%, casein 10.0%, butter 5.0%, skim milk powder 10.0%, calcium carbonate 1.5%, sodium chloride 1.0%.

TABLE 1. LIST OF POISONS, THEIR SOLUBILITY IN WATER, MINIMAL FATAL DOSE, AND NUMBERS AND KINDS OF RATS USED

Poison and Source	Approx. LD50 Norway Rats[1] Dom.	Approx. LD50 Norway Rats[1] Wild	Approx. Minimum Fatal Dose Man[2]	Solubility in Water (Room Temperature)[3]
	mg. per kg.	mg. per kg.	mg. per kg.	mg. per 100 ml.
1. Strychnine sulphate (Merck)	6	5	1	3200
2. Mercuric chloride (Merck)	40	40	0.5	6900
3. Phenyl thiourea (Eimer and Amend)	3	9	Not known	260
4. Thiosemicarbazide (Eastman Kodak Co.)	15	10	Not known	1000–2000
5. Red Squill Extract (Penick) Powder (Prentiss)	200 90	130♀ 275♂	Not known	Not known Not known
6. Alpha-naphthyl thiourea (ANTU) (du Pont)	5	7	Not known	6
7. Arsenic trioxide (Merck)	175	138	1.5–15	3700
8. Barium carbonate (Baker)	900	1480	800	Insoluble
9. Zinc phosphide (Fish and Wildlife Service)	45	40	40	Insoluble
10. Sodium fluoroacetate (1080) (Monsanto)	5	0.5	2	11,000
11. Thallium sulphate (Am. Smelting & Refining Co.)	18	16	20	4870

[1] Determinations made in this laboratory. (Red Squill extract toxicity from Penick and Company.)
[2] Ward and Spencer: 1947. Food Technology, Vol. I: 51–55.
[3] Various sources in the literature.

tently preferred, regardless of its position in the cage. Thereafter, up to the limits of solubility of the compound or the death of the rat, the concentration of poison was increased daily as indicated in the figures. If the rat started consistently to drink less from the bottle containing the poison solution and correspondingly more of the distilled water, we concluded that it was able to taste and reject the poison. The concentration at which the rat first began to reject the poison solution and to drink more distilled water (from the bottle that was originally less pleasing) was taken as the "taste threshold" for that particular poison. If, however, the intakes of the poison solution and of distilled water remained at constant levels, or if they decreased simultaneously, the results were interpreted as indicating that the rats did not distinguish by taste between the water and the solution of poison.

The poison solutions were always prepared on the day before use and allowed to stand overnight at room temperature as was the distilled water, thus making certain that both bottles had the same temperature when offered to the rats.

A total of 70 adult male domestic Norway rats from our stock colony was used for these tests.

The taste of these same compounds to human subjects was determined as follows: 1 cc. of a given solution was offered in a small medicine glass, and the subject was instructed to swirl it around in his mouth and to taste it as carefully as possible. For the five very soluble compounds concentrations were used which were well above the taste thresholds found for rats for these compounds. For the less soluble compounds, such as phenyl thiourea and ANTU, "saturated" solutions were used; these were prepared by allowing water to stand overnight at room temperature in contact with an excess of the solids in finely divided form. The various poisons were also offered as powders: a small amount of each (not more than three mg.) was picked up on the end of a flat toothpick and placed on the middle of the protruded tongue. In all instances the subjects were asked to report whether they could taste the compound; and if so, to describe the taste sensation.

The subjects were not told anything about the nature of the compounds, but from the bitterness of some of the powders as well as from a knowledge of the experimenter's interests, they may well have suspected their toxic nature. The vials and bottles were kept under a counter, out of view, but the subjects were not blindfolded. With the exception of squill, zinc phosphide and ANTU, the poisons were all white powders, reduced with mortar and pestle to approximately the same particle size. Red squill is, as its name implies, a reddish powder, while ANTU is greyish, and zinc phosphide dark grey.

To avoid a carry-over of the taste sensation from one solution to another, some of the subjects were tested with only one poison each day; other subjects were given several of the poisons each day but in different order from person to person, a close watch being kept on the effects that one poison might seem to have on the taste of the one that followed it. In most instances we tried to start the tests with a compound likely to be tasteless.

A total of 60 adult human volunteers was used for these observations: 13 assistants and helpers in the laboratory and 47 enlisted men and officers at the Army Chemical Center at Edgewood, Maryland. Most of the subjects were tested with all of the compounds.

Results

Taste Tests on Rats

The taste threshold tests showed that the rats were able to taste seven of the eleven poisons and were unable to detect the remaining four compounds in solution. Figure 1 gives the average taste threshold

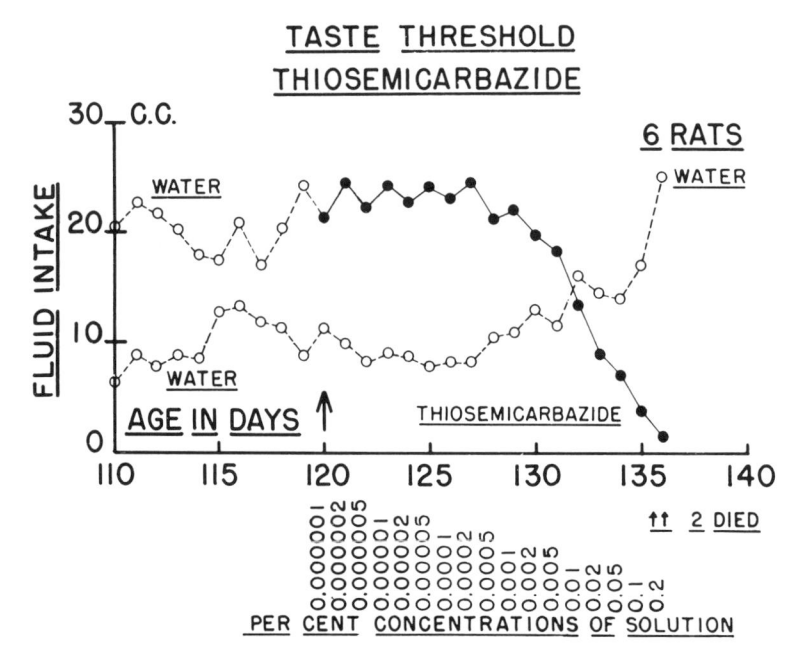

Fig. 1. Average Taste Threshold Curves for Six Rats on Thiosemicarbazide. Ordinates give the fluid intake in cc; abscissas, age in days.

Taste and Solubility in Poisoning of Rats and Man

curves for the six rats on thiosemicarbazide. The ordinates give the daily intake from each of the two bottles in cubic centimeters; the abscissas give average age in days as well as the per cent concentration of the solution offered each day. For the first 10 days (age 110-119 days inclusive) both bottles contained distilled water (open dots). Then on the 120th day an exceedingly dilute solution of thiosemicarbazide was introduced into the preferred bottle (solid black dots). For eight days, that is until the concentration reached 0.0002 per cent, the rats continued to take as much from each bottle as they had during the control period. However, with the next higher concentration, 0.0005 per cent, they started to drink less of the poison solution and more water—and after eight further daily increases of concentration their drinking was confined almost entirely to the distilled water. The average concentration at which the rats first indicated that they could distinguish between the water and the solution of thiosemicarbazide fell at 0.0005 per cent. This concentration, then, is the average taste threshold of domestic rats for thiosemicarbazide.

Figure 2 gives the average taste threshold curves of six rats tested with an extract of red squill. The curves are essentially the same as those obtained with thiosemicarbazide. Strychnine sulphate, mercuric chloride, phenyl thiourea and arsenic trioxide all gave similar taste threshold curves. The curves obtained with ANTU are slightly different

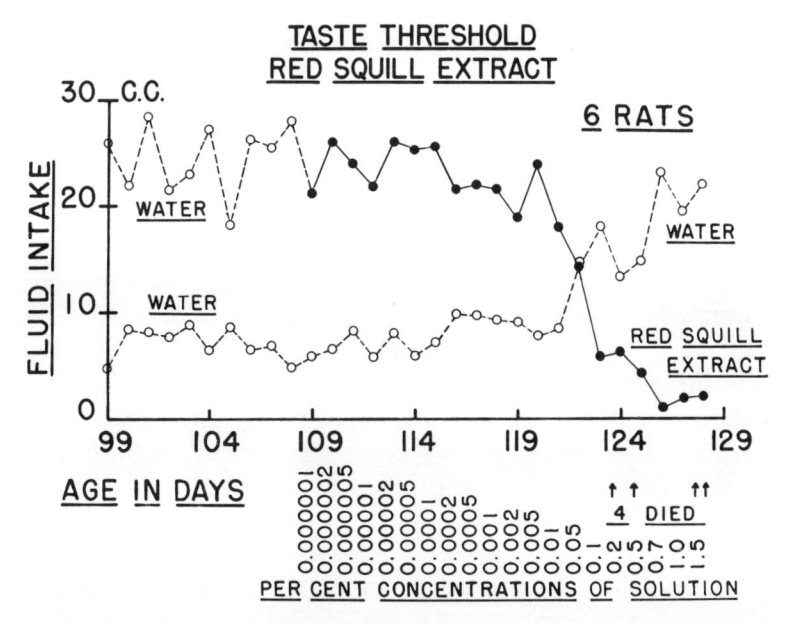

Fig. 2. *Average Taste Threshold Curves for Six Rats on Red Squill Extract (Prentiss). Arrows indicate when rats died.*

TASTE THRESHOLD ANTU

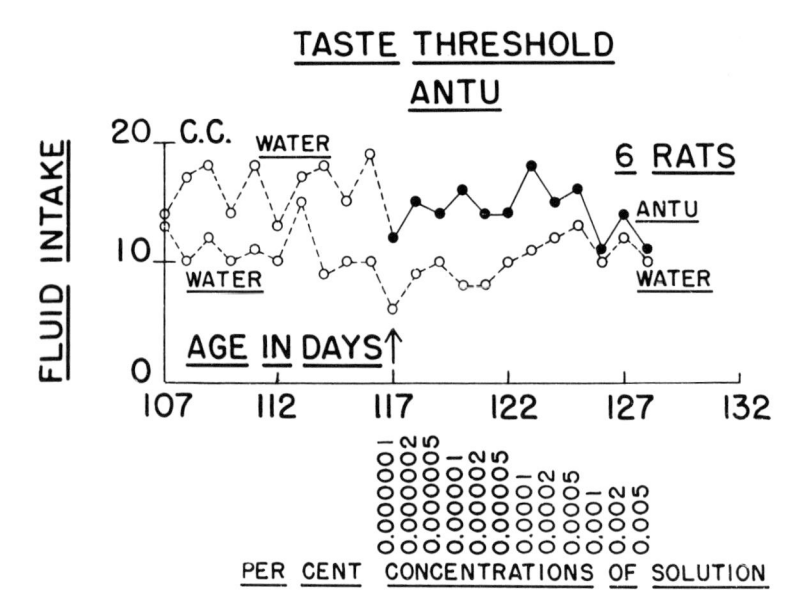

Fig. 3. Average Taste Threshold Curves for Six Rats on ANTU.

(figure 3), as owing to the low solubility of this substance the experiment had to be terminated just after the rats began to recognize and reject the solution.

Table 2 lists the taste threshold concentrations for each individual rat on the seven poisons that they were able to detect by taste. It is not clear why the rats showed a much narrower range of variation in taste threshold for some compounds than for others. The taste thresholds were lowest for phenyl thiourea and highest for red squill. Two of the six rats failed to taste ANTU while one of six rats was apparently unable to taste red squill solution.

Table 2 shows further that two rats on thiosemicarbazide, four rats on red squill extract, one on arsenic trioxide, died even though they had definitely begun to reject these poisons. The arrows in figures 1 and 2 indicate when the rats on thiosemicarbazide and red squill died.

Two of the remaining poisons, barium carbonate and zinc phosphide, had such low solubilities in water that the regular taste threshold experiments could not be carried out.[7] "Saturated" solutions of the two compounds were tested with six rats each and no discrimination observed.

---

[7] Barium carbonate and zinc phosphide are not in themselves toxic, but they react with hydrochloric acid in the stomach to produce barium chloride and the gas phosphine both of which are poisonous.

TABLE 2. TASTE THRESHOLD FOR INDIVIDUAL RATS
CONCENTRATIONS OF SOLUTIONS IN PER CENT

Rat No.	Strychnine Sulphate	Rat No.	Mercuric Chloride	Rat No.	Phenyl Thiourea	Rat No.	Thiosemicar-Bazide	Rat No.	Red Squill (Extract)	Rat No.	ANTU	Rat No.	Arsenic Trioxide
1	0.005	1	0.001	1	0.0001	1	0.0005	1	0.001–D	1	0.0005	1	0.0002
2	0.005	2	0.002	2	0.0001	2	0.0005–D	2	0.002	2	0.001	2	0.0002
3	0.005	3	0.003	3	0.0006	3	0.0005–D	3	0.01–D	3	0.001	3	0.0002
4	0.005	4	0.006	4	0.0008	4	0.002	4	0.05	4	0.002	4	0.003
5	0.01	5	0.007	5	0.0009	5	0.005	5	0.1–D	5	—	5	0.005–D
6	0.02			6	0.0009	6	0.005	6	— –D	6	—	6	0.005
				7	0.007							7	0.005
				8	0.008							8	0.01
												9	0.01
												10	0.01
												11	0.01
												12	0.02

D—indicates that before the completion of the experiment the rat died.

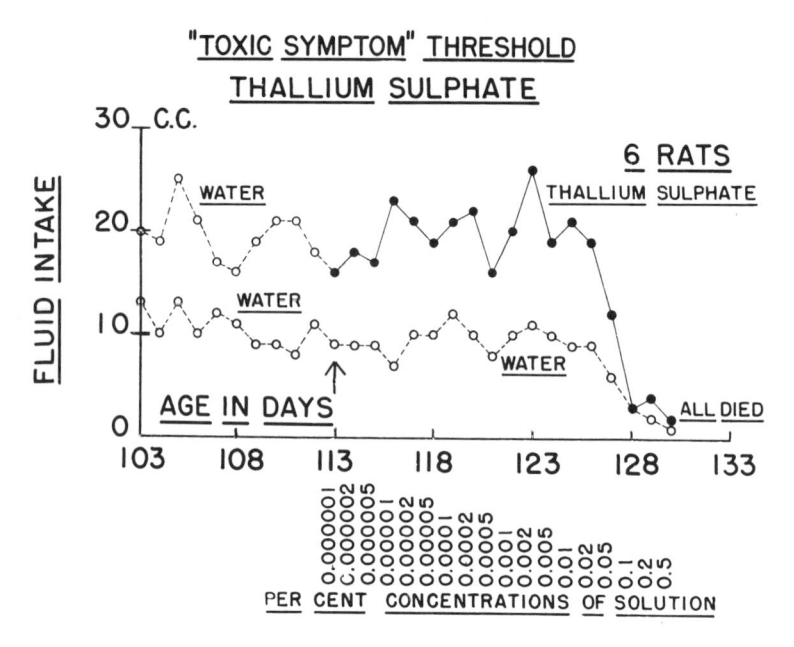

Fig. 4. Average "Toxic Symptom" Threshold for Six Rats on Thallium Sulphate.

Figure 4 shows the average intake curves for six rats on thallium sulphate, one of the other two poisons that the rats did not taste. The rats continued to drink essentially the same volume of the first 14 concentrations offered (solid black dots) as they had previously taken of distilled water from the same bottle. On the 15th day, however, which was obviously when they were beginning to feel the injurious effect of the poison, they began to drink less from both bottles and continued to do so throughout the next four days, when they all died. These results give clear indication that the rats were unable to distinguish between distilled water and solutions of thallium sulphate. The fact that the total fluid consumption decreased so abruptly indicates that they were reacting to the toxic effect of the thallium compound.

Figure 5 represents the average curves for six rats on compound 1080. They are similar to those obtained with thallium sulphate.

The concentration at which the rats began to take less of both the poison and the distilled water can be referred to as the "toxic symptom" threshold. Table 3 shows the individual "toxic symptom" threshold for six rats each on thallium sulphate and on compound 1080. For thallium sulphate the values range from 0.02 to 0.1 per cent and for compound 1080 from 0.0002 to 0.005 per cent. The great difference between the toxic threshold of these two compounds may be explained

"TOXIC SYMPTOM" THRESHOLD
1080

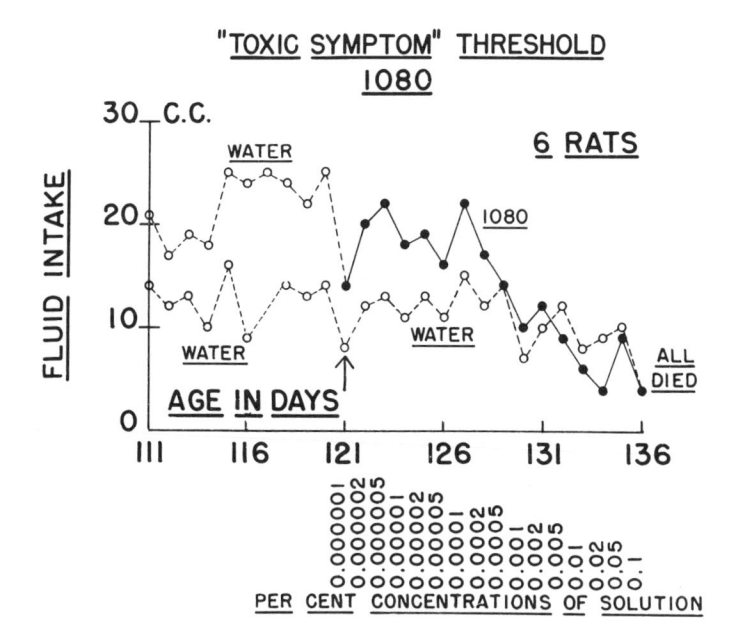

Fig. 5. Average "Toxic Symptom" Thresholds for Six Rats on Compound 1080.

in part by the slow action of the thallium sulphate (2–4 days) and the fast action of 1080 (10–20 minutes), and in part by the lower toxicity of thallium sulphate. See table 1.

Taste Tests on Human Subjects

Table 4 divides the eleven poisons according to whether rats are or are not able to detect them by taste. It shows the number of human subjects that were tested with each poison and the number reporting a positive taste sensation. It also gives a description of the taste sensations

TABLE 3. TOXIC SYMPTOM THRESHOLD
CONCENTRATIONS OF SOLUTIONS IN
PER CENT

Rat No.	Thallium Sulphate	Rat No.	"1080"
1	0.02	1	0.0002
2	0.02	2	0.0005
3	0.05	3	0.001
4	0.1	4	0.001
5	0.1	5	0.001
6	0.1	6	0.005

TABLE 4. TASTE OF POISONS TO HUMAN SUBJECTS

Compound	Total No. of Subjects	No. Reporting a Taste	Slightly Bitter	Moderately Bitter	Bitter	Very Bitter	Extremely Bitter	Astringent	Dry
A. Poisons rats are able to taste									
Strychnine sulphate									
Solution (0.05%)	52	52	2	5	14	16	15	0	0
Powder	20	20	0	1	6	8	5	0	0
Mercuric chloride									
Solution (0.05%)	31	29	6	0	7	2	0	11	3
Powder	21	20	2	0	7	0	0	10	1
Phenyl thiourea									
Solution (ca. 0.26%)	31	31	2	5	7	10	7	0	0
Powder	51	44	9	7	13	15	0	0	0
Thiosemicarbazide									
Solution (0.05%)	9	7	0	0	2	4	1	0	0
Powder	15	12	1	2	5	4	0	0	0
Red squill									
Extract (undiluted)	13	13	1	2	5	5	0	0	0
Powder	22	22	6	6	6	4	0	0	0
ANTU									
Solution (ca. 0.006%)	29	22	6	4	7	5	0	0	0
Powder	52	20	18	2	0	0	0	0	0
Arsenic trioxide									
Solution (0.05%)	14	10	10	0	0	0	0	0	0
Powder	52	1	1	0	0	0	0	0	0
B. Poisons rats are unable to taste									
Barium carbonate									
Powder	21	0							
Zinc phosphide									
Powder	25	16	11(garlic, 1 sulphur, 2 phosphorus, 2 illuminating gas)						
1080									
Solution (0.5%)	25	0							
Powder	21	0							
Thallium sulphate									
Solution (0.1%)	24	0							
Powder	21	0							

TABLE 5. TASTE OF POISON: PER CENT OF TESTED
SUBJECTS THAT TASTED POISONS

	Rats	Humans	
Poison	Solutions	Solution	Powder
Strychnine sulphate	100	100	100
Mercuric chloride	100	93	95
Phenyl thiourea	100	100	85
Thiosemicarbazide	100	78	80
Red squill	83	100	100
ANTU	67	76	38
Arsenic	100	71	2
Barium carbonate	0		0
Zinc phosphide	0		61(Odor?)
1080	0	0	0
Thallium sulphate	0	0	0

reported. All of the 31 subjects tasted phenyl thiourea in solution while only 85 per cent (44 of 51) tasted it in powder form. The closely related, equally toxic but less soluble ANTU was tasted by 76 per cent (22 out of 29) in solution and by only 38 per cent (20 out of 52) in powder form. Arsenic trioxide in solution was tasted by 71 per cent (10 out of 14) while only 2 per cent (1 out of 52) tasted it in powder form.

It is well known through the work of Blakeslee (2) that not all individuals are able to taste phenyl thiourea[8] and that the inability to taste this compound is inherited as a Mendelian recessive. The present results show that a large number of individuals are not able to taste the related compound ANTU, particularly in powder form. The inability of some individuals to taste another closely related compound, thiosemicarbazide, may rest on the same basis.

Table 4 shows further that none of the individuals tested was able to taste the compound 1080 or thallium sulphate when offered in solution or in powder form. They were also unable to taste barium carbonate in powdered form. Sixteen of 25 individuals tested with powdered zinc phosphide reported a taste; judging, however, from the way the taste was described it would seem likely that these individuals were reacting to the odor of phosphine, which is inevitably formed when zinc phosphide is dissolved in water.

Table 5 demonstrates a very close relationship between the ability of rats and of human subjects to taste these eleven compounds. Compounds that were not tasted by the rats were also not tasted by the

---

[8] It is interesting, however, that the taste threshold concentration of phenyl thiourea for rats fell below that of strychnine sulphate by about a factor of ten.

human subjects, with the possible exception of zinc phosphide; likewise the compounds that were tasted by the rats were also tasted by most of the human subjects.

Discussion

The results show that no general relationship exists between water solubility and the taste of these poisons (see tables 1 and 5). Some of the most soluble compounds are not tasted by either humans or rats, while one substance with a low solubility (ANTU) has a definite taste to some rats and to some human subjects. The results indicate, however, that within a closely related group of chemical compounds such as the thioureas, greater solubility is associated with increased taste, but presumably only because a larger amount of the compound goes into solution before the saturation point is reached.

The finding that such highly toxic soluble substances as thallium sulphate and compound 1080 have no taste to rats or man came as a definite surprise. Whether any other highly toxic substances exist that have no taste we do not know. One reason for this lack of knowledge may be that students of the chemistry of taste have almost of necessity focused their attention on substances with a definite taste, rather than those without taste. A compilation and study of soluble tasteless substances, particularly the highly toxic ones, would help throw more light on this relationship.

Tasteless toxic substances could not have existed widespread in nature in readily available forms at any time in evolutionary history, since in the absence of a taste warning every animal or man that ingested them would have perished. It is more likely that they belong to a group of compounds to which, in evolutionary history, man and animals have never been extensively exposed: that is, substances that are not commonly present in plants or in the bodies of other animals, or in the streams, lakes, springs, and other sources of drinking water; or they may belong to a group of man-made compounds which do not occur in nature. Thallium compounds are not widely distributed in nature and they are not present in the body. Fluoroacetates occur naturally only in certain plants and not in the bodies of animals. All of the essential nutrients that we have tested so far have proved to have definite tastes in solution, by which rats are able to recognize them and thus make beneficial dietary selections.

It also appears that the relationship between taste and rodenticidal efficiency is not simple. Table 6 lists the eleven poisons according to

TABLE 6. RELATIONSHIP BETWEEN TASTE AND RODENTICIDAL EFFICIENCY

	Maximum Kill at Any Conc. in Water (Dom. Rats) %	Maximum Kill at Any Conc. in Yellow Corn[2] (Wild Rats) %	Lowest Conc. in Water Giving 100% Kill[1] (Dom. Rats) %	Lowest Conc. in Yellow Corn Giving 100% Kill[2] (Wild Rats) %
Poisons rejected by rats and disliked by man				
1. Strychmine sulphate	0	63	None	None
2. Mercuric chloride	0	0	None	None
3. Phenyl thiourea	71	75	None	None
4. Thiosemicarbazide	100	100	0.25	1.0
5. Squill Extract (Penick & Co.) Powder (Prentiss)		50		None
6. ANTU		100		0.5
7. Arsenic trioxide	100	100	1.0	4.0
Poisons not tasted by rats or man with possible exception of zinc phosphide				
8. Barium carbonate		88		None
9. Zinc phosphide	100	100		0.2
10. 1080	100	100	0.1	0.2
11. Thallium sulphate	100	100	0.025	0.1

[1] Data from this Laboratory.
[2] Dicke, S. H.: 1948, Proc. Soc. Exp. Biol. & Med. 69: 593.

whether or not they are tasted by rats and man, and gives the rodenticidal efficiency when used as a water poison for domestic rats and as a food poison for wild rats. In general, the poisons that have no taste—compound 1080, thallium sulphate, zinc phosphide, barium carbonate—are readily accepted in lethal amounts when mixed in baits; poisons that have a bitter taste—strychnine sulphate, mercuric chloride, and phenyl thiourea—are not accepted and hence are poor rodenticides. However, three poisons that taste bitter to man, and which rats can detect in solution—ANTU, arsenic trioxide and thiosemicarbazide—are readily accepted by rats in lethal amounts and thus are effective as rodenticides. Red squill powder is accepted by some rats in spite of its bitter taste. It will be recalled that some of the rats died during the taste threshold tests on arsenic trioxide, red squill extract and thiosemicarbazide.

A difference in degree of bitterness may explain the acceptance of these poisons, especially since in our tests on human subjects, when the various poisons were tested one after another in different orders, the subjects almost always reported strychnine to be more bitter than any other poison. It is also possible that bitterness may differ in quality. Thus, rats voluntarily drink riboflavin solutions which have a bitter taste, but refuse strychnine solutions which also have a bitter taste. Presumably the essential nutrient qualities of the vitamin, as contrasted with the toxic nature of the alkaloid, determine the respective acceptance and rejection of these compounds by the rats.

As might have been anticipated, the ability of both rats and human beings to taste a given substance is often affected by the form in which the compound is offered: whether powdered or in solution. In general, the powders are more often tasteless. This was most notably true of arsenic trioxide, which in a dilute solution was readily tasted by both rats and human subjects, but in powdered form was tasted by only one of 52 human subjects. It should be added, that while this compound is soluble to the extent of 3.7 parts per 100, solution takes place only very slowly. Another factor of undoubted significance is that of the relative solubilities of the substances in water and in saliva. This requires further investigation.

Special Observations on the Taste and Acceptance of Red Squill Solution

In the taste threshold studies made with red squill extract or with filtered solutions of the raw powder, it was found that some rats died before the highest concentrations were reached. See figure 2. This indicated that the rats drank the red squill solution in lethal amounts in spite of its taste, and suggested that it might possibly be used as a water poison.

Preliminary tests showed that a 2 per cent concentration of a red squill extract when offered to four domestic rats killed three, while the same solution killed all of four wild Norways, and one of seven wild Alexandrines. It would thus appear that a solution of red squill is quite as effective as the dried powder even when the powder is fortified with red squill extract. To our knowledge red squill has not previously been used as a water poison for rats. It is possible that the good results obtained by Boulenger and Mitchell (3) with watery mash mixtures of red squill may have been obtained on this basis. That the toxic principle in red squill powder is water soluble was reported in 1922 by Claremont (4), while Munch, Silver and Horn reported in 1929 that it is not soluble in water (18).

Since completing these experiments we have learned that the toxic principle of red squill recently has been identified and given the name scilliroside by a chemist, A. Stoll and his collaborators (27). Stoll found that scilliroside is soluble in water and has a toxicity of 2 mg. per kg. for domestic rats. Its action closely resembles that of the cardiac glucosides. The use of red squill as a water poison might have some economic significance since extraction of the toxic constituent in the region where squill is grown would obviate transporting the bulky bulbs, in addition to providing a far more concentrated effective product.

Summary

1. A study was made on rats and on human subjects of the characteristics that make some toxic substances effective food and water poisons. For this purpose eleven substances were used:

1. Thallium sulphate
2. Sodium fluoroacetate (1080)
3. Thiosemicarbazide
4. Arsenic trioxide
5. Alpha-naphthyl thiourea (ANTU)
6. Zinc phosphide
7. Phenyl thiourea
8. Barium carbonate
9. Red squill
   (fortified powder and extract)
10. Strychnine sulfate
11. Mercuric chloride

The first six of these substances are effective rodenticides when offered in baits and the first four are also effective when dissolved in water.

Red squill powder is non-effective, while red squill extract is quite effective for the control of Norway rats.

2. A study was made of the ability of rats and men to taste these different toxic substances. For the rat the taste threshold method was used; for man a verbal report test. A good correlation was found between the ability of the two species to detect these substances by taste.

3. No definite relationship was found between taste and solubility in water of the poisons. Although some of the insoluble compounds have no taste and some of the soluble ones have a very bitter taste, notable exceptions were found. ANTU, which is not readily soluble, was found to have a bitter taste to some rats and human subjects, while compound 1080 and thallium sulphate, both very soluble, were found to have no taste at all either to rats or human subjects.

4. Although four of the highly effective rat poisons have no taste, four others—ANTU, thiosemicarbazide, arsenic trioxide, and red squill extract—are accepted by rats in spite of the fact that they can readily detect these substances in dilute solutions.

5. The poisons had less taste in powdered form than when offered dissolved in water; arsenic trioxide had a bitter taste in solution and no taste at all as a powder.

6. Poisons that have no taste may be either naturally occurring substances with which man and animals have had little or no contact in evolutionary history, that is, those compounds that are ordinarily not present in plants, in the bodies of animals or in streams, springs or lakes; or compounds made in chemical factories by man.

References

1. Abu Mohammed Abdallah Ben Ahned: Grosse Zusammenstellungung über die Kräfte der Bekannten Einfachen Heil—und Nahrungsmittel. Translated into the German by Dr. Joseph von Sontheimer, II, 216, Stuttgart, 1942.
2. Blakeslee, A. F.: Genetics of sensory thresholds: Taste for phenyl thio carbamide. *Science*, 1931, 74:607.
3. Boulenger, E. G. and Mitchell, P. C.: Report on methods of rat destruction. *Proc. Zool. Soc. Lond.*, 1919, 227–244.
4. Claremont, C. L.: Notes on the analysis and use of red squill in rat poisons. *Analyst*, 1922, 47:60–67.
5. Crampe, H. M.: Bewährte Mittel gegen Feldmäuse. *Dtsch. Landw. Presse*, 1878, 5(79):530.
6. Crampe, H. M.: Mittle gene Feldmäuse. *Jber. Agr. Chem.*, 1878, 1:347.
7. Danzel, L. A.: La "Rati-Scille", Scille Rouge Raticide. *Ann. Hyg.*, 1935, 13: 677–701.

8. Grandi, G.: Alcuno nitizio sui topi campagnoli che infestano le terre dell' ltalia meridionale e sul modo di combatterli. *Ministero dell' Agricultura e delle Foreste,* Boll., 1912, 11:20–23.
9. Kalmbach, E. R.: "Ten-Eighty," A war-produced rodenticide. *Science,* 1945, 102:232.
10. Lamy, M.: Rapport sur un mémoire de M. Lamy, relatif au thallium. *C. R. Acad. Sci.* Paris, 1862, 55:866–872.
11. ———: Sur les effets toxiques du thallium. *C. R. Acad. Sci.,* Paris, 1863, 57:442–445.
12. Lantz, D. E.: *The house rat.* Year Book U. S. D. A. 1917, 235–251.
13. Lewin, L.: *Die Gifte in der Weltgeschichte.* Berlin: Julius Springer, 1920.
14. ———: *Gifte und Vergiftungen,* 4. Ausg. Berlin: George Stilke, 1929.
15. Marais, J. S. C.: The isolation of the toxic principle "Potassium Cymonate" from "Gifblaar," *Dichapetalum cymosum* (Hook) Engl. *Onderstepoort J.,* 1943, 18:203–206.
16. ———: Monofluoroacetic acid, the toxic principle of "Gifblaar" *Dichapetalum cymosum* (Hook) Engl. *Onderstepoort J.,* 1944, 20:67–73.
17. Mascall, L. M.: *A booke of engines and traps to take polcats, buzardes, rattes, mice and all other kinds of vermine and beasts whatsoever, most profitable for all warriners, and such as delight in this kind of sport and pastime.* London: John Wolfe, 1590.
18. Munch, J. C., Silver, J. and Horn, E. E.: Red squill powders as rodenticides. *U. S. D. A. Tech. Bull.,* No. 134, 1929.
19. Munch, J. C. and Silver, J.: The pharmacology of thallium and its use in rodent control. *U. S. D. A. Tech. Bull.,* No. 238, 1931.
20. Orfila, M. P.: *Traité des Poisons Tirés des Règnes Minéral, Végétal et Animal ou Toxicologie Générale, Considérée sous les Rapports de la Physiologie, de la Pathologie et la Medicine Legale,* 2d ed. 2 vols. Paris: Crochard, 1818.
21. Personal Communication. Extensive laboratory tests on its toxicity and action have been made. Dieke, S. H.: Thiosemicarbazide: A new toxic derivative of thiourea. *Proc. Exp. Biol. & Med.,* 1949, 70:688–693. The Fish and Wildlife Service have started field tests.
22. Recommendation of the Subcommittee on Mammalogy of the Chemical Biological Coordination Center, National Research Council, Washington, D. C. Revised October 1948 with addendum January 1949.
23. Richter, C. P.: Salt taste thresholds of normal and adrenalectomized rats. *Endocrinology,* 1939, 24:367–371.
24. Richter, C. P. and Clisby, K. H.: Phenylthiocarbamide taste thresholds of rats and human beings. *Amer. J. Physiol.,* 1941, 134:157–164.
25. Richter, C. P.: The development and use of Alpha-Naphthyl Thiourea (ANTU) as a rat poison. *J. A. M. A.,* 1945, 129:927–931.
26. Steyn, D. G.: Gifblaar poisoning. A summary of our present knowledge in respect of poisoning by *Dichapetalum cymosum,* 13th and 14th Reports, Director of Veterinary Education and Research, Union of South Africa, 1928, pp. 185–194.
27. Stoll, A. and Renz, J.: Cardiac glucosides. XVIII. Scilliroside. *Helv. Chim. Acta,* 1942, 25:43–64.
28. Stoll, A., Renz, J. and Helfenstein, A.: Über die Struktur des Scillirosids. *Helv. Chim. Acta,* 1943, 26:648–672.
29. Witthaus, R. A. and Becker, T. C.: *Medical Jurisprudence, Forensic Medicine and Toxicology,* Vol. 4, 1896.

Part V   PHILOSOPHY AND SCIENCE

EXPERIENCES OF A RELUCTANT RAT-CATCHER
THE COMMON NORWAY RAT—FRIEND OR ENEMY?

The Norway rat is undoubtedly hated and feared by more people and in more countries in the world than is any other animal. These people see in it a filthy animal, destroyer of property, spoiler of food, carrier of bubonic plague and many other terrible diseases, attacker of human beings, particularly defenseless babies.

A small number of people—mainly scientists—however, believe that the rat's virtues far outweigh its evil doings. They regard it as one of the world's most valuable animals. Actually at this moment scientists are housing, feeding, and caring for several million Norway rats of the albino variety in laboratories throughout the civilized world. Scientists use them for experiments in almost every field of biological research— nutrition, endocrinology, neurology, pharmacology, and many others; and it is generally agreed that most of our knowledge in these fields, particularly nutrition and endocrinology, has come from observations on this animal. There can be little doubt but that few people living in the world today have not profited in one way or another, or actually have been kept alive, by what has been learned from studies on the rat.

The Norway rat was the first animal to be domesticated for strictly scientific purposes. Domesticated rats were first used in Europe for scientific studies over one hundred years ago. They were brought over from Europe (the Department of Zoology at the University of Geneva) to this country in 1890 for studies on the brain by Adolf Meyer, then a newly arrived Swiss neuropathologist, later Professor of Psychiatry and

---

This paper was originally published in the *Proceedings of the American Philosophical Society*, Vol. 112, No. 6, December 1968. Reprinted by permission.

Head of the Phipps Psychiatric Clinic at the Johns Hopkins Hospital and long time Dean of American Psychiatry. When H. H. Donaldson, Professor of Anatomy at the University of Chicago, first saw Meyer's rats, he at once recognized their possibilities for scientific research in general, and later established the famous colony of albino rats at the Wistar Institute in Philadelphia that until recently supplied rats to laboratories all over the world.

The Norway rat has many advantages for scientific studies. To mention just a few: its dietary needs are very nearly the same as man's. This explains how observations made on it can so readily be extrapolated to man. Our pioneer in nutrition, the late Professor E. V. McCollum, first used rats for nutrition studies in 1907. All of his well-known discoveries of the nutritive value of vitamins were made on this animal. It took him a long time to convince the authorities that much more could be learned from this "economically" useless animal, than from cows and pigs that up to then had been the favorite animals for nutrition studies. It is very stable and reliable. This means that results obtained on one day can be observed repeatedly under the same conditions. It lends itself to almost every form of surgical interference—except perhaps in relation to the vascular system. Its high resistance to infection makes it ideal for surgical and physiological studies. It reproduces readily and is just the right size for all kinds of anatomical and physiological studies. Its short life-span—of about three years—makes it possible to study factors involved in growth, development, and aging. Finally, and not least of all, contrary to popular belief it is a very clean animal. Given opportunity it will keep itself perfectly clean. It is only when the wild rat is crowded in filthy human surroundings that it gets unclean and covered with vermin. Brought into the laboratory it frees itself of vermin in a very short time.

During my almost half-century in behavioral and neurological research I have chiefly used rats, but also many different animals such as cats, dogs, monkeys, sloths, rabbits, beavers, porcupines, honey bears, alligators, and others. If someone were to give me the power to create an animal most useful for all types of studies on problems concerned directly or indirectly with human welfare, I could not possibly improve on the Norway rat.

I mention this because for almost three years of my life—during World War II—I was forced to think of the Norway rat as Man's arch enemy and was responsible in one way or another for the killing of a million or more.

This role developed in the following way. After the start of World

War II, it was discovered that the country's sources of rat poison had been cut off, partly because occupation by Axis powers of the Mediterranean seaboard, particularly the northern coast of Africa, ended supply of a bulb from which the common rodenticide, red squill, was prepared, and partly because manufacture of other rodenticides involved critical materials and so had to be stopped. There was an urgent need for a new poison for general use in eradicating rats and also for protecting ourselves in case the Axis powers started rat-borne germ warfare.

In 1942 the National Research Council at the National Academy of Sciences in Washington gave me the task of trying to remedy this situation. I was chosen for two reasons: one, I had just found that the chemical phenyl thiourea, also known as phenyl thiocarbamide, which had been widely used by psychologists and geneticists for taste tests, was very toxic to Norway rats and was readily accepted by them in lethal amounts; and two, it was thought that my experience with dietary self-selection and nutrition studies on rats would help in finding a good bait in which to mix this poison.

This job developed in many unexpected ways and I suddenly found myself heading a city-wide experimental rat control campaign in Baltimore—so far as I know, the first of its kind. I, and the many workers associated with me, remember it with pleasure as a most interesting and challenging undertaking. We learned a great deal about wild Norway rats, poisons and poisoning, traps and trapping; about city officials— mayors and members of the City Council; about people in general and their reactions to rats; and finally we learned from exact counts the incredibly large number of rats that may share space in an American city with human beings, not only in impoverished but in well-to-do residential areas. To date my associates and I have published fifty-seven papers in scientific journals on various aspects of this venture.

The project was later carried on under support from the Office for Scientific Research and Development (OSRD), the agency responsible for all wartime research. Dr. A. N. Richards, Director of OSRD and one of our leading scientists, gave the work his constant enthusiastic help and encouragement.

History of Phenyl Thiourea and Discovery of Its Toxicity

This account must start with our finding that phenyl thiourea, which had not even been suspected of any toxic property, is highly toxic for the Norway rat. This compound had been used by du Pont de Nemours & Co. at some stage in the process of the vulcanization of rubber. In 1931 Dr. Herbert Fox, a research chemist at du Pont, observed that as this chemical, in the form of a fine dust, was blown through his laboratory, some fellow-workers complained of a very bitter taste while most of them denied tasting anything at all. In testing a large number of persons, Fox found that although about 85 per cent could not taste this compound, even in large amounts, about 15 per cent found it extremely bitter. After making tests on many more persons, including members of the same families, he found that the ability to taste phenyl thiourea is inherited as a Mendelian recessive. Fox's findings stimulated observations by geneticists on members of various races all over the world. Many such studies are still in progress at the present time.

In 1939 this substance became of special interest to me in relation to results of my dietary self-selection studies, which showed that the rat has an extraordinary ability to select beneficial substances and avoid harmful ones. These studies demonstrated that the rat's appetite is a good guide to its nutritional needs; that in fact it is reliable enough to use in determining nutritive values of various food-stuffs; that it helps the rat to avoid harmful or non-nutritive substances—which is of particular importance in view of its inability to vomit. Results of these studies indicated that taste of food-stuffs—natural or chemically purified—plays an important part in dietary selections, determining chiefly whether or not an animal will ingest a substance. It naturally interested me to determine the extent to which observations on the role played by taste in dietary selections in rats can be transferred to man—whether man and rats have similar taste abilities.

Thus, when I first heard that phenyl thiourea has such a bitter taste to some people while having for others no taste at all, I wondered whether likewise some rats would taste it and others not. Ability to taste it was tested in a simple experiment. A minute amount of phenyl thiourea powder—as much as can be put on the small end of a toothpick—was placed on the tongues of six rats. The rats were then watched for signs of distaste—attempts to get rid of the powder with their paws or tongues. After watching for over half an hour, I decided that even if they could taste it they did not find it very bitter. To my great surprise the next morning all six rats were dead. They were found to have died of massive pulmonary edema and pleural effusion. Their chests and lungs were filled with fluid. Later, systematic tests showed that as little as 1–2 milligrams sufficed to kill a rat, and that when phenyl thiourea was mixed in food in small amounts, 1–2 per cent, our laboratory rats ate it freely and died. Thus it was demonstrated for the first time that phenyl thiourea is highly toxic to rats, and that rats will eat it in toxic amounts.

Observations of Phenyl Thiourea as a Poison for Wild Rats

This then was the status of our observations in January 1942, when the National Research Council gave me a small grant to determine whether phenyl thiourea could be used as an effective rat poison. At that time, I and my small group of assistants had no experience at all with the possible ultimate consumer, the wild Norway rat in streets, alleys, yards, and cellars. Nor did we even have any idea where to find wild rats in the city. In retrospect this seems unbelievable, since within a few months we were to find that many a block within good residential districts in Baltimore harbored 300 or more rats. From a member of the Sanitation Department we learned that rats could be found on city dumps and in some grocery stores. This officer offered to take me to one of the large city dumps in a suburb of Baltimore. I shall never forget this first introduction to the Norway rat. This officer was a young man dressed in a very natty blue uniform with a corps cap and well-shined leather puttees. In walking over the dump, we saw a number of rats scurrying about even though it was in the mid-afternoon. Suddenly he asked whether he should catch one for me. Before awaiting my answer, he dashed down a slope, leaping about like a young gazelle over old cans and piles of rubbish in pursuit of a rat. He chased it from under one can or box after another; then suddenly I heard a loud squeal as he held the rat up in his hand. He obviously had had a close acquaintance with wild rats—in spite of his natty uniform. I never found anyone to duplicate this performance.

For the first tests phenyl thiourea was mixed with bread crumbs and other foods and placed at different locations on one of the city dumps and in a few grocery stores where we saw obvious signs of presence of rats. The results were not encouraging. In most instances the rats apparently had refused to eat the poisoned food, and in others they apparently had not eaten sufficiently large amounts to kill them.

It became clear that we could not learn much about poisoning when working under complicated conditions in the field. We decided to start therefore with controlled conditions in the laboratory to determine whether wild rats are equally susceptible to the poisoning, whether they are able to taste the poison or not. Furthermore it became clear that we had to learn more about baits in which to mix the poison and what concentrations of poison to use.

To make such studies a wild rat laboratory was opened in the Carnegie Building of the Johns Hopkins Medical School. Our first problem was to find out where and how to get wild rats. We bought traps of every design available on the market and tried them out in yards and alleys near the Johns Hopkins Medical School. Only small numbers of rats were caught with any one of them. Then we found that a man near the Hospital had been catching rats in a large wooden rabbit trap with good success. He brought his trap in for inspection. We decided to have some built with a few modifications and simplifications. These traps gave excellent results at once. We began getting more rats than we could use at that stage. Later on, several thousands of these traps were made for us by boys in several public schools at $1.00 apiece. We found that horse-feed (mixture of alfalfa, corn, and molasses) spread on the floor of the trap enticed rats to enter. Then, more or less incidentally, in their exploration of the traps, the rats pulled on the baited (apples, potatoes, cantaloupe) trigger or bumped into it, releasing the trap-door, and so became trapped. The traps were so efficient that we caught four or five rats at one time, and in some instances as many as nine. We found that traps made of undressed lumber gave better results than traps made with dressed lumber since rats are apt to shy away from shiny objects. Use of these traps gave us for the first time an inkling about the great magnitude of the rat population in Baltimore.

At this point I must call attention to the fact that with very few exceptions rats caught or later recovered after poisoning were so-called Norway or brown rats. Only a few of the closely related but distinct roof or ship rats (otherwise known as black or Alexandrine rats) were trapped. Next to Norways, these rats, usually found quite near the seaboard, are the most common rats in the world. Comparisons of the two strains brought out many differences in habits, anatomy, and physiology. When released in a room together they separate like milk and cream—Norways remaining on the floor and Alexandrines taking to the ceiling or rafters. One sure source of roof rats when we needed them for special studies on poisons was a large office building near the harbor. Why they happened to be located only in this building we never found out. It may just have been its proximity to the waterfront. We collected many dead rats from fumigated foreign and native ships in the harbor, and in all instances these were roof or ship rats.

We were next confronted with the problem of handling and housing wild rats—what kind of cage to use, how to transfer them from cage to cage, how to catch and hold them for injection or tube feeding of poisons. With time we developed various devices that made it possible to handle unanesthetized wild rats without danger of being bitten, quite as readily as was possible with our tame domesticated rats. In the beginning we worried about the fleas carried by these rats, so all rats were fumigated in special chambers. The fleas dropped off into pans of water and so could be counted. Most of the rats actually did come in with fleas, in some instances as many as 20–30 each. We soon found, however, that this defleaing process was unnecessary, since almost at once after coming into clean surroundings rats defleaed themselves, so thoroughly indeed that I have never seen a flea on any of the many hundred wild rats brought into my laboratory from the outside during the past twenty-five years, nor on one of the thousands of domesticated rats that at one time or another were housed in the same room with the wild rats.

It should be mentioned here that we all learned to have a high regard for the wild rat—its aggressive fighting spirit, high intelligence, and alertness. This meant that in working with them, holding them for injection or tube feeding or putting them under ether, we had to be on guard every second, which made it very exciting. Despite all our care, most of us got at least a bite or two when off guard.

After all these preliminaries I can now report that our tests by intraperitoneal injection or tube feeding showed that phenyl thiourea has the same toxicity for wild as for domesticated rats. This indicated that in our field tests, wild rats failed to die because the bitter taste of phenyl thiourea had kept them from eating adequate amounts of the poisoned food.

Finding of Alpha-Naphthyl Thiourea, an Effective Thiourea Compound

Clearly then what we needed was a thiourea compound with the same physiological effects and high toxicity as phenyl thiourea, but with little or no bitter taste. I discussed this situation with Dr. Kennerley Marshall, Professor of Pharmacology at the Johns Hopkins Medical School. He suggested that I take the problem to Dr. Herbert A. Lubs at the du Pont de Nemours Co. in Wilmington, Delaware. Dr. Lubs was very cooperative and almost at once started sending samples of over two hundred related thiourea compounds from the company's shelves.

These compounds were tested first by tube feeding on domesticated rats for gross toxicity levels. Promising compounds were tested in smaller doses on both domesticated and wild rats. Compounds with a high toxicity (killing 100 per cent in doses of 2–3 milligrams per rat) were then tested for acceptance. One powdered compound was accepted readily in lethal amounts, even by unstarved rats, when mixed with ground yellow corn. This was alpha-naphthyl thiourea. This compound had possibilities as a rat poison since its manufacture did not involve use of any critical materials or any complicated or expensive chemical processes. Later (December 11, 1945), after several years' usage in our campaign, it was patented by the OSRD as ANTU.

During the same period of time that we were screening these various thiourea compounds, we were also making extensive tests to find the most attractive bait in which to offer the poison—that is, a food that would be accepted readily by all rats, regardless of whether they had had any prior experience with it. One hundred different foods were tested under controlled conditions in the laboratory. Outstanding was ground yellow corn, which was eaten in large amounts by all rats on first exposure and aroused no suspiciousness whatsoever. Interestingly from the point of view of the rat's ability to select nutritive foods, it was found that rats grow well, thrive, and reproduce on a diet limited to yellow corn supplemented only with minute amounts of cod-liver oil. In contrast, on a diet limited to white corn, rats develop nutritional deficiencies even with cod-liver oil supplement. Thus, in our experience, rats get along better on yellow corn than on any of the other grains, and eat it in large amounts even on first exposure. Fresh yellow corn on the cob was also found to be a very attractive bait.

Choice of an Entire City Block as the Smallest Unit for Field Tests. Our First Trial with ANTU

At the same time that we were testing ANTU in the laboratory and trying to find the bait that would be most attractive to rats, I was giving much thought to problems connected with testing ANTU on wild rats in the field. I spent much time looking for signs (burrows, runways, droppings, etc.) of rats in alleys, yards, houses, cellars in different parts of the city; also in talking to people who had a rat problem. I became impressed with the disregard rats show for human boundary lines such as fences and walls. Rats seemed to circulate freely between yards and alleys and often between houses and cellars, but rarely between blocks.

Experiences of a Reluctant Rat-Catcher

They did not seem to cross streets except under very special circumstances—after a fire, following demolition of a house, or when driven out by a dog or cat. From these various observations I decided that the smallest unit that we could use for field tests of ANTU would be an entire block. All of our later experiences proved the correctness of this decision.

Eight blocks of typical Baltimore row houses in the vicinity of the Johns Hopkins Hospital were selected for our first test. Boy scouts did the baiting. They distributed small piles of ground yellow corn mixed with ANTU (one per cent) and small sections of fresh corn on the cob dusted with ANTU powder in cellars, yards, and alleys. Results of this operation were quite encouraging. Many rats were killed, and inhabitants of the blocks concerned reported seeing only a few rats afterwards.

Development of a Method for Quick Eradication of Rats

More extensive tests now seemed warranted. In October 1942 the city, through the then Mayor Howard B. Jackson, contributed $5,000 to hire men to help in baiting and trapping. The OSRD in Washington provided ANTU and bait. In the Eastern Health District, a heavily populated and rat-infested area near the Johns Hopkins Hospital, 200 blocks were selected for the first large-scale test. Poisoned bait in small one-inch paper lily cups was distributed in alleys and yards of each block and supposedly in homes and cellars. Dead rats were collected on the following days. A house-to-house survey was made several weeks later for reports from residents on persistence of rats. Detailed records were kept for each block. Results again were encouraging. Failure to kill all rats could be explained at least in part by presence of garbage and by hasty distribution of poisoned food by unreliable crew members. Furthermore, we found that not all hideouts of rats had been discovered and that baits had not been placed in all houses or cellars.

We now felt that we were ready to start an intensive campaign in a small trial area, making use of all we had learned in these previous trials. We selected for this purpose a heavily rat-infested residential area of 28 blocks, again of typical old Baltimore row-houses about a mile from the center of town.

Fifteen young, enthusiastic air-raid wardens in the area volunteered for this job. They were briefed on details of the operation by myself and assistants. We all took an active part. We decided to treat only a few blocks each week (largely because the air-raid wardens could only work on weekends) and roughly adhered to the following schedule.

Early in the week an effort was made to notify all inhabitants of a block that their rats would be poisoned on Saturday afternoon. This was done by (1) posting warning placards printed in large red letters on posts and poles at corners of the block and at the alleys; (2) distributing by hand to each tenant personally a typewritten notice and making certain of his full cooperation. Notices carried information about the schedule of operations, asking everyone to clean their cellars and yards; to have all trash ready for collection by city crews within the next few days; to have garbage ready for collection on Saturday morning; to remove all sources of food and water; to unlock all gates and cellar doors during the week to enable volunteers to survey for signs and locations of rats and on Saturday afternoon to let them distribute poisoned bait. Any inhabitant who refused to cooperate was reported to city inspectors. On Saturday afternoon we distributed yellow corn meal mixed with ANTU (one per cent) or corn on the cob, sliced sweet potatoes and apples, all dusted with ANTU powder, to every yard, cellar, garage and alleyway that showed any signs of rats. Small, flat pans containing water dusted with ANTU (which, being insoluble in water, remained as a film on the surface) were placed with poisoned bait in all closed areas—garages, sheds, and cellars. Every effort was made not to miss a single rat hideout. On Sunday morning dead rats were collected and counted. This was always an exciting occasion for all workers.

On the following days, all holes were firmly closed and uneaten food was removed. The block was then inspected at regular intervals by the warden in charge of the block for signs of rats. Surviving rats were either poisoned a second time or trapped.

Detailed records were kept of the poisoning operation, number of dead rats recovered and number of surviving rats.

In each of the 28 blocks used for this intensive campaign, reports indicated that the rat population had either been eliminated or reduced to just a few rats. Some blocks apparently remained rat-free for over two-and-a-half years without any further attention. How heavily infested this area was is shown by the fact that in one block 367 dead rats were recovered. Many more must have died underground. Results of this campaign demonstrated that with our technique and a single treatment with ANTU, a rat population can be struck down within a few days in case of emergency.

Further Tests on Larger Areas—Start of Rat Population Studies

It was then decided to make further tests in larger areas, using patterns set in our earlier tests, in an effort to work out methods for permanent control. Emphasis was placed on simplifying procedures and problems of personnel.

At this point it became clear that we needed to know much more about population dynamics of rats: how to recognize presence of rats, how to estimate numbers of rats per block and how to follow re-growth of populations after poisoning or trapping. I was fortunate in getting Dr. John T. Emlen, one of our leading younger naturalists and an expert on animal population dynamics, to join our group of workers. Using our live traps, he trapped many blocks to the last rat, giving us for the first time accurate knowledge about rat populations: number of males, number of females (non-pregnant, pregnant, nursing), number of juveniles, young adults, and old rats. He retrapped many blocks months afterwards in order to determine how long such blocks remained rat-free. He trapped, marked and released rats, and then later retrapped them to learn more about their home range. Results of Dr. Emlen's observations added immeasurably to our knowledge about rat populations and animal populations in general.

In May, 1943, the City of Baltimore, through Mayors Howard B. Jackson and Theodore R. McKeldin, contributed $55,000 for an eighteen-month period for this project. The city opened "Rodent Control" offices in City Hall and in the field and provided office help, field workers, a health inspector, a clean-up crew and technical assistants. Rodent control was removed from the jurisdiction of the Health Department and made a separate sub-department of the Department of Public Works under my direction.

During this period 1,360 city blocks were treated with ANTU by city crews—a motley bunch of intelligent and not so intelligent characters. Results were good but not perfect: 90–95 per cent of rats were eliminated in most blocks and 100 per cent in a few. All efforts were made to eliminate surviving rats either by a second poisoning or by trapping. Emphasis was placed on the development of methods that could be used effectively by ordinary citizens.

First Efforts to Work Out Program of Permanent Control

At the end of 1944 I withdrew from active participation in the control program to resume full-time work on another wartime project and on my own research. The latter, as a result of this rat-control experience, included studies on the behavior and physiology of wild rats and effects of domestication on the Norway rat. The control program was placed under the direction of Dr. John T. Emlen.

At this time the city appropriated $49,000 for another year for the purchase of grain and for salaries of city personnel while the OSRD still continued to supply the ANTU. By the end of the year over 5,000 blocks had been treated with ANTU and had been incorporated into a system for periodic resurvey and treatment.

Through our efforts (particularly those of my secretary, Mrs. Martha Schaffer) the city provided a number of inspectors who reported all persons who failed to keep their yards clean and garbage cans covered. Offenders were taken to court and fined. Newspapers carried notices about people thus fined. This had a far-reaching effect in getting residential areas cleaned up.

In still another way Dr. Emlen contributed to the success of a permanent control operation. He lectured on rat control to children in city schools, to members of various civic groups, clubs, and church associations in all parts of the city. His lectures dealt with every aspect of the rat-control problem, placing emphasis on elimination of sources of food and places of shelter for rats. He also emphasized the importance of showing people how to help themselves and where to find advice and assistance when needed. His lectures, I am sure, had lasting effects in keeping the rat population down over the years, long after our active work had stopped.

During this same period, much work was being done on buildings in the business district and particularly in the city markets. Over 900 rats were killed in a single night's poisoning in the city's large Lexington Market, and many hundreds in the other markets. Furthermore, routine checks every week showed that the markets remained essentially free of rats for many months even without any further treatment.

At one point we found that a lack of knowledge about Baltimore sewers hampered progress of our operations. A study of the sewage system revealed the interesting fact that sewers in different parts of the city were originally operated by various small companies that were not linked together until fairly recent times. Some of the sewers crossed at angles through blocks apparently following early pathways. This interest in sewers later took me to visit the sewers of London and Paris. In London I walked in high boots through miles of sewers under guidance of the Chief Officer of the Port of London. There the great tiled-in sewers followed the small rivers that originally fed into the Thames. Of interest was that the rats that came into the beam of our flashlights were all very thin and obviously underfed. In Paris I was taken through the sewers in a barge. I saw no rats. It was, however, a very instructive experience since I saw that all of the public services of Paris—electricity, gas, telegraph, telephone, potable and non-potable water were exposed on the vaulted ceiling of the sewer. All of the service carriers were accessible right into each house or building. This meant that nowhere were any of the services covered. An elegant solution of an important problem of city planning.

By the middle of 1946 an additional 5,574 blocks had been treated. At this time the number of rats killed per block averaged 75. During the four years, by actual count well over a million rats were recovered after poisoning. Many thousands were trapped, and many more may have died underground. There can be no doubt that, despite the unevenly efficient help of the volunteers, the rat population of Baltimore was thus reduced to a mere fraction of the 1942 level.

Later in 1945 Dr. Emlen left the operation in order to head the new Department of Population Dynamics in the School of Hygiene and Public Health of the Johns Hopkins University. The importance of his studies impressed me so much that I went to the Rockefeller Foundation to ask for funds for Dr. Emlen to make a special study of population dynamics, not only on rats but also on other animals and birds. The International Health Division very kindly provided a generous sum for this purpose. This is still a very productive and flourishing department, and has attracted many able men.

After Dr. Emlen left the control operation, it was taken over by the City Public Works Department. Sometime later it reverted to the Health Department, where it is now just one of the many divisions of this department. No effort was made to keep up the organization started by us, largely because the rat population had been reduced to such a low level that it did not present a problem. Over the years the population has built up again, so I understand that it has again become a problem.

Our relations with the Head of the Health Department, Dr. Huntington Williams, were friendly but somewhat complicated. I mention this because of the debate as to whether or not rodent control belongs in the Health Department. At the start of our work, Dr. Williams gave only hesitant cooperation, more or less denying that Baltimore had a rat problem at all. The "non-existent" rat problem was made obvious some months later when we began recovering several hundred rats from a single block, and we also found that over one hundred individuals, mostly children, had been bitten by rats over a four-year period within a radius of one mile of the Johns Hopkins Hospital. This indicates only that a highly successful health commissioner still may not be particularly interested in or know much about the problem of rats. These observations hold true for any department already functioning as part of a city's program. Rat control cuts across the lines of too many departments to be placed under any given one with good results. Then too, even if a department head were concerned about rodent control, priorities already established would probably leave little time and few workers available for a control program. It is thus in my opinion necessary to set up a rodent control office which is independent of other departments and which is responsible directly to the Mayor and City Council. It should be run by full-time personnel trained to handle this problem. The director must be a man who is willing to step out into the field to check for himself results of active control measures, and who is not content to sit in his office simply dispensing advice about the importance of eliminating sources of food and places of harborage.

A Few General Remarks about Poisoning and ANTU

In my opinion, poisoning, supplemented by trapping, would be the method of choice for quick eradication of rats. For permanent control, elimination of sources of food and places to shelter is important, although this by itself has only limited value since it is difficult to eliminate all sources of food such as plants, roots and flower seeds, and rats always seem to find new hideouts. Rat proofing is another possibility, but it may be very expensive and in many cases unnecessary. Choice of methods will depend of course on the type and size of city: whether old with many dilapidated tenement buildings, whether new with comparatively few hiding places for rats; whether small and easily encircled, whether large and widely scattered.

Results of our campaign demonstrated the effectiveness of ANTU when used as a one-time poison, even without prebaiting, so long as a careful job was done in covering every possible infested part of a block. ANTU, which kills rats in 16–30 hours, has a great advantage in that workers—either civilian or hired crews—see the results of their efforts almost immediately. This is of great importance when volunteer workers are doing the job. Our experience showed that ANTU is perfectly safe to use. Many tons of it were used during our campaign. Twenty or more men were exposed to the dust and to ANTU-poisoned food for five years or more; hundreds were exposed for shorter periods; none showed any ill effects. As will presently be seen, results of clinical therapeutic observations showed that most thiourea derivatives can be given to patients in high amounts over long periods, without toxic results.

Poisons that kill rats only after long exposure—ten days or more—have the shortcoming that the poisoned food may deteriorate or be washed away, and further that workers do not see immediate results. In these long intervals rats may learn to avoid the poisoned food. Fortified red squill, the most commonly used rat poison, was found to be ineffective both in our laboratory and field tests. Because of its low toxicity, rats have to ingest 10–20 times as much poisoned food for a fatal dose as is the case with ANTU-poisoned food.

However, rats that have survived one ANTU poisoning do appear to develop a tolerance which lasts about thirty days. A second poisoning, therefore, may be only partially effective. The fact that ANTU was not yet on the public market and that therefore at the time of our campaign none of the rats had ever been exposed to it may explain in part the generally excellent results. Its chief use is in the block- or city-wide operations. It may be used by isolated individuals, but then preferably with careful prebaiting to ensure a 100 per cent kill on the first attempt. In a prebaiting operation, unpoisoned food is put out for several days beforehand to get the rats accustomed to eating the particular food that later will be poisoned. Of importance when using ANTU in a block- or city-wide operation is the elimination of all avoidable disturbances during the night of poisoning, to make certain that the rats are not scared away before having ingested a lethal dose. This means keeping dogs and children away from areas where the poison has been laid. It is also important not to embark on an operation in face of threatening inclement weather.

There can be little doubt that poisoning or trapping of a block or any confined area is useless without a follow-up—a search for signs of surviving rats and further treatment with poison or traps—aimed to get rid of the last rat. This may require time and effort, but both are well spent, because blocks treated in this way may remain rat-free for years. Elimination of only 60–80 per cent of rats is in my opinion next to useless.

Laboratory Studies Carried on during Various Field Tests

While these various operations were in progress, active research was being carried on, in my laboratory in the Hospital and in the Carnegie Building, on ANTU, other thioureas, and other rodent poisons. This work was carried on mainly with Dr. Sally Dieke, a mathematician and chemist. She contributed in many ways to the success of our venture and to our general knowledge about chemistry and toxicity of thiourea derivatives.

For various reasons we wanted to know the toxicity of ANTU for other rodents, particularly the roof or ship rats, and also for animals such as dogs and cats, pigs and chickens. Studies were also made on monkeys, but no observations were made on man. ANTU was also found to be toxic for Alexandrine or ship rats, but much less so than for Norway rats. This fact definitely limited its general usefulness as a rodent poison since, as I said earlier, the roof rat, next to the Norway, is the most common rat in the world. In view of ANTU's lower toxicity for Alexandrines, it was fortunate that Baltimore had only a very small number of them.

ANTU shows the most extraordinary and interesting species differences in toxicity: while it is very toxic for Norway rats, and fairly toxic for dogs and pigs, it is almost non-toxic for monkeys and chickens. It can be given to them almost in spoonfuls without producing any untoward effects. In spite of its toxicity for dogs, it is surprising that so few were killed, considering the fact that our operation covered practically the entire city and many dogs must in spite of our precautions have had access to poisoned food. This could be explained in part by the fact that dogs, unlike rats, are able to vomit.

Much research was done on toxicity, modes of action, and acceptance of all the common rodenticides. Laboratory acceptance tests showed that under controlled conditions baits containing 5 per cent ANTU or 5 per cent thallium sulfate killed 100 per cent of rats; 0.1 per cent 1080 (sodium fluoroacetate) killed 96 per cent; 5 per cent phosphate killed 95 per cent; 10 per cent arsenic trioxide killed 88 per cent; and 10 per cent fortified red squill only 28 per cent. Warfarin, Pivat and other poisons now available appeared only after the end of our campaign so we have no data on their comparative toxicities.

To obtain a better idea about how the various poisons taste to the rat we determined how they taste to human subjects. The poisons were administered in small non-toxic amounts as a powder or in solution. Strychnine and arsenic trioxide were tasted in small concentrations by all subjects. A few individuals found that ANTU had a just perceptible bitter taste, while the highly toxic poisons—sodium fluoroacetate and thallium sulfate had no taste whatsoever to any subject. Taste threshold tests on all the common poisons were made on many rats and many human subjects. In all instances rats and human beings had the same thresholds—all of which further demonstrates that rats and man have much the same taste ability.

Many studies were made in the laboratory on acceptance of ANTU and other poisons. We wanted to determine the most effective concentration of the poisons; also the best methods of offering the poisons: for instance whether dusting a powedered form of a poison on food is more effective than mixing it into the food; whether poisoned water is more effective than poisoned food. For this purpose we used two large circular observation pens, made of metal, 14 feet in diameter and 4 feet high. Twenty-five freshly-trapped rats were daily released in each pen in the morning without food or water. They quickly took refuge in a small round sheet-iron shelter in the center of each drum where they remained throughout the day. The rats entered the shelter through eight small openings on the sides. In the late afternoon just before dusk small piles of food or dishes of poisoned water—preparations to be tested for acceptance—were placed at equidistant intervals around the shelter and midway to the wall of the drum. After dark we took up positions on comfortable chairs with our elbows resting on the wide flange on top of the drum and sat as quietly as possible. The room had a dim light just bright enough to make it possible to observe the rats. Normally within 10–15 minutes the rats began to emerge inch by inch, literally flat on their bellies, very cautiously at first, ready to withdraw into the shelter in a flash. Gradually they got confident enough to reach the food and begin eating. In this way we could see not only how they reacted to the poisoned food but to each other, and their behavior in this situation could not have been more interesting or instructive. Similar observations were made in the field. One of our favorite places was a poultry shop just across the street from the city's largest market. Just after dark we placed chicken parts on the floor of a large shipping room and then settled ourselves in a good observation spot. Usually within 10–15 minutes the rats began to appear, just as cautiously as in the pen; sometimes as many as 75 by actual count. Constant sparring and bickering between them added to the interest of this extraordinary scene.

Now to return to our specific studies on ANTU. One of our chief interests was of course development of an effective antidote for use in case of accidental poisoning of human beings or pets. Although all evidence indicated that ANTU is not toxic for human beings, we nevertheless felt that an antidote must be found. This search meant that we had to know in the first place just how ANTU acts—how fluid gets from the bloodstream into the lungs and thoracic cavity. This turned out to be a complicated problem, and one of great medical interest. Before long, therefore, members of various departments of the Medical School—pathology, physiology, pharmacology, medicine—became involved. It was found that within 10–15 minutes after poisoning, fluid seeps through the lung capillaries into the perivascular spaces in the lung; not too long after that, fluid begins to collect in the thoracic cavity. Finally, fluid fills the thoracic cavity under pressure to make it larger than normal. Respiratory surfaces in the lungs become reduced until the animal no longer is able to get adequate amounts of oxygen and dies. Some of the best help in this problem came from Dr. Cecil Drinker, Professor of Physiology at Harvard and an authority on action and function of the lymphatic system. When I first told him about our problem and suggested that the lymphatics might play a part, he expressed great doubt. He agreed however to try ANTU out on a dog, his favorite breed of animal for studies on lymphatics. What he saw impressed him so much that for a long time he used ANTU for his own studies, and I spent many hours working with him trying to track down the underlying mechanisms. Much was found out by the workers in the various fields about the action and mechanisms of ANTU. We did not find an antidote. Much can still be learned from the action of ANTU and the various thiourea derivatives that may be of help in throwing light on production of lung edema and pleural effusion in man.

We found that ANTU and related thioureas have a number of interesting effects, quite apart from their production of pulmonary edema and pleural effusion. I have already mentioned that du Pont de Nemours & Co. sent me about 200 thiourea derivatives for testing. Alerted to our needs, a number of other chemical companies also sent thioureas from their shelves; some companies even made new thiourea compounds for us. As a result, I probably have the largest and most complete collection of thiourea compounds available anywhere. We have actually studied in detail only phenyl thiourea (our original compound), alpha-naphthyl thiourea (ANTU), thiourea and a few other derivatives, but other thioureas have been studied extensively elsewhere. When given in small concentrations in food or water for several months, both phenyl thiourea and ANTU have remarkable physiologicl and anatomical effects. Some of these effects can best be seen in freshly clipped black rats. Both chemicals remove all pigment from the skin, leaving it as pink as in an albino. ANTU also completely stops hair growth. Phenyl thiourea has no effect on hair growth, with the result that emerging new hair, lacking all pigment, is white. Thus, in a short time a black rat can be turned as white as an albino except for pigmentation of the eyes. A few days after discontinuation of treatment of an animal with phenyl thiourea or ANTU, its skin becomes flooded with black pigment, just as though ink had been poured on it; hair growth is resumed, and soon the animal is as black as before.

When given in food or by tube-feeding over long periods, phenyl thiourea and ANTU block formation of the thyroid hormone. The thyroid glands become markedly hyperplastic as a result of efforts of the pituitary gland to stimulate the thyroid to secrete adequate amounts of thyroxin. This antithyroid effect of the thioureas has been widely used clinically, particularly by Dr. T. S. Astwood, formerly of the Johns Hopkins Hospital and now Professor of Medicine at Tufts Medical School, in the treatment of hyperthyroid patients. Several thiourea derivatives are now used for this purpose in high amounts, thus demonstrating their non-toxicity for human beings. Of special interest to me in relation to my present studies on biological clocks was the finding that prolonged treatment of rats with thiourea and various derivatives brought out activity and behavior cycles of 30—40 days in length that in many ways resembled those of periodic catatonic-schizophrenic patients. We believe this indicates that these patients may be suffering from a thyroid deficiency. Undoubtedly the thioureas in our collection still harbor many other interesting physiological actions, or even a more effective rat poison than ANTU. A thiourea derivative with absolutely no taste or smell would undoubtedly make an ideal rat poison. Such a compound would have all the advantages of the highly toxic and effective sodium fluoroacetate (1080) and thallium sulfate, in having absolutely no taste, but without the disadvantages of being highly toxic to man as well as rats.

Studies on Effects of Domestication and Civilization

Of most lasting interest to me in this experience was the opportunity that it offered of studying effects produced by domestication on animals and indirectly effects produced by civilization on man.

The Norway rat, as was said before, is the first rat to have become domesticated for strictly scientific purposes. This process started about one hundred years ago. Domesticated rats are now available in large numbers throughout the world.

Their wild ancestors are also available in large numbers throughout the world. It thus becomes possible for the first time to compare living specimens in large numbers of a domesticated animal with their wild ancestors. In his pioneer study on domestication Darwin was almost entirely dependent for his ancestral forms on paleontological specimens from animals long since dead. His knowledge was limited to strictly anatomical details; further he had only a limited knowledge—mostly anatomical—of the domesticated forms. In contrast more is known not only about the domesticated rat's anatomy, but also its physiology and behavior, than about any other animal; and much is known about its wild ancestor's physiology and behavior. Furthermore, the short life span of the Norway rat—3–5 years—and early age of maturity make it possible to follow the various characteristics throughout many generations within only a few years.

For this purpose I have made it a practice to use equal numbers—whenever possible—of wild and domesticated Norways in all of our experiments regardless of the fields—whether in studies on the brain, endocrine glands, or behavior. Almost without exception differences in anatomy, physiology and behavior have come out of these observations. It will not be practical to review all of the differences at this time. I would like, however, to call attention to just two differences—the first concerns the adrenal glands; the second the sex glands. The adrenal glands—secretions of which play such an important part in the ability of an organism to meet stress—are much larger in wild Norways—3–8 times as large. Loss of adrenals completely incapacitates wild Norways, but has only a small detectable effect in domesticated Norways. In contrast the sex glands—the ovaries and testes—develop earlier in the domesticated rats and in general play a more important part in their lives. Domesticated rats mate earlier and more often. Castration has a profound effect on domesticated Norways, making them almost totally inactive, whereas it has only a small effect on wild Norways.

So far we have been able to explain many of the differences in terms of natural selection. In the wild state it is the strong, fierce and aggressive rats—that is, animals with the largest adrenals—the fittest for that type of environment—that survive; whereas in the laboratory it is the tamer, more tractable, gentle animals—animals that breed most readily—the fittest for that type of environment that survive. I have been interested in determining to what extent the changes in anatomy, physiology, and behavior that have occurred in the rat during its transition from the wild to the domesticated state can be followed in man during his transition from the primitive, wild state in which he had to fend for himself to the civilized state, characteristized by weaker, milder, better adjusted individuals. Results of these observations and speculations were summarized in 1959 in the paper on "Rats, Man and the Welfare State."

Epilogue

Not long after the end of our campaign Dr. Emlen left Baltimore to become Professor of Zoology at the University of Wisconsin. Over the years since then he has carried on population studies on various wild animals in different parts of the world—most notably on gorillas in Africa. He has stimulated interest in population studies in his students— among them George Schaller (*Year of the Gorilla*). I know very little about the fate of ANTU. It apparently has become just one of the various old and new rat poisons that are now available on the market. I have not heard that it has ever again been used in a city-wide campaign of our type.

Papers Resulting Directly or Indirectly from This Rat-Catching Experience

1. Richter, C. P., and K. H. Clisby. 1941. Phenyl-thiocarbamide Taste Thresholds of Rats and Human Beings. Amer. Jour. Physiol. 134:157.
2. Richter, C. P., and K. H. Clisby. 1941. Graying of Hair Produced by Ingestion of Phenylthiocarbamide. Proc. Soc. Exp. Biol. & Med. 48:684.
3. Richter, C. P., and K. H. Clisby, 1942. Toxic Effects of the Bitter-Tasting Phenylthiocarbamide. Arch. Path. 33:46.
4. Griffiths, W. J., Jr. 1944. Absence of Audiogenic Seizures in Wild Norway and Alexandrine Rats. Science 99:62.
5. Emlen, J. T. 1944. Device for Holding Live Wild Rats. Jour. Wildlife Manag. 8:264.
6. Dieke, S. H., and C. P. Richter. 1945. Acute Toxicity of Thiourea to Rats in Relation to Age, Diet, Strain and Species Variation. Jour. Pharmacol. & Exper. Therap. 83:195.
7. Richter, C. P. 1945. Incidence of Rat Bites and Rat Bite Fever in Baltimore. Jour. Amer. Med. Assn. 128:324.
8. Richter, C. P. 1945. The Development and Use of Alpha-Naphthyl Thiourea (ANTU) as a Rat Poison. Jour. Amer. Med. Assn. 129:927.
9. Richter, C. P., and J. T. Emlen, Jr. 1945. A Modified Rabbit Box Trap for Use in Catching Live Wild Rats for Laboratory and Field Studies. Pub. Health Rep. 60:1303.
10. Dieke, S. H., and C. P. Richter. 1946. Age and Species Variation in the Acute Toxicity of Alpha-Naphthyl Thiourea. Proc. Soc. Exp. Biol. & Med. 62:22.
11. Dieke, S. H., and C. P. Richter. 1946. Comparative Assays of Rodenticides on Wild Norway Rats. I. Toxicity. Pub. Health Rep. 61:672.
12. Richter, C. P., and J. T. Emlen, Jr. 1946. Instructions for Using ANTU as a Poison for the Common Norway Rat. Pub. Health Rep. 61:602.
13. Anderson, W. A., and C. P. Richter. 1946. Toxicity of Alpha Naphthyl Thiourea for Chickens and Pigs. Vet. Med. 41:302.
14. Rogers, Philip V. 1946. Relation Between Sex Hormones and Changes in Susceptibility of Domestic Norway Rats to Alpha-Naphthyl Thiourea. Proc. Soc. Exp. Biol. & Med. 63:38.

15. Richter, C. P. 1946. Biological Factors Involved in Poisoning Rats with Alpha-Naphthyl Thiourea (ANTU). Proc. Soc. Exp. Biol. & Med. 63:364.
16. Dieke, S. H. 1947. Pigmentation and Hair Growth in Black Rats, as Modified by the Chronic Administration of Thiourea, Phenyl Thiourea and Alpha-Naphthyl Thiourea. Endocrinol. 40:123.
17. Dieke, S. H., G. S. Allen, and C. P. Richter. 1947. The Acute Toxicity of Thioureas and Related Compounds to Wild and Domestic Norway Rats. Jour. Pharmacol. & Exp. Therap. 90, 3:260.
18. Griffiths, W. J., Jr. 1947. Audiogenic Fits Produced by Magnesium Deficiency in Tame Domestic Norway Rats and in Wild Norway Rats. Amer. Jour. Physiol. 149:135.
19. Latta, H. 1947. Pulmonary Edema and Pleural Effusion Produced by Acute Alpha-Naphthyl Thiourea Poisoning in Rats and Dogs. Bull. Johns Hopkins Hosp. 80:181.
20. Emlen, J. T., Jr., and A. W. Stokes. 1947. Effectiveness of Various Rodenticides on Population of Brown Rats in Baltimore, Maryland. Amer. Jour. Hyg. 45, 2:254.
21. Emlen, J. T., Jr. 1947. Baltimore's Community Rat Control Program. Amer. Jour. Pub. Health 37, 6:721.
22. Richter, C. P., and C. E. Hall. 1947. Comparison of Intestinal Lengths and Peyer's Patches in Wild and Domestic Norway and in Wild Alexandrine Rats. Proc. Soc. Exp. Biol. & Med. 66:561.
23. Rogers, P. V., and C. P. Richter. 1948. Anatomical Comparison Between the Adrenal Glands of Wild Norway, Wild Alexandrine and Domestic Norway Rats. Endocrinol. 42:46.
24. Richter, C. P. 1948. Physiology and Endocrinology of the Toxic Thioureas. Recent Prog. in Hormone Research 2:255.
25. Dieke, S. H. 1948. Effect of Removing Various Endocrine Glands on the Hair Cycles of Black Rats. Endocrinol. 42, 4:315.
26. Hall, C. E. 1948. Comparison of the Preputial Glands in the Alexandrine, the Wild and the Domestic Norway Rat. Proc. Soc. Exp. Biol. & Med. 69:233.
27. Dieke, S. H. 1948. Comparative Assays of Rodenticides on Wild Norway Rats. II. Acceptance. Proc. Soc. Exp. Biol. & Med. 69:593.
28. Dieke, S. H. 1949. Thiosemicarbazide: A New Toxic Derivative of Thiourea. Proc. Soc. Exp. Biol. & Med. 70:688.
29. Richter, C. P. 1949. The Use of the Wild Norway Rat for Psychiatric Research. Jour. Nerv. & Ment. Dis. 110, 5:379.
30. Richter, C. P. 1949. Domestication of the Norway Rat and Its Implication for the Problem of Stress. Proc. Ass. Res. Nerv. & Ment. Dis. 29:19.
31. Richter, C. P. 1950. Taste and Solubility of Toxic Compounds in Poisoning of Rats and Man. Jour. Comp. Physiol. Psychol. 43:358.
32. Richter, C. P., P. V. Rogers, and C. E. Hall. 1950. Failure of Salt Replacement Therapy in Adrenalectomized Recently Capture Wild Norway Rats. Endocrinol. 46:233.
33. Dieke, S. H. 1951. Influence of Alpha-Naphthyl Thiourea on Gastric Evacuation. Proc. Soc. Exp. Biol. & Med. 76:788.
34. Mosier, H. D., Jr. 1951. Responses of the Rat Adrenal to a High Salt Diet. Abstract in Johns Hopkins Bullctin 89:44.
35. Richter, C. P. 1951. The Effects of Domestication on the Steroids of Animals and Man. Proc. Nat. Acad., November 1951.
36. Richter, C. P. 1951. The Effects of Domestication on the Steroids of Animals and Man. Symposium on Steroids and Behavior (Ciba Foundation, London).

37. Richter, C. P. 1952. The Physiology and Cytology of Pulmonary Edema and Pleural Effusion Produced in Rats by Alpha-Naphthyl Thiourea (ANTU). Jour. Thoracic Surg. 23:66.
38. Richter, C. P. 1952. Domestication of the Norway Rat and Its Implication for the Study of Genetics in Man. Amer. Jour. Human Genet. 4:273.
39. Richter, C. P. 1952. Stress and Structural Change. Seventh Annual Menas S. Gregory Lecture. May 1, 1952, New York University—Bellevue Medical Center, New York City.
40. Richter, C. P. 1953. Experimentally Produced Behavior Reactions to Food Poisoning in Wild and Domesticated Rats. Annals of the New York Academy of Sciences 56:225.
41. Richter, C. P., G. E. S. Jones, and J. W. Woods. 1953. Behavior Cycles Produced in Rats by Thyroidectomy, Injection of I^{131}, or by Feeding Sulfamerazine. Meeting of the Endocrine Society, May 28, 29, 30, 1953. New York City.
42. Woods, J. W. 1953. Differences in Adrenal Response to Adverse Conditions in Wild and Domesticated Norway Rats. Fed. Proc. 12, 522.
43. Richter, C. P. 1953. Behavioral Regulation of Homeostasis. Symposium on Stress. March 16, 17, 18, 1953. Army Medical Service Graduate School, Walter Reed Army Medical Center, Washington, D.C.
44. Richter, C. P., and H. D. Mosier, Jr. 1954. Maximum Sodium Chloride Intake and Thirst in Domesticated and Wild Norway Rats. Amer. Jour. Physiol. 176:213.
45. Richter, C. P., and E. H. Uhlenhuth. 1954. Comparison of the Effects of Gonadectomy on Spontaneous Activity of Wild and Domesticated Norway Rats. Endocrinol. 54:311.
46. Woods, J. W. 1954. Effects of a Chronically Cold Environment on Endocrine Organs of Wild and Domesticated Rats. Fed. Proc. 13, 555.
47. Richter, C. P. 1954. The Effects of Domestication and Selection on the Behavior of the Norway Rat. Jour. Nat. Cancer Institute 15:727.
48. Baker, S. P. 1954. Anuria Produced by Alpha-Naphthyl Thiourea. Amer. Jour. Physiol. 179:457.
49. Wood, D. E. 1955. Hypophysectomy and Domestication in the Norway Rat. Bull. Johns Hopkins Hosp. 97(2):178.
50. Richter, C. P. 1956. Salt Appetite of Mammals: Its Dependence on Instinct and Metabolism. Contribution to L' instinct dans le comportement des animaux et de l'homme (Paris, France).
51. Karli, P. C. 1956. The Norway Rat's Killing Response to the White Mouse: An Experimental Analysis. Behaviour 10:81.
52. Mosier, H. D., Jr. 1957. Comparative Histological Study of the Adrenal Cortex of the Wild and Domesticated Norway Rat. Endocrinol. 60:460.
53. Richter, C. P. 1957. Phenomenon of Sudden Death in Animals and Man. Psychosomatic Med. 19:191.
54. Woods, J. W. 1957. The Effects of Long-Term Exposure to Cold Upon Adrenal Weight and Ascorbic Acid Content in Wild and Domesticated Norway Rats. Jour. Physiol. 135, 2:384.
55. Mosier, H. D., Jr., and C. P. Richter. 1958. Response of the Glomerulosa Layer of the Adrenal Gland of Wild and Domesticated Norway Rats to Low and High Salt Diets. Endocrinol. 62:268.
56. Richter, C. P. 1959. Rats, Man and the Welfare State. Amer. Psychologist 14:18.
57. Mosier, H. D., and C. P. Richter. 1967. Histologic and Physiologic Comparisons of the Thyroid Glands of the Wild and Domesticated Norway Rat. Anat. Rec. 158:263.

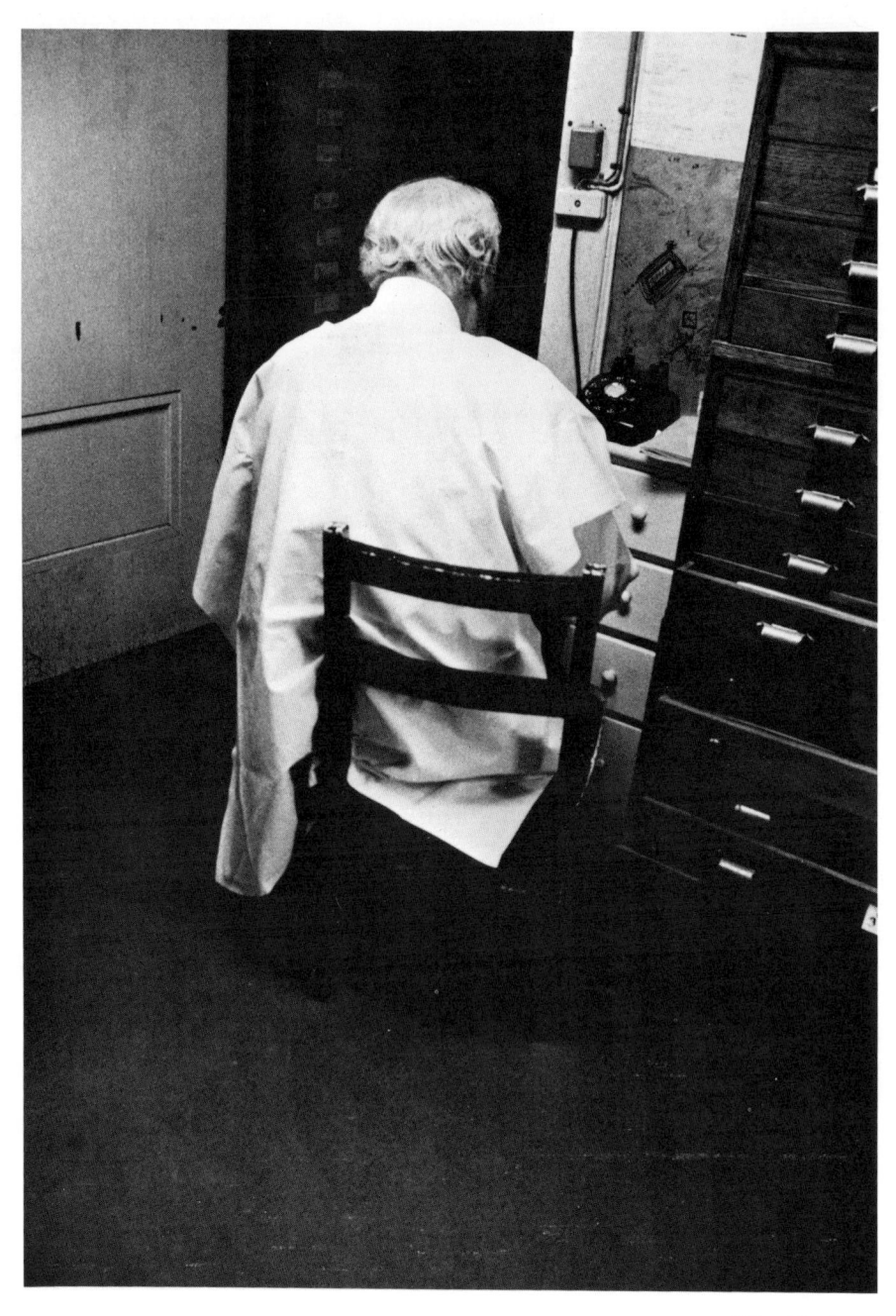

Elliot M. Blass

APPENDIX:
COMPLETE BIBLIOGRAPHY OF CURT P. RICHTER

Carter, E. P. Richter, C. P., and Greene, C. H. A graphic application of the principle of the equilateral triangle for determining the direction of the electrical axis of the heart in the human electrocardiogram. *Johns Hopkins Hospital Bulletin.* 30:162–167, 1919.

Richter, C. P. A behavioristic study of the activity of the rat. *Comp. Psychol. Mongr.* 1:1–55, 1922.

Richter, C. P., and Wada, T. Method of measuring salivary secretions in human beings. *J. Lab. and Clin. Med.* 9:2–4, 1924.

Richter, C. P. Action currents from the stomach. *Am. J. Physiol.* 67:612–633, 1924.

Richter, C. P. The sweat glands studied by the electrical resistance method. *Am. J. Physiol.* 68:147, 1924.

Bagley, C. J., and Richter, C. P. Electrically excitable region of the forebrain of the alligator. *Arch. Neurol. and Psychiat.* 2:257–263, 1924.

Richter, C. P. Some observations on the self-stimulation habits of young wild animals. *Arch. Neurol. Psychiat.* 13:724–728, 1925.

Wang, G. H., Richter, C. P., and Guttmacher, A. F. Activity studies on male castrated rats with ovatian transplants, and correlation of the activity with the histology of the grafts. *Am. J. Physiol.* 73:581–599, 1925.

Richter, C. P. The significance of changes in the electrical resistance of the body during sleep. *Proc. Nat. Acad. Sci.* 12:214–222, 1926.

Richter, C. P. A study of the effect of moderate doses of alcohol on the growth and behavior of the rat. *J. Exper. Zool.* 44:397–418, 1926.

Richter, C. P., and Bartemeier, L. H. Decerebrate rigidity of the sloth. *Brain* 49:207, 1926

Gillespie, R. D., Richter, C. P., and Wang, G. The oculo-cardiac reflex; its clinical significance. *J. Mental Sci.,* 72:321–325, 1926.

Richter, C. P. New methods of obtaining electromyogram and electrocardiogram from the intact body. *J. A. M. A.* 87:1300, 1926.

Richter, C. P., and Wang, G. H. New apparatus for measuring the spontaneous motility of animals. *J. Lab. and Clin. Med.* 12:289–92, 1926.

Richter, C. P. A study of the electrical skin resistance and the psychogalvanic reflex in a case of unilateral sweating. *Brain.* 50:216–235, 1927.

Richter, C. P. On the interpretation of the electromyogram from voluntary and reflex contractions. *Quart. J. Exper. Physiol.* 18:55–77, 1927.

Richter, C. P. Animal behavior and internal drives. *Quart, Rev. Biol.* 2:307–343, 1927.

Richter, C. P. The electrical skin resistance. *Arch. Neurol. Psychiat.* 19:488–508, 1928.

Richter, C. P., and Ford, F. R. Electromyographic studies in different types of neuromuscular disturbances. *Arch. Neurol. Psychiat.* 19:660–676, 1928.

Richter, C. P. The dependence of the electromyogram from voluntary contractions on the anterior horn cells. *Am. J. Physiol.* 85:403, 1928.

Wang, G. H., and Richter, C. P. Action currents from the pad of the cat's foot produced by stimulation of the tuber cinereum.*Chin. J. Physiol.* 2:279–284, 1928.

Richter, C. P., and Wislocki, G. B. Activity studies on castrated male and female rats with testicular grafts in correlation with histological studies of the grafts. *Am. J. Physiol.* 86:651–660, 1928.

Richter, C. P. Pathologic sleep and similar conditions. *Arch. Neurol. Psychiat.* 21:363–375, 1929.

Richter, C. P. Physiological factors involved in the electrical resistance of the skin. *Am. J. Physiol.* 88:596–615, 1929.

Richter, C. P., and Brailey, M. E. Water-intake and its relation to the surface area of the body. *Proc. Nat. Acad. Sci.* 15:570–578, 1929.

Richter, C. P. Nervous control of the electrical resistance of the skin. *Bull. Johns Hopkins Hosp.* 45:56–74, 1929.

Richter, C. P. The galvanic skin-reflex in spinal animals. *Proc. and Papers Ninth Internat. Cong. Psychol.*, 357–358, 1929.

Richter, C. P. Thirst: A function of body-surface. *Proc. and Papers Ninth Internat. Cong. Psychol.*, 358–359, 1929.

Richter, C. P. Biological approach to manic depressive insanity. *Proc. Assoc. Res. in Nerv. and Mental Dis.* 11:611–625, 1930.

Richter, C. P. Experimental diabetes insipidus. *Brain.* 53:76–85, 1930.

Richter, C. P. Galvanic skin reflex from animals with complete transection of the spinal cord. *Am. J. Physiol.* 93:468–472, 1930.

Richter, C. P. High electrical resistance of the skin of new-born infants and its significance. *Am. J. Dis. Child.* 40:18–26, 1930.

Langworthy, O. R., and Richter, C. P. The influence of efferent cerebral pathways upon the sympathetic nervous system. *Brain.* 53:178–193, 1930.

Richter, C. P., and Wislocki, G. B. Anatomical and behavior changes produced in the rat by complete and partial extirpation of the pituitary gland. *Am. J. Physiol.* 95:481–492, 1930.

Richter, C. P., and Shaw, M. B. Complete transections of the spinal cord at different levels. *Arch. Neurol. Psychiat.* 24:1107–1116, 1930.

Richter, C. P. Sleep produced by hypnotics studied by the electrical skin resistance method. *J. Pharmacol. and Exper, Therap.* 42:471–486, 1931.

Tower, S. S., and Richter, C. P. Injury and repair within the sympathetic nervous system. I. The preganglionic neurons. *Arch. Neurol. Psychiat.* 26:485–495, 1931.

Richter, C. P. The grasping reflex in the new-born monkey. *Arch. Neurol. Psychiat.* 26:784–790, 1931.

Richter, C. P., and Paterson, A. S. Bulbocapnine catalepsy and the grasp reflex. *J. Pharmacol. and Exper. Therap.* 43:677–691. 1931.

Richter, C. P., and Paterson, A. S. On the pharmacology of the grasp reflex. *Brain.* 55:391–396, 1932.

Richter, C. P. IV. Biological foundation of personality differences. *Am. J. Orthopsychiat.* 2:345–354, 1932.
Tower, S. S., and Richter, C. P. Injury and repair within the sympathetic nervous system. II. The postganglionic neurons. *Arch. Neurol. Psychiat.* 28:1139–1148, 1932.
Tower, S. S., and Richter, C. P. Injury and repair within the sympathetic nervous system. III. Evidence of activity of postganglionic sympathetic neurons independent of the central nervous system. *Arch. Neurol. Psychiat.* 28:1149–1152, 1932.
Richter, C. P., and Hines, M. Experimental production of the grasp reflex in adult monkeys by lesions of the frontal lobes. *Am. J. Physiol.* 101:87–99, 1932. (Proceedings).
Richter, C. P. The role played by the thyroid gland in the production of gross body activity. *Endocrinology.* 17:73–87, 1933.
Paterson, A. S., and Richter, C. P. Action of scopolamine and carbon dioxide on catalepsy produced by bulbocapnine. *Arch. Neurol. Psychiat.* 29:231–240, 1933.
Richter, C. P., and Langworthy, O. R. The quill mechanism of the porcupine. *J. f. Psychol. u. Neurol.* 45:143–153, 1933.
Langworthy, O. R., and Richter, C. P. The cerebral motor cortex of the porcupine. *J. f. Psychol. u. Neurol.* 45:138–142, 1933.
Richter, C. P. The effect of early gonadectomy on the gross body activity of rats. *Endocrinology.* 17:445–450, 1933.
Richter, C. P. Cyclical phenomena produced in rats by section of the pituitary stalk and their possible relation to pseudo-pregnancy. *Am. J. Physiol.* 106:80–90, 1933.
Buchman, E. F., and Richter, C. P. Abolition of bulbocapnine catatonia by cocaine. *Arch. Neurol. Psychiat.* 29:499–503, 1933.
Richter, C. P. Cyclic manifestations in the sleep curves of psychotic patients. *Arch Neurol. Psychiat.* 31:149–151, 1934.
Richter, C. P., and Hartman, C. G. The effect of injection of amniotin on the spontaneous activity of gonadectomized rats. *Am. J. Physiol.* 108:136–143, 1934.
Richter, C. P., and Hines, M. The production of the "grasp reflex" in adult Macaques by experimental fronal lobe lesions. *Proc. Assoc. Res. Nerv. Mental Dis.* 13:211–224, 1932.
Richter, C. P., and Benjamin, J. A., Jr. The third ventricle: Conformation of the floor and its relation to the meninges. *Arch. Neurol. Psychiat.* 31:1026–1037, 1934.
Richter, C. P. The grasp reflex of the new-born infant. *Am. J. Dis. child.* 48:327–332, 1934.
Richter, C. P. Experimental diabetes insipitus: its relation to the anterior and posterior lobes of the hypophysis. *Am. J. Physiol.* 110:439–447, 1934.
Richter, C. P. Pregnancy urine given by mouth to gonadectomized rats: its effect on spontaneous activity and on the reproductive tract. *Am. J. Physiol.* 110:499–512, 1934.
Richter, C. P., and Benjamin, J. A., Jr. Ligation of the common bile duct in the rat. *Arch. Path.* 18:817–826, 1934.
Levine, M., and Richter, C. P. Periodic attacks of gastric pain accompanied with marked changes in the electrical resistance of the skin. *Arch. Neurol. Psychiat.* 33:1078–1080, 1935.
Richter, C. P. The primacy of polyuria in diabetes insipidus. *Am. J. Physiol.* 112:481–487, 1935.

Richter, C. P., and Eckert, J. F. Further evidence for the primacy of polyuria in diabetes insipidus. *Am. J. Physiol.* 113:578–581, 1935.

Richter, C. P., and Hines, M. Increased activity produced by brain lesions in monkeys. Second Internt. Neurol. Cong. 1935.

Richter, C. P. Increased salt appetite in adrenalectomized rats. *Am. J. Physiol.* 115:155–161, 1936.

Richter, C. P. The spontaneous activity of adrenalectomized rats treated with replacement and other therapy. *Endocrinology* 20:657–666, 1936.

Richter, C. P., and Eckert, J. F. Behavior changes produced in the rat by hypophysectomy. *Proc. Assoc. Res. Nerv. Mental Dis.* 17:561–571, 1936.

Richter, C. P. The pituitary gland in relation to water exchange. *Proc. Assoc. Res. Nerv. Mental Dis.* 17:392–409, 1936.

Cannon, Engle, Richter, Hoskins, Lee. An appraisal of endocrinology. Report to the Directors of the John and Mary R. Markle Foundation, 1936.

Richter, C. P., and Eckert J. F. Increased calcium appetite of parathyroidectomized rats. *Endocrinology* 21:50–54, 1937.

Richter, C. P., and Levine, M. Sympathectomy in man. *Arch. Neurol. Psychiat.* 38:756–760, 1937.

Richter, C. P., and Eckert J. F. The effect of hypophyseal injection and implants on the activity of hypophysectomized rats. *Endocrinology* 21:481–488, 1937.

Richter, C. P., Holt, L. E., Jr., and Barelare, B., Jr. Vitamin B^1 craving in rats. *Science* 86:354–355, 1937.

Richter, C. P. Hypophyseal control of behavior. *Cold Spring Harbor Symposia on Quantitative Biology* 5:258–268, 1937.

Richter, C. P., and Hines, M. Increased general activity produced by pre-frontal and striatal lesions in monkeys. *Trans. Am. Neurol. Assoc.*, 63rd Meeting, 107–109, 1937.

Richter, C. P., Holt, L. E., Jr., and Barelare, B. Jr. The effect of self-selection of diet—food (protein, carbohydrates, and fats), minerals and vitamins—on growth, activity, and reproduction in rats. *Am. J. Physiol.* 119:388–389, 1937.

Richter, C. P. The work of the psychobiology laboratory. Contributions dedicated to Dr. Adolf Meyer, ed. by S. Katzenelbogen, 81–85, 1937.

Barelare, B. Jr., and Richter, C. P. Increased sodium chloride appetite in pregnant rats. *Am. J. Physiol.* 121:185–188, 1938.

Langworthy, O. R., and Richter, C. P. A physiological study of cerebral motor cortex and decerebrate rigidity in the beaver. *J. Mammal.* 19:70–77, 1938.

Richter, C. P., and Eckert, J. F. Mineral metabolism of adrenalectomized rats studied by the appetite method. *Endocrinology* 22:214–224, 1938.

Richter, C. P., and Hines, M. Increased spontaneous activity produced in monkeys by brain lesions. *Brain* 61:1–16, 1938.

Richter, C. P. Two-day cycles of alternating good and bad behavior in psychotic patients. *Arch. Neurol. Psychiat.* 39:587–598, 1938.

Richter, C. P., Holt, L. E., Jr., and Barelare, B. Jr. Nutritional requirements for normal growth and reproduction in rats studied by the self-selection method. *Am. J. Physiol.* 122:734–744, 1938.

Richter, C. P. The integration of the grasp reflex. *Trans. Am. Neurol. Assoc.*, 64th Meeting, 128, 1938.

Richter, C. P. Factors determining voluntary ingestion of water in normals and in individuals with maximum diabetes insipidus. *Am. J. Physiol.* 122:668–675, 1938.

Richter, C. P., and Barelare, B., Jr. Nutritional requirements of pregnant and lactating rats studied by the self-selection method. *Endocrinology* 23:15–24, 1938.
Barelare, B., Jr., Holt, L. E., Jr., and Richter, C. P. Influence of vitamin deficiencies on appetite for particular foodstuffs. *Am. J. Physiol.* 123:7–8, 1938.
Richter, C. P. Animal cages. *Am. J. Physiol.* 123:170, 1938.
Richter, C. P., Holt, L. E., Jr., Barelare, B., Jr., and Hawkes, C. D. Changes in fat, carbohydrate, and protein appetite in vitamin B deficiency. *Am. J. Physiol.* 124:596–602, 1939.
Richter, C. P. Salt taste thresholds of normal and adrenalectomized rats. *Endocrinology* 24:367–371, 1939.
Richter, C. P., and Barelare, B., Jr. Persistence of 4- to 5-day activity cycles in vitamin A deficient rats with constant cornification of the vaginal epithelium. *Endocrinology* 24:3764–366, 1939.
Richter, C. P., and MacLean, A. Salt taste thresholds of humans. *Am. J. Physiol.* 126:1–6, 1939.
Langworthy, O. R., and Richter, C. P. Increased spontaneous activity produced by frontal lobe lesions in cats. *Am. J. Physiol.* 126:158–161, 1939.
Richter, C. P., and Eckert, J. F. Mineral appetite of parathyroidectomized rats. *Am. J. Med. Sci.* 198:9–16, 1939.
Richter, C. P., and Hawkes, C. D. Increased spontaneous activity and food intake produced in rats by removal of the frontal poles of the brain. *J. Neurol. Psychiat.* 2:231–242, 1939.
Richter, C. P., and Barelare, B., Jr. Further observations on the carbohydrate, fat, and protein appetite of vitamin B deficient rats. *Am. J. Physiol.* 127:199–210, 1939.
Richter, C. P., and Schmidt, E. C. H., Jr. Behavior and anatomical changes reproduced in rats by pancreatectomy. *Endocrinology* 25:698–706, 1939.
Richter, C. P. Transmission of taste sensation in animals. *Trans. Am. Neurol. Assoc.*, 65th Meeting, 49–50, 1939.
Richter, C. P., and Campbell, K. H. Sucrose taste thresholds of rats and humans. *Am. J. Physiol.* 128:291–297, 1940.
Richter, C. P., Honeyman, W., and Hunter, H. Behavior and mood cycles apparently related to parathyroid deficiency. *J. Neurol. Psychiat.* 3:19–25, 1940.
Wilkins, L., and Richter, C. P. A great craving for salt by a child with corticoadrenal insufficiency. *J. A. M. A.* 114:866–868, 1940.
Richter, C. P., and Campbell, K. H. Alcohol taste thresholds and concentrations of solution preferred by rats. *Science* 91:507–508, 1940.
Richter, C. P., and Campbell, K. H. Taste thresholds and taste preferences of rats for five common sugars. *J. Nutrit.* 20:31–46, 1940.
Richter, C. P., and Hawkes, C. D. The dependence of the carbohydrate, fat and protein appetite of rats on the various components of the vitamin B complex. *Am. J. Physiol.* 131:639–649, 1941.
Richter, C. P., and Schmidt, E. C. H., Jr. Increased fat and decreased carbohydrate appetite of pancreatectomized rats. *Endocrinology* 28:179–192, 1941.
Richter, C. P. Behavior and endocrine regulators of the internal environment. *Endocrinology* 28:193–195, 1941.
Richter, C. P. The internal environment and behavior. Internal secretions. *Am. J. Psychiat.* 97:878–893, 1941.
Richter, C. P. Alcohol as a food. *Quart. J. Studies on Alcohol.* 1:650–662, 1941.
Schmidt, E. C. H., Jr., and Richter, C. P. Anatomic and behavior changes produced by partial hepatectomy in the rat. *Arch. Path.* 31:483–488, 1941.

Richter, C. P. The nutritional value of some common carbohydrates, fats and proteins studied in rats by the single food choice method. *Am. J. Physiol.* 133:29–42, 1941.
Richter, C. P. Biology of drives. *Psychosomatic Med.* 3:105–110, 1941.
Richter, C. P. Sodium chloride and dextrose appetite of untreated and treated adrenalectomized rats. *Endocrinology* 29:115–125, 1941.
Richter, C. P., and Clisby, K. H. Phenylthiocarbamide taste thresholds of rats and human beings. *Am. J. Physiol.* 134:157–164, 1941.
Richter, C. P., and Birmingham, J. R. Calcium appetite of parathyroidectomized rats used to bioassay substances which affect blood calcium. *Endocrinology* 29:655–666, 1941.
Richter, C. P. Changes produced by sympathectomy in the electrical resistance of the skin. *Trans. Am. Neurol. Assoc.*, 67th Meeting, 157, 1941.
Richter, C. P., and Woodruff, B. G. Changes produced by sympathectomy in the electrical resistance of the skin. *Surgery* 10:957–970, 1941.
Richter, C. P. Decreased carbohydrate appetite of adrenalectomized rats. *Proc. Soc. Exp. Biol. and Med.* 48:577–579, 1941.
Richter, C. P., and Clisby, K. H. Graying of hair produced by ingestion of phenylthiocarbamide. *Proc. Soc. Exp. Biol. and Med.* 48:684–687, 1941.
Richter, C. P., and Clisby, K. H. Toxic effects of the bitter-tasting phenylthiocarbamide. *Arch. Path.* 33:46–57, 1942.
Richter, C. P. Increased dextrose appetite of normal rats treated with insulin. *Am. J. Physiol.* 135:781–787, 1942.
Richter, C. P. Physiological psychology. *Ann. Rev. Physiol.* 4:561–574, 1942.
Richter, C. P., and Woodruff, B. G. Facial patterns of electrical skin resistance— their relation to sleep, external temperature, hair distribution, sensory dermatomes and skin disease. *Bull. Johns Hopkins Hosp.* 70:442–459, 1942.
Richter, C. P., and Rice, K. K. The effect of thiamine hydrochloride on the energy value of dextrose studied in rats by the single food choice method. *Am. J. Physiol.* 137:573–581, 1942.
Richter, C. P., and Birmingham, J. R. Decreased fat appetite produced in rats by ligation of the common bile duct. *Am. J. Physiol.* 138:71–77, 1942.
Richter, C. P. Total self regulatory functions in animals and human beings. *Harvey Lectures Series.* 38:63–103, 1942–3.
Whelan, F. G., and Richter, C. P. Electrical skin resistance technique used to map areas of skin affected by sympathectomy and by other surgical or functional factors. *Arch. Neurol. Psychiat.* 49:454–456, 1943.
Richter, C. P. The self-selection of diets. *Essays in Biology*, in honor of Herbert M. Evans, University of California Press, 1943.
Richter, C. P., and Rice, K. K. Depressive effects produced on appetite and activity of rats by an exclusive diet of yellow or white corn and their correction by cod liver oil. *Amer. J. Physiol.*, 139:147–154, 1943.
Richter, C. P., and Whelan, F. G. Sweat gland responses to sympathetic stimulation studied by the galvanic skin reflex method. *J. Neurophysiol.* 6:191–194, 1943.
Rice, K. K., and Richter, C. P. Increased sodium chloride and water intake of normal rats treated with desoxycorticosterone acetate. *Endocrinology* 33:106–115, 1943.
Richter, C. P., and Katz, D. T. Peripheral nerve injuries determined by the electrical skin resistance method. I. Ulnar nerve. *J. A. M. A.* 122:648–651, 1943.
Richter, C. P., and Rice, K. K. Effects produced by vitamin D on energy, appetite, and oestrous cycles of rats kept on an exclusive diet of yellow corn. *Am. J. Physiol.* 139:693–699, 1943.

Richter, C. P., Woodruff, B. G. and Eaton, B. C. Hand and foot patterns of low electrical skin resistance: their anatomical and neurological significance. *J. Neurophysiol.* 6:417–424, 1943.

Richter, C. P., and Helfrick, S. Decreased phosphorus appetite of parathyroidectomized rats. *Endocrinology* 33:349–352, 1943.

Richter, C. P., and Rice, K. K. Comparison of the nutritive value of dextrose and casein and of the effects produced by their utilization by thiamine. *Am. J. Physiol.* 141:346–353, 1944.

Fish, H. S., Malone, P. D., and Richter, C. P. The anatomy of the tongue of the domestic Norway rat. I. The skin of the tongue: the various papillae; their number and distribution. *Anat. Rec.* 89:429–440, 1944.

Richter, C. P., and Rice, K. K. Self-selection studies on coprophagy as a source of vitamin B complex. *Am. J. Physiol.* 143:344–354, 1945.

Richter, C. P., and Rice, K. K. A comparison of the nutritive value of dextrose and sucrose and of the effects produced on their utilization by thiamine hydrochloride. *Am. J. Physiol.* 143:336–343, 1945.

Dieke, S. H., and Richter, C. P. Acute toxicity of thiourea to rats in relation to age, diet, strain, and species variation. *J. Pharmacol. and Exper. Therap.* 83:195–202, 1945.

Richter, C. P. Nutritive value of dextri-maltose determined by the single-food choice method. *Proc. Soc. Exp. Biol. and Med.* 59:260–263, 1945.

Richter, C. P., Schmidt, E. C. H., Jr., and Malone, P. D. Further observations on the self-regulatory dietary selections of rats made diabetic by pancreatectomy. *Bull. Johns Hopkins Hosp.* 76:192–219, 1945.

Richter, C. P. Incidence of rat bites and rat bite fever in Baltimore. *J. A. M. A.* 128:324–326, 1945.

Richter, C. P., and Woodruff, B. G. Lumbar sympathetic dermatomes in man determined by the electrical skin resistance method. *J. Neurophysiol.* 8:323–338, 1945.

Richter, C. P., and Malone, P. D. Peripheral nerve lesion charts. *J. Neurosurg.* 2:550–552, 1945.

Richter, C. P. The development and use of alpha-naphthyl thiourea (ANTU) as a rat poison. *J. A. M. A.* 129:927–931, 1945.

Richter, C. P., and Emlen, J. T., Jr. A modified rabbit box trap for use in catching live wild rats for laboratory and field studies. *Pub. Health Rep.* 60:1303–1308, 1945.

Richter, C. P. A comparison of the nutritive values of dextrose and of corn syrups and of the effects produced on their utilization by thiamine. *Am. J. Physiol.* 145:107–114, 1945.

Richter, C. P., and Otenasek, F. J. Thoracolumbar sympathectomies examined with the electrical skin resistance method. *J. Neurosurg.* 3:120–134, 1946.

Bruesch, S. R., and Richter, C. P. Cutaneous distribution of peripheral nerves in Rhesus monkeys as determined by the electric skin resistance method. *Bull. Johns Hopkins Hosp.* 78:235–1946.

Richter, C. P. Instructions for using the cutaneous resistance recorder, or "dermometer," on peripheral nerve injuries, sympathectomies, and paravertebral blocks. *J. Neurosurg.* 3:181–191, 1946.

Dieke, S. H., and Richter, C. P. Age and species variation in the acute toxicity of alpha-naphthyl thiourea. *Proc. Soc. Exper. Biol. and Med.* 62:22–25, 1946.

Dieke, S. H., and Richter, C. P. Comparative assays of rodenticides on wild Norway rats. I. Toxicity. *Pub. Health Rep.* 61:672–679, 1946.

Richter, C. P., and Emlen, J. T., Jr. Instructions for using ANTU as a poison for the common Norway rat. *Pub. Health. Rep.* 61:602–607, 1946.

Anderson, W. A., and Richter, C. P. Toxicity of alpha-naphthyl thiourea for chickens and pigs. *Vet. Med.* 41:302–303, 1946.

Richter, C. P. Biological factors involved in poisoning rats with alpha-naphthyl thiourea (ANTU). *Proc. Soc. Exper. Biol. and Med.* 63:364–372, 1946.

Fish, H. S., and Richter, C. P. Comparative numbers of fungiform and foliate papillae on tongues of domestic and wild Norway rats. *Proc. Soc. Exper. Biol. and Med.* 63:352–355, 1946.

Dieke, S. H., Allen, G. S., and Richter, C. P. The acute toxicity of thioureas and related compounds to wild and domestic Norway rats. *J. Pharmacol. and Exper. Therap.* 90:260–270, 1947.

Richter, C. P. Cutaneous areas denervated by upper thoracic and stellate ganglionectomies determined by the electrical skin resistance method. *J. Neurosurg.* 4:221–232, 1947.

Richter, C. P., Biology of Drives. *J. Comp. and Physiol. Psychol.* 40:129–134, 1947.

Richter, C. P., and Hall, C. E. Comparison of intestinal lengths and Peyer's patches in wild and domestic Norway and in wild Alexandrine rats. *Proc. Soc. Exp. Biol. and Med.* 66:561–566, 1947.

Rogers, P. V., and Richter, C. P. Anatomical comparison between the adrenal glands of wild Norway, wild Alexandrine and domestic Norway rats. *Endocrinology* 42:46–55, 1948.

Richter, C. P. Physiology and endocrinology of the toxic thioureas. *Recent Progress in Hormone Research* II:255–276, 1948.

Bordley, J. E., Hardy, W. G., and Richter, C. P. Audiometry with the use of galvanic skin resistance response. *Bull. Johns Hopkins Hosp.* 82:569, 1948.

Richter, C. P. Effect of galactose on the utilization of fat. *Science* 108:449–450, 1948.

Richter, C. P. Nutritive value of fructose for rats and effects produced on its utilization by thiamine. *Am. J. Physiol.* 154:499–505, 1948.

Richter, C. P., and Whelan, F. G. Description of a skin galvanometer that gives a graphic record of activity in the sympathetic nervous system. *J. Neurosurg.* 6:279–284, 1949.

Richter, C. P. The use of the wild Norway rat for psychiatric research. *J. Nerv. and Ment. Dis.* 110:379–386, 1949.

King, A. B. and Richter, C. P. Spinal subdural abscess due to a congenital dermal sinus and accompanying changes in the autonomic nervous system. *Bull. Johns Hopkins Hosp.* 85:431–439, 1949.

Richter, C. P., Rogers, P. V., and Hall, C. E. Failure of salt replacement therapy in adrenalectomized recently captured wild Norway rats. *Endocrinology* 46:233–242, 1950.

Richter, C. P. An ideal preparation for the dissection of spinal, peripheral and autonomic nerves of the rat. *Science* 112:20–21, 1950.

Mirick, G. S., Richter, C. P., Schaub, I. G., Franklin, R., MacCleary, R., Schipper, G., and Spitznagel, J. An epizootic due to pneumococcus type II in laboratory rats. *Am. J. Hygiene* 52:48, 1950.

Richter, C. P. Taste and solubility of toxic compounds in poisoning of rats and man. *J. Comp. Physiol. Psychol.* 43:358–374, 1950.

Richter, C. P. Domestication of the Norway rat and its implications for the problem of stress. *Proc. Assoc. Res. Nerv. and Ment. Dis.* 29:19–47, 1949.

Richter, C. P. The physiology and cytology of pulmonary edema and pleural effusion produced in rats by alpha-naphthyl thiourea (ANTU). *J. Thoracic Surg.* 23:66–91, 1952.

Richter, C. P. The effects of domestication on the steroids of animals and man. *Proc. Nat. Acad.*, 1951.

Richter, C. P. The effects of domestication on the steroids of animals and man. *Symposium on Steroids and Behavior*, Ciba Foundation, London, 1951.

Richter, C. P., Jones, G. E. S., Woods, J. W. Behavior cycles produced in rats by thyroidectomy, injection of I^{131}, or by feeding sulfamerazine. *Endocrinology*, 1953.

Richter, C. P. Stress and structural change. Seventh annual Menas S. Gregory Lecture. May 1, 1952, New York University-Bellevue Medical Center, New York City.

Richter, C. P. Experimentally produced behavior reactions to food poisoning in wild and domesticated rats. *Annals N. Y. Acad. Scs* 56:225–239, 1953.

Richter, C. P. Domestication of the Norway rat and its implication for the study of genetics in man. *Am. J. Human Genetics* 4:273–285, 1952.

Richter, C. P., and Wood, D. E. Hypophysectomy and domestication in the Norway rat. *Fed. Proc.* 12:378, 1953.

Richter, C. P. Behavior cycles in man and animals. *Nat. Acad. Sci.* 1953.

Richter, C. P. Free research versus design research. *Science.* 118:91–93, 1953.

Richter, C. P. Behavioral regulation of homeostasis. Symposium on Stress. Army Medical Service Graduate School, Walter Reed Army Medical Center, Washington, D. C. 1953.

Park, E. A., and Richter, C. P. Transverse lines in bones: The mechanism of their development. *Bull. Johns Hopkins Hosp.* 93:234–248, 1953.

Richter, C. P. Alcohol, beer and wine as foods. *Quart, J. Studies on Alcohol* 14:525–539, 1953.

Richter, C. P., and Mosier, H. D., Jr. Maximum sodium chloride intake and thirst in domesticated and wild Norway rats. *Am. J. Physiol.* 176:213–222, 1954.

Richter, C. P., and Uhlenhuth, E. H. Comparison of the effects of gonadectomy on spontaneous activity of wild and domesticated Norway rats. *Endocrinol.* 54:311–322, 1954.

Pfaffmann, C., Young, P. T., Dethier, V. G., Richter, C. P., and Stellar, E. Preparation of solution for research in chemoreception and food acceptance. *J. Comp. Physiol. Psychol.* 47:93–96, 1954.

Tan, E. M., Hanson, M. E., and Richter, C. P. Swimming time of rats with relation to water temperature. *Fed. Proc.* 13:498, 1954.

Richter, C. P. Behavioral regulators of carbohydrate homeostasis. *Acta Neurovegetativa* 9:247–269, 1954.

Richter, C. P. The effects of domestication and selection on the behavior of the Norway rat. *Jour. Nat. Cancer Institute* 15:727–738, 1954.

Richter, C. P., and Rice, K. K. Comparison of the effects produced by fasting on gross bodily activity of wild and domesticated Norway rats. *Am. J. Physiol.* 179:305–308, 1954.

Richter, C. P. Self-regulatory functions during gestation and lactation. Gestation-Transactions of the Second Conf. Princeton, New Jersey. Pages 11–93. 1955.

Richter, C. P. Nutritional factors. 17th Ross Pediatric Research Conference on Growth and Development of Dental and Skeletal Tissues, Boston, Mass. Pages 22–30, 1955.

Richter, C. P. Experimental production of cycles of behaviour and physiology in animals. *Acta Medica Scandinavica*, Suppl. 307: 36, 1955. (International Society for the Study of Biological Rhythms) Basal, Switzerland, Sept. 1953.

Richter, C. P. Salt appetite of mammals: its dependence on instinct and metabolism. Contribution to *L'Instinct dans le Comportement des Animaux et de l'Homme*. Paris, France, 577–632, 1956.

Richter, C. P. Loss of appetite for alcohol and alcoholic beverages produced in rats by treatment with thyroid preparations. *Endocrinol.* 59:472–478, 1956.

Richter, C. P. Behavior and metabolic cycles in animals and man. *Proc.* 45th Annual Meeting of the Am. Psychopathological Assoc. *Experimental Psychopathology*, Hoch and Zublin, eds. Grune and Stratton, New York, 34–54, 1955.

Richter, C. P. Phenomenon of sudden death in animals and man. *Psychosomatic Med.* 19:191–198, 1957.

Richter, C. P. Hunger and appetite. *Am. J. Clin. Nut.* 5:141, 1957.

Richter, C. P. Production and control of alcoholic cravings in rats. *Trans. 3rd Conference in Neuropharmacology.* Princeton, New Jersey. (H. A. Abramson, ed.) The Josiah Macy, Jr. Foundation, New York, 39–146, 1956.

Richter, C. P. Ovulation cycles and stress. *Transactions 3rd Conference on Gestation.* Claude A. Villee, ed. Pages 53–70. Princeton, New Jersey, 1956.

Richter, C. P. Hormones and rhythms in man and animals. *Recent Progress in Hormone Research*, 13:105–159. Gregory Pincus, ed. New York: Academic Press Inc., 1957.

Richter, C. P., and Rice, K. K. Experimental production in rats of abnormal cycles in behavior and metabolism. *J. Nerv. and Ment. Dis.* 124:393–395, 1956.

Richter, C. P. Loss of appetite for alcohol and alcoholic beverages produced in rats by treatment with thyroid preparation. Sym. on Alcoholism-Basic Aspects and Treatment, Atlanta, Georgia. H. E. Himwich ed. Publ. No. 47 of the Am. Assoc. Advanc. Sc. 1957.

Richter, C. P. Permanent damage done to rats by prolonged feeding of several common therapeutic drugs and hormones. *Nat. Acad. Sci.* 126:1234, 1957.

Richter, C. P. Abnormal but regular cycles in behavior and metabolism in rats and catatonic-schizophrenics. 2nd International Congress of Psychiatry, *Psychoendocrine Symposium with Special Reference to Schizophrenia.* Zurich, Switzerland, 1957. 4:326–327, 1959.

Richter, C. P. Decreased appetite for alcohol and alcoholic beverages produced in rats by thyroid treatment. Symposium on hormones, brain function and behavior. *Proc. Conf. on Neuroendocrinology*, pages 217s,n220. Harriman, N. Y. H. Hoagland, ed. Academic Press, Inc. New York, 1957.

Mosier, H. D., and Richter, C. P. Response of the glomerulosa layer of the adrenal gland of wild and domesticated Norway rats to low and high salt diets. *Endocrinol.* 62:268–277, 1958.

Richter, C. P. Abnormal but regular cycles in behavior and metabolism in rats and catatonic-schizophrenics. *Psychoendocrinology*, pages 168–181. Max Reiss, ed. Grune and Stratton, New York, 1958.

Richter, C. P. Neurological basis of responses to stress. *A Ciba Foundation Symposium on the "Neurological Basis of Behaviour"* (In commemoration of Sir Charles Sherrington), pages 204–217. G. E. W. Wolstenholme and Cecilia M. O'Connor, eds. J. & A. Churchill Ltd. 104 Gloucester Place, London W.1, England, 1958.

Richter, C. P. Diurnal cycles of man and animals. *Science* 128:1147–1148, 1958.

Richter, C. P. On the phenomenon of sudden death in animals and man. *Psychopathology—A Source Book*, pages 112–125. Charles F. Reed, Irving E. Alexander and Silvan S. Tomkins, eds. Harvard University Press. Cambridge, Massachusetts, 1958.

Richter, C. P. The phenomenon of unexplained sudden death in animals and man. *Physiological Bases of Psychiatry.* Compiled and edited by W. Horsley Gantt. pages 302–313, 1958. (Article read at the 25th anniversary of the Pavlovian Laboratory, Phipps Psychiatric Clinic, Johns Hopkins Hospital.)

Richter, C. P. Rats, man and the welfare state. *Amer. Psychologist,* 14:18–28, 1959.
Richter, C. P., Jones, G. S., and Biswanger, L. Periodic phenomena and the thyroid. I. Abnormal but regular cycles in behavior and metabolism produced in rats by partial radiothyroidectomy. *Arch. Neurol. and Psychiat.* 81:233–255, 1959.
Richter, C. P. Lasting after-effects produced in rats by several commonly used drugs and hormones. *Proc. Nat. Acad. Sci.* 45:1080–1095, 1959.
Kline, A. H., Sidbury, J. B., Jr., and Richter, C. P. The occurrence of ectodermal dysplasia and corneal dysplasia in one family. *J. Pediatrics* 55:355–366, 1959.
Richter, C. P. Biological clocks in medicine and psychiatry: Shock-phase hypothesis. *Proc. Nat. Acad. Sci.* 46:1506–1530, 1960.
Kline, A. H., Sidbury, J. B., Jr., Richter, C. P., and Billingsly, J. Mode of transmission of familial ectodernal dysplasia. (Abstract) Americal Pediatric Society, 1958.
Richter, C. P. Biological clocks in medicine and psychiatry. Thomas William Salmon Lectures at the New York Academy of Medicine, 1959.
Richter, C. P. Biological clocks in infants and children. Annual meeting of the American Pediatrics Society, 1961.
Richter, C. P. Biological clocks. Presented at the annual meeting of the American Philosophical Society, Philadelphia, Pennsylvania, 1961.
Richter, C. P. Biological clocks and the endocrine glands. Proceedings of the Second International Congress of Endocrinology, London, England. Pages 119–123, 1964.
Fries, J. F., and Richter, C. P. Lung cancer. Detection by use of electrical skin resistance method. *Arch Int. Med.* 113:624–634, 1964.
Richter, C. P. Behavioral and physiological changes produced in rats by removal of the superior colliculi of the brain. Presented at the National Academy of Sciences autumn meeting, University of Wisconsin, Madison, Wisconsin. October 12, 13, 14, 1964. *Science* 146:429, 1964.
Richter, C. P. Psychopathology of periodic behavior in animals and man, pages 205–227, *Comparative Psychopathology.* American Psychopathological Assoc., Grune & Stratton, Inc., 1967.
Richter, C. P. Sleep and Activity: Their relation to the 24-hour clock. *Procs. Assoc. Research Nerv. and Ment. Dis.* 45:8–29, 1967.
Richter, C. P. Biological clocks. Presented at the Ciba Foundation meeting, 41 Portland Place, London, England in honor of Professor Bernhard Zondek. July 27, 1966. Edited by G. E. W. Wolstenholme. J. & A. Churchill, Ltd., London, England, 1967.
Richter, C. P. *Biological Clocks in Medicine and Psychiatry.* Charles C Thomas. Springfield, Illinois, 1965.
Richter, C. P. A hitherto unrecognized difference between man and other primates. *Science* 154:427, 1966.
Mosier, H. D., Jr., and Richter, C. P. Histologic and physiologic comparisons of the thyroid glands of the wild and domesticated Norway rat. *Anat. Rec.* 158:263–274, 1967.
Richter, C. P., Langworthy, O. R., and Park, E. A. An ideal preparation of animals (on single-food-choice diet) for dissection of nerves and glands and for bone growth studies. *Proc. Nat. Acad. Sci.* 57:265–272, 1967.
Richter, C. P. Clock mechanism esotropia in children—alternate-day squint. *Johns Hopkins Med. J.* 122:218–223, 1968.
Richter, C. P. Inherent twenty-four hour and lunar clocks of a primate—the squirrel monkey. *Comm. Behav. Bio.* part A, 1:305–332, 1968.

Richter, C. P. Experiences of a reluctant rat-catcher. The common Norway rat—friend or enemy? *Proc. Phil. Soc.*, 112:403–415, 1968.

Richter, C. P. Periodic phenomena in man and animals: their relation to neuroendocrine mechanisms (a monthly or nearly monthly cycle). *Endocrinology and Human Behaviour*, Richard P. Michael, ed. Oxford University Press, London, 1968. (Presented at the proceedings of a conference held at the Institute of Psychiatry in London, May 9–111 1967.)

Richter, C. P. Inborn nature of the rat's 24-hour clock. *Proc. Nat. Acad. Sci.* 61:1153–1154, 1968.

Richter, C. P. Blood-clock barrier: Its penetration by heavy water. *Proc. Nat. Acad. Sci.*, 66:244, 1970.

Richter, C. P., and Duke, J. R. Cataracts produced in rats by yogurt. *Science* 168:1372–1374, 1970.

Richter, C. P. Dependence of successful mating in rats on functioning of the 24-hour clocks of the male and female. *Comm. Behav. Biol.* Part A, 5: No. 1, September 1970.

Richter, C. P. Yogurt induced cataracts: Comments on their significance to man. *J. A. M. A.* 214:1878–1879, 1970.

Richter, C. P. Inborn nature of the rat's 24-hour clock. *J. Comp. Physiol. Psychol.* 75:1–4, 1971.

Riley, L. H. Jr., and Richter, C. P. Uses of the electrical skin resistance method in the evaluation of patients with neck and upper extremity pain. 1975. *Johns Hopkins Med. J.* 137:69–74, 1975.

Richter, C. P. Astronomical references in biological rhythms. International Society for the Study of Time, Second World Conference, Lake Yamanaka, Japan, *Study of Time II.* Springer-Verlag. New York. 1975.

Richter, C. P., and Warner, C. L. Comparison of Weigert stained sections with unfixed, unstained sections for study of myelin sheaths. *Proc. Nat. Acad. Sci.* 71:598–601, 1974.

Richter, C. P. Part played by taste in self-selection of diets as determined by six common sugars. Conference on the Development of Sweet Preference sponsored by the National Institute of Dental Research, Bethesda, Maryland, June 1974. (In press.)

Richter, C. P. Deep hypothermia and its effect on the 24-hour clock of rats and hamsters. *Johns Hopkins Med. J.* 136:1–10, 1975.

SUBJECT INDEX

Activity, human spontaneous
  at birth, 8
  hunger directed, 47–49
  regularity of recurrence, 8, 9
  relation to stomach, 36, 37, 43, 54–56, 60, 61
  two-hour rythm, 54–56
Activity, rat spontaneous
  and age, 7, 8, 23–30
  defection, 83–86
  drinking, 83
  experimental approaches, 5, 7, 13, 34, 52
  external temperatures in relation to, 16–19
  food, relation to, 8–16; development of feeding habits, 63–67; difference with age, 11, 13, 15, 54, 64; relation to time of feeding, 11, 12, 14, 141; starvation, 10
  four-day rhythm, 67–80, 89
  grooming, 46, 57
  heat regulation in relation to, 16, 90
  hunger in relation to, 44–49, 58
  illumination in relation to, 19–23
  multiple activity in relation to, 91, 93
  nest building, 86–90
  origin, 34–44
  periodicity, 7, 8, 23–30, 371
  running in relation to, 70–73, 75, 76, 77
  sex hormones, dependence on, 78
  stomach, relation to, 35–49
  urination, 83, 86
  withdrawal of rhythmic stimulus, 30–34
Activity, spontaneous
  cat, 66
  Convoluta roscoffensis, 34
  dog, 37
  frog, 39, 59
  guinea pig, 53
  phosphorescent organisms, 34
  pigeon, 59, 60
  rabbit, 66
  turtles, 39
  See also Human spontaneous activity; Rat spontaneous activity
Adaptation. See Domestication
Addison's disease, 164, 221, 222, 289
Adrenalectomy, 135, 157–164, 167, 179, 182–185, 191–193, 195, 196, 202, 211
  See also Selection; Self-regulation
Adrenals, 80, 295, 314, 372
  differences between wild and domestic rats, 304, 305, 312, 315
Age and activity, 7, 8, 23–30
Alcohol, 223
Alexandrine rat, comparison with Norway rat, 358, 368
ANTU (alpha-naphthyl thiourea), 332, 335, 337, 338, 343, 346–348, 360–371
Apparatus and cages:
  Aktograph, 7
  combined food and activity, 44, 45, 56
  drinking, 83, 84, 143

389

electrodes: skin resistance, 278
fighting chamber, 308
food choice, 61, 62, 204
gross movement, 6, 52
hunger contractions, 54
mineral appetite, 196
multiple activity, 91, 92
multiple food choice, 169, 204
nest-building, 87, 198
revolving drum, 24
running, 67
sleep and activity, 127, 130, 131
starvation, 33
swimming, 322
taste threshold, 196
urination and defecation, 84, 85
wild rat handling, 324
Appetite and nutritional needs, 107, 186
See also Selection
Arsenic. See Poisons
Atropine, 279, 280
Autophagia, 217, 218

Barium. See Poisons
Behavior: definitions, 3–5; as integration of function, 3
Biological clocks (human), 96–127
 central, 118, 121, 125
 evolution, 121
 homeostatic, 118, 119, 121, 125
 independence of external influences, 109, 124
 inherent cycle, 109, 125
 manifestation under pathological conditions, 97–109, 119–121, 124
 mental and emotional symptoms, 102–107, 116, 371
 peripheral, 117, 120, 125
 physical symptoms, 97–102, 111, 112, 113–117, 120, 122, 123
 presence of several clocks, 116
 shock-phase hypothesis, 122–125
Biological clocks (rat) (24-hour clock), 129–147
Birds. See Chicken; Pigeon
Blindness. See Eye
Blood cells, 100–101, 115, 123
Brain lesions. See Self-regulation
Brodmann, divisions of the frontal lobe, 265, 266
Breeding, rat, 291
Bullfrog. See Frog

Cages, 6, 33, 45, 52, 62, 72, 83–85, 87, 91–93, 129–131, 199, 204
 See also Apparatus and cages
Cancer tissue, 217
Cat: activity, 66; reflex, 245, 250, 251, 253, 255–257
Catatonia, 105, 115–116, 285
Cattle, 216
Chicken: activity, 66; selection, 167, 216, 218
Coatimundi: self-stimulation, 148, 149
Cod liver oil, 220
Compound 1080. See Sodium fluoroacetate
Convoluta roscoffensis, 34
Coprophagy, 217, 227. See also Selection, rat, coprophagy; Selection, rat, Vitamin B deficiency
Copulation, 78
Cow: selection, 216, 218
Craving, food. See Selection, human
Cyclicity of behavior. See Biological clocks

Death, psychogenic (human), 319–321, 328, 329
Death, psychogenic (rat), 321–323, 325–328
Defecation, 83–86
Depression, 105–107
Diet:
 McCollum, 9, 169
 stock, 205, 229, 291, 333
Diet, self-selection of. See Selection
Diurnal activity, rat, 19–23
Dog: activity, 37; reflex, 245; selection, 217
Domestication, human, parallels with rat, 315, 316, 372
Domestication, rat:
 anatomical changes, 290, 292–304, 314, 372
 behavioral changes: aggression, 290, 308, 309, 313, 321
 controlled domestication, 312, 313
 genetic selection, 314, 315
 physiological changes, 290, 304–308, 311, 312, 315
 scientific purposes of, 353, 354
 stress of captivity, 311
Drinking, 83, 84, 143, 311–312
Drive. See Activity, spontaneous

Subject Index

Drugs, effects on biological clock, 136, 137, 145
Duodenal ulcers, 102

Eye, effect on biological clock, 131–134

Feces. *See* Coprophagy
Feeding habits, rat. *See* Activity, spontaneous; Selection
Ferret: selection, 216
Fever, 102, 111
Food selection. *See* Selection
Fright, behavior of rat, 93
Frog: activity, 39, 59
Fruit fly: biological clocks, 122

Guinea pig:
  activity, 53, 66
  reflex, 245
  selection, 216

Heat conservation, 90
Hodgkin's disease, 101, 114, 115, 123
Homeostasis, concept of, 128, 194, 224
Horse: selection, 218
Hunger and activity, 44–49
  See also Activity
Hunger contractions, 54–56, 65
  See also Stomach
Hydrarthrosis, 98–100, 108, 113–114
Hypophysectomy, 135
Hypothalamic lesions, 136, 143, 146
Hypothermia. *See* Temperature

Insulin, 212
Intelligence, rat, relation to multiple activities, 91

Kinkajou, self-stimulation, 150

Light and activity, 19–23
  See also Eye

Macaque: reflex, 267–275
Magnesium deficiency, 307
Mercury. *See* Poisons
Metabolic equilibrium, 39, 40
Minerals, 233, 235, 237, 238
  See also Selection
Mink: selection, 216

Monkey:
  reflex, 245, 261, 262, 280, 283
  selection, 216, 217
  self-regulation, 224
  self-stimulation, 151
Mouse, selection, 167

Nest-building, rat, 26, 27, 86–90, 199, 200
Nocturnal behavior, rat, 19–23
Norway rat:
  behavior, 360
  bites, 365
  cleanliness, 354, 359
  dietary needs resemble man's, 354
  fleas, 359
  life span, 354, 372
  poisoning. *See* Poisoning, rat; Poisons
  population studies, 363
  resistance to infection, 354
Nursing, 47–48
Nutrition. *See* Selection

Ovaries, 72, 73, 77, 86
Ouronodypsia, 217
Ovulation, 69, 70

Parathyroid, 222
Parkinsonism, 265
Phenyl thiourea. *See* Poisons
Phosphorescent organisms: activity, 34
Pig: selection, 166, 167, 216
Pigeon:
  activity, 59, 60
  selection, 216
  sudden death, 328
Pinealectomy, 135
Pituitary, 118, 299
Poisoning:
  human, 330, 335, 341–344, 346, 348, 356, 368. *See also* Selection
  rat, 331, 332, 335–338, 340, 341, 344, 346, 360–366, 368. *See also* Selection
Poisons:
  alpha-naphthyl thiourea (ANTU), 332, 335, 337, 338, 343, 346–348, 360–371
  arsenic, 216, 331, 337, 343, 346–348
  barium, 331, 338, 343, 346, 347
  distribution in nature, 344, 348

mercury, 202, 216, 333, 337, 346, 347
phenyl thiourea (phenyl thiocarbamide), 219, 223, 332, 337, 338, 343, 344, 346, 347, 355–358
sodium fluoroacetate (Compound 1080), 332, 340, 343, 344, 346–348, 368, 371
solubility, 344
squill, red, 331, 335, 337, 338, 346–348, 355, 368
strychnine, 331, 333, 337, 346, 347, 368
thallium, 331, 340, 341, 343–348, 368, 371
thiosemicarbazide, 333, 337, 338, 343, 346–348
zinc phosphide, 331, 335, 338, 343, 346, 347
Pregnancy and activity, 71

Rabbit:
 activity, 66
 self-stimulation, 152
 sudden death, 328
Rat first used in laboratory, 290, 353, 354
 See also Alexandrine rat; Norway rat
Reflex, cat (decerebrate animals):
 contraction, 259
 red nuclei, 255–257
 standing, 245, 256
Reflex, human:
 electrical resistance changes, 278–284
 extensor rigidity with brain lesions, 261
 grasping, 261, 263–265, 274, 275
Reflex standing in decerebrate dog and guinea pig, 245
Reflex in macaque:
 ablation technique, 266
 frontal lobe lesions, 267
 lesions resulting in hanging response, 268–270
 interpretation of results of lesions, 271–275
 production of grasp reflex, 264–276
Reflex, monkey, 261, 262, 245, 280, 283
 See also Reflex in macaque

Reflex, sloth:
 in decerebrate animals, 250–259
 normal postures, 248, 249
Rhythms of activity, 30–34, 52–61
 See also Activity

Salt appetite. See Selection, rat, sodium; Selection, human, sodium
Selection:
 chicken, 167, 216, 218
 cow, 216, 218
 dog, 217
 ferret, 216
 guinea pig, 216
 horse, 218
 mink, 216
 monkey, 216, 217
 mouse, 167
 pig, 166, 127, 216
 pigeon, 216
 sheep, 216, 218
Selection, human, 167, 223
 calcium, 222
 carbohydrate, 219
 dependence on taste, 223, 224
 iron in pernicious anemia, 222
 poisons, taste thresholds, 219, 223
 sodium in disease, 164, 186–191, 193, 221, 222
 sodium taste thresholds, 219
 total caloric intake in hyperthyroidism, 222
 vitamin D (cod liver oil), 219–221
 water in diabetes, 222
Selection, rat
 adrenalectomy effect, 156–164, 167, 179, 182–185, 191–193, 195, 196, 202, 211
 autophagia, 217, 218
 calcium, 167, 168, 170, 173, 174, 192, 197, 207, 213, 214
 carbohydrate, 169, 170, 173, 175, 197, 198, 201, 208, 209, 211, 212, 219
 coprophagy, 217, 227–229
 dependence on taste, 201
 fat, 169, 173, 175, 208, 209
 multiple food choice, 171–175, 177, 205, 208, 210
 ouronodypsia, 217
 parathyroidectomy effect, 197
 phosphorus, 170, 173, 174, 197

Subject Index

poisons, 201, 202, 216, 219
potassium, 170, 173, 174, 208, 214
pregnancy, effect, 208
protein, 170, 173, 208
single-food choice, 214–216
sodium, 170, 173, 174, 180–182, 184, 200, 201, 219
vitamin B complex, 171, 175, 206, 207, 209, 227–241
vitamin C, 175
vitamin D, 171, 174
vitamin E, 171, 175
water, 198, 199
in wild and domestic rats, 309, 313
Self regulation, 195, 199, 200, 203, 223, 224
  See also Selection, rat
Self selection (of foods). See Selection
Self stimulation: 148, 149, 150–152
Sheep:
  selection, 216, 218
  sudden death, 328
Shrew, sudden death, 328
Sleep, 43, 55, 60, 61, 104–105, 128–147, 150, 277–286
  See also Reflex, human, electrical resistance changes
Sloth, three-toed (*Bradypus, griseus griseus*), 247
  See also Reflex, sloth
Sloth, two-toed (*Chloepus didactylus, Linn.*), 247
  See also Reflex, sloth
Sodium fluoroacetate. See Poisons
Spontaneous activity. See Activity, spontaneous
Squill, red. See Poisons
Starvation, 10, 30–34, 136, 142
Stomach contractions, 35–43, 46–49, 54–61

Stress, 321, 325
  and domestication, 289–318
Strychinine. See Poisons
Suicidal behavior, 103

Taste, 201, 223, 224. See also Poisoning; Poisons
Temperature (body) rhythms, 97–99
Temperature and activity, 16–19, 199–200
Temperature and biological clocks, 136
Testes, 76
Thallium. See Poisons
Thiosemicarbazide. See Poisons
Turtle: activity, 39

Ulcers, duodenal, 102–103
Urination, 83, 84, 86
Urine drinking. See Ouronodypsia

Vitamin B. See Selection
Vitamin C. See Selection
Vitamin D. See Selection
Vitamin E. See Selection
Voluntary activity. See Activity, spontaneous
Voodoo death. See Death, psychogenic, human

Water. See Selection
Wild rat. See Alexandrine rat; Norway rat; Domestication

Yeast, 231–233, 238

Zinc phosphide. See Poisons

AUTHOR INDEX

Abbott, O.D., 226
Abramson, H.A., 386
Abu Mohammed Abdallah Ben Ahned, 348
Addison, T., 316
Adie, W.J., 265, 271, 276
Aiginger, J., 126
Akert, K., 141, 143, 147
Alexander, I.E., 386
Allen, G.S., 374, 384
Anderson, W.A., 373, 384
Arey, L.B., 127
Aschoff, J., 126
Atchley, D., 225

Bagley, C.J., 377
Baker, B.M., 100, 125
Baker, S.P., 375
Barelare, B., 167, 178, 194, 225, 241, 380, 381
Bartemeier, L.H., 245, 377
Basedow, H., 319, 329
Bazett, H.C., 250, 252, 263
Beach, F.A., 226
Bechterew, W.V., 265, 276
Becker, T.C., 349
Benjamin, J.A., 379
Bernard, C., 128, 147, 194, 195, 224
Best, C.H., 329
Billingsly, J., 387
Birmingham, J.R., 194, 225, 382
Biswanger, L.T., 126, 387
Blakeslee, A.F., 223, 226, 343, 348
Blum, M., 224, 226

Bohn, G., 34, 49
Boinet, E., 290, 316
Boldireff, V.N., 54, 94
Boldyreff, W., 49
Bordley, J.E., 384
Boulenger, E.G., 331, 347, 348
Bradford, N.M., 127
Brailey, M.E., 378
Brantigan, O.C., 100, 125
Brett, W.J., 127
Brobeck, J., 224, 226
Brodmann, K., 265, 276
Brown-Sequard, C.E., 289, 316
Bruce, V.G., 127
Bruesch, S.R., 383
Buchman, E.F., 379
Bugbee, E.P., 73, 94
Bünning, E., 127
Bykow, K.M., 126

Campbell, K.H., 194, 225, 226, 317, 381. *See also* Clisby, K.H.
Cannon, W.B., 35, 37, 39, 46, 49, 55, 94, 128, 147, 194, 195, 223, 224, 319, 320, 325, 328, 329, 380
Carlson, A.J., 35, 37–39, 46–49, 54, 59, 60, 94
Carter, E.P., 377
Casper, J., 265, 271, 274, 276
Castle, W.E., 313, 316
Chambers, 278, 286
Claremont, C.L., 347, 348
Clark, A.S., 329
Clay, J., 178

Clisby, K.H., 194, 225, 226, 289, 315, 317, 349, 373, 382. *See also* Campbell, K.H.
Cohen, E., 289
Cohen, J., 316
Coon, C.S., 147
Corner, G.W., 127
Covian, M.R., 289, 304, 316
Cowgill, G.R., 240, 241
Crampe, H.M., 331, 348
Critchley, M., 265, 271, 276
Croll, H.M., 240, 241
Crosby, P.T., 265, 276
Culbertson, C.C., 225

Danzel, L.A., 348
Danziger, L., 126
Darley, W., 184, 185
Darwin, C., 290, 316
Davies, E.R., 127
Davis, C.M., 167, 178, 186, 193, 219, 226
Day, H.G., 226
del Castillo, E.B., 127
Dethier, V.G., 385
Dewan, J.G., 126
Dieke, S.H., 289, 306, 316, 349, 368, 373, 374, 383, 384
di Paola, G., 127
Doan, C.A., 184, 185
Donaldson, H.H., 178, 290, 292, 296, 298, 299, 317, 354
Donaldson, J.C., 295, 317
Dove, W.F., 167, 178
Duke, J.R., 388
Dutcher, R.A., 227, 240, 241

Eaton, B.C., 383
Ebbecke, 281, 286
Ebstein, W., 102, 125
Eckert, J.F., 168, 178, 185, 193, 194, 224, 380
Eglitis, A., 126
Ellsworth, R., 193
Elvehjem, C.A., 206, 225
Embleton, D., 101, 125
Emlen, J.T., 291, 317, 363–365, 373, 374, 383
Engle, E., 380
Evans, H.M., 69, 94
Evvard, J.M., 166, 167, 178, 216, 225

Fairchild, T.E., 167, 178, 216, 225
Farmer, 278, 286

Feuchtwanger, E., 265, 274, 276
Firor, W.M., 158, 165
Fish, H.S., 289, 302, 303, 317, 383, 384
Fleischmann, W., 186, 193
Ford, F.R., 378
Fox, A.L., 223, 226
Fox, H., 356
Francis, E., 240, 241
Franck, U.F., 127
Franke, K.W., 217, 225
Franklin, R., 384
Freeman, W., 265, 276
Fries, J.F., 387
Froehlich Fried, W., 49
Fulton, J.F., 271, 275, 276

Gantt, W.H., 386
Garlock, B., 240, 241
Garrod, A.E., 99, 125
Gaunt, J.H., 157, 165
Gaunt, R., 157
Gillespie, R.D., 377
Ginsburg, H., 60
Giragossintz, G., 158, 165
Gjessing, R., 105, 108, 126
Godden, W., 216, 225
Goldstein, K., 265, 274, 276
Gornall, A.G., 126
Grandi, G., 349
Green, H.H., 218, 225
Greene, C.H., 377
Griffiths, W.J., 289, 306, 317, 373, 374
Grollman, A., 158, 165
Guerrant, N.B., 227, 241
Guttmacher, A.F., 74, 76, 95, 377

Halberg, F., 127
Hall, C.E., 289, 295, 296, 302, 304, 314, 317, 318, 374, 384
Hamilton, L.D., 126
Hammett, F.S., 308, 317
Hanson, M.E., 385
Hardy, W.G., 384
Hargreaves, F.J., 178
Harriman, N., 386
Harris, L.J., 176, 178
Harrop, G., 193
Hartman, C.G., 127, 379
Hatai, S., 317
Hawkes, C.D., 194, 225, 226, 241, 381

Author Index

Helfenstein, A., 349
Helfrick, S., 383
Heller, H., 127
Heller, V.G., 240, 241
Hench, P.J., 316, 317
Hill, J.H., 143, 147
Himwich, H.E., 386
Hines, M., 226, 264–266, 276, 379, 380
Hitzig, W.H., 97–99, 125
Hoagland, H., 386
Hoch, 386
Hollander, W.F., 216, 225
Holt, E.B., 3
Holt, L.E., 167, 178, 194, 214, 225, 241, 380, 381
Honeyman, W., 106, 126, 381
Horn, E.F., 347, 349
Hoskins, R.G., 52, 75, 76, 94, 380
Howard, J.E., 186, 193
Howell, 277, 286
Hunter, H., 106, 126, 381
Hutton, M.K., 168, 178

Irving, L., 329

Jacobsen, C.F., 271, 275, 276
Jahiel, R., 103, 126
Janischewsky, A., 265, 276
Jones, G.S., 126, 375, 385, 387
Jones, L.G., 225

Kajdi, C.N., 214, 225
Kalmbach, E.R., 332, 349
Kalmus, H., 127
Karli, P.C., 375
Katz, D.T., 382
Keeble, F., 34, 49
Keller, A.D., 276
Kendall, E.C., 317
Kennard, M.A., 271, 275, 276
Kennedy, C., 241
Kinder, E.F., 51, 87–89, 94, 194, 225
Kindwall, J.A., 126
King, A.B., 384
King, H.D., 317
Kleist, K., 265, 276
Kline, A.H., 387
Kohlschütter, 277, 284, 286
Kon, S.K., 167, 178
Krick, E.T., 157, 165, 193
Kutz, R.L., 157, 165

Lamy, M., 349
Langworthy, O.R., 226, 378–381, 387
Lantz, D.E., 331, 349
Lashley, K.S., 318
Latta, H., 374
Lee, M., 380
Leonard, K., 126
Levine, M., 379, 380
Lewin, L., 331, 349
Lhermitte, J., 265, 276
Liddell, E.G.T., 259, 263
Lindsay, J.S.B., 126
Lipton, M.A., 206, 225
Loeb, R.F., 193, 202, 225
Long, J.A., 69, 94
Lubs, H.A., 359
Luckhardt, A.B., 39, 49

MacCallum, W.G., 203, 225
MacCleary, R., 384
McCollum, E.V., 9, 217, 218, 225, 226, 354
McElroy, C.H., 240, 241
McKeown, T., 157, 165
MacLean, A., 194, 226, 315, 318, 381
MacWilliam, 284, 286
Magnus, R., 255, 256, 262, 263
Mall, G., 126
Malone, P.D., 383
Maloney, M.A., 126
Mannering, G.J., 206, 225
Marais, J.S.C., 349
Martin, C.J., 90, 94
Martin, C.L., 54, 55, 94
Mascall, L.M., 331, 349
Mayer, C., 276
Mendel, L.B., 167, 178, 240, 241
Meyer, A., 4, 245, 353
Michael, R.P., 388
Michelson, 277, 286
Mirick, G.S., 384
Miller, A., 126
Mitchell, H.S., 167, 178
Mitchell, P.C., 331, 347, 348
Moadié, J., 127
Monninghoff, 277, 286
Moore, B., 34, 49
Moore, C.U., 241
Moritz, A.R., 329
Mosier, H.D., 289, 374, 375, 385, 387
Moss, F.A., 52, 94
Muhammed Elgabaki, 331
Munch, J.C., 347, 349
Mursell, J.L., 176, 178

Nash, C.B., 218, 225
Nelson, E.M., 240, 241
Neumayer, E., 126
Nevins, W.B., 225
Nichols, J., 312, 313, 317

O'Connor, C.M., 386
Ogden, D.P., 316
Olmstead, J.M.D., 158, 165
Orent-Keiles, E., 217, 225, 226
Orfila, M.P., 331, 349
Orr, J.B., 216, 218, 225
Osborne, T.B., 167, 178, 240, 241
Otenasek, F.J., 383

Palmer, L.S., 241
Papanicolaou, G.N., 69, 78, 95
Park, E.A., 96, 385, 387
Parsons, H.T., 168, 178
Paterson, A.S., 276, 378, 379
Patt, H.M., 126
Patterson, T.L., 59, 65, 94
Pearl, R., 167, 178, 216, 225
Pencharz, R.K., 158, 165
Penfield, W.G., 250, 252, 263
Pfaffman, C., 385
Philipeaux, J.M., 290, 317
Phymate, H.B., 241
Pieper, 278, 286
Piesbergen, 277, 286
Pilez, A., 107, 126
Pincus, G., 386
Pineas, H., 276
Pittendrigh, C.S., 127
Polley, H.F., 317
Potter, van R., 217, 225
Price, W.A., 216, 225

Rademaker, G.G., 255, 256, 262, 263
Reed, C.F., 386
Reimann, H.A., 108, 126, 127
Reiss, M., 386
Renz, J., 349
Rice, K.K., 96, 106, 126, 194, 225,
    227, 311, 317, 382, 383, 385
Riddoch, 261
Riley, L.H., 388
Robinson, L., 264, 276
Rogers, F.T., 54, 55, 60, 94
Rogers, P.V., 289, 295, 304, 314, 318,
    373, 374, 384
Roscoe, M.H., 227, 240, 241
Rowe, A.H., 98, 125, 127

Rubin, M.I., 157, 165, 193
Ruch, T.C., 224, 226

Sadovnikova-Koltzova, M.P., 308, 318
Sahyoun, P.F., 127
Schaub, I.G., 384
Schipper, G., 384
Schmidt, E.C.H., 194, 225, 381, 383
Schuster, P., 265, 271, 274, 276
Sell, M.T., 240, 241
Selye, H., 157, 165, 315, 318
Semerdjian, S., 127
Shaw, M.B., 378
Sherf, L., 127
Sherrington, C.S., 259-263
Sidbury, J.B., 387
Silver, J., 347, 349
Simond, A.E., 73, 94
Slocumb, C.H., 317
Slonaker, J.R., 26, 49, 52, 69-73, 80,
    94
Smith, A.H., 240, 241
Smith, H.W., 127
Snedecor, G.W., 225
Snell, M.G., 225
Snyder, L.H., 223, 226
Soffer, L.J., 193
Sohar, E., 127
Spitznagel, J., 384
Stahl, J., 225
Starobinski, A., 126
Stearns, G.L., 216, 225
Stellar, E., 143, 147, 385
Steenbock, H., 240, 241
Steyn, D.G., 349
Stockard, C.R., 69, 78, 95
Stokes, A.B., 126
Stokes, A.W., 374
Stoll, A., 347, 349
Stone, C.P., 52, 95, 308, 314, 318
Sweet, C., 167, 178, 220, 226
Szymanski, J.S., 7, 13, 49, 95

Tan, E.M., 385
Taylor, N.B., 329
Theiler, A.H., 218, 225
Timme, W., 102, 103, 125
Tobin, C.E., 157, 165
Tomkins, S.S., 386
Tower, S.S., 378, 379
Tracy, H.C., 52, 95
Trescher, J.H., 193
Turro, R., 176, 178

Author Index

Uhlenhuth, E.H., 375, 385

van Potter, R. *See* Potter, van R.
Viljoen, P.R., 218, 225
Villee, C.A., 386
Voegtlin, C., 225
Voshell, A.F., 100, 125

Wada, T., 8, 9, 36, 37, 43, 49, 51, 60, 61, 95, 377
Waletzky, E., 333
Waller, 278, 286
Walshe, F.M.R., 261, 263
Wang, G.H., 8, 48, 51, 67–70, 73–75, 94, 95, 163, 165, 377, 378
Ward, A., 178
Warner, C.L., 388
Washburn, A.L., 55, 94

Watson, C., 295, 318
Weiss, S., 329
Whelan, V., 240, 241
Wilkins, L., 186, 193, 222, 226, 381
Williams, R.G., 126
Wilson, S.A.K., 261, 263
Wislocki, G.B., 76, 94, 245, 378
Witthaus, R.A., 349
Wolstenholme, G.E.W., 386, 387
Wood, D.E., 375, 385
Woodruff, B.G., 382, 383
Woods, J.W., 289, 375, 385

Yerkes, R.M., 308, 314, 318
Young, P.T., 385

Zamchek, N., 329
Zublin, 386